A HUNDRED YEARS of TEXAS WATERFOWL HUNTING

NUMBER TWENTY-THREE: GULF COAST BOOKS,
SPONSORED BY TEXAS A&M UNIVERSITY—CORPUS CHRISTI

John W. Tunnell Jr., General Editor

A list of titles in this series is available at the end of the book.

*Publication of this book
was generously underwritten
by Anita and George H. Rau Jr. '69
in recognition of generations of Texas waterfowlers,
including their son, George H. Rau III,
and their irrational dedication to birds, dogs, and inclement mornings.*

★ ★ ★

A HUNDRED YEARS of TEXAS WATERFOWL HUNTING

THE DECOYS, GUIDES, CLUBS, AND PLACES, 1870s TO 1970s

R. K. SAWYER

Foreword by Matt Kaminski

TEXAS A&M UNIVERSITY PRESS

College Station

Copyright © 2012 by R. K. Sawyer
Manufactured in the United States of America
All rights reserved
First edition

The author gratefully acknowledges Lee Smith, who provided technical reconstruction of the historical photographs used in this book.

This paper meets the requirements of ANSI/NISO Z39.48-1992 (Permanence of Paper). Binding materials have been chosen for durability.

Library of Congress Cataloging-in-Publication Data

Sawyer, R. K. (Robert Knowlton), 1956–
   A hundred years of Texas waterfowl hunting : the decoys, guides, clubs, and places, 1870s to 1970s / R. K. Sawyer ; foreword by Matt Kaminski. — 1st ed.
      p. cm. — (Gulf Coast books ; no. 23)
   Includes bibliographical references and index.
   ISBN-13: 978-1-60344-763-8 (cloth : alk. paper)
   ISBN-10: 1-60344-763-6 (cloth : alk. paper)
   ISBN-13: 978-1-60344-773-7 (e-book)
   ISBN-10: 1-60344-773-3 (e-book)
1. Waterfowl shooting—Texas—Gulf Coast—History.
I. Title. II. Series: Gulf Coast books ; no. 23.
SK331.S34   2012
799.2'4409764—dc23
                          2012003946

CONTENTS

Foreword, by Matt Kaminski vii
Acknowledgments ix

Introduction 1

PART ONE
TEXAS WATERFOWL HUNTING

1. Sport Hunting in Texas 7
2. Decoys and Duck Calls 23
3. Hunting Laws: Rules of the Game 51

PART TWO
COASTAL TEXAS HUNTING CLUBS, GUIDES, AND PLACES

4. Sabine Estuary 59
5. East Bay 87
6. Trinity River Delta 127
7. San Jacinto River 145
8. West Galveston Bay 161
9. Brazos and San Bernard Rivers to the Gulf 173
10. Matagorda Bay 185
11. Espiritu Santo and San Antonio Bays 205
12. Copano and Aransas Bays 221
13. South Bay to Corpus Christi Bay 255
14. Laguna Madre 279

PART THREE

NORTH, WEST, AND EAST—INLAND SPORT HUNTING

15 Big Prairie and Eagle Lake   299
16 Katy Prairie   325
17 Short Stories from Farther Afield   343

Epilogue   361
Notes   367
Index   391

FOREWORD

The sport of waterfowl hunting began, for many of us, at an early age. As summer green turned to fall orange, we put on our boots and went afield with fathers, uncles, brothers, friends, and sometimes we went alone. I was introduced to waterfowl when my parents put a Flambeau bluebill decoy in my bathtub. From the tub I migrated to the garage, where I helped with cleaning and plucking duties, pulling the wax off of our harvest of fat mallards. Even before I was old enough to shoot a gun, my dad made sure I understood that duck hunting was not a right, but a privilege.

My love for waterfowl—its conservation, management, and the hunt—was nurtured by my family. Near my hometown of Starkville, Mississippi, my dad leased property, a mixture of former soybean fields and bottomland hardwoods, that seasonally flooded from the backwaters of the Noxubee River. For us, the waterfowl season was a year-long affair. Each spring we pulled boards from water control structures to encourage growth of millet and smartweed and planted willow trees we made into duck blinds before each hunting season. Summer was a time to fight mosquitoes, cottonmouths, and the ever-persistent beaver. During fall we walked our oak flats to check on the year's acorn production from a great stand of willow and cherrybark oaks, which provided food for wintering mallards and wood ducks. We prepped our willow blinds by adding natural vegetation, and as the days got shorter and cooler we awaited the northern fronts that would stir the humid air and bring the winter rains. When the rain ran off the hills and began to fill the bottoms, we began to anticipate the arrival of the ducks. Our first hunt was rewarding not only for the ducks we harvested, but also for the unforgettable sight of hundreds of birds rising, returning, and decoying to the habitat we constructed. Months of preparation had come full circle.

Like countless young boys before and after me, I grew up on the rich legends and lore that make up the history of waterfowl hunting. I remember how my dad described the rafts of bluebills on Lake Michigan near his hometown of Manitowoc, Wisconsin, during the 1950s and 60s. He told me how he measured these "slicks" in miles and how he hunted the open water for the "butterballs." He explained how these ducks traveled from their prairie and boreal forest breeding grounds to staging areas on lakes in the upper Midwest before heading to the Atlantic or Gulf Coast.

Stories like these have entertained and influenced hunters young and old across North America's wetlands, and that is what *A Hundred Years of Texas Waterfowl Hunting* presents to waterfowl hunters, watchers, historians, and other enthusiasts. It brings the reader back in time to when waterfowl hunting was a way of life and highlights how communities were connected to the land and marsh. This book provides a rich and detailed reflection on the people, the communities, the habitat, and the multitude and diversity of waterfowl and waterfowl hunting on the Texas Gulf Coast. *A Hundred Years of Texas Waterfowl Hunting* clearly affirms that waterfowling is more than the sport—it is the passing of heritage from generation to generation.

Matt Kaminski
Ducks Unlimited, Texas

ACKNOWLEDGMENTS

THE ONE AUTHOR'S NAME ON THE BOOK COVER IS MISLEADING, as the effort results from contributions by a great many people. First and foremost are those who provided written material, both published and unpublished, oral histories, and family photographs. They are the ones who wrote the book. Special gratitude is also extended to Cliff Fisher for providing photographs from the John Winter Collection. It was these images, first shared with me by Chet Beaty, which provided the spark that set the idea afire. I am particularly indebted to retired Texas Parks and Wildlife Department (TPWD) biologist Charles Stutzenbaker, who filled the pages with rich observations from his years on the Texas coast and edited many sections.

Jefferson County came alive from the contributions of Charles Stutzenbaker; Jim Sutherlin; Bobby, Billy, and Craig LeBlanc; Rosine McFaddin Wilson; E. G. Gerry Cordts Jr.; E. J. Fournet; Bill Quick; Mark, Randy, Leo, and Coty Foreman; Hayes Mendoza; James "Cowboy" Fernandez; Randy and Brook Chatagnier; Lillian Chatagnier Richard; Greg Keddy; Bill Wilson; Wayne Stupka; and Mike Cooper. Yvonne Sutherlin and the Port Arthur Public Library and Judy Linsley of the McFaddin-Ward House provided research and photographs.

The history of Chambers County was told by Jim Bob Jackson, Freddie and Mary Jean Abshier, Joe Whitehead, Jean and Janet Lagow, Jack Holland, Karla Jackson Dean, Quinten Jackson, Arthur Jackson, Felix Jackson, Gene Campbell, Ralph Leggett, Shannon Tompkins, J. Steve Kole Jr., Mary Margaret Lytle, Palmer and Talley Melton, Chet and Will Beaty, Peter Stines, Doug McLeod of the Moody Foundation, Bill Gammel, and Kevin Ladd at the Wallisville Heritage Center. Special thanks are owed to Dave Wilcox, Justin Teltschik, and Jason Holmes. The author is indebted to Melanie Wiggins, Forrest West, Clyde "Boots" Faggard, Joe

Faggard, Claud Kahla, Thelma Berwick Black, and Joe Doggett for their assistance with Bolivar Peninsula.

Trinity River Delta hunting history is the product of Kendon L. Clark, Johnnie Dutton, Sylvia Lamb, Walter Besser, John Kemp, Prentice Holder, and Buddy Davison. A very deep appreciation goes to Dr. Royce A. Strickland of Baytown for access to his extensive collection of photographs and interviews and his friendship.

For San Jacinto River, West Galveston Bay, and Brazoria, resources were generously provided by Mary Jean Romero, Mike Leebron, Bill Womack, Gordon LeCompte, James Smock, Bill Stransky, Larry Goodbread, Brian Marshall, Liston Roberts, Steve Parker, Mike Wicker, Gary Cole, and David Hailey. Research assistance was provided by Michael Bailey and Jamie Murray of the Brazoria County Historical Museum.

I am indebted for Matagorda Bay history to Ted Bates Jr., Jim Dailey, Ducks Unlimited's Todd Merendino, TPWD's Marc Ealy, Forrest Hawes, and Captain Raymond Cox. From the Matagorda County Museum Archives Department in Bay City, Jennifer Rodgers compiled and donated photographs, and Barbara Smith provided historical accuracy.

Contributions to the sporting history of Lavaca Bay, San Antonio Bay, and the Guadalupe Delta were made by J. C. Melcher, Carlos Smith, Jim Mills, Cocoa and Will Blackbird, Joe Ray Custer, Jimmy Wayne Johnson, Stewart Campbell, Steve Fisher, Ronnie O. Luster, James B. Tennant, Chris Martin, and Harvey Evans. Historical photographs were provided by Dean Johnstone and by George Ann Cormier of the Calhoun County Museum.

In Rockport, Ed Duvall made it possible for the author to prowl the hallowed halls of the Port Bay Club and to interview members. I am grateful to Al Johnson, David M. and Jim Herring, Jo and John Silberisen, Elaine Vandeveer, Jerry Lynn Ayers, Betty Armstrong Adams, Johnny Atwood, Fred Close, John Warren, James Fox, Alex Halff, Jeff Kuchera, Mary Martha Culpin, and C. H. "Burt" Mills for their contributions. Research was facilitated by Janie White of the Aransas County Historical Society and Barbara Armstrong and Iris Sanchez of the Aransas County Public Library.

Contributions to the history of the Ingleside, Aransas Pass, and Port Aransas areas were made by Byrd Lee Minter Jr., Rick Pratt of the Port Aransas Museum, Barney Farley III, Pat Farley, Bruce Baker, Brian Preston, Jamie and Gordon Spears, Mark Creighton, J. Guthrie Ford, and Bertha Nell of the Blackland Prairie Museum, Taft.

In the Corpus Christi Bay area, thanks are extended to Billy Sheka Jr., Doug Bird, Murphy Givens, Mack Ray, David Coover Jr., and Dr. John Pettigrove. Jim Moloney kindly made available the entirety of his extensive photographic collection. Photographs were provided by Bell/Whittington Library, Portland, with help from RoseAleta Laurell, the Corpus Christi Public Library by Gerlinda Riojas, and the Institute of Texan Cultures in San Antonio.

For the Laguna Madre area to Brownsville the author is indebted to Norm Rozeff, Bill Kiel, Caesar Kleberg Research Institute's Bart Ballard and Tim Fulbright, Lisa Neely and Butch Thompson of King Ranch, Walt Kittelberger, and Barry Batsell.

The story of Eagle Lake and Garwood was told by Jerry Sims, Agnes Reel Strauss, Davis Waddell, Clifton Tyler, Louis Schorlemmer, Bill Blair, Charlie Braden, Alex and David Wolff, Barry Lewis, Gervais Bell, Sydney Struss, Jodie Socha, Bill Appelt, Morris Howland at the Prairie Edge Museum, the staff at the Eula and David Winterman Library, and David Todd. For the Katy Prairie, thanks go to Lyle and Pat Jordan, Jim Warren, Larry Gore, David Lobpries, Jim Longtin, James Prince, Doug Pike, and Al Bisbey.

In the chapter "Short Stories from Farther Afield" I am indebted to Hilmar G. Moore, Orin Covell of the George Foundation, Bill Kiel, Rich Flaten, Andrea Weddle from James Gilliam Gee Library, Texas A&M University–Commerce, Jonathan Gerland of the History Center in Diboll, historian James Conrad, and Walter and Brenda Martin.

In addition to photographs provided by many of the interviewees, additional images were provided by Aryn Glazier of the UT–Austin Center for American History; Bill Stein of the Columbus Nesbitt Library; Joel Draught of the Houston Public Library; Dreanna Belden at the University of North Texas; Tom Shelton and Patrick Lemelle of the Institute of Texan Cultures in San Antonio; Brian Collins of Dallas Public Library; the Library of Congress in Washington, DC; Jeff Pelaya of the Canvasback Gallery in Easton, Maryland; Joe Walsh, also from Easton; Victoria College/University of Houston–Victoria Library; and Darrell Appelt. Photographs from the Rosenberg Library at Galveston were facilitated by Casey Greene.

Texas decoys came to life under Ron Gard, senior consulting specialist of Sotheby's American Folk Art Department. Additional contributions to the history of Texas decoys and calls were provided by Johnnie Dutton, Chester Barker, Chuck Barry, Gordon Stanley, Gary Chambers, Bill Provine, Dr. Thomas Hutson Nelson, and Thomas Andrew Nelson.

Thanks go to Todd Steele and retired game wardens Doc McCallum and Jim Stinebaugh for their help. Mary Botes, Harold Burgess, and Dave Morrison provided assistance with swans and cranes. The contacts, camaraderie, and patience extended to me by outdoor writers Shannon Tompkins of the *Houston Chronicle* and David Sikes of the *Corpus Christi Caller-Times* will always be remembered.

This book exists as a result of the vision of Shannon Davies of Texas A&M University Press, and if in parts it appears that I have used good English, then the credit should go to reviewer Rudy Rosen and editors Thom Lemmons and Noel Parsons.

Last, but not by any means least, I am indebted to my wife, Wendy, and daughter, Christen, who both spent too many days without a husband and father while I endeavored to bring this story to print.

A HUNDRED YEARS
of TEXAS
WATERFOWL HUNTING

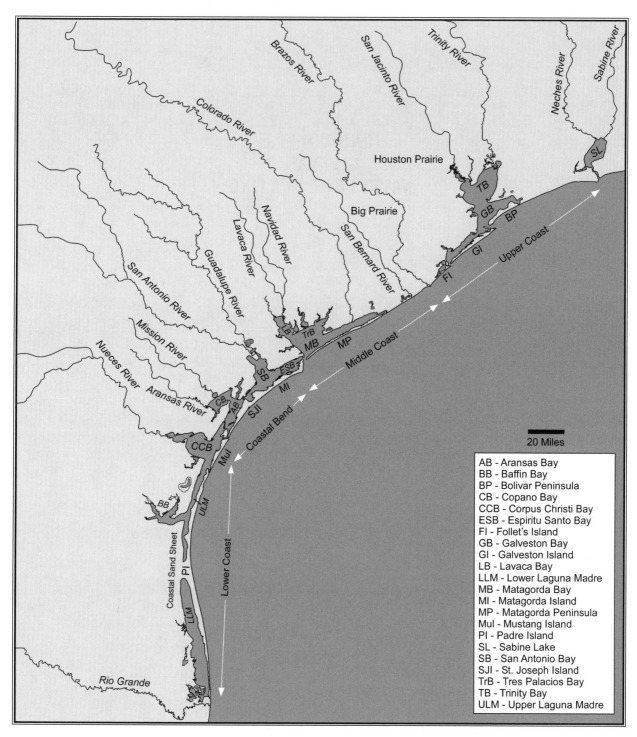

Coastal Texas *bays, rivers, and landforms.*

INTRODUCTION

WATERFOWL HUNTING HAS BEEN AN INTEGRAL PART OF NEARLY two hundred years of Anglo Texas settlement, first as sustenance, then market hunting, followed by recreation or sport hunting. *A Hundred Years of Texas Waterfowl Hunting* attempts to bring to life the trinity of wildfowl, man, and sport hunting. The book covers the state's spectacular wintering waterfowl habitat, hunting clubs, guides, and decoys, and the sportsmen who played a role on nature's stage. The story focuses on, but is not limited to, the period between the 1870s, when the first private hunting clubs were founded by sportsmen from growing Texas cities, and the 1970s, when the proliferation of clubs and guides was so great their documentation would require a separate tome.

Aboriginal Indians, followed by the Spanish, French, and Mexicans, first trapped or hunted ducks and geese on the Gulf Coast for sustenance or barter. Waterfowl were just as important to the next wave of settlers, the Anglo-American frontiersmen, planters, and immigrants and their slaves, who lived on what they gathered from land and sea. For them the fall waterfowl migration provided a change in diet and a time for replenishment of the homestead with feathers for pillows and rendered lard for cooking.

Anglo-Americans were the first in what would become Texas to look upon nature as a commodity, finding a place for it in local then later national economies. They were the market men—commercial hunters and merchants—who made their living by killing and selling waterfowl for profit. Not only meat made its way to the marketplace, but also plumage, skins, and eggs from a host of wading birds and shorebirds. Sport hunting paralleled market hunting for several decades until the latter was outlawed in Texas in the early 1900s.

Sport hunters came from all walks of life. Many hunted to put food on the family table, while for others hunting was an essential outdoor recreation. Dallas writer Nick Hardy explained the virtues of duck hunting to the Texas businessman in 1909. Daily stress, he opined, "tends to wear on his system and tear down his tissues," but after only a few days in pursuit of ducks, "he will return to his labors with more vim and vigor than before he left" and "look and feel years younger."[1]

Waterfowl hunting was deeply embedded in the state's culture, a feature in large- and small-town newspapers even before Texas independence. By the late 1800s, newspapers published sporting accounts in great detail, and the information weighed as heavily as did stories of who had married or died. This lasted until the 1930s, when recreational hunting, no longer featured on the front page or the society pages, moved to the sports section and the pens of the first Texas outdoor writers.

Texas waterfowl hunting was used to promote tourism and land development. Postcards that featured contented sportsmen with big harvests were mailed throughout the country from the Texas coast. One from Rockport, for example, showed two men who shot sixty-three ducks in just a couple of hours. Another, promoting the new town of Port Arthur, featured hunters in suits posing with hundreds of ducks they killed during a two-hour shoot around Sabine Lake. Glossy brochures from Corpus Christi at the turn of the century proclaimed, "Even a novice can bag all the ducks the law allows," and carried photos of sportsmen with great hauls of ducks, Canada geese, and sandhill cranes.[2]

Sportsmen were enticed to visit the Lone Star State by hyperbole, as in *Field and Stream* magazine's 1893 proclamation, "Texas today is the finest and best hunting and fishing ground in the United States," and another that called the Texas Gulf Coast "the greatest sporting discovery of the age." Visiting sportsmen helped develop a significant outdoor industry, providing income to guides, farmers, boat captains, restaurateurs, and hotels whose "sporting solicitors" arranged hunts for their guests.[3]

An important sport hunting institution was, and remains, the private hunting club. First organized in the 1870s by urban sportsmen from the state's largest cities, notably Galveston, Houston, San Antonio, Waco, and Dallas, early hunting clubs followed the railroads. These clubs, often called hunting preserves, owned or leased their land and were usually incorporated, filing charters with the state and having a board of directors and elected officers. Early club memberships were exclusive, made up of prominent businessmen and politicians who had both money and leisure time and knew the value of mixing business with pleasure.

Proprietors of private clubs carved out comfortable, sometimes luxurious, accommodations from a mostly hostile environment, employing groundskeepers, lodge staff, guides, boat captains, and gamekeepers. Gamekeepers, whose main job was to keep local hunters off the shooting preserves, were also called fence riders or game wardens, the latter easily confused with lawmen who in the early 1900s came to be known by the same name.

Texas hunting clubs of the 1800s held regular shooting competitions that usually pitted one prominent club against another from a nearby city. Live pigeon and glass ball shoots were popular, as were prize hunts, contests to kill the greatest number of wild birds on the wing. Prize hunts were organized with various bird species assigned point values; the scorecard usually included snipes, rails, bitterns, curlews, plovers, woodcocks, prairie-chickens, ducks, owls, hawks, geese, and sandhill cranes.[4]

Prize hunt tallies can only be taken in the context of a different time, when wild game appeared to be unlimited and conservation was a concept still in the future. The Houston Gun Club's 1884 prize hunt in Hockley resulted in a kill of nearly 1,000 birds. Competing in a "grand prize hunt," two Galveston teams killed 4,000. A Houston match with twenty-six shooters to each team brought in 4,600 snipes. In "an amiable spirit of rivalry," the Houston Gun Club challenged Galveston sportsmen to a match on neutral territory at Clear Lake in 1889. There were twenty-five participants from each city, and rail cars were filled with friends and family to watch the event. With a total of 542 birds harvested, the Houston team won, the Galveston team supplying the traditional oyster and champagne dinner.[5]

Plovers and snipes were the target for big-volume prize hunts in the inland cities of San Antonio, Waco, Dallas, and Fort Worth. These were day-long social affairs with food and music, and the shooting squads consisted of men, women, boys, and girls. On the prairies north of Dallas, two six-man teams killed 1,055 plovers, and again the low-scoring team bought the celebratory supper. The contestants distributed all of the birds to townspeople.[6]

The great flocks of wildfowl that once animated the Texas sky are gone. Sport hunters were not the cause, although they might have been without early-twentieth-century laws to curtail their excesses. Recreational hunters have borne witness to the changes in habitat and bird numbers. Yet each fall they return to the field, their passion for the sport largely unabated from the days when there was no daily limit on the number of birds that could be killed, to the present, when many species of wildfowl cannot be harvested at all. Sport hunters, too, have seen the evolution from muzzle-loading shotguns to repeating, semiautomatic guns and have watched as canvas sails were replaced by gasoline engines and horse and wagon by the automobile. Texas waterfowlers adapted to all the changes, and this book celebrates their story.

The account presented here is largely from two sources: the media and interviews with people who individually or with their families have been an integral part of the land and its wildfowl resources. Sometimes what is printed in media, and what people remember, is inaccurate. Some of what the author has interpreted from both sources may also be incorrect. None of these inaccuracies are intentional, and the strengths and weaknesses are best summed up as a gumbo of fact, legend, and lore that is Texas waterfowling history.

PART ONE

TEXAS WATERFOWL HUNTING

CHAPTER I

SPORT HUNTING in TEXAS

Early Texans found a vast, unbroken coastal marsh that extended from the Sabine River on the Louisiana border to the Lavaca River, punctuated by the rich estuaries of Sabine Lake and Galveston, Matagorda, and Lavaca Bays. To the south, where fewer rivers provided freshwater input than on the upper coast, the middle and lower coastal waters of San Antonio, Copano, Aransas, and Corpus Christi Bays were more brackish to saline. More saline still were Baffin Bay and Laguna Madre, the latter stretching along more than a hundred miles of Texas coast and into Mexico.

West of Galveston Bay were Houston and Big Prairies, where copious inland freshwater habitat extended near to the headlands of Lavaca Bay. Miles of pristine river floodplains crossed the state, providing water to a large number of natural freshwater lakes. Some lakes held water year-round, as did Caddo and Green Lakes, while others, such as the uncountable playa potholes of West Texas and the Texas Panhandle, were seasonal.

TEXAS WINTERING WATERFOWL

The diverse habitat of the Gulf Coast was—and remains—the principal wintering area for great flocks of wildfowl that migrate south from summer breeding grounds along the inland corridor of the Central Flyway. Each fall, Texans awaited their arrival, and the volume and diversity of cranes, swans, geese, ducks, and shorebirds they saw were immeasurable. The favored puddle ducks over the decoys and on the table were mallards, which, in their vernacular, Texas sportsman always called greenheads. Northern pintails they called sprigs, and the resident mottled ducks they usually called black or summer mallards. Big early-fall flights of blue-winged teal, with later green-winged teal and occasional cinnamon teal, also commonly filled hunters' bags. Gadwalls, northern shovelers or spoonbills, and wigeons—in the early years always called baldpates—were plentiful but not as favored on the table. The colorful wood duck was a staple for hunters in flooded timber. Black-bellied and fulvous whistling-ducks were abundant summer residents of the Rio Grande delta, with the range of the fulvous species extending as far north as Louisiana.

Diving ducks, which prefer more open water than do most puddle ducks, were traditionally hunted on bays and large inland lakes. Central Flyway diving ducks included redheads and lesser scaup (the latter usually called bluebills), canvasbacks, ring-necked ducks, ruddy ducks or butterballs, buffleheads, common goldeneyes, and mergansers. Although the Texas Gulf Coast held far more redheads and bluebills, the canvasback was king. It was the way it decoyed—and tasted on the table—that eclipsed all other ducks in popularity.

Snow geese in Texas, called white brant or brant, were considered by many as "fishy and worthless." Before the mid-1900s, grey or even black brant was the common name for lesser white-fronted geese, also known as specklebellies or specks. Gray brant was also used for the dark phase of the snow goose, the blue goose. The Texas coast and interior were winter home to all varieties and sizes of Canada geese. The largest, what sportsmen today call the greater Canada goose, usually weighed eight to twelve pounds. Historically in Texas the big Canadas were nearly always called ringnecks, or sometimes honkers. The smaller varieties, informally known as lesser Canadas, were sometimes called Canada geese, but usually just geese.[1]

No one was counting geese in Texas before the mid-1900s, but qualitative accounts from naturalists and sportsmen show remarkably consistent trends. Snow geese were certainly the most abundant geese on the coast, but there were also large numbers of greater Canada geese, considered by ornithologists at the turn of the century to be abundant east of Rockport. Biologist Bob Singleton in 1953 confirmed what the hunters knew: the largest Canada goose populations were in coastal Chambers, Matagorda, and Brazoria Counties, St. Charles Bay, and on the Laguna Larga of the King Ranch Laureles Division. Until the 1940s they were the only goose seen on the Lissie and Katy Prairies.[2]

It was the opposite for the blue-phase snow goose and Ross's goose. The blue goose was so uncommon in Texas that ornithologist Henry P. Attwater celebrated his good fortune to collect one in 1891. The US Biological Survey and Audubon Society found only three blue geese in Texas in 1910—one at Lake Surprise and two in Matagorda County. A steady increase occurred from the mid-1940s as they shifted laterally from the Mississippi Flyway. Freddie Abshier, growing up in the rice fields of northern Chambers County, says, "We never knew what a blue was. They kept driftin' further this way, following the Ross's geese that had come a little earlier." The Ross's goose historically wintered in southern California until the 1940s, when the little geese increasingly followed snows to the Gulf Coast. California's loss was coastal Texas's gain.[3]

At the turn of the century there were probably fewer white-fronted or specklebelly geese wintering on the Texas coast than are observed today. It was 1932 before state game warden Tom Waddell saw his first specklebellies around Eagle Lake, and he counted thirty-two birds. Connie Costabile in 1939 saw the largest flock of specklebelly geese supposedly ever seen on Bolivar Peninsula to that time: seventeen birds. Specklebelly geese were reported along the Rio Grande as early as the 1850s, but according to Elizabeth Smith, the South Texas wintering population numbered only a few thousand prior to the 1950s. By 1952 the King Ranch shoreline on Upper Laguna Madre alone held as many five thousand. That year the numbers around Eagle Lake rose to as many as fifty thousand.[4]

It is not possible to determine early population trends for lesser Canada geese. Naturalists in 1911 believed the small goose was abundant east of Galveston Bay but rare to the south, and it was not until 1914 that the geese showed up in the rice fields around Eagle Lake. But dozens of photographs, taken only a few years later in places as far south as Aransas Pass, give the impression that this goose was fairly common.[5]

Hunters once harvested both trumpeter and tundra, or whistling, swans from Sabine Lake to the Rio Grande delta and all bodies of inland water across the state. As late as 1912, John Strecker in *The Birds of Texas* reported that the whistling swan wintered abundantly between Galveston and Corpus Christi Bays, with trumpeter swans considered common. Legend has it that when Brazoria County hunters killed a whistling swan in 1970, it appeared in the *Freeport Facts* with the caption "greater snow goose." The rare sightings of the great white birds today are a cause for celebration.[6]

The Texas coast was home to both whooping cranes and sandhill cranes. Called "noble and majestic targets" by hunters, whooping cranes were a challenging quarry due to "their superior height and great . . . timidity." English sportsman and market hunter Captain Frank Wilden Flack confessed he didn't kill more than fifteen in his years pursuing them along the Texas coast. Sandhill cranes, the smaller cousins of the whooper, were described by one outdoorsman as having an unmistakable call "resembling the sounds made by a block when hoisting a sail." Rarely taken on the wing in the 1800s, sportsmen preferred to shoot them with rifles from horseback or "by decoying [them] with pasteboard figures, cut to proper size and shape and painted."[7]

Sometimes shorebirds came down the Central Flyway in such numbers in nighttime darkness that their silhouettes blotted the light of the moon for hours. While the most commonly hunted shorebirds were snipes, plovers, and curlews, all species were fair game in the field and on the table. Those who hunted shorebirds called them by a wide range of names. The upland sandpiper or plover was called the grass plover. In the Rio Grande Valley the upland sandpiper and

HUNTERS' NAMES FOR CENTRAL FLYWAY WATERFOWL

Common Name	Texas Hunters' Name
Mallard	Greenhead
Northern Pintail	Sprig, Sprig tail
Mottled Duck	Black or summer mallard
Northern Shoveler	Spoonbill
American Wigeon	Baldpate
Lesser Scaup	Bluebill, Blackhead
Ruddy Duck	Butterball
Snow Goose	White brant or brant
Snow Goose (dark phase)	Blue goose, Gray brant
Lesser White-fronted Goose	Specklebelly, Speck, Gray or black brant
Greater Canada Goose*	Ringneck, Honker
Lesser Canada Goose**	Canada goose
Tundra Swan	Whistling swan
Upland Sandpiper (Plover)	Grass plover
Upland and Wilson's Sandpipers	Papabot (Rio Grande Valley)
Killdeer	Ringneck plover or plover
Wilson's Snipe	Jack snipe

*Branta canadensis   **Branta hutchinsii*

Wilson's plover were both called papabot. Any ploverlike bird went by local names such as gray plover, prairie plover, sand-snipe, yellow-shanked tattler, prairie-runner, spring plover, tilt-up, beach bird, prairie pigeon, or prairie snipe. Killdeers were ringneck plovers or just plovers. The Wilson's snipe was nearly always called the jack snipe, mistaken for its European cousin. The name tattler or telltale was given by waterfowlers to some species of plovers, lesser yellowlegs, and willets for their shrill alarm call at the approach of a hunter.[8]

GETTING TO THE DUCKS

Before the 1870s, sportsmen who followed waterfowl south to Texas arrived by steamer or schooner, their journey always long and entirely at the whims of the weather. Only the hardiest of waterfowlers braved the vagaries of the journey before expansion of Texas's railroad network after the Civil War. With trains, recreational hunters could access points along the Texas Gulf Coast in a matter of days and in relative comfort. Private hunting clubs and guiding services grew along the tracks of the railroads, the trains delivering sportsmen from the Lone Star State's growing cities, the United States, and the world.

Sportsmen from all walks of life depended on trains. Private rail cars were the preferred means of travel for men of wealth. Typical in the 1890s was a Tennessee hunting party that journeyed to Rockport on the San Antonio and Aransas Pass Railway (SA&AP). They leased a private Pullman car, the *Isaak Walton*, fitted with

> The San Antonio and Aransas Pass Railway is the
> Popular Line to Galveston and East,
> Waco and North.
>
> # A POINTER!
> ## "Shoot Johnny, Or Give Up the Gun."
>
> Duck, Geese, and Brant Hunting is About On.
> Take a few Days' "Outing" along the line of the Aransas Pass Railway. Game of all kinds in abundance.
> Thirty Day Excursion Tickets on Sale to Corpus Christi, Rockport, Portland and Aransas Pass.
> Elegant Parlor Cars on all trains to and from Houston and Corpus Christi.   ALLEN IRWIN, Ticket Agent
> E. J. MARTIN, General Passenger Agent

(Modified from *San Antonio Sunday Light,* Nov. 17, 1896)

kennels, gun racks, a large dining room, parlor, kitchen, pantry, refrigerator, and observation room. The Pullman Company provided the excursionists with "an experienced French cook, an expert pantry man, and its most efficient porters." The train made stops along the way to allow hunters to shoot prairie-chickens, quail, and deer.[9]

At the turn of the century, railroad magnate Colonel T. J. Anderson organized a hunting and fishing expedition to cover, by rail, a thousand miles of Texas coastline. Guests included magazine and newspaper editors from throughout the nation, governors of two states, and thirty or more prominent northern and eastern businessmen. The Texas press vigorously promoted the trip, anticipating calling attention "to the vast undeveloped resources of the section traversed."[10]

Sportsmen of average means also relied on the rail network. Retired TPWD biologist Charles Stutzenbaker says, "My Dad told me that when he was a young man, you could get on a train anywhere along the Texas coast and make arrangements with the conductor to stop the train at any point that you wanted, and he'd let you off. It was common for people to take their camping supplies and get off the train and hunt for a couple of days, and when it came time to go home, they'd walk the railroad tracks, and flag the train down."[11]

Trains were often a part of the hunt. Passengers on the Gulf and Inter-State Railway between Galveston and Beaumont watched out the windows for ducks, and the engineer stopped to allow hunters and crew to sneak the birds as spectators cheered or jeered the hunters' success. Mallards were usually the quarry when the Gulf, Colorado, and Santa Fe train rolled to a stop on the route between Galveston and Richmond. In South Texas, ducks rising along the track of the Rio Grande Railway bridges between Point Isabel and Brownsville were shot from

SAILING SCHOONERS, *sloops, and cat-rigged sailboats were used on Texas waterways even after popularization of the inboard diesel engine. Shown is Palacios's Ted Bates Sr. on the stern of the sloop* Helen B. *The Bates family towed pulling skiffs they built from cypress. Note the cut brush for duck blinds in the closest skiff. (Courtesy Ted Bates Jr.)*

windows of the slow-moving passenger cars, after which the engineer stopped the train to allow the gunners to retrieve their kill.[12]

Trains got visiting sportsmen near the shooting grounds; the remainder of their—or any waterfowl hunter's—journey depended on whether shoots were over water or land. For transportation on shallow lakes, ponds, and shorelines, waterfowlers used locally built rowing skiffs and small cat-rigged sailboats. The broad waters of Texas's bays were crossed by sloops, schooners, and wood-burning steam launches. Schooners were the backbone of bay hunting, with captains and crews available for hire in every port town on the coast. Excursions lasting days and even weeks at sea became immensely popular with northern sportsmen. San Antonio's L. F. Meyers, planning a hunt in 1893, explained, "We will be out from two to four weeks. We shall sleep right on the schooner and have our cook and everything complete."[13]

E. T. Martin traveled each winter from Illinois, hiring a schooner and crew in quest of big canvasback concentrations. Renowned author Emerson Hough came for the once abundant greater Canada geese. On a hunt in the late 1890s his captain found the big birds on sandbars in Matagorda Bay, where the hunters dug pits in the sand and staked harvested birds as decoys. Of life aboard the schooner, Emerson was impressed by "Jim, the negro cook . . . [who] knows what he can do in his little galley down under the schooner's deck with a Texas winter goose."[14]

Inland and coastal prairie hunters relied on horses, mules, and oxen for transportation, with wooden carts for hauling. Farmers who had seen their livestock walk to within a few feet of resting birds began to use trained oxen for the hunt. Controlling the steer with a halter and stick, hunters walked behind the big animals and into resting waterfowl until they were close enough to fire. Hunter Bill Ward says he rested his fowling pieces on the steer's back, and even after the shot the ox never stopped feeding.[15]

Visiting sportsmen were often dismayed at the success of these hunts. Kem Dean II, who moved to Houston in the early 1920s, described a hunt south of the city in which he "rented for the morning a trained ox which has been in the hunting game for years and is the chief source of his owner's income. This animal has been trained to walk around in circles, apparently grazing, gradually coming nearer and nearer to the birds, while we kept on his far side. He can get very close in this way and we got all the duck we wanted in a couple of hours, and more than we could eat. We fired several times right in the old bull's ear but he must be stone deaf."[16] The use of trained hunting steers as moving blinds was common across the upper coast from Sabine Lake to Matagorda. While the practice was not unique to Texas, by the 1920s it had become so widespread that the importance of hunting steers in Texas was not unlike that of the sculling boat to sportsmen on the Great Lakes and that of the sink box on Chesapeake Bay's Susquehanna Flats.

Introduction of the horseless carriage, like the arrival of the railroads, again changed the way sportsmen got to the hunt. Traveling shell, gravel, and sand roads, automobiles allowed sportsmen to get to their destinations more quickly than they ever imagined possible and took them to remote places once only reachable by horseback or sail. Legend has it that Colonel Edward H. R. Green brought the first automobile to Texas from Saint Louis in 1894, leaving a trail of frightened horses in his wake. Mass-produced automobiles appeared after the turn of the century, and by 1910 there were 14,267 automobiles in the state. Three years later they were so numerous that the *Dallas Morning News* worried that wild game, even at great distances from the city, had been hunted out.[17]

It took wildfowl time to adjust to the automobile. At first birds did not flush from the noisy contraptions and were easily approached and killed from a car. Driving at night west of Houston, an Aldine farmer hit a flock of low-flying ducks, killing several blinded by the lights. One startled motorist watched as a mallard dove headlong to the asphalt pavement in front of his car, evidently convinced the new roadway was a canal.[18]

Boats with internal combustion engines put an end to steam power and wind-filled canvas sails. The first were powered by naphtha engines in the 1880s, but

TRAINED STEERS *were commonly used to hunt waterfowl on Texas prairies until outlawed in the 1940s. Shown is Henry "Hank" Jordan's Katy Prairie hunting steer in the 1920s with Leonard Jordan (left), Chester Jordan (center), and Hank Jordan (right). (Courtesy Lyle and Pat Jordan)*

ORANGE COUNTY *hunters displaying ducks, shorebirds, rabbits, opossums, and deer in 1912. Automobiles made it easier to get to the hunt, and it was common for sportsmen to return home with their harvest prominently displayed across their vehicles. (William Temple Hornaday Papers, Library of Congress, File No. PR 13 CN 1985)*

OUTBOARD MOTORS *revolutionized travel on waterways, replacing sails and oars. Ed Bond is standing with thirty mallards from Lost Lake on the Trinity River, Chambers County, by a soft-chined skiff powered by an Elto Ruddertwin in 1921. (John Winter Collection, courtesy Cliff Fisher)*

their habit of exploding kept their popularity low. By the turn of the century one- and two-cylinder gasoline inboards with giant flywheels made their appearance. Cameron B. Waterman invented the outboard, or "detachable rowboat motor," in 1905, but it was another fifteen or so years before they were widely available and considered by Texas sportsman as a "worthy gadget." Houston's Marshall Hayes says, "When people started getting boats, that freed us." Like the automobile, power boats got sportsmen quickly to the hunt.[19]

The rapid growth in the popularity of sport hunting after World War I was fueled by the internal combustion engine. Sportsmen no longer had to spend days or weeks in the field; they could make a day hunt, as it came to be called, in which they hunted and returned home in the same day. Sport hunting was curtailed when the roaring twenties came to crashing halt with the Great Depression in 1929 and, a year later, the beginning of the Dust Bowl, a killing drought with a dramatic effect on waterfowl populations. The Second World War brought rationing that made it nearly impossible for sportsmen to find tires, gasoline,

SPORT HUNTING IN TEXAS → 15

MULES AND HORSES *were made increasingly obsolete by marsh buggies in the 1920s. Shown is a Model T marsh buggy with wooden slat wheels on Pipkin's Ranch, Jefferson County, in the 1930s. A turning plow on the back was used to build pirogue trails for access by fur trappers and hunters. The ladder was used to see over high sea cane. (Photo by Dan Lay, courtesy Charles Stutzenbaker)*

A FORMIDABLE *Beaumont marsh buggy, 1935. (Courtesy USFWS, Elkins, WV, File No. NCTC-D 4175)*

ammunition, and guides, who left duck blinds all across Texas for Europe and the Pacific.

After World War II sport hunting was propelled into a very big business by a burgeoning postwar economy and even more modernized machinery. Gasoline engines expanded to marsh buggies and airboats. Marsh buggies started as a backyard cottage industry with modifications made to Model Ts and As that, by the 1950s, had evolved into sophisticated machines of all shapes and sizes, some with balloon tires and others with mud tracks. Airboats made their appearance in Jefferson County in the late 1920s, and by the 1940s and '50s hunters in Brazoria County, Port O'Connor, Rockport, Corpus Christi, and Laguna Madre had em-

By the 1950s *tracked marsh buggies were popular. Shown is the "Jones boys" marsh weasel at Needmore Ranch, Jefferson County, 1950. It is hard to find any other duck on their strap other than a mallard.* Left to right: *Casey Jones, Caldwell McFaddin, Harold Fiegleson, B. Bryant, and Pete Cordts. (Courtesy McFaddin-Ward House, Beaumont, Texas)*

Henry LeBlanc *with his Bruno Schulz airboat at Port Arthur Hunting Club, late 1920s to early 1930s. (Courtesy Bobby LeBlanc)*

braced the noisy machinery. By the 1970s airboats were to coastal Texas hunters what the horse and sailing sloop had been a hundred years earlier.[20]

The earliest known airboats built in Texas were from Port Arthur. Henry LeBlanc of the Port Arthur Hunting Club had a heavy cypress airboat built by Bruno Schulz at the Gulfport shipyard in the late 1920s. Like most early models, it had no cage around the wooden airplane propeller, and the engine was started by hand-cranking the propeller. Port Arthur's Lucien Fournet and his family put together their first airboats in the late 1920s. Son E. J. says those early boats "were planked with Model A Ford motors on them. I can remember hearing that an

SPORT HUNTING IN TEXAS

uncle of mine was killed in a airboat they were trying out." He remembers, too, "the prop came off the airboat sometimes, and it once cut through the hull."[21]

TOOLS OF THE TRADE

Whether alone in the field or as part of a club, sport hunters traversed a wide variety of habitat, covering inland prairies, agricultural fields, river bottoms, coastal marshes, lakes, bays, and barrier islands. The logistics of their hunt were a reflection of the land and water and vastly different across the state. While many sportsmen used decoys, duck blinds, and retrievers, about the only things Texas hunters all had in common were shotguns, and in the early days, rifles.

The evolution of firearms from muzzleloaders to repeating guns with smokeless powder was a major catalyst to the growth of sport hunting. With muzzleloaders, hunters had to haul chilled or soft shot in kegs or pouches, a powder horn, and paper wadding to the field. Loading was a time-consuming affair with primer, an exact amount of black powder, shot, and wadding tamped down the barrel into the chamber by ramrod. In all muzzle-loading guns, powder had to be kept dry—no small achievement in Texas waterways and weather. For a hunter in the 1860s who depended on his guns for food, it was always a problem "not being able properly to use them in consequence of the rain."[22]

Breech-loading shotguns, developed before the Civil War, and hammerless shotguns in the 1870s were a vast improvement. Though they still used black powder, weapons no longer had to be loaded in the field; sportsmen could pack preloaded shells they either loaded themselves or purchased in advance. Not everyone welcomed the new shooting technology. Muzzleloaders remained popular in Texas into the late 1800s, the new breechloaders considered by some as a Yankee invention of "no earthly consideration" and looked upon with "hate and suspicion." Muzzle-loading guns were headed for extinction in the 1880s and '90s with the mass production of repeating shotguns, and later semiautomatics, that used smokeless powder.[23]

Early gunners crouched in the grass on a bank or dug into a sandbar. They shot from skiffs surrounded with cut brush and even from sloops anchored next to shore. Hunting clubs were among the first to build fixed wooden blinds and cut brush before hunting season—sea cane on the upper coast, bay brush on the lower—a fall ritual. A few of the bigger hunting operations also employed the labor-intensive method of sink box shooting.

Hunting from sink boxes, a technique in which the hunter lay prone in a narrow floating box below water level with only the top of the box exposed, was popularized on Chesapeake Bay's Susquehanna Flats. The sink box operation required a schooner or sloop and a large crew, but the phenomenal kills that could be made justified the effort. In Havre de Grace, Maryland, the sink box fleet

DUCK BLINDS *at the Fin and Feather Club of Dallas, high and dry during the statewide drought of the early 1950s. (Texas/Dallas History Archives Division, Dallas Public Library, File No. PA76–1/11582.2)*

returned from a single day's shoot with 15,000 canvasbacks; one gunner alone killed 540.[24]

Accounts of Texas sink boxes exist from the San Jacinto River at Galveston Bay, Lake Surprise in Chambers County, and Harbor Island between Aransas Pass and Port Aransas. The Harbor Island operation used a rig described as a watertight box two feet wide, six feet long, and one foot deep, with sixteen-foot side boards fastened to each side. Sportsmen stayed on the outfitter's schooner for up to five days at a time, the crew rising each day before dawn to set huge decoy spreads and the shooting box. Hunters with five hundred to one thousand rounds of ammunition were rowed to the box. A cat-rigged sloop tacked downwind to pick up the kill.[25]

Sink box shooting in coastal Texas never reached the level of popularity it did on the East Coast. Harris Brown wrote, "The sink box, so indispensable on the Chesapeake Bay, is almost unknown to the duck hunter along the Texas coast," as "there are so many easier and equally profitable methods of securing an abundance of game."[26]

Retriever dogs were uncommon in Texas before the 1950s; most sportsmen and guides fetched their own birds. Retriever references that do exist mention mostly Chesapeake Bay retrievers, the hard-headed, untiring dogs bred on the East Coast. Retrievers gained popularity with a growing awareness of conservation—a well-trained dog reduced the number of lost birds—and with the arrival of a dog relatively new on the sporting scene, the European-bred black Labrador retriever. The trainability and handling of the black lab quickly made it

EXAMPLE OF *a sink box rig from Chesapeake Bay. The shooting box was below the surface and weighted down with iron decoys on the wing boards. (Photo by A. Aubrey Bodine, Jennifer B. Bodine Collection, courtesy Jeff Pelayo, Canvasback Gallery, Easton, Maryland)*

ONE OF ONLY *a few known sink box photographs from Texas, this image shows a portable rig in route to Cedar Bayou, near Baytown. Note duck decoys on the folded wing boards. (John Winter Collection, courtesy Cliff Fisher)*

the four-legged star of retriever clubs that sprang up in cities from Beaumont to Brownsville.[27]

Not every part of Texas was suitable for gunning over retrievers. Oyster reefs cut paws and legs to the bone, and more than a few sportsmen learned the hard way that retrievers and alligators were not a good mix. Too, most retrievers were only as good as their owners. Lyle Jordan, who guided as many city hunters as any man alive on Katy Prairie, says, "I've seen a lot of good ones, and a thousand sorry ones." Mostly retrievers found a warm place in sporting hearts as the unfailing companion who shared the hardship and reward of the hunt. In 1929, when E. H. Paulk of Palacios lost his dog in San Antonio Bay, he went looking for it and froze to death trying. Searchers found the dog standing dutifully over the missing hunter's body.[28]

HARDSHIP

Whether on land or water, sport hunters had chosen a hobby often uncomfortable and sometimes deadly. A long litany of things could go wrong in the protracted logistical march to hunt ducks. Weather had the biggest influence, with heat on the south wind before a cold front and driving rain and freezing temperatures on the back side. The worst of the cold fronts was the norther, and when it roared across the land it could, in a matter of hours, drop temperatures by as much as fifty degrees. Accompanying gale-force winds frequently blew the water from shallow bays, leaving behind a fleet of boats beached on the flats.

Not enough wind was an adversary as well. Boat captains and their charges often spent days becalmed at sea, sometimes within sight of land. By no means the exception were sportsmen on the sloop *Magenta,* stranded for three days heading to Bolivar Peninsula in 1878, or the party of fifteen hunters who drifted for two days in a chartered schooner at Brazos Santiago in 1906. When thick fog blanketed the coast it could strip the senses of all geography. The words of Chambers County's Freddie Abshier ring true for most sportsmen when he says, "In the fog, I don't care what kind of marshman you are, you're gonna get lost. The man that tells me he's never been lost in the fog, he's just never been in the fog."[29]

Texas hunters contended with water moccasins, or cottonmouths, and rattlesnakes. Chambers County's Peter Stines says when his grandfather, market hunter Captain Will Stines Sr., was bitten by a water moccasin, he cauterized the wound by lighting black gunpowder in it. Mosquitoes were the great plague of the sport. A Galveston Bay hunter after the Civil War described them as "winged tormentors" that "almost drove me crazy [every] morning, when I could scarcely see out of my eyes, so swollen was my face." One nine-day mosquito plague on the shores of Sabine Lake made the sun appear to be in eclipse. In 1902 the swarms of mosquitoes around Alvin were "a burden to both man and beast and forced suspension of all kinds of work."[30]

Duck hunters died. They drowned when boats sank or capsized in rivers and bays. Exposure killed hunters stranded when shallow bays, deep enough for schooners a few hours earlier, turned to mud flats as the wind blew the water to the Gulf. Others died when they got lost in high sea cane, and if they were found alive, the disorienting cane maze sometimes made them crazy. Mostly duck hunters shot each other and themselves. When partly ignited black powder sizzled in gun chambers, the delay in discharge could be as deadly as worn steel gun barrels could explode in a gunner's hands. Loaded guns in wooden boats carelessly handled or the swing of a gun barrel across a companion added to the toll. The number of hunters killed or injured in pursuit of the sport was staggering. As late as 1930, in just one sporting season, forty Texas hunters died and another thirty-five were injured.[31] Not everyone would understand why Texas sport hunters kept returning to the field.

CHAPTER 2

DECOYS and DUCK CALLS

WHILE WAGONS, SAILBOATS, SHOTGUNS, AND OTHER PARAPHERnalia were critical to early hunters, only wood decoys and game calls were entirely unique to the sport, their sole purpose to bring waterfowl within range of a hunter's gun. Carved duck decoys and duck calls are a thoroughly American folk art and have become collectibles that, throughout the United States, reflect the people and their geography. Before wooden decoys there were live decoys, and before duck calls, hunters imitated ducks and geese with their mouth.

There wasn't always a need for decoys. From prairie to marsh, many hunters went to the fowl under conditions often so trying that they hauled nothing out that was not absolutely necessary. Chambers County's Freddie Abshier says his family was like many who, "the first duck they killed they broke a spunk bean twig off, stuck it down in the mud, [and] put his bill over that. That was your first decoy. [They] didn't haul no decoys at all." His neighbor Joe Whitehead says, "I crawled a lot of ducks. We never did a lot of hunting over decoys." For others, however, decoys were as indispensible as a trusted shotgun.[1]

LIVE DECOYS

Nothing compared to a flock of live ducks on the water to attract "flying ducks within range of the sportsman's rifle." Live duck decoys in Texas were usually mallards, called English callers, and were purchased from catalogs, hardware stores, and breeders. On East Texas's Caddo Lake, hunters put out as many as forty to fifty live decoys, creating a demand that supported dozens of people in nearby towns who raised and sold live decoys.

> MALLARD DECOY DUCKS — Genuine stock; carefully reared; excellent callers; half regular price; eggs for sale. FRED COOK, La Marque, Tex.

(Modified from *Galveston Daily News,* Feb. 16, 1932)

> SEAVIEW HOTEL, High Island, Galveston County, now open for accommodation of hunters; boats, team and automobile service; live decoy Mallard ducks for hunting purposes; long distance phone in hotel; call me up; I meet all trains. GEORGE H. CARPENTER, Prop.

(Modified from *Galveston Daily News,* Nov. 6, 1921)

> **Hunters!**
> Are you having any Luck?
>
> You always have luck if you use our live decoys. They are "talkin' fools."
>
> Live Duck Decoys—one doz. per day $3.
>
> Canadian Geese per day, each $1.
>
> We are open ALL THE TIME and have all kinds of guns, boats, for rent.
>
> Steve Ridlage can make your gun as good as new, too.
>
> **ARGONNE HUNT CLUB**
> 608 W. 6th   Ph. 2-2762

(Modified from *Amarillo Globe,* Oct. 30, 1930)

On Galveston Bay, Fred Cook advertised that his live mallard decoy ducks were "excellent callers, carefully bred, reared and shot over." A San Antonio dealer promoted his birds with, "If you can hit 'em you can get 'em." English mallard callers called "wonderful workers" were sold during the 1920s in downtown Dallas at the Central Bank Building. George Carpenter, proprietor of the Sea View Hotel on Bolivar Peninsula, loaned live mallard decoys at no cost to his patrons. Live birds could even be leased; the Argonne Hunt Club in Amarillo charged three dollars a day for English callers and a dollar a day for geese.[2]

Clubs and guiding operations kept flocks of live birds in wooden duck pens. For the hunt, ducks and geese were collected then put in boxes or canvas tow sacks with their heads poking out. A pair of tow sacks were often tied together and tossed over a horse's back, one bag to a side. In the field, the birds were prevented from escaping by a neck collar tethered to a stake or heavy lead weight. In later years, the neck collars were replaced by a snap attached to the duck's leg and fastened to a staked line. While most birds were returned home the same way they got to the field, guide Jack Holland's uncle, Will Cox, removed the string and weights from his decoys and tossed them into the air. They then flew back to the home farm pond, although he lost more than a few to hunters along the way.[3]

Live decoy stories are a vanishing part of Texas waterfowling lore. Jefferson County's Charles "Smitty" Smith had three English callers, two hens and a drake. He reminisced, "I'd stake the hens out in a pond and put the drake where they

$10.00 REWARD
Any information as to whereabouts of my flock of English Caller Mallard ducks, strayed from ten miles down the Island.
GEO. REEG,
1402 15th St.

(Modified from *Galveston Daily News*, Aug. 5, 1927)

LIVE DECOY *duck cage from Smithers Lake, George Ranch, Fort Bend County. (Courtesy George Ranch Museum Collection, File No. 2000.082.024)*

HUNTING OVER *live mallard decoys at Pine Island on Highway 90 between China and Beaumont, about 1916. (John Winter Collection, courtesy Cliff Fisher)*

couldn't see him. Those hens called the drake and other ducks that came around." When Paul Winter of Port Arthur staked out his decoys, "they would set up a loud clamor each time flocks of wild ducks passed over, but they never attempted to fly away and join their brethren."[4]

Retired TPWD biologist Charles Stutzenbaker says, "I talked to one of the old hunters who kept his ducks in the blind with him. When ducks would start flyin', he had a metal pie pan with some corn in it, and he'd shake that corn, and those ducks would start that feed call." Game warden Tom Waddell once told his great-nephew Davis Waddell "to put a hen outside the decoys and a drake inside the blind. Every time that drake let out a little quack, that hen would reply [with a highball]."[5]

A DUCKING BOAT *provides a resting spot for live decoys after a John Winter hunt at the mouth of Cross Bayou, Trinity River delta, about 1920. (John Winter Collection, courtesy Cliff Fisher)*

LIVE MALLARD *decoys, a prominently displayed outboard motor, and a stringer of pintails, canvasbacks, and Canada geese from Calhoun County, probably in the 1920s. Hunters are W. P. Regan (left) and P. K. Dudgeon (right). (Jan Regan Collection, courtesy Dean Johnstone, Spoonbill Gallery, File No. 0679)*

Trinity Bay sportsman Lindsey Dunn Sr. once lost his best hen mallard on a hunt. Son Lindsey Jr. said, "Well, late that night [my father] heard a terrible commotion outside his window. He jumped out of bed, grabbed his lantern and shotgun and ran out on the porch in his nightshirt. There was the little hen just sitting there.... As he shined the light out in the yard he saw that she had brought home about seventy-five wild mallards with her."[6]

Fred William Bates's *live Canada and snow geese shared his Palacios yard with domestic fowl. (Courtesy Ted Bates Jr.)*

Houston's Henry "Peg" Melton raised mallard decoys behind his house. His son Palmer remembers, "Dad had these live callers in a cage. And they were heading to JHK Ranch [in Chambers County] down Main Street in Houston. Somewhere around the Rice Hotel—it was about six o'clock in the morning—that cage fell out of that Model T and busted open on the street, and those live callers got loose and they were chasing 'em down Main Street tryin' to catch 'em. They couldn't fly, their wings were clipped. They were squawkin', and of course people didn't have any air conditioning so everybody's windows were open." Palmer says for a time his father fed his live callers leftovers from their family meals, but "he took 'em hunting and he put 'em out and he noticed they were getting lower and lower in the water. They were sinking from no oil in the feathers."[7]

Snow geese and greater Canadas, the latter called tollers, were common as well. While live duck decoys were raised and sold commercially, geese were usually secured by wounding a few during the hunting season. H. M. Brown of Harwood kept a crippled Canada goose for years until the bird met an untimely demise when, struck by lightning, it was "instantly broken to pieces." Palacios's Ted Bates Sr. had a favorite greater Canada goose named John, and son Ted Bates Jr. recalls that it started calling as soon as it was staked out. In the agricultural fields near Austwell, J. Howard Mills of Mills' Wharf added snow geese to his spread of silhouette decoys. Along the Rio Grande delta, the "father of Harlingen," Lon C. Hill, raised two greater Canada tollers he named Tom and Jerry.[8]

During the off-season, tame ducks and geese shared the barnyard with domesticated fowl. Sometimes duck eggs were collected from the wild and hatched by chickens. Jack Holland remembers how flustered the family's setting hens got as their hatchlings broke off from the chicks and headed for water. The Hollands

DECOYS AND DUCK CALLS

LIVE SNOW *goose decoys from St. Charles Bay Hunting Club, Lamar Peninsula, in the 1920s. Geese were transported in tow sacks (in front, at bottom). Shown are manager Howard Mills (left) and club member R. Harmon (right). The boy is unidentified. (Courtesy Aransas County Historical Society)*

hatched a few resident mottled ducks that way, but the mottled duck as a live decoy, for them, failed. They never became tame, as mallards did, and "would blare distress calls to run every duck out of the marsh."[9]

Federal regulations in 1931 limited the number of live decoys that could be used to ten, but because of public outrage, the next year the limit was raised to twenty-five. Live decoys were outlawed entirely in 1935. An unnamed sportsman complained that, without live decoys, much of the romance of waterfowl hunting was gone. Many Texans, unable to break old habits, kept using live birds. Earl Porter on the Trinity River said of his English caller, "We'd slip her out there in a bunch of carved ducks and let her work a bunch of ducks in. Then if somebody come up, you had to kill her. That's what was bad."[10]

WOOD DECOYS

Pintails, redheads, and mallards were the most common wooden decoys carved in Texas, their quality ranging from elegant to offensive. Along the upper coast, decoys were usually made from cypress and sometimes tupelo. Cypress knees produced a heavy, durable decoy, and cypress roots a lightweight decoy. Freddie Abshier relates that, in the 1920s and '30s, "different [hunters] would hew 'em out of cypress knees and whatnot. They'd chop 'em out, whittle 'em out. Just anybody would make 'em that had a hacksaw or any kind of little old saw. They'd paint 'em themselves." On the middle and lower Texas coast, balsa and driftwood appear to have been the most common materials.[11]

Not many Texas decoys remain today. Some were swept from boathouses and sheds along the coast by hurricanes. Others were simply discarded or used as firewood, as were the Eagle Lake Rod and Gun Club's wooden decoys that, when plastic decoys became available, were tossed on the fire pit. The scarcity of locally carved decoys also stems from a lack of interest by collectors. William F. Mackey wrote that Gulf Coast decoy workmanship "does not compare with that of decoys [from the East Coast], which are generally recognized as collectible. Hundreds of the crude Gulf coast cypress duck decoys have been reviewed and found wanting." Hunting clubs often did not even look to Texas for their decoys, instead ordering them from prominent East Coast and midcontinent carvers and later from decoy factories. Texans who carved decoys often made only enough for their own use, and none are known to have reached a commercial volume that matched that of midcontinent or East Coast carvers.[12]

Like the decoys, the names of most of the Texas carvers have been lost to history. A little is known of upper coast carvers from the twentieth century. Nothing is known of middle coast carvers, only that Carlos Smith's Port Lavaca family had decoys that the men at the Saluria lifesaving station on Matagorda Island "carved between shipwrecks." Nearly all of the Smiths' wooden decoys were lost during hurricane Carla in 1961. Much more is known about the twentieth-century carvers from Coastal Bend and some about inland Texas carvers, but decoys made between Corpus Christi and Brownsville await discovery.[13]

The names of very few carvers from Jefferson County are readily available. One not lost to history is Port Arthur's Andy Vaughn, who made lightweight cypress decoys as early as the 1920s that he sold for sixty cents apiece. Becky Stutzenbaker remembers that Andy, a rugged and independent individual, built and painted pirogues in the middle of his living room, and "if you went to his place in a suit or carried a briefcase, he'd tell you to get off his property."[14]

On the Trinity River in Chambers County, Wallisville guide Morgan LaFour started carving decoys when live decoys were outlawed. For his own gunning rig he made cypress root decoys, but in duck blinds used by his day hunters he filled tow sacks with crude blocks made from cypress knees. Several generations of the Harmon family of duck hunting guides carved decoys from cypress knees, eventually accumulating so many that they filled a shed behind Homer Harmon's house in Old River.[15]

Joe Maley, of Cove, carved duck and even swan decoys. His grandson, Kendon L. Clark, says, "Grandpa Maley had two professions, cotton farming and carpentry. The latter, including furniture and coffins for local folks, was all done with hand tools, as he passed away three years before electricity came to Cove." Kendon's father, guide Manson Clark, carved cypress decoys, and Kendon says over the years he painted and repaired those decoys so many times that "I became 'personally familiar' with every one of them."[16]

Amos Tilton, from Old River, made elegant cypress and tupelo decoys, probably beginning in the 1940s. Most of his decoys were small, ranging from ten to fourteen inches long, and since Tilton didn't like to paint, he left many their

DECOYS AND DUCK CALLS

JACKIE CLARK *with Joe Maley's hand-carved swan decoys, mid-1930s. (Damon McKay Collection, courtesy Royce Strickland)*

natural wood color. Tilton whittled his decoys in the caretaker shack in back of the Champion Paper Company lodge from wood he collected along the Trinity River.[17]

East of Cedar Bayou on Trinity Bay, Johnnie Dutton learned how to carve from his father, Doris Daniel Dutton. Doris in the mid-1930s used live English mallard decoys, and when they were outlawed, he started carving. He turned cypress knees into fine working decoys with only a handsaw, hatchet, and pocketknife.[18]

Baytown, between the Trinity River delta and Houston, had a number of decoy carvers, the best known of whom was Rudolph "Rudy" J. LeCompte. Born in 1910, Rudy came to Texas from Bourg, Louisiana, in 1936. He got his carving start from Louisiana's Mark Whipple, and according to Rudy's son Gordon, Rudy first learned first how to paint because "Whipple could carve, but not paint so good."[19]

Rudy sold his first cypress root decoys in the late 1920s in Louisiana for a dollar each. When he moved to Texas, Gordon says, Rudy walked the cypress bottoms along the Trinity River, marking trees with roots suited for two or three decoys, returning later with a saw. All his body and head work was done "with a hatchet, Case knife, and a hand plane," bringing his birds to life with nothing more elaborate than house paint, a mixture of flat and enamel colors.[20]

Carver Walter Brewer explained to Baytown's Royce Strickland how Rudy made his counterfeit birds ride so well in the water. First he poured melted lead into a split bamboo mold then flattened the lead weight on each end to fit flush against the decoy base. Next, he secured the weight with rubber bands and floated the decoy in a washtub, moving the weight around until the decoy rode perfectly.

The ballast was secured with copper nails, and in the last step a brass or stainless steel eyelet was secured to the base for attaching the anchor line.[21]

Rudy first sold his decoys in Texas at Crystal Bay in the 1930s, and by the 1950s a Rudy LeCompte working decoy carried a four dollar price tag. Most years Rudy carved an average of eighty to one hundred decoys, a pace he maintained for nearly forty years. In his most prolific year, with carving friend H. B. "Bowie" Creekmore, the two produced sixteen dozen decoys that made them four hundred dollars. Rudy carved all big ducks until 1967, when he made his first blue-winged teal and mottled ducks for son Gordon to use at Brazoria County's Freeport Boating and Hunting Club.[22]

After his beloved wife, Cecile Hays, died in 1966, Rudy lost interest in making decoys, and he later quit painting birds when he lost sight in one eye. The LeCompte carving style was synonymous with Baytown decoys for many decades through the works of H. B. Creekmore, Walter Brewer, and Deer Park's Oliver Townsend. Rudy mentored them all.[23]

Other examples of upper coast decoys include the only known decoy from Colonel Moody's Lake Surprise hunting preserve, a lightweight pintail with a high back that is part of Joe Whitehead's collection. Joe and Shannon Tompkins both have identical mallards from Chambers County, wrapped in canvas and sealed with wax. Nothing is known about their origin. Sportsman Marshall Hayes still has a couple of balsa decoys carved by Houston's J. D. Grant, who made several hundred in the 1940s and '50s and painted them all one color with gray house paint. West of Houston, contemporary carvers J. L. Finley, Charles "Red" Meitzen, and George Garcia produced outstanding decoys that date back to the late 1960s.[24]

In the shed behind his Mills' Wharf fishing and hunting guiding business on Lamar Peninsula, J. Howard "Cap" Mills carved more than sixteen hundred decoys, his pintails filling club skiffs for thirty years starting in 1931. None of his decoys are known to exist today. Rockport guide Willie Close carved hundreds of balsa decoys in the 1930s and '40s. His blocks had a space carved into the bottom just large enough for a detachable head. Manager Dave "Bubba" Davis carved the last stool of wooden pintail decoys used by Rockport's Port Bay Club, with the first ones probably made in the 1950s and the last ones in the 1970s.[25]

Gordon Stanley has preserved some of Rockport's decoy heritage. His collection includes heartwood cypress decoys carved by a Mr. Maclin in the 1930s and George Ratisseau's pintails and redheads carved for Jolly Roger Hunting Club about the same time. Others include guide Les Sontag's layered decoys made from wooden shotgun shell boxes and Jim Frandolig's flat-bottomed balsa decoys from the 1950s. Frandolig drilled holes in the decoy base with a brace and bit, then poured lead in for weight. The dowel affixing the head to the body was extended below the base to attach the decoy line. According to Gordon, other area carvers included Guy Hanks and the Wright brothers.[26]

Some of the sixteen hundred working wooden duck decoys carved by Howard Mills. The goose silhouettes were cut from tin. (Courtesy Aransas County Historical Society)

In Port Aransas, John G. Mercer, chief of the US Life Saving Service, made lightweight pintails from beach driftwood before the turn of the century. The few that survive were given to writer and museum curator Rick Pratt by Eva Mercer.[27]

In the 1970s Ron Gard embarked on a mission to find and document Texas carved working decoys. He found decoys from two inland carvers, W. C. Wells and Dr. Thomas H. Nelson, that he says compare with those of the great decoy makers from the East Coast. Ron is one who would know—he is senior consulting specialist of Sotheby's American Folk Art Department and founder of the Texas Decoy Collectors Association. W. C. Wells was a Fort Worth carver who sold his laminated wood and cork decoys to hunters from the 1920s to the 1960s. To date, Ron has found mallards, bluebills, and pintails, although it is likely Wells made other species as well.[28]

Dr. Thomas H. Nelson grew up in New Orleans and started hunting in 1943 at age eleven. His father, whose working decoys earned a mention in Charles Frank's *Wetland Heritage: The Louisiana Duck Decoy,* was a worthy mentor to the boy, who carved his first bird the next year. In 1960 Tom moved to Dallas, where, between his profession as a doctor and duck hunting, he found time to produce hundreds of working decoys.

Tom's blocks cover the gamut from some with rounded or partly rounded bottoms to others that are flat-bottomed, the design depending on species and hunting conditions. Using mostly cypress root or tupelo gum, and sometimes cedar, he has made nearly every species of duck on the Central Flyway. Ron Gard says Tom's blending of paint colors reminds him of the technique of the Ward Brothers and Elmer Crowell, both famous East Coast decoy makers.

Tom has carved whole decoy stools, most of which he gave away to friends and family. Passionate about duck hunting, son Thomas Andrew Nelson attributes his father's prodigious volume of carving as his way of dealing with the months when he couldn't hunt ducks. Between seasons, Thomas says, "he carves. When he is finished, he carves more. When he runs low, he seeks tupelo gum or cypress root to carve again." That zeal extended to building other wooden objects to hunt with, including layout boats, more than fifty pirogues, and custom-built duck blinds that can be found in waters from Dallas to Caddo Lake.

Tom's boys, Thomas Andrew and David, grew up hunting over their father's decoys, a priceless experience tempered only by the reality, as Thomas puts it, of hauling "sixty pounds of splendid working floaters, a tiring ordeal when walking a long way in hip boots." They don't question, however, that the memories were worth every painful footstep.[29]

Examples of Texas-made goose decoys are rarer than duck decoys. The most common goose decoy in the early 1900s was the silhouette, as it was easy to make and transport. Smith Point's Ad "Buddy" Whitehead made his own Canada goose silhouettes in the 1940s, cutting them from tin and attaching them to stakes with lead nails. In the 1930s, Mills' Wharf had dozens of silhouette Canada goose decoys made from tin by J. Howard Mills, who later invented and patented a folding goose decoy.[30]

There were probably quite a few homemade floating goose decoys whose makers, like the decoys, are lost to history. One collection that remains is from upper coast carver Doris Daniel Dutton, who made twenty-five floating cypress goose decoys, including snows, specklebellies, and Canadas, between the late 1930s and early '50s. Ron Gard has a rare wood "flying" goose decoy with tin wings made by an unknown carver from Orange in the early 1900s.[31]

FACTORY DECOYS

Decoys made by labor-saving woodworking machinery were available after the Civil War. By the early 1900s some of the best known factory decoys were from the Mason and Dodge factories in Michigan, and by the 1920s a number of factories opened in Pascagoula, Mississippi. Texas can claim a small part of the wooden factory decoy business with sporting goods merchant Charles W. Grubbs. Born in 1847, Grubbs followed the supply of pop ash and tupelo gum down the Mississippi River from Chicago in 1918, establishing the first wooden decoy factory in Pascagoula. Grubbs frequently visited Texas, peddling his sporting wares to hunters on the Trinity River and in Galveston and Port Lavaca between 1907 and 1924.[32]

In 1928 Grubbs moved his Charles W. Grubbs Manufacturing Company to Gray Street in Houston, distributing his products nationally through the *C. W. Grubbs Catalog of Sporting Goods*. He sold half a dozen species of machine-lathed balsa decoys, duck calls, grass blinds, and grass duck-hunting suits and provided a decoy repair service. Grubbs, still "hale and hearty" owing "to his outdoor life," was eighty-one years old when the Port Aransas Club hired him to repair and repaint their thirty dozen decoys and organize duck calling classes for club guides. The last *C. W. Grubbs Catalog of Sporting Goods* featured a drawing on the cover from Cove. It was 1933, and Grubbs died that year.[33]

The weight and high maintenance of wooden decoys led to their demise as wood was increasingly replaced by synthetic materials developed during World War II. Chambers County's Freddie Abshier was glad to see wooden decoys disappear, remembering, "You couldn't carry very many because they were so bunglesome. You couldn't put but ten, twelve in a tow sack. But back then you didn't need no whole lot of decoys." The era of the plastic decoy was born with synthetic decoys that were lightweight and collapsible and that evolved into molded plastic and other synthetic compounds.[34]

Houston had two commercial decoy factories in the mid-1900s. Armstrong Featherweight Decoys Inc., started by Charles L. Armstrong and partner Constant A. Oliverus, manufactured lightweight decoys made from printed canvas cloth wrapped around a cork or kapok body with a wooden bill and glass eyes inserted in the head. Between 1938 and 1945 their line included bluebills, mallards, black ducks, redheads, pintails, and Canada and snow geese. The Armstrong Company sold tow sacks with the company logo and an ingenious canvas vest with layered pockets to carry their decoys. Constant Oliverus started the Oliverus Manufacturing Company in 1941 and for ten years carried a line of Duc-Em Zephyr pintail, mallard, and Canada goose decoys very similar to Armstrong's.[35]

THE TEXAS WHITE RAG SPREAD

The 1950s growth in commercial rice field hunting for geese and ducks brought a new decoy, the white rag spread, loosely defined as hundreds of pieces of anything white placed on the ground to resemble a flock of feeding snow geese. The white rag spread in Texas started with newspapers. In a 1928 article in the *Galveston Daily News,* Commissioner William J. Tucker of the Game, Fish, and Oyster Commission suggested that goose hunters try using scraps of newspaper with a wad of mud piled on top. A year later, J. C. Enright was featured in the *Port Arthur News* for his success killing ducks and geese over newspapers and magazine pages. Bob Brister remembered that one of his first articles as an outdoor writer for the *Houston Chronicle* was titled, "The Geese that Read the Chronicle," a reference to geese decoying to newspapers on the Katy Prairie.[36]

Baytown's Jim Nelson and William Read are credited with developing the earliest white rag spread made from cloth. Baytown's Prentice Holder says that Nelson and Read Moss were hunting over a shell decoy spread in the 1940s when flocks of snow geese, ignoring their conventional decoys, swirled into an adjacent field where discarded newspapers were blowing in the wind. It gave Nelson and

A Jimmy Reel *white spread on Eagle Lake Prairie, 1961. (Agnes Reel Strauss Collection)*

Read the idea of creating white cloth rag decoys that could also move with the wind. Jim Nelson made his first "all white" hunts between 1941 and 1943, creating enough of an impression that in 1953 he was featured in a *Life* magazine article titled "Ghostly Goose Hunters in Texas."[37]

Houston's Alex Wolff relates a similar version of the first white spreads in Texas. He says: "The story goes that some guy from New Orleans was hunting down here and reading the *Times Picayune* when the wind blew it all over the prairie. He noticed geese started coming in to the blowing papers. Soon everybody started using newspapers. That's the way I always heard it told." Alex saw his first rag spread in Chambers County at Jackson Ranch in the mid-1940s, and when he started leasing land from Jimmy Reel in Eagle Lake a few years later, he made his own white spreads. Wearing navy-issue white jumpers, he experimented with white pith helmets and bleach bottles and finally settled on rags bought from Houston rag man Sam Seagle. Alex remembered that Jimmy couldn't understand why they wanted to hunt snow geese but changed his mind when he saw how the many pintails decoyed to Alex's white spreads.[38]

The cloth rag spread rose from a local practice to an institution when it was embraced by Jimmy Reel and another acclaimed Colorado County guide, Marvin Tyler. Jimmy made his very first white spread from surplus dance hall posters, then newspapers and paper plates that, in a stiff wind, his hunters chased all over the fields. He next moved to cloth rags with a spread of two hundred diapers bought from Houston's Neiman-Marcus department store. By the late 1950s Jimmy adorned his clients in surplus US Army ski uniforms. At that time the white spread was still rare enough, according to Bob Brister, that cars passing along the road slowed down, staring in dismay at grown men "in white coveralls in the middle of a bald prairie."[39]

Marvin Tyler first used white objects that moved in the wind in 1951. They were famously remembered as consisting of napkins and tablecloths from his

Altair restaurant. Sitting at a dining table in Marvin's Blue Goose Hunting Club, Bob Brister first met Marvin when Marvin walked up to his table and snatched the white tablecloth out from under him. A startled Brister nearly slugged the intruder. The next morning Bob hunted over every "dirty napkin, tablecloth, washrag, and dirty towel from Marvin's steakhouse."[40]

Marvin's son Clifton Tyler says a friend of his father's, Joe McKenzie, first "suggested using those tabletops from the restaurant when they were fun hunting." Clifton remembers that the restaurant linen that doubled as decoys was the property of Houston's Martin Linen Company, and their delivery men "complained about all the rice straw, so he had to start cleaning the linen before they'd pick it up." Marvin eventually put in a laundry, where "we had four washers and a dryer, and during hunting season we ran them twenty-four hours a day." Marvin's first rag spreads were small, no more than fifty cloth decoys, and over time grew to three hundred, then to a thousand.[41]

Cloth rag spreads by the late 1950s became the standard for Texas rice field goose hunting. Guides left them in piles in the field, and according to Clifton, "we left the rag spreads out and took the hunters out to 'em. At the Vineyard [in Eagle Lake] we had five spreads that we left out. We went out in the morning and just fluffed 'em." Doug Pike worked for Lyle Jordan, the man responsible for bringing the Texas white spread to Katy Prairie, and remembers that when they located the piles of rags in the dark, he always approached downwind "to make sure there wasn't a skunk sleeping in there."[42]

It was hard work to place hundreds of pieces of linen over rice stubble, but when the fields were wet, the weight of a load of muddy, wet cloth decoys could be unbearable. In 1973 one of Marvin Tyler's guides came up with the idea of replacing white cloth rags with lightweight, inexpensive DuPont plastic banquet cloth cut into three-foot squares. While these lightweight rags were preferred by Marvin's guides, Marvin hated the shiny plastic and preferred that his guides use nothing other than cloth.[43]

In the early 1970s the commercial wind sock decoy was introduced. The patent for tying pieces of white plastic to a stake belongs to Katy's Chuck Barry. Chuck is quick to credit, as well, guide Bobby Hale, "who figured out how to make it better." While various types of wind socks had been used for many years, it was Barry who mass-produced a decoy that imitated a feeding goose yet was light enough that guides could carry hundreds at a time. Wind socks quickly became the product of choice for most goose hunters. Chuck was working for Marvin Tyler when he started Texas Hunting Products to distribute his Texas wind sock decoys, and he shared many of his ideas with Marvin. Chuck says, "I showed him one of my decoy bags that was thirty inches by forty inches, but Marvin said, 'It's too small.' Almost as a joke, I showed him one that could haul a thousand rags. He said, 'It's perfect.'"[44]

THE TEXAS *white cloth spread became big enough business for manufacturers to advertise diapers as decoys* (Houston Chronicle, Oct. 22, 1967).

WHITE OUTFITS *used in snow goose spread hunting at Hebert Ranch, Jefferson County, in the 1950s are worn by Prentice Holder (left) and Asa Moss. (Prentice Holder Collection, courtesy Royce Strickland*

DUCK AND GOOSE CALLS

For years many Texas hunters made their own duck calls. Port Arthur's Charles "Smitty" Smith, who learned to call ducks by listening to his flock of live decoys, made his first call from a piece of cane and a brass shotgun shell. For the reed, he hammered the brass into a long sliver and plugged it with a piece of cork. Billy LeBlanc used cane for his first duck call, carving and sanding the reed from a plastic comb. He won first place in several calling contests in the early 1940s, and seventy years later that call still sounds very much like a mallard duck. Chambers County guide Ralph "Sonny" Baughman whittled calls from sea cane, practicing with mallards he raised in his backyard. George Marion Harrell, manager of Rockport's Port Bay Club in the 1940s, made pintail whistles from hollowed sweet bay trunks with the reed made from a sweet bay leaf.[45]

As early as the 1860s hunters who did not make their calls could order them. F. A. Allen made calls after 1863, Charles W. Grubbs in 1868, and Petersen and Charles Ditto calls were available by 1870. The most popular calls across the upper and middle coast appear to be those made by Grubbs, who personally delivered them to Texas hunters as early as 1907. Grubbs hunted the Trinity River delta in the 1920s with Lindsey Dunn Sr., who had two of his calls made from cedar and birch with German silver reeds. Popular later manufactured duck calls were Olt, Perdew, Cajun Calls, and Faulk.[46]

No one knows who made the first commercial duck call in Texas. It might have been Eagle Lake's A. L. Townley, who marketed a mallard call in 1905. Townley crafted his calls at his Eagle Lake machine shop, where at the turn of the twentieth century he built cypress cisterns and offered blacksmith and horseshoeing services. Eagle Lake's Davis R. Waddell has one of his calls and says Townley "would go to Houston and would walk up and down the streets blowing the calls, and he would sell 'em." In the 1920s Townley sent samples to the *Galveston News,* and the newspaper informed its readers that they had been "tested by local hunters, who declare them to be as fine as any they ever heard." Made from cedar with a reed described as "a silver tongue," the calls cost two dollars and could be ordered by writing "Mr. Townley at Eagle Lake." In 1933 Townley's vocation had cost him half of his fingers on both of his hands, but, undaunted, he said he "still got enough fingers left to bait a hook."[47]

Houston had two commercial duck call manufacturers before World War II: Armstrong Featherweight Decoys Inc. between 1938 and 1945, and the Oliverus Manufacturing Company from 1941 to 1951. Armstrong carried a single line of plastic duck calls, while Constant A. Oliverus carried several designs under the brand name Duc-Em that were marketed by L. L. Bean, Montgomery Ward, and Sears.[48]

By the second half of the twentieth century there were a number of duck call manufacturers in Texas. Many were only available locally, but some, such as

> **Announcement—**
>
> C. W. Grubbs, inventor of the Duck Call, wishes to meet all sportsmen, especially the duck hunters. He will be at Lyons Hardware Co.'s store on Jan. 7 and 8 and will give free instructions on calling and hunting ducks each day.
>
> ## Lyons Hardware Co.
> 2219 Postoffice St.   Phone 132

(Modified from *Galveston Daily News,* Jan. 6, 1924)

COWBOY FERNANDEZ (right) *of Yentzen and Sure Shot game calls at Port Arthur Hunting Club with Bobby LeBlanc* (middle) *and Dick Connerly* (left). *(Courtesy Bobby LeBlanc)*

Johnny Stewart Game Calls in Waco and George Yentzen and Cowboy Fernandez in Jefferson County, grew into notable commercial ventures.

George Yentzen in the 1940s was well known in Jefferson County, but his fame was not from duck calls but from his Nederland Bakery, the largest in the county. Yentzen produced ten thousand loaves of bread a day, delivered by his fleet of trucks to Port Arthur, Port Neches, and Beaumont. Yentzen the baker cut his first black walnut duck call on a band saw on his back porch in Nederland in the early 1950s and with his young assistant James "Cowboy" Fernandez designed and patented the first double-reed duck call, with its reeds joined together by rivets. Yentzen's double- and triple-reed calls dominated the local and national market for the next twenty years.[49]

DECOYS AND DUCK CALLS

Yentzen's protégé, Cowboy Fernandez, was born to parents from Spain who settled first in Georgia and then in Texas. In 1930 the first of the family born in Texas was given the nickname "Cowboy" in honor of their adopted state. After George Yentzen died in 1957, Cowboy took over his business, navigating the explosion in popularity of Yentzen duck calls, and its successor company, Sure Shot Game Calls. Cowboy remembers, "In the first year, I made 55 calls and sold all 55 of them. The next year I made 555. [From] January 20th to December the 4th, it took me all that time in the garage, one [call] at a time. I sold all 555."

Cowboy entered calling contests across the Gulf Coast and in 1959 won the Gulf Coast championship in Port Arthur, followed by the Texas Open, the World Duck Calling Championship in Stuttgart, and the International Duck Calling Contest held in Crowley, Louisiana. He says,

> When I won the World, I got a call from a company called A. T. Lloyd and another company called Bush Caldwell, out of Little Rock, Arkansas. They asked me if I would come over and demonstrate the calls to them. I drove up there, all day long, to Little Rock. There was an old man sittin' on the front row that was a salesman for the Bush Caldwell Company, and he asked me if that thing would blow "wet" like I say it will. So I went and filled that call up with cold water, and I took it and I poured it out. "Cack, cack, cack, cack, cack." Well, that ol' man said, "I believe I can sell a hundred of them, in fact, a bunch of 'em."

It was Cowboy's third year in business, and the man in the front row ordered one thousand calls.[50]

The Arkansas order put the duck call maker from Groves over the threshold: "I needed an order for 1,084 calls, 'cause that's what it was going to take me to get a mold made, just like you see it today." To pay for it, he took out a bank loan for fifteen hundred dollars, putting up for collateral a 1955 Dodge, golf clubs, shotguns, a boat, a motor, and a trailer. His wife was ready to kill him.[51]

Cowboy marketed the calls himself. He remembers when he traveled to Houston to convince Ansell Oshman to carry his calls at Oshman's Sporting Goods: "I talked to the salesman that was on the sales floor. 'What will it take to get Mr. Oshman to buy my calls?' He said, 'Well, it's a no to start with. But if you make him smile, he'll buy just a few, but if you can make him laugh, he'll buy a whole bunch of your stuff.'" Cowboy pulled his trousers up over his belly, waltzed into his office doing his best Red Skelton imitation, and introduced his product. "He laughed and said, 'Come in here, I'm gonna buy everything you got.' That's the gospel truth. And he bought calls from me until he died."[52]

Cowboy's Yentzen calls in the 1960s did not just compete in the market, they conquered it. Charles Stepan of Port Arthur won the World Championship in

1960 with a Yentzen call. Billie Domingue held a five-year winning streak in the women's division of the World Contest with her Yentzen. Yentzen calls were used to imitate mallard ducks by twenty-eight out of forty-two contestants in the Oklahoma State Duck Calling Contest in 1966, and four out of five of the top winners were blowing Yentzens.[53]

Cowboy Fernandez developed several famous calls over the years and traveled the country to give calling seminars for Ducks Unlimited. One of his favorite memories is the time he put on a class in Minnesota, where six hundred kids attended the first day and another six hundred the next day. Every one of them was blowing a Yentzen Sure Shot duck call.[54]

Unlike most duck callers, many of the guides who called geese learned to imitate their sounds by mouth, a skill honed by listening to the birds every day while they fished and trapped the marsh. Sabine Pass guide O. D. LaBove learned his craft by calling to birds while he was skinning muskrats. O. D was like many who reached a level of proficiency rarely replicated by commercial calls, and it was said that he could mouth call geese in so low "you could catch them with a net."[55]

Collector Gary Chambers of Baytown says Charles Grubbs manufactured a combination duck and goose call at his Houston store in 1933, but it wasn't until the early 1960s that commercial volumes of goose calls were made in Texas by Dwight Thomas in Fort Worth and Jack Ray of East Texas. Katy Prairie guide Lyle Jordan says Texas hunters used Louisiana native Dudley "Dud" Faulk's calls, the first that could "break," imitating the yodel of the specklebelly goose. Lyle remembers the first speck call he saw made in Texas was the product of federal game warden Frank Clarkson, who in 1960 made the reed from a rubber baby doll. Altair's Marvin Tyler used a Lohman brand call in the 1950s and sold so many from his sport shop at his Blue Goose Hunting Club headquarters that Lohman started manufacturing the Marvin Tyler Model XXXX.[56]

CALLING COMPETITIONS

Duck and goose calling competitions are hugely popular in Texas and throughout the country. The first waterfowl calling contest held in Texas may have been at the National Democratic Convention in Houston in 1928. It was the idea of Charles Grubbs, who challenged the 1924 national title holder to a grand championship duck calling contest on the floor of the Houston convention center. It is not known whether Al Smith, Herbert Hoover's opponent for the presidency in the year before the Great Depression, actually shared the floor with Grubbs and his mallards duck call.[57]

It was another twenty years before calling contests were regularly held in the state. The first, in 1947, was sponsored by the Houston chapter of Conservation of Texas Fish and Game, Inc. (COTFAG). One of the main movers behind the contest was *Houston Press* writer Andy Anderson, who helped raise one thousand dollars of prize money. Between 1947 and 1949 COTFAG events were held at the San Jacinto High School auditorium in Houston, and all three years the contest was won by Baytown's Rudy LeCompte. In 1950 the contest was moved to the Floyd Breedlove VFW Post in Katy and dubbed the VFW-COTFAG Hunters Party and State Championship Duck Calling Contest.[58]

In the contest's formative years, Texas towns jockeyed for the popular event. The Houston COTFAG chapter wrested the state championship contest away from Katy in 1951. Beaumont's George T. Camp raised the ante in 1953, moving the contest to Jefferson County with an endorsement from Texas governor Allan Shivers, who "officially blessed the Beaumont deal as a bona-fide Texas duck calling proposition." With Beaumont's hold on the 1955 contest questionable, Governor Shivers again stepped in, deeming the Beaumont contest the only officially designated Texas contest. Duck and goose calling competitions—local, regional, and state—soon spread throughout Texas.[59]

There are good duck callers in Texas. But maybe because of the once big numbers of mallards and mottled ducks along the upper coast, callers from that region hold most of the titles. Cowboy Fernandez once said that Jefferson County boasted some of the best callers in the country, and he swore that when he put a mallard duck in a local competition one year, it finished seventh.[60]

Typical Texas primitive style of decoy, this one by an unknown carver from Wallisville and the Old River area, late 1940s. (Royce A. Strickland Collection, photo by Royce Strickland)

Front: *Port Arthur–area working green-winged teal decoy carved by Andy Vaughn.* Rear: *The pintail drake and mallard hen were made by Charles Stutzenbaker. (Charles Stutzenbaker Collection, photo by R. K. Sawyer)*

Trinity River delta bluebill decoy, 1920s. The words on the bottom read, "Blue bill drake—Made by an Indian—La Fleur on Lake Charlotte—used at Clark's Duck club at Cotten Lake, Texas, ca. 1920." (Ron Gard Collection, photo by Todd Steele)

Amos Tilton cypress mallard decoys, Trinity River delta. (D. A. Tilton Collection, photo by Royce Strickland)

Working decoys carved by Baytown's Rudy LeCompte. (Mike Leebron Collection, photo by R. K. Sawyer)

Examples of working teal decoys from Baytown's Rudy LeCompte. (Mike Leebron Collection, photo by R. K. Sawyer)

Hen mallard carved by H. B. Creekmore, Baytown. (Prentice Holder Collection, photo by Royce Strickland)

Mottled duck decoy carved by Walter Brewer of Baytown. (Royce A. Strickland Collection, photo by Shannon Tompkins)

Deer Park's Oliver Townsend carved these pintails. (Royce A. Strickland Collection, photo by Shannon Tompkins)

Nothing is known about the origin of this matched pair of Chambers County mallards, wrapped with canvas and sealed with wax. Note the replacement head on the hen. Market hunter Addison Whitehead's brass 10-gauge shell is to the left for scale. (Joe Whitehead and Shannon Tompkins Collections, photo by R. K. Sawyer)

Contemporary carver Red Meitzen's mottled duck and wigeon decoys. (Rick Pratt Collection, photo by R. K. Sawyer)

Working wooden decoys from Rockport's Port Bay Club, a combination of Pascagoula style and ones made by club manager Bubba Davis. (Port Bay Club Collection, photo by R. K. Sawyer)

Front: *Rockport Maclin pintail decoy carved from heartwood cypress, 1930s.* Rear: *Mason-style canvasback decoy with a replacement head. (Gordon Stanley Collection, photo by R. K. Sawyer)*

Les Sontag pintail decoy, Rockport. Sontag carved decoys from 1930 to 1960 using the ends of wooden gun shell crates; the layers of wood are visible along the front. He used copper screen tacks for eyes. (Gordon Stanley Collection, photo by R. K. Sawyer)

Jim Frandolig's balsa pintails, Rockport, 1950s. Lead was poured into three holes drilled in the base with brace and bit. (Gordon Stanley Collection, photo by R. K. Sawyer)

These lightweight pintails were carved from beach driftwood by John G. Mercer, chief of the US Life Saving Service, before the turn of the century. (Rick Pratt Collection, photo by R. K. Sawyer)

W. C. Wells pintail decoys, 1929. (Ron Gard Collection, photo by Todd Steele)

Dr. Thomas H. Nelson wood duck decoy, 1976. (David Nelson Collection)

Dr. Thomas H. Nelson ringneck duck decoy, 1976. (David Nelson Collection)

Smith Point's Ad "Buddy" Whitehead made his Canada goose silhouettes in the 1940s from tin, with the stakes attached by nails. (Joe Whitehead Collection, photo by R. K. Sawyer)

Canada, specklebelly, and snow goose decoys carved from cypress knees by Baytown's Doris Daniel Dutton during the late 1930s to early 1950s. (Johnnie Dutton Collection, photo by R. K. Sawyer)

Flying snow goose decoy from an unknown Orange carver, early 1900s. (Ron Gard Collection, photo by Ron Gard)

Factory-made mallard decoys from Charles W. Grubbs Manufacturing Company, Houston, lathed between 1928 and 1933. (Chester H. and Beth Barker Collection, Blue Goose Antiques, photo by R. K. Sawyer)

Mallard decoys made by Armstrong Featherweight Decoys of Houston in the period 1938 to 1945. The stitching across the top characterizes Armstrong decoys from those of his partner and later competitor, C. A. Oliverus. (Ron Gard Collection, photo by Todd Steele)

A Townley duck call, made in Eagle Lake from 1905 until about 1930. (Davis Waddell Collection, photo by R. K. Sawyer)

Houston's Constant A. Oliverus made these duck calls during the 1941–50 period. The original Oliverus-brand Duc-Em call is on the left; the others were marketed under different names. (Chester H. and Beth Barker Collection, Blue Goose Antiques, photo by R. K. Sawyer)

CHAPTER 3

HUNTING LAWS: RULES of the GAME

DECLINES IN ALL GAME SPECIES, NOT JUST WATERFOWL, BROUGHT conservation to the national conscience in the late 1800s. The market hunter was widely blamed for the declines, although that is an oversimplification. The first laws, penned by an unlikely coalition between newly emerging conservation groups and sport hunters, were aimed at his livelihood. In Texas, the main players were members of the Texas Audubon Society, sportsmen's clubs, and local Game Protective Associations.

Passage of the Permanent Game Law and Game Warden Act by the Texas legislature in 1907 provided for enforcement new state hunting regulations by the Texas Game, Fish, and Oyster Commission (GFOC). With roots that went back to 1879 as the Fish and Oyster Commission, the agency was the forerunner of today's Texas Parks and Wildlife Department (TPWD). As the sun set on commercial hunting between 1903 and 1918, laws enforced by the GFOC and later TPWD began to shift from market hunting and entirely towards recreational hunting.[1]

Game laws were hardly popular, and as state and federal restrictions proliferated, a Corpus Christi writer spoke for many when he complained that to comply, "a man is going to have to be an expert ornithologist, an awful good shot and something of a mathematician and memory specialist, too." Particularly complicated was the period from 1918 until 1939, when Texas hunters were regulated by both state and federal laws, which were not always the same.[2]

One of the earliest state laws aimed at sportsmen was the "Sunday law," which made it illegal to hunt on the Sabbath within half a mile of any church, school, or private residence. In 1903 warrants were served on a dozen hunters at Rock Island on the West Fork of the Trinity River when local citizens complained that the countryside was overrun with Sabbath breakers. In Galveston, authorities in

1908 warned that the law was to be strictly enforced, as gunfire surrounding the city on Sunday mornings had reached unbearable proportions.[3]

Hunting licenses were mandated in 1909 but at first were not required in the county in which the hunter lived or in any adjoining counties. Five thousand "non-resident county" hunting licenses were printed the first year. Rules on the back stated that the bearer "may kill, in all seasons of the year, ducks, geese, robins, wild pigeons, jack snipe, curlew, Mexican pheasant, with a bag limit of 25 in any one day." The license did not restrict hunting at night but prohibited use of a lantern.[4]

The federal goverment legislated the first waterfowl hunting season in 1913, and its intent was mainly to curtail spring shooting. Called the Weeks-McLean Law, and later renamed the Federal Migratory Bird Act, the law was challenged the next year as a violation of states' rights. To complicate matters, game wardens in Texas, a state with no hunting season, did not have the authority to enforce federal laws, and when the law first passed, there were no federal wardens in Texas. Many hunters considered the new rules an inconvenience and ignored them.[5]

The Texas legislature got into the hunting season business in the 1920s, with split seasons and bag limits set by hunting zones within the framework of the Migratory Bird Treaty Act of 1918. Texas hunting zones were divided along lines that followed the track of the International Great Northern Railroad between Laredo and Texarkana. By 1927 sportsmen had to know their railroads, as legal hunting zones were delineated by six different railways and one river between Del Rio and Nacogdoches. It took a long time for the hunting season message to reach hunters in some parts of Texas. When an Alvin duck hunter was arrested in 1937 for shooting 325 ducks, he had never heard of a hunting season.[6]

Early game laws dealt with technologies of the time, and few foresaw the role gasoline engines would occupy in killing game. The Permanent Wild Life Protection Fund lobbied to outlaw hunting from an automobile in 1916. Two years later the federal government made it illegal to shoot wildfowl from a motorized boat. The state, however, did not pass the law, so only federal game wardens had the authority make arrests. In 1910, the "possibility of utilizing the aeroplane in duck shooting was demonstrated by experiments" in Southern California, and by 1918, aerial bird shooting was a popular sport in Texas. State lawmakers outlawed the killing of migratory birds from the air in 1921.[7]

The earliest law restricting the number of migratory birds that could be killed was passed in 1907, setting the daily bag limit at twenty-five, with a possession limit of seventy-five. The law was not mandated by the federal government but by the state, and its passage was a result of the decades-long battle waged in the "war on the market hunter."[8]

Declining wildlife resources were the issue when the Federal Migratory Bird Act of 1913 made it illegal to kill whooping cranes, sandhill cranes, swans, curlews, and most species of shorebirds. All other species of migratory birds could still be hunted in Texas as long as the amount did not exceed twenty-five a day. The twenty-

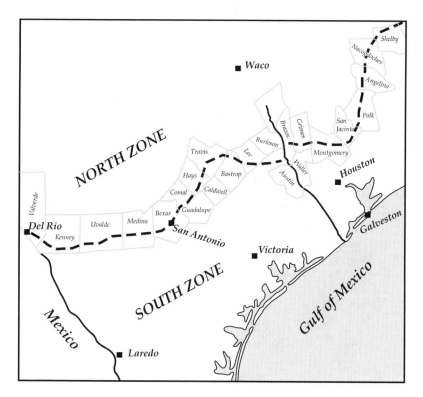

DIVISION OF *the first Texas hunting zones, north and south, mandated by the state Game, Fish, and Oyster Commission in 1927. (Modified from* Dallas Morning News, *Sept. 4, 1927)*

five-bird limit was challenged in 1925 when Texas legislator Dr. A. R. Shearer of Mont Belvieu proposed a bag limit of fifteen ducks. Shearer was outraged to learn that more than one thousand wild ducks were shot in his native Chambers County each day over forty consecutive days. Those forty thousand birds, he said, were "slaughtered in the name of sport" by scores of men "coming down from Houston and taking back 75 ducks a day for each man in each automobile."[9]

It took a great cloud of dust—the Dust Bowl—to realize Shearer's goal of a reduced bag limit. The drought that started in 1930 decimated nesting areas of the mid-continent and Canada, and the federal government's response to rapidly declining waterfowl populations was immediate. The daily bag limit was reduced to fifteen in 1930, and the limit on geese dropped from eight to four. More years of drought and more dust followed. By 1934, for the first time, the number of waterfowl shooting days was restricted to only three days a week. The season was shortened to two months, with another reduction in the bag limit to twelve ducks a day.[10]

The following year there was a debate on whether to close the 1935–36 hunting season. A thirty-day season was eventually approved, with the bag limit on ducks again reduced, this time to ten. There was, however, no open season on wood ducks, buffleheads, Ross's geese, or swans, canvasbacks, and redheads. That year was also the first in which certain species of ducks, with the exception of the wood duck, had been protected on the Central Flyway.[11]

CHARLES STUTZENBAKER *of the Texas Parks and Wildlife Department holding mallards, pintails, and blue geese from some of the estimated two thousand birds that died of lead poisoning in Jefferson County marshes during the 1960s. (Courtesy Charles Stutzenbaker)*

The Dust Bowl of the 1930s brought dramatic regulations, and they were not well greeted by a large part of Texas sporting society. But there was more to come. In 1936 the use of any form of bait to attract waterfowl was prohibited, and restrictions were placed on sink boxes and sneak boats. Live duck and goose decoys were banned, and a three-shell limit was placed on the magazine capacity of repeating shotguns. No gun larger than a 10-gauge was allowed, and waterfowl could only be shot from 7:00 a.m. to 4:00 p.m. All across Texas sportsmen put their guns away, for good.[12]

In 1941 the US Fish and Wildlife Service, in a step back in technological time, outlawed shooting ducks and geese from behind trained oxen. One of the first arrests was in 1946, when federal warden Frank Clarkson ticketed farmer Leo de Bellvieu, west of Winnie, for "using a sort of trained horse to approach a concentration of snow geese and kill seven of them, three more than the bag limit."[13]

Compared to the 1930s, the 1950s to 1970s were relatively quiet legislative times. Hunting seasons and bird limits waxed and waned, but only a few laws, such as restrictions on taking redheads and canvasbacks during the 1960s, were

DAVID LOBPRIES (right), *shot the first duck in Texas with steel shot—a drake pintail—on an experimental hunt with TPWD's Charles Stutzenbaker (left) at Murphree Wildlife Management Area, Port Arthur, during the 1979–80 season. (Courtesy Charles Stutzenbaker)*

controversial. That changed in the late 1970s when the state considered a ban on the use of lead shot, which was to be phased out over a several-year period. Lead had been the preferred shot from the inception of the scattergun, but it came with consequences: waterfowl that ingested lead pellets died from lead poisoning.

The effects of lead poisoning were known as early as the 1890s, when market hunters poured so much shot into Chambers County's waterways that the Galveston city inspector "condemned as unfit for food a lot of ducks offered for sale by a hunter from the vicinity of [Stephenson's] Lake." Speculation was that "at the time they departed this life they were either victims of lead-poisoning or were suffering from its effects." San Antonio conservationist and sportsman Oscar Guessaz remarked, "Assuredly; a great many ducks are found daily on that lake stone dead, and without shot marks, and if one takes the trouble of investigating further it will be found that the gizzards of the birds are filled with shot, which they have picked up on the bottom of the lake while feeding." *Forest and Stream* published an article on lead poisoning at Stephenson Lake and Lake Surprise in 1894, calling it "self-poisoning of ducks," noting that in addition to lead shot, some gizzards contained old percussion caps.[14]

Seventy years later, TPWD's Charles "Stutz" Stutzenbaker, walking the marshes of Jefferson County in late winter, came upon large numbers of dead and flightless birds. His supervisor, Bob Singleton, suspected lead poisoning. He was right—analysis of their gizzard contents showed they had ingested varying numbers of highly toxic lead pellets. Biologists across North America documented other bird die-offs from lead poisoning during that time, including significant losses of Canada geese on Lake Puckaway in Wisconsin and mallards in South Dakota.[15]

An appeal for a substitute nontoxic shotgun pellet was slowly voiced. Laws mandating the use of nontoxic shot followed, and they were unpopular with many. Ammunition companies were reluctant to embrace nontoxic shot because of the perceived increased manufacturing costs. In 1981, when nontoxic shot was required in Texas from Orange to Freeport, a Brazoria County hunting club filed a lawsuit against the state. They lost. Today lead shot has been banned for waterfowl hunting throughout the United States.[16]

PART TWO

COASTAL TEXAS HUNTING CLUBS, GUIDES, and PLACES

CHAPTER 4

SABINE ESTUARY

In the early 1800s settlers found the Sabine and Neches Rivers a "dense solitude of unbroken timber" and Sabine Lake an untouched estuary. To the south, fresh and saline waters collided at Sabine Pass, blocked to deep-draft ships by a huge oyster reef. Adjacent marshes and sloughs were rimmed by ancient beach terraces, called cheniers, their sands originating in the Appalachian and Ouachita Mountains, carried to the coast by rivers, and shaped by alongshore currents. Coastal wetlands paralleled the Gulf of Mexico west for nearly thirty miles into what later became Chambers County, its landscape a maze of river channels, oxbow river meanders, distributary channels, and coastal potholes. The freshwater upper marsh was marked by cordgrass, saltgrass, bulrush, spikerush, millet, and *Phragmites* (reed), and the more saline lower marsh by three-square grasses, saltgrass, saltmeadow cordgrass, and marsh cordgrass.[1]

From the river bottoms to the coast, flocks of waterfowl at times covered the horizon. The great flocks were sustenance to the early settlements of Jefferson and Orange Counties, and by the late 1800s, were a source of income to market hunters and to those who guided wealthy sportsmen.

Sabine Lake in the 1870s and '80s was a hard destination for visiting sportsmen to reach. They first traveled by train to Houston, switched carriers to the Southern Pacific as far as Beaumont, then journeyed by sailboat to the edge of the lake, where they waded ashore in a cloud of mosquitoes. The trip was easier after Arthur Stilwell's Kansas City Southern Railway connected the fledgling town of Port Arthur with the US interior in 1897. The new railroad brought large numbers of sportsmen to Sabine Lake and the southeast Texas coast.[2]

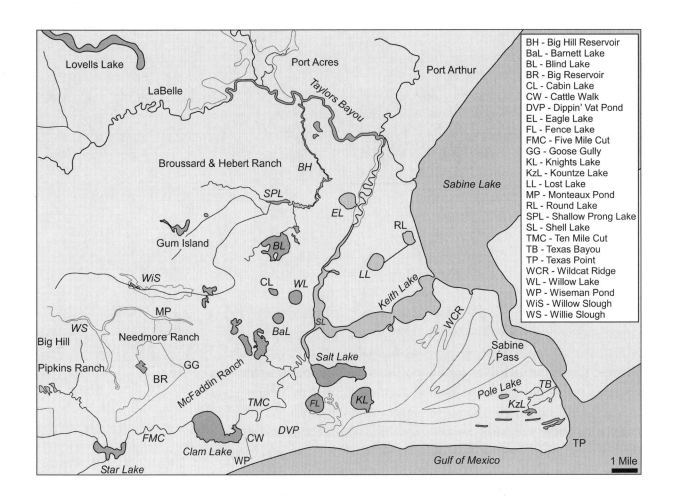

SABINE ESTUARY *and surrounding lands as they looked before the Intracoastal Canal and ship channels to Beaumont and Port Arthur.*

Sport hunters embarked from sloops, steamers, and naphtha launches that lined the wharves in Orange, Port Arthur, and Sabine. They hired captains and guides such as George Pastre, who took hunters to Taylor Bayou and Clam Lake on his launch *Jennie,* and Beaumont's G. M. Oliver, "one of the oldest citizens of the county, [who] is known at every farm house for his expert shooting and jovial disposition." Popular sporting vessels in Orange were the steamer *Nellie* and the elegant *Robert E. Lee.* One Kansas City party returned from an 1893 hunt on the *Robert E. Lee,* declaring, "brant [snow geese] and ducks had never been seen in the area in such numbers, and were thick on ponds, on the burns, and wherever acorns are to be found."[3]

One of the greatest challenges posed to sportsmen was returning home safely after the chase. The winter storm of 1892, for example, left a litter of sailing vessels and hunters strewn across Sabine Lake. One was an Orange hunting party that spent several days beached aboard the pilot boat *Star of the East,* passing their time shooting ducks and snipes. H. J. Lutcher was left stranded in the marsh when high seas forced his hired sloop to return to port. He was eventually retrieved by the steamer *Fannie,* found in good health with 250 ducks and an uncountable number of snipes.[4]

COASTAL TEXAS HUNTING CLUBS, GUIDES, AND PLACES

In 1896, Orange duck hunters crossing Sabine Lake at night on the sloop *Wild Duck* faced gale force winds, and with waves sweeping over the boat, they bailed all night to keep the vessel afloat. The next morning a mistake in navigation put them into the mouth of Bessie Marsh, where, with no food or water, they remained for several days. After limping back to harbor, the party confessed they never shot a duck. Land could sometimes be as challenging as water. Beaumont hunters in 1884 lost their bearings in high sea cane along the edge of Sabine Lake and wandered all day and into the black of night. With no moon to guide them, they drove their wagon into a slough. Wet and covered in mud, they abandoned their mule and the day's ducks and walked all night back to Beaumont.[5]

MORE THAN JUST SPORT

Despite the potential for calamities, recreational waterfowl hunting grew in popularity and became a critical part of advertising schemes used to attract investors to the upper coast. In an effort to advance his new town of Port Arthur, Arthur E. Stillwell built the plush, forty-three-room Windsor Hotel at Sabine Pass to accommodate hunting and fishing parties. Sporting solicitor C. W. Barker was hired to arrange hunting parties, always on the ready with a "supply decoys and waders free of charge and [to] chaperone parties who are here for a good time." One of his Kansas City parties was dropped off by horse and wagon along a continuous line six miles long, and they described Sabine Pass skies as "absolutely clouded" with ducks and their guns "hot from the incessant firing."[6]

According to historian Bill Quick, duck and goose hunting was also used by the Kountze brothers to promote their new town of Sabine in the early 1900s. Waterfowl were so abundant near town that when the first carbide arc lights illuminated the night sky at the Union Sulphur Company docks in 1905, hunters shot ducks all night long from the swarms attracted to their beams.[7]

Legend has it that Port Arthur grew from one house to a modern city as a result of a duck hunt, when John Warne Gates killed nine hundred ducks in a morning as a guest of Arthur Stilwell in 1899. Gates, the story goes, was so impressed with the hunting that he decided to stay, building on Sabine's Lakeshore Drive a magnificent two-story colonial mansion that he referred to as his hunting lodge.[8]

The colorful Gates, who grew wealthy as his brand of barbed wire stretched across the Texas range, had the same passion for duck hunting that he did for business. At his Gates Club southwest of Sabine Lake he created an artificial impoundment almost half a mile long named Round Lake and built the three-story Big Cypress Lodge on its banks. Each fall Gates traveled down the Mississippi River from Chicago aboard the *Roxana,* an elegantly fitted one-hundred-foot steam-powered yacht with a crew of maids, valets, chefs, and stewards. Gates met guests in New Orleans before boarding his private rail car bound for Port

The Windsor Hotel

SABINE PASS, TEXAS

Rates $2.00 and $2.50 per Day—New and Modern

Finest house in Southeast Texas. Situated on Sabine Pass, overlooking the Gulf. Sportsman's Paradise for Water Fowl and Feathered Game. Elegant Fishing. Correspondence solicited.

JAMES FURLONG, Manager.   I. E. OSBORN, Chief Clerk.

(Modified from *Houston Daily Post*, Nov. 18, 1897)

A PROMOTIONAL *postcard featuring Beaumont's J. M. Beaty with the results of a few hours of duck hunting near Port Arthur, early 1900s. Identifiable are mallards, teal, shorebirds, and a specklebelly goose. (Courtesy Port Arthur Public Library, File No. 3071-A)*

Arthur. He built a spur road off the main Kansas City Southern line that led to the clubhouse, where family and friends stepped directly from their rail car into the comfort of the lodge.[9]

Jim Sutherlin, area manager for the J. D. Murphree Wildlife Management Area (WMA), which now encompasses Lost Lake Preserve, says Gates had a canal dug for rowboat access between Round Lake and his Lost Lake shooting ground. Canvasback shoots at Lost Lake were probably equaled only by those at

Lake Surprise in Chambers County. Big flocks of diving ducks were attracted to 267 acres of sago pondweed and banana water lily that Gates supplemented with plantings of wild celery, rice, and other crops.[10]

Gates courted investors, businessmen, and politicians from throughout the United States at Lost Lake Preserve. Isaac Ellwood, another barbed wire tycoon, was a guest who, like Gates, decided to remain in Port Arthur and built the luxurious Pompeiian Villa on Lakeshore Drive as a hunting retreat in 1900. It stood in marked contrast to most hunting lodges, with a pink exterior and guest rooms that opened to a central veranda. J. A. Edson, president of the Kansas City Southern Railway, made frequent winter trips, such as one in 1909 on which, with a group of New York investors, he met his private yacht *The Whim* at the preserve for several days of hunting before traveling for a shoot in Rockport.[11]

Gates and his son Charles were hosted by an equally prominent southeast Texas business family, Galveston's Colonel W. L. Moody and his son, W. L. Moody Jr., at Lake Surprise in Chambers County. Moody's telegram of invitation assuring Gates of plentiful canvasbacks was followed by a trip to East Bay aboard the *Roxana,* where the group killed four hundred. Gates had such a fine time that he offered to purchase Lake Surprise, to which Moody replied, "It is beyond price."[12]

When Gates died in 1911, only twelve years had passed since his visit to the place in the marsh that would become Port Arthur. Change had come quickly to the shores of Sabine Lake. The great Spindletop Oil Field discovery in 1901 brought jobs and people to Jefferson County at a dizzying pace; the population had more than doubled between 1900 and 1910. The endless sea cane near Gates's Lakeshore Drive "hunting lodge" was replaced by a bustling Port Arthur, its wharves jammed with schooners and steamships and a medley of masts and smokestacks.[13]

McFADDIN RANCH

The marshes of McFaddin Ranch, part of the extensive landholdings of William McFaddin and his son William Perry Herring (W. P. H.) McFaddin, seemed a world away from Port Arthur. From north to south the ranch covered Taylor Bayou to the Gulf of Mexico, and east to west it stretched from White's Ranch in Chambers County to Fence Lake, where it took a jog to the north to Keith Lake. Jim Sutherlin says the ranch was so large, and parts so remote, that the only way fur trappers along the waterways would hear of family news and world events was from a rider who patrolled the perimeter year-round. Waterfowl biologist Charles Stutzenbaker puts it succinctly when he says, "McFaddin land covered what was probably the most important waterfowl habitat in the state."[14]

The twelve-thousand-acre Needmore Ranch was summer headquarters for W. P. H. McFaddin's cattle operations and where the extended McFaddin family hunted each winter. The Needmore ranch house south of Willow and

GREATER CANADA *and snow geese with a few mallards and pintails, Needmore Ranch, 1939. Left to right: George Gaines, unidentified, Caldwell McFaddin, and ranch foreman Robert Chesson. (Courtesy McFaddin-Ward House)*

Willie Sloughs overlooked unbroken sea cane as far as the eye could see, its only landmarks the small motte of trees known as Big and Little Persimmon Ridges. Puddle ducks congregated on nearly every waterway, and greater Canada geese came to roost where the high prairie gave way to marsh at Goose Gully, a place that remained long in the lore of Jefferson County hunters.[15]

When the Intracoastal Canal (IC) crossed Needmore in the late 1920s and early '30s, it cut off the supply of fresh water and sediment, allowing saltwater to invade the upper marsh. According to McFaddin heir Bill Wilson, that fresh water was crucial for rice crops and cattle, and to try to reverse the damage, the family built levees, dams, and pumping stations. Improvements created new hunting habitat, places that were not on any earlier maps. There were Big Reservoir and Willie Slough, where W. P. H.'s son Big Perry hunted; Boggy Slough, where son Caldwell shot over his rig of hand-carved balsa decoys; and Monteaux Pond, frequented by family member Pete Cordts.[16]

Caldwell's daughter Rosine McFaddin Wilson recalls, "When duck season came along everything else in my family came to a halt." The family hosted Beaumont businessmen, politicians, and sports figures such as 1930s and '40s baseball star Bobby Wolf and his friend Dizzy Dean. Rosine Wilson says regular guest Smythe Shepard lives on in family lore for the time he was burning vegetation around a duck blind and the fire got out of control, "sweeping across acres of prairie and burning fences and a couple of duck blinds. Caldwell called him Smokey from then on, and that's how his name appears on the lease records." Guests, she says, stayed at the ranch foreman's house, sleeping in a room with bunk beds and no heat.[17]

Needmore had boat blinds for many years, and to get to them in the early days, hunters walked. By the 1940s they used a marsh tractor, and by 1950 an old army "weasel" with oak slat–covered steel tracks. Big Perry's Chesapeake Bay retrievers Mutt and Jeff often tagged along behind whoever came to the ranch. Gerry Cordts recalls, "If [the guests] were shooting birds, the dogs would retrieve them, but if they didn't, the dogs would wander away bored."[18]

McFaddin land always attracted poachers. They stole cattle, particularly during the Depression and during World War II rationing, and they came to hunt. Curtailing trespassers was one of the reasons W. P. H. Sr. began leasing land to hunting clubs, and it factored into the family's decision in 1957 to sell to the Texas Game and Fish Commission the eighty-four-hundred-acre Big Hill Bayou part of the ranch—now the J. D. Murphree WMA.[19]

PORT ARTHUR HUNTING CLUB

The first of the McFaddin Ranch hunting clubs was Port Arthur Hunting Club, arguably the largest and most influential of the Jefferson County sporting clubs. Club founder Henry Joseph LeBlanc, who was born in Louisiana in 1893, followed the oil business to Port Arthur, where he started Standard Brass Manufacturing Company. Henry loved to hunt ducks and geese, and the camp his brother Oliver built from driftwood and a corrugated tin roof in the dunes on McFaddin Beach became his winter weekend retreat. What Henry didn't already know about the marsh he learned from Oliver, better known as Mutt, who earned his living by trapping furs, fishing, and crabbing.[20]

The history of Henry LeBlanc and Port Arthur Hunting Club lives on through two of Henry's sons, Billy and Bobby LeBlanc. Bobby says his father had permission to hunt McFaddin Ranch from W. P. H. McFaddin but wasn't allowed to bring guests. He only broke that rule once, and when he did, word spread among his customers "like a marsh fire in front of a north wind." Port Arthur duck hunters were serious about their sport, and Henry knew he had a problem. One of his clients was so mad that he told Henry that until he took him duck hunting, they weren't going to do any more business.[21]

Conscious of the importance of those duck hunts to Standard Brass customers, Henry asked W. P. H. McFaddin if he could lease some land to start a hunting club. McFaddin was reluctant, but when he saw Henry's list of proposed members, which included executives from the area's major oil companies, he began to think it could be in his best interest as well. There were other motivations. The family for years had tried to evict a squatter and trapper, known as the Swede, from McFaddin Beach. Too, the federal government in the mid-1920s announced plans to construct the IC, and McFaddin figured his land, sliced nearly in half by the waterway, would be accessible to more trespassers. According to son Billy, Henry was granted thirty thousand acres, with W. P. H. stipulating: "I'm gonna lease it to you if you'll stop the trespassing and get rid of that Swede."[22]

NOTICE TO HUNTERS

All land of the McFaddin Trust bordering on the south side of the Intracoastal Canal has been leased to the Port Arthur Hunting Club and is posted to the water's edge. This land is being patrolled and trespassers will be prosecuted.

(Modified from *Port Arthur News*, Nov. 26, 1937)

HENRY LEBLANC SR., *patriarch of Port Arthur Hunting Club, at Star Lake in 1948. Note dead ducks staked as decoys in the background and his stool of wooden Padco decoys. (Courtesy Bobby LeBlanc)*

Port Arthur Hunting Club opened in 1926 and was incorporated seven years later by founding members Henry LeBlanc, Bob Stafford of Sabine Lumber Co., and Gulf Oil's Charles R. Stevenson. Club members were assigned areas to hunt and given membership cards to identify themselves to state game warden and club patrolman Keller Hines. Long-time hunting partner and mechanic Arnold Rode kept the club machinery running, and Standard Brass's Jake Anderson was the club handyman for more than forty years.[23]

For Henry, nights spent with mosquitoes and cold north winds that seeped through the cracks of Mutt's trapping shack came to an end when he built the Breeze Inn. Located on the beach near McFaddin's corral, Breeze Inn was built high on pilings with wide front steps that led to a screened porch. Here, visitors shook off mosquitoes before entering the roomy building with its bar, dance floor, and big kitchen that served great seafood. The family sold the oasis on the beach before World War II, when the government took it over to use as a patrol station.

Customers, friends, and family later stayed on Henry's fifty-foot yacht *Bonnie Lee* until, in the 1940s, he built the Standard Brass Camp, located on the south side of the IC. Henry dredged a big reservoir in the front where guests fished after a morning hunt and a big afternoon meal. When the first Standard Brass Camp was destroyed by Hurricane Carla in 1961, Henry built a new camp east of the Shell Oil Company Road by Clam Lake. That second camp remained as

BOBBY LEBLANC *with mallards, pintails, and gadwalls in front of the first Standard Brass camp. (Courtesy Bobby LeBlanc)*

GULF OIL *yacht* Ada *tied up at Sabine Towing's houseboat* Gertrude *at the Star Lake lease pier, 1930s to 1940s. (Courtesy Bobby LeBlanc)*

headquarters for the McFaddin National Wildlife Refuge long after Port Arthur Hunting Club closed, demolished by Hurricane Ike in 2008.

Other Port Arthur Hunting Club members with camps in the marsh included Bruno Schulz, Alton Angelle, Gene Ohmstede, and Gulf Oil on Star Lake. Gulf brought clients down the IC on their Mathews-built yacht *Ada* and first lodged them on the houseboat *Gertrude,* which Sabine Towing Company rented to them for a dollar a year. Later they built two camps, the first a one-story, four-bedroom structure on the north side of Star Lake. When it floated across the IC in one piece during Hurricane Carla, they hauled it back.

SABINE ESTUARY

As the Port Arthur Hunting Club membership expanded after World War II, Henry carved out his own lease on McFaddin Marsh for Standard Brass. The decision over which part of the marsh to choose was solved by sons Billy and Bobby when they found the sky over a senna, or "coffee bean," flat near Clam Lake thick with greenhead mallards. The next morning the boys and their guests shot forty-two, all greenheads except one. Although they had to suffer their father's wrath when they showed off their mallards to an important customer with a mixed bag of spoonbills, teal, and gadwalls, the Standard Brass lease was born from that great hunt.

What Henry knew about habitat management he perfected at the eight-thousand-acre company lease east of Clam Lake. He constructed a levee system around the entirety of the property and installed a large rice field pump. In summer he pumped brackish canal water into the marsh to kill unwanted vegetation, then let it drain out when the north winds blew the tide out. With gates closed, fall rains brought in fresh water, and fresh water meant ducks. Each October he burned areas of the prairie to promote new grass shoots, and family and friends remember the thousands of geese and pintails that often covered those burns during winter.

Henry and the early club members reached the edge of McFaddin Marsh on the shell-packed beach road that became Highway 87. Getting off the main track was risky, as the combination of rain and cattle could turn the side roads into a quagmire. One club member who drove a Ford pickup truck with balloon tires to the Dipping Vat Ponds mired it in mud up to the frame. Bobby says he couldn't pull it out, so he gave the keys to Henry's brother Mutt, with, "It's yours. I give up." The old marshman got it out and drove it until it rusted away. Besides the beach road, club members reached the marsh in boats of all sizes along the IC.

Getting to the marsh was one thing, but getting to the ducks quite another. Henry first traveled by horseback, then by a marsh buggy he built from an old Model T flatbed truck with foot-wide balloon tires and chains. Access was improved with his first airboat. With a hull twenty feet long constructed from three-quarters-inch cypress, the boat was powered by a water-cooled Curtis OX5 aircraft engine started by a hand crank through a hole in the radiator. The engine had to be shut down periodically to allow oil to be squirted on exposed rocker arms, and because there was no guard over the wooden propeller, standing behind the boat was ill advised. Bobby recalls that the boat was designed with a water rudder that would kick up when it ran over hard objects such as driftwood or mud flats and even "large garfish or alligators."

At the end of each hunting season, Henry and a work crew drove a two-ton flatbed truck to the marsh to prepare the airboat for the summer. They unbolted the engine and mount and hoisted them in the truck. The cypress boat would crack during warm summer months, so they would scuttle the hull and leave it submerged until August. They would then return each fall to haul it out, wash it,

Henry LeBlanc's *right-hand man, Jake Anderson, next to one of the club's alligator buggies. (Courtesy Bobby LeBlanc)*

caulk the bottom with cotton and oakum, and let it dry. With new canvas decking and a coat of green paint, Henry's airboat would be ready for duck season.

Henry and Port Arthur Hunting Club members experimented with nearly every type of marsh transportation. There were crawlers, or alligator buggies, that looked like a boat with two huge wheels and that had a ladder welded to the frame to allow hunters to look over the tall sea cane. They also used a Ford tractor with half-tracks to pull a "gypsy wagon" fitted with large combine tires and filled with hunters and their gear. Club member Howard Perkins even built a marsh buggy out of pure copper that looked good but was so heavy that it sank before it ever reached the marsh. For years the LeBlancs used a lightweight fourteen-foot plywood airboat from Port Arthur's Clint LeBlanc and powered it with a 190-hp Continental aircraft engine. Henry improved access on the Standard Brass lease with numbered boat ditches so guests could better find their way to the duck blinds. He bought a new fleet of aluminum jonboats and built a boathouse to house them.

The LeBlanc brothers all made their first duck hunts at the Star Lake Island blind. Billy was ten years old on his first hunt in 1936 and remembers the details as if it were yesterday:

When we left the houseboat there was a big blue sky across the whole north part of the country. Well, we got to the blind and I've never seen the likes of the ducks. My brother Henry [Jr] was with us. We got some shooting in and that norther came through, a blue cold one, and the temperature dropped to I don't know how cold. And it rained like hell. We were all soaked. He [Henry LeBlanc Sr.] had a duffle bag that he carried everything in. He had a little can of saw dust with a little coal oil in it, and waded across from Star Lake Island and got some fence posts and cow dung, and built a fire and dried our clothes for us. He put us back in shape. We were waiting for the airboat to show, and it wasn't going to show for a while.

On his first trips to the marsh, Billy wore only socks and tennis shoes, and the initial predawn step into the freezing mud and water, he says, "was almost too much to bear."

The mix of men, machinery, and marsh provides plenty of fodder for LeBlanc family story-telling. Bobby remembers when, after a norther had blown most of the water out of the marsh, Henry and mechanic Arnold Rode stuck the old cypress airboat on a mud flat. It stayed there for two days and took a crew of eight men to pull it off. Running an airboat up Five Mile Cut on a cold morning, his older brother Henry Jr. found the water covered with a sheet of ice that sliced the sides out of the boat. Bobby once made a high shot on a goose that fell into his motorized pirogue and cracked the thin plywood bottom. The only way he got home was by adjusting the load to keep the damaged part of the boat out of the water. Henry Sr. was launching his boat when his new car followed it into the canal; handyman Jake Anderson couldn't swim a lick but went in after him.

Decoys and duck blind stories are also part of the Port Arthur Hunting Club lore. The hunters often set their spreads of heavy wooden Pascagoula decoys simply by heaving them as far as possible, and once a poorly aimed toss hit Hugh Wagner in the head and nearly knocked him unconscious. Cans of insect repellent for mosquitoes and spray paint used to touch up duck blinds were traditionally left on the blind seats where guests could find them. When Standard Brass vice president Fred Wilson and customer Earl James went to a blind before daylight, they were greeted by clouds of mosquitoes. Reaching for a can of insect repellent, they sprayed each other head to toe. Billy says, "So here's Daddy's V.P. with his hot shot customer and they say 'Ol' Henry thinks of everything, even got us some bug spray here.' But they'd grabbed the spray paint, and daylight comes and they look at each other and they were all green."

There were outstanding duck hunts at Standard Brass, and old LeBlanc family photographs capture the days when hunters posed with large numbers of ducks, many of them mallards and pintails. Plenty of geese flew low over club duck blinds, but following them by foot across the marsh was often too much work for

Henry's customers. It was never too much effort for Bobby, who spent long hours getting to hard places to hunt them. He once scouted a flock of greater Canadas on Wiseman's Pond on a growth of green grass from a recent rain. With only three goose decoys, nine Canadas decoyed in, and he and his guests shot all nine. The biggest Canada goose he ever shot weighed ten pounds field dressed. To get that bird, he crouched on a frozen prairie with both knees and a hand in the water, a twelve-gauge shotgun balanced on the back of his neck.

The most unusual goose hunt Bobby made was from the front porch of the first Standard Brass camp. As a group of five geese headed for the reservoir next to camp, Bobby and Billy started "hollering," or mouth calling. Bobby relates, "We had a trash pile on the far side of the front yard, and those geese were heading for some white papers the wind had scattered." The brothers kept calling, and the geese kept coming. Billy and Bobby shot four from the front steps, and guest Charlie Serefina ran out the side door and shot the fifth one.[24]

Jim "Cowboy" Fernandez was a member of the Port Arthur Hunting Club in the 1960s and, like Bobby, worked hard to hunt geese. He came up with the idea of making goose decoys from discarded metal newsprint plates he collected from the *Port Arthur News*. He cut 750 decoys, and he jokingly says it took him "ten thousand gallons" to paint them. He says one plate was never very heavy, but "750 plates was plenty heavy. But you couldn't keep the geese out of them. When the geese were working your part of the marsh and they saw all those decoys, it was cherry pickin' time."[25]

While the name Henry LeBlanc is best known in sporting circles for the club he ran for more than fifty years, he was a man equally passionate about conservation. He was a Texas game and fish commissioner from 1953 to 1959, president of the Sportsmen's Clubs of Texas, a director for the National Wildlife Federation, and a member of Ducks Unlimited and the Big Hill Bayou Conservation Club. The Texas Sports Writers Association voted him outstanding sportsman and conservationist three years in a row, and Governor John Connally recognized his service to conservation in 1967. Henry LeBlanc died in 1988 at ninety-five years of age.[26]

The Port Arthur Hunting Club remained in existence until the late 1970s, when its land became part of McFaddin National Wildlife Refuge. Henry and his sons had all left a little earlier: Bobby in 1965 and Billy in 1974. Bobby later organized White Ranch Salt Grass Hunting Club and stayed for fourteen years before starting Box Slough Hunting Club on Hebert Ranch with his son Craig. Bobby died as this book was going to press.

E. D. FOREMAN AND THE FOREMAN CAMP

The first of three generations of Foreman waterfowlers, Ezra D. "Easy" Foreman Sr., came to Port Arthur from Louisiana in 1931 to work at the Texaco refinery.

Easy and his brother Rufus teamed up with renowned duck caller Charles "Smitty" Smith, hunting between Port Arthur Hunting Club and Spindletop Reservoir. Theirs was a long run in the dark down the IC, watching for tugboats. Although the return trip was safer, it sometimes took longer; Coty Foreman says if his father, Rufus, didn't already have his limit of twenty-five mallards when it was time to quit, "he would stop at every coffee bean flat on the way back and jump shoot mallards until he got them."[27]

At Easy, Rufus, and Smitty's duck camp south of Willow Slough, they had a long-standing rule that whoever shot the first spoonbill of the season washed all the dishes for the rest of it. From camp they watched the skyline over Goose Gully for greater Canada or "ringneck" geese, and it became Easy's favorite goose hunting spot. He passed it on to the next generation of Foreman hunters, and before long the lone figure of son E. D. Jr. could be seen on his belly sneaking up on those geese with a retriever that learned to get down and crawl beside him.[28]

E. D. became one of the best known Port Arthur duck hunters, his waterfowling exploits featured in Bill Thomas's *Lone Star* hunting and fishing shows and by outdoor writers across Texas. His legacy is still fresh with his extended duck hunting family: son Leo, nephew Randy, Rufus's son Coty Foreman, with his sons Mark and Kirk, and family friend Hayes Mendoza. They remember that although E. D. always had a good lease, there was no way to keep him on it. He had to go where the birds were, and to get there, he walked. Son Leo recalls, "It wasn't nothing to walk two miles in the marsh. We'd go where the ducks were. That's the way we hunted." Coty says that more than once "E. D. like' to walk me to death. He made me drink marsh water a few times, my mouth dry like cotton."[29]

Hayes Mendoza worked with E. D. at the Texaco refinery and became his regular hunting partner largely because he fulfilled two important requirements—he could walk the marsh, and he could shoot. On Hayes's first hunt, he says, "We went out to one of his blinds. E. D. asked me how many shells I brought, and I said, 'I got a box—can't kill but ten.' So E. D. watched me shoot for a while, and I said, 'E. D. aren't you gonna shoot?' He said, 'No, I'm just gonna watch.' And E. D. didn't shoot. I had to borrow one shell from E. D. to get our limit of twenty ducks.[30]

E. D. was an accomplished duck caller. *Port Arthur News* outdoor writer Ed Holder sat in the high roseau cane one morning with E. D., who, with no decoys set out, called in flock after flock of mottled ducks and mallards that, with necks straining, landed only a few feet away. Holder had him repeat the performance on the duck calling record *Secrets of Duck Calling,* produced by Waco's Johnny Stewart Wildlife Calls. E. D. and son Leo stunned another sportswriter by mouth calling flock after flock of geese. Leo was only twelve years old.[31]

The extended family moved to Foreman Camp on Star Lake in 1952 when Dr. Darrell Perkins and Roland Foreman leased the tract from the Port Arthur

E. D. FOREMAN *with greater Canada geese and a few mallards from Goose Gully on McFaddin's Needmore Ranch, 1958. (Courtesy Leo Foreman)*

Hunting Club. Roland taught his sons Garrett and Randy how to hunt there, and Randy remembers, "He put me out there when I was five or six, and Daddy told me to shoot everything with a green head. And I shot every spoonbill there was. When he come back, he said, 'Don't you ever shoot a spoonbill again.'" Randy learned his lesson, adding, "The next morning I got in a blind with Darrell Perkins, and I shot nothing but mallards."[32]

Each year they burned the prairie, after which the new, green growth attracted geese and swarms of pintails. "Daddy and Darrell," Randy says, "would tie cut grass to their belts and lay down in the burnt field. Soon we did too. Aunt Nora [Montaux], Easy's sister, made us these shell vests that would hold sixty-four shells with straps that you could stick cane into. We would walk into the slough and get down on our knees. We didn't move until the geese were right on us." When E. D. Jr. joined his brother Roland at Star Lake in 1964, he built an eighty-acre reservoir and a roosting area. E. D., like Henry LeBlanc before him, managed water levels and salinities. Randy adds, "The reason we had such good hunting was that we took care of our land. We burned it. We let it dry. We knew when to put the water on. We would test everything. We would let water in from

SABINE ESTUARY

the IC in February. Then we'd turn around and cast net and catch thousands of pounds of shrimp. Then we let it in again during equinox, the high tide. Leo and I still look at equinox [today]."[33]

For the working man in Port Arthur's refineries, hunting was an expensive hobby. Coty says, "Back then, we were lucky to have a fourteen-foot boat and a broken-down motor." The barter system, where they negotiated for camp supplies, marsh buggy parts, and heavy equipment, helped cover costs. Rather than pay bills to keep their machinery running, they gave mechanic "Old Man" Ellis Labbit a club membership, and he stayed for more than twenty years.[34]

The Foremans covered other expenses by selling rabbits, $1.25 for a "swamper" and $1.00 for a cottontail. Leo says, "There were lots of rabbits back them. We'd kill hundreds of 'em to help pay for the waterfowl season. We'd go back to Port Arthur, the west side, and sell 'em." Hayes adds that they "always had to leave a foot on 'em, so they wouldn't think it was a cat." They guided as well, often helping out Gulf Oil manager Metcalf. Randy says, "He'd call Daddy and say, 'We got sixty people we need to hunt, and Daddy would hunt 'em. We helped them and they helped us." The Foremans gave Gulf camp caretaker Earl Litton "a hundred ducks and geese every day," and he in turn loaded them up with food for their camp. E. D. guided hunters during the week for five dollars a day, getting free advertising in columns by his regular guests, outdoor writers Buddy Gough, Ray Sasser, and Ed Holder.[35]

The last years of Port Arthur Hunting Club were the years of ten-point pintails, and a typical Foreman Camp hunt was nine "bull" sprigs (northern pintails) and one drake mallard. Coty remembers that "E. D. shot his gun so much the barrel went thin." When Randy reflects on those years, he says, "We didn't overshoot, but we didn't undershoot, either. Word was out the Foremans were killing ducks," and it attracted some attention. Federal game warden Doc McCallum knew Randy "on a personal basis" and once came swooping in on them by helicopter during a hunt. State game warden Bob Heitman was "after Roland and after everybody." When Heitman's boat broke down, and he spent a long night on Star Lake, Randy made sure that the fox watching the henhouse had a key to their clubhouse in case it ever happened again. He had trouble explaining to E. D. and his father why that was a good idea.[36]

OTHER PRIVATE JEFFERSON COUNTY CLUBS

While few Jefferson County hunting and fishing clubs had as long a history as the Port Arthur Hunting Club, there were earlier ones. The first may have been a hunting lodge built at the Keith Lake Gully Bridge for visiting sportsmen in 1897. John Gates's Lost Lake Preserve followed, then the Port Arthur Tarpon Club in 1902. The Tarpon Club held their meetings at the venerable Sabine Hotel and hunted Keith Lake, where the captain of the club's launch positioned the boat at

JOHN GATES's *Lost Lake Preserve* still held large numbers of canvasbacks in the 1920s. Shown are thirty-two drake canvasbacks on the top row and about forty hens on the bottom row in back of Port Arthur's Rose Hill mansion. Rome H. Woodworth is believed to be on the right. (Alva Carr Collection, courtesy Port Arthur Public Library)

water's edge to use as a "shooting box." Sportsmen shot passing ducks in comfort and did not have to set foot in the marsh.[37]

Carrying on the tradition of John Gates's Lost Lake Preserve, Port Arthur's J. L. Boyd in 1913 organized a "millionaire sportsmen's club," complete with a new "commodious clubhouse commensurate with the wealth of the club members." John Gates's son Charles was invited to personally select fifty to one hundred members. Boyd thought the moneyed members could turn Lost Lake into a recruiting ground for the museums, as "some of the rarest birds known to the American Continent" are found in the "wildness of these waters and swamps." In the late 1920s Mary Woodworth bought Gates Hunting Preserve as a private family retreat and built a new hunting lodge.[38]

Local game warden J. A. Lawler incorporated Lawler Boating, Fishing, and Hunting Club in 1915, and its twenty members built a clubhouse on two thousand acres near the Bessie Marsh. The Rainbow Outing Club formed in the 1920s with annual dues of ten dollars, which covered a clubhouse with telephone service. Orange Hunting Club was incorporated in 1922 and built a camp on the IC; Judge Kenesaw Mountain Landis, major league baseball commissioner, was a member. John R. Adams Hunting Preserve opened about the same time, with its clubhouse on a high bluff overlooking the Sabine River.[39]

A. J. LeBlanc offered a "fine, exclusive" duck hunting club in 1924, leasing thirty thousand acres of the Broussard and Hebert Ranch near Gum Island on Taylor's Bayou. LeBlanc advertised a game warden and sheriff on the property to assure "protection from outsiders," and he limited the number of members from Port Arthur and Beaumont because, he thought, local sportsmen killed too many birds. Longtime caretaker Louis Broussard ran some of the other hunting operations on Broussard and Hebert Ranch, and the family's Labelle Hunting Club was run by Joe Broussard.[40]

SABINE ESTUARY

Nederland baker and duck call maker George Yentzen was a founder of the Port Arthur Hunting Preserve, which was chartered in 1929. Club members launched boats on Taylor Bayou at Port Acres and hunted about four thousand acres on Big Hill Bayou. The Gulf Coast Rod, Reel, and Gun Club was established in Beaumont as a sportsmen's club in 1932 with a large club building on Gulf Street. Organized by Bruce Wiggins of Bruce's Sporting Goods and sports writer Everett Brashear, it had more than four hundred members at its peak. High Island guide Charlie Faggard of Gilchrist arranged much of the club's fishing and hunting in the 1950s.[41]

South Texas Fishing and Hunting Club was founded in Port Arthur in 1939 and held its meetings at the yacht club. Port Acres Sportsman's Club opened its doors in 1943, leasing nearly ten thousand acres on Broussard and Hebert's Ranch at Blind Lake. Founded by Tolbert Crowder and later run by Walter J. Stone, Port Acres Sportsman's Club had twenty-five airboats, and, according to Bobby LeBlanc, "when they started all those airboats before daylight, the club grounds sounded like World War II Flyin' Tigers were taking off." In Orange, Orange Outboard Motors opened Greens Bayou Hunting Camp during the 1940s. Reservations covered transportation, boats, guides, and lodging at the camp.[42]

By the 1950s the number of private Orange and Jefferson County hunting clubs was nothing short of exceptional. Henry LeBlanc's original Standard Brass lease alone was surrounded by no fewer than fourteen clubs, their rosters reading like a who's who of Jefferson County politics, civic groups, and business. The law firm of Tatum, Camp, and Ball formed Old Cabin Lake Hunting Club in 1952. Organizer George T. Camp promised W. P. H. McFaddin he would hire a patrolman and "place him in the trapper's shack west of Cabin Lake and . . . furnish him with a boat and motor." Cliff Cooper of the Pure Oil Company ran North Star Hunting Club for members mostly from Port Neches and Beaumont, with their lease at the end of Shell Lake Road on McFaddin's Needmore Ranch.[43]

Taylor's Bayou Hunting Club had forty-five members from Port Arthur, Groves, Nederland, Port Neches, Port Acres, and Beaumont. The Firemen's Lease, north of the IC, was run by Harry A. Hebert, president of the Port Arthur Fire Department. Bruno Schulz of Gulfport Boiler and Welding Works bought the old Gates Hunting Preserve on Lost Lake until it was condemned by the government for a drainage project. Jefferson County sheriff Charles H. "Charley" Myer ran the Sheriff's Lease until 1961, when a large cash gift delivered in a brown paper bag resulted in a federal indictment.[44]

Shell Lake Hunting Club on Pintail Flats on the edge of Keith Lake was formed in the early 1950s by Dick Connerly and was later managed by Dr. E. C. McCrea. Cowboy Fernandez helped run the club with its twenty-nine members in the early years and remembers Keith Lake still held clouds of canvasbacks. Cowboy was sitting in Bill Martin's duck blind one morning before dawn and

HUNTING CLUB LEASES JEFF. COUNTY RANCH				
NAME OF CLUB:	APPROX. ACRES:	PRICES OF LEASE: OLD	NEW	LEASE EXPIRES:
PORT ARTHUR HUNT CLUB	35,000	$ 10,000	$ (*)	-
✓DOTSON LEASE	750	750	750	-
✓BOBBY WOOLFE LEASE	300	250	250	-
✓HOWELL & MAIER LEASE	750	750	750	-
SHERIFF'S LEASE	2,600	1,500	2,000	-
✓LONE STAR LEASE (COOPER)	1,000	1,500	1,500	1960.
✓FIREMAN'S LEASE	1,000	500	500	1960
✓MALLARD HUNT CLUB	1,900	1,500.	1500	-
✓SMOKEY SHEPPARD LEASE	750	500	500	-
CHAS. SMITH LEASE	500	400	400	-
D.P.CONNERLY LEASE	8,000	3,500	3,500	1961
PORT ACRES HUNTING CLUB	2,950	1,500	2,000	-
✓TAYLOR'S BAYOU HUNT CLUB	1,700	1,000	1,000	1960
SHUEY LEASE	-	100	100	-
TOTALS -	57,200	$ 23,750	($1,000)	-

(*)(RAISE TO $12,000 TO BE DISCUSSED)

Bruno Schultz - 350 -

A LONG LIST of clubs leased McFaddin Ranch in the late 1950s.
(Courtesy Bobby LeBlanc)

smelled something musty. He shined his light and found he was sharing his blind seat with a water moccasin as thick as his arm.[45]

Many of the clubs that opened in the 1940s and '50s remained in business through the '60s and the early '70s, when the quantity of clubs in Jefferson County reached numbers that no one has ever tried to count. By then eighty years had passed since sloops first tacked down narrow Sabine Pass to the hunting lodge on its shores.

DAY HUNTING RANCHES AND GUIDES

Alternatives to joining private clubs included guided hunts and day hunting ranches, where sportsmen paid a daily or seasonal gate fee for access to private land. According to guide Greg Keddy, Pipkin's Hunting Ranch was the first day hunting operation in Jefferson County. Covering Big Hill and the north part of Star Lake, habitat on the eighteen-thousand-acre Pipkin's Ranch included fresh and salt wetlands, prairie, rice fields, and reservoirs. Pipkin's had a long sporting history. Beaumont's Everett Myers hunted the ranch in the 1910s, driving his Model T Ford through sea cane "higher than a house" as far as he could before he got stuck. Myers described shoots near Big Hill, where, still using black-powder shells, he took as many as two hundred mallards, most of which he gave to an orphanage.[46]

Beaumont's S. W. "Steve" Pipkin opened the ranch to the public in the late 1920s, and it remained in business for more than fifty years. By the 1950s ranch hunting was run by John and Bruce Pipkin, and in the 1960s by Mickey Winters. Local guides Albert Schmidtke and Bruce Goates of Groves provided decoys, blinds, and airboat transport to and from the blinds for a fee of $7.50 per hunter in the 1970s.[47]

Several day hunting operations opened in Sea Rim Marsh near Texas Point and McFaddin Beach. Sea Rim had long been a popular gunning destination, first by boat and then by car with construction of the shell road from Port Arthur that became Highway 87. So many duck hunters wound their way down the road in the 1920s that an enterprising man in 1922 built a toll gate across it, demanding a fee of one dollar, payable only by duck hunters. His scheme was short-lived, as outraged sportsmen had the deputy sheriff close it down.[48]

The road to Sea Rim Marsh was still shell when Wilson LaBove opened Sea Rim Hunting Club in the 1930s for a gate fee of a dollar a day. Wilson went overseas during World War II and turned the club over to Mrs. R. D. Rutherford, who advertised two-dollar daily permits or twelve dollars for the season. Dupre and Albert Cessac started Cessac's Sea Rim Hunting Club in 1943 on eighteen thousand acres of the McFaddin and Doornbos Ranches. Out-of-town hunters had some trouble finding the gatehouse, described only as "just beyond the first cattle guard after leaving Granger's Place on the road to Sabine." Permits cost a dollar a day, with season passes for ten dollars.[49]

Outdoor writer Ed Holder thought the worst thing about Cessac's Sea Rim Hunting Club was traversing the "deceitful, man-killing [mud of the] marsh called the Sea Rim." His words were not hyperbole. A long time before, in 1898, a search party looking for a missing hunter found him dead, stuck in the mud near Sabine Pass. Sea Rim hunting was best near the beach, but it was also the most inaccessible. Dupre and his nephew Preston Cessac solved the problem in the late 1950s with two "Cat-A-Gators," huge machines powered by a twenty-horsepower air-cooled engine with wheels that ran on rubber tracks. Cowboy Fernandez and Charles "Smitty" Smith built their first marsh buggy in the 1960s, and Cowboy says "it was the biggest in the country and could go anywhere—except Sea Rim Marsh. That's the only place I got it stuck."[50]

Most of Sea Rim Marsh was sold in 1969, and in 1973 TPWD created Sea Rim State Park. That year Dupre Cessac ran a terse ad in the *Port Arthur News* notifying sportsmen he had lost his lease and thanked them for thirty years of patronage. Some of the land not involved in the sale was run by Cowboy Fernandez as the seven-thousand-acre Sea Rim Hunting Club with permits at $150 a season. By 1977 the state allowed public duck hunting at Sea Rim State Park one day a week.[51]

Other day hunting operations in Jefferson County included Dutch Joe's 320 acres near Needmore Ranch that, according to Gerry Cordts, had "legendary, good hunting. His day hunters would often drift over to Needmore Ranch, but back in those days no one cared much." John Wilfert had a day hunting opera-

> CESSAC HUNTING CLUB, Sea Rim Marsh, Sabine Pass, Texas; one-day pass, $2; season pass, $10. Apply at Hunting Club.

(Modified from *Port Arthur News,* Oct. 31, 1943)

tion near Big Hill, with permits sold by his daughter-in-law. Goose hunters frequented Sea Breeze Hunting Ranch and its Fontenot's Reservoir next to Pipkin's Ranch.[52]

On quiet fall mornings, waterfowl biologist Charles Stutzenbaker often heard a fusillade of shots in the distance that were followed by a series of single "cripple" shots. Stutz always knew the source: O. D. LaBove was hunting geese on one of his two sand ridges: Goose Knoll or Sandy Crossing. Astounding numbers of geese came to ingest grit—necessary to their digestion—and those old cheniers were one of the few places where Sabine marsh mud was interrupted by hard sand. Customers who followed the plywood sign with its big arrow pointing to Back Ridge Road and LaBove Shooting Resort often told animated stories of what it was like to be on the receiving end of great tornadoes of decoying snow geese.[53]

LaBove was a third-generation muskrat trapper, alligator hunter, and duck hunter. By the time he was twelve he had developed his mouth calling to such a high degree that private hunting clubs begged the young boy to guide their preferred customers. O. D. was fourteen years old when he headed off on his bicycle from the family's Nederland home, determined to move to Sabine Pass and closer to the birds. His father soon tracked him down and hauled him home. O. D. realized his goal in the late 1950s when he opened LaBove Shooting Resort on part of Hebert and Broussard Ranch south of Keith Lake. Initially offering only guided hunts, O. D. added day hunting in 1968 and opened a lodge next to his boat docks in 1970.[54]

Grit and geese were what separated LaBove Shooting Resort from other guiding services. The best known of LaBove's gritting blinds, near Keith Lake south of Wildcat Ridge, held up to twenty hunters. Its floor was carpeted with oyster shell sacks, and its frame brushed with oleanders. It was there that O. D. and his guides waited for as many as a thousand geese to light on the bar before they called the shot. After one of their withering volleys the number of dead and crippled geese on the water could approach a hundred. LaBove had other frame blinds at the Goose Knoll gritting pond and duck blinds spread across the marsh, including one with carpeting, a bar, and cushioned seating.[55]

O. D. was an impressive outdoorsman. He walked the marsh, moving effortlessly in tennis shoes he wrapped with salt marsh grass. Sports writers from throughout the state paid him homage, with one writing how he brought ducks and geese down so low with his mouth calling that you could catch them with a net. O. D. was active in Jefferson County sportsmen associations and often appeared on the *Lone Star Sportsman* television show. In his trademark faded overalls, he discussed the future of LaBove Shooting Resort with reporter Susan Lindee of the *Port Arthur News* in 1977: "We're more concerned than we've ever been before about wildlife," he said, "so we're following the rules." O. D. died six years before a 1988 undercover operation splashed the name LaBove across television, magazines, and newspapers throughout the United States for gross violations of federal game laws.[56]

A COLORFUL CULTURE

With the outdoors close by, fishing, hunting, and trapping were a way of life in Orange and Jefferson Counties. In Port Arthur, for example, townspeople during the 1920s braved a January freeze to collect scores of live ducks they found locked in the ice. On the main reservoirs on the edge of town in 1927, dozens of hunters killed so many ducks they couldn't retrieve that engineers were concerned about contamination of the city's drinking water supply, and the city hired guards to enforce a new no trespassing ordinance. When Port Arthur residents found dozens of crippled ducks inside city limits, Mid-County Hunting Club was held accountable, and a legal effort was made to move the club outside of town.[57]

Before it was Port Arthur's Highway 365, it was Peek Road, and in the 1930s and '40s it passed through freshwater marshes where, according to Lillian Chatagnier Richard, "we had duck hunting right behind the house. Where the drive in-theatre is now is also where [my husband] Roland would shoot mallards. Son Brook says, "Before Daddy would go to work in the morning he'd ask Momma how many ducks she wanted for supper, and she'd say 'Get me three or four mallards' and he'd go out and kill the ducks and go to work."[58]

Before work each day at the Gulf Oil refinery, Tolbert Crowder fired up his airboat to hunt ducks at Mud Lake, afterwards driving the boat up on the refinery yard. It was the same for Lucien Fournet. Born in 1900 in Louisiana, he moved to Port Arthur in 1920 to work at the Texaco refinery, and after each shift he hunted ducks behind the plant at Taylor and Salt Bayous. Son E. J. says, "My father hunted five days a week and ran airboats until he was 78, when the land was no longer available to lease."[59]

Brook Chatagnier hunted between shifts at the DuPont plant, crossing Sabine River to Johnson Bayou by crew boat or water taxi from Pleasure Island. He says, "If I wanted nothing but mallards, I knew just where to go. If I wanted wigeons and pintail, I knew where to get them. And there were always geese on the high ridge by Sabine Lake and Lighthouse Lake." On three foggy mornings in a row he killed 108 geese and used them to barter a trip back to Port Arthur on an Army Corps of Engineers boat.[60]

Automobiles made it easier for sportsmen to get to the ducks. Shown here are John Winter (right) and two unidentified Beaumont hunters in 1916 with forty-four mallards and teal taken in China, Jefferson County. (John Winter Collection, courtesy Cliff Fisher)

Several generations of family members spent time together in the marsh. In the early days of the automobile, Holden Granger, with an assortment of relatives, loaded cars with gear and headed to Gum Island, west of Big Hill Bayou. When the old Model A Fords got stuck, everyone pushed. Wives and daughters maintained their tent camps while the men walked prairie ponds, shooting a few birds along the way to stake as decoys. They killed seventy-five to one hundred ducks a day as well as an "uncountable number of geese" and, in the days before portable refrigeration, had to eat as many birds as possible.[61]

A big part of the outdoors culture was the muskrat shack, camp, or lodge. It is impossible to estimate the number of structures once standing in Jefferson County marshes. There were so many camps on Big Hill Bayou that in 1931 fifty-five Port Arthur hunters filed a joint suit forcing W. P. H. McFaddin to remove a fence he had constructed across the bayou that kept them from motoring up the waterway. By the 1950s there were about fifty camps on Big Hill Bayou, another two dozen on the Shallow Prong Lake part of McFaddin Ranch, and many more stretching along the IC.[62]

Charles "Stutz" Stutzenbaker says, "In the 1930s and '40s, Frank Duhy and his wife would take their children out of school during the winter muskrat trapping season and stay at his father's camp on the Intracoastal. They brought along chickens and a couple of pigs that were fed muskrat carcasses." For other food, they bartered. "They would stick a cane pole in the mud along the banks of the waterway and tie a half dozen ducks on a string. When the tugs came by and took the ducks, the crew tossed a bag with whatever they had to barter—fresh fruit

SABINE ESTUARY   →   81

was common—onto the bank or in the water. In those days Port Arthur would [even] deliver mail to 'rat trappers."

Stutz remembers that at Fletcher White and his son Buddy's camp, "they didn't want the geese eating up the forage for the muskrats, and they'd go in and kill a couple hundred snow geese. [Buddy] said they'd take and breast 'em out and partially fry 'em and put 'em in big crocks. They'd cover them with melted lard and let it solidify. That was meat for the rest of the winter. When they wanted meat they'd get them a big spoon and just dip out a goose breast and fry it up."[63]

E. J. Fournet's family had camps at Big Hill Bayou and Blind Lake. The camps had no heat, and E. J. remembers as a boy nights so cold he put newspapers between his socks and boots for insulation. Once he caught a four-foot catfish under the camp that had been feasting on cleaned duck parts all season, and in its stomach he found fifty-six bright red mallard legs. Because they had no way to keep ice, it was fourteen-year-old E. J.'s job to take the ducks they didn't eat at camp to town, making the twenty-five-mile trip by boat often late into the night.[64]

The waterfowling culture of the Orange, Beaumont, and Port Arthur areas was—and to some extent remains—like no other region in Texas. The uniqueness, says Jim Sutherlin, is due largely to the "Louisiana influence on the city attitude. It's pretty much what's fun to do and livin' off the land." The outdoors culture started early, with boys taught hunting protocol before they first stepped into a duck blind. Craig LeBlanc, grandson of Port Arthur Club's Henry LeBlanc, says, "You learned to brush blinds. You were told blind manners—who shot first and all. I was given a duck call and told that before I could go out with 'em, I had to learn how to blow it. I practiced it every day." Randy Foreman remembers, "When we weren't blowing a duck call, we'd be at uncle's shooting corks they tossed in the air with a BB gun. For thirty minutes every day after school, we shot corks, and you didn't skip it either, or you didn't have supper."[65]

E. J. Fournet, like many others, spent as much time as possible in the marsh as a boy in the late 1940s and early 1950s. He rented a rowboat for a dollar a day from Pop Sonnier at his Taylor Bayou tar paper shack, where, with no windows, its open sills were covered in big piles of chewing tobacco. E. J. spent two weeks each year hunting during the Christmas holidays, carrying so many ducks over his shoulder that before he could return to school his mother had to delouse him. Money was tight, and his father told him never to shoot only one teal with one shot; it was too expensive. Like a lot of hunters in the 1950s, he paid for shotgun shells with ducks he wrapped in butcher paper and sold for two dollars to three dollars a pair.[66]

Jim Sutherlin remembers Port Arthur's "hunters rights" law, which allowed, "as long as you were going hunting or fishing, you could stop at a red light and if no one was coming, just go on through. It was legal." Sportsmen could attend the duck hunter's Mass, held on Sunday mornings early enough that they could still

A BIG PART *of the upper coast culture was the rat shack, camp, or lodge. Shown is Fletcher White's fur trapping and hunting camp on the south shore of Johnson Lake, Sabine Pass. (Fletcher White Collection, courtesy Charles Stutzenbaker)*

be in the marsh by dawn. There was a priest whose congregation bought him a four-wheeler so that he could hunt in the morning and return in time for mass. Cowboy Fernandez sometimes traveled down the highway to Keith Lake in his two-ton marsh buggy. "We'd crank that baby up and go right down the highway. We didn't have any sense at all. The highway patrol would look at us and they would shake their heads. We'd leave from right here at the shop [in Nederland], and go right through town, then down Highway 87. Most people get put in jail."[67]

At Peck's Bakery in Port Arthur the aroma of baked bread mixed with the smell of duck gumbo. Lillian Chatagnier Richard says the Chatagnier men dropped their ducks off at the bakery, but they had to get there early, before Andy the baker could "get drunk as a lord and pass out." Alone on a hunt in the late 1950s at Keith Lake, Murphy Chatagnier returned to the bakery with forty or fifty ducks and went back for another thirty. It was one of his best days of hunting, and son Randy says he put his shotgun away and quit hunting that day. Murphy was in the merchant marine, and he recalled that "the officers who had charge of ocean going tankers would always use Port Arthur boys to man the machine guns 'cause they knew how to lead."[68]

Claude Romero, who ran the houseboat and hunting for Sabine Towing on Shallow Prong Lake, was puzzled about a bird killed years before and asked Charles Stutzenbaker about it. "Claude said, 'You know, back in 1938 we were farmin' rice over there in LaBelle [Taylor's Bayou] and this big white bird came in the ricefield. Grandpa went out there and shot 'im. We cooked 'im and ate 'im and he was really good. Never seen one like that. He was a big tall bird, had a big red top knot and a long bill. White like a snow goose and had black wing tips.'" Stutz says he nearly fell out of his chair. "I'm convinced that Claude's grandfather killed one of the last whooping cranes from the remnant Louisiana breeding population of the White Lakes marshes, probably displaced by the 1938 storm."[69]

In the culture of Jefferson County, politics and duck hunting were never widely separated. Rosine Wilson relates the story of her grandfather W. P. H. McFaddin, who, concerned about the outcome of an election, "opened his ranch for a free day of duck hunting for any who wanted it. The south county hunters flocked to the hunt, bypassing the election," and, she writes, "the offending proposition" was not passed.[70]

Henry LeBlanc in the 1930s was host to nearly the entire Port Arthur city government—commissioners, clerks, the tax collector, and other city officials—on hunts at Port Arthur Hunting Club. Henry, along with the local Chamber of Commerce and a host of oil executives, later organized the Annual Governor's Hunt for state political officials. Popular events for nearly twenty years, the festivities in 1950 were attended by Governor Allan Shivers "with more than half the members of the legislature's upper body." Bobby LeBlanc says guests stayed aboard the Texas Company (Texaco) yacht *Ava,* where they enjoyed great food and drink, and sometimes too much of both. He says one guest felt so bad in the morning that he told the porter to just put the decoys around his bed, because he was going to hunt right there.[71]

A SPLIT DOWN THE MIDDLE

The outdoor passion that permeated Jefferson County was evident in the 1970s when marshlands long cherished by the sporting community were targeted by state and federal agencies as wildlife refuges. Few had objected to the 1957 TPWD purchase of the eighty-four-hundred-acre Big Hill Bayou WMA, later J. D. Murphree WMA, but it was a different matter when the state announced intentions to acquire Sea Rim Park in 1973. Orange, Beaumont, and Port Arthur sportsmen organized in opposition, collecting nearly ten thousand signatures on a petition presented to the Texas Parks and Wildlife Commission. State officials closed the area to hunters the next year.[72]

There was more to come. Three years later the US Fish and Wildlife Service (USFWS) announced plans to create a national wildlife refuge from fifty-five thousand acres of former McFaddin Ranch lands south of the IC and twelve thousand acres of the Sea Rim Marsh near Texas Point. The first sparks of what would become the fire of public opposition were struck in an article outlining the proposal by *Port Arthur News* outdoor editor Ray Sasser in May 1977. In a matter of days a deep rift developed in the Jefferson County hunting community.[73]

On one side were people who faced losing shooting grounds that had served generations of duck hunters. Billy LeBlanc says, "There's two things you don't mess with—a man's wife or his hunting lease." The highly organized opposition to the refuge proposal included Beaumont lawyer Ned Johnson and many remaining members of the Port Arthur Hunting Club. Letters and thousands of signatures in opposition filled Port Arthur and Beaumont newspapers.[74]

The annual *Senator's Hunt at Port Arthur Hunting Club*, year unknown. Far right is believed to be Lamar University president F. L. McDonald. Senator Jep Fuller is second from right. On the far left is Alton Angelle, and next to him is one of the club guides. Others in the photo are unknown. (Courtesy Bobby LeBlanc)

On the other side were those concerned with preserving the marsh from development, including an increasing use of wetlands for burying hazardous waste materials. Port Arthur's Tolbert Crowder quickly formed the Wetlands Preservation Committee to organize support from Texas environmentalists. Other supporters included TPWD's Charles Stutzenbaker, Anahuac Refuge manager Russell Clapper, and the Texas branch of the Nature Conservancy. The two sides converged at the first public hearing on the proposed purchase, attended by 150 "vocal sportsmen," in June 1977 on Pleasure Island. Ray Sasser described the mood as hostile, and Leo Foreman remembers "it was a wild west."[75]

Members of the Port Arthur Hunting Club did everything they could to keep hunting and even attempted to purchase some of the property from new landowners Planet Oil and the Horizon Corporation. Cowboy Fernandez says, "I was the one that went up to Dallas to negotiate and got shot down by the CEO of Planet Oil." Randy Foreman publicized that the Port Arthur Hunting Club would allow anyone voting against the proposal to hunt with them.[76]

The Jefferson County Commissioners Court cast a unanimous vote in opposition to the USFWS purchase. In the roll call, each vote of the court as opposed was met by applause from the standing-room-only crowd. The final hurdle was crossed when Governor Dolph Briscoe sided with the commissioners and local sentiment, rejecting the sale.[77]

The sporting community had won the battle but lost the war. That fall, Ray Sasser wrote, "Locked gates greeted the [Port Arthur Hunting Club] during the September teal season" in a poorly disguised retaliatory move against those who had organized opposition to the refuge purchases. Then, in 1979 the Nature Conservancy announced transfer of the old McFaddin Ranch lands and Sea Rim Marsh to the USFWS, with Russell Clapper named as manager of the new wildlife refuge. Two years later, sixteen thousand acres were made available for public hunting. "You know," says Greg Keddy, "a lot of us were opposed to this refuge. But now it seems like a pretty good thing." More than thirty years later, not everyone agrees.[78]

It's fall again in Jefferson County. Small flights of teal and gadwalls cross the upper prairie against a horizon of endless saltgrass on one side and glistening vertical and horizontal steel stacks and pipes of equally endless refineries on the other. In the distance, marsh fires are burning as they have for 150 years, the flames lit by ranchers to promote new growth for their cattle. After the flames come thousands of geese that often get to the green shoots first. With pride, Jim Sutherlin and Charles Stutzenbaker echo a similar sentiment: "You'll never meet a community like this one was."[79]

CHAPTER 5

EAST BAY

West of Sabine Lake, horse and oxcart trails led across fifty miles of unbroken prairie along the Atascosita Road to Liberty and Anahuac. With its northern edge an irregular boundary of longleaf pine forests, the prairie route was dissected by small streams and pothole depressions filled with mallards, teal, and pintails, particularly after hard winter rains. To the south, East Bay, separating the mainland from Bolivar Peninsula, was an easier destination to reach by sail than by land.[1]

WHITE'S RANCH

The Atascosita Road crossed the upper part of White's Ranch, founded in the 1830s by Louisiana's James Taylor White. The ranch adjoined McFaddin Ranch on the east and East Bay Bayou to the west and extended south to the Gulf of Mexico, where it covered Mud Lake, Doe Island salt dome, also known as the High Islands, and the brackish water potholes of the Knoll Ponds. Geese roosting in the East Bay marshes first began to feed on fresh green shoots and roots when White, the "Cattle King of Texas," started the practice of burning native coastal prairie grass for his stock.[2]

White's Ranch had an early sport hunting history, at least as early as the 1890s, when the High Island Hunting Club was organized by the Selkirk family of Galveston. In the club's first years members traveled on the Gulf and Inter-State Railway (G&I), which crossed the wooden barge between Galveston Bay and Bolivar Point, and completed their journey by rented horses. Later they hired a driver with a Model T at Bolivar Point, on the drive down the beach jumping driftwood

> **Notice to Sportsmen**
>
> On Nov. 10 we will open a new resort for hunters, to be located at Whites Ranch Station, on the G. & I. Railway, forty miles from Galveston. This is the best duck and goose range in Texas, and the ducks and geese are in now. Parties are accommodated only on reservation, so arrange your dates and make your reservation now if you want a good hunt this season.
>
> For full information write or see
>
> **J. U. (DOLPH) ROGERS.**
>
> **Phone 368.** **Galveston, Tex.**

(Modified from *Galveston Daily News,* Nov. 11, 1920)

logs and other hazards that produced "punctures, blowouts, broken axles, and bodily hurts."[3]

With three thousand acres leased east of High Island, the High Island Hunting Club built several lodges, two of which were destroyed by the 1900 and 1915 hurricanes. Thomas Selkirk wrote of a hunt not three hundred yards from one of the lodges, where, from sunken blinds barely visible in towering sea cane, there were "mallards, high, mallards, low, mallards in the azure as far and as high as the eye could see." A single volley by two guns produced twenty-seven mallards, with snipes so thick that dozens were unintentionally killed by the fusillade aimed at the ducks. Returning to the Galveston rail depot after one hunt, and covered in mallards, snipes, and greater Canada geese, they marched "triumphantly through an admiring Sunday crowd."[4]

The G&I stopped at the White's Ranch depot on its once-a-day trip from Galveston to Beaumont and opened the ranch to more sportsmen. Their success was so great it attracted the attention of game warden Forest E. White, who in 1910 announced he would vigorously patrol the ranch in an effort to enforce the legal limit of twenty-five birds. Galveston businessmen opened a hunting resort at White's Ranch Station in 1920, promoting it as the "best duck and goose range in Texas." Run by J. U. "Dolph" Rogers, the club offered guided hunts with accommodations, their hunters often shooting a limit of twenty-five mallards early enough to return on the 8:30 train to Galveston.[5]

In the 1930s and '40s, Dave Brown ran Brown's Camp, a day hunting operation on White's Ranch, where his one-dollar-a-day fee covered a guide and horses. Permits were available at "the trapper's camp" on the IC and at Brown's Camp on the beach, or could be purchased in advance from Port Arthur's Bailey Motor Company and K.C.S. Wood Yard. Customers arriving by car via Winnie

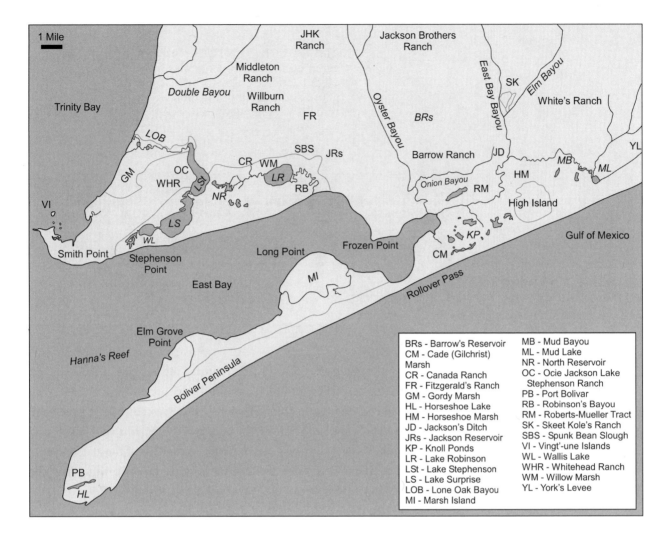

East Bay *and surrounding lands as they looked before the Intracoastal Canal.*

were instructed to look for a green house with Brown's sign on the front. If they came by boat, they could buy a ticket for Ned Prutzman's ferry service; his motor cruiser *Princess of Beaumont* ran from the drawbridge at High Island in the 1940s. When Brown's closed in the mid-1940s, the operation was next run by Barney Kahla of High Island, who sold permits from a shack on the beach road between Sabine Pass and White's Ranch.[6]

White's Ranch public day hunting ended in the 1950s with a shift to mostly private leases. Beaumont oilman George Dishman of Gulf Supply Company had six thousand acres between York's levee and Mud Lake, with a camp in Gilchrist that slept forty guests. High Island's Claud Kahla ran the club in the 1950s and early '60s and remembers that each fall he built and maintained fifty to sixty blinds and brought in two eighteen-wheeler trucks filled with decoys. Army surplus "weasels" were used to transport hunters and gear, and Billy Ray and Burl, two local African American boys, helped Claud with the labor and guiding duties.[7]

Claud Kahla hunted a marsh that looked very different from the way Selkirk's High Island Hunting Club sportsmen had seen it. The tall sea cane was

> NOTICE DUCK HUNTERS—Brown's camp on the beach, 4½ miles from High Island at Cedars is open; good goose and duck hunting; horses for rent. Beach highway is now open.
>
> (Modified from *Port Arthur News,* Nov. 21, 1935)

LETTERHEAD FOR *Bolivar Peninsula's "great summer and winter resort,"* Sea View Hotel, 1902. (Courtesy Melanie Wiggins)

disappearing, a casualty of subsidence and nutria, and instead of mallards the ducks that most often sailed into Claud's huge decoy spreads were pintails. One thing that hadn't changed was the thick mud. Mud Bayou and Mud Lake were once described as "some very bad marshy country . . . which is very boggy, and numbers of animals have drowned in its crossing." Claud hiked the marsh in only tennis shoes, sometimes through ice and snow, other times "turning into the wind to get a breath of air [because] the mosquitoes were so thick."[8]

Other private leaseholders on White's Ranch during the 1960s leased their land from T. T. Taylor in Port Arthur, who advertised seasonal hunting leases for twenty dollars per year. Bobby LeBlanc of Port Arthur leased an eight-thousand-acre tract from Jamie White near Mud Bayou in 1965, and Texaco hunted on six thousand acres between the IC and the beach east of Mud Lake, with the company's camp run by John Briggs and his son Marty.[9]

BOLIVAR PENINSULA

Bolivar Peninsula was the last strip of land between the upper coast marshes and the Gulf of Mexico, where myriads of waterfowl gathered to "thrive to a fattening point" before crossing to Central and South America at the end of their migration. Circling mallards, mottled ducks, sprigs, and teal could be seen from the High Island salt dome over intermittent potholes surrounded by coastal Bermuda grass in Horseshoe Marsh and the Knoll Ponds. Down the peninsula at Rollover Pass, swans and geese came to grit on the beach until, after the turn of the century, the swans disappeared and the geese, mostly snows and greater Canadas, moved deeper into the East Bay marsh.[10]

Where the peninsula terminates at Bolivar Point was once said to be "alive with every species of known duck, from the stout canvas-back to the diminutive teal. So thickly do they strew the water, in fact, that when they arise to fly it appears as though some great black cloud had suddenly risen." Huge flocks of ducks passed over the light of the first lighthouse lamp, constructed in 1848—so many that the lighthouse keeper was forced to cover the top of the structure with a wire frame "for protection against wild fowl, which fly headlong at the light when under its bewildering illuminence." Adjacent to the lighthouse, great flocks of ducks rose from the thick reeds of Horseshoe Lake.[11]

Proximity to Galveston made Bolivar one of the city's favorite gunning destinations. Periodicals called Bolivar a fish and game resort with "innumerable ponds and sufficient protection to hide and creep on game unawares." Popularity increased enough that, as early as 1885, Bolivar gunners complained of ten hunters to every bird. Most sportsmen came by sail from Galveston, hiring Bolivar captains such as the master of the popular sloop *W. H. Starks*. When the G&I connected Galveston with Bolivar in 1896, sportsmen boarded rail cars loaded on a barge for the Galveston Bay crossing, then flagged the train down at the end of the hunt.[12]

Hunting camps, small hotels, and boarding houses were available in communities that, between hurricanes, existed at Frenchtown, Patton, Caplen, Rollover, Gilchrist, and High Island. Best known was C. T. Cade's three-story Sea View Hotel, built in 1897 at High Island and managed by "fat, gray and jolly" J. F. Borden. Cade promoted his hotel by claiming that "winter shooting surpasses that of Florida." Typical of his customers was a party of forty from the Missouri-Kansas-Texas Railroad Company that arrived by train from Katy for a week's stay in 1905, spending their days "hunting and seining, and everything that was not tied down at both ends was captured by the jolly bridgemen."[13]

Guiding was an important source of income to Bolivar families. Author Melanie Wiggins, great-granddaughter of the C. T. Cade, collected their stories in *They Made Their Own Law*. She wrote of R. C. Bouse Jr. with his hunting camp at Caplen, west of Rollover, who took Galveston hunters to Cade Marsh, another name for the Knoll Ponds. Bouse's quote, "All I did for years was hunt," could have been uttered by almost anyone in Bolivar.[14]

Guide Monroe Kahla Sr., nephew of part-time market hunter Fred Kahla, remembered, "We used to go out about dark and kill all the game we wanted, but there weren't no iceboxes so we just shot as many as we could eat the next day." The Shell family had a one-room hunting shack on Bolivar when Kate Shell Hughes was a girl, and she recalled: "The wealthy men from Galveston would come over to spend the weekend and shoot ducks and geese—all they could kill, because there wasn't any limit then."[15]

In the 1920s hunters descended on Bolivar by car, driving from Houston or from Beaumont on the new shell road or sailing from Galveston on the *Silver King* gasoline launch that ferried passengers twice a day. The influx of winter sportsmen numbered in the hundreds. One of the more popular places for hunters was Kahla's High Island Hotel, which opened in 1924. Many of the local guides met at Cessac Café, later renamed High Island Café, a tradition that continued until at least the 1960s.[16]

In the 1930s the *Silver King* was replaced by an automobile ferry, electricity came to High Island and lit the derricks of the new High Island Oil Field, and the IC was dug across the back of the peninsula. Despite the changes, Bolivar, according to Claud Kahla, was still "all cane ponds" and still full of mallards. After the Second World War the best known commercial guiding families on Bolivar Peninsula were the Berwicks and Faggards.[17]

The extended Berwick family of guides operated hunting camps between Johnson Bayou and Bolivar beginning in the late 1800s. One was Jim Berwick, who hunted and trapped around Sabine Lake at the turn of the century. His sons Walter and Luther later guided at Barrow's Ranch, Oyster Bayou, and the Knoll Ponds, making trips across East Bay from a fishing boat berthed at the High Island bridge. The Berwick brothers didn't advertise, "you just called their home and booked hunts." Another Bolivar guide was Edward "Ed" Berwick Sr. His granddaughter, Thelma Berwick Black, says Ed guided colorful General Edwin Walker when Walker was young boy. Years later the general wrote Berwick a letter recalling those days, and the old guide promptly responded, arranging a hunt with his son-in-law, Richard Black. Walker later went on to become a controversial political figure and survived an assassination attempt by Lee Harvey Oswald.[18]

Coming from Alabama in 1929, Clyde "Pop" Markham Faggard was the first resident of Gilchrist, the town built over the remains of Rollover after it disappeared in the 1915 hurricane. A commercial crabber, fisherman, and duck hunter, Pop opened Faggard's Place with a bait stand, boat slips, and cottage. He opened the Sportsman Club in the early 1940s, and by 1945 it had seventy-five members, with guides available by request.[19]

Son Charley Faggard followed in his father's footsteps, in 1947 opening Faggard's Mud Lake Day Camp and Faggard's Hunting Camp on Cade Marsh, where he kept an eye on the land and cattle in trade for the hunting rights. Hunters looked for a row of cedar trees on Highway 87 where Charley had his permit shack, his three-dollar day fee covering one of twenty duck blinds. The price was the same at Faggard's Hunting Camp, with another four dollars for marsh buggy transportation to and from one of his forty blinds. Guided hunts cost six dollars, with permits purchased at Faggard's store in Gilchrist.[20]

Older brother Joe Faggard, Bolivar Peninsula constable for twenty years, ran the operation in the 1970s. He was ninety years old when he looked back on the days when, as a boy, he made the long walk with his father to the Cade Marsh Knoll Ponds. He later got there by horseback, remembering once being thrown

Guide Forrest West *at Barrow's Ranch, 1960s. (Courtesy Jack Holland)*

through the ice on Mud Bayou. Wet, cold, and muddy, he kept hunting. Youngest son Clyde "Boots" Faggard carried on the family tradition as a guide for Forrest West.[21]

The hunting exploits of Forrest West were a favorite subject for outdoor writers from the 1960s and for the next nearly four decades. Even if you didn't know him, you knew the reputation. He was the guide in High Island with the giant marsh buggies and big retrievers and a Model 12 Winchester pump with sawed-off, cylinder-bored barrels. He was also the man who produced amazing hunts from flooded timber, marshes, and rice fields.

When Forrest's father died early, he was raised by an aunt and uncle in East Texas. He says his family wasn't poor; they just lived without many frills—such as electricity. The lights were turned on when Forrest was in the eighth grade, about the time the family got refrigeration by surreptitiously tapping into a natural gas line from the East Texas oil field. Forrest learned the ways of field and stream on Caddo Lake, and in 1956 he headed to Venice, Louisiana, where he paid nine dollars to a justice of the peace to marry Gayle, his wife of over fifty years. It was there, at the mouth of the Mississippi Delta, that Forrest learned to mouth call geese using newspapers for decoys.

Forrest moved to the upper Texas coast to work for Diamond Shamrock, hunting Smith Point in Chambers County with coworker Sonny Baughman. The two young men often left the marsh loaded with geese, and Joe Lagow of Barrow's Hunting Ranch was watching. He asked them if they would be interested in guiding, and they both said no. The tenacious Lagow called their wives and convinced them their husbands ought to be guiding at Barrow's Ranch, and before they got home, Forrest and Sonny were guides. Working on weekends, Forrest in the early 1960s earned thirty-five dollars a day for two hunters with another five dollars for a third or fourth gun.

By Forrest's own admission, he and Sonny should have been working instead of using their time on the clock at Diamond Shamrock to fabricate three thousand plastic cone-shaped goose decoys. It was, Forrest says, a short-lived victory. "I started putting them out at 11:00 one night for clients that I had the next morning. A cold front came through that night, with wind like I had never seen before. We were getting calls from people who found decoys as far away as seven or eight miles. We lost the entire spread."

Forrest's supervisor, a duck hunter, always covered for Forrest's "part-time" waterfowl exploits to Smith Point, Barrow's Ranch, and the Trinity River bottoms. His next supervisor was not as understanding and offered him a choice between duck hunting and his job. The rest is history. In 1977 Forrest embarked on a full-time guiding career that he called Los Patos Guide Service, and Diamond Shamrock executives were among his first customers.[22]

The Los Patos name originated from Forrest's first lease on the Trinity River bottoms at the Los Patos Lodge on Champion Lake. The phenomenal timber mallard hunting came to an abrupt end when Champion Paper was sold and the oaks on the high ground were logged as houses began to line the lakeshore. Forrest West needed another place to hunt. Melanie Wiggins knew Forrest's reputation, and for three years she called him, offering to lease her grandfather's Cade Marsh land. Always Forrest's answer was no, but after he lost the Champion lease, it was Forrest who called Melanie. They met at a coffee shop and, when the meeting was done, Los Patos Guide Service at High Island, Texas, was born.[23]

Clients and season hunters stayed at the red cottages on Bolivar until the ten-thousand-square-foot Los Patos Lodge, with its dozen private rooms, dining room, and decks, was built on the beach in 1983. Forrest built his operation up to almost ninety thousand acres with twenty-five guides, and his properties included the fifteen-thousand-acre Cade Marsh and its famous Knoll Ponds, part of Mud Lake, Middleton Ranch, and Jefferson County's Pipkin's Ranch. For a time Forrest had exclusive rights to two thousand acres of Joe Lagow's Home Ranch, where he and Sonny guided Joe's favorite clients.[24]

Forrest got permission to hunt Dave Middleton's land in Chambers County when "Dave came up to me at a DU dinner and said, 'Forrest, I've got goose problems [on the ranch]. You can hunt 'em for nothing.'" Middleton joined Forrest on his first hunt, and Forrest remembers "a pick-up truck slowed down on the farm road. Dave recognized it, and said 'get down quick.' The guy gets out of his truck with a high-powered rifle. I looked at Dave kind of puzzled, but when I heard the first bullet go by, I did what he said." Sheepishly, Middleton admitted that the shooter was a neighbor he had asked to help drive geese off his fields, and he had mistaken their spread for a flock of live geese.[25]

Customers were rarely short of stories about Forrest West's retrievers, described by *Houston Chronicle*'s Joe Doggett as "great, vicious black dogs known for intimidation and tyranny in the field. Not surprisingly, West got along famously with these terrible beasts." Field champion Boncho hated other dogs and was banned for life from field competitions for failing the "steadying" test, in which a quacking hen mallard was tossed but another dog was sent for the mark. The young dog that made the retrieve, according to Forrest, was "nailed in midair" by Boncho. Joe wrote that Boncho not only broke, he "hurled himself onto the other dog, killing it instantly in front of the horrified gathering of judges and handlers." The kind of discipline Boncho needed at times was once administered by the stock of one of Forrest's 12-gauge guns "during a disagreement over blind etiquette." Forrest says proudly, "He was a super dog."[26]

Then there was Bo. Paul McDonald of Thunderbird Hunting Club says Forrest and Bo had an unwritten rule that the dog could always eat the first duck shot. Forrest called it "Bo's percentage." The dog weighed over one hundred pounds, and Forrest warned his hunters to "never, ever touch him when there was a duck in his mouth. He would bite, for keeps." He bit Boots Faggard, and as for Joe Doggett: "Bo chased me from a levee on a September teal hunt, forcing me to huddle half-soaked on a fire ant bed while he ate my birds."[27]

On quiet mornings in Gilchrist and High Island Marsh, the only noise louder than the breaking Gulf of Mexico surf was the sound of huge flocks of ducks and geese. Chet Beaty says that during a heavy north wind, birds stacked up on the Knoll Ponds before making the Gulf crossing, but to shoot them meant contending with the marsh's thick black muck. Forrest's solution to the problem was a fleet of eight-ton marsh buggies with six-foot tires, and it wasn't long before his legacy with the machines matched the tales told of his dogs.[28]

Joe Doggett was on a hunt when one of the machines came to a grinding halt, sinking in a five-foot hole in the middle of a pond. He and Forrest scrambled through the water and mud while West's black lab Jefferson Davis swam in circles around the "shipwrecked marsh mariners." Another time Forrest ran a marsh buggy off a steep bank and into a canal. Hearing these stories again, Forrest says, "You know, Joe still blames me for his back injury. All he was doin' was pullin' a jonboat over a levee." One gets the feeling that Joe's version would be terribly different.[29]

In a forty-plus-year waterfowl guiding career that ended in 2006, Forrest West was featured in numerous newspaper articles and a dozen ESPN shows. He still runs a dove, quail, and deer guiding service from his ranch in West Texas west of Abilene. Forrest has picked his retirement date carefully and gladly conveys that it's the day he dies. Son Jimmy West learned the trade from his father and continues to run the operation today.[30]

Across East Bay from Bolivar Peninsula, native hackberry and willow and groves of oaks planted by early settlers mark the high ground of Ingleside Ridge, which separates Lone Oak Bayou and Double Bayou on Trinity Bay from East Bay. The landward expression of the ridge ended at a string of oyster reefs—Bird Island and the Vingt'-une Islands—that crossed Trinity Bay to Dollar Point on the mainland before they were dredged. Cattle driven across the bay along the reefs had to swim only across the old Trinity River channel.[31]

South of Ingleside Ridge was a twenty-mile swath of fresh and brackish water marsh parallel to East Bay. In its web of bayous and ponds, hidden deep in the sea cane, were four large water bodies famous to sportsmen: Lake Robinson and the chain of three lakes known as St. Claire Lake, Lake Surprise, and White's Lake. In later years, St. Claire was called Blue, Little, or Wallis Lake, and White's Lake began to appear on maps as Lake Stephenson. Lake Surprise was the pearl in the chain, its one-and-one-half-mile length covered in banana water lily, wild celery, and, in winter, uncountable numbers of canvasbacks.[32]

During the late 1800s in this part of Chambers County, the original ranching families were still struggling to earn a living from cattle and farming when, each fall, new neighbors arrived in the form of moneyed sportsmen. Most came from Galveston to open private hunting preserves on land they bought or leased around the chain of three lakes. The best known of the Chambers County sporting preserves was Colonel Moody's Lake Surprise.

LAKE SURPRISE AND THE CHAIN OF LAKES

When Colonel William Moody bought Lake Surprise in 1893, his purchase was considered "maybe the best canvasback duck preserve in the United States." For politicians and businessmen in Moody's inner circle, the 1890s and early 1900s were heady times at Lake Surprise. Guests set sail from Galveston on Moody's steam yacht *Pherobe,* complete with a galley and French chef, and docked at Moody's nearly quarter-mile-long pier on East Bay. There they were met by a team-drawn wagon for the short journey to Moody's "colonial mansion" between the bay and the lake. Guides rowed hunters out to one of about a dozen duck blinds, depositing each with a case of shotgun shells, lunch, and water. Moody, with one of his English Purdy, Westley Richards, or W. W. Greener shotguns, took his place in his Old Home Blind, complete with a rocking chair.[33]

Moody's Lake Surprise guest list was a who's who of Texas men of influence. It included New York's John W. Gates, who had his own private shooting resort at Lost Lake in Jefferson County; Texas governor Thomas Campbell; a plethora of state Democratic party leaders, businessmen, bankers, and judges; and Texas railroad officials. William Jennings Bryan, popular orator, statesman, and three-time presidential candidate, made the trip every year, and his shooting prowess was discussed for over twenty-five years in Texas newspapers. One newsman quipped, "Texas ducks were apparently as fond of Colonel Bryan as are Texas voters," where ducks "appeared to be desirous of being accorded the distinction of

THE MOODY yacht Pherobe in Galveston harbor about 1900. (Moody Foundation Collection, courtesy Doug MacLeod)

going into the Colonel's capacious [game] bag." Bryan remained a guest of the Moody family after the colonel's death in 1920.[34]

Frequent guest Texas governor James H. Hogg once swore to the press he would never hunt again at Lake Surprise. He complained of a hunt during which he was caught in a blizzard and another when he faced a "cyclonic sea" in Galveston Bay. As the *Galveston Daily News* described the second adventure, the battered statesman reached Galveston's Pier 19 but "had separated from his cabbage and buttermilk," and the sorry-looking patriot headed directly for the nearest outgoing train. The others in the party found respite at the Tremont Hotel, where they "did not hesitate to drown their past sorrows."[35]

Lake Surprise guests were afforded some of the finest waterfowl hunting on the Texas coast. Governor Hogg shot 300 canvasbacks and puddle ducks on a hunt in 1895. Isaac W. Morton of Saint Louis killed 235 in about six hours in 1898. During the winter of 1899, Moody and guests killed in excess of 10,000 canvasbacks as well as uncountable "common ducks," geese, and snipes, and on one hunt in 1901, Moody and party harvested 350 ducks.[36]

A legion of stories describes how the economical Moody divided the spoils of the hunt. Sport hunting ran parallel to Moody's commercial hunting operation until 1903, but the volumes of harvested birds were worth more money in the marketplace than as gifts to his guests. Smith Point's Forest McNeir, who with his brother Pascal managed the Lake Surprise preserve for two years in the 1890s, wrote that visitors anticipating a celery-fed canvasback after a hunt were sorely disappointed. Canvasbacks were all shipped to market, while shovelers, teal, and gadwalls were prepared for camp meals. Richmond mayor Hilmar Moore shares the story of family member John Milton Moore, a guest in the 1890s. "He killed

EAST BAY 97

> WANTED—A man to take charge as keeper of my Lake Surprise property in Chambers County. Apply at bank of W. L. MOODY & CO.

(Modified from *Galveston Daily News,* Feb. 23, 1913)

25 sprigs. After the hunt, he went in and changed clothes, cleaned up, 'cause they always prepared your ducks to take with you, and they handed him a package. He said, 'Well I had 25.'" The helper replied, "Mr. Moody says five is enough for anybody. He sells the rest of them."[37]

After Colonel Moody died, sons Shearn and W. L. Moody Jr. continued to host men important to the family's political and business interests. One was Texas governor Pat Neff, who, when he sat down one morning to breakfast, found a wooden duck decoy on his plate. It was explained that each guest was to eat what he had shot the day before, to which Neff is said to have retorted, "The report that I never fired a gun almost cost me my governorship. Now my expert marksmanship is about to rob me of my breakfast."[38]

A sombre chapter in the Lake Surprise saga was the death of Houston assistant district attorney E. R. Waraken. Weather had often plagued the bay crossing from East Bay to Galveston's Pier 22, where the Moodys berthed their yachts, but there had never been a fatality, not from the days of the coal-fired *Pherobe,* the "trim power yacht" *Nancy Ann,* or the gasoline yacht *Elizabeth.* That changed in 1926 when the Moody speedboat *Anico* exploded on a hunt hosted by Shearn Moody for Houston mayor Oscar Holcombe and C. J. Lilley, editor of the *Houston Press.* The party jumped overboard into frigid January bay waters, and the exposure was fatal to Waraken.[39]

Canvasbacks on Lake Surprise had been hunted for market and shot for sport and died in large numbers from lead poisoning, but none of these were the cause of the bird's disappearance from Lake Surprise. It was saltwater, which destroyed the bird's mainstay diet of wild celery. During the killer hurricane of 1900, several feet of Gulf water inundated Lake Surprise, and the next year sportsmen shot only redheads, bluebills, and "black ducks." Some wild celery returned, only to succumb to storms in 1908 and 1915. It came back intermittently through the 1940s, and each time it did, the white, black, and red divers returned. But by then the Moody family was hunting more often at their shooting paradise on the shores of Espiritu Santo Bay in Calhoun County. W. L. Moody Jr. donated part of his favorite duck hunting spot as a wildlife preserve in 1954.[40]

Colonel Moody shared the chain of lakes with several other private clubs. In the late 1890s Isaac W. Morton and W. L. Huse of Saint Louis leased Wallis Lake, adjacent to Lake Surprise. Morton built a lodge on the lake with lumber brought

Colonel Moody Jr.'s *1947 Christmas card shows one of the last years of abundant canvasbacks on Lake Surprise.* (Moody Foundation Collection, courtesy Doug MacLeod)

by sail from Galveston and hauled through the marsh by horse and cart by Smith Point's Forest W. McNeir. Morton's daughter was a notable sportswoman who created a stir among "bachelor hunters in these parts" during her annual winter visits. The Morton family lodge did not survive the 1900 hurricane.[41]

White's Lake Hunting Resort was organized in 1906 by Newt Rogers and Galveston oyster merchant Dolph Rogers. The club's hunting and fishing clubhouse was built northeast of Lake Surprise on White's Lake, the early name for Lake Stephenson. In 1909 Galveston baseball legend Elias Kaphan managed the grounds, living in the clubhouse for the entirety of each hunting season.[42]

JHK RANCH

James Jackson founded JHK Ranch in the mid-1800s, settling on the banks of Double Bayou with his reluctant fourteen-year-old bride, daughter of cattleman James Taylor White. By the time he died in 1895, Jackson's landholdings extended from Frozen Point on East Bay to Double Bayou and from the mouth of Oyster Bayou to Lake Robinson.[43]

In *Home on the Double Bayou,* author Ralph Semmes Jackson wrote that in the late 1800s they shot ducks and geese not for sport but for food and feathers. When the prairie sky went black with geese, family and ranch hands hooked up a team and wagon and drove to within a couple hundred yards of the birds, then got down on their bellies to "crawl" them. Young boys sometimes flushed geese by circling a pond in an attempt to drive the birds toward waiting guns. The Jackson family also hunted over a trained steer, "the resulting slaughter of birds . . . tremendous." At night, roosting geese were approached on open lakes in small

Houston's Henry Palmer "Peg" Melton with his Model T and canvas tent attachment on a wet prairie, JHK Ranch, 1922. (Courtesy Palmer and Talley Melton)

A Peg Melton JHK Ranch hunt in 1927 that produced mallards, teal, pintails, and some specklebellies. The man standing in front of the trapper's rat shack is thought to be Cuz Milligan. (Courtesy Palmer and Talley Melton)

rowboats with a kerosene flare on the bow. Quietly sculling into the big flocks, several hunters would rise to fire a volley, usually filling the boat with geese.[44]

Sport hunting on JHK Ranch grew as sail and steam were replaced by gasoline engines. Houston mayor Richard Fonville brought his young nephew Henry Palmer "Peg" Melton from Kemah by motorboat in 1915 for Peg's first hunt. Peg found at JHK "numberless Canada honkers, mallards, and sprigs," and his party of eight killed four hundred birds. Peg never heard another gun or saw another hunter on the edge of East Bay.[45]

A few years later, Peg Melton determined to hunt the JHK Ranch by automobile, although his Model T got stuck on several attempts before he made it. The year was 1919, and it began a thirty-year tradition in which family and friends left Houston on Friday and returned from the hunt on Sunday. With no hotels or guest houses, they slept in muskrat trapper shacks or camped on the prairie, hunting ten thousand acres of salt grass marsh on East Bay west of Oyster Bayou.

JAMES BERT JACKSON SR. *of JHK Ranch, 1930s, with son James Bert Jr. and daughter Mary Jean Jackson Abshier. (Courtesy Mary Jean Abshier)*

JHK RANCH *shooting preserve license, 1935. (Courtesy Mary Jean Abshier)*

Younger son Talley Melton says, "That marsh was hell. It was an effort to get from where we camped to the sloughs."[46]

As automobiles brought more sportsmen during the 1920s, James Bert Jackson, grandson of the ranch founder, opened JHK to day hunters. Daughter Mary Jean Jackson Abshier says visitors paid a gate fee at the family ranch house and signed a permit book. JHK's ranch hands, mostly African Americans from Double Bayou, who worked as guides included Buster Humphreys, Clark North, Desiree "Sweet" Johnson, and Matt and Freddie Johnson.[47]

Without guides, hunters got lost and they got stuck. JHK was reached by White's Ranch Road between Smith Point and High Island, and it was sand until the late 1940s. Freddie Abshier says, "The drier it got the worse it got. People got stuck all the time. Everybody had teams of mules and pull 'em out." If they negotiated the route in, they next had to contend with ranch roads. Jackson and his cowboys employed a team of mules to locate lost hunters and pull others out of rice fields, ditches, and mud. Jim Bob Jackson remembers a hunter who arrived at his doorstep late at night, face and hands swollen from mosquitoes after a long walk from a stuck vehicle, professing, "I have never been so tortured by rain,

EAST BAY → 101

cold, heat, mud and mosquitoes and swear I will never come back to Chambers County."[48]

Sometimes it was worse. In 1926 two duck hunters driving across the field in the predawn hours spotted a shape, eyes gleaming in the headlights. Certain it was a wolf, one of the hunters aimed his rifle and squeezed the trigger. Their wolf turned out to be Houston's D. C. Lillard, his eyes reflecting the light of his pasture campfire. Lillard was rushed to the Jackson ranch house, then driven to Devers and loaded on the G&I train bound for Houston, where he died. On a cold November day in 1932, newly appointed Beaumont deputy game warden Mark W. "Pete" Hargrove and companion Louis Bond Jr. froze to death on a hunt.[49]

The twenty-six-thousand-acre JHK day hunting operation brought sportsmen from throughout Texas and the United States. Mary Jean Abshier recalls the excitement when pioneer aviator Wiley Post and social commentator Will Rogers came to hunt in the 1930s, and the sadness shortly after when they died in an airplane crash in Alaska. Big-city businesses and hotels, including Houston's swank Shamrock Hotel, provided JHK day hunting permits to clients and customers in the late 1940s and '50s. Jackson's day hunting operation outgrew the family home, and he moved it to a one-room shack run by gatekeeper Johnny Wilson and later Jim Bob Jackson.[50]

The Jackson family also leased to season hunters with private camps built by family and friends. One was Clifton "Pappy" Hebert, proprietor of Hebert's Ritz Restaurant on McGowan Street, who leased one of Judge Guy Cade Jackson's ponds in the 1940s with Houston's Alex Wolff. Alex says Hebert always brought his African American cook from the restaurant, who was tasked with driving Hebert's jeep as far back in the marsh and as close to the blind as possible, carrying Hebert's Belgian-made 10-gauge, and with retrieving downed ducks. Hebert eventually lost the JHK lease. A devout Catholic, he sponsored a weekend youth hunt for boys from the Houston Catholic church. Alex Wolff says, "The altar boys kinda tore up the place, and Judge [Guy Cade] Jackson kicked us off."[51]

Rancher, oilman, and author Jim Bob Jackson chronicles his years at JHK in *JHK Ranch from the 1940s to the 1960s*. The ranch, deep in the East Bay marsh, was a prime destination for illegal hunters. Jim Bob writes that James Jackson had a number of run-ins with a regular bunch from High Island, whose logic was that "God made the ducks and God made me, so I can go wherever the ducks go." One night James approached a group shooting snow geese by moonlight, and they tried to shoot him. From then on James carried a single-action Colt .45 revolver during hunting season. "He said they'd never run him off his own land again."[52]

Guy Cade Jackson Jr., Jim Bob's father, started the private Jackson Hunting Camp on JHK Ranch in the early 1940s. Not fancy, it was constructed by moving some old houses together, including a bunkhouse, cookhouse, and guide shack. Dalton LaFour and Wilber "Guts" Kindle managed it, with Sherman Gill

```
          HUNTING PERMIT     00531
       HOUSTON SHELL LEASE (JACKSON RANCH)

            W. Ed Brown          , has Shamrock Accomoda-
tions for the evening of  Monday 27 December 1954    ,
and hunting privileges for the morning of    Tuesday    ,
    28 December 1954          , from Sunup until 11:00 A.M
                    Haulton Nesrsta
as a guest of                                            ,
Houston Shell & Concrete Company.

This permit is issued subject to the regulations of the lease

This permit is to be surrendered to the gatekeeper upon
departure.
                         J. Reynaldo
                        Issuing Agent,
                    Houston Shell & Concrete Co.

Hunting Station
Blind No                          McBride
```

JHK Ranch *hunting passes, sponsored by the Houston Shell and Concrete Co., were available to guests of the Shamrock Hotel. (Courtesy Mary Jean Abshier)*

The JHK Ranch *gatehouse, with gatekeeper Johnny Wilson (seated, right); and two others unidentified. (Courtesy Jim Bob Jackson)*

EAST BAY

A GOOD DAY *at Guy Cade Jackson's hunting camp with mallards and pintails, 1950. Left to right: Donny Smith, Pete Walker, and Jim Bob Jackson. In the background is the cook's shack. (Courtesy Joe Whitehead)*

the camp cook after the first cook quit, chased by a "brimmer" bull to the top of his car. Guides and local boys plucked all the ducks, and neighbor Joe Whitehead remembers on weekends "four or five of us would pick 100 to 150 ducks a day."[53]

At Jackson Hunting Camp, Guy Cade, a county judge with oil, cattle, and farming interests, entertained Texas and Washington, DC, businessmen and politicians, with regular guests the Pew family of Sun Oil. Mary Jean Abshier remembers when one guest, a vice president of a well known bank in Beaumont, shot too many geese. "He didn't want to waste them, so he drove up to the front of the Hotel Dieu hospital in Beaumont, piled up all the geese, rang the bell, and took off!"[54]

Jim Bob says some guests "drank all night, played poker, didn't feel like gettin' up in the morning, and Joe Whitehead and I shot ducks for them." Local ranch hands guided those with the gumption to make a morning hunt. The most colorful and revered was trapper and cowboy Matt Johnson. He loved the bottle and took a shot every morning before a hunt, then brought a pint with him. It eventually killed him.[55]

Guy Cade hunted the eighty-five-acre Jackson Reservoir with its wooden walkways to the blinds, and the Cane Hole north of the reservoir, a long and narrow pond surrounded by sea cane. Joe Whitehead says the Cane Hole was reserved for special guests, and on a hunt he made there, "Ducks were coming out of the northeast and were just falling into the decoys. I had one box of twenty-five shells and I had killed twenty-three ducks with the first twenty-four shells. I passed up two or three bunches to get a shot at a double and finally got my chance. I had one shell left and I didn't make the shot. I got too greedy. That is the best I ever shot, killing twenty-three ducks with twenty-five shells." Guy Cade abandoned his rustic Jackson Hunting Camp in the 1950s. He next moved the Pine Island schoolhouse to the ranch to use as a clubhouse for his Fin and Feather Club, but it was only open for a couple of years.[56]

Private clubs, day hunters, and family members at JHK Ranch enjoyed spectacular waterfowl hunting. Joe Whitehead as a boy hunted a big mud flat below the Jackson Reservoir often covered with pintails, but the only way to reach them was by crawling through the mud. On one hunt a muddy Joe and Bud Joeffrey shot forty-two sprigs, and he says, "It was way into the night before we got through picking them. Never heard so much complaining in your whole life."[57]

One of Freddie Abshier's favorite spots "was a big slash, about half a mile long and three hundred yards wide. It was a goose roost, where snow geese used the north end and Canadas the south end. That's the way we'd find it every morning." Another was Spunk Bean Slough, or Cane Bayou, north of Robinson Lake. Freddie says, "After a two-inch rain you couldn't shoot the ducks out of that slough. There were thousands of 'em. Big ducks, ten, fifteen, twenty in a bunch, would come in late after returning from the rice fields. One big mass of ducks would get up that had covered any of those natural ditches for maybe half a mile."[58]

During the days of rice threshers, Freddie shot geese from big piles of rice straw "forty to fifty feet wide and up to fifteen feet high. We'd dig us out a hole in the edge of it. The geese and ducks, especially if it was wet, they would go right into them straw stacks. That just made for easy hunting. We'd kill all we could pack out of there, that's for sure. Everybody done it, there wasn't no game wardens or nothin.'"[59]

Once a year the Jackson family allowed local boys to kill snow geese for Andy Anderson's Annual Wild Game Dinner for Disabled Veterans in Houston. Joe Whitehead remembers:

> The snow geese stayed down in the Oyster Bayou area where they ate the rat grass. Six of us went down one afternoon to kill a few. We killed about 30 when I decided to crawl the bunch. I got on my stomach in about four inches of water and rat grass waist high. I crawled right into the bunch and shot three times. I picked them up and put them on a muskrat bed. The geese did not go too far, so I crawled them again and again and shot them three more times. Out of the two bunches I killed 80 snow geese. Everybody else had to come to help carry them out of the marsh. One person could carry between 15 and 20, and it was nearly dark before we got out of the marsh. We had 120 [geese] to send to Houston.[60]

Palmer and Talley Melton hunted greater Canada geese as boys on JHK Ranch with their father, Peg. They remember hunting a pasture with a flowing water

TWENTY CANADA *geese, mostly greaters, taken on JHK Ranch in 1939, with Punk Cummins (left) and Houston's Henry Palmer "Peg" Melton. (Courtesy Palmer and Talley Melton)*

well, where "every year a group of Canadian honkers would come in and water at the well, and they would be there most of the winter. It was about three or four dozen at a time. My dad and his buddy would go over there and kill one or two apiece and then get out of there and let 'em alone." One day their father allowed a guest to hunt there, advising him to shoot only a couple. "Then Dad started hearing all this shooting. This guy had killed twenty-three of them. It never was any good anymore after that. My dad griped about that all the rest of his life."[61]

During World War II the Army Corps of Engineers targeted Jackson Ranch for use as a bombing range, and Guy Cade and James Jackson bartered a case of whiskey for their reconsideration. It was going to take more than whiskey when, in the early 1960s, the federal government approached Guy Cade intent on purchasing JHK for a national wildlife refuge. Jim Bob was there when the government lawyer from Albuquerque told his father, "'Mr. Jackson, we've been looking at this land since the '30s as a refuge for ducks,' and he says 'We want it. Now there's two ways to negotiate, friendly and hostile. You pick which one you want.'" Hunters' guns were silenced in 1963 when almost ten thousand acres of JHK Ranch became the Anahuac National Wildlife Refuge.[62]

The entrance to Anahuac NWR replaced James Jackson's day hunting shack, and nearby, Guy Cade Jackson Jr.'s Jackson Reservoir is now called Shoveler Pond. For thirty-seven years, Freddie Abshier continued to walk his beloved marsh, but not as a hunter. He was an employee of the refuge, and instead of carrying a gun, he carried surveying equipment.

BARROW'S RANCH AND JOE LAGOW

Bears were more common than cattle on the east side of Galveston Bay when Benjamin Barrow founded Barrow's Ranch on the forty-eight-hundred-acre Home Place land grant in 1836. Ralph J. Barrow ran Barrow's Ranch in the early 1900s, raising cattle and produce he sold to Galveston by way of market boats.

CAMPING IN *the sweet gum trees at Ralph Barrow's Home Place Ranch, 1917. Some of John Winter and Lindsey H. Dunn Sr.'s fifty-four mallards hang from the branches. (John Winter Collection, courtesy Cliff Fisher)*

Ralph's granddaughters Jean and Janet Lagow say that times were so lean the family came close to losing the ranch, and when Ralph opened Barrow's Ranch to day hunters in 1928, he did it because he needed the income. Ranch lands grew a few years later when Ralph inherited fourteen thousand acres from John Henry Jackson. The land was known to the family as the Big Ranch, but hunters came to know it as Barrow's Hunting Ranch.[63]

Day hunters who drove White's Ranch Road kept an eye out for the wooden cattle gate and shack where they paid the gate fee. High Island hunters came by boat, purchasing hunting permits at trapper Henry Hildebrant's Oyster Bayou shack set on tall pilings with wooden cisterns and no screens on the shuttered windows. Henry got most of what he needed by hunting or fishing, his only companionship "a bunch of pet skunks."[64]

The two-dollar Barrow's Ranch permit covered a guide who took customers into the "high prairie" by a cart harnessed to an ox. Freddie Abshier says in those days there were so many ducks they didn't have to go far into the marsh. "Wherever you could find the first water, as a rule, well, you could set up business right there." Decoys were rarely used because of the extra weight, with early guides preferring to stake out dead geese or ducks.[65]

Times were better for Ralph Barrow and Barrow's Ranch after World War II, and Janet and Jean Lagow can still picture their grandfather in his first motorized skiff, with two outboards on the back, driving madly through the ranch canals and bayous, wide-eyed visitors clinging to anything bolted down. In the late 1950s he bought an airboat. Janet remembers: "He'd tell an unwitting victim, 'Come on, I can put you right on a bunch of ducks and geese.' So he'd take off and he'd hit

JOE LAGOW *of Barrow's Ranch, late 1940s. (Courtesy Janet and Jean Lagow)*

it really hard to make a sharp turn and see those guys go flyin' off and just laugh! And he'd say, 'I'll pick you up on the way back! But now you watch out for those alligators!'" Jean adds, "You know, everybody would only ride with Mr. Barrow once. Nobody ever rode twice."[66]

Ralph couldn't throw future son-in-law Joe Lagow from his boat, and it impressed him. Born near Dallas in 1908, Joe first visited Barrow's Ranch in the 1930s while at Rice Institute. On one hunt he brought back a crippled snow goose he tried to nurse back to health in his dorm bathroom—until a classmate came running out naked, hollering about a goose in the shower. Joe was in the Army Air Corps during World War II, and when the military brass needed a weekend of entertainment, he knew a duck hunting spot in Chambers County. Locals craned their necks to watch the big planes with a crew of generals and colonels land on the grass strip next to Ralph J's ranch house. Only once did the plane overshoot the landing area, ending up in the fence along the road to Smith Point.[67]

Joe Lagow married Elizabeth Barrow in 1944 and took over the Barrow's Ranch hunting business. Long-time friend Bob Brister of the *Houston Chronicle* provides a vivid description of his first visit to Barrow's Ranch and the man who ran it:

> At 4 a.m. one foggy morning in 1953, with the sky shrieking with cries of snow geese, I walked past a half mile of parked cars full of hunters toward the lights of a little building beside a blacktop road southeast of Anahuac. This was the entrance to the famed Barrow's Ranch, thousands of acres of wild marsh full of waterfowl, and I was there for the same reason as all those other people. It was a place we could afford to hunt.
> ... Hovering in [Lagow's] face, chattering like a magpie, was some intoxicated woman making a scene because he wouldn't accept her license or hunting money. In the middle of the melee he glanced up at

The original Barrow Ranch's gatehouse. (Courtesy Jean and Janet Lagow)

Advertisement for Barrow's Ranch, probably 1960s. (Unreferenced newspaper clipping, Jean and Janet Lagow Collection)

me, eyes twinkling. "So you're the new outdoor writer at the *Chronicle?*" he asked loudly enough for everyone in the room to hear. "Just step aside a minute until I can tell you and your girlfriend here where to hunt."[68]

Joe's gatehouse was the heart of the hunting ranch, with stuffed birds and wooden decoys that hung from the ceiling, its walls covered in hunting photos and the certificate of Jack Holland and Martin "Bubba" Wood's fifty-year-old snow goose that was banded in Russia. Joe was usually behind his desk, on the telephone with newspapermen from Beaumont to Waco or a first time hunter—or it might just as well have been Governor John Connally, Governor Dolph Briscoe, Senator Phil Gramm, or Congressman Richard Kleberg.[69]

Joe manned the gatehouse every day except Christmas for hunters who made the pilgrimage from across Texas, the line of cars at the entrance growing every year. On the opening day of the 1950 season 113 hunters passed through the gates, and the number doubled within two years. On Saturday mornings son Donny and twin daughters Jean and Janet helped handle the crowd, filling out hunting permits and checking licenses and duck stamps. His daughters say as Joe eyed hunters driving through the gate with new, store-bought gear, he'd chide them with, "You're gonna have to shed off at least half of that if you're gonna walk in our marsh," or, "You know, you're gonna sink out of sight if you don't take some of that off!"[70]

At the 'rat shack inside Barrow's gate, hunters could get their ducks cleaned by Freddie Johnson or some of the other ranch hands. Nearby was an assortment of travel trailers that served as part-time homes to guide Jack Holland, winter Texans Roy Williams and Arley Welch, and Bud Baggs with his boudin and jambalaya. Friends of the family sometimes camped inside the gate. Baytown's J. W. Gammel brought renowned decoy carvers Rudy LeCompte and H. B. Creekmore, their limit of morning mallards simmering in the gumbo they cooked around the campfire that night. The rest of their mallards were hidden in a tow sack in the marsh, and after dark they went back to pick them up. Gordon LeCompte remembers there were so many geese it was sometimes too noisy to sleep.[71]

Barrow's Ranch was once endless sea cane dotted with prairie ponds and bayous. Hunters got lost, often wandering in circles. Sometimes it was amusing, as was the time Houstonian Grant Ilseng "left a trail of discarded ducks, geese, cartridges, coats, and sweaters, crawling when he became too exhausted to walk." Lagow, who picked it all up later, told him "he'd found it 'in a pregnant alligator's trail.'" Sometimes it was deadly, as in 1939 when twenty-three-year-old Howard Trinkle of Beaumont, lost and wandering for hours, died from exposure.[72]

Ox cart trails through the sea cane were replaced by cattle walks and later a shell road. Some hunters launched small skiffs on Oyster or East Bay Bayou or came across East Bay from Bolivar. Sooner or later, though, they had to walk the marsh to hunt, and, according to Bob Brister, they faced "a wild vastness of gumbo mud and cordgrass where you drove as far as you could without getting stuck, then slogged into a vastness of sulphur-stinking marsh water and potholes protected by towering cane." When Rudy LeCompte brought his brother for a hunt, the Barrow's Ranch walk provoked the Cajun to exclaim, "This place is from the devil!"[73]

Hunters, however, all came for the same reason. Barrow's Ranch, says Jack Holland, was a waterfowl mecca, where rising flocks of ducks and geese blackened the sky. The deep marsh held large concentrations of mallards as late as the 1960s. Goose Roost Slough, in the middle of the ranch, was an ancestral Canada goose roost that still held the giant birds as late as the 1970s as well as thousands of snows and specks.[74]

Every sportsman had their favorite spots. Guide Forrest West had three ponds in the back of the ranch near Elm Bayou and Joe's Home Place reservoir. Jack Holland held court on the west side, priding himself with limits of pintails and geese. Shannon Tompkins hunted Jackson's Ditch where it ran into Onion Bayou and Mueller's near East Bay Bayou. Gene Campbell hunted Goose Roost Slough for several years. Anahuac's Dave Wilcox, with his father and grandfather, hunted what they called Meat Pond and Wilcox Pond, which they found by trudging after flocks of ducks spotted on the horizon from a cattle walk. Years earlier, Beau-

Dizzy Dean (bottom left), *Joe Lagow* (bottom right), *Max Babineaux* (top left), *and Jack Holland's father, Lee Roy* (top right), *after a Barrow's Ranch hunt. (Courtesy Jack Holland)*

mont's Max Babineaux and baseball legend Dizzy Dean had found those two ponds the same way.[75]

Sea cane was high enough in Ralph Barrow's days that hunters never had a need for duck blinds. In the late 1950s the grasses began to disappear, a casualty of subsidence accelerated by transplanted nutria. In 1962, Joe was forced to start building the first blinds, the number reaching fifteen on the Home Place and more than forty on the Big Ranch, available on a first-come basis. Lagow raised the $4.00 day permit price to $5.00 in the 1960s, then $5.50. The $5.50 figure, according to rice farmer Aubrey Jones, "was the worst thing Joe ever did 'cause he never had change. After one year, he went back to $5.00."[76]

Joe's ability to walk Barrow's Ranch was legendary. His daughters say he liked to take athletes hunting and needle them about their ability to keep up with him. "Daddy would take them out to the deep marsh, and he'd say, 'Now if you're in really good athletic shape, why you huffin' and puffin' like that?' Daddy was only five foot, eight inches, but no one could cross a marsh like him. He was like a little purple gallinule." Freddie Abshier remembers, "That man left many a foot track in the marsh."[77]

The last year the entire ranch was in operation was 1979, when a staggering twenty thousand hunters passed through the gate and killed 19,643 geese and eighteen thousand ducks. That year the original gatehouse was moved west in anticipation of the sale of over twelve thousand acres of the Big Ranch for inclusion in Anahuac NWR. Fifty years of day hunting came to an end, although guided hunts were still available at the renamed Barrow's Hunting Preserve. Lagow manned the new gatehouse for a short time, with an increasing role from family members and guides Jack Holland and Gene Campbell.[78]

Joe Lagow left footprints in more than just the marsh. As a conservationist, Joe was an early supporter of Ducks Unlimited and established the first Chambers County DU chapter. In 1952 he popularized the idea of restricting shooting to the hours from sunrise to noon, and it wasn't long before that practice of morning only shooting spread across much of coastal southeast Texas. He developed and practiced innovative land use and wildlife restocking. At the Home Place reservoir in front of his house Joe nursed crippled waterfowl back to health, and it was home to Francis the pet deer and an assortment of otters, opossums, nutria, rabbits, and alligators.[79]

Joe's footprints extended to the Anahuac community as well. He was a Chambers County commissioner for twenty-four years and served on numerous boards. When Anahuac needed a new doctor, Joe offered as enticement a lifetime of hunting and fishing at Barrow's Ranch. Dr. Leonidas Andres answered the call, and decades later he is still at the hospital and still hunting and fishing. Lagow offered Barrow's Ranch to worthy research efforts, including early lead poisoning studies by Rice University biologist Dr. Frank Fisher and TPWD's Charles Stutzenbaker.[80]

Joe Lagow died in 1996 at age eighty-eight. A handwritten note on the last page of one of his scrapbooks lists the men he wanted as pallbearers at his funeral. It included Russell Clapper from Anahuac NWR and Dr. Andres. Despite years as a state conservationist and county politician, the remainder of the list was made up entirely of his favorite duck hunting guides.

BARROW'S RANCH GUIDES

Some of the guides who cut their teeth at Barrow's Ranch were, and some still are, among the best in Texas. The names of the African American men who led the first hunting parties into the marsh by ox cart for Ralph Barrow are mostly lost to history except for one, Elmer "Crack Corn" Jackson. Crack Corn was from Double Bayou and started guiding at the age of twelve. The most requested guide on the ranch, he was the first to leave the gate in the morning and the first to return, nearly always with full limits. A broken arm that never set well forced him, in his later years, to shoot a .410, and with that small-gauge gun he still outshot just about every other hunter. Gordon LeCompte can still picture Crack Corn quietly watching flights of greater Canadas, then finding a ridge to pass shoot them. Crack Corn guided well into his seventies.[81]

Other guides included Crack Corn's nephew, Rufus Jackson, a third-generation waterfowler from Anahuac who mouth-called geese and shot nothing larger than a 20-gauge. Forrest West and Sonny Baughman both got their

IN THEIR OWN HAND: *Barrow's Ranch guides from the 1970s. (Courtesy Jean and Janet Lagow)*

start with Joe Lagow in the 1960s. Other well-known guides were Jack Inmon, Harry Fair, Earl "Bluebill" Sanders, and Nathon "Spoonbill" Byrom. Guide Gene Campbell went out on his own in 1982 and later opened Oyster Bayou Hunting Club, and Mike Ladnier started Bay Prairie Outfitter and Lodge in Midfield. Shannon Tompkins, who guided at Barrow's Ranch when he was in college, says Joe always made sure he had a weekend party to help him earn money for expenses.[82]

Jack Holland was another Barrow's Ranch guide who gained a national following. Jack was born in Hayes, Louisiana, and he says as a young boy his family hunted to eat. Jack's half-century of guiding started at Barrow's Ranch in 1964, and it was an inauspicious beginning. He says, "There were two groups of people that Joe Lagow tried to keep out of Barrow's Ranch—cattle rustlers and poachers." Jack Holland was a poacher.

Young Jack the poacher launched a flat-bottomed boat on the road between Smith Point and White's Ranch to run the bayous to the back side of Barrow's Ranch. He says, "I'd go in there and I'd kill all these birds and go back and talk to people at the shack and show 'em. And Joe [Lagow] said, 'Where you killing all those birds?' and I said, 'Barrow's Ranch.' He said, 'Well, I never seen you come through this gate.' So Joe told me if 'I ever catch ya back in there I'm gonna file trespassing charges on you.' 'Yeah, Mr. Joe, but you'll never catch me.'"

Jack was wrong. He was hunting Jackson's Ditch in 1964, and, he recalls,

I'm sitting out there with some friends of mine and we were blastin' away and here comes a hunter. And of course we never seen any day hunters, we never saw anybody back there 'cause it was too far. It was six miles from the main gate up there. In the marsh it would be at least two miles and two miles in the marsh is a long way. This guy kept on coming and finally he got pretty close. I was hollerin' "Man, move, you're gonna get hit!" He just kept his head down and kept on walking, and it was Mr. Lagow. "I told you I was gonna catch ya!"

Lagow told Jack to meet him at the gatehouse. "So I went by that shack and he said, 'You know I hate to turn you in, but I told you I was gonna turn you in.' I figured I was in trouble. He said, 'I'll tell you what I'll do. Can you hunt in the morning? I got some people here that want to kill ducks and geese on the same hunt.' I said, 'Well, if I take 'em out for you, then I'll be free?' 'Yeah, but I better not catch you back there again.'" The party, from Dallas, had a good hunt, and Jack was asked to return, this time for a fee.

Joe Lagow was fifty-six years old when he walked the part of the marsh where few other hunters ventured, and it started Jack Holland's guiding career. The next year Jack opened Green Head Guide Service, taking clients to Lake Conroe, the Trinity River near Dayton, and his regular spots on Barrow's Ranch. Customers included such notables as pioneering heart surgeons Michael DeBakey and Denton Cooley, outdoor radio show host Bob Stephenson of station KTRH, Nolan Ryan of the Houston Astros, and Phil "Scrap Iron" Gardner when he was a Los Angeles Dodger.

Jack guided Boston Red Sox baseball legend Ted Williams, an outstanding shot with a reputation at the end of a fusillade for claiming most of the birds on the water. Jack says, "I was instructed by Williams's buddies that when we downed several ducks they would claim them and I would take what was left—leaving Williams shooting zero." Jack called the shots, congratulating the others on their fine shooting. A frustrated Williams saw a flock of ducks approaching the spread, stood up, and downed three ducks at fifty-five yards before anyone else could shoot. He yelled a few choice words that left his amused friends no doubt who killed the ducks—and for that matter most of the morning's bag.[83]

Passionate about waterfowl hunting, Jack taught hunting, fishing, and dog training classes at North Harris County College for sixteen years. His friends cannot agree which was better—his retrievers and their eight-hundred-yard marks, or his marksmanship. Long-time friend Walter Besser recalls he "wore out two or three Browning A-5 automatics." Jack laughs, "Yeah, they're supposed to be a gun of a lifetime."[84]

From the early days when Jack the poacher squirmed uncomfortably as Joe Lagow pondered his punishment for trespassing, Jack is proud of how, sixteen years later, he helped run Barrow's Hunting Preserve for the family. He sold Green Head Guide Service to Will Beaty of Central Flyway Outfitters in 1998, bringing about the end of his thirty-three-year operation. For a time he hunted

A HUNT *at Barrow's Ranch, 1975, guided by Jack Holland* (top right). *(Courtesy Jean and Janet Lagow)*

and guided on the north side of Lake Livingston, then he moved to Estes Flats near Rockport, where he still hunts every day of the season.[85]

JOE WHITEHEAD AND WHITEHEAD RANCH

Joe Whitehead was born in 1933 and until he died in 2012, lived on the ranch near Smith Point first settled by his great-grandfather, Joseph. Arriving in Galveston from England in 1871, Joseph purchased land sight unseen on East Bay and built a house on the rise of an old Indian mound. As the structure washed away during the hurricane of 1875, the family climbed into their bois d'arc sailboat, and the little vessel carried them inland on the storm surge. When the boat came to rest on the only land protruding above the water—Ingleside Ridge—Joseph Whitehead bought it. Five generations of Whiteheads have since weathered hurricanes on the Whitehead Ranch.

Whitehead Ranch covers part of Wallis Lake to the north shore of Lake Surprise. The prairie between is a green sea of cutgrass, cordgrass, and saltgrass, the water's edge marked first by cattails and then bulrushes and sea cane. Waterways boil with shrimp, blue crabs dart from the shallows, and redfish "tail" on calm mornings beneath a sky filled with herons, egrets, roseate spoonbills, and pelicans. On the northwest edge of Lake Surprise small mounds of clam and oyster shells with pottery shards mark where Native Americans first saw the great flocks of canvasbacks, and in the distance the small white structure on pilings was once Moody's place.

It was here that Addison Whitehead, Joe's grandfather, hunted ducks for the market, fetching a dollar a pair, which paid for the construction in 1898 of the house that stands today. His son Buddy, or Ad, was the first of the Whiteheads who could afford the luxury of hunting for sport, and on a narrow slough east of

Lake Surprise he built a concrete blind that the family used for over seventy years. Joe made his first hunt in that blind at four years old, and it was where his father made his last hunt nearly fifty years later.[86]

Joe Whitehead documented his family's hunting lore in an unpublished memoir he titled "Ducks," and it is as entertaining as it is a rare window to a vanished time of mallards, canvasbacks, and big ringneck Canada geese on the upper Texas coast. In those days there were only a few specklebelly and blue geese, Joe says, but plenty of snow geese. As a boy, little about the hunt had changed from the days of his grandfather. Joe still got to the marsh by horseback and crawled through the marsh for ducks instead of using decoys. Since he didn't own waders, a morning hunt was always wet and often cold.

Joe traversed all the great East Bay ranches. He remembers as a boy when his father hunted a small hole in the sea cane on nearby Canada Ranch "and came out of the marsh with forty-five mallards, all drakes with one hen." Joe was six years old when, with his full-choke .410 shotgun, he shot his first greater Canada "ringneck" goose:

> Daddy was helping Mr. Canada rebuild a cow shed that had blown away in a hurricane that summer. About a hundred and fifty yards out in the pasture was an artesian well. It was a dry fall and all the ringnecks were watering there. The grass was about three-feet tall, and when they lit I picked out one where I could see the head sticking up above the grass. He was too big to carry so I had to drag it back to the shed. I went back and killed another one, and had to drag him too. They would not let me kill anymore as the season was not open.

Joe hunted ringnecks on the south side of Trinity Bay and remembers, "Daddy and I would go after a norther, and with the tide out, the geese would come over to pick up gravel. We would build a blind in the bluff bank with logs and would put out 12 tin decoys that Daddy had made. I killed two greater Canada geese there that weighed 20 pounds a piece, and they were too heavy to carry." On another hunt, "the geese came just after sunup. We had 13 come in to us and killed nine with six shots."[87]

Ducks on the East Bay marshes once gathered in flocks so large that at times the mist under rising birds was too thick to see through. For boys like Joe, those birds were sport, but for their families they were food on the table. Joe says the most ducks he killed out of one bunch, by himself, was on Robinson Bayou during a hard norther. With high sea cane on the bank, "I didn't have to crawl at all. I had a 12-gauge, 32-inch barrel, and a full choke. I shot three times and I had cripples going in all directions." When Joe ran out to pick up the ducks, "their wings stuck to the mud, and I got every crippled duck, nothing got away. They were sprigs and teal and I picked up 38 ducks."[88]

JOE WHITEHEAD *with mallards and greater Canada geese—"ringnecks"—at the Smith Point Whitehead Ranch, 1941. (Courtesy Joe Whitehead)*

Joe watched as great changes came to East Bay and Lake Surprise. He said, "Maybe in the last 15 years I've seen one bunch of canvasbacks. And we don't even see redheads anymore. Maybe two or three pair of black mallards now is all you'll ever see. There's no food." But as the fourth-generation Chambers County rancher reflected on his lifetime as an outdoorsman and waterfowler, he said "It's been a good trip."[89]

FREDDIE ABSHIER

Like Joe Whitehead, Freddie Abshier has a long attachment to the land and the waterfowling heritage of Chambers County. Born in Hankamer on the Trinity River, he is a gifted storyteller, a link to the days when mallards were the most common duck on hunters' straps, and a witness to the change. As a boy Freddie retrieved ducks for the family. He says, "I was a bird dog for many years. My dad was of a family of thirteen, and ten of 'em was boys. Daddy and one of the brothers had wagons pulled by mules or horses, and they had a box built where three people could sit and whatever decoys they had. In about 1934, when I was seven, eight years old, they'd put me in the box with them. You wouldn't have to go more than a mile from the house and it was duck hunting country. Wherever you run into the first slough in the prairie, that's where you set up camp."

On a morning shoot his father and uncles sometimes killed close to a hundred birds, and for their bird dog it was frantic work. Freddie says, "It got to where if I was pickin' 'em up and they were still alive, first thing I did is just put their head in my mouth and bite 'em through the head. The head would crush. That's the reason my teeth aren't as good now. There ain't no tellin' how many hundred of duck I have bit. That kills 'em instantly, something about that brain. It's the fastest way, rather than wring his neck, or hit 'em over the gun barrel or the stock. A lot of us done it."

The kill was hauled from the field in tow sacks made of lightweight burlap. They were called 220s or 110s, named for how many pounds of rice they held. "We'd stuff those birds in these sacks, one, two, three sacks of ducks. Sometimes when we emptied them out there would be one or two still alive get up and fly off. We talked about that a whole lot."[90] When Freddie started shooting, his first gun was a double-barreled 16-gauge Lefever Nitro Special. He loaded two shells in the chambers and held a third one in his mouth. "I killed a many a three ducks that way." He wore old tennis shoes because he couldn't afford waders, and "the water did get cold."

Freddie moved to Anahuac after World War II, married James Jackson's daughter Mary Jean, and began guiding at JHK and the adjoining Barrow's Ranch. Freddie says, "We didn't take money, we took it in something to hunt with," usually shotgun shells or boots. "The first good pair of hip boots we ever owned was when Dizzy Dean and Judge Ben Connally brought 'em to us. And then when Red Ball come out with their hip boot they brought us a couple pair. That was the first time we ever got to hunt dry-footed every day, because we had a spare pair of boots." Freddie remembers:

> Two of our good people was black undertakers out of Dallas, and they'd come in here in a big black Cadillac, and they'd have two or three cases of whisky and a gun and cases of beer and hip boots. Shotgun shells by the case. They'd sit right there at the car on the levee and drink beer and eat corned beef sandwiches and never change out of their house shoes into their boots. They never would fire a cap. They had a good time drinkin' and eatin,' and we were having a good time hunting. We'd go out there three hundred yards to a big pond where it wasn't no problem with killing a limit in forty-five minutes, and I mean pick the ducks, greenheads, pintails, nothing but the males. Don't shoot no females. We'd kill 'em two limits of ducks and they'd have a big ice chest there. When they left, they'd leave us six, seven cases of shotgun shells.

Freddie guided five-star general Henry "Hap" Arnold and Texas writer Hart Stilwell, who liked to hunt snipes. "I'd locate a good bunch of jack snipe where they were roostin,' and he'd wander around in the boggy marshes. The overflow around these windmills were ideal places for jack snipe. You could just walk a hundred yards around that watering trough and shoot jack snipe all day long."[91]

Regular hunting partners were mechanic Jack Chambliss and *Houston Chronicle* outdoor writer Bob Brister, and in the days before marsh buggies, a day's hunt meant a long walk. "By the durn time you got a limit, you [had walked] back in mile, mile and half back in that marsh, and you had all the load you wanted to

FREDDIE ABSHIER *in 1957 with the marsh buggy he built with Jack Chambliss and Bob Brister in the 1950s. There are not very many hen pintails in the picture. (Courtesy Mary Jean Abshier)*

come out of there with. But I don't even know whether we even paid any attention to a limit back in those days. Old man Frank Clarkson was the only federal warden, and sometimes we knew where he was at and sometimes we didn't."

The long walk in the marsh ended when Freddie and Jack Chambliss built one of the first marsh buggies in Chambers County from an old army four by four truck. "Bob Brister was one of the backers 'cause he knew people and he could get parts, he could get stuff. He brought us a twenty-five-horse upright Kohler [air-cooled engine]. We stripped that buggy but kept the transmission and rear end. Somebody had a connection that got us these C-46 airplane tires. So they brought us four of those. We modified the wheels to fit the buggy. We was in business. The traction wasn't no good, the tires were smooth, so we got three-quarter-inch chains and welded hooks onto the rims. We got over them marshes like you wouldn't believe."

Freddie hunted the days when mallards were plentiful in Chambers County. He remembers

> this one slough about sixty yards wide and a quarter mile long. And when the mallard ducks would be coming out of the rice field to the north, their old throat would be big around, puffed out, full of rice, and their old head reared back, and we'd get 'em to break, it might be seven, eight, nine, ten, eleven in the bunch and whenever they set their feet right on top of the water, well that's when we go to work on them. That ol' greenhead and that bull sprig, he was the top dog on that marsh. And the fellow who killed the most of 'em, well, he was kinda in the top dog bunch.

With his regular cronies there wasn't much they had to discuss about blind etiquette. "You're gonna take 'em on the right and I'm gonna take 'em on the

EAST BAY → 119

left. If there's more greenheads on my side, well don't come over on my side. You didn't cross over just because you run out of mallard drakes over on your side. You just shut down; you didn't come over here and help. And you don't want to kill no hens, either."

The only things that ever troubled Freddie in the marsh were fog and water moccasins. "In the fog, I don't care what kind of marshman you are, you're gonna get lost. The man that tells me he's never been lost in the fog, he's just never been in the fog. I'd look for a windmill for marker. Sometimes I'd end up all the way at East Bay or even on the road in. Lost, just as lost." Of water moccasins, or cottonmouths, Freddie says, "I had dogs bit by 'em. I had to pack those dogs three hundred or four hundred yards. Choking to death was common until we started takin' those collars off 'cause their neck swelled up. I've lost two or three dogs that way. I guess the most cottonmouths I ever killed in one spot was probably twenty or twenty-five. I mean just as big as they grow."

Freddie remembers the days when "we've had [as many as] ten mallards come in a bunch, and after we shot, there might be one, two, three ducks fly away. There'd be lots of times we'd had seven, eight, nine drakes feet first on the pond. That's not braggin,' that's just telling you the way it was. It's just like it happened yesterday. Now you could go down there and look for a shot like that and I'd spend the rest of my life and never get a shot like that again." From family bird dog to guide, Freddie Abshier looks back on his lifetime of waterfowl hunting and says only two words: "I'm satisfied."[92]

JACKSON BROTHERS RANCH

Felix, Arthur A., and Ocie Jackson hold a special place in the hunting lore of East Bay. Their father was Double Bayou's John Henry Jackson, their mother Charlotte Lewis, a nurse from Louisiana who likely came to Double Bayou during the 1877 smallpox epidemic. As Karla Jackson Dean tells the story, Charlotte Lewis "was a mixture of Karankahua Indian and possibly other races. She had a choice. She could be thought of as a black person, a descendant of slaves, or a savage [Indian] that ate people." She chose the former.[93]

When John Henry died, his three sons inherited the ranch lands on the east side of Oyster Bayou just as the Felix Jackson No. 1 well, spudded in 1937, discovered the giant Oyster Bayou Oil Field. With the flow of oil came money, and the Jackson Brothers, who everyone assumed were black, became wealthy men during a time when color and money were an uncommon combination. Karla Dean says, "Felix managed the ranch and [the oil] field, and my grandfather Arthur A. was the financier." Ocie, born in 1904, was almost twenty years younger than his brothers and was as comfortable working cattle on the ranch on horseback as he was in the Lamar University boardroom.[94]

JACKSON BROTHERS *Ranch, 1950, showing L. B. Lewis* (far left), *Felix Jackson* (with his arm on the fence post), *and Ocie Jackson* (behind and to Felix Jackson's right). *Others are unidentified. (Courtesy Arthur and Quentin Jackson family)*

Arthur James Jackson says that, in the years before oil, "Our grandfathers would hunt every day. They lived off of the game they killed. They didn't do it for it sport." The brothers hunted a marsh where "the cane was so high, twelve feet in areas, and the ducks so low, that you could reach up and touch them." They crossed the marsh by horseback and often hunted over mules, as "mules weren't afraid of the gun shot. A horse would jump and run. The mule served as [both] a blind and as an animal to pack the birds out."[95]

With oil, hunting was no longer a necessity. The Jacksons could afford to hunt for fun and built a ranch house for family and business entertaining. They no longer had to fetch their own ducks; they hunted over retrievers, mostly English spaniels or Ocie's Chesapeake Bay retrievers. Guests were guided by ranch cowboys, who trapped and plucked ducks to supplement their income and kept Jackson visitors out of trouble. Quinten Jackson says, "There's places in our marsh where if you don't know where you're goin' you'll disappear. We had floating turf and alligator holes. We had a motto that we always used: 'If the water was black, you don't step there, 'cause you'll disappear.'"[96]

The guest list at the ranch was extraordinary. Guide Jack Holland remembers "seeing fancy cars from as far away as New York and California pull in." Arthur James recalls visits by Willie Mays, Wilt Chamberlain, and football players from the Dallas Cowboys and New York Jets, including Joe Namath. Ball player Gus Holloman took home more than just a limit of ducks when he married a local girl.[97]

Of the brothers, Ocie Jackson was well known to the community as a benefactor who, Karla Dean says, "Put kids through school with scholarships that would not have been able to go because of color or money. He gave those kids

EAST BAY → 121

opportunity."[98] But he never lost his connection with the land. A family member says of Ocie that in his later years he missed two calves in "pick-up" rodeo, and he never roped again. The man who was a very good shot also knew when it was time to stop hunting. "He missed three geese one day, and he never hunted again."[99]

CANADA RANCH AND EAST BAY LODGE

The ranch of colorful George R. "Ray" Canada, west of JHK Ranch, covered parts of Robinson Bayou and Willow or Gordy Marsh. Crossing the prairie on horseback, Joe Whitehead hunted with the Canadas and the ranch's next owners, the Ezer family, shooting ducks from sunken barrel blinds along Robinson Bayou. He remembers, "You'd ride up the bayshore bank and by the time you got to Robinson Bayou, there'd be two or three hundred [greater Canadas] in front of you and they'd get up, and then [you'd jump] another two or three hundred."[100]

In 1956 the west side of Robinson Lake to Lake Stephenson became the exclusive Brown and Root Company East Bay Lodge. Brown and Root founder Herman Brown lived for business and loved to hunt, and East Bay Lodge served both purposes well. Herman accessed his lodge, with its huge fireplace and commercial kitchen, by a private landing strip and constructed a clay target and live pigeon shooting area on the grounds. Central Texas rancher Ralph Leggett was brought in to manage the operation. More comfortable in cattle country than in East Bay marshes, Ralph had never seen an alligator or a muskrat when he first arrived, and for him it "was a different world."

Ralph says in those days the North Reservoir at Lake Stephenson still had quite a few canvasbacks, and surrounding marshes held "lots of Canadians and mallards. There were only a few blue geese, and I'll bet there weren't ten specklebellies." Ralph, the man at first more suited to Central Texas's bluestem prairie, learned his coastal craft well. He managed water levels and salinities and studied the types of foods that attracted ducks, planting sago pondweed and Japanese millet. Knowing that nearby Lake Surprise once held wild celery, he tried to plant it, but it never grew.[101]

Ralph, who shared guiding duties with Ralph Holmes and Cecil "Copy" Carrington, remembered the time neither one of them showed up for a morning hunt. "Sheriff Buster of Harris County was hunting with us, and I said, 'Buster, call the damn jail and see if they're in jail.' And they were." Copy Carrington guided at East Bay for forty years.[102]

Chambers County farm roads, usually traversed by old pickups and tractors, were filled during hunting season with black Cadillacs heading to East Bay Lodge. Lyndon Johnson and Governor John Connolly hunted here with many other politicians and businessmen of the period, and Ralph, who guided them, says, "You didn't really guide Johnson. He was in command." On Johnson's visits, the Secret Service took over the lodge. But they couldn't control the farm roads; Johnson "would drive ninety [mph] in his Lincoln [or] Cadillac. The secret service couldn't keep up."[103]

Ralph says, "I never will forget we had Governor Connally and a group of them down. It was all political. Early that next morning we put 'em all out in their blinds, we got 'em set, and about 8:30 or 9:00 and here comes every policeman and game warden in the county. And then the helicopter came in with frogmen. Governor Connally was hunting up there in the goose preserve where the ringnecks came in. And they landed the helicopter there and blew his decoys all over the place. They tried to catch us everywhere they could. Governor Connally said, 'I'm not putting up with this.' There were some telephone calls being made." Joe Whitehead watched as the lawmen confiscated all their ducks, then three days later the helicopter returned to give them all back.[104]

Some of Brown and Root's guests were evidently more suited to the halls of power than the duck blind. Cecil Carrington once told the story of a group of hunters who said they didn't need a guide, then spent the morning shooting pelicans they mistook for snow geese. With a sly grin, Leggett said, "We sent 'em home with them. We even had them cleaned." When the Brown and Root era ended in the 1960s, Ralph leased the land and lodge as a private club. Waterfowling lost Ralph Leggett in 2010.[105]

KOLE FARM

The calls of greater Canada geese echoed across the prairie at sunset as the big geese headed for "the goose roost," two hundred acres of water that collected in a natural depression where Elm Bayou met East Bay Bayou in eastern Chambers County. It was originally part of the extensive White Ranch, then in the mid-1940s it was purchased by Port Arthur resident James Stephen "Skeet" Kole Sr., who raised eleven children in the house he built among his rice fields.

Eldest son Steve Jr. recalls most area rice farmers bought their water from canal companies, but his father built his own pumping station on East Bay Bayou and often ran it "non-stop for six weeks, turning it off long enough only to change the oil." That water filled the five-hundred-acre Kole Reservoir, built on the site of the old goose roost that local newspapers described as little more than "200 acres of wasteland marsh."[106]

The Kole Reservoir displaced the goose roost but created duck habitat. Huge flocks of circling ducks inspired Skeet to start a private hunting club, the first of three clubs on Kole Farm over the past seventy years. He built a boat shed and ten numbered boat blinds, and since telephones did not reach the farm until 1958 he posted a schedule in one of the outbuildings so members could keep track of their location. Son Steve says the hunting was as much about barter as it was about income. With eleven children, "Daddy traded hunting for doctors and even for things like dry cleaning."[107]

Skeet Kole *in the early 1940s on the Kole farm with greater Canada geese. (Courtesy Skeet Kole family)*

Storm surge from Hurricane Carla in 1961 breached the Kole Reservoir levees and killed its freshwater vegetation. Damage was so extensive that Skeet closed the hunting club and converted Kole Reservoir to cropland. "Carla," Steve says, "ended an era." Skeet died the next year at fifty-two years of age.[108]

The Kole family later sold the farm to Chuck Jones and Bobby Allen, who restored Kole Reservoir and leased the hunting rights to Houston's Pilant Club. The club was founded on the Hale Ranch in Fort Bend County, but when it made the move to Chambers County, it stayed for thirty years. Pilant Club members over the decades witnessed the mallard slowly giving way to pintails, and the greater Canadas to snow and specklebelly geese.[109]

When Will Beaty and his partners in Winnie's Central Flyway Outfitters bought the Jones and Allen farm, they dreamed big, re-creating the days of plush, private East Bay hunting clubs with carefully constructed habitat. By then Skeet Kole's reservoir had grown up in acres of bulrushes and cane, with little open water. Working with Ducks Unlimited, Marsh Point owners restored the reservoir and adjacent properties, providing several ponds for year-round mottled duck habitat. By 2008 they had a total of sixteen DU projects underway, and their long-term plan included donating the conservation easements to DU in perpetuity.[110]

Then came Ike. The hurricane, in one furious moment, sent a twelve-foot wall of water across the prairie, leveling Marsh Point lodge, buildings, and habitat infrastructure. Hurricane Ike, like Carla nearly fifty years earlier, could have spelled the end of the Marsh Point club, but it didn't. On the back of the property a new pumping station is running almost nonstop to pump fresh water into a freshly repaired levee system. A flock of mottled ducks rises from the site of the two hundred acres between Elm and East Bay Bayous that, for almost a hundred years, was called the goose roost.

CHAPTER 6

TRINITY RIVER DELTA

North of East Bay, past the narrow, tree-lined harbors of Lone Oak Bayou and Double Bayou and the wharves at Anahuac, hunters in the 1800s found the mouth of the Trinity River a pristine delta wilderness. From the river's headlands in the central interior plains, over four hundred miles of Trinity River fresh waters terminated at Trinity Bay, forming, like fingers on a hand, lobes of rich, clastic sediment. Trinity River delta building processes created river meanders such as Old River Lake; lakes in the timber bottoms such as Turtle Bay, Lake Charlotte, and Mud Lake; and the wetland lakes of Lost Lake, Cotton Lake, and Wet Marsh Pond.

The delta was a paradise for wildfowl, earning mention in the 1883 *Sportsman's Gazetteer and General Guide,* which cataloged prolific gunning locations in the United States. There were times when ducks covered the entire horizon over Trinity delta. Near the turn of the century Smith Point's Forrest McNeir killed more than one hundred ducks one morning without missing a shot, dropping every one in a little alligator hole.[1]

Large concentrations of geese frequented the gravel bars of Southwest Pass. Cove guide Damon McKay recalled that there were no blue geese in the early 1900s, but there were plenty of "the white ones and Canadas." He said that gunners only had to sit down "by a log and wait for 'em to come in, they'd come in and light pert' near on you if you didn't move." The delta passes also held large numbers of swans. On a steamboat in 1866, English hunter Frank Flack wrote that he was "astonished to see vast numbers of swans. . . . We estimated that at least two thousand were in sight from the deck." Swans were hunted on the Trinity River delta until the early 1900s.[2]

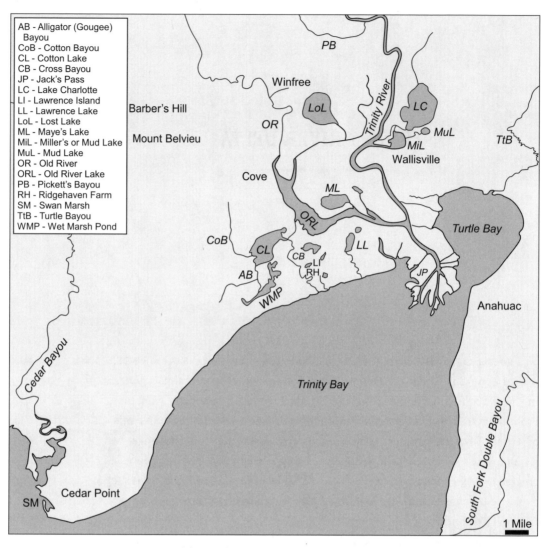

TRINITY RIVER *delta as it looked in the early 1900s. The entirety of the Wet Marsh Pond (WMP) disappeared with construction of a Houston Lighting & Power Company cooling pond.*

HUNTERS MADE *Trinity River delta crossings on small wooden ferries. Shown here in 1921 is the Jack's Pass ferry, which Houston's John Winter used as camping headquarters. (John Winter Collection, courtesy Cliff Fisher)*

128 ← COASTAL TEXAS HUNTING CLUBS, GUIDES, AND PLACES

THE TRINITY RIVER *delta produced phenomenal hunts for Houston sportsmen in the 1920s. Pictured are John Winter (left) and Ralph B. Lechenger in front of the C. L. and Theo Bering Hardware and Sporting Goods with 186 ducks, mostly mallards and pintails, after a Cove hunt in 1921. (John Winter Collection, courtesy Cliff Fisher)*

Snipe hunting, too, was a big sport on the delta. In the late 1800s the captain of the steamer *Kate* kept his crew and guests entertained on Trinity River passages by shooting snipes and plovers from the bow of the boat. Fred Badger, a sportsman and writer traveling throughout North America in the late 1800s, spent weeks aboard a sailboat on the Trinity River Delta shooting snipes on the "burnt prairie."[3]

Hunters crossed Trinity River Delta waterways by horse-drawn and wooden ferries and rented cypress plank skiffs at most of the ferry landings or at Charles T. Joseph's general store on the west bank of Old River. By the 1910s automobiles turned Trinity River hunting into big business. Houston was only a sixty-mile drive on roads north to Dayton then south through Mont Belvieu to Cove, although with rain and mud the drive could take all night.[4]

HUNTING CLUBS AND GUIDES

According to Cove historian Kendon Clark, the old guides "looked with some suspicion as the hunting clubs from the cities opened in the area." The earliest was probably the Potlikker's Club, organized in the late 1910s on Wet Marsh Pond on Lawrence Marsh. Cove Hunting and Fishing Club was started in 1922 by Harris County sportsmen, who purchased land from M. E. "Ras" Stubbs north of Old River Lake. Houston oilman Lindsey Dunn Sr. was an early club president.[5]

Winfree's Cove, later just called Cove, was the center of Trinity River delta sport hunting. Perched on a bluff west of the river, the community overlooked Old River Lake, with Lost Lake to the east, Cotton Lake to south, and a maze of

TRINITY RIVER DELTA → 129

Lost Lake *in 1921. Shown are a duck boat, a motorized skiff loaded with mallards, wooden factory decoys, and wooden silhouette duck decoys on a fanning rod, with Ed Bond (left) and an unidentified hunter. (John Winter Collection, courtesy Cliff Fisher)*

Charles Wilburn *(right) with Lindsey H. Dunn Jr. in Cove, November 1946. (Lindsey H. Dunn Jr. Collection, courtesy Royce A. Strickland)*

bayous, ponds, potholes, and marshes between. Early Cove area guides included Ras Stubbs, who, with his one-cylinder inboard boat, guided on Old River Lake in the 1910s, and Freeman McKay, Wellington "Wellie" Harmon, Vic Fannett, and Seaf and George Wilburn.[6]

Most delta guides shot pumps and side-by-side double barrels. Vic Fannett, who hunted Lawrence Marsh, shot a traditional side-by-side that held only two shells, but "every time a bunch of ducks come in, he got off four shots." George Wilburn preferred semiautomatic shotguns, and his held eleven shots. Once, after pushing up on a mud bank, he opened fire with plovers on both sides of his boat and picked up ninety-three.[7]

ROBERT FREEMAN MCKAY (right) *and son Arnold at Lindsey Dunn Sr.'s Ridgehaven camp, 1937. The lodge burned down in 1960. (Damon McKay Collection, courtesy Royce A. Strickland)*

OLGA MCKAY, *future Cove guide Damon McKay (the little boy), and Leda McKay, 1920. (Courtesy Royce A. Strickland)*

According to Cove guide Damon McKay, his father, Robert Freeman McKay, began guiding "when the cars came out." Robert, who went by his middle name Freeman, took hunters to Mesquite Pond and Backridge or Back of the Ridge Bayou, later Dunn's Bayou, on the north side of Lawrence's Island. With his Remington pump six-shot 12-gauge, Freeman in 1922 killed a hundred ducks every day for seventeen straight days except on Sundays, when he went to church.

Son Damon was born in Cove in 1916 and with his brothers Arnold and Arlie helped with the family guide business. When part of the Lawrence property was sold, they hunted Cotton Lake and Mullet Slough on Trinity Bay. Fifteen-year-old Damon made the long journey to their duck blinds with a one-horsepower

Johnson outboard. He set out about thirty-six wooden factory decoys at each blind and quit using live decoys, he said, because "they kept trying to get up into the boat, and I gave up."[8]

Guide Wellington "Wellie" Harmon was born in 1882. During the 1915 hurricane, when floodwaters floated his Cove house into Old River Lake, he hauled it back with a mule team. Wellie's son Homer was born the year of the hurricane, and the family later moved to a cypress-plank home in Old River–Winfree. Homer started guiding for his father at ten years old in flooded cypress at Lost River and Lost Lake and along the shoreline of Trinity Bay. In an interview with Royce Strickland, Homer described a Trinity River delta still occasionally visited by swans and big flocks of canvasbacks, a sky that filled with ducks ahead of a big norther, and flocks on the water of four to five thousand at a time.

In his first years of guiding, Homer couldn't afford hip boots, using instead rubber ankle boots with a prayer he wouldn't sink over the top, but he almost always did. He rowed customers to blinds in a flat-bottomed, narrow-keeled cypress pulling skiff made by Cove boat builder Quince Icet. In 1930 his father purchased an inboard cabin boat to tow skiffs filled with hunters. That year Homer got his first outboard, a three-horsepower outboard that could pull seven skiffs, even in a strong wind. When their sense of direction was obliterated by fog, the Harmons tied all their boats together, navigating from one blind to the next by memory.[9]

At each blind the Harmons used twenty-five or thirty decoys that they made from cypress knees. The shed next to Homer's house was stacked with them. One day Houston's Barney Smith arrived in his Model T carrying an English calling hen mallard. The Harmons were so impressed with that duck that they added a live decoy to every blind. Homer remembered, "Sometimes the decoy duck would see a flock of ducks before we did," and he learned to watch the tame decoy as often as the horizon.[10]

After federal regulations silenced the calling of live decoys, Homer used a black plastic Olt call for ducks and called snow geese and greater Canadas by mouth. He shot a 12-gauge Winchester pump with a full-choke thirty-two-inch barrel, and Earl Porter, who guided for Homer in the 1940s, says he "wore out I don't know how many. Used to get 'em for fifty-seven dollars and forty-seven cents. [He] used to take his plug out so he had seven shells. One morning these teal come in. I said, 'Now, they's seven out there, lets see what you can do.' He killed two on the water and killed the other five that got up. And he still had one shell in his gun."[11]

In the 1950s Homer Harmon charged four dollars for a hunt. His customers met him at four in the morning near Barber's Hill, but they were never able to call ahead because he had no telephone. Homer hunted the years when huge numbers of mallards wintered on the delta and guided until the early 1970s. By then the combination of nutria and diversion of the Trinity River had destroyed the

OLD RIVER–WINFREE *guide Homer Harmon* (right) *in the late 1930s. (Courtesy Royce A. Strickland)*

sea cane, and the clear fresh water between Lost and Old River Lakes had turned brown with silt. Homer stopped seeing his mallards.[12]

Guide Larenzie Aubrey Williams, nicknamed Dee, was born in Cove in 1911, one of ten children. Like the McKay family of guides, he guided duck hunters on Lawrence Marsh, and the seven dollars he charged paid for his first shotgun. Decades later he recalled a fall day when the river came up, turning the delta landscape into a continuous sheet of shallow water. "Sprigs would be solid when the river was up on the flats, and that's what we saw when we went to the lake. We threw our decoys out, and before we could even build a blind, sprig just covered the pond. We cut our cane real quick and stuck it all around us for a blind. We had nine boxes of shells and shot every one of 'em. I killed fifty-one ducks. All sprigs."

Dee could shoot six ducks with six shells, but "I could never get that seventh duck, I wasn't quick enough." Once he snuck up on a large group of snow geese on Southwest Pass with Charles Joseph, and "when they got up, they were so thick it was like shooting at a wall." After the smoke cleared, the water was white with geese.

Scouting ducks got easier for Dee in the 1950s when Cove got its first telephone service, a party line, each family with a different series of rings. Dee said, "Vic Fannett of Old River carried out hunters, and we knew his tone. When we heard

TRINITY RIVER DELTA → 133

it was his phone, we'd pick it up and listen in on all his calls. Sometimes when the Houston duck hunters would call, he'd say, 'Oh, we killed our limit today,' but we knew he hadn't killed a one."[13]

One of the most renowned early-twentieth-century Trinity River guides was Manson Clark, whose exploits as an alligator hunter, trapper, fisherman, and duck hunter were the subject of a book by his son, Kendon L. Clark, titled *Marshman! Wildlife Experiences of Manson L. Clark of Cove, Texas.* Set in a backdrop of freezes and hurricanes, water moccasins and alligators, it is the story of the waterman's way of life on the Trinity River. Manson was born in 1905 and lived his entire life in Cove on the edge of Old River and Cotton Lakes. At age thirteen, with Cotton Lake frozen over, he waded barefoot through the mud and ice pulling a wooden skiff behind him, filling it with half-frozen fish he caught by hand to sell at market. Manson quit school the next year, determined to scratch out a living fishing, trapping, and hunting.[14]

When the first automobile came to Cove around 1910, Manson heard it—then smelled it—before he ever saw it. The new form of transportation brought Houston sport hunters, who rented cypress skiffs from his father, William, paying the young boy as much as three dollars a day to row them across Cotton Lake to Wet Marsh Pond. Manson once faced an unexpected norther that nearly killed one of his parties of Houston hunters. With water rushing out of Cotton Lake and rain turning to sleet, the barefoot boy rowed for hours to get his hunters to the safety of the family's boat landing before they froze to death.[15]

Manson got his guiding start on Cotton Lake when he turned fourteen, charging fifty cents a day, and in the late 1920s he opened Clark's Duck Hunting Service. Customers met at the family's house in Cove, then headed to the wharves at Clark's landing, where as many as fourteen skiffs were loaded with thirty wooden decoys, oars, and two to three hunters for the tow to the blinds. Son Kendon worked for his father in the 1950s and '60s, remembering how father and son sat on the bluff overlooking the lake, watching as inexperienced gunners sometimes fired away at a seagull, pelicans, or the silvery flash of mullet that leaped between decoys.[16]

Manson earned a waterfowling reputation without equal in an area known for good hunters. As a roughneck near Lost Lake, he scouted the marsh for ducks from the top of the Pure Oil derrick, feeding the drilling crew with ducks he shot for the rig galley. Alone on a shoot at Back of the Ridge Bayou, he killed forty "big" ducks with thirty-three shells fired from a single-barrel shotgun. Hunting alone between guided hunts during the 1932–33 season, he shot one thousand ducks. Manson never needed much to be comfortable in the marsh, bringing with him only a sweet potato, a jar of water, sometimes a French harp, and a compass to use for rowing in the fog.

During the winter of 1960 Cotton Lake froze over, and the ice destroyed every one of Manson's twenty duck blinds. Ice, however, was to be the least of his

Marshman Manson Clark, 1947. (Courtesy Kendon Clark)

Manson Clark's *skiffs at Clark's landing on the north side of Cotton Lake, 1948. (Courtesy Kendon Clark)*

problems. Interstate 10, which split the little town of Cove in half in the 1950s, made it easier for city hunters to reach Cotton Lake, and often when Manson pulled up to one of his duck blinds he found it already full. Then in 1976 a public launch opened on Cotton Lake, and the noisy flotilla of jonboats, bass boats, and airboats made it impossible to shoot ducks. After nearly fifty years, Manson closed Clark's Duck Hunting Service. Manson was featured on the television show *The Eyes of Texas* and in *Houston Chronicle Magazine* and continued hunting, fishing, and trapping until he died in 1986.[17]

TRINITY RIVER DELTA → 135

Doris Daniel Dutton and sons Gene, Avery, and Johnnie lived on Trinity Bay south of Cotton Lake. Doris hunted the Potlikker's Club in the mid-1930s and with his 12-gauge Winchester Model 12 shot only drake mallards and pintails over decoys he made from cypress knees. Doris's sons followed their father's footsteps. Gene guided for Manson Clark, Avery built cypress pulling-skiffs, and Johnnie carved decoys and decorative birds from his home near Baytown. The family ate ducks twice a day during the days before household refrigerators, hanging their ducks outside in tow sacks that kept the flies off.[18]

Johnnie remembers that ducks and geese roosting on Cotton Lake and Wet Marsh headed west to feed in rice fields, the flocks so huge that "the sky was just full." The Duttons hunted the southwest shoreline of Trinity Bay, and Barber Hill's Earl Porter, who hunted with them, says, "Every one of 'em [the Dutton men] shot different size shot. Now you let two or three of 'em be in a blind, and have all of 'em shoot at a duck? Well, the autopsy started then. The one that had the most shot in 'im, he got the duck or the goose."[19]

The mallard and pintail flyway of the north Trinity River delta converged with the canvasback and bluebill flyway to the south at the extraordinary wetlands of the 5,000-acre Lawrence's Marsh. Houston oilman Lindsey Dunn Sr. hunted there with guide John Winter in the 1910s and later as president of Cove Hunting and Fishing Club. In the mid-1920s Dunn bought 1,750 acres of Lawrence Marsh, naming the property Ridgehaven Farm for the long shell ridge known to locals as Lawrence's Island. Ike Handy once stood in the yard at Ridgehaven at sundown, and for as far as the eye could see, ducks, mostly mallards, were coming and going from the marsh to rice fields where they fed at night.[20]

Dunn created new wetland ponds by constructing levees in the 1930s. The places he hunted mixed old and new vernacular; Lawrence Marsh was called Wet Marsh, Back of the Ridge Bayou was renamed Dunn's Bayou, and the lake that ran into it was called Dunn's Lake. Dunn's hunters got to these places by mule and cart, on horseback, and by foot before Dunn Sr. built a marsh buggy from a 1929 Model A Ford truck, appropriately named the *Muskrat*. In 1931 Dunn built his first lodge, a two-story cypress lapboard house on the shell ridge next to Cross Bayou, which he reached from Cove by the cabin cruiser *Black Mallard*.[21]

It was a fall day when a young boy climbed atop the water tower by the lodge, watching as thousands of ducks descended into the marsh at sunset. His name was Lindsey Dunn Jr., and he told historian Royce A. Strickland, "The thing that stands out in my mind is during the winter, late in the evening, the ducks would come from the bay, and flew over the house. I would get on the water tower and watch, and it was amazing. Just as far as you could see, from east to west, a solid line of ducks. It was fantastic. They did that for several years and then they just stopped. Never did it again."[22]

Lindsey Jr. was born in 1916 and started hunting alone at age seven, crossing Old River in an old inboard cabin boat. Royce Strickland first hunted with

Lindsey H. Dunn Sr. *with forty-five ducks from Mesquite Pond, Ridgehaven, in 1933. In the background is the cypress lapboard Ridgehaven camp. (Lindsey H. Dunn Jr. Collection, courtesy Royce A. Strickland)*

Getting ready *for a hunt at Ridgehaven. Seif Wilburn (left) and Lindsey Dunn Jr. haul a wooden duck skiff with a detachable rowboat motor to the marsh by mules and cart. (Lindsey H. Dunn Jr. Collection, courtesy Royce A. Strickland)*

The Muskrat, *a converted 1929 Ford Model A, in 1933 at Ridgehaven. (Lindsey H. Dunn Jr. Collection, courtesy Royce A. Strickland)*

Lindsey in 1960. Many years later Dunn's widow gave him access to the detailed hunting, fishing, and trapping notes and photographs her husband had compiled. In *Ridgehaven and a Dunn Marsh Legacy: Photojournal of a Texas Coastal Outdoorsman Lindsey H. Dunn, Jr.,* Royce tells the story of Lindsey Jr. and the last days of skies black with ducks over the Trinity River delta.

Royce's collection of stories includes Lindsey's hunt during the big Chambers County freeze of January 1940 and days when flocks of sprigs and teal "stretched out east and west as far as you could see." Lindsey's least favorite duck, and one he never admitted he shot, was the scaup, or bluebill. Yet he always seemed to have some and was always trying to give them away, "going house to house at the Old River boat ramp." One lady who answered the knock on her door took a look

LINDSEY H. DUNN (left) *with C. B. Delhomme in front of Ridgehaven lodge, 1937. The pair took thirty-six ducks in blind no. 27 on Lindsey's twenty-first birthday. (Lindsey H. Dunn Jr. Collection, courtesy Royce A. Strickland)*

METICULOUS *record keeper Lindsey H. Dunn Jr. in the 1993–94 season. Inspection of his records proved this was actually his 999th mottled duck. (Lindsey H. Dunn Jr. Collection, courtesy Royce A. Strickland)*

at his ducks, poor culinary specimens in a country rich with mallards, and "shut the door in his face."[23]

Lindsey Jr. admitted he hunted five mornings in a row one season and never shot a duck, not even a bluebill. On a sixth hunt with plenty of ducks, he shot well over his limit, explaining to Royce, "I'm not trying to be greedy, just tryin' to make my average for the season." Lindsey also tried not to shoot teal, only "big" ducks. There is a photograph of Dunn holding a sign with the words "1,000th Black Mallard." Legend has it that when he checked his records, he was distraught to learn it was really only number 999, so he promptly went out to get another.

Lindsey was running late on one of Royce's first hunts with him, the sun coming up fast. The hurried command, "Get those chunks [decoys] out here," created a little tension in the boy, who was eager to impress, and he swung around and hit Lindsey in the face with an oar. Returning later to the dock, property caretaker Rudolph Krajka inquired about the injury. Lindsey looked away, mumbling, "That young boy hit me in the face with a paddle." Forty years later the boy with the poorly aimed paddle was responsible for preserving the culture of the Trinity River delta guides and the Dunn family.[24]

Lindsey Dunn Sr. sold Ridgehaven to C. B. Delhomme and partners in 1941. Delhomme, best known to Houstonians for Delhomme Marina and as organizer of the annual Houston boat show, built his new Delhomme Reserve into a world-class hunting operation. In the late 1950s he dug a system of canals from the lodge to the main waterways. Boats, featuring Evinrude outboard motors he sold at his dealership, took hunters directly and easily from lodge to blind. Next, he purchased what Ike Handy called "an airplane motored boat," or airboat. The days of carrying decoys and building a blind from cut sea cane were over; permanent blinds were built with decoys that no longer had to be hauled out before each hunt.[25]

When the original Dunn Sr. house burned in 1960, Delhomme constructed a stone lodge with six bedrooms on Cedar Island. The mortar was barely dry when Hurricane Carla weaved towards the delta in 1961. Caretaker Rudolph Krajka, convinced that the stone structure was a safe retreat, prepared to ride out the storm. Neighbors couldn't budge him, but evidently C. B. Delhomme did. With winds freshening before the storm, Delhomme, in a suit and necktie, piloted his yacht up the bayou to extricate the reticent caretaker. Nothing but the north wall remained of the lodge upon their return after the storm. The lodge was replaced by one equally elegant, with eight bedrooms, air conditioning and heat, and its walls covered in old photographs and bird mounts.[26]

Delhomme Reserve was donated to Houston's Methodist Hospital in the 1970s and was later acquired by the Ducks Unlimited Foundation before being purchased by a private outfitter. Steve Wilburn, property manager in those later years, remembers dropping an overly confident party off at one of the blinds, and when he returned they asked him to recover a number of snow geese they had dropped in the marsh. Wilburn dutiful retrieved every bird, and each turned out to be a pelican.[27]

Remaining members of the original Potlikker's Club chartered the Chambers County Club in 1942, and they still hunted at the club's original Wet Marsh lease west of the Trinity River. Angleton's Walter Besser, who first hunted at the club in the late 1950s, is a keeper of its history. Walter says that Cove hunter, trapper, and fisherman Linzie Griffith managed the operation and built blinds, guided, and "ran out the poachers." Club staff included an African American cook whose husband, Junior, picked all the ducks. By the 1960s the club had thirty-six members, most from Houston, who paid a $255 initiation fee and $250 annual dues. Women and children were allowed to visit only on Tuesdays.

Walter remembers that "the marsh in those days was solid cane. You had to follow trails to find the duck blinds. And it was mean. You might go five to six miles out. If you got stuck, Linzie [Griffith] would come get you. He never went home until after everybody came in." Walter saw some big changes during his time at the club. The first was the nutria, which he says "took down all the cane, and today it is just salt marsh. Those nutria, they'd eat anything. We kept our decoys out all season, and had to switch to chain decoy lines because the nutria ate all the string line. We had a sign in the club that said, 'Don't shoot the alligators because they eat nutria.'"

In the early 1970s Wet Marsh was bought by Houston Lighting and Power Co., and its intricate mix of wetlands and bayous was inundated for a massive cooling pond. The club moved in 1972, transporting a few of their original buildings to Butsy Edmund's land on Lone Oak Bayou, east of Trinity Bay. From its beginnings after the turn of the century as the Potlikker's Club, the Chambers County Club lived on until the Lone Oak land was sold in 2005.[28]

East of the Trinity River, hunters from the settlement that grew around Fort Anahuac in the 1830s first aimed their guns toward the skyline over the large freshwater body of Turtle Bay, its shores rimmed to the north and east by forests and to the west by the delta. The only Turtle Bay sporting club whose name remains to history is Hargraves Hunting Camp, operated by Sam Hargraves Sr. and his family during the 1950s and '60s. Customers met Hargraves at the City Café in Anahuac, and as late as the 1950s they still bagged mallards, redheads, and canvasbacks from one of fifteen duck blinds. David Wilcox remembers the Hargraveses "just owned that lake. They hunted it and fished it every morning."[29]

North of the mouth of the Trinity River delta, sea cane marsh gave way to flooded timber bottoms. The largest of the timber lakes, Lake Charlotte, was once crystal clear, its surface a checkerboard of widgeon grass, the shoreline and small tributaries rimmed with cypress and tupelo and dotted with Indian mounds. Sportsmen knew Lake Charlotte for its mallards and later for the man who hunted them there, Morgan LaFour, whose highball mallard call could be heard ringing through the cypress trees.[30]

Morgan was born in 1905 and started guiding at the age of seventeen. As a boy he proved his prowess early by shooting 109 mallards in one morning. Sportsman Harvey Evans recalls Morgan once told him of those outlaw days: "You don't shoot when they first light. You wait till they swim together and you stand up and whistle at 'em so they stick their heads up, and that's when you get the shot."[31]

The LaFours were a family of outstanding Trinity Bay watermen. Father Emmet was a market hunter, and the family he raised made a living by hunting, trapping, and fishing. Morgan trapped muskrats in High Island marsh and ran trotlines and hoop nets on Trinity River, selling his fish at the family's outdoor stall in Wallisville. Sylvia Lamb, LaFour's niece, remembers seeing him come downriver some days with hundreds of pounds of catfish, the skiff so low in the water she could barely see its gunwales. "You know," Sylvia adds, "Uncle Morgan lived his whole life on the water and couldn't swim a lick."

Guiding sportsmen during winter was a family affair. Morgan's brother, Otis Sr., had a guiding business in Old Wallisville with sons Dalton and Otis "Punk" Jr. Morgan had his twenty-five duck blinds mostly in the flooded timber of Lake Charlotte, called "the Big Lake," with others built on "Little Lake." Son Buddy

CHAMBERS COUNTY *Club member Donald Matranga, late 1940s, with pintails and mallards. (Courtesy Walter Besser)*

GUIDE MORGAN LAFOUR, *about 1970. Morgan hunted Lake Charlotte, north of Wallisville, for more than fifty years. (Courtesy Sylvia Lamb)*

helped out with guiding duties, and Morgan's sister Zelma LaFour Conklin made breakfast for his hunters. LaFour's predawn meal was not standard fare; according to Sylvia, "He'd start each day with a raw egg mixed with Four Roses [bourbon]."[32]

Hunters who came from Houston in the days before Interstate 10 had to take the long way to Morgan LaFour's Guide Service, traveling on Highway 90 from Houston to Crosby, then on to Liberty. At the end of the drive was the large red arrow on the sign "Duck Hunting—Morgan LaFour Guide Service" pointing to a small white house with its screened front porch by the side of Wallisville–Liberty road. On Saturday mornings the road was lined with cars. The drive and the wait were usually worth it, as a hunt with LaFour almost always meant a morning of greenhead mallards.

Morgan also offered day hunts with transportation to his blinds. Houston's Cliff Fisher says, "For his day hunts, he provided a taxi service. You tied your skiff rope to the big boat or the next skiff in line, and ran out through canals dug around the property." Walter Besser made some of his first Chambers County hunts with LaFour. He says: "We couldn't afford a guided hunt, so we did day hunts. Morgan was charging five dollars a day in the late 1950s. You know," he adds, "Morgan was well liked. Not all of those guys were."[33]

Morgan learned how to call ducks by listening to his flock of live English caller decoys. His duck calling was so good, and he brought mallards in from such heights, that their cupped wings made a whistling sound that reminded *Houston Chronicle*'s Bob Brister of "incoming bombs." Cliff Fisher remembers sitting in a blind a long way off from LaFour on Lake Charlotte. "His calling sounded just like music. It sounded like a symphony over there and you'd just watch them take a shot at some mallards, and Morgan would start callin' and I'd watch 'em come back again!"[34]

When Bob Brister wrote about Morgan LaFour, he used such phrases as "a deadly efficient hunter" who "does not miss at all." The last accolade was from someone who knew good shooters. Once on a foggy morning son Buddy stood in the bathtub of their Wallisville house and called out the window to a flight of snow geese that came in so low Morgan killed three off the porch. Morgan quit shooting in 1976, complaining he just couldn't see anymore. Mickey Lamb was with him on one of his last hunts and says of the man who couldn't see that he pulled up and killed two overhead mallards before anyone else even knew they were there. Morgan LaFour died in 1981. Brister provided a fitting epilogue, calling him "one of the greatest duck hunters and callers in the legends and lore of the upper coastal marsh country."[35]

If mallards weren't in Morgan's Lake Charlotte, they were probably in the hardwood bottoms on the west Trinity River, in Liberty County, at Stubbs Bayou, Wooten Lake, Day's Lake, and Champion Lake. From the late 1800s until as late as the 1970s, mallards that roosted by night in flooded timber on the west side of the river left in huge waves every morning for rice, returning again at sunset.[36]

The abandoned river meander that became Champion Lake, on the road between Old River–Winfree and Dayton, was intermittently dry much of the year. That changed when Big Caney Creek was dammed at its confluence with Pickett's Bayou, forming seven hundred acres of backwater in the standing timber. Shannon Tompkins painted a vivid picture of Champion Lake with its "cypress, tupelo, willows and buttonbushes, back in the dark, wet places beyond the edge of a watery opening in the flooded river bottom." So many mallards and wood ducks came to this stretch of Trinity River that hunters who witnessed it remember the deafening sound as they rose from the shallow water.[37]

Texas subsidiaries of Champion Paper and Fibre Company started Casa de los Patos on Champion Lake as a private hunting retreat in the 1940s, hiring Old River's Amos Tilton as manager and guide. The company built a spectacular lodge with log cabin outbuildings at the end of a two-mile dirt road that followed the Champion Lake shore through stands of oak and pine trees. The "grand old log cabin back in the woods," as writer Joe Doggett called it, had tongue-and-groove hardwood floors, pine wood ceilings, and wall panels joined by wood

MALLARDS FROM *Old River in the 1940s, shot by Walter Green* (left) *and Champion Lake proprietor Amos Tilton. (Courtesy Royce A. Strickland)*

dowels. Gun lockers flanked the entrance, which led to a large central room with an eight-foot-wide fireplace.[38]

Renowned guide Forrest West kept the original Casa de los Patos name when he leased the Champion Paper Company lodge as his first commercial hunting operation in the early 1970s. Joe Doggett made his first hunt in the flooded black oaks and cypresses with Forrest and Bob Brister in 1972, and he jokes that Forrest knew a lot about those mallards before he ever leased the place; like many young men before and after him, he poached the area. Joe says Forrest's wife, Gayle, "dropped us off before daylight on the blacktop," and they walked in. Both Bob and Joe were featured on Forrest's promotional brochures, their photos beneath the title "The Best Timber Shooting This Side of Arkansas." Forrest built wooden platform tree blinds, with one of them, the High Blind, a giant affair immortalized in John P. Cowan's 1978 painting of the same name.[39]

Southeast of Champion Lake, Pickett's Bayou Hunting Club members shot ducks that poured through the cypress trees on Ash and Stubbs Lakes. With about sixteen members, the club was small, but it had a giant reputation, earned in part from the hunting and from larger-than-life founders Abe and Babe Badgley of Baytown and Joe Matthews of Mont Belvieu.[40]

Before she died at ninety-two years of age, Abe's wife, Nowyta, told how her husband used to post himself in the limbs of a tree to shoot ducks, filling an extended magazine tube so he didn't have to climb down for more ammunition. Brother Babe Badgely often stayed at camp entertaining guests with hunting stories. Babe did most of his hunting in February, when there was no gunning pressure, and after he filled his two camp freezers with mallards, he was done hunting for the year. Club cofounder Joseph E. Matthews hunted ducks from a pirogue nearly every day of the season until he was almost ninety. Shannon Tompkins remembers Matthews as the epitome of the Texas hunter-conservationist, a staunch advocate for wetlands preservation who fought Trinity River drainage projects and dams. Wetlands and waterfowl, Shannon says, were his life.[41]

Pickett's Bayou Hunting Club built box blinds at water level and often positioned another hunter in a cypress tree over the blind. Prentice Holder remembers hunting thirty feet in the air in a metal lawn chair, pulling gear up behind him by rope. In other trees they hung metal drums and according to Bill Gammel one of the Badgely's metal drum blinds can still be seen hanging behind Ash Lake. Pickett's Bayou Club once used the best decoys in Texas, given to them by Baytown decoy carvers Rudy LeCompte and H. B. "Bowie" Creekmore after they were invited as guests. Rudy later brought them eight cypress pirogues built in Louisiana.[42]

Some of Champion Lake is today a Texas state park. Although logging and houses have changed much of Champion Lake's shoreline, parts of that special backwater will, for future generations, look as it did in the days, not so long ago, when rising ducks blackened the sky.

CHAPTER 7

SAN JACINTO RIVER

WEST OF THE TRINITY RIVER DELTA, THE SAN JACINTO RIVER met Galveston Bay by way of Clopper's Point, later Morgan's Point. Wintering flocks of shorebirds, ducks, geese, and swans were an important resource for watermen, market hunters, and guides in the river and upper bay communities of Harrisburg, Houston, Lynchburg, and William Scott's Bay Town settlement. By the early 1900s Houston and later Baytown grew into two of Texas's most influential sport hunting communities.

BUFFALO BAYOU TO MORGAN'S POINT

At the headlands of Galveston Bay, the city of Houston was founded on an elaborate prairie and woodland drainage system made up of Greens, Whiteoak, Buffalo, Brays, and Sims Bayous and the San Jacinto River a short distance to the east. Sporting guides in the 1800s listed waterfowling localities near Houston that are places now unrecognizable: Johnson, Coleman, and Westheimer Sloughs, McClure's Prairie, and Hooker's Flat, now called Montrose. The *Galveston Daily News* in 1891 advised that the best duck hunting in Harris County was at the mouth of Buffalo Bayou. Flocks of geese landed right in the middle of the city by the bayou in 1893, and as late as 1909, geese were still shot from backyards by residents of Houston Heights.[1]

Hunting lodges were built along all the major bayous on the edge of Houston. The Houston Gun Club, founded in the 1870s, built an eight-thousand-acre game preserve on Buffalo Bayou at Deepwater Rice Farm. In 1906 its fifty members erected a finely appointed clubhouse, built an artificial lake, and hired a game warden to manage the grounds. Now within Houston city limits near the

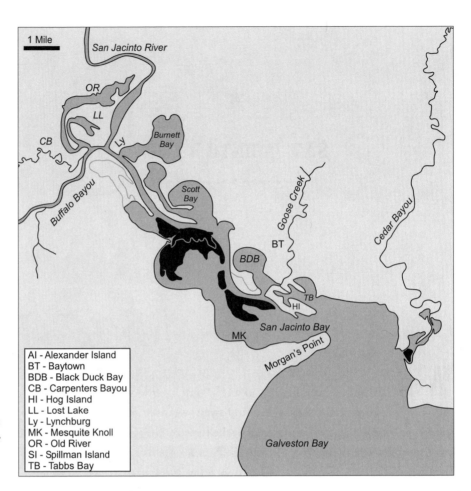

THE SAN JACINTO RIVER *and San Jacinto Bay as they appeared in the late 1800s.*

intersection of Interstate 610 and Westheimer Avenue, the property once held so many waterfowl that "the whir of wings has been described as resembling the sound of exhaust of a steam engine."[2]

There were at least two prominent clubs on Brays Bayou: Brays Bayou Gun Club and Brays Bayou Hunting Club. Other early Houston clubs included Houston Hunting Club, founded in the 1870s, and Harris County Hunting and Fishing Club, which built a dam and private lake south of town in the early 1900s.[3]

East of town Houston hunters found puddle ducks and huge concentrations of canvasbacks and redheads on the lower reaches of the San Jacinto River and San Jacinto Bay. Typical was a group in the late 1800s that hauled a skiff in a horse-drawn wagon to Lynchburg ferry and rowed up the north shore, killing ninety-eight ducks. The steam launch *Ruby* docked on Buffalo Bayou, taking hunters on excursions to Greens Bayou and along San Jacinto River. Sportsmen on longer hunts followed the river further south to Burnett and Scott Bays and the mouth of the river at Morgan's Point.[4]

San Jacinto River fresh water converged with the brackish water of Galveston Bay in the narrows by Tabbs Bay. Here, "dazzling in their whiteness," were the sand shoals of Clopper's Bar and Swan Reef, sometimes submerged and at other times exposed, that held flocks of pintails often several miles long, uncountable numbers of canvasbacks, and huge rafts of swans in late winter. The adjacent promontory of Clopper's Point was renamed Morgan's Point for its famous resident, Colonel James Morgan. Mexican General Santa Ana, on his march to San Jacinto in 1836, burned Morgan's estate to the ground and seized his mulatto servant Emily West Morgan, known in Texas lore as the Yellow Rose of Texas.[5]

Colonel Morgan was an avid duck hunter, the sails of his schooner a familiar site on the shallow oyster reefs and shoals of Trinity and Galveston Bays in the 1840s and '50s. Shouldering an old muzzleloader, he hunted flocks of teal in early fall, late winter canvasbacks, and found the gritting places of greater Canada geese and swans. Morgan wrote letters with his fowling observations to local papers, such as the report published by the *Houston Telegraph and Texas Register* in 1845: "Important to Sportsman—We learn that many of the inlets of Galveston Bay are literally filled with wild ducks, brant, geese, etc. Several thousand are often seen in a single flock. Colonel Morgan informs us that one of his slaves lately killed sixty-five ducks in about two hours." A visitor to Colonel Morgan's estate in 1859 wrote that it was "an earthly paradise . . . filled with geese, ducks and swans." When the sixteen-hundred-acre estate was advertised for sale in 1865, the colonel apologized that it would be "inconvenient to answer any communications in writing." He was nearly blind. Morgan still went hunting, alone, and the nearly blind sportsman twice saved himself from drowning when his boat overturned on Trinity Bay. Morgan died at his home in 1866.[6]

Part-time market hunter Edward T. Martin gunned at Morgan's Point before the turn of the century. On one hunt with a commercial outfitter he killed 186 pintails, wigeons, and mallards from a "zinc-lined shooting box." On another he hired "John the Decoy Boy," who set 175 wooden decoys and sailed the waterways to keep birds stirred. Martin shot so many rounds he had to dunk his gun in bay water to cool the barrels, and his line of dead ducks reached to the shoreline. Snow was nearly a foot deep on Morgan's Point during a winter storm in 1886 when Martin and another gunner killed 318 ducks.[7]

The prominent Left-Hand Hunting, Fishing, and Carnival Club purchased property on Morgan's Point in 1894. With Houston headquarters in the old opera house and later Travis Street, its membership boasted merchants, lawyers, judges, and politicians such as Governor Hogg. The club's specially fitted "palace barge" was berthed at the foot of Fannin Street and from there towed down Buffalo Bayou by steam launch for weeklong hunts, the barge joined by finely appointed private yachts. Gatherings of the Left-Handers were a celebration of oyster roasts, Christmas parties, parades, and brass bands, such as the one that serenaded them back to Houston after a duck hunt aboard the steam launch *Richmond* in 1900. Club members hunted from Seabrook to the Trinity River delta. On a turn-of-the-century steamer trip to the delta, they boarded small skiffs at Wallisville wharf, and they returned "with a fine supply of canvas back ducks."[8]

Other Morgan's Point clubs included Redfish Boating, Fishing, and Hunting Club, with their steamer *Hiawatha;* the short-lived Metropolitan Fishing and Hunting Club, which disbanded after five years because "game was no longer plentiful"; and the Morgan Point Hunting and Fishing Club. Morgan's Point was so popular with winter hunters and summer fishermen that a resort hotel was built there in 1893.[9]

Houston and the San Jacinto River remained a premier gunning ground through the first half of the 1900s. Celebrated outdoor writer Nash Buckingham, who hunted canvasbacks and redheads on San Jacinto Bay, remembered his trips as "priceless." Thousands of duck blinds lined the river's north shore from Burnet Bay to Black Duck Bay. Near the then still pristine shoreline of the San Jacinto battlegrounds, the Old River Club opened in 1920, its 150 original members a who's who of Houston's business and sporting community. Old River was promoted as a family club with by-laws that precluded gambling, intoxicants, and "undesirable characters." Members built a modern lodge with a water well, sewage disposal plant, and eighty-foot wharf to accommodate twelve new pleasure boats. Club manager Kavanaugh handled the grounds and the main building, with sleeping quarters limited to a dozen beds, but members could bring their own tent.[10]

The numbers of wildfowl around Houston began to decrease in the early 1900s, and one of the main causes was drainage. At first only small plots of prairie were converted to agriculture, mostly rice fields, through drainage channels and burning. As the pace increased at the turn of the century, one of the consequences was that smoke from prairie fires blanketed the area for days at a time. Hunters rendered invisible by fires between Houston and Spring in 1909 killed large bags of ducks disoriented by the haze. Several clubs, including the venerable Houston Gun Club, were forced to relocate in the 1920s when thirty-three thousand acres of prairie between Brays and Buffalo Bayous, "which had been a hunters paradise, were drained and made tillable."[11]

As the city grew, sportsmen began to locate their new clubs further afield, the automobile providing them with access to areas as far away as the Trinity River delta, West Galveston Bay, coastal Brazoria County, and the Katy and Lissie Prairies. A 1906 article in *The Horseless Age* described Houston with "fine macadamized or shell roads [that] radiate from the city in every direction" through the heart of hunting country. The virtues of automobile hunting were extolled with stories such as, "Last spring plover shooting from automobiles was extensively practiced. [Plovers] pay no attention of the car, and will not fly from it."[12]

The center of Houston hunting was on Capitol Ave. at C. L. and Theo Bering Hardware and Sporting Goods, founded by Colonel C. L. Bering. An avid sportsman, Bering was a member of Eagle Lake Hunting Club and an original incorporator of Seabrook Hunting and Fishing Club in 1907 and the Old River

HUNTERS AND *their Model Ts crossing the San Jacinto River east of Houston on the Lynchburg Ferry, 1919. (John Winter Collection, courtesy Cliff Fisher)*

HOUSTON HUNTERS *often returned to the city with their automobiles loaded with game, as in this 1927 photo with greater Canada geese. (Courtesy James Smock)*

Club in 1920. He was also a member of the Houston Gun Club and one of the best trap shots in the state.[13]

C. L. and Theo Bering Hardware and Sporting Goods carried all the necessary supplies for the modern waterfowler: leather live decoy neck collars, wooden duck boats, preloaded smokeless powder shotgun shells, and the latest Winchester and Remington shotguns. Sportsmen traveled long distances to get to Bering's. At the beginning of each season Trinity River delta guides loaded into

SAN JACINTO RIVER → 149

Renowned sportsman *Maj. C. L. Bering (at the wheel) with 150 ducks from a Cove hunt in 1918. (John Winter Collection, courtesy Cliff Fisher)*

Model Ts for the trip to the city, and guide Damon McKay remembered Bering's four-foot-long table piled high with duck calls. Colonel Bering arranged guides and hunts for city sportsmen, and his store employee John Winter became the best of the guiding lot.[14]

John Winter's parents brought him from Germany as a child, immigrating to Houston through the Port of Galveston in 1898. John as a boy couldn't resist the wild banks and waterways of San Jacinto River and Cedar Bayou east of the city, which he reached on horseback. Traveling to the farming community of Clodine, west of Houston, by train, he shot his first ducks in 1913. Those five mallards taken from huge flocks on Williford pasture lit a waterfowling fire in John that he never extinguished.[15]

John left Houston for his first job in Beaumont, where he worked as a window decorator for E. L. Wilson Hardware Co. Early photographs show him hunting with his side-by-side Parker shotgun on McFaddin Ranch, Village Creek on the Neches River, Pine Island, and China Marsh west of Beaumont at Langham's Ranch, where, before it was drained for agriculture, mallards and pintails fed on the clear-water aquatic grasses and adjacent rice fields.[16]

In 1915 John returned to Houston to arrange window displays for C. L. and Theo Bering Co. Hardware and Sporting Goods. Bering's store was the starting place for sportsmen on hunting excursions who, returning days later, had their pictures taken along with the fruits of their efforts. The ritual was no small affair, as passers-by crowded around, measuring the worth of the sportsmen by the size

HOUSTON HUNTERS *took the SA&AP train to hunt farming communities west of the city. Shown is John Winter at the Clodine depot with a good bag of mallards and teal from a hunt in 1913. The area has now been absorbed by the city of Houston. (John Winter Collection, courtesy Cliff Fisher)*

of their kill. John Winter soon became both their guide and the man who took their photographs after the hunt.

The places John guided in the 1910s reflect a mostly vanished Texas: a pond near a motte of trees at Barrow's Ranch in Chambers County, the Vingt'-une Islands oyster reefs in Trinity Bay, marsh ponds at High Island on Bolivar Peninsula, the aptly nicknamed Camp Mosquito at St. Louis Pass on Galveston Island, the cypress-studded waters of Lake Charlotte, the deep marsh at Jack's Pass in the Trinity River, Lost and Old Rivers at Cove, Cedar Bayou, Burnet Bay at Lynchburg on San Jacinto River, the wooded shores of Buffalo Bayou, Alief on Brays Bayou on the prairie west of Houston, Orchard Lake in Fort Bend County, the high-standing prairie grasses and knoll ponds that were once the Lissie and Katy Prairies, and last, Eagle Lake.[17]

In 1917, John's two best guided hunts produced 339 ducks at Cove, with another shoot of 54 mallards in an evening at Ralph Barrow's ranch. In the 1917–19 season he hunted thirty-two times and brought home 1,720 ducks, his best shoot producing 150 ducks at Cove on the Trinity River delta. Highlights of 1919–20 included 216 ducks on three more hunts at Cove and 210 ducks at Eagle Lake. John

JOHN WINTER (left) and A. J. Jolmson are well dressed for their photograph in front of Bering Hardware. The hunters are pictured with eighty ducks, mostly teal, mallards, pintails, and diver ducks, from Cove's R. A. Bond Club in the early 1920s. (John Winter Collection, courtesy Cliff Fisher)

Winter, however, did not just write down the number of birds he killed; he built scrapbooks, filling their pages with words and pictures of what he saw between 1906 and the 1950s. He hauled his camera, a Revolving Back (RB) Tele Graflex, with him wherever he went, and he went places often very hard to get to.[18]

Ford Model Ts and As got John near the places he hunted. His were automobile convoys hauling canvas tents, camping equipment, retrievers, crates of live decoys, tow sacks filled with wooden ones, rowing skiffs, duck boats, sometimes a small sink box, and never less than a case of shotgun shells. Waterways were crossed on narrow wooden plank bridges or by one of the many wooden ferries still common in coastal Texas. When mud kept him from getting close to the shooting grounds, he loaded the mounds of hunting gear into horse-drawn carts.[19]

Other times John relied on transport by boats, traversing Trinity and Galveston Bays in cat-rigged sloops or long, narrow boats with one-cylinder gasoline motors and a big flywheel that, to start, were cranked by hand. Hard-chined, narrow, pointed rowboats were hauled behind tow boats. In the early 1920s John and his hunting partners had the latest technology—outboard motors manufactured by Ole Evinrude and Lockwood—attached to the transoms of their wooden skiffs.[20]

Like Texas hunters for a hundred years before him, John Winter faced the many things that could go wrong in marshes and bays. He was not the first

WIVES AND CHILDREN *join sportsmen John Winter (seated, right) and Lindsey H. Dunn Sr. (standing, right) at Cedar Bayou, near Baytown. Note the trailer used to haul hunting and camping gear. (John Winter Collection, courtesy Cliff Fisher)*

sportsman marooned in the middle of a bay, but his experience may be the best documented. His party was sailing on the single-masted oyster lugger *Erett* between Smith Point and Galveston when the boat grounded on the Vingt'-une Islands oyster shell reefs during a norther. They spent three days on one of the islands, which he dubbed Camp Compac, passing the time collecting oysters and shooting diving ducks that ventured too close to the beached boat.

Hunts with John Winter began with afternoon trips to locate birds for the next morning's shoot. They retraced their route in the predawn darkness, cutting brush along the way that they pushed into the mud to hide their boats. They then put out decoys, a combination of carved wooden ones, Johnson-brand silhouettes on a wooden fanning rod, and live mallards raised in John's backyard.[21]

John spent hours listening to the tame decoy ducks, imitating their sounds with his mouth and with a duck call. He learned his craft well; Houston newspaper columnist Jimmy Lingan called him the best mallard duck caller he ever heard, "able to lure ducks away from other nearby hunters with larger decoy spreads ... Johnny Winter used to call them to us when they were neither hungry nor lonesome." According to Cedar Bayou Kennel's Chet Beaty, the only duck call John ever used was a Charles Ditto call from Illinois.[22]

John was a popular guide with military officers during World War I. Scrapbook entries from the 1918 and 1919 season show a litany of war hero generals, colonels, and majors, including famous Brigadier General Billy Mitchell. He also guided a long list of prominent, mostly Houston businessmen. Houston oilman Lindsey Dunn Sr. was a client and later bought the land he hunted near Cove, which became the famous Ridgehaven and Delhomme hunting preserve.[23]

The early 1920s was the watershed period when the tools of the past were being made obsolete by the machinery of the future. For duck hunters, one of the most important inventions was the "detachable rowboat motor," and John embraced it so completely that he designed and built his own boat around it. The result was the *Ankle Deep,* a motorized canoe initially used to pull hunting skiffs. Within a few years he rebuilt the boat several times, and in 1925 the sleek inboard *Ankle Deep II* was capable of reaching seventy mph.

With faster boats and faster automobiles, John in 1921 began hunting Matagorda County, hired as the Houston representative for W. W. Hunt's Port O'Connor Hunting and Fishing Lodge. On his first hunt he and his companions killed 191 pintails, gadwalls, and teal. That year he shot canvasbacks and redheads and had another hunt of 100 pintails at Redfish Bay. He continued to frequent Cove, Lost Lake, and Trinity Bay with his usual success, bagging a total of 282 ducks in four hunts. John returned to Matagorda the next season and made a 150-duck hunt at Oyster Lake near Collegeport.[24]

John next learned to fly, and with his Ace biplane there was no more bogging down on muddy roads between Houston and Matagorda County and no more long boat rides from the mainland to Matagorda Island. Scrapbook entries for his 1923 "Palacios by plane" hunts include 115 and 125 ducks on two trips and, after landing on the beach at Matagorda Island, a hunt that produced 132 ducks and 32 geese.

Traveling the Texas coast, despite the increasing use of gasoline engines, was not without its hazards. On one airplane hunt to Cove, John collided with another biplane landing in a pasture. In January 1924 John and his party were nearly sunk crossing Trinity Bay in the *Ankle Deep.* The wind came up, heavy waves crashed over the boat, and sleet froze to both boat and men. The sportsmen spent a cold night camping near Anahuac, but recovered well enough to shoot a limit of two hundred ducks over two days.[25]

John also contributed numerous sporting articles to Houston-area newspapers. His articles in the 1930s reported on duck populations from surveys he made himself, and he wrote a popular five-part newspaper series on duck hunting in the 1940s that was reprinted in 1946 in the publication *Sports Round-Up* under the title "Hints to Duck Hunters."[26]

John Winter was a man of his time, often well ahead of it. In a short period he had become an accomplished photographer, marksman, guide, naturalist, fisherman, boat builder and racer, writer, and aviator. To visit John's garage at his Bur Street house in Houston was to hear the sounds of mallards clucking in the backyard, the sawing and sanding of wood while he worked on a sink box or a new design for his *Ankle Deep,* or an engine idling while John was doing something to make it go faster. The yard fell silent in 1954 when John Winter died of heart failure, and the quiet was heard in the sporting world from Cove to Matagorda Island.

PILOT JOHN WINTER *chronicled his "Palacios by plane" hunt in 1924. Shown are Sam Kaiser (far right) and mechanic Ralph B. Lechenger next to Kaiser. The other men and the woman are unidentified. (John Winter Collection, courtesy Cliff Fisher)*

Henry Palmer "Peg" Melton was another well-known Houston hunter in the 1920s and '30s. Born in Houston in 1902, Peg was twelve years old when, while trying to jump onto a moving train, he fell and lost a leg. It didn't seem to slow him down; he was the first Eagle Scout in Harris County, a Rice University ball player, Texas state skeet shooting champion, and captain of the US Olympic shooting team in the 1930s. Peg was also a hunter and an early conservationist.[27]

Peg made his first hunt in 1915 at Jackson (JHK) Ranch, reaching it by boat and then by Model T. For many of his early years the limit was twenty-five ducks, and more times than not Peg Melton returned home after a three-day hunt with seventy-five birds. Sons Palmer and Talley remember those birds all too well—they had to help pluck them. "We picked them as kids until we couldn't stand to look at them, and sometimes our backyard in Houston would look like a feather factory." Those children also ate a lot of ducks—so many that "all of us broke out in a rash. We went to the doctor. Dr. York said, 'What have you kids been eating?' And we went, 'Duck.' And he said, 'How often?' We said, 'Three times a day. We have fried teal for breakfast with an egg, we have a duck sandwich for lunch, and we have baked ducks at night.' He said, 'No wonder y'all are broken out.' He told our father, 'Peg, you cannot feed these kids ducks like this.'"[28]

In 2000, *Houston Chronicle* writer Shannon Tompkins introduced Peg Melton to a new generation of sportsmen. Peg, he wrote, embraced the theme of conversation in its early days, putting his ideas into words in an influential 1935 radio address. Peg had seen the number of ducks and geese decline in a two-decade period and voiced concern that "the supply of game has gradually been reduced until now at times it is necessary to remain in our blind quite a bit longer than was necessary some years ago in order to obtain our limit." Causes, he thought, included draining and plowing of the breeding range and "the complete network of hard surface roads to practically all isolated places." He heralded the Bureau of Biological Survey's "vast program of inviolate waterfowl refuges," funded from proceeds of recently mandated duck stamps.[29]

Peg, according to Shannon, left a legacy of hunting tales and photos to his children, and they told of a world of giant Canada geese and skies filled with mallards and sprigs. During his lifetime Peg Melton gunned at Clear Lake, the prairie of Matagorda County, and the Bill Ramin Lake east of Rosharon. He shot prairie-chickens at Almeda Road, where the Astrodome was later built, and on the dirt road to Sharpstown that became Bellaire Boulevard. One wonders what Peg would think of a drive to his old gunning haunts today.[30]

After World War II, Houston hunters had joined clubs and leases on all points of the compass; they formed conservation organizations, retriever clubs, and skeet and trap clubs; and they religiously following their sports in local newspapers. The first Houston outdoor feature columnist was probably Jimmy Lingan of the *Houston Chronicle* in 1934, followed closely by *Houston Post*'s Bill Walker and Andy Anderson of the *Houston Press.* Later well-known and long-lived columnists were Harv Boughton; Stan Slaten, "the guides outdoor writer"; and the legendary Bob Brister. The zenith of Houston outdoor writing was perhaps reached in 1990 when sportsmen could choose from columns written by Bob Brister, Joe Doggett, Doug Pike, and Shannon Tompkins in the *Houston Chronicle.*[31]

Bob Brister started writing for the *Houston Chronicle* in 1954 when, as he described it, Houston was a "whiskey and trombone town" with hard-living, hard-drinking newspapermen. His hero was writer Hart Stilwell, and Bob once wrote that "I learned a good bit from him, including how to pick up his hefty bar tabs." The fodder for Bob's rich storytelling was gleaned from sporting forays at Barrow's Ranch in Chambers County with Joe Lagow, in the cypress swamps of the Trinity River with Morgan LaFour, on prairie rice fields with Jimmy Reel, Marvin Tyler, and later Larry Gore, and on the flats around Matagorda Island with Stewart Campbell. His stories appeared in print for almost forty years as well as the mid-1960s *Outdoors with Brister* television show, which he filmed, wrote, and produced.[32]

Brister reached national prominence as *Field and Stream* shooting editor between 1971 and 1985, and his resume included documentary outdoors films, freelance writing, a Pulitzer nomination, and his publications *Shotgunning: The Art and the Science* and *Golden Crescent,* a celebration of coastal Texas sporting with art by John Cowan. Brister is credited with bringing sporting clays to the United States from England.[33]

Bob was a celebrated wing shooter; legend has it that his winnings from pigeon shooting competitions paid for a Houston home. Guide Forrest West says,

"We called him 'the Old Gray Possum,' and he was the best shot I ever saw. I had a hunt where Bob was shooting a .410 and still out shot C. B. Delhomme and Grant Ilseng." That was not a simple feat. Ilseng was an exhibition shooter who held national skeet and trap titles and coached celebrities who included entertainment stars Gary Cooper, Fred McMurray, and Clark Gable.[34]

GOOSE CREEK AND BAYTOWN

In the 1800s, the north Trinity Bay shoreline by the San Jacinto River mouth was lined with cedar, pine, and magnolia trees. The only communities on the forested shores were William Scott's Bay Town settlement and Cedar Bayou, with the waterfront between them speckled with fishing villages and hunters' shacks. One of these, the small settlement of Busch Landing at Goose Creek, was where Henry T. Busch hunted ducks, geese, snipes, and plovers. It was here the first well of the hundred-million-barrel Goose Creek Oil Field was drilled in 1908. Within a decade a forest of wooden derricks sprouted over Busch's hunting spot, and it was followed by a Humble Oil refinery in 1917 and the company town of Baytown. Oil brought jobs, and the men who lived in Baytown's tent communities in the early 1920s hunted ducks every afternoon when they got off work.[35]

Baytown by the mid-1900s was a small town with a big waterfowl hunting culture. Duck and goose hunting reports were among the most essential news published in the *Baytown Sun*. Hunters traded yarns at Jim Nelson's Sporting Goods on North Main Street or at the Trophy Barber Shop on East Texas Avenue, its walls covered with game trophies owner Jimmie Carpenter collected from around the world with hunting companion Babe Badgely. Baytown's waterfowl culture produced some well-known names. At the top of the impressive list is Rudy LeCompte.[36]

Rudy LeCompte came to Texas in 1936 from Bourg, Louisiana, to work as a chemist at Baytown's Esso refinery. While best known to Gulf Coast collectors for his decoys, Rudy was an equally accomplished hunter and guide. He won three state duck calling championships between 1946 and 1949 and placed in three international events in Crowley, Louisiana. Rudy's cousin Nolan LeCompte made all of his duck calls from bamboo with an Ace comb reed, and Rudy's son Gordon can still picture his father with one of Nolan's calls hanging around his neck, the end of the barrel charred brown from the fire as he leaned over it to burn pin feathers while cleaning ducks.[37]

Learning to call ducks better than just about anyone else was a family affair, and father and son together crushed all comers in local Baytown calling contests. Gordon became the better goose caller in the family and remembers he got his start when Rudy brought the twelve-year-old boy to the 1955 international contest in Crowley. Quebec Cree guide Ernest Meaux, a champion mouth caller, invited youngsters onstage to learn his craft, and Gordon was the first on the stage. He

BAYTOWN DECOY *carver Rudy LeCompte in the 1930s or '40s. (Courtesy Gordon LeCompte)*

says, "I went home and for six years hunted nothing but geese to practice. He ruined me!"[38]

After Gordon moved to Freeport, father and son were regulars in the Brazoria County marshes until 1970, when they moved to Sargent Ranch and started the small private club that later became the Goose Roost Hunt Club. Long-time friend Mike Leebron, who now runs the operation, remembers that Rudy and Gordon watched him for a year before inviting him to join them on a hunt. On their first morning together in a blind, they watched a flock of teal land in the decoys at first light. Mike waited. In his thick south Louisiana accent, Rudy asked, "Wassa matta, you don't shoot duck? You want 'em to quit swimmin' or what?"[39]

Mike says Rudy was close to eighty years old when they made that hunt. "He was a gentle soul with a stout sense of humor. After a good hunt, ol' Rudy liked a big tug of whiskey from his flask, which he carried in case of snake bite." Gordon LeCompte now lives in Arkansas, spending his winters calling mallards as his father once did. A couple of times each year he returns to Sargent Ranch, where his calling is still music to snow geese and specklebellies. There's an old Cree mouth caller who would be proud.

Jim Nelson was another of Baytown's larger-than-life waterfowlers. The Nelson family farmed land between Trinity Bay and Cedar Bayou, moving to Baytown in 1919 when Jim was five. He and his brother Joe started hunting early, finding plenty of canvasbacks feeding on banana water lilies at Ash Lake on Cedar Bayou. Along with W. A. Read, Jim was the subject of a 1953 *Life* magazine article on snow goose hunting with white decoys; their white hunting outfits were considered, at the time, very unusual hunting attire.[40]

Baytown outdoorsmen relied on Jim Nelson for their fishing and hunting reports. They visited him at his Nelson's Sporting Goods store, a fixture in the outdoor community from 1947 until 1978, and read his columns "Fishing Facts and Fiction" and "Outdoors" in the *Baytown Sun.* Jim, for his whole adult life, carried over one hundred pellets in his foot from the time his brother Joe accidentally shot him.[41]

Baytown's Prentice Holder was, like Jim Nelson, an avid goose hunter who shot over some of the earliest Texas white spreads. At ninety-five years of age he recalled with unfailing clarity how, in the early 1950s, he and jeweler Bill Bailey designed their early white spread using a wire support system over which they stretched white cloth cut from shirts, pillowcases, and sheets. They gave the lady who sewed all the decoys a silver serving set for her work and convinced their wives to sew them white hunting coats and scarves.[42]

Elbert "Watty" Watkins, who moved to Baytown in 1929 from Louisiana, made duck calls by hand, learning to call ducks by listening to birds in the rice fields at night. Baytown had a number of talented decoy carvers, including H. B. Creekmore, Walter Brewer, and Oliver Townsend, all mentored by Rudy LeCompte. Globetrotting sportsmen and Pickett's Bayou Hunting Club founders Abe and Babe Badgely lived in Baytown. Jim Nelson once wrote a yarn about Babe, who, he said, as a young boy often shot so many geese he couldn't haul them home. He solved the problem, the tale goes, by learning how "to shoot them on one side or the other and [to] just break a wing." When Babe had all the geese he wanted, he got behind them and herded them back to his house."[43]

Baytown outdoorsmen relished tall tales such as the one about Babe. There were a number of good local storytellers, but the undisputed champion was master storyteller Jeff Harbour. Jeff, who operated Harbour's Fish Camp on Trinity Bay, had dozens of his fables published in the local newspaper. In one, he advised putting decoys in deep mud because landing birds would get stuck in the mire and could be caught by hand. In another, he suggested hunters run as fast as they could into a flock of geese, as it would shock the birds, and in their confusion they would break wings running into each other. Legend has it that one day Jeff presented a single goose foot to a salesman at Nelson's Sporting Goods, explaining that he had called a lonesome honker down so low he reached up and grabbed it by the foot.[44]

The landscape of the old gunning clubs from Cypress Creek to Morgan's Point and across San Jacinto River to Busch Landing at Goose Creek is today unrecognizable, the once impenetrable tangle of prairie, thicket, and forest replaced by an equally impenetrable jungle of urban development and heavy industry. As early as the 1920s so much oil floated on the water at Baytown that the river caught fire. Bob Brister wrote that in the 1950s the Houston Ship Channel "was so polluted that chemicals were damaging the propellers of big ships, and some owners of early fiberglass boats were hesitant to use them . . . for fear they might dissolve."[45]

From a car window on the interstate, three canvasbacks float on the river by Lynchburg, the last vestige of the huge flocks that once roosted on the San Jacinto River. No one has seen a swan in maybe a hundred years. Names of the waterways—Black Duck Bay and Goose Creek—are all that remain as a historical glimmer of a once rich waterfowling culture.

CHAPTER 8

WEST GALVESTON BAY

Sportsmen who frequented the extensive wetlands and prairies between San Jacinto River and Galveston Bay in the early 1800s were mostly from Houston and Galveston. By the mid-1800s they were joined by hunters from a growing number of small coastal communities and, as railroads crossed the west side of the bay, by gunners from prairie depot towns that sprang up along the tracks. Waterfowl and the hunters who pursued them shared a diverse ecosystem where the freshwater prairie met Galveston Bay by way of estuaries such as the appropriately named Clear Lake and bays such as Dickinson, Moses, Swan, and Jones.

CLEAR LAKE TO VIRGINIA POINT

Sportsmen traveled to the west side of Galveston Bay between Houston and Galveston as early as the Civil War on the Galveston, Houston and Henderson Railroad, and in the late 1870s on the Gulf, Colorado and Santa Fe Railway. Weekend excursionists filled passenger cars with guns, gear, and even boats for hunts between Clear Lake and Virginia Point. Guides met the train, providing hunters with horses and ponies. One customer, Joe Murphy, kept his "prairie cowboy" guides amused when he shot fifty rounds and downed only one duck in 1873.[1]

During winter, Clear Lake in the late 1800s could be covered with teal, canvasbacks, and mallards, although weekend hunters were advised that "these aquatic fowl generally swam out to the middle of the lake with the advance of the sun." Trips to Clear Lake by sportsmen and their families were outdoor social affairs with week-long camping trips on the bluffs of Seabrook Peninsula. Camp Squall, later called Camp Comet, remained a popular tent community into the 1900s.

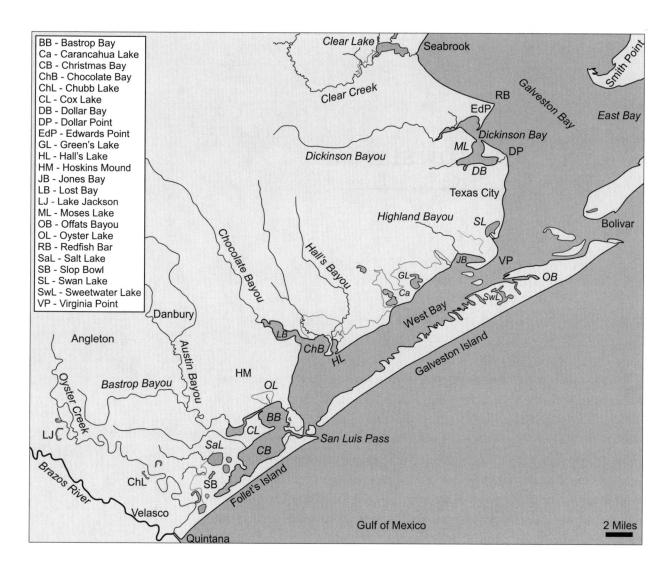

West Galveston Bay and West Bay before the Intracoastal Canal.

Less rustic accommodations were available at Mamie Repsdorph's Seabrook Hotel on Clear Creek in the 1890s, and nearby, fledgling League City boasted plenty of hotels to accommodate "lake country" sportsmen.[2]

The early 1900s were the heyday for organized hunting clubs in Clear Lake. Houston sportsmen formed Seabrook Fishing and Hunting Club in 1906 and built a clubhouse and wharf connected by oyster shell walkways. The venerable Houston Fishing and Hunting Club, established in the late 1880s, moved their clubhouse to Seabrook in 1907, and Lone Star Fishing and Hunting Club in Seabrook was incorporated the same year.[3]

The fishing village of Shoal Point, between Dickinson Bay and Virginia Point, was a popular sporting locality in the late 1800s. A number of watermen guided hunters in winter—the best known of them Captain Sam Sparks. The Myers brothers from Minnesota shot so many ducks on a trip to Shoal Point in 1891 that they decided to stay, changing the name of their adopted town to Texas City.[4]

> WANTED—Responsible party to conduct and manage the Seabrook Fishing and Hunting Club's clubhouse at Seabrook. For further particulars, write CHAS. E. PARKER, Chairman House Committee, 904 Texas Avenue, Houston, Tex.

(Modified from *Galveston Daily News,* Sep. 8, 1908)

The Wooden Shoe Hunting and Fishing Club built a lodge in the late 1800s on the southern tip of the Galveston County mainland at Virginia Point, hunting Highland Bayou where it drained into Jones Lake. Club members returning to Galveston boarded private rail cars or waited for the Houston train, which stopped on the bridge over West Bay, signaling sportsmen it was time to board with five whistle blasts.[5]

Galveston hunters rode the Gulf, Colorado and Santa Fe Railway—the Santa Fe line—to inland communities between Hitchcock and Arcola, walking out on the prairie for late morning shoots and returning on the evening train. Boarding the train with their guns and dogs, hunters monopolized the smoking cars as they waited to be dropped off along the route between Virginia Point and Alvin. The engineer often slowed down along the route for passengers to shoot prairie-chickens, snipes, ducks, rabbits, and deer from the car windows. Patient travelers in 1879 waited while one passenger shot two dozen mallards before returning to his car.[6]

The volume of Sunday hunters descending on Alvin raised the ire of church-going residents in the 1880s. Sensing an opportunity, nearby Hitchcock advertised its tolerance of Sabbath-breakers and quickly usurped Alvin as a Sunday shooting destination.[7]

GALVESTON ISLAND

Galveston sport hunting goes back to the days of the Republic of Texas and was featured as early as 1843 in the *Civilian and Galveston City Gazette,* which let residents know, "Wildfowl are becoming abundant, and the hunters have fine sport." In those same years the *Houston Telegraph and Texas Register* advised hunters where they could find big concentrations of fowl around Galveston Bay. Visiting from England in the 1840s, Matilda Houstoun wrote several anecdotes on Galveston sport hunting. For trips afield, she and her husband usually paid half a dollar a day to rent a horse and carriage. On one snipe shooting foray to the edge of town, Matilda said her husband was "fast filling his pockets with those birds." She preferred to eat ducks rather than geese, which, she wrote, "are not worth eating, for no keeping makes them tender, and they taste much more of fish than fowl."[8]

Separated from the mainland and Galveston Bay by West Bay, city sportsmen did not have to travel far for extraordinary sport. In the 1840s and '50s hunters shot ducks in a slough where today Broadway Street crosses 32nd Street. West Bay between Offats Bayou and the flats at Tenchman's Point were black with fowl, and nearby Sweetwater Lake, with its luxurious growths of wild celery, held "black mallards" and canvasbacks. A short voyage by sloop brought hunters to Pelican Island, Bolivar Point, Virginia Point, or down Galveston Island. With favorable winds, it was only a day's sail to East Bay, north Galveston and Trinity Bays, and to the west, the mainland from Jones Bay to Carancahua Bay. Carancahua Bay in the 1880s was called a "very desirable locality for ducks, geese, brant, and snipe," although sportsmen were warned of its deep mud and abundance of alligators.[9]

After the Civil War, Galveston was the largest of Texas's cities, with hunting a fashionable pastime for men of business. An entire industry grew up around the demand for the shooting sports. City hotels arranged hunts with guides such as Captain Fred Allen on his steam tug *Justine* and the sloop *Pelican,* which set sail from Pier 23 for Half Moon Reef, Carancahua Bay, and West Bay. The Tremont Hotel had its own captain and boat, the tug *Hygeia,* kept berthed at the hotel pier. In September and October, captains and crew returned to Galveston harbor with their decks piled high in blue-winged teal, mottled ducks, and early migrating pintails. By November they added mallards, bluebills, and wigeons to the kill. Late winter saw the arrival of more mallards, canvasbacks, greater Canada geese, and swans.[10]

Local hunting clubs were an integral part of Galveston's late 1800s social fabric, their activities a regular feature of Galveston society pages. Clubs organized dances, lectures, oyster roasts, boat regattas, fishing tournaments, and trap shoots, and they built floats and rode in parades, with many raising money for orphans and war veterans. Music was a big part of the entertainment; one 1870s sporting club called itself the Amateur Fishing, Hunting and Serenading Club.[11]

The august Galveston Gun Club opened in the 1870s, holding glass ball shooting exhibitions at the club grounds on Avenue H and 6th Street. The Bucktail Club in the late 1800s sponsored annual duck hunting excursions between Orange and the San Bernard River, its members traveling in a specially fitted rail car and camping in tents for as long as two weeks. The Galveston Tarpon Club formed in 1899, and by 1902 it boasted it had retired its fleet of sailboats for a large vessel powered by both sail and steam.[12]

In the late 1800s, a Galveston sportsman fired two shots into the "animated air," and it "rained ducks." With fowl littering the ground, he said, "I picked up as many as I could and started back toward the horses, leaving as many more crippled or dead upon the ground." His name was Joseph Cline, meteorologist with the US

A RARE PHOTOGRAPH *of a swan harvested on Galveston Bay. Note the rattlesnake at the bottom of the photo. The year and the hunters are unknown. (Rosenberg Museum Collection, Rosenberg Library, Galveston, File No. G-928-5)*

Weather Bureau, and he made history along with his brother Isaac as the weather forecasters who raised the warning flag before the fury of wind and sea of Galveston's great 1900 hurricane.[13]

In the months after the 1900 storm, ducks migrated to a debris-covered wetland around Galveston Bay. But many of the area's famous duck hunting haunts had gone quiet. Duck hunters making their way through the marsh grass on the south side of Pelican Island found eight storm victims. That fall, dozens more were discovered on Deer Island, Pelican Island, Virginia Point, San Luis Pass, Chocolate Bayou, and Carancahua Lake.[14]

The next year a healing city went duck hunting again. Galveston Hunting Club was founded with one hundred original members who constructed a large hunting lodge. The Pastime Hunting and Fishing Club opened about the same time, later trading their sails for a gasoline-powered boat with a twenty-horsepower engine, cook room, and eight sleeping berths. Other new clubs included Booth Hunting Club, Santa Fe Hunting Club, and Gulf Coast Hunting Club.[15]

The Booth, Santa Fe, and Gulf Coast clubs combined to form an alliance that eventually controled land from Galveston Island to Fort Bend County, where the dizzying pace of rice production along the Brazos River was attracting clouds of ducks. Club members who traveled inland packed Galveston's Union Depot each Friday evening, a spectacle of doctors, clerks, and lawyers "arrayed in their

> **SPECIAL NOTICE**
>
> Applications for membership on the CANVAS-BACK CLUB, SWEETWATER LAKE, will be received by the undersigned. Membership limited. Price $25 for the season.
>
> GEO. G. CLOUGH,
> Manager.

(Modified from *Galveston Daily News,* Sep. 8, 1908)

hunting jackets and caps, with boots and guns." The Santa Fe line took them as far as Thompson's Switch, where they were met by wagons for the ride to Booth and George Ranches. One Galveston Gun Club member returned from Smithers Lake on George Ranch in 1901 with eighty ducks, "embracing nearly all the known varieties."[16]

Two private game preserves, the Sweetwater Lake Hunting Club and the Canvasback Club, opened on Galveston's Sweetwater Lake in the early 1900s. With its wild celery irresistible to canvasbacks, Sweetwater Lake had long been a favorite location among city gunners. Weekend mornings saw a parade of hunters who made the six-mile journey from the city to the lake by horse and buggy and in wagons. Public access was curtailed when Sweetwater Lake Hunting Club and the Canvasback Club hired game wardens to patrol the shooting grounds. In 1908, Canvasback Club dues were twenty-five dollars a year. Its membership of between thirty and fifty sportsmen saw to it that recently promulgated game laws "are observed on their preserves and that game is not wantonly slaughtered."[17]

Galveston hunters wasted no time adopting the gasoline engine. As early as 1908, outdoor writer Nick Hardy boasted that sportsmen with automobiles could leave the city after office hours, speed to the end of the island for a hunt the next morning, and return to the city in plenty of time for business. An entire newspaper column was dedicated to Thanksgiving weekend in 1916, when the *Galveston Daily News* estimated a thousand Oleander City residents traveled as far as fifty miles to hunt and fish. With the opening of the ferry to Bolivar Peninsula to motoring sportsmen in 1930, a new hunting ground was "thrown open to Galveston nimrods," who found marshes filled with mallards and "Canadian honkers."[18]

Inboard and outboard motor boats after World War I took sportsmen east to High Island and Double Bayou, down the island to San Luis Pass, and, launching at Art LaFrance's fishing camp on Highland Bayou, to the mainland on West Bay. W. D. McMillan provided a charter boat service from Virginia Point to his public Sportsman's Pier's fishing and hunting club at Carancahua Lake. Each morning his boat, the *Sankaty,* left the pier at 6:30 a.m., and it returned at 5:00 in the afternoon. With Prohibition the law of the land between 1919 and the early '30s, duck

A GENTEEL *Galveston hunter with his automobile and a display of snow geese, pintails, and a spoonbill, early 1930s. (Rosenberg Library, Galveston, File No. G-928-9)*

> **Boats, Launches, etc.**
> MOTOR BOATS FOR SALE— Sportsmen, you have found that you can not reach the ducks by automobile this season. You need a motor boat. I have them, all sizes and prices, J. A. PAULETTE. Offats Bayou Marine Ways.

(Modified from *Galveston Daily News,* Jan. 21, 1923)

hunters shared the remote west end of the island with bootlegging operations. The wooden skiff rowing to shore in the predawn darkness was as likely stacked with bottles of contraband as it was with wooden decoys.[19]

It was said that every available body of water on Galveston Island was controlled by a hunting club in the early 1900s. Newspaper society pages followed duck camp culture with the same vigor with which they once reported on the coming and going of excursionists by sea and by rail. Hunting lodges, ranging from fancy to crude fishing shacks, extended all the way down the island to San Luis Pass. The newspaper classified sections were jammed with jobs for cooks, groundskeepers, and guides. Typical was a classified ad run by Galveston's US National Bank Hunting Club in 1929 that read: "Medium age, white couple without children, for hunting camp on Galveston Island. Woman must cook: man must be active and willing worker. References required. None but steady, willing and sober couple need apply."[20]

By the 1920s the nucleus of waterfowl hunting had shifted away from hotels and the harbor. The new guide in town was the downtown hardware store,

WEST GALVESTON BAY

with Lyons Hardware Co. and John Christensen & Co. the largest in the city. One Galveston "ammunitions dealer" who sent fifteen hunting parties out in 1923 reported that his customers had killed nearly four hundred birds. Hardware stores evolved into sporting goods stores, and by the 1930s Galveston's center of waterfowling was on Tremont Street at A. J. Rasmussen & Sons sporting goods, which carried everything from guns to live decoy collars, leg bands, and anchors. By the early 1940s hunting supplies were available from Johnny Junker of Rasmussen's, at Charner Skains's sporting goods store, and from Harry Feigle of Feigle Sporting Goods.[21]

When the *Galveston Daily News* hired Ike Walton as its first full-time outdoor writer in the late 1920s, sportsmen no longer had to sail or motor the waterways to know when mallards filled West Bayou, West Bay, Cow Bayou, Greens Bayou, or Carancahua "reef": they read it in the comfort of their homes. Walton's "Fishing and Hunting on Treasure Island" ran from the 1920s to the 1940s, with hunters later following the birds in columns by Jack Proctor and, in the late 1940s, by A. C. Becker Jr. in his "Daily Sporting Roundup" and "Fin and Feathers" columns. The nephew of a Galveston County market hunter, Adolf C. Becker used the initials A. C. because, according to historian Kevin Ladd, "Adolph was not a popular name in 1940s America." Becker, whose career spanned forty years, authored *Waterfowl in the Marshes, Game and Bird Calling,* and *Decoying Waterfowl* as well as several books on sport fishing.[22]

The barrier island city in the 1940s and '50s had become more urban, and the change was reflected in Galveston's waterfowl hunting. The era of the private hunting club had passed. Only two new ones were advertised in the early 1940s: West Bay Hunting Club and Treasure Island Fishing and Hunting Club on Offats Bayou. Offats in the predawn hours was still a bustling place where sportsmen launched or rented boats at more than half a dozen fishing camps, but, like much of the area around Galveston, Offats was soon entirely engulfed by the city.[23]

Galveston Island still prickled with hundreds of duck blinds, but the largest concentrations of birds were increasingly found on West Bay, around Carancahua Lake and Greens Bayou. Most of the mallards were on Bolivar, and nearly all of the sprigs had moved to the island's west end by San Luis Pass. At the start of the 1948–50 season, one thousand Galveston duck hunters took to the marsh for opening day. But like duck hunters in other growing Texas cities, they started moving further from the city for a good hunt.[24]

CHOCOLATE BAY

Named for an Indian word for a pepper plant that once grew along the shore, Chocolate Bay in east Brazoria County was reached by Galveston hunters who set a course by sail in the mid- to late 1800s for its black mud shoreline and fringing *Spartina* grasses. Punctuated by Hall's Lake and Hall's, New, and Chocolate

RIP SMOCK's *Chocolate Bay fishing shack, 1940s*. Left to right: *Marion Polka, Harry Matell, Walter "Rip" Smock, and Adam Edward "Ed" Polka with ducks, geese, and one rattlesnake.* (Courtesy James Smock)

Bayous, its marshes held geese and flocks of pintails measured by the mile. Mallards filled nearly every freshwater slough and pothole, and flocks of diving ducks—bluebills, redheads, and buffleheads—at times covered the open bay.[25]

Writer Ned Hardy in 1928 wrote that Chocolate Bay was "accessible to autos or boats," and over it "ducks fly regularly twice a day." Hardy saw the future, as camps and private and public hunting clubs began to line West and Chocolate Bays. Houston's Rip Smock was typical of many of the motorized sportsman in the years between the world wars. He and his Houston companions built a shack on Chocolate Bayou, launching runabouts and fishing boats at Peterson Landing for the long ride down the twisting bayou to Chocolate Bay. In good weather they crossed West Bay, sleeping in tents on the bay side of Follett's Island. Expelling rattlesnakes from their shack and camps was a weekend ritual.[26]

Smock family photographs from the 1940s show harvests of dozens of mallards and pintails along with snow, blue, and lesser Canada geese. Son James Smock says his father's hunts were not so much about recreation but "both a way of life and a way to provide substantial food for the family. He didn't waste a thing." During World War II Smock and his companions saved gas rationing coupons to fill truck and boat tanks for their hunts, sometimes walking the neighborhood in army uniforms, trading fish and fowl for gas rationing cards.[27]

With easy access by cars and boats from Houston and Galveston, day hunting grew in popularity, with hunters motoring in for a morning shoot and returning home the same day. Hall's Bayou was headquarters for the new mobile sportsmen, who frequented Franks Hunting Camp on lower Hall's Bayou, and Hall's Bayou Ranch.[28]

Unwanted guests *rounded up from Rip Smock's Chocolate Bay hunting and fishing shack, 1940s. (Courtesy James Smock)*

Bob Briscoe of Briscoe Irrigation Co. opened Hall's Bayou Ranch to day hunters in the 1940s. With twenty-one thousand acres of rice, prairie, and marsh between Carancahua Lake and Hall's Bayou, Hall's Bayou Ranch grew into one of the largest public day hunting operations on the coast. Hundreds of hunters in the 1950s and '60s lined up to pay the five-dollar gate fee at the permit shack on Farm to Market Road 2004. In the 1960s the gatekeeper was Ronnie La Rue, and Houston's Marshall Hayes remembers the fence by his gatehouse was often covered with rattlesnakes killed by sportsmen on their morning shoots.[29]

Houston Chronicle outdoor writer Bob Brister was a frequent Hall's Bayou visitor, often with his crony Stewart Campbell. Bob was teaching Stewart to mouth call geese while they were driving on a winding dirt road to the ranch, and Stewart says, "We were hollerin' away, and a cop pulled up beside us. He stopped and looked at us and thought we were complete loonies." Hall's Bayou Ranch day hunting ended in 1982, but the ranch today remains in operation as a popular private club.[30]

Chocolate and West Bays ended at the Big Pass, later called San Luis Pass, by way of Mud Island and Titlum Tatlum Island, or Moody's Island. Here the Moody family built a private lodge in the early 1900s and entertained the sporting wealthy with fishing and hunting trips in the same tradition as Colonel Moody once did at Lake Surprise.[31]

Although the swans, Canada geese, and most of the mallards are gone, parts of Chocolate Bay look as they did a hundred years ago. Others are hardly recognizable. Native prairie grasses were displaced by rice, but now most of the rice fields are fallow, choked by Chinese tallow trees that extend from the upper prairie all the way up the mallard holes along the tracks of the old Santa Fe route. Houston has covered Clear Lake, Galveston and Virginia Point, and heavy industry, Texas City. Sludge pits replaced wetlands on the side of Carancahua Lake, and at night, lights of the Chocolate Bayou petrochemical complex illuminate a sky where waterfowl, and the hunters who followed them, once saw only stars in the blackness.[32]

CHAPTER 9

BRAZOS and SAN BERNARD RIVERS to the GULF

S PLIT ROUGHLY DOWN THE MIDDLE BY THE BRAZOS RIVER, Brazoria County covers a wide range of habitats: tidal marshes on West Galveston Bay, inland prairie, Brazos River bottoms, and, to the west of the river, wetlands that fringe the Gulf of Mexico. The region provided sustenance to the earliest of Texas settlers and, after the mid-1800s, unrivalled sport for gunners from throughout the United States.

On its east side, coastal Brazoria County begins where West Bay struggles with its identity between land and water behind Follett's Island. Here, below an ancient beach terrace, the shoreline once formed a three- to five-mile-wide band of lower marsh with a complex web of knoll ponds and larger, nearly circular ponds called Oyster, Alligator, Lost, Cox, Salt, Wolf, and Nick's Lakes. Before the IC it was a single, contiguous wetland where upper-prairie fresh water of Bastrop Bayou, Austin Bayou, and Big Slough mixed with the tidal waters of Bastrop, Christmas, and Drum Bays.

Hunters reached this corner of Brazoria County by wagon and sail, pursuing snow geese, greater Canadas, and late winter swans that at times came right to the edge of the Velasco town limits. They moored their sloops on the banks of Rattlesnake and Christmas Points, shooting puddle ducks as they moved to and from the marshes and diver ducks that crossed promontories jutting into broad waters. In the 1890s gunners at Christmas Point were said to be "slaughtering geese and all sorts of game."[1]

Names of many of the waterways changed over time. Oyster Bay, easily confused with neighboring Oyster Lake, was renamed Christmas Bay. Lost Lake was named for an earlier body of water drained in 1922 by a precursor to the IC. Nick's Lake was named for its resident waterman, Nick Jones. Coastal wetlands adjacent

A Mr. Wright *on the deck of his sloop, Brazoria County, with a mallard, a canvasback, and a snow goose. (Courtesy Brazoria County Historical Museum, File No. 2002.016p.0051)*

to Salt Lake were called the lower end of Ranch Prairie until the early 1900s, when it was better known by sportsmen as the Slop Bowl.[2]

West of the Brazos River mouth, much of the wetlands was part of James F. Perry's Peach Point Plantation. Waterfowl fed the plantation's planter culture of cotton and sugarcane, and the Perry boys and slaves hunted "on a regular basis, and venison or wildfowl often found their way to the Peach Point kitchen." Wintering waterfowl filled natural freshwater depressions that circled Bryan Mound salt dome, the *en echelon* lakes of Jones Creek, and, to the west, Cedar Lake and Cow Trap Lake.[3]

Cedar Lake paralleled the Gulf shoreline for six miles. Because of its landward edge of black marsh mud and thick cordgrass, access to it was easiest from the Gulf side, although hunters suffered clouds of mosquitoes as they picked their way through rattlesnakes stretched out to sun on the beach. Adjacent Cow Trap Lake, part of the Pool Ranch, was a seemingly endless succession of circular, freshwater wetland ponds in the lower prairie. The lake got its name for cattle that perished by bogging down in is bottomless muck, leaving a landscape littered with bones. If they could walk it at all, hunters got lost and, like cattle before them, they got stuck.[4]

Velasco and Quintana, located where the Brazos River met the Gulf, were Brazoria's main destination for sportsmen in the 1800s. Town piers were crowded

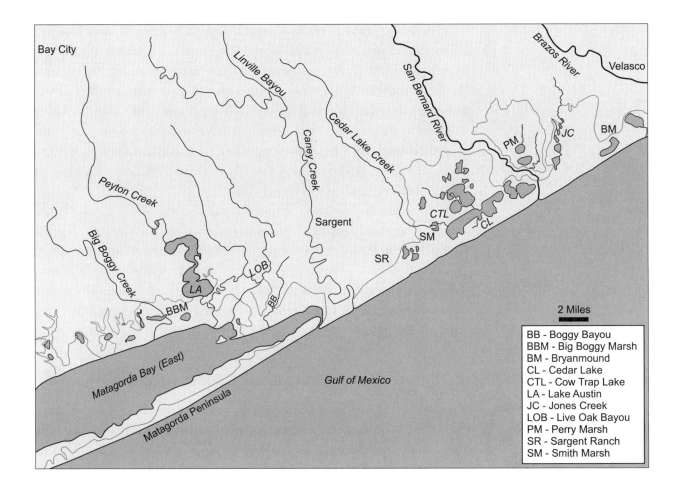

Brazoria County *and what became East Matagorda Bay as it looked in the early 1900s.*

with sloops, schooners, steamers, and launches whose captains ferried clients east and west and up the Brazos River. Hotel sporting solicitors arranged fishing and hunting excursions for their patrons. Many of their customers were railroad men, such as the Pacific Express Company and International Great Northern employees who hunted and camped on the beach at Cedar Lake in 1895. When Fred Brock hosted O. H. Springer from Detroit on a duck hunt in 1896, the party arrived aboard what may have been the first steam yacht in Brazoria County. By the 1890s a direct route to Velasco was available with completion of the Velasco Terminal Railway.[5]

By the turn of the century, sportsmen frequented the new Velasco Hotel, a magnificent four-story building with its own electricity, sewage system, cold storage, and ice plant. Overlooking the Gulf, visitors could hardly see the sand for waist-high driftwood that covered the beach. The hotel arranged transportation upriver by horse-drawn buggies to land it leased on Oyster Creek, Lake Jackson, Buffalo Camp Bayou, and the five-thousand-acre Lake Jackson Place plantation. Returning in the evening, the sportsmen's bounties of fish and wild game were prepared by the hotel chef and served in the hundred-foot-long dining room.[6]

West of Quintana to the San Bernard River a number of small boarding houses catered to fishermen and hunters. Some were crude affairs, offering little more than respite from fall mosquitoes and winter cold fronts. Others were tourist destinations in their own right, such as Frenchman Laurent Ducroz's boarding house, described in 1893 as one of the most pleasant resorts for fishing and hunting on the coast. The Ducroz family operated the rope ferry across the river, the staging spot for sportsmen who came for a bounty of mallards, teal, and "black ducks" between Jones Creek, Cow Trap Lake, and the Cedar Lakes and for geese and sandhill cranes in the upper prairie.[7]

It didn't take long for ducks to find Brazoria County's first rice crop, planted in 1907 along Bastrop Bayou. That year shooting was "very fine, and ducks in the rice fields are as thick as the rice birds were in harvest time." The writer added, "It would be a world of fun if it was not for the pesky mosquitoes, which were never more plentiful or annoying." By 1917 the few hundred acres of rice that were under cultivation in the county attracted ducks thick enough that they "attempted to take over the consumption of it."[8]

COASTAL BRAZORIA HUNTING CLUBS

There were only two known private clubs at the turn of the century: Velasco Fishing and Hunting Club and Velasco Gun Club, with fifteen charter members. Then came sulfur. Using a rope cable ferry to cross the Brazos River and ox teams that mired in Bryan Mound mud, Freeport Sulphur Company extracted the first commercial sulfur in 1912. The town of Freeport followed. Freeport Sulphur wasted no time in capitalizing on Brazoria County's sporting opportunities, the next year opening the Tarpon Inn as a company hunting and fishing resort. In the inn's early years, hunting parties boarded the hotel yacht berthed at a pier near the beach, and the captain navigated the coast on trips for geese and ducks. Freeport's Tarpon Inn remained a sporting entity until 1956.[9]

Freeport grew after more sulfur was discovered at Hoskins Mound in the early 1920s. Sportsmen from the growing town had great waterfowl hunting only a short distance away. Six miles to the northeast, the marsh at the lower end of Ranch Prairie east of Stratton Ridge—the Slop Bowl—was home to many of Freeport's hunting clubs. Part of the Slop Bowl's popularity was due to its proximity to town, and part because it was "20,000 acres of the best duck hunting to be found anywhere along the Texas Gulf Coast," a place where discriminating sportsmen could, in a single morning, choose to shoot limits consisting of only mallards or canvasbacks.[10]

In the Slop Bowl the mud was thicker and the bayous more tortuous than anywhere else in Brazoria County. It did its best to claim duck hunters, as it had cattle for over a hundred years. Freeport's Frank Brazill drove a rebuilt Model A Ford across the marsh to build duck blinds on a warm fall day. When he hadn't

(Modified from *Galveston Daily News*, Oct. 8, 1913)

Sportsmen returned *from the Slop Bowl in Brazoria County and Cove with 250 ducks. The photograph was taken in front of C. L. Bering Sporting Goods and Auto Supply, Houston, probably in the late 1920s. (Houston Public Library Metropolitan Research Center, File No. MSS 0100-932)*

returned by sunset, Brownie Rhodes found him stuck in the marsh, "hardly recognizable through the swarms of mosquitoes" and confined to his vehicle by hordes of rattlesnakes. When former Angleton mayor Neal Giesecke got lost, he walked so long he was hospitalized, unconscious. Graham Scott, of Freeport and Houston, was rescued three times between 1945 and 1952.[11]

The Slop Bowl was home to Freeport Boating and Hunting Club, incorporated in 1944 with 110 members. In its first year the club leased nine thousand acres and built permanent blinds, shell roads, and a hunting lodge. It was a duck hunters club, one that measured its prominence less by title or money and more by the reputation of the sportsmen it attracted.[12]

The Freeport Boating and Hunting Club was an important part of the local community. Members organized charities and raised money for a number of worthy causes, including programs for wounded World War II veterans. Club member M. C. Raney wrote a regular outdoor column for the *Freeport Facts* that kept sportsmen informed of local hunting and fishing news in the 1940s. Lake Jackson's C. A. "Rube" Tracy maintained a report on the numbers of ducks and geese harvested at the club, compiling the results for the State Game, Fish, and Oyster Commission to use in their annual waterfowl surveys. When outdoor feature filmmaker Ronnie Luster Sr. produced a color movie of Texas duck hunting in 1946, he chose the Slop Bowl and Freeport Boating and Hunting Club. Host O. C. Wallace delivered Ronnie and club members Raymond Carlton and Edna Callaway to the marsh in something new to the area—his "swamp buggy."[13]

> **Membership In The HUGHES HUNTING & FISHING CLUB**
> 1 year in "Slop Bowl" 10,000 Acres $25.00
> Membership must be paid by August 15th.
> **BILL EDGAR**
> Freeport   Ph. BE 3-3203

(Modified from *Brazosport Facts,* July 21, 1959)

On the northern edge of the Slop Bowl, part of I. C. Hoskins's extensive holdings covered the prairie adjacent to Bastrop Bay and the topographic high, later known as Hoskins Mound, at the head of Ranch Prairie. Natural prairie lakes that ringed the dome attracted puddle ducks, canvasbacks, and redheads. Even after mining operations displaced natural drainage with artificial impoundments, ducks still came in large numbers. Employees of the Freeport Sulphur Company opened the Sulphur Company Club in 1946, hunting both Hoskins Mound and a hundred-acre lake west of Freeport at Bryan Mound sulfur dome. By 1948 the original hundred members grew to three hundred, with annual dues of three dollars.[14]

Brazoria County saw a large increase in the number of hunting clubs between the 1950s and 1970s. East of the Brazos River, Hughes Hunting and Fishing Club opened in the 1950s with an annual membership fee of twenty-five dollars, and leased ten thousand acres in the Slop Bowl. Muldoon Hunting and Fishing Club, run by H. R. Berry, opened in the 1960s. Members hunted the Slop Bowl and later constructed a freshwater lake, called Canvasback Lake, near their lodge on Otter Slough. Hoskins Mound and the grounds of the old Sulfur Company Club were purchased by Texaco, and the company's corporate hunting was managed by Bud Mize. When Al Bisbey hunted there in the 1960s, he remembers, "You had to walk backwards because of the mosquitoes. That was the only way you could breathe."[15]

West of the Brazos River, Perry Ranch in the late 1960s hosted Sweetwater Lake Club, run by W. H. Flessner and Hank Lippold, with a fifty-dollar annual membership fee. Angleton's M. Gardner managed another club with thirty-five members on part of Perry Ranch. Pool Ranch, covering Cow Trap Lake, was leased to a private hunting club. Members included B. H. "Hardy" Carlton and his wife, Clara, who in the 1950s had to abandon a morning shoot because of rattlesnakes. Clara killed twenty-five from her duck blind that morning before she fled.[16]

ON THE BANKS OF THE BRAZOS

The Brazos River, with Oyster Creek to the east and the San Bernard River to the west, was only a short distance from the tidal flats and fringing lakes of the coast, but the duck shooting was entirely different there. Called the Columbia bottomlands, it was almost a million acres of coastal floodplain forest where repeated lateral changes in the river's course formed meandering oxbows, sloughs, lakes, and flooded stands of oaks, sweetgum, hackberry, ash, elm, and hickory in a tangle of yaupon and palmetto. As early as 1860, Houston hunters got as far as East Columbia on the Houston Tap and Brazoria Railroad, then journeyed by riverboat, returning with barrels of acorn-fed mallards and wood ducks.[17]

The Brazos River cut through miles of bluestem prairie interspersed with bayous and lakes and extending to the west to Great Prairie Canebrake near the San Bernard River. Around the time of the Civil War, sportsman and commercial hunter Frank W. Flack rode through the grassland, killing hundreds of Canada geese as they fed on burns with fresh grass sprouts. Huge flights of wigeons between Oyster Creek and Old Caney Creek in Matagorda County provided the English visitor with what he called "capital sport." Near East Columbia, Flack crawled a flock of blue-winged teal and wrote of the reward: "We emptied our right-hand barrels. Fifteen of the teal were killed or wounded, and the surviving pair were stopped by two shots from the left-hand barrels of our guns."[18]

Up the Brazos River, past the antebellum towns of Brazoria and East Columbia, are Maner and Eagle Nest Lakes. For time seemingly eternal, alligators slipped from their banks and water moccasins stood their ground on the giant cut-grass and bulrush-covered shoreline. The mast of moss-covered oak trees once attracted mallards in such numbers that their rising was deafening, and late winter canvasbacks were drawn to sago pondweed that grew in clear, open water. Those ducks, along with the lake's fish and alligators, fed landowners and slaves as part of James Austin's extensive Osceola Plantation. In 1878 Osceola Plantation was purchased by T. L. Smith and the Womack family.[19]

The countryside had hardly changed when Jack Renfro leased the plantation lakes in 1923 and opened his Eagle Nest & Maner Lake Fish and Game Preserve. Renfro remained the patriarch of duck hunting on Maner and Eagle Nest Lakes for the next forty years, later renaming the club, with its alternative spelling, the Manor Lake Hunting and Fishing Club. The story of Jack Renfro and his club live on through his granddaughter, Mary Jean Romero, whose recollections are augmented by trunks of memorabilia that include club member Walter H. "Stag" Steigerwald's diaries kept from 1918 until 1952. Steigerwald's words provide a rich image of club life against a backdrop of fried frog legs, calico bass, Glen McCarthy oil wells, Brazos River floods, and the first graveled roads across the Columbia bottomlands.[20]

EAGLE NEST *and Maner Lake Fish and Game Preserve's Jack Renfro* (left) *and Frank O. Perry* (right) *with greater and lesser Canada geese, 1923. The seated man is thought to be a guide. (Courtesy Mary Jean Romero)*

John Roger "Jack" Renfro followed the oil rigs from his North Texas home to West Columbia with his wife, Mary Estelle, "May," about 1919. Oil money and city men were a good mix for the gambling side of Renfro, who opened Palace Café in West Columbia with a hidden poker room in back. Four years later he used his winnings to open Eagle Nest & Maner Lake Fish and Game Preserve on the south side of Maner Lake. He chose a site in a stand of oak trees to construct half a dozen wood-frame guest cottages, a main dining hall, a couple of cabins for employees, and the Renfro house. Visitors in the days between the world wars were hosted by club foreman Otto Poppendorf and his wife, Betty, who ran the kitchen with long-time employee "Aunt" Louisa. On the grounds were a large vegetable garden, milk cows, and Jack's herd of Hereford cows, the source of big, thick T-bones, sirloins, and porterhouse steaks served at breakfast and supper.[21]

The culture of Manor Lake Hunting and Fishing Club was a reflection of its organizer, Jack Renfro. With his ever-present pipe and hat, broad smile, and confident swagger, he nurtured an atmosphere of big southern hospitality with great hunting and fishing. Members brought their families, from children to grandparents, and Mary Jean remembers the club "as the kind of a place to take your wife. The men dressed up to hunt. On Sundays they had special dinners."[22]

Poker remained Jack Renfro's passion, and he built one of the Maner Lake guest cabins larger than the others for evening high-stakes card games. During World War II rationing, when shotgun shells were as precious as greenbacks, West Columbia's Cap McMurrey paid one of his gambling debts with shotgun shells, and another wager pit shells against a yearling heifer.[23]

Most of Renfro's club members represented the new middle class that was defining Houston in the first half of the twentieth century. Some memorable names were Walter Steigerwald; Dr. Carl Robertus; dredging and mining engi-

GUEST CABIN *and Model Ts at Jack Renfro's Eagle Nest and Maner Lake Fish and Game Preserve, 1920s. (Courtesy Mary Jean Romero)*

neer Howard B. Kenyon, who owned Kenyon Island in Calhoun County; Jacob S. Oshman of Oshman's Sporting Goods; Joe Weingarten of Weingarten's Grocery; and C. F. "Bert" Hess, manager of the Houston Auditorium Hotel in Houston. Many on the roster remained active in sporting circles long after Renfro's club closed. E. D. Peden of Peden Iron and Steele Co. later formed a private hunting club in Rockport, Joseph A. Tennant Sr.'s family moved south to the Hasselmann Bay Club in Port O'Connor, and C. G. Pillot of Henke and Houston's Pillot grocery stores joined Eagle Lake Rod and Gun Club.[24]

Manor Lake Hunting and Fishing Club was open year-round. Spring and summer members fished for white perch they called calico bass, largemouth bass or black bass, and bream and bluegills. Winter brought ducks. Club fishing and hunting guides were called polers, and all were African Americans who lived on farm roads around Maner and Eagle Nest Lakes. Steigerwald's diary mentions polers Johnny Walker and Leon "Too Too" Jones; the last names were lost for guides Earnest, Ira, Alec, Ike, Becky, John, "a tall, dignified, and extremely polite old darky," and Garfield, "one of Jack's dusky top hands." The best known and most requested guide was Jocko Washington from Eagle Nest Lake. After the club closed, Jocko remained as Renfro's right-hand man until he died.[25]

Morning hunts started at the screened-in porch by the dining hall, where anxious members were matched with guides and blinds by drawing from a hat filled with poker chips. Then they drove to the pier at Eagle Nest Lake, where skiffs were loaded and poled to the blinds. Sometimes hunters had to watch their step; more than one duck blind was built on what was thought to be solid turf until someone stepped entirely through it. There were times when hunters watched as these floating islands, up to an acre in size, would blow past them, sometimes carrying away the decoy spread.[26]

Wooden decoy stools brought a variety of birds, including teal, pintails, mallards, wigeons, gadwalls, bluebills, spoonbills, and an occasional greater Canada

LONG-TIME *Maner Lake hunting and fishing guide Jocko Washington, 1940s. (Courtesy Mary Jean Romero)*

goose. Ducks moved inland from the coast before cold fronts, and sometimes thousands stacked up on the skyline from every point on the compass, with hundreds decoying at a time. Mallards returning from nearby rice fields at times covered the shores of Eagle Nest Lake.[27]

In the mid-1940s, Renfro turned management of the club over to the membership, and he later sublet it to American General Insurance Company. In 1949 he leased it to Brown and Root, and the new tenants brought Texas's top power brokers to Maner Lake. Legend has it that Renfro secured his retirement income around the poker table from those who did business with Herman and George Brown. Jack Renfro died in 1965, playing poker.[28]

Brown and Root, later part of Halliburton, still maintain Jack Renfro's Maner Lake lease. Eagle Nest, once the better of the two duck hunting lakes, was reshaped by Brown and Root earth moving machinery during the 1956 drought, when its irregular shoreline was smoothed, contoured, and cleared of vegetation. When prevailing south winds turned clear lake waters brown with suspended sediment, most of the aquatic vegetation disappeared, and with it, most of the ducks.[29]

Halliburton club manager Mike Wicker says that when he started in 1974, some of the original guiding families were still on the lake, and they "preferred the old cypress boats to the new fibreglass ones, and still poled them." A few years later, airboats replaced skiffs. The Halliburton lodge sits near where Renfro's dining hall once stood, and a couple of the original cabins remain on the grounds.

THERE WERE PLENTY *of ducks on Maner Lake in 1923, the first year of Jack Renfro's Eagle Nest and Maner Lake Fish and Game Preserve. (Courtesy Mary Jean Romero)*

Guides at the boathouse still tell alligator stories, such as that of the reptile alleged to have snapped off the lower unit of an old Brown and Root outboard motor. Too, the ninety-year-old traditional question—Which will retrieve a downed duck first, the alligator or the guide?—is still asked on Maner Lake.[30]

Probably every inland Brazoria County pond and oxbow held one club or another during the twentieth century, and the names of some of the later ones remain for posterity. In the 1940s, Dow Chemical built their exclusive Dow Reservoir with mallard and wood duck hunting in the flooded timber by invitation only. C. F. Mann in the early 1950s built levees around a topographic low called Mann, or Mallard, Lake, near East Columbia on the Brazos River, which became home to Mallard Lake Hunting Club and Brazos River Hunting Club. Houston's G. C. "Cleve" Moses founded the Brazos River Club with both flooded timber and open-water hunting. West of Angleton in the 1960s, Angleton Hunting and Fishing Club built a lodge, cabins, and eighteen duck blinds on two lakes. Member Gary Cole recalls that blinds were high enough to hide his boat under, and after a hunt, "you pulled your boat up to the dock, and the caretaker cleaned your boat and your ducks."[31]

BRAZORIA'S SPORTING CULTURE

Brazoria County residents didn't have to join a club to hunt; most landowners and ranchers willingly gave them permission. Bill Gunn, for example, never charged hunters in the 1950s and '60s for access to his Gunn Ranch on Jones Creek. Many of the local boys hunted at French Lake, later called Long Pond, which was right behind Freeport and close enough for them to walk to it in the early morning hours.[32]

Families and friends spent weekends hunting, their sloops and tents relegated to the past in the mid-twentieth century by fishing boats, airboats, and houseboats. The Brazoria County outdoors culture ran deep, its passion reflected in activities such as Paul Webber's Duck School, started in 1976 at Alvin Community College as a continuing education program. Classes included waterfowl identification and calling, for a fee of ten dollars, and over the years the popular program featured instructors Doug Clemons of Houston, Rudy LeCompte of Baytown, and Sabine Pass's O. D. LaBove.[33]

The sporting passion bubbled to the surface when the community had to contend, as had Jefferson County on the upper coast, with the loss of treasured hunting grounds to federal and state wildlife refuge programs. It started in 1967 when 6,367 acres of the Slop Bowl were incorporated into Brazoria National Wildlife Refuge. The next year San Bernard National Wildlife Refuge was formed from the 14,000-acre Pool Ranch. The pace accelerated in the 1970s when USFWS and TPWD acquired another 2,235 acres of the Slop Bowl, Smith Ranch, the McNeill Tract in east Matagorda County, Perry Marsh, Hoskins Mound, and Hall's Bayou. In another acquisition in the mid-1980s, with funds from the sale of Texas duck stamps the state added Peach Point Wildlife Management Area.[34]

Resentment of federal and state acquisitions never reached the fever pitch it did around Port Arthur, but the bitterness in some quarters remains many years later. One of the biggest controversies was the forced closing of long-established hunting clubs. Another was that, while most of the refuge program land was acquired by willing sellers, some landowners saw their property condemned. On the positive side, public hunting opportunities were created for a large number of sportsmen who might not have been able to afford to hunt. Too, industry was hovering over the Brazoria County coastline, planning, among other things, hazardous waste dump sites and, off Peach Point, a deepwater port with construction of pipelines and oil storage facilities. So far, that hasn't happened.[35]

CHAPTER 10

MATAGORDA BAY

It was Spanish then French explorers who first flushed endless flocks of waterfowl from Matagorda Bay, once called San Bernardo Bay, between the mainland and Matagorda Peninsula. There was no East Matagorda Bay; the Colorado River drained directly into Matagorda Bay and formed a continuous, almost fifty-mile-long estuary from Caney Creek to the port town of Indianola. Tres Palacios, Carancahua, Keller, and Lavaca Bays defined the bay's northwest shoreline, with Matagorda Peninsula its southern boundary.[1]

East of the Colorado River between San Bernard River and Caney Creek, the Great Prairie Canebrake extended north for seventy miles nearly to Eagle Lake. Hunters had to know the land to reach—and return from—Canebrake River, better known as Caney Creek. While its lower reaches were accessible by small skiffs, the upper river was an impossible snarl of bamboo cane that grew to twenty feet. Hunters on foot were easily disoriented, walking in circles through a land of canebrake rattlesnakes, cougars, wolves, and bears. Those who braved it found the entire length of the narrow river covered with ducks, and where Caney Creek approached the Gulf, mallards came for acorns among great growths of oak trees.[2]

George Sargent raised cotton and cattle on the high ground by Caney Creek before he was drowned in the hurricane of 1875. Near the town that bears his name, the first ridge out of the marsh was an ancestral roosting area for greater Canada geese. Between Sargent and the Colorado River were the extensive tidal marshes or "hog wallow lands" with appropriately named waterways such as Boggy Bayou and Big and Little Boggy Creeks, where sportsmen moored sloops on muddy shoreline banks to pass shoot flocks between bay and roost. To the west the fresh waters of Lake Austin were part of Colonel William Hawkins's sugar plantation, its wintering ducks, geese, swans, and cranes sustenance to Hawkins's slaves.[3]

A delta wilderness formed where the Colorado River met Matagorda Bay, its winding river branches dissecting the wedge of sediment into Selkirk, Wild Cow, and Baxter Islands. Like Caney Creek to the east, the delta was covered in high-standing cane but added impenetrable snags of trees brought downriver. When Captain William Sterling settled on the delta in 1845, he found Karankawa Indians still living in rude huts and prairie-chickens so abundant they roosted with domestic fowl in his barnyard.[4]

In the bluestem grasses and canebrakes upriver, the crossroads of Bay Prairie became Bay City in 1894. Bay City's founder, Colonel David Swickheimer, was a devoted waterfowl hunter who traveled from Denver by train and horse-drawn wagons to his new town for week-long waterfowl hunts. When Swickheimer arrived, only isolated patches of the once extensive canebrake remained, and native prairie grasses were disappearing, making way for rice crops. Rice brought ducks, which swarmed inland from the coast for the new grain. After the Cane Belt Railroad reached Bay City in 1901, railroad men reported rice fields with huge numbers of birds, "very fat and very fine." The next year sportsmen said the volume of ducks was so great "they obscure the light of the sun," and it was no sport "to get a wagonload of them in a very brief space of time." Bay City hunters in 1908 saw a single flock so large it covered the entire horizon.[5]

Steamers navigated the Colorado River as far as Austin until the early 1860s, when a logjam dammed the river's West Branch. The log drift grew to nearly twenty miles, extending upstream to within two miles of Bay Prairie. Behind the logjam, a twelve-mile-long lake formed, inundating over a hundred thousand acres. Called Jennings Lake, it became an oasis for nearly every species of puddle duck along with geese, cranes, and shorebirds. Sportsmen who went there to hunt found that Jennings Lake could be a dangerous place; river waters that swept downstream collided at the dam with its confusion of submerged logs, and silt deposits in places formed a quicksand below swirling eddies.[6]

The seventy-five-year-old inland sea disappeared when Howard Kenyon removed the logjam and dredged the Colorado River from Wharton to the Gulf in 1927. Lodged behind the dam was a slurry of sediment, along with cottonwood, cedar, and pine logs that poured into Matagorda Bay at the mouth of the river. Dredge boats were kept busy trying to keep the river navigable until it was decided in the 1930s to extend the river channel to Matagorda Peninsula and the Gulf, dividing Matagorda Bay. East Matagorda Bay was born.[7]

West of the Colorado River delta, sportsmen sailed the long, white sand and shell shoreline to Palacios Point and Tres Palacios Bay. There were subtle differences in the wetlands they passed along their route. Fresh water dominated both Brandt Lake, its edges covered in bulrushes and cattails, and Cane Lake, fifty acres of nearly solid sago pondweed. Crab Lake, Hollybroke Marsh on Robbins

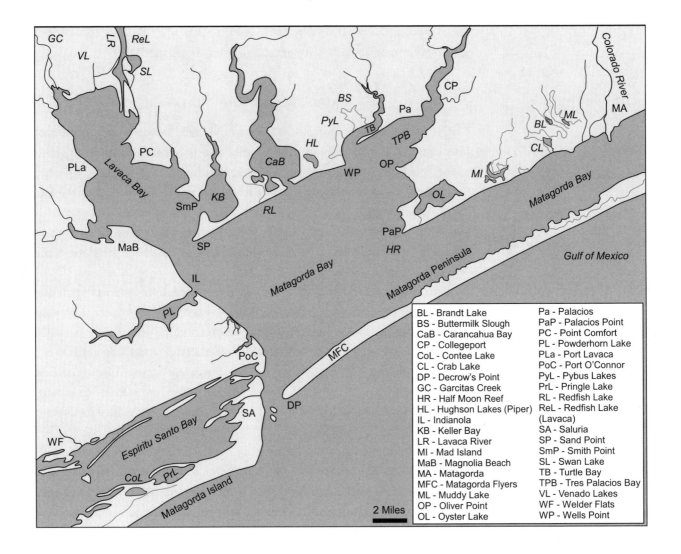

Matagorda Bay *as it appeared before the Intracoastal Canal and diversion of the Colorado River to the Gulf.*

Slough, and the south part of Mad Island were tidal, their muddy substrate covered in widgeon grass. On the peninsula between Matagorda and Tres Palacios Bays, cutgrass gave way to oyster shell flats dotted with *Salicornia* at Oyster Lake. Considered a "favorite resort for sea fowl" in the 1800s, the banks of Oyster Lake were at times lined with sloops loading salt, which was gathered in bushel baskets, as well as oysters and ducks destined for Galveston market stalls.[8]

Across Matagorda Bay, gunners in the 1800s shared Matagorda Peninsula's nearly fifty miles of sand and back-barrier marshes with rattlesnakes, horseflies, and mosquitoes. There were no settlements on the peninsula; even the once thriving port town of Decrow's Point was gone, its buildings swept from their foundations during the hurricane of 1875. Travel to the narrow ribbon of sand by sail was a challenge. From the east, vessels had to be large enough to navigate the Gulf of Mexico but nimble enough to negotiate Pass Cavallo. On the bay side, captains had to reckon with the Colorado River delta and its constantly changing shoals, bars, and shallow oyster reefs. On Half Moon Reef, between Oyster Lake and the peninsula, a Mr. Hubby grounded his sloop while hunting in 1906 and spent several days aboard the vessel until a rising tide floated it off.[9]

MATAGORDA SPORT HUNTING

Matagorda Bay's first seaport resort town, with hotels, boarding houses, and able boat captains, was Matagorda, on the banks of the Colorado River. In the mid-1800s, sportsmen made their way to Matagorda from across the United States. Sail and steam were the only ways to reach Matagorda Bay well into the late 1800s. When wealthy Joseph Leiter came for a winter gunning trip, he and his guests traveled by train from Chicago to Galveston, where they met his steam yacht *Riva,* which had set sail from New York. In the weeks they spent afield, the young millionaire killed a thousand ducks.[10]

Before rail reached Bay City, the nearest depots were in El Campo and Louise. There, Southern Pacific agents provided sportsmen traveling to the Colorado River with saddle horses, but they warned that no hunting guides were available. That changed when the Cane Belt Railroad linked Bay City and Matagorda at the turn of the century. By 1901, sporting excursions were arranged from the new Matagorda Hotel and from the Gulf View Hotel on Matagorda Peninsula in 1903. A weekly rate of eight dollars at the Gulf View included hunts guided by Captain H. D. Hill.[11]

Texas newspaper sporting columns and periodicals were usually rich with waterfowling accounts from Matagorda Bay. One from the *Galveston Daily News* in 1901 read: "Last week a party of three returned from Matagorda Peninsula with 85 large geese and 40 ducks. More could have been killed had not the stock of ammunition run short." The *San Antonio Express* told its readers Matagorda Bay was the place to visit for huge flocks of canvasbacks, redheads, teal, and "green and black mallards." Texas newspapers were buzzing when Governor Campbell mysteriously disappeared from the state capitol in 1909. It was rumored that he was planning a secret inspection of Texas convict camps; he was instead hunting, and he and his party of state officials returned from the coast with seven hundred ducks and geese.[12]

Texas railroad executives founded Matagorda County's earliest private hunting clubs. The Southern Pacific Transport Company was first, with their behemoth hunting preserve at the turn of the century. The resort covered seventy-eight square miles, encompassing Selkirk Island, the coastline of the Palacios Townsite Company, Caney Creek, and pasturelands near Van Vleck. Their largest lease was on the fifty-thousand-acre ranch of Bay City's W. F. Box—a place, Box extolled, with thousands of ducks at the railroad men's disposal.[13]

Unprecedented promotion followed the announcement by Southern Pacific's Houston passenger agent, Colonel Tom Anderson, that the company was planning a grand six-week hunting excursion in 1905, dubbed by the press "the great hunt." The colonel invited fifty guests from a dozen states, the list including politicians such as Texas governor Lanham, judges, lawyers, businessmen, more than a dozen newspaper reporters, and a photographer. After boarding a private Pullman car in Houston, the entourage headed to Bay City, then traveled to the field on horseback and in mule-drawn cane wagons. Wharton's Judge J. G. Barbee had charge of the seven professional hunters who guided shoots for bears, deer, panthers, "leopard cats," small game, and waterfowl in a still wild Matagorda County.[14]

There was unexpected backlash. The first game laws had just been passed in Texas, and the hunt touched raw nerves. The Wharton correspondent to the *Galveston Daily News* wrote: "Considerable unfavorable comment is heard on all sides regarding the Southern Pacific's projected hunting tour into this county." The article continued, "Commercializing such a scheme is looked upon as little short of an outrage . . . when a railroad advertises to haul the outside world in to slaughter." Southern Pacific countered, reminding the public of the benefits from visiting men of prominence and wealth who, without the shooting sports, "could not otherwise be persuaded to come [to Matagorda]." Texans were assured these men would invest in the county. Although it had been envisioned as an annual outing, 1905 was the last year of the Southern Pacific great hunts.[15]

Trains brought more clubs to Matagorda's shores in the 1910s. Sam A. Kendig, agent for the Santa Fe Railroad, organized Coast Country Shooting and Hunting Club as a "pleasure club" for founding members from Temple and Brenham in 1906. Chicago sportsmen founded the extravagant Matagorda Bay Hunting and Fishing Club on Lake Austin and in 1911 built a lakeside lodge surrounded by cottages for two hundred charter members. Matagorda County rancher A. H. Wadsworth, with F. H. Jones of Bay City and J. V. Brasfield from Chicago, founded the Bull Calves Hunting Club on Wadsworth's Portsmouth Ranch in 1921. The elegant Collegeport home of Theo Smith was purchased for their clubhouse.[16]

Matagorda Bay Hunting and Fishing Club was short-lived, and in 1923 it was converted by E. W. Turner Rice & Irrigation Co. into a commercial hunting and fishing operation Turner opened to the public. Called Mad Island Game Preserve, it was managed from Collegeport by E. L. Montgomery. The new club advertised that "it is a settled fact, known to all hunters within a radius of 100 miles or more, that Mad Island and Oyster Lake have no equal in the United States for fishing, oyster fishing, or duck and geese hunting." Hunters were advised to "come on train if roads are bad."[17]

Matagorda's roads were bad. They were narrow, either shell or dirt, and city sportsmen in their Model Ts and As often spent long hours digging the cars out of sand and mud. Richmond mayor Hilmar Moore hunted at Mad Island with Houston oilman Dan Harrison in the late 1930s and says he always got stuck. But the volume of ducks made it worth the effort, and automobiles continued to bring sportsmen to Matagorda Bay. In just one weekend in 1922, a group of

Returning from *Oyster Lake, on A. H. Wadsworth's Portsmouth Ranch, in 1922 with 150 ducks, mostly pintails and mallards, and a couple of greater Canada geese. The hunters are towing the second vehicle. (John Winter Collection, courtesy Cliff Fisher)*

hunters in cars killed one thousand ducks, donating the birds to the Matagorda County Shrine Club for a banquet in Bay City.[18]

Willie Parker and Peg Melton were like many who drove their Model T from Houston to Bay City in search of ducks. Peg wrote in his scrapbook that they met rice farmer Otis Beatty and asked to hunt his farm. Beatty told them no. It was the days of Prohibition, and Peg wrote that, after they presented Beatty with a quart of liquor, he immediately "turned his whole farm and house over to us, and got a fence rider to permit us to hunt on a [private] club." They killed 150 ducks and sixteen geese. Peg Melton returned many more times, always a welcome visitor at Beatty's house.[19]

A number of public hunting operations were available to sport hunters between the 1930s and 1950s. Former sheriff Henry Hejil operated a bait camp on Lake Austin's Chinquapin Bayou, where he rented rowboats for a dollar a day. Fishing guide Raymond Cox remembers a Mr. Gollott, who had a shack on the LeTulle holdings west of Mad Island and charged hunters a five-dollar gate fee for rice field shooting. Slim's Hunting Club opened in Sargent during the 1950s, his hunters seeing some of the last of Matagorda's greater Canada geese.[20]

A number of private sporting clubs opened on the old Portsmouth Ranch around Mad Island. On the east side of Mad Island Lake, the Clive Runnels family built A.P. (Armor-Pearce) Hunting Club and later leased it to Dresser Industries. The Runnels family donated the lodge and the land to the Nature Conservancy in the 1980s. In the late 1950s Houston oil and real estate man R. E. "Bob" Smith bought Mad Island Slough and the central part of Mad Island Lake.[21]

Much of the Mad Island Slough wetlands was once part of a freshwater ecosystem where two creeks provided natural drainage and rice tailings. Construction of the IC in the 1940s brought saltwater, and hunters accustomed to seeing huge blue catfish swim through their decoys started seeing redfish instead. Bob Smith brought the fresh water back by constructing a levee road across the slough as a saltwater barrier. Guests could peer over the north side of the levee into clear fresh water thick with aquatic vegetation, then look to the south and see saltgrass and tailing redfish. Alligators liked both sides of the levee, and visitors often had to wait as they crossed the road.[22]

Bob built his first camp on the north side of the lake in 1963, mistakenly situating it on LeTulle property. The Smiths paid a dollar a year in rent for their oversight until Bob and his wife, Vivian Leatherberry, constructed the two-story Mad Island Hunting Lodge. The grounds and buildings were managed first by a retired Houston policeman, who lived aboard an old forty-foot cabin cruiser docked on the IC, then by Palacios's Pat Jewel.[23]

On morning shoots of mallards, pintails, teal, and occasional redheads and canvasbacks, Bob provided his guests with trained retrievers so they didn't have to fetch their own ducks. Afternoons were spent goose hunting on the prairie south of the lodge from galvanized pit blinds over aerially seeded rye grass. Vivian at times preferred to hunt geese from the comfort of the lodge, and a snow goose she shot from the second floor wearing not camouflage but a fur coat was mounted and hangs in the upstairs dining room. Bob Smith died in 1973, and today the family uses the property for fundraisers and other charitable events. Bob's freshwater slough is now mostly grown over with cattails and bulrushes, but visitors driving his levee road still have to stop and wait for alligators to cross.[24]

In 1922, "the latest system in duck hunting"—a biplane—touched down in Matagorda. The US Army fliers, from San Antonio's Kelly Field, killed a string of ducks and geese as long as the plane's wingspan. Biplanes roared over Matagorda Bay again when aviators from the Third Attack Group, based at Fort Crockett in Galveston, organized Matagorda Peninsula Hunting Club in 1928. They leased a large tract of land and built a landing strip on the southwest side. In 1929 they were ordered to stop circling over duck camps, as a number of complaints were being filed by sportsmen outraged by low-flying planes that scared off ducks.[25]

Most hunters did not have planes, and for them travel to Matagorda Peninsula required a long bay crossing by fishing boats and later, outboard motorboats. The Bates family of Palacios hunted the peninsula beginning in the 1920s, towing pulling skiffs across the bay behind their fishing boat. Rowing to shore, they

UNIDENTIFIED *Matagorda Bay hunters with greater Canada geese, mallards, and pintails, early 1900s. (Courtesy Matagorda County Museum Archives, File No. 1989.09.130.2)*

brushed skiff and standing blinds with *Baccharis* bushes and oleanders to hunt giant Canada geese, pintails, redheads, and mallards. Ted Bates Jr. remembers, as a boy, seeing ducks rise from one end of the bay to the other as they crossed from Palacios to the peninsula.[26]

As late as the 1960s and '70s, the only signs of civilization on Matagorda Peninsula were dilapidated buildings of the old army fliers' landing field and ranch houses of the family of wildcatter Hugh "Roy" Cullen. Jim Mills was Roy and Harry Cullen's guide in the mid-1960s and piloted them from the Colorado River to Port O'Connor to hunt ducks. Raymond Cox hunted with Cullen family member Isaac Arnold right behind the Cullen houses, one of the best pintail spots on the peninsula.[27]

Greater Canada geese were one of Matagorda Bay's prized quarries, with the largest numbers on Matagorda Peninsula and south of Sargent. Hilmar G. Moore recalled that the big birds came over the marsh at the same time every day. "You could set your watch by 'em." They began to disappear by the 1960s, and one sportsman remembers when, south of Sargent, there were only about two dozen remaining, and "they passed unmolested over the prairie. No one would shoot them." Gordon LeCompte, with upper coast guides Forrest West and Sonny Baughman, made a trip to Sanborn Ranch near Sargent in the 1960s. Lying on a cactus-covered ridge, they shot limits of lesser Canada geese and in the distance saw some of the last of the greater Canadas. By 1975, Gordon says, they were gone.[28]

UNIDENTIFIED *Palacios hunters in the early 1900s with a harvest of greater and lesser Canada, snow, and specklebelly geese along with a string of mallards, snipes, wigeons, and pintails. (Courtesy Matagorda County Museum Archives, File No. 1989.09.260J.1)*

RETURNING TO *Palacios harbor after a successful hunt of geese, sandhill cranes, whooping cranes, mallards, and teal, probably between 1904 and 1913. The hunters are unidentified. (Courtesy Dean Johnstone, Spoonbill Gallery, Port Lavaca, File No. 0630)*

PALACIOS

Matagorda Bay terminates abruptly to the west where the town of Indianola once stood. To the north, the bay shore makes a right-angle turn into Tres Palacios, Carancahua, Keller, and Lavaca Bays. The town of Palacios, on Tres Palacios Bay, was incorporated in 1902 in part of a bull pasture owned by Abel H. "Shanghai" Pierce. Good duck and goose hunting was close to town on the promontory of Hamilton Point, the shallow sand point of Turtle Bar by Turtle Bay, and Wells Point. To the west big numbers of wildfowl roosted on the coastal marshes of Buttermilk Slough, later called Castle Roost; Pybus Lakes, renamed Sartwelle Marsh; and Hughson Lakes, later called Piper Roost.[29]

Rail, which arrived in Palacios in 1903, was followed by the opening of the Bay View Hotel, later the Hotel Palacios. Advertising "wild ducks, geese . . . only

PALACIOS GUIDE *Bob Price, about 1920, with a day's harvest of greater and lesser Canada geese, pintails, and mottled ducks. Note the cut brush for blind building on the top deck. (Courtesy Matagorda County Museum Archives, File No. 1968.31.260J.7)*

a short distance away," the hotel was immediately popular with traveling sportsmen. A Wisconsin sporting entourage in 1907 included former governor George W. Peck and George A. Lougee, one of the largest hotel owners in the state. Hunts were made aboard the yacht *Novice,* their guide likely Captain H. D. Hill, the best known Palacios guide in the early 1900s.[30]

The large volume of rice planted around Palacios in the 1920s brought ducks inland to feed by night, the birds resting on the bay by day. Hunters stood in a line on the shoreline to shoot them as they passed, with so many wigeons and mallards they could "reach their bag limit in ten minutes." Bob Price was the town's best known guide in those years, taking customers on hunts in the comfort of his inboard cabin cruiser. Price ran a hardware store, and Ted Bates Jr. remembers that he "would break open a box of shells and sell us a quarter's worth," leaving the box open on the counter for the next youngster.[31]

Ted Bates Jr. hails from the Bates family of watermen with their nearly one hundred years of Palacios waterfowl hunting history. In the 1920s, he says, the family hunted from their Alabama-built sloop *Helen B,* which was fitted with both sails and a ten-horsepower, one-cylinder inboard engine. The Bates family built cypress pulling skiffs they used to hunt the shallows on Matagorda Peninsula and around Tres Palacios Bay. Ted recalls how, at the end of each trip, ducks and supplies were off-loaded from horse-drawn wagons on Palacios's East Bay pier. He remembers too that almost no one in the fishing community had refrigeration, and families canned ducks to eat all summer.

Ted's father was the first commercial shrimper in Palacios, and in late fall "the family would shrimp until it got cold, then we'd get home from school and Daddy would say, 'Well, its time to paint the decoys.'" Then they would touch up their three hundred wooden decoys, mostly pintails, with white house paint and

Mostly mallards *and pintails from a 1932 hunt at Turtle Bay aboard the* Helen B. *Note the tow sacks used for decoys.* Left to right: *Fred Franklin Bates, Raleigh Bates, Ted Bates Sr, and Herschell Gollott, later a Freeport fishing guide. (Courtesy Ted Bates Jr.)*

Ted Bates Sr. *with mallards, pintails, and a fourteen-pound greater Canada goose on a 1930 hunt at Turtle Bay, Palacios. (Courtesy Ted Bates Jr.)*

replace the twine weight lines. Ted Jr. was six when he shot his first duck on Turtle Bar, between Turtle Bay and Matagorda Bay. "We had a skiff blind on Turtle Bar, and a black [mottled] duck lit in the decoys. Daddy said, 'Okay. I'll let you shoot 'im.' That gun liked to kicked me off of the seat."

At fourteen, Ted rode his bicycle to the post office to pick up his first gun, a Stevens 12-gauge with a three-foot-long barrel. "Momma used to take me to the dead end road [at Camp Hulen, near Turtle Bay] after school. I'd put a sack of wooden decoys on my shoulder and I'd put shells in my pocket. And I'd walk down there and just pull me up a log in that grass, put me a sack of decoys out. She'd come back when it was dark, and I'd throw the ducks and my decoys in the trunk of the old car."[32]

Dan Barber was a Palacios guide in the 1960s and 70s. Port Lavaca's Marvin Strakos remembers Dan sometimes brought clients to sit by a bush in his yard. As geese came off nearby roosts around Tres Palacios Bay, he started mouth-calling. He sounded so much like a goose that, even with no decoys out, "the cackling Canadas [Lesser Canadas] would come right to him—they were looking for the sound."[33]

CARANCAHUA AND KELLER BAYS

Carancahua and Keller Bays, between Palacios and Port Lavaca, were popular destinations for schooner excursions in the late 1800s. Two dozen hunters who chartered a boat in 1895 hired servants and cooks to tend to their campsite on Carancahua Bay. The party returned from the comfortable hunt with hundreds of ducks. Fort Worth and Chicago businessmen the same year hired the Port Lavaca schooner *Little Charlie* for an extended hunt on Keller Bay, making their camp at the Swedish settlement of Olivia.[34]

Sand Point Ranch, on the strip of land between Keller and Carancahua Bays, has been in the Smith and Bauer families of Port Lavaca for several generations. Carlos Smith grew up hunting ducks on Redfish Lake by Carancahua Bay, and greater Canadas in the marsh behind Sand Point. Crawling geese one morning, Carlos came face to face with a coiled rattler. "After that," he says, "I didn't do any more crawlin.'" There were so many rattlesnakes on that sandy strip of beach that his father killed 103 of them in three days, "filling a No. 3 washtub full of them."[35]

PORT LAVACA

It is almost a right angle between Sand Point at Keller Bay and Lavaca Bay. With the final demise of Indianola in 1886, the town of Port Lavaca, on the western shore of Lavaca Bay, held title as the largest town between Matagorda and Rockport. Close to town, sailboats and wagons took the town's sportsmen to the bay's headlands in flats along the Lavaca River, adjacent Chocolate Bay, and inland creeks and prairie.

Swan Lake and the sinuous chain of Venado Lakes are located at the head of Lavaca Bay, and, according to TPWD biologist Jim Dailey, the area had "some of the finest duck hunting in the world, holding wigeons, gadwalls, teal, sprigs, and mallards." Little about the way Jim hunted it had changed in a hundred years. "We took the boat up the Lavaca River at dawn then walked in. But you couldn't get back up in there if a hard norther was blowing because it blew out dry. There were several times when I got caught up in a little bayou. The bayou was deep, but the lake would be completely dry, so we'd push the boat through the mud and hold on to it."[36]

An easier location to reach was manmade Lake Placedo, on the west side of Garcitas Creek and the Lavaca River. In the early 1900s, Clark Rice and Irrigation Company used a team of horses to construct an earthen dam for a twenty-two-hundred-acre reservoir for rice irrigation. Shouldering heavy 8- and 10-gauge guns, Port Lavaca sportsmen, along with hunters from the small farming town that grew along Lake Placedo's shores, lined the banks to shoot "ducks, geese, and other water fowls which come in untold numbers." Today the lake and town that shared its name are gone.[37]

BEACH HOTEL *on the bay, Port Lavaca. C. U. Yancy, owner of the hotel, stands on the right; all others are unidentified. (Courtesy Calhoun County Museum, File No. 0453)*

Waterfowl began to move inland from Lavaca Bay when the first small rice plots were etched into the prairie around the turn of the century. According to J. C. Melcher Jr., a third-generation Port Lavacan, "Ninety acres and a mule was a true saying. People simply didn't have the ability to farm large areas of land." Some of the early rice fields fed more fowl than people. At Clark's rice farm on the edge of town, neighbors assisted in the slaughter of hundreds of wild ducks, geese, rice birds, and prairie-chickens in 1903 in an effort to save Clark's uncut rice from total destruction. Calhoun County farmers were concerned that their crops might suffer a similar fate during the "main southern migration."[38]

Port Lavaca grew into a popular destination for traveling sportsmen during the late 1800s. By 1888 it was listed in *The Sportsman's Guide to the Hunting and Shooting Grounds of the United States and Canada,* whose editor counseled that although the town had no professional guides, "volunteers can be had." Both visiting and local sportsmen found so many ducks in Lavaca Bay that some "enjoyed the sport for a while, but found it too easy to be interesting," and those that did not hunt for market "had more difficulty in giving away their game than in killing it."[39]

Railroad tracks that had once sent barrels of ducks north to market increasingly brought recreational hunters south. By the turn of the century, hotels that catered to sportsmen included the Seaside Hotel and the Beach Hotel, where proprietor Lish Stevens was kept busy handling correspondence from northern sportsmen. The San Antonio & Aransas Pass (SA&AP) rail company hired Dr. Harry Redan to manage its booming Port Lavaca resort business in 1905.[40]

Waterfowl hunting was a critical card played in the growth of Port Lavaca in the early twentieth century. When Houston's Alamo Beach Investment Company

C. W. Grubbs *hunting party, Port Lavaca, probably 1907. Grubbs (front right) was one of the first commercial duck call manufacturers. (Courtesy Calhoun County Museum, File No. A0123)*

opened their Alamo Beach development in 1907, they sponsored two days of sporting festivities at the Beach Hotel. Visitors from throughout the United States who descended on the town were "entertained with duck hunts and yacht trips over the bays." Famous decoy and duck call manufacturer C. W. Grubbs gave the welcoming address. Festivities included a target shooting competition at Port Lavaca Gun Club. The list of contestants featured Grubbs, former wild game merchant H. W. Warrach Jr., and local sportsman W. P. Regan. The winner received land worth four hundred dollars in the "new resort city" of Alamo Beach.[41]

Private hunting clubs flourished along the shores of Lavaca Bay in the early 1900s. One of the biggest was Alamo Beach Game Preserve, started by the National Game Preserve Association at Alamo Beach. Club manager Colonel S. M. Scott sold shares for twenty-five dollars, and the popular enterprise quickly boasted a one-hundred-room hotel and clubhouse overlooking Lavaca Bay along with a large wharf and pavilion. Club members hunted four hundred acres of prairie and three hundred acres of fresh water on the south side of Chocolate Bay.[42]

The Port Lavaca Fishing and Hunting Club opened in 1912. Port Lavaca physician Dr. W. G. Peterson was its organizer and brought members from Victoria, San Antonio, Port O'Connor, Cuero, and Beeville. From their new beachfront clubhouse and wharf, the launch *Jamie* ferried hunters to shooting grounds on Magnolia Beach, Old Indianola, and Powderhorn Lake.[43]

The members of the Port Lavaca Gun Club were mostly locals and included the Smith family of waterfowl guides and Ed Melcher of Melcher's Hardware. J. C. Melcher, who runs his grandfather's hardware business today, says members of Port Lavaca Gun Club traveled by wagon over roads that, in those days, were oyster shell and dirt. They spent "two or three days at a time [in the field], going

PORT LAVACA *Gun Club members W. H. "Will" Smith Jr.* (standing, center), *S. E. "Stanley" Smith* (seated, far right), *and Ed Melcher* (kneeling, far right), *owner of Port Lavaca's Melcher Hardware, in 1910. Others are unidentified.* (*Courtesy Calhoun County Museum, File No. 009PL*)

MORE THAN FORTY *Canada geese and a pile of ducks shot by Ganado sportsmen from Port Lavaca, early 1900s. The schooner* Leonora *was plying Gulf waters at least as early as the 1890s.* (*Courtesy Calhoun County Museum, File No. A0274*)

from one pasture to another," where they snuck geese from a horse or crept potholes for ducks. The club was still in existence in the 1930s.[44]

Boat captains made good winter income guiding hunters on trips that lasted from several days to weeks at a time. One was Captain Singer, who, when he wasn't guiding, delivered mail from Port Lavaca to Olivia on his two-masted schooner *Leonora*. Hordes of hunters converged on the town in the early 1900s, and boats and their captains were in demand. In the early 1920s newspaper reported that "all of the hunting boats are engaged for the season by different parties."[45]

Captain Frank Bauer, the first game warden in Calhoun County, guided hunts from the Lavaca Hotel. Houston sportsman A. C. Burton, who traveled to Port Lavaca on his private yacht *Captiva II,* was one of Bauer's regular clients in the late 1920s and early '30s. On one excursion, Bauer and Burton "brought down

MATAGORDA BAY → 199

GUIDES *Owen Smith (left) and W. H. "Will" Smith (right) with mallards, pintails, and Canada geese taken at Magnolia Beach, 1908. The others are unidentified.* (Courtesy Calhoun County Museum, File No. 0385PL)

PORT LAVACA'S *Smith guiding family with thirty-five Canada geese and a few pintails.* Left to right: *Harry C. Smith, Owen Smith, W. H. "Will" Smith, and Fred Ullrich. The photo was taken in front of the Port Lavaca lumberyard, 1911.* (Courtesy Calhoun County Museum, File No. A0124)

a duck with a metal band attached to its leg," an early reference to Biological Survey's migratory bird banding program. Captain Frank's son, William "Bill" H. Bauer, followed in his father's footsteps as a guide and game warden. With Sheriff Leonard Fisher, Bill made one of the last legal whooping crane hunts, the big bird's range then still extending into San Antonio Bay.[46]

The Port Lavaca guiding family the Schmidts, or Smiths, came from Germany by way of Indianola in 1845. By the early 1900s the Smiths opened a number of seafaring, merchant, and construction businesses. One was boat building, with their shop located on Port Lavaca's waterfront at the appropriately named Smith Harbor, and another was guiding. The Smith family of hunting guides included brothers Harry, Owen, William "Will" Henry Jr., and sometimes S. E. "Stanley" Smith.[47]

Harry C. Smith started guiding in the early 1900s, taking customers along the coast for a week at a time in his fifty-foot boat, the *Lurline*. Built by Owen Smith as a two-masted schooner, the *Lurline* was later converted to a launch, with the mast and sails replaced by a three-cylinder Atlas diesel engine. Hunters spent comfortable days and nights aboard the cruiser with its pilothouse, aft cabin, and galley below deck. For years, Ben Phillips was the galley hand and made extra income by cleaning ducks for Harry's clients.[48]

Harry covered a lot of ground in the *Lurline,* sailing from Tres Palacios Bay to Aransas Bay with most of his hunts on Matagorda Island by Espiritu Santo Bay. The *Lurline* towed as many as three skiffs built from solid cypress planks by the Smith family. One hundred wooden decoys "made up north" were loaded into the skiffs along with spaniel retriever dogs and a case of shells, with bay brush for blinds stowed under the seats. Harry usually hunted two men to a blind, poling them ashore, and Harry's son Carlos says, "He'd shove the boat on the edge of the bank, and he'd take the sweet bay and build a blind all the way around it."[49]

Most Smith family clients were from Dallas. Best known was Colonel Albert E. Humphreys, the "oil king of Mexia," who reserved the first week of every season. On a hunt near Port O'Connor, Colonel Humphreys and the Smiths killed five hundred ducks and one hundred geese, returning in a skiff so loaded with birds that no freeboard remained between gunwales and sea. Carlos remembers that local black families who wanted to earn money would watch for the return of the *Lurline,* then run down the bluff to the harbor to help clean, ice, and pack ducks. Ducks were packed in wooden barrels from Bauer's barrel factory behind Melcher's Hardware store, then loaded on the train for shipment.[50]

Substantial labor went into preparing for the gunning season each fall. The huge volume of brush needed to cover duck blinds was cut on the Welder Ranch near Port O'Connor. "Mr. Welder would let [my father] go on the site, and he'd cut the sweet bay, load it on a truck, bring it back home, [then he'd] lay it out in the yard, and lay boards on it so it was flat." Carlos helped repair decoys before each season, and remembers: "We'd spread 'em out on the floor of the shrimp house and repair 'em. Paint 'em, put weights on the bottom, put string on 'em, and put new heads on if they needed them. That was a yearly ritual."[51]

Harry gave up guiding in the 1930s when game laws sharply reduced the season's length and daily limits. By then his favorite gun, a 12-gauge Remington, had been used so much "that the receiver went thin and cracked, and I don't know how many stocks he beat off of that gun." Harry and his brothers continued hunting, but only for sport. On Sundays, when the military planes over Matagorda Island were silent, the family went to Saluria Bayou on their big company barge with a canopy on it, spending their nights "with a cot and a mosquito bar." Carlos remembers one hunt on the island when "we built a blind out of driftwood, and we shot sprigs only. We were using 20-gauge Remington Model 11s, and we ran out of shells at 11:00. We shot 138 ducks."[52]

Photographs of the Smiths and the extended Bauer and Ullrich families provide a window to an extraordinary time on the middle Texas coat. There are Will and Owen in black rain slicker suits readying for a hunt, their cypress skiffs loaded with gear behind one of Owen Smith's launches, which has a Star gasoline engine, a tunnel stern for shallow water, and a steering lever. In other pictures the family is standing with side-by-side shotguns and Remington humpbacks by dozens of greater Canada geese, sandhill cranes, and pintails. The volume of birds, like the boats and buildings in the background, is today relegated to history.

INDIANOLA AND POWDERHORN LAKE

Indianola, between Lavaca Bay and the southwestern shoreline of Matagorda Bay, was one of the largest Texas coastal cities in the mid-1800s. Town residents, with Matagorda Bay on one side and Powderhorn Lake on the other, shot waterfowl from their back doors. Within range of their shotguns and rifles were rafts of bluebills, goldeneyes, buffleheads, redheads, and canvasbacks on broad water and teal, wigeons, pintails, snow geese, Canada geese, and swans congregated on the flats. To the southwest, freshwater Coloma Creek held mottled ducks year-round. During the Civil War, the crew of a Yankee privateer took respite from their plunder of Confederate blockade runners, as "the immense quantity of geese [and] ducks in the vicinity . . . invited some of the crew ashore for a day's sport."[53]

In 1886 Indianola was erased from the shores of Matagorda Bay by its second major hurricane in a decade. Within a few years the abandoned town was overgrown by a thicket of cactus, mesquite, and yucca, with pilings all that remained of the once busy shipping wharves. The *Galveston Daily News* noted that, where once stood a prosperous city, there was only a blank spot on the map, a place good for nothing more than "the rendezvous of myriads of waterfowl." For the next half-century, sloops and schooners from Port Lavaca, Seadrift, Rockport, and later Port O'Connor followed birds to the blank spot on the map that they called "old Indianola."[54]

Port Lavaca hunting clubs that gunned Powderhorn Lake in the early 1900s had largely disappeared after the Depression, their power launches replaced by rowboats rented by Ed Bell. There were private hunting reserves around the lake, most notably Powderhorn Ranch on the south shore, managed by deputy game warden Jack McCarley and his wife, Bess, in the 1950s. Next to Powderhorn Ranch, former Calhoun County sheriff turned oilman Leonard Fisher leased Cedar Dam Ranch and entertained business clients in the 1940s with an old houseboat for lodging. Grandson Steve Fisher remembers as a boy driving farm roads at full speed to intercept snow geese coming off Powderhorn Lake.[55]

Ed Bell remained a fixture on Powderhorn for almost forty years and sold his fishing business in 1972. Jack Brewer opened Indianola Fishing Center on the site, guiding customers who, like the Indianola townspeople a hundred years before, shot ducks on Powderhorn Lake. They found plenty of pintails, bluebills, teal, and snow geese, but a lot fewer canvasbacks and mottled ducks. They sometimes saw greater Canada geese, but the swans had been gone for a half-century or more.[56]

CHAPTER 11

ESPIRITU SANTO and SAN ANTONIO BAYS

Extending from Matagorda Bay to San Antonio Bay, and tucked between the mainland and Matagorda Island, narrow Espiritu Santo Bay is six miles across at its widest point. The estuary makes a bend at Welder Flats into San Antonio Bay where, at its north end, the rich Guadalupe Delta is fed by the San Antonio and Guadalupe Rivers. Sloops and shallow-draft steamers once connected the early port landings and town of Alligator Head, later Port O'Connor, the German settlement of Upper Mott near what became Seadrift, and the seaport of Saluria on the north end of Matagorda Island.[1]

PORT O'CONNOR

Port O'Connor is perched at the edge of a marvelous ecosystem. To the east is Matagorda Bay and Matagorda Peninsula, to the southwest Espiritu Santo Bay, and across the bay, Matagorda Island. This corner of Calhoun County was once Alligator Head Ranch, owned by Victoria's Thomas O'Connor. O'Connor hosted San Antonio and Victoria hunters throughout the 1890s, his ranch wetlands holding sprigs, redheads, teal, and canvasbacks in flocks sometimes numbering over fifty thousand. Alligator Head began to compete with Port Lavaca for the attention of northern sportsmen when it became Port O'Connor in 1909. Sportsmen's headquarters was the LaSalle Hotel, which opened in 1910. Its proprietor, Joe Mathews, chartered hunting parties for seven dollars a day on Charles Kertel's gasoline launch.[2]

Hunting parties arrived each day by rail, and Texas newspapers boasted of their large numbers. One of the more prominent visiting sportsmen was Chicago's Fred H. Teeple, who came by yacht in 1909 and leased seventy thousand

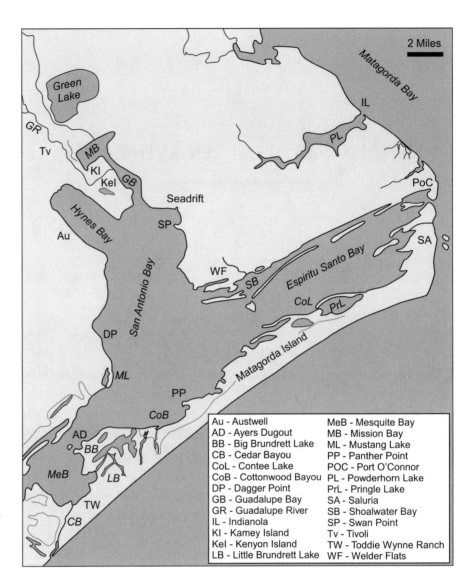

San Antonio and Espiritu Santo Bays as they looked in the early 1900s.

acres of O'Connor land as his private hunting preserve. Each winter Teeple entertained guests such as Texas governor-elect O. B. Colquitt and Fish and Game Commissioner R. H. Wood for weeks at a time on his yachts *Bunco* and *Bunco 2*. A group of seven northern sportsmen visited Port O'Connor in 1914 and returned home with enough ducks and geese "to fill six large barrels." Joseph Pulitzer of Saint Louis arrived in the Pulitzer yacht to hunt Port O'Connor in 1920.[3]

New duck hunters came to town in 1925 when Shearn Moody purchased fourteen thousand acres of the LaSalle Ranch on Espiritu Santo Bay west of Port O'Connor. The Moodys hosted politicians and businessmen from throughout Texas and the United States at their new private game preserve with its opulent LaSalle Lodge. They hunted freshwater windmill ponds on the shore, and Stewart Campbell, a later owner of part of LaSalle Ranch, says, "Those ducks had to wait in line to get into that fresh water."[4]

A MORNING'S HUNT *of mostly pintails at LaSalle Ranch, Calhoun County.* Left to right: *Fred B. Markle, Will H. Ford, Robert A. Lyons Jr., and Shearn Moody. (Moody Foundation Collection, courtesy Doug MacLeod)*

After World War II, cars brought even more sport hunters to Port O'Connor. Harvey Evans made the drive almost every weekend from Houston, hunting First and Second Boggy Creeks by walking the shoreline from town. He says he could have gone by power boat outside the jetties, "but the bay could be so rough in the wintertime that the shrimpers, they used to sit in that little ol' café that's almost to the [Port O'Connor] jetties and make book on whether the duck hunters were gonna make it that morning or not."[5]

A number of guiding operations catered to the growing volume of hunters. One of the best known was Payne Boat Docks, opened by Houston's Ed Payne and partner Frank Flood. With several cottages and a restaurant, by the late 1950s Payne booked as many as forty hunters a day. Everything about Ed Payne was big—his pot belly, ten-gallon hat, airboat, and way of hunting. He put clients deep into the mud flats on Espiritu Santo Bay with tunnel-sterned skiffs and his large, covered airboat called *Sprig*. Stewart Campbell remembers *Sprig* as "a great big, old, horrible airboat. It got stuck a lot." By 1960, with new partners, Ed Payne's place was renamed Lewis Marine Station. Payne lost every boat and structure in Hurricane Carla in 1961, but within a year he had rebuilt. After Payne died in the mid-1960s, guides J. D. and Howard Lewis took over Lewis Marine Station.[6]

Former Houstonian Lee Richter guided hunting and fishing parties from Richter Marine in the 1970s. A man with a sense of humor, he and Port O'Connor's Jimmy Crouch once posed for a picture holding two sandhill cranes they painted to look like whooping cranes, and the photograph hung on the wall of a trailer in Hurricane Junction they rented to weekend sportsmen. Beaumont's Wayne Stupka remembers that picture, with "Two guys holding 'em up and they were doctored up to look just like whoopers. Underneath was the caption that read, 'Tastes Just Like Chicken.'" Richter and Crouch were soon visited by USFWS agents, who were not amused.[7]

ESPIRITU SANTO AND SAN ANTONIO BAYS

TPWD's Jim Dailey recalls, "Over in Port O'Connor, the people who loved to hunt would leave their decoys out. Nobody'd bother them. We'd be working and watch 'em go out and bag a limit of ducks anytime of the day. It was something to behold. Nowadays it is nothing to what it was, and that was in my lifetime."[8]

MATAGORDA ISLAND

When La Salle sailed between Matagorda Island and Corpus Christi Bay in 1685, he found the barrier island of Matagorda "was not cheering, with its barren plains, its reedy marshes, its interminable oyster-beds, and broad flats of mud bare at low tide." One hundred and fifty years later the seaport of Saluria established its short-lived hold on the shifting sands across from Pass Cavallo, on the north side of the island. For a time it was a vibrant town with steamer and sail traffic. Hunting excursions were arranged for visitors as early as the 1850s by Saluria's S. S. Givens, proprietor of the Sea Breeze Hotel. After the Civil War and hurricanes in 1875 and 1886, most of the buildings at Saluria were gone. At the dawn of the twentieth century the only sign of life on Matagorda Island was the ranches of Judge J. W. Hawes and the Brundrett family and the coast guard station built near the remnants of Saluria lighthouse.[9]

Punctuated with mangrove, cane, and *Spartina* grasses, Matagorda Island wetlands paralleled the bay and high barrier island dunes the length of the island to Cedar Bayou. Names of its waterways familiar to generations of waterfowlers include Pringle and Contee Lakes, Panther Point, Cottonwood Bayou, and Big and Little Brundrett Lakes. Although gasoline launches made the island more accessible in the early 1900s, little else had changed. The web of waterways continued to fool even skilled watermen, and northers still turned bayous into mud flats and churned Espiritu Santo Bay waters into a dangerous froth. The first advertised outfitters in the era of the gasoline engine were San Antonio's Dr. Frank Kent, who offered island hunts for five dollars a day in the 1920s, and Wilkins W. Hunt's Camp Hunt, which opened a few years later.[10]

Wilkins W. Hunt opened his Port O'Connor Hunting and Fishing Lodge, better known to sportsmen as Camp Hunt, in the 1930s. He built a lodge on the mainland in Port O'Connor and advertised that the twelve-mile bay crossing was made in "seaworthy boats" to docks on the bay side, where "fast autos" took customers to the island ranch house headquarters.[11]

Many of Wilkins's clients were from Houston, and their excursions were arranged by the club's "Houston representative," former Cove guide John Winter. Clients hunted dozens of freshwater ponds, where Wilkins built roomy, comfortable sunken blinds. Houston's George Vogt wore a tuxedo to one of these pit blinds and never got it soiled. According to Port Aransas writer and historian Rick Pratt, Wilkins dried and flooded ponds, built culverts, and installed pumps to control water and manage his habitat.[12]

Port O'Connor *Hunting and Fishing Lodge duck blind on a freshwater pond, Matagorda Island, early 1920s. (John Winter Collection, courtesy Cliff Fisher)*

Late 1920s *photo with 132 ducks and thirty-two geese from Port O'Connor Hunting and Fishing Lodge. John Winter is on the far right; the others are unidentified. (John Winter Collection, courtesy Cliff Fisher)*

The hum of the first military biplane over Matagorda Island was heard in the late 1920s, when Army Air Corps officers from San Antonio's Brooks Field landed in a pasture by the old coast guard station. They liked what they saw. Airmen were assigned to rebuild the plank coast guard building and haul over a one-ton truck and twenty-foot flat-bottom boat for the new Brooks Field Hunting and Fishing Lodge. Master Sargeant Al Granger of the Eighth Attack Squadron at Fort Crockett in Galveston was assigned to supervise the fishing and hunting, and two privates were given duties as full-time caretakers and lived on the grounds. Renamed Matagorda Island Lodge, by the 1930s it had gained a reputation as a playground for military brass from throughout the state.[13]

During World War II the US government condemned nineteen thousand acres of Matagorda Island for use as a military bombing range. Landowners were given seven dollars an acre and ten days to relocate, and the public was banned from fishing and hunting on much of the island. As gunnery facilities expanded, the old coast guard station and Camp Hunt's Port O'Connor Hunting and Fishing Lodge were burned. John Winter, who had guided military brass around Texas for three decades, wrote to Major General G. C. Brant in 1943 about the hunting ban. In his reply, the general said it was out of military control; the Texas Game, Fish, and Oyster Commission had recently ruled that no shooting of migratory birds would be allowed on any military reservations, but, he wrote, "I am in hopes we may be able to get this ruling changed."[14]

Evidently the general was successful. Matagorda Island became the premier sporting destination for air force officers and, for the next thirty years, a very sore subject in Texas. The air corps built a new landing strip using dredge material from the bay, after which the dredge site became the well-known winter fishing spot called the Army Hole. Nearby were over twenty dog kennels filled with pointers and retrievers. Duck ponds were built with fresh water pumped by new windmills, and a network of new roads ensured that military personnel could reach the blinds in the comfort of jeeps. If hunting was slow, ducks were rounded up from Matagorda Bay with helicopters.[15]

The military did not make good neighbors. The roar of aircraft and live ordnance was bad enough, but in 1951 the air force petitioned for a fifty-yard easement around the entirety of the island. The move was ostensibly for military secrecy, but it was perceived as a way to preserve the best Texas hunting and fishing for the "fly boys." It took Senator Lyndon Johnson and Governor Allan Shivers to vote it down. What they couldn't do with legislation, the air force did with construction. To prevent sportsmen from accessing the island by water, the "Bridge to Nowhere," too low to pass beneath, was built across the upper bayou of Pringle Lake, and spent artillery shells were driven into the mud as a barrier to accessing Panther Lake. Parts of both structures remain today.[16]

In a 1956 letter to the *Advocate,* Calhoun County Judge Howard Hartzog fumed at the public's lack of access and the use of government funds for entertainment. Hartzog was ahead of his time. It was another twenty years before Senator William Proxmire of Wisconsin demanded a Pentagon report on the cost of the "officer's hunting and fishing resort" on Matagorda that, in 1972, had provided recreation to nearly two hundred officers and enlisted men at taxpayers' expense. Proxmire, aided by the National Audubon Society, which was concerned that bombing threatened the endangered whooping crane, won the day. The next year the air force declared Matagorda Island "surplus." Matagorda Island belonged again to Texas, but not to families like the Haweses, whose land was condemned but never returned. They had survived the Civil War and hurricanes, but not the US government.[17]

Stewart Campbell came from Houston in the 1950s and spent years figuring out how to hunt Espiritu Santo Bay. Prowling the shorelines of East Matagorda Bay and Welder Flats and the backside of Matagorda Island with an old outboard, he found that Calhoun County duck hunting wasn't like the sport on the upper Texas coast he'd grown up with. Campbell admits that at first he didn't know what he was doing, but "there were so many ducks it didn't matter." He says, "Nobody was hunting over here, we had it all to ourselves." His only neighbors were the military, which sometimes dropped bombs on him while he was hunting.

The few hunters who did share the back side of Matagorda shot from platform blinds, but Stewart put in sunken blinds. "The first ones we built were galvanized fifty-five-gallon drums, but in the saltwater they didn't last. Then we built individual concrete blinds. They weighed eight hundred pounds apiece. We first built a floating barge to haul them out, but loading and unloading was hard. So then we carried 'em out using airboats with platforms we built on." Stewart got the idea of using fiberglass, but the lightweight blinds popped out of the mud. He next designed ones that flared at bottom, and they worked; some are still on Contee Lake today. "We would sink 'em right to water level. At one point we had forty to fifty blinds, and they were all sunken. After those sunken blinds we had ducks that would decoy ten feet away." By then, "We had the duck hunting here down to a science. We had to compete with big rafts of ducks, so we imitated them with large decoy spreads."

Stewart's were hard places to get to, made easier in the late 1950s when he built his first wood-planked airboat with a four-cylinder Lycoming engine. His hunting partners in those days included Houston outdoor writer Bob Brister, who he met when Brister wrote an article about the painted twenty-four-ounce tin juice cans he used as decoys. Stewart in those days couldn't afford store-bought decoys, and Brister was curious to know if they worked. They did, and the story started a lifelong friendship. Stewart and his band of Houston hunters slept on a houseboat docked at Charlie's Place, later Bob and Leonard's fish camp, and another bunk was filled when Brister brought artist John P. "Jack" Cowan for a hunt in the 1960s.[18]

Stewart's days pursuing greater Canada geese on Panther Point and Welder Flats were immortalized in *The Golden Crescent,* Brister and Cowan's literary and artistic tribute to the Texas outdoors. In it, Stewart is the thinly disguised Stu Walters in the story of an airboat, its throttle wide open in the darkness when it hit a mud flat, throwing hunters, dogs, and gear aloft and into the marsh. They hunted anyway, and despite the mud and the blood, they were rewarded with the big honkers. Nearly half a century later, Stewart added simply, "We had water [there] the day before."[19]

Stewart and his style of hunting were featured in a number of Cowan paintings. The subject of "Pickle Barrels" is Campbell's sunken fiberglass blinds, and in the artist's notes Cowan fusses about bailing them and sharing the confined space with snakes. But he didn't complain about the ducks. The blinds are barely visible in the painting, with Cowan remarking, "It would probably take an archeologist to find them." But Stewart knew where every one was. Other Cowan works show the houseboat, the airboats, the areas they hunted, and the ducks. There is one Cowan painting not kept in Stewart's house but in his garage. It is an airboat Jack camouflaged with individual grass blades painted on the hull, his brush marks punctuated by shorebirds and raccoons peering from the vegetation. There is undoubtedly not another airboat like it in the world.[20] Duck hunter and fishing record holder Stewart Campbell died in 2010.

As a customer of Rockport guide A. J. "Moose" Adolphus, Dallas oilman Clinton Murchison first hunted southern Matagorda Island after the Depression, and by 1941 he had accumulated eight thousand acres from the Brundrett family. Murchison built a ranch complex on Cedar Bayou with a twenty-bedroom main house, outbuildings, and a boathouse and dock on the bay side. He flew into a landing strip made from packed oyster shells, and they hunted "everything from geese to rattlesnakes."[21]

In 1943 business associate Toddie Lee Wynne took over the land, renaming it Star Brand Ranch and enlarging it to over nine miles of barrier island. Visitors arrived in his plush DC-3 with hand-polished chrome propellers, landing on a new paved airstrip with a large hangar. At the lodge, with its well-tended lawn, rows of palm trees, and white fence, Wynne's guests were well tended by a full-time wait staff hired from black families who lived on the island. Trips on the bay were made on Wynne's World War II–vintage PT boat and a hundred-foot barge.[22]

Wynne built an extensive freshwater network for his cattle, and Al Johnson, who worked Star Brand as a ranch hand, says, "He had a windmill on every pasture, and there was an artesian water source on the island. Toddie Lee pumped out the low country to get it dry enough for cattle grazing. You couldn't do that now." In other areas he built reservoirs. "We brought over junk vehicles on the barge and unloaded with a winch truck, and we used them to impound water."

Wynne's fresh water brought ducks, but hunting the sandy island between the marsh and the Gulf of Mexico was, according to Al, "a tough environment." There were times when the "mosquitoes were so bad you'd have to move from the back side to the windward side. Anything you picked up on the island you learned to pick up away from you because of the rattlesnakes." Wynne and his staff consulted the Air Force bombing schedule to determine when it was safe to travel. Even so, "they bombed one of his windmills, and another time one fell near the ranch house."[23]

For years, the bunkhouse of the Hasselmann Bay Club, high on pilings overlooking the water on a line of oyster reefs on the bay side of Matagorda Island, was an Espiritu Santo Bay landmark. The private club was started by Karl Hasselmann, president of Salt Dome Oil, with most of the membership in the 1940s and '50s from Houston. Seadrift's Chris Martin remembers the club had a tradition they called Duck Eve: the night before duck season, when tuxedoed hunters were picked up by yacht at Bob and Leonard's in Port O'Connor. Some of the hunts at Hasselmann Bay Club were a little too good. In 1940, ten Houston guests and members were fined for shooting forty more ducks than the legal limit. Hasselmann paid all the fines.[24]

Chris Martin says that Matagorda Island outfitters over the past forty years have abided by a gentleman's agreement: "The Rockport guys stayed to the south and Seadrift hunters to the north." It's still a hard destination to reach. Seadrift hunters, Chris says, cross fifteen miles of open San Antonio Bay waters. "It takes years of experience to cross those bays in the dark. Then, it's a myriad of little cuts and bayous. It's like a maze. We use halogen lights and . . . run two boats with dual tanks."[25]

Rockport hunters coming from the south brave an Aransas Bay crossing before squeezing through narrow passes in Mesquite Bay and into shallow Matagorda flats. David and Mike Nestleone guided on Big and Little Brundrett Lakes from the late 1960s. Al Johnson sometimes joined them, and he remembers how hard it was to find the little feeder creeks in the dark, a journey made in a 22-foot skiff pulling an airboat on a 150-foot tow rope. He says, "You had to have a full tank of gas to get over there. Everything from fuel to decoys had to be brought over." When Al hunted with the Nestleones, they had competitions to see who could shoot the heaviest Canada goose. "We always accused them of putting lead weights in their birds.[26]

SAN ANTONIO BAY

On the mainland corner where Espiritu Santo Bay meets San Antonio Bay, tidal marshlands of Shoalwater Bay and Welder Flats in the late 1880s were part of the ranch of Victoria businessman and rancher John J. Welder. Welder's Bone Lake and Cane Pond were hidden deep in high cane, but sportsmen knew how to find them by watching huge circling flights of pintails and redheads attracted to the fresh and brackish water. Acres of adjacent tidal flats made Welder Flats one of the grand coastal Texas wintering areas for greater Canada geese and sandhill cranes. Though the hunting spots were nearly impossible to reach, the variety and volume of birds there made it impossible not to try. Early gunners took skiffs as far as they could into the marsh with a prayer for high tides and south winds. Without both, they mired in mud while oyster shells cut their boots open as they tried to pull their skiffs out.[27]

Then came airboats. Stewart Campbell, who had one of the first airboats in the area, remembers, "We had great hunts on Welder for greater's [Canada geese]. The Cane Pond was the only fresh water down in that area. Sometimes we used to walk over there and sit and watch the ducks. And probably it was about five acres of pond. And there were so many ducks goin' to that fresh water, they literally would be circling around up there waitin' for some to get out so others could come in. You couldn't believe what it was like. Ducks came to fresh water by the thousands and thousands."[28]

Chris Martin hunted greater Canada geese at Welder Flats in the 1970s and swore he'd return. That day came in 1998 when he opened Bay Flats Lodge in

Mrs. R. Bindewald *with a Canada goose she shot in her backyard, Seadrift, 1915. (Victoria Regional History Center Collection, Victoria College/ University of Houston–Victoria Library, File No. 300)*

Seadrift. With blinds on Bone Lake, Shoalwater Bay, and Cane Lake, he says even today "we'll see tens of thousands of redheads." But he no longer sees Welder's once famous Canada geese.[29]

North of Welder Flats, in a grove of oak trees called Lower Mott, the town of Seadrift grew from 120 residents in the late 1880s to 1,250 by 1914. Between running alligator lines, tonging oysters, and seining fish, local watermen set sail as wildfowl guides to visiting sportsmen. No one in town advertised until Collins-Branch F.O. and Co. built a lodge on Turnstake Island in 1917 that provided customers with "a fast boat, fine new decoys and good blinds."[30]

Louie Walker, who started hunting ducks and alligators in 1915, ran Louie Walker's Bait Camp near Long Mott. Louie guided duck hunters and also ran a towboat service, hauling wooden skiffs behind his work boat to duck blinds on Guadalupe and Mission Bays. Port Lavaca's J. C. Melcher remembers that in the 1950s, for $0.50 to $1.00, "You'd stay all day, and he picked you up at night." By the late 1950s Al Moulton offered airboats, lodging, and three meals for $12.50 a day at his Seadrift Hunting Club.[31]

GREEN LAKE

Across from Seadrift, along the floodplain of the Guadalupe River, Green Lake is thought to be the largest natural freshwater lake in Texas. Early sportsmen found it was an irresistible destination for waterfowl that roosted in San Antonio Bay's brackish and saltwater marshes. Floodplains on the south and west held mottled ducks, mallards, pintails, and teal. On its east side were high bluffs covered in knockaway (anacua), ash, and oak trees, the oaks extending to the shore, where mallards gorged on their bounty of acorns. Canada geese and sandhill cranes roosted on the mud flats of the northwest corner and, averaging a little over four feet deep, the middle of the lake was covered in rafts of bluebills, redheads, and canvasbacks.[32]

Waterfowl were a source of food for Virginia farmers who settled the area and a source of sport for the resort community of Green Lake, founded by the 1840s. After the Civil War, horses and wagons brought recreational hunters, particularly from Victoria, who camped for days to weeks on the lakeshore. Victoria papers carried stories of the hunt, like the large party in 1896 that returned to the city with "plenty of game and fish and all had a jolly time." John J. Welder and W. B. Traylor owned much of the shoreline in the late 1800s, each fall entertaining business guests with hunts by horseback and skiffs. Traylor grew weary of sharing Green Lake with market hunters, but because there were no laws to control them, he instead persuaded local authorities to arrest them for trespassing.[33]

Illinois businessman George W. DuNah purchased one thousand acres around Green Lake in 1908 and opened a sporting resort called the Custom Cutter's Plantation, its main purpose to promote land sales to members of the Custom Tailor's Association. When DuNah planted peanuts in old Green Lake settlement cotton fields, the skyline over the edge of the lake turned black with mallards and Canada geese. Welder and Traylor descendants had another new neighbor when the state awarded the entirety of the lake bottom to Elmer Yates in 1918, and later to Houston's Howard Kenyon.[34]

In the first half of the twentieth century, most who hunted Green Lake were family and friends of Tom P. Traylor and his son-in-law Clyde Bauer. By the 1960s the lake's east side was the private hunting preserve of John E. Kilgore of the Singer Company, with other investors. Kilgore had intended to use the site for industrial development, but with his passion for duck hunting, he somehow never got around to it. Kilgore built two camp houses and hired retired game warden David Fredericks to watch the grounds.[35]

Cattleman and waterman Jimmy Wayne "J. W." Johnson is today a link to the special ecosystem that was Green Lake. First learning its ways half a century ago when his father caught catfish to market across the country, J. W. is one of the few who can describe the lake in years it went nearly dry, as it did during the 1930s, or when it filled with saltwater from storms such as Hurricane Carla in 1961. He has seen, too, how during floods the Guadalupe River leaves its banks near Bloomington and washes over into Old River and Black's Bayou, the sheet flow crossing Green Lake into Mission Bay.[36]

GUADALUPE RIVER DELTA

Where the Guadalupe River meets San Antonio Bay, mud- and nutrient-rich sediments created an eight-mile-long birds-foot delta separating the estuary into liquid compartments of Mission Bay to the north, Guadalupe Bay to the east, and Hynes Bay to the west. The delta formed a spectacular ecosystem, partitioned by branches of the Guadalupe River into what became Kamey and Kenyon Islands and, to the south, a brackish-water and saltwater marsh called Guadalupe Flats.

Kamey Island was named for the J. S. M. McKamey family that, after the turn of the century, settled the nearby farming community of Kamey. No one remembers why he did it, but family member John W. McKamey built a giant wooden goose decoy so large it took a wagon to move it. He kept it in a vacant lot next to his Kamey residence, and one day in 1921 a lone Canada goose circled the town, set its wings, and landed next to the giant counterfeit. It was immediately dispatched by John W's rifle.[37]

The family's land on the Guadalupe Delta wasn't an island until 1938, when Traylor's Cut was dug. No one suspected it at the time, but the narrow gash of Traylor's Cut changed the course of the Guadalupe River, shifting it from the Guadalupe Delta to Mission Bay. Seadrift hunters, family, and friends gunned Kamey Island until the private Palmetto Lodge hunting club was built in the late 1970s. Nearby Pintail Lake, with its water lilies and sago pond weed, became a favorite place for canvasbacks, for hunters who sometimes shot too many of them, and for game wardens who every so often kept count.[38]

What became known as Kenyon Island was, in the 1800s, a nameless tract of land known only as the "island at the mouth of the Guadalupe River." Its terrain was nearly impenetrable to travelers, a tangle of dense willow and ash trees, cypresses, vine-covered shrubs, high cane, and palmettos, its waterways sometimes choked with log rafts, an ideal habitat for water moccasins, coral snakes, rattlesnakes, alligators—and ducks.[39]

By 1890, nine families scratched out a living on the nameless land, but all of them abandoned their shacks and moved away when the river flooded. For the next few decades it was home only to squatters, fishermen, market hunters, and Joe Duncan's cattle. The island was finally given the name Adler Island for owner H. C. Adler in the early 1900s, a time when the only vestiges of civilization were a few houseboats and W. H. Thornton and P. F. Robideaux's hunting and trapping shack. Guadalupe Delta was a rough place, a sanctuary for rum runners and outlaw market hunters, and sometimes people disappeared there. Adler Island was renamed Kenyon Island in the early 1930s by its new owner, Houstonian Howard B. Kenyon. The island nearly changed hands again when, in the 1940s, the man running cattle on the land got drunk and wagered half of an island he didn't own on a poker hand he didn't win.[40]

Over its long history only one private gunning club was built on the island, the Kenyon Island Duck Club, founded by Corpus Christi's William C. Triplett in the 1940s. Kenyon has been, instead, the place where four generations of the extended Howard Kenyon Sr. family have come to enjoy the outdoors. Howard Sr.'s granddaughter Coco Amerman Blackbird grew up hunting there with her father, A. E. Amerman Jr., and uncle, Howard Kenyon Jr. They were, she says, "maniac hunters and fishermen" who camped on the island to hunt teal, pintails, mottled ducks, and the fattest mallards she has ever seen.[41]

When A. E. taught his daughter how to shoot, she practiced by poking a gun from the window of their Houston Brays Bayou home, with snakes her most common quarry. She was thirteen when her father first hauled her across the narrow Guadalupe River on the hand-drawn barge to Kenyon Island. It was the 1940s, and she remembers the alligators had all been trapped out, but there were lots of snakes. One, a blue indigo "as big as an alligator," remains vividly in her memory.[42]

Howard Kenyon Sr. farmed cotton on the island, every summer burning areas of dense vegetation to create open water for fall hunting. Today those cotton fields are water, a result of diversion of the Guadalupe River at Traylor's Cut that cut off the supply of silt and mud. The shoreline, once covered in cypress, is now open to the bay; a few dead cypress trees still stand sentinel by the sea. Kenyon's old irrigation canals and levees are submerged beneath Big Lake, a shallow body of brown water over a black mud substrate dissected by a maze of alligator runs and ridges, its shore a wall of giant cut grass and sea cane interspersed with wolf weed and water hemp, locally called blood weed.[43]

The toe of the delta south of Kenyon Island, called Guadalupe Flats, was once nearly four thousand acres of tidal and freshwater marsh adjacent to the bay. Subtle topographic variations marked where *Salicornia* flats graded into saltwater Bermuda grass and stands of cut grass. Cattails ringed coffee-colored freshwater ponds, natural oases in a landscape of bulrushes and sea cane. Sky and grass were interrupted in only one place, where cypress trees surrounded a clearwater lake. The flats were a celebration of birds; waders, stalkers, skimmers, shorebirds, pelicans, ducks, geese, swans, and cranes. Bobcats stalked flocks of geese, and the scream of a panther could be heard in the palmetto scrub on the edge of the high ground.[44]

At the turn of the century it was Duncan Ranch, owned and worked by rancher Joseph Wesley Duncan. According to Duncan heir Joe Ray Custer, the family lost their land when a Victoria bank seized it over a delinquent grocery bill. The bill was paid by Orange and San Antonio businessman H. Lutcher Brown in 1946, who renamed the place Swan Lake Ranch. It was property Brown knew well before he bought it, having hunted it for years with Seadrift hunting guide Louie Walker.[45]

H. Lutcher's daughter Carolyn was an avid sportswoman who first hunted waterfowl with her father as a young girl at the family's Louisiana lodge and around Orange from his yacht *Emily Brown.* She was a San Antonio debutante, and when the Alamo City's socially prominent ladies chirped off a list of things they were thankful for during Thanksgiving of 1939, most provided quips about God and family. These were not for young Carolyn, who was thankful for "turkey, rain, and duck hunting." Carolyn's famous last name changed to one equally prominent when she married globetrotting hunter and angler William Negley. As Mrs. Negley, she became the matriarch of Guadalupe Delta duck hunting on Swan Lake Ranch.[46]

Local guides Marvin Strakos, Joe Ray Custer, and Jim Mills ran Swan Lake Ranch for Mrs. Negley, and each has a favorite story. Jim says Mrs. Negley, at four feet, nine, carried "two 12-gauge shotguns that went with her everywhere she went. She had one for geese and one for ducks." Marvin adds: "Those two guns were both Remington 1100s, and she always took the plugs out. It was my job to keep them loaded for her." Her Christmas card one year pictured her, pistol in hand, climbing a hoist with a suspended alligator twice her height. A favorite tale of Carolyn Negley's pluck was a standoff with well-known Seadrift poachers. She had Jim pilot the airboat into their decoys, demanding they leave the property. They wouldn't budge. They threatened to shoot her; she lit a cigarette. When they fired a volley over the bow, she kept smoking. They left.[47]

H. Lutcher Brown's and the Negleys' family and guests hunted places such as Mr. Brown's pond, with his one-man, round concrete blinds, and Refuge and Swan Lakes, which filled with flocks of late-season ducks. At the twelve-person goose blind built on the edge of Big Lake, Mrs. Negley sometimes brought her maid, whose main job was to fill hunters' wine glasses. Jim Mills says the hardest part of his guiding duties on those hunts "was telling them when to shoot."[48]

Subsidence and saltwater have had a dramatic impact on this last piece of land before San Antonio Bay. The cypress tree lake is gone, the tangle of remaining roots today called Cypress Stump Lake. Saltwater has claimed the route where hunters drove the marsh on a road along Big Bayou. But the Guadalupe Flats remain a special place. Jim Mills can still stand on the bank at Lucas Lake on a cold night as the sun sets, watching pintails and gadwalls pour into the marsh behind him. With Hynes Bay to his west, San Antonio Bay in front, and Guadalupe Bay to his east, at moments like these everything is all right with the duck hunting world.[49]

HYNES BAY

If there are two birds that once defined the Hynes Bay shoreline next to the Guadalupe delta between Tivoli and Austwell, it would be canvasbacks and greater Canada geese. *Forest and Stream* writer Emerson Hough wrote of the "very heavy bags" of Hynes Bay canvasbacks in the 1890s, when the white, black, and red birds were followed by schooners and sloops from Rockport, Port Lavaca, Seadrift, and as far away as Galveston. Captains had to watch the weather, as winter northers often blew the water from the bay, leaving in its wake huge mud flats and beached boats. A schooner party in the 1890s was like many that

MILLS WHARF *goose hunt between Tivoli and Austwell, Hynes Bay. Bundles of cut millet were used for temporary blinds and surrounded by a couple of dozen tin silhouette Canada goose decoys. (Courtesy Aransas County Historical Society)*

couldn't even reach the shooting grounds when, with a howling headwind, the captain was unable to tack into the bay's narrow confines.[50]

Greater Canada geese, joined by swans, sandhill cranes, and whooping cranes, roosted in the Guadalupe Delta, depressions on the headlands of Hynes Bay, and down San Antonio Bay shoreline to Tomas Pond and Mustang Lake on Blackjack Peninsula. Part of what brought them was a shoreline that provided abundant grit, particularly the ancient dune field called Sand Mounds at Dagger Point. Sportsmen frequented the nearby promontory of McDowell Point between Hynes and San Antonio Bays, where, if they could refrain from shooting into the sometimes never-ending flocks of ducks and shorebirds, they were usually rewarded with bags of the big geese.

By the early 1900s hunters traveling between the Guadalupe Delta and Blackjack Peninsula could stay at the Austwell Hotel, whose proprietor was a renowned hunter and trapper known only as Mr. Brexhauer. The two-story wooden building on the beach was welcomed by sportsmen, who in the decades before had slept aboard sloops and in tent camps. By then, the number of canvasbacks on Hynes Bay was declining as rapidly as that of the greater Canada geese was increasing. There were a host of reasons for the changes in canvasback populations, but only one for geese: prairie grasses around this part of Refugio County, a seemingly endless food source next to a major roosting area, were being turned under to make way for corn, millet, and milo.[51]

Rockport's Johnny Attwood remembers the waves of Canadas that made their way to his grandparents' farm between Tivoli and Austwell. His family planted corn, Johnny says, and "back then they left the crops standing. Hunters would get permission to hunt by trading my grandfather smoking tobacco or beer." Private Rockport hunting clubs started shooting geese in the area in the 1920s.[52]

By 1931 the king of the goose hunting hill was John Howard "Cap" Mills of Mills' Wharf on Lamar Peninsula. Cap Mills first brought goose hunters to the area when he was manager of St. Charles Bay Hunting Club, and the big flights of geese became a mainstay of his Mills' Wharf day hunting business for the next nearly twenty-five years. Refugio County goose hunting was some of the best in Texas. Newspapers reported on it with the same vigor they would later use to describe snow goose hunting in Eagle Lake and Katy Prairie. As late as 1950, greater and lesser Canada geese were said to have "smothered Hynes Bay, Mission Lake [Bay], Tivoli, and Austwell areas."[53]

Then, like the canvasbacks a half-century earlier, the geese disappeared. Cap Mills speculated that hunting pressure had driven them away, while others blamed the drought of the early 1950s. In 1956 snow and specklebelly geese began to return, but there was something missing—the greater Canadas. A decade or so later all the geese left. Locals say their disappearance coincided with a change in agricultural practices; farmers had begun to till their fields each fall, turning under the seeds and fresh sprouts that once sustained the great flocks through winter.[54]

CHAPTER 12

COPANO and ARANSAS BAYS

Inland prairie meets water at Copano Bay, its drainage system made up of Copano Creek, Mission River, and the Aransas River. Fresh water around Copano Bay was always magic to wintering waterfowl, and one of those special ecosystems was Fennessey Ranch. Here, east of the coffee-colored waters of Mission River, oak-covered riverbanks gave way to mesquite and then to acres of cordgrass before spring-fed Fennessey Flats and McGill Lake. It was one of the few places sportsmen could shoot canvasbacks and wood ducks in a single morning.[1]

Lamar and Live Oak Peninsulas form the geographic boundary between Copano and Aransas Bays, and adjacent to Lamar is St. Charles Bay by Blackjack Peninsula. To the south, Rockport was a busy town after the Civil War, with fish and oyster houses, turtle pens, and its wharves built on the edge of Aransas Bay. Shallow sea grass flats extended from Fulton and Rockport to Traylor Island, their waters rippled by the wakes of redfish digging and crushing clams in summer and covered by a riot of waterfowl in winter. Across the bay was St. Joseph Island, its high line of dunes cut only by Cedar Bayou, a natural pass deep enough for sloops to pass before the twentieth century.[2]

EARLY ROCKPORT AREA GUNNING

Every Central Flyway species of shorebird, puddle duck, diver duck, goose, swan, and crane was found somewhere in the Aransas and Copano Bay estuaries. In 1879, abundant acorns in live and pin oak flats around Rockport attracted "great swarms of ducks, especially mallards." In an 1896 account, Rockport waters were "alive with ducks, geese, and brant. . . . Here in town the citizens are becoming so accustomed to the honk of geese that they are not kept awake all night, as

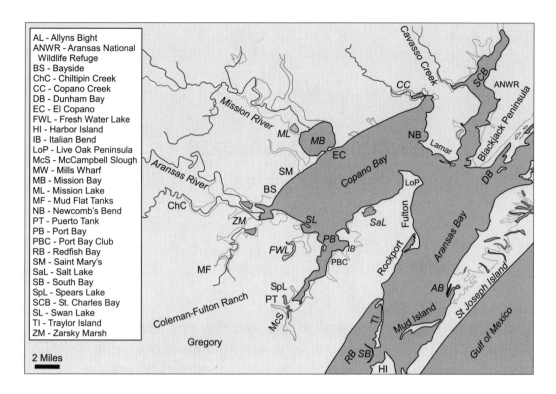

Copano and Aransas Bays as they appeared in the early 1900s.

earlier in the season." As recently as the late 1800s, whooping cranes, later critically endangered, were still a common sight in hunter's bags on St. Charles Bay.³

San Antonio businessmen were among the first urban Texans to look to Rockport for sport hunting. An early entry into Rockport's hunting diary were three San Antonio sportsmen who, after the Civil War, returned by horse and buggy from a three-day hunt with a wooden barrel full of redheads, sprigs, and mallards. Three other San Antonio hunters sent a wagonload of ducks and geese home "as trophies of their prowess."⁴

Rockport's George W. Fulton, a founder of the Coleman-Fulton Pasture Company (CFP), promoted his business interests in the late 1800s through duck hunting. From the elegant Fulton mansion, Fulton took guests to CFP's Rincon Pasture on the south side of Copano Bay. There, he built five dams on Chiltipin Creek with more than two dozen wells, the freshwater tanks attracting enormous concentrations of shorebirds, ducks, geese, cranes, and swans. Fulton's Mud Flat Tank was three miles long, and he covered its length in a wagon drawn by four horses, a gun storage locker under its seats.⁵

The long trip to Rockport by horse, ox cart, or stagecoach ended in the 1880s when the SA&AP railroad reached Rockport and nearby Gregory. Sport hunting ran parallel to commercial hunting until the turn of the century, with the SA&AP sending ducks to market one direction and bringing recreational hunters the other. Railroad promotional material advised that the "Pleasure Resort" of Rockport was a healthy place to hunt, with no foul or standing water "to cause fevers or malarial complaints." But it wasn't the lack of standing water that brought

> **S. A. & A. P. R'y.**
> Now is the time for Duck Shooting at Our Gulf Coast Points.
> **SPLENDID SPORT.**
> MARDI GRAS Tickets to New Orleans on sale in February. Take it in. Our county is a good place for Homeseekers—send them down our way.
>
> **E. J. MARTIN,** Gen'l Passenger Agt. San Antonio, Texas.
>
> **GEO. F. LUPTON,** A. G. P. A. San Antonio, Texas.

(Modified from *San Antonio Daily Light*, Jan. 18, 1898)

hunters to the shores of Copano and Aransas Bay, it was wildfowl, and their numbers set in motion a vigorous sporting industry.[6]

The heart of 1800s Copano and Aransas Bay hunting was Rockport's hotels and schooners. Headquarters in the 1870s were the Congdon and the three-story Aransas Hotel, later renamed the Del Mar Hotel. When the Shell Hotel opened in the 1880s, northern sportsmen often booked every room and set sail for hunts from the hotel wharf on the schooner *Sedalia*. New Yorkers who kept apartments at the Del Mar spent "most of their time aboard [Captain Armstrong's] yacht *Alice*, which they have chartered for the winter, in quest of redheads and canvasbacks." A single day in February 1898 gives a sense of the popularity of Rockport hunting, when a Denver hunting party was aboard the schooner *Oriole*, visitors from Michigan and Shanghai, China, had chartered the yacht *Connie* on a several-week "duck chasing tour," and Captain William Armstrong was guiding New York City hunters on the *Alice*.[7]

Rockport boat captains, who owned their vessels or had charge of schooners belonging to wealthy syndicates, delivered some impressive hunts. One party on a three-day shoot killed 700 ducks, mostly canvasbacks and redheads. Another had phenomenal one-day shoots of 1,100 and 1,500. On a six-day cruise in 1893, Kansas City sportsmen shot only canvasbacks, killing 84 on St. Joseph Island before sailing to Copano Bay for bags of geese, curlews, and swans. Austin businessman E. J. Nalie chartered *Alice* for a week in 1899, returning to harbor with nearly 800 canvasbacks and redheads. San Antonio sportsmen on a hunt with Captain W. Y. Sedam of the sloop *Lady Gay* killed 450 ducks, mostly sprigs and redheads.[8]

One of the earliest Rockport duck hunting guides was Captain C. L. Dean. Legend has it Dean was "the first actual settler" in Rockport, arriving long before the Civil War when he was "put off a boat at [Live Oak] Point to die, having tuberculosis." Dean survived and was later given charge of the schooner *Oriole*, owned by San Antonio philanthropist Colonel George W. Brackenridge. With the colonel's prominent guests such as Texas governor Hogg, Dean often set a course behind St. Joseph and Matagorda Islands for the colonel's favorite hunting area, the Guadalupe delta. Brackenridge later gave his beloved *Oriole* to Dean, and its days as a "finely fitted schooner" were over, as Captain Dean never again gave it a coat of paint.[9]

Theodore "Charlie" Johnson was born in 1836 and made his way to the Coastal Bend in 1851 after surviving a shipwreck. Washed up on Bolivar Point, he was rescued by Captain Peter Johnson. Both Johnsons later settled on St. Joseph Island, where they ran the schooner, stage line, and ferry boat service connecting St. Joseph with the mainland. Captain Charlie's vocation provided him an intimacy with every oyster reef, shifting sandbar, and body of water around Aransas County. Most of all, his work allowed him to watch the ducks.[10]

During the Civil War, Captain Charlie moved to Lamar and guided gunners from his three-masted mail service schooner *Francis*. A visiting Galveston sportsman wrote of a hunt on which Captain Charlie "staked a couple of crippled ducks as decoys, and killed 43 ducks, mostly sprig [pintails], with 16 rounds." The *Francis*, its canvas sails among the most recognized on the bay, was scuttled in 1898. The old sea captain and hunting guide died in 1921, his legacy living on through son Rob Johnson, an early manager of the St. Charles Bay Hunting Club.[11]

Captain William Armstrong, born in 1857, followed the sea all his life. From his schooner *Alice*, named for his daughter, he plied waterways from Corpus Christi Bay to Espiritu Santo Bay. In the years before game laws he worked for the Fish and Oyster Commission, his $150 annual salary covering use of the *Alice* to oversee oyster harvests. Armstrong shot ducks for the market and was one of the best known hunting guides of 1800s Texas.[12]

Writer W. B. Leffingwell, with a group of Chicago and Dallas sportsmen, chartered Armstrong's *Alice* and *White Rose* schooners in the late 1890s for a trip between Rockport and Hynes Bay. The Leffingwell party hunted redheads and pintails from wooden skiffs along shorelines covered in thousands of ducks and hundreds of swans and geese. On a hunt behind Matagorda Island, Armstrong watched as greater Canada geese dropped into a freshwater pond. He brought the party ashore, hired a mule team and wagon, and took hunters, gear, ropes, and chains for a two-mile journey through marsh grass, cactus, and sand. They could hear the pounding Gulf surf as they dug pit blinds on a shallow mud flat where ducks and geese poured in all afternoon. With dead birds staked out as decoys, they killed seventy-three geese, forty-one ducks, two cranes, and a "wildcat."[13]

Captain Armstrong lived long enough to see sails give way to gasoline engines. Down the beach from his home, the Bludworth family of craftsmen were still building duck-hunting sloops in 1899, but within a decade watermen could not replace canvas sails fast enough. Rockport's winter sportsmen the Merrill brothers traded their Bludworth-built sloop in the 1910s for the "palatial" power boat *Beatrice*. Armstrong's son Clarence followed, taking the masts off the venerable *Iris* and converting it to a gasoline launch.[14]

Joseph Pulitzer's *yacht* Grenada II *was captained by Rockport's Clarence Armstrong. The person on the bow is unidentified. (Keith Farley Collection, courtesy Port Aransas Museum, File No. 20)*

Armstrong made one of his last hunts in 1915 with sons Clyde and Clarence on the *Nereid* and *Iris*. Their customers, from the Kansas City Southern Railway, returned to their private car the *Geraldine* with six hundred ducks. William Armstrong died two years later at age sixty-one.[15]

Captain Clarence Armstrong guided as many famous clients as his father had. Excursions with Joseph Pulitzer Jr. of the Saint Louis and New York publishing family may be the best documented, as his trips were richly chronicled by Saint Louis newspaper correspondent Clark McAdams. Hunts in 1911 were made by sail aboard the *Iris* and *Nereid,* but in 1918 Pulitzer arrived in his motor yacht *Granada II*. Powered by two forty-five-horsepower inboard engines, it was one of the most modern yachts of the time.[16]

McAdams wrote of trips well tended by a crew and cook, with feasts of boiled crabs, gumbo, trout, oysters, and roasted ducks. Sailing between Corpus Christi and Aransas Bays, McAdams saw tens of thousands of ducks, with one flock nearly three miles long and in places a mile wide. One afternoon Armstrong scouted tens of thousands of pintails and redheads feeding on a shallow oyster bar. He set anchor and lowered the yacht's launch and a "lighter boat" loaded with one hundred wooden decoys, guns, gear, and Brownie, a Chesapeake Bay retriever. Their launch, piloted by "a dusty" who "whistles at sprigs and sputters at redheads," secured the boat on the shallow flats and surrounded it with sweet bay branches for the afternoon shoot.[17]

Most of Pulitzer and McAdams's hunts with Captain Armstrong produced limits of twenty-five ducks each, and on their ten-day excursion they saw only one other gunning rig between Corpus Christi and Aransas Bays. Clarence Armstrong later moved to Corpus Christi, where he worked as a tugboat and pilot boat captain and died in 1955.[18]

ROCKPORT HUNTING CLUBS AND GUIDES

The first gunning clubs founded on Copano and Aransas Bays in the 1890s were open to the public. Two of the earliest were Kemp's Duck Preserve on Puerto Bay and Sorenson's Camp, both located on the south shore of Copano Bay. The area's first private club was probably Oak Shore Hunting Preserve, which opened in 1905. It was followed by the Rockport Sportsman's Club, founded by Rockport developers between 1905 and 1910. Located on Salt Lake, Rockport Sportsman's Club was touted as "the finest, most modern and complete sportsmen's club house in the entire south." For reasons unknown it was short-lived.[19]

Fred Kemp's Duck Preserve on Puerto Bay had already established a national following as early as 1895, with customers from San Antonio, Dallas, Waco, and as far away as Chicago and Milwaukee. Kemp's $2.50 fee covered transportation from the Gregory SA&AP depot, accommodations, food, and a day-long hunt. Kemp had twenty-two duck blinds on Swan Lake, between Port and Copano Bays, where customers shot redheads and canvasbacks passing from saltwater feeding grounds to freshwater marsh.[20]

San Antonio sportsmen were often critical of Kemp's Place. In the *San Antonio Light,* one wrote that Kemp's was not for gunners "inclined to be lazy and afraid to work," as they had to row to the blinds and handle their own decoys. Another thought Kemp's required "the constitution of a mule" and complained of the poor condition of Kemp's boat, its sails nearly rotten. The last known account of Kemp's Place was in 1901, when two SA&AP railroad men drowned while hunting Swan Lake.[21]

Andrew "Pop" Sorenson, an immigrant from Denmark and cattleman for the Coleman-Fulton Pasture Company (CFP), founded at least four Rockport-area hunting clubs. He was also a conservationist, and over his lifetime he worked with the Waco-based Texas Game Protective Association and served for forty-one years with the Texas Game, Fish, and Oyster Commission. Sorenson the outdoorsman shot and mounted an eastern brant that, in 1911, was the only one ever known from Texas waters.[22]

Sorenson first guided hunters in the 1890s from his Sorenson's Camp, later Sorenson's Lodge, across from Kemp's Place at Clubhouse Point on Copano Bay. San Antonio's Oscar Guessaz brought "a syndicate of capitalists" from Memphis to

ANDREW SORENSON (right) with "Jim" at Sorenson's Camp, Rockport, ca. 1920s. (Houston Public Library Metropolitan Research Center, File No. RG1118-0084)

SORENSON'S CAMP, *later Swan Lake Hunting Club, Rockport, 1924, with Andrew Sorenson* (standing, right) *and San Antonio's Alex Halff by his Packard.* (Houston Public Library Metropolitan Research Center, File No. RG1118-0085

hunt in 1895, arriving by private Pullman car, their culinary needs met by a French cook whose elaborate meals included Swan Lake canvasbacks. Sorenson's Camp hosted sportsmen for another thirty-five years, although the name changed in the mid-1920s to Swan Lake Hunting Club. During those years, Sorenson opened the Port Bay Club on the old Kemp Place, and in 1916 he purchased and renovated the old Shell Hotel, headquarters for the private Oak Shore Club.[23]

The Oak Shore Club, originally called Oak Shore Hunting Preserve, was founded in 1905 by Major John T. Wheadon and Frank P. Holland and located on the grounds of the Shell Hotel in Fulton. Dallas and Fort Worth members, who

COPANO AND ARANSAS BAYS → 227

THE SHELL HOTEL *and Oak Shores Club on Aransas Bay, 1906. The hotel is to the left, and club member cottages are on the right. (Courtesy Jim Moloney)*

built cottages among the oak trees, enjoyed a lavish Oak Shore Club menu that featured breakfasts of wild quail on toast and dinners of buffalo and beef supplied by rancher Charles Goodnight. Christmas festivities in 1906 had a supper table set for fifty guests with venison, wild turkeys, geese, ducks, jack snipes, quail, fish, and oysters supplied by "the gentlemen members of the club."[24]

The club changed its name in 1912 to the Oak Shore Outing Club and grew to accommodate 150 guests. That year club founder and newspaper editor Holland hosted the first annual meeting of the influential Texas Editorial Association, and for weeks afterwards embellished stories of each fish and duck the newspapermen harvested appeared in major Texas tabloids. The Oak Shore Club's Shell Hotel changed owners several times, and by the late 1910s it was owned and managed by Port Bay Club's Andrew Sorenson, and then later by his son James B. Sorenson. In 1923 the hotel was sold and converted into a private residence.[25]

Andrew Sorenson's Port Bay Club was, and is, renowned for bay flats pintail and redhead hunting, holding title as the oldest continuously operating hunting and fishing club in Texas. The club got its start in 1909 when Sorenson bought the grounds of Kemp's Duck Preserve on Puerto Bay. He turned it into a private club in 1912.[26]

In its early years, club members traveled to it on the SA&AP railroad. From the Gregory depot they reached the club by horse and wagon and later by Charles Cleveland's jitney service—a Model T enclosed with isinglass windows. As they crossed scrub pasture, the humming of tires on the shell road gave way to the racket on the worn wooden boards of the one-lane causeway over Port Bay. To the north they saw the shimmering waters of Copano Bay. Ahead was the Port Bay Club boat dock, duck cleaning shed, and, finally, tin roof, white clapboards, and wooden cisterns of the main building.[27]

If they came instead from Rockport, after Market Street they followed the deeply rutted clay road before turning onto the mud track of the old Sinton Highway, now Port Bay Drive. Sometimes coyotes, bobcats, or rattlesnakes crossed their path. Always there were the horned lizards, "horny toads," that ducked beneath mesquite and yucca scrub and prickly pear cactus. Ahead were the decoy storage shack, the guides' quarters, and then the club building outlined by salt cedars.

In its first year Port Bay Club sold shares at $150 each to one hundred members from Texas, New York, Chicago, Saint Louis, Cincinnati, Atlanta, Wisconsin, and Massachusetts. Almost immediately, trips to the club by persons of note from throughout the United States and Texas, mostly Waco, Dallas, and San Antonio, were a regular feature of newspaper society pages.[28]

Charter member and former Wisconsin governor G. W. Peck often stayed at the club all winter, shipping his stacks of salted ducks in wooden barrels home by rail. Charter member Ed Rand was well known in San Antonio sporting circles as a founding member of San Antonio's Blue Wing Club and was an early advocate of efforts to pass state game law legislation. I. C. Thurmond, from Oklahoma City and Amarillo, built one of the first cottages at Port Bay Club. Thurmond said at Port Bay "ducks would fly over the bay about 10,000 at a time, almost blackening the sky. You could shoot in any direction and hit them." In a blind on Swan Lake he killed forty-two ducks with five shots.[29]

Rear Admiral Albert Mertz spent weeks each winter at the club. On a hunt in 1929 he shot a banded redhead, which was featured in the *Galveston Daily News* article "Letter Gives Unique Angle on Migration," explaining waterfowl migration and the Bureau of Biological Survey's banding program to its readers. The admiral kept detailed records of the geese and ducks he killed, reaching the ten thousand mark in the late 1920s.[30]

Other early members were Connie Mack of the Philadelphia Athletics; Max Fleischman, the margarine magnate; Tris Speaker, manager and outfielder for the 1920 world champion Cleveland Indians; and G. N. Pierce of Pierce-Arrow automobile fame. Robert A. and Fred W. Chesebrough of the Vaseline Company sailed south each fall from New York on their private yacht. The Moodys of Galveston held memberships, along with Dr. W. L. McBride, who moved from Kansas City to retire at his club cottage.[31]

After only six years, the entrepreneurial Andrew Sorenson—immigrant, cowboy, hunting guide, private club owner, and hotelier—turned the reins of the Port Bay Club over to Arthur Richard Curry, who managed it from 1918 until 1943. Curry lived in Fulton, delivering mail, groceries, and passengers by boat between Port Aransas and Rockport. Elaine Curry was three years old when her parents

I. C. Thurmond *of Oklahoma (left) by his Port Bay Club cottage, 1920s. The guide and children are unidentified. (Courtesy Port Bay Club)*

Retired US Navy *rear admiral Albert Mertz (left) and his favorite Port Bay Club guide, Walter Gray, in front of one of the club's wooden cisterns, 1920. (Courtesy Port Bay Club)*

moved to the club, and she lived there until 1937. Her recollections as Elaine Curry Vandeveer at ninety-two years of age provide a rich history of the early days of the club.[32]

Port Bay, Elaine recalls, was a long way from Rockport when she and her brother Maurice were growing up. The family raised a few pigs and two cows, selling milk, cream, and butter. "Daddy had a huge garden. Mother raised chickens and turkeys. I remember we always canned vegetables, and even canned ducks." Arthur Curry maintained the grounds and buildings, managed the guides, built and brushed blinds, built hunting skiffs, and piloted the tow boat, a duty he shared with Rockport's Edwin Ballou.

During hunting season many of the club guides lived on the grounds. In addition to their salary, they cleaned ducks for ten cents apiece. Ducks were hung and cured in the duck house, which was originally an open room with screens until Curry in the 1950s built wooden refrigerator chests that held hundred-pound blocks of ice delivered from Rockport. African American families worked at the club each winter. Elaine remembers that "all of the help was from Hockley. Nora and John Riley worked every hunting season for at least twenty years, driving a car down from Hockley with the dishwasher and maid. Nora cooked over a large cast iron wood stove with two ovens. John would wait on the members' tables, and I remember he always had a fine suit jacket and white linen draped over his arm."

ARTHUR CURRY, *Port Bay Club manager, returning with wooden skiffs after the hunt. (Courtesy Elaine Curry Vandeveer)*

PINTAILS TAKEN *at Port Bay Club, late 1920s. Club manager Arthur Curry is second from the left. Elaine Curry Vandeveer and her brother Maurice are seated. The house in the background is the Chandler house, one of the original club cottages. (Courtesy Port Bay Club)*

The Curry family remained at the club during the 1919 hurricane. "Daddy brought his boat, the *Nereid,* with him to the club and lost it in the 1919 storm. The only way we knew it was coming was that Daddy had his barometer, and he kept watching it fall. He'd never seen it drop like that." With water rising in the living quarters, Curry put Elaine on his shoulders and waded to the guides' quarters, the highest ground on the property. They emerged after the storm to find every structure on the grounds damaged or destroyed, but Curry had the club ready for the 1919 fall season.[33]

When Elaine and Maurice Curry left for college in the 1930s, their education was paid for by club members who had created a fund for their expenses. Arthur Curry left Port Bay in 1943 to become sheriff of Aransas County and died in 1951.

George Marion Harrell succeeded Curry in 1943 and ran the club until 1949, when he became Aransas County constable. He was followed by his son Milton Harrell, who remained at the club helm for the next twenty-eight years.[34]

When Milton Harrell took charge, Port Bay buildings were still painted white with green trim and gray wood porches, and they were still surrounded by a white picket fence. The wooden cisterns, a fixture for nearly fifty years, came down in 1958 when the club got its first piped water. The four original private members' cottages changed ownership; I. C. Thurmond's house was sold to Andrew Sorenson's grandson Jimmy Sorenson, and next door the original Chesebrough cottage was bought by Charles "Pappy" Schneider of San Antonio, whose grandson George King is still a club member. The other two houses were owned by the families of a Dr. McKeever and a Dr. Miller.[35]

Milton's daughter Jerry Lynn Ayers grew up at Port Bay Club in the years after World War II. "Daddy and Bubba Davis," she says,

> built all the wooden skiffs. I don't think they even had power tools. And they made cast nets. I can remember every summer Daddy would sit and paint decoys. They had all these little tomato sauce cans of paint all lined up. In September, Daddy started building blinds and cutting sweet bay brush on Blackjack Peninsula and around Austwell, and the trucks would just be loaded. Then they had to load the launches. They would come in tired and cranky and Mother would say, "Here they come, you girls be good." Everything had to be ready and just perfect for that opening day of hunting season.

Jerry's mother, Ophelia Harrell, ran the kitchen and dining room. The wintertime staff

> all lived in Waller and Prairie View, and every year, we'd take a ride up there and ask them if they wanted to work this year, and we'd round 'em all up. They would come live at the club. There was Sambo and the cook Elizabeth. Later, Jonnie V was the cook. She lived in Refugio, and I remember she couldn't read or write. Willie B was the porter. Oris Young was one of Daddy's guides for many years. He rode the bus to the club at the beginning of every hunting season. He slept all season in the guide room, and always wore striped overalls and a white shirt.[36]

The club's two power launches, one named *Jerry* and the other *Linda Sue*, after Jerry's younger sister, towed up to eight skiffs to the channel, where as late as the 1960s guides still rowed to the blinds. Airboats made their appearance in the mid-1960s but were quickly prohibited. Jerry remembers, "Jerry Wendell had some of the first airboats in Rockport. He came up to the pier one day to show my father, and I remember how loud it was. Well, he turned that thing around, and it just sucked the raincoat off of somebody on the pier, and it went through the prop and came out the other side just all torn up. Daddy said 'You get that thing out of here!'"[37]

Milton Harrell retired in 1977. Looking back, Jerry says, "I wish I could hear Daddy walk in early in the morning just one more time and call out 'Board' and see him pass his cap for the drawing of numbers to form the line of small skiffs behind the big motorboats going out to be dropped off at the hunters' blinds."[38]

When Dave "Bubba" Davis replaced Harrell in 1977, he was only the fourth Port Bay manager in a span of sixty-five years. A Rockport waterman, Davis had been a guide at both the Port Bay Club and St. Charles Bay Hunting Club. He carved many of the wooden decoys still used by the club and always hunted ducks with a single-shot 12-gauge. He never wasted anything he shot; even as a boy, when he shot a pelican at St. Joseph Island, his mother made him eat it. Davis's tenure lasted until 1997 and again from 1999 to 2001. In the two years between, the club was run by Rob Atkins, and since 2005 by Baffin Bay fishing guide Jeff Kucera.[39]

Members keep the club lore alive. Second-generation member Ed Duvall was there the day the launch *Jerry* sank, and from his Swan Lake duck blind he could see the lone figure of Captain Charlie Lowe clinging to the bow. Bubba Davis's retriever went out for a duck on the shallow flats, returning not with a fowl but with a thrashing redfish. George King had a reputation for cutting every trotline on Port Bay because, with low water, their hooks hung head-high to club members making night crossings in club skiffs.[40]

Port Bay Club nearly became a victim of the 1980s banking and oil collapse and declined to only thirty dues-paying members. The tenacity of its membership during those trying times was reflected by people such as Dr. Ed Futch of Galveston, who told the board, "As long as I am alive, this club will not go out of business." Futch's legacy lives on not just at Port Bay, but through a fellowship grant to Ducks Unlimited's Institute for Wetland and Waterfowl Research. John Cook came up with the Adopt a Project idea, a creative way to pay for improvements to the lodge that was embraced by the membership.[41]

The club today maintains about forty blinds in the bay, with another twenty in the marsh at Italian Bend called the Lease. Port Bay continues to use a motor launch to tow skiffs to the shooting grounds, but small outboards replaced oars in the early 1960s. Wooden skiffs were traded for fiberglass, the club using a mold designed by Bubba Davis. Redheads still rise from Port Bay in small knots, and pintails circle high over the flats. Only pilings remain of the causeway that brought members from the Gregory depot. Pop Sorenson's once unobstructed view of Copano Bay is now interrupted by buildings, and some of the duck blinds, with a century of history, are being abandoned to housing developments on the shore. When the Italian Bend marsh was recently offered to developers, a group

A WELL-MAINTAINED *Rockport hunting operation in 1927, complete with a cook trailer. It is possible this was part of the Peninsula Club. (Courtesy Jim Moloney)*

of club members rose to the challenge, and it remains, as it should be, part of Port Bay Club.[42]

A decade after Port Bay Club was founded, Dallas, Fort Worth, Waco, Austin, and San Antonio sportsmen opened the Peninsula Club and Hotel as a "modern haven of rest for the businessman, and a paradise for the sportsman." Promoted as modern in every way, the club advertised a radio receiving station with a radius of two thousand miles and featured hunting guides with motorized skiffs. A fleet of larger boats included a high-powered motor boat "capable of crossing the bays at 30 mph." The club disappeared in the mid- to late 1920s.[43]

St. Charles Bay Hunting Club, on the east side of Lamar Peninsula, has a long sporting tenure, and like Port Bay Club, remains in operation today. The rich history of the club has been preserved by its members and guides. David Herring wrote an account titled "Duck Hunting in the Old Days," with anecdotes from guides Jimmy Silberisen and Glenn DeForest. San Antonio's Alex Halff published *St. Charles Bay Hunting Club: Sport, Tradition, and Camaraderie.*

St. Charles Bay Hunting Club was founded in 1923 by original incorporators Armstrong B. Weakley, H. N. Moore, and A. L. Huber. Twenty-four of the club's original twenty-five charter members were from San Antonio, and the first president, Charles Steffler, and the next two presidents were former members of Rockport's Port Bay Club. In its first year the club charged annual dues of twenty-five

> **NEW HUNTING CLUB.**
>
> **San Antonio Sportsmen Organize St. Charles Bay Club.**
>
> A new hunting club known as the St. Charles Bay Club has been organized by four of San Antonio's leading sportsmen. The new club will be situated at Lamar, Texas, in the best hunting grounds of any bay on the Texas Coast.

(Modified from *San Antonio Express*, Mar. 28, 1923)

dollars and hired John Howard "Cap" Mills, who had run a fishing camp on Lake Medina northwest of San Antonio, as club manager. In those days the club could only be reached from Rockport and Fulton by boat, with the journey completed by Model T over dirt and sand roads through live oaks. At the end of the road was the club's assortment of buildings, which included a mess hall, manager's house, servant's quarters, and duck house. Several structures were assembled from existing buildings on Lamar Peninsula and dragged to the club grounds by a team of mules.[44]

Club members in the 1920s and '30s hunted northern Copano Bay, St. Charles and Dunham Bays, Aransas Peninsula, Goose Island, and the western shore of St. Joseph Island. Shoal grass and widgeon grass were so thick in the bays that guide James Fox remembers he couldn't even wade through it. There were no other gunners as far as they could see—only ducks. A Chicago club member shipped a barrel of ducks to business associates across the nation every day he hunted. Manager Cap Mills, with his wife and son, shot ninety-three ducks in one afternoon. Member Doc Hausinger regularly got his limit of sprigs with a Winchester .410. As late as the 1940s, the club's season total reached well over six thousand birds.[45]

Cap Mills was replaced as club manager in 1931 by Rob S. Johnson, who guided the club through the Depression and World War II shortages of guides, shotgun shells, and gasoline. Management stayed in the family after Johnson retired and son-in-law Walter Heldenfels took over in the 1940s. Club guides Jim and David Herring remember how Johnson and Heldenfels safely navigated the launch around shallow bays "in the dark and the fog with just a compass and a watch," towing as many as a dozen fourteen-foot skiffs in a line, each loaded with guns, gear, sixty to ninety heavy wooden decoys, a guide, and hunters.[46]

Club captains often had to make a run all the way up to the head of St. Charles Bay, and the trip could take over an hour one-way. David says they knew how

HOWARD MILLS (left), first manager of St. Charles Bay Hunting Club and later owner of Mills Wharf, and Alex Halff of San Antonio, 1925. (Houston Public Library Metropolitan Research Center, Collection No. RG 1118-0002)

ST. CHARLES BAY *Hunting Club cottage. Club member J. W. "Jack" George poses with greater Canada and snow geese on the porch, 1930s. (Courtesy John Warren)*

OKLAHOMA *oil man Tom Slick and Charles Urschel at St. Charles Bay Hunting Club, 1927. In the photo are Rockport's J. Howard Mills, son Harry Mills, Rob Johnson, and Henry Ballou. (Courtesy Aransas County Historical Society)*

long each leg of the journey should take "and adjusted it for wind. And when they blew the foghorn, guides headed for shore and unfailingly came upon a blind." The foghorn signaled it was time for the guide in the next-to-last boat to untie the last skiff. Working in the dark, rain, and cold in a small skiff loaded with hunters and gear, the guides used a simple slip or "guide" knot that could be quickly untied with a jerk on the free end. A delay releasing the skiff meant the tow boat had to slow down and led to humiliating catcalls from the often long line of guides and hunters impatiently waiting to get to the next blind.[47]

St. Charles Bay Hunting Club was served by a long list of local guides, mostly Rockport watermen who made a living fishing and hunting year-round. Many continued to have an influence on the sport years after they left the club. Jimmy Silberisen and Henry Ballou were two early guides who later went on to operate their own guiding businesses. Ballou, according to Rockport's David Herring, "was an excellent shot. He always used a .410-gauge double-barreled gun, tightly choked, and when Henry shot, a duck fell." Manager Cap Mills's sons Harry and Herb cut their guiding teeth at the club before the family opened their Mills' Wharf fishing and hunting operation in 1931.[48]

Guides worked hard. With no outboard motors, they rowed or poled then pushed their skiffs into blinds framed with sweet bay branches stuck into the mud. After the decoys were put out, if no ducks were working that part of the shoreline, they picked up and moved—and set out the decoys again. Guides watched for ducks, told the hunters when to shoot, and were the bird dogs who

COPANO AND ARANSAS BAYS

LAUNCH LEAVING *the pier with wooden skiffs for an afternoon hunt at St. Charles Bay Hunting Club, 1920s. (Courtesy Aransas County Historical Society)*

picked up the kill and chased cripples. At the end of the hunt, they rowed the skiff back out to deep water near the channel to await the return of the tow boat.[49]

In the 1940s guides were paid $3.50 for a day that started at 4:30 a.m. and lasted until late afternoon. The club limited the guide's tip to no more than $1.00 per day, and for extra cash guides picked and cleaned birds. Jim Herring says the rate was "ten cents for a duck and a quarter for a goose, and we had orders to save the gizzards." Gizzard stew was the mainstay of the guide's diet, and they got so tired of eating it that "if you had time you'd pick and clean your ducks on the way in, you'd make sure the gizzard went over the side." Brother David says that it took a rebellion in the mid-1940s to stop the flow of stewed innards.[50]

The Herring brothers remember well their days on Lamar Peninsula. Ducks were plentiful and decoyed well. Guides whistled for sprigs or raked a shell across the checkered forearm of their pump guns to attract the attention of passing redheads, although "you could stand up and holler at 'em and they'd still come in." David's first day as a guide was in 1944, and he says that, after he made the long, ninety-minute tow to the head of the bay, his "sports" killed thirty ducks and ten snow geese. It took the fourteen-year-old boy all afternoon to pick those birds.[51]

Gulf Coast weather played an important part in day-to-day hunting. Fog that rendered land and water invisible presented a challenge, like the time disoriented hunters were lost until late in the day and eventually collected in skiffs spread from Key Allegro to the Causeway. Blue northers pushed water from shallow bays and built huge swells in the main channels. One of these winter storms nearly killed club guide Henry Ballou. Making no headway as he poled against the wind and sea, he climbed out of the skiff to pull it. Waves broke over him, and he was chilled to the bone. Other members in the party covered him, sick with cold, in a pile of dead ducks at the bottom of the skiff. After they made landfall, Henry was warmed by the ubiquitous duck gizzard stew, and it was one time the meal tasted pretty good.[52]

Change came rapidly to St. Charles Bay Hunting Club after World War II, with electricity, refrigerators, game ice boxes, and the first telephone. The annual spring ritual of hauling out the wooden skiffs to scrape, sand, caulk, and paint them ended with purchase of aluminum skiffs, although it was another thirteen years before the club bought five eighteen-horsepower outboard motors. The ceiling on the guide's tip was raised to two dollars, and former guide Johnny Atwood says they made thirty-five cents for each cleaned duck and a nickel a gizzard by the 1950s.[53]

St. Charles Bay Hunting Club had new neighbors when Aransas National Wildlife Refuge was established in 1937, but it was an uneasy marriage from the start. Separated by only narrow St. Charles Bay, the harvesters of migratory waterfowl were but a stone's throw away from the protectors. Added to the mix were the last vestiges of the population of whooping cranes, one of the most endangered bird species in North America, which wintered on the refuge. Almost immediately, the club was prohibited from hunting on the east side of St. Charles Bay.[54]

In 1973, Houston Audubon Society visitors were horrified to see duck blinds on the west shore of the bay and petitioned to close that area to migratory bird hunting. With friends in the right political places, the club thwarted their efforts. The government considered closing all of St. Charles Bay to hunting in 1983, but club members who went to Washington, DC, and lobbied on their behalf again prevailed. Then, as *Houston Chronicle* outdoor writer Bob Brister put it, "Just as hunters were showing they indeed can be the good guys, somebody shot an endangered whooping crane."[55]

In January 1989, Houston's Mario Yzaguirre was hunting as a guest on St. Joseph Island when he pulled the trigger on a white bird in the sky above him, certain it was a goose. It wasn't. In Alex Halff's telling of the tale, the closest guide "saw the guy shoot the whooping crane and he jumped in the airboat and ran down to the blind. And the guy is holding it up and he says 'I don't think this is a goose.'" The guide told him, "'I know it's not a goose. What it is, [though] is probably going to get you three years in the penitentiary.'" Club manager Wade Callam convinced the guest to turn himself in, and soon, Wade said, "all hell broke loose. Newspapers were calling and *Newsweek* magazine wanted to interview me. . . . The guide was offered six thousand dollars to give an exclusive interview with *Field and Stream*." A quarter-century later, versions of the whooping crane legend are still told from Beaumont to Port Isabel.[56]

Housing developments encroach, but as yet do not smother, the St. Charles Bay Hunting Club grounds on Lamar Peninsula. Members still shoot redheads

> **MILLS' WHARF**
> DUCK HUNTING—FISHING
> Boats for hire, hunting, fishing. Guides, decoys, fishing tackle. Only open club this vicinity. Lamar, end new Copano bay causeway. Phone, wire Moores Service Station, Rockport.

(Modified from *Corpus Christi Times*, Nov. 13, 1931)

MILLS' WHARF *main building with a launch used for fishing and towing skiffs* (foreground) *to the duck blinds. Cap Mills put the dummy on the roof, complete with a pith helmet and fishing pole, as an advertising gimmick. At the left corner of the building is the pole used to display porpoises.* (Courtesy Al Johnson)

and pintails, just not as many as they once did. The gizzard stew is gone. Club members still hunker down in a blind as a blue norther approaches. In the distance, the hunters spot a flock of whooping cranes, flashes of brilliant white against the darkening, lead grey sky. No one mistakes them for geese.

John Howard "Cap" Mills, the first manager of St. Charles Bay Hunting Club, started Mills' Wharf on Lamar Peninsula as a public fishing and day hunting operation in 1931. Cap's timing was perfect: the club's opening coinciding with completion of the first causeway across Aransas Bay that connected the towns of Fulton and Lamar. Family lore has it that the crews who constructed the causeway drove the pilings for Mills' Wharf piers and the main building, and it cost Cap only barbecue and beer.[57]

The big white Mills' Wharf building on bartered pilings became a local landmark. Passengers in cars negotiating the narrow two-lane bridge across the bay always took a second look at the building; on its high-pitched roof over the water Cap fastened a life-sized dummy with a pith helmet and fishing pole, and he hung a pair of five-hundred-pound porpoises from a winch pole outside the building as an advertising gimmick.[58]

Most visitors stayed at the adjacent Wells Court, walking next door to the main building where each morning fifty to sixty hunters crowded into the main

A MILLS' WHARF *hunting trip to St. Joseph Island by plane, including Cap Mills* (center), *son Harry Mills* (left), *both with hunting dogs, and Lamar Peninsula's Rob Johnson, manager of the St. Charles Bay Hunting Club* (far right). *Others are unidentified.* (Courtesy Jim Mills)

GUESTS AFTER *a Mills' Wharf hunt, probably in the 1940s or early 1950s.* (Courtesy Aransas County Historical Society)

room to draw for guides and duck blinds. After the draw, duck hunters drove to the club launch at Holiday Beach for a tow to blinds on Copano Bay, while goose hunters followed the Mills' Wharf pickup truck north to Austwell and Tivoli. During the 1940s, two airplanes were added to the club fleet that shuttled hunters across Aransas Bay to St. Joseph and Matagorda Islands.[59]

Mills' Wharf grew from 281 customers in 1936 to a little over 1,000 by 1939 and at its peak employed fifty hunting guides. The number of guides was far fewer

COPANO AND ARANSAS BAYS → 241

during World War II. Guides were so hard to find that Bill Biss and Woodie Owen were the only two available for eighty hunters on the opening day of the 1943 season. Besides Cap Mills's sons, one of the longest tenured club guides was Joe "Uncle Billy" Sontag, who guided for thirty years, a tradition carried on by his son Les. For an all-day hunt, guides made $2.75 on top of Mills's $4.50 fee.[60]

Cap Mills carved the club's sixteen hundred wooden decoys, mostly pintails, and made all his own silhouette goose decoys. He was also a collector and loved nature's eccentricities. In 1939 he was featured in Ripley's *Believe It or Not* holding a redhead that drowned when an oyster closed on its foot. The redhead remained at the club for years, mounted on the wall "just above the gila monster cage." Mills's collection also included a mounted surf scoter, the only one ever taken on the Texas Gulf Coast up to that time. After World War II, Mills opened up a shop behind the main building where he sold his hand-made decoys and fishing tackle, turning the fishing and hunting operation over to sons Harry and Herb.[61]

Harry and Herb were extraordinary watermen. Harry Mills, according to his son Jim, always decoyed his birds in close and never used anything bigger a $7\frac{1}{2}$ lead shot size for ducks or geese. Harry never used a duck call, he just whistled, and he could sound like exactly like a wigeon or a pintail. "Whenever the redheads came by, he'd take an oar and beat on the side of the boat; all you had to do was get their attention."[62]

The brothers' decoy spreads sometimes included live mallard ducks and geese, even after it was no longer legal, and there is a story that they quickly added tame mallards to their bag once when they thought they saw a game warden. Another time Harry was visited by a game warden behind the club, and, thinking he had an empty gun, teasingly took an imaginary lead on a very real seagull and pulled the trigger. He killed it stone dead. The bird sailed down directly into the back of the game warden's truck, providing Harry little room to squirm out of the ticket the warden was writing him.[63]

Jim began guiding for his father in 1949. The club still used the big launch to tow boats to the blinds, and the releasing of each rowboat was a test of their seamanship. "If it was foggy," Jim says, "they'd just toot the horn, and that guy better get that knot undone, because otherwise that guide's gonna have a long row to the blind." At the end of the hunt "a party would give you an extra tip if they got their limit early, and instead of waiting for the tow boat to come by, I rowed them across the bay." The club had only two outboard motors, a Mercury and an Evinrude, both seven and one-half horsepower. "The guides drew straws to see which one would not get that Merc. That Evinrude always ran. You could catch it on fire, and unhook it and dump it in the water, put it back on the boat and then start it again."[64]

There were a lot of ducks and geese to clean at Mills' Wharf. Jim says, "I could get in the [tow boat] line and all the other guides would throw me their ducks and I could pick on the way in, and get that twenty-five cents a duck extra." They also

J. Howard Mills *with the redhead that drowned when an oyster closed on its foot. The story was featured in Ripley's "Believe It or Not." (Courtesy Al Johnson)*

had duck picking contests, and Harry Mills held the record for cleaning a duck in fifty-seven seconds. Sometimes Dick the handyman would pick ducks, impressing Jim that "he could chew tobacco and drink beer at the same time." Herb's son, Aransas County Judge C. H. "Burt" Mills Jr., remembers two local African American families who helped out, along with Frankie Roe's picking house in Rockport.[65]

A big part of the reputation of Mills' Wharf came from world-class goose hunting on agricultural fields around San Antonio Bay. Jim remembers a spot on Austwell's Oaker farms, across the fence from Aransas National Wildlife Refuge, they called Coffin Corner. "To get to the refuge," he says, "the geese came from Bergantine Lake, and they had to go over that corner. That would be the place to get." One time in the fog Jim and another club guide fired only three shells and picked up thirty geese. Herb's son Burt remembers a hunt when geese flew so low over the fence that his dog nearly caught one by the foot.[66]

Cap Mills died in 1960, the year Mills' Wharf was sold to Dallas oilman Toddie Lee Wynne and Burt Mills Jr. Mills' Wharf was renamed the Sea Gun Inn, and in 1963 it was rebuilt to include motel units, a restaurant, fishing charter boats, private duck blinds, and a marina. The "multi-million-dollar . . . Texas-size playground" became an exciting destination for more than just sportsmen. Hollywood movie stars and entertainers such as Frank Sinatra and the Rat Pack were said to have made their way to the "flashy oasis" on Lamar Peninsula. Hunting remained big business, with Harry Mills managing the operation and guiding goose hunters until he died in 1965.[67]

Jimmy's Duck Hunting Camp, and the waterfowling legacy of its proprietor, Jimmy Silberisen, lives on through his son John and John's wife, Jo, who generously provided most of the material used here. Jimmy first guided at St. Charles Bay Hunting Club, then started his own guiding business, open to the public, just

JIMMY SILBERISEN *in 1936 during his guiding days at St. Charles Bay Hunting Club. (Courtesy Jo and John Silberisen)*

before the Depression. Business was so slow he wondered if he was going to survive, until one day the phone rang, and it was a man from "up north" who wanted to know if he was available to guide for a few weeks. He was.

For the excursion Jimmy leased the Corpus Christi yacht *Japonica,* the largest vessel at the time on local waters. His customers were comfortably situated as he plotted a course to hunt ducks on the bays, geese on the agricultural fields, and quail behind the sand dunes on St. Joseph Island. When the *Japonica* docked, Silberisen's efforts were rewarded with a seven-hundred-dollar tip, an extraordinary amount of money during the Depression. Jimmy never gave much thought to who his customer was, even when the man told Jimmy to "look for his name in the paper." They shook hands, and Mr. Pulitzer returned home.[68]

Jimmy, like most Rockport guides in the late 1930s, met his hunters at City Café in downtown Rockport, and as business improved, he hired more guides. One of them, Jim Herring, says he made his first hunt the day the Japanese bombed Pearl Harbor. "I started out guiding for Silberisen in 1941. I was out there on December the seventh, 1941. I never will forget it. Butterfly day, bright and sunny, no ducks."[69]

Jimmy's business moved from the City Café in the 1940s when he opened Jimmy's Duck Hunting Camp on forty-eight acres of Redfish Bay and Estes Flats shoreline. Son John says, "It was not an impressive looking location, but it proved to be a good place to go if you wanted good duck hunting." Located at the end of a quarter-mile rutted road off Highway 35, the grounds had a large old building from an earlier duck hunting club that Jimmy converted into a café and family living quarters. They had outdoor toilets and a water supply from gutters that led to a cement cistern covered by screen wire to keep snakes out, and they hauled drinking water by mule from Dad Chaney's property on Estes Flats. A turning basin was built for their twenty-six-foot tow boat and twenty-four wooden skiffs.[70]

Jimmy and son John built nearly fifty wooden skiff blinds, and to brush them each fall they cut and bundled enough sweet bay branches to fill a long trailer. For as long as he was in business, Jimmy never ran a phone line to the camp, and to book a hunt customers had to find him at home. By the 1950s hunters paid ten dollars a day for a skiff loaded with thirty wooden decoys and tow-boat service to the blind. John Silberisen recalls Aransas Bay was at times almost completely black with ducks, so many it could be hard to see any water between swimming birds. With the first shot in the morning, a cloud of ducks rose that included pintails; wigeons; redheads; bluebills; gadwalls; canvasbacks; mallards; blue-winged, green-winged, and cinnamon teal; goldeneyes; hooded mergansers; and an occasional goose.[71]

John made his first guided hunt when he was twelve. The morning was an unusually warm day as he loaded his three clients into a club skiff and motored to the blind. He was setting out the decoys when the customers set their watches back an hour, hoping to fool the youngster into some extra shooting beyond his father's standard quitting time. By late morning the skyline was giving hints of bad weather to come. John recognized it and told his party it was time to go ashore. They protested that it was too early, "Just look at our watches." The young boy had been taught good manners and remained silent even as he saw his father's big boat in the distance pulling the other parties across the bay towards camp.

John suspected that the devil of all winter weather systems, a blue norther, was bearing down on them. With the sky turning purple, then black, he jumped from the blind to pick up the decoys. The men were still protesting when a wall of wind and rain converged, causing the sea around them to leap and lurch. With visibility reduced to only a few feet, John pulled the crank on the outboard. It wouldn't start. As the boat began to blow down the bay, John jumped overboard, grabbed the bow rope, and started pulling. As he stooped low from the weight of the boat, tall, triangle-shaped waves broke over his head. As he pulled, one step forward, two steps back, the bay floor beneath his feet was sometimes soft to the ankles with silt, sometimes hard with oysters. With each step he had but a brief moment to feel for firm footing, hoping there wasn't a deep hole or drop-off. He knew, too, that somewhere—if he took a bad turn—was the deep channel.

John pulled long enough that the leading edge of the front passed, and on its back side the temperature dropped to nearly freezing. He pulled long enough that the sky turned to darkness; long enough that the men hunkered down in the skiff had grown very quiet. John thought he saw a light in the distance and pulled towards it. He heard voices and wanted to cry out, but he couldn't. He was exhausted. The men in the boat yelled out, and a father splashed into the water to reach a son. Jimmy was almost unable to pry his son's fingers from the rope he had held for so many hours. It was midnight, and John had pulled the boat across the bay for nearly seven hours. So it was that a twelve-year-old boy put his face into the teeth of a blue norther on Redfish Bay.[72]

When the Intracoastal Canal was dredged south of the Rockport shoreline, it spelled the beginning of the end to Jimmy's Duck Hunting Camp. He sold it to a developer who built City by the Sea in 1965. When Jimmy started guiding, the limit was twenty-five birds, and by the time he shuttered his club doors, the limit was five per hunter. Many days, on the bay once black with ducks, it was hard even to see that number.[73]

The Close family was another with a well-known reputation as Aransas Bay watermen and waterfowl hunters. Family patriarch William Sherman "Big Willie" Close was a commercial fisherman who, by the time he died in 1950, was thought to have caught more fish than anyone else on the Texas Gulf Coast. Grandson Fred Close says Big Willie didn't hunt for sport: "Back in the '30s and '40s down here we were hunting to eat," and he adds, "It was very hard during the Depression and even during the War, because German subs made it hard to fish. During the day we couldn't get out of sight of land, and nights were blacked out—no lights anywhere on the coast." Fred ate so many ducks as a young man that "even today I don't hardly ever eat a duck—that's all we had to eat."[74]

Fred's father, William Frederick "Little Willie" Close, guided at Port Bay and St. Charles Bay Hunting Club during the 1930s. When Little Willie started guiding day hunters on his own, his was a business he never had to advertise. He took hunters to St. Joseph by shrimp boat, hunting mostly at Mud Island and Allyn's Bight. Rockport guide James Fox says when Little Willie traded his wooden decoys for his first plastic Victor ones, he didn't like the factory colors and repainted all 144 himself. As a waterman, he was a perfectionist as well, building his own wooden skiffs using dowels instead of nails.[75]

A. J. "Moose" Adolphus, who came to Rockport from Port Arthur, opened Adolphus Pier as a public operation in the late 1920s or early '30s. Located where the Causeway was later built at Live Oak Point, Adolphus Pier had a bunkhouse and boathouse with a beer joint on the top, and at the end of the long fishing pier was a bait shack and cleaning area. Moose guided two customers who were so impressed with Coastal Bend that they purchased large pieces it. One was Dallas oilman Clint Murchison, who bought a ranch on Matagorda Island, and the other Fort Worth's Sid Richardson, who purchased St. Joseph Island. Adolphus Pier closed when Moose died in 1941.[76]

Other Rockport-area day hunting operations included Sportsman's Haven, which opened by 1934 and provided hunters half a dozen one-room white cot-

> BEST TROUT AND RED FISH-
> ING AND DUCK HUNTING ON
> TEXAS COAST
> # Adolphus Pier
> Nine Mile Point
> ROCKPORT, TEXAS
> PHONE 99   P.O. BOX 46

(Modified from *Corpus Christi Times*, Aug. 25, 1936)

tages on Aransas Bay. George A. Ratisseau ran Jolly Roger Hunting and Fishing Club on Redfish Point north of Live Oak Point from the early 1930s. George's wife, Thelma, managed it after he died in 1947, and it remained in business into the mid-1950s. Across Copano Bay neck at Holiday Beach, school bus driver Slim Suttles had a day-hunting operation with blinds that extended from the causeway bridge to Newcomb Bend.[77]

In the late 1940s and '50s sportsmen hunted at Heard Courts, Glenn's Hunting and Fishing Camp, Red's Fish Camp, and Calhoun Courts, where proprietor Lem Calhoun towed skiffs behind his shrimp boat to one of twenty blinds on north Copano Bay and Mission Bay. Former St. Charles Bay Hunting Club guide Henry Ballou was still guiding day hunters for a fee of ten dollars, but since he had no telephone, sportsmen wrote him a letter or went to his house to arrange a hunt.[78]

Rockport's private clubs and public hunting operations employed hundreds of men and boys from the fishing villages around Aransas and Copano Bays. Fred Close says, "During duck season down here we almost used to shut down school so the boys could guide." When Jim Mills skipped football practice, he was not alone; most of his team was duck hunting, and the coach quit. College weekends for David Herring were not spent at a football game; instead, he caught a ride from Austin every Friday with St. Charles Bay Hunting Club members and guided.[79]

Those guides hunted a Rockport very different from today's. Former St. Charles Bay Hunting Club guide Johnny Atwood remembers: "There were inland lakes on Fulton Road, and we would stand on the running boards of cars in the 1940s, and drive up to [shoot ducks]." Little Bay, now surrounded by the town, was once "full of grass, and held at least five thousand or ten thousand ducks in the early fifties." Frandolig Island, now the Key Allegro subdivision, had great pintail and redhead hunting but "was a snake haven. You did not get off the beach." Fred Close as a boy hunted pintails on freshwater springs in the dunes and scrub oaks of Estes Flats. The ducks disappeared when the United Carbon Company carbon black plant was built, turning "all the brush downwind solid black. Even the cows were black."[80]

ST. JOSEPH ISLAND

Separating Aransas Bay from the Gulf of Mexico, the barrier island of St. Joseph extended from Cedar Bayou to the always shifting flats of Aransas Pass. St. Joseph was one of the main sporting destinations for Rockport ship captains in the 1800s, called by Captain W. Y. Sedam "the best point on the gulf coast for duck shooting." On the bay side, clouds of pintails rose from the tidal fan delta behind Cedar Bayou. Flocks of redheads congregated at the shallow, northwest-southeast-trending Long Reef and Deadman's Island, which, traversing Aransas Bay, had claimed more than their share of sailing vessels. To the south, arcuate fingers of water extended down the bay side to Blind Pass and Mud Island, jutting into the water before Lydia Ann Island and the Lydia Ann Channel by Aransas Pass. Between sand dunes the island interior was dotted with natural freshwater lakes covered in smartweed, where hunters followed the birds by mule and wagon.[81]

By the late 1800s little remained of the settlements founded on the island before the Civil War. The hardships endured by those early settlers were largely forgotten as the gilded sporting era was ushered in with Colonel Edward H. R. "Eddie" Green's Tarpon Club in 1898. Green envisioned a private club that catered only to the most elite of Americans. When the last schooner load of cypress lumber was delivered to the southern end of the island across from Aransas Pass, the *Dallas Morning News* gushed that rising from the sand was "one of the most beautiful club houses on the continent."[82]

The two-story building had eighteen sleeping rooms, servants' quarters, a tramway, a pavilion, and an observatory. It was modern in every way, with water pumped from a twenty-six-thousand-gallon, thirty-foot cistern and piped into the kitchen and bathrooms. Copper screens covered every window. The kitchen served an "educated palate" in the well-appointed dining room, which was cleared each evening for a dance floor. A power plant run by a naphtha engine provided electricity that brought lights to all the rooms and verandas; people traveling on the train to Aransas Pass could see the glow of the Tarpon Club from across the bay.[83]

The board of directors, mostly from San Antonio and Dallas, with E. H. R. Green from Terrell, hired A. R. A. Brice as club manager. The venture in its first year boasted three hundred members, whose "wealth combined reaches into the hundred millions." By the next year, the growing membership was dubbed the "First Four Hundred Sportsmen of America," a privileged group with "more politicians and businessmen than in any other similar organization in the United States." The list included Grover Cleveland and President McKinley.[84]

Colonel Green brought members from the mainland by a gasoline launch, the first in Coastal Bend. James "Ed" Cotter was hired to pilot it, with Green sending him to Chicago to "learn about the combustion and ignition of gasoline engines."

THE GRAND TARPON *Club, St. Joseph Island. (Courtesy Jim Moloney)*

Rockport was soon a busy place, with dignitaries arriving at the rail depot before making their way to the harbor. It didn't take long before Ed Cotter's yacht was joined by other vessels, and the business of transporting guests created a small flotilla on Rockport's wharves, with sail, wood-burning, and motor boats that included Green's personal yacht *Mabel*.[85]

Tarpon Club members came for the opulence, to rub shoulders with others of their economic stature, and for world-class sport. Green had situated his club on a prolific triangle of waterfowling habitat between Mud Island and Harbor Island that covered Lydia Ann Peninsula, Quarantine Shore, and island freshwater ponds where there were "clouds of canvasback, redhead, mallard, blue-winged teal, green-winged teal, pintails, wigeons, and other varieties of duck. There are wild geese of all kinds, and 30 species of snipes. The air is alive with them and their wings make a continuous hum."[86]

The *Dallas Morning News* explained that the huge volume of birds harvested by the Tarpon Club members was justifiable, as "members of the club are not market-gunners, they kill mercifully and scientifically." Not everyone believed the hyperbole that followed the moneyed sportsmen. A market hunter from Harbor Island watched disdainfully as club members, "including a state senator," spent a calm, clear day firing high-powered rifles into the resting flocks on the bay. He added that club hunters "picked up only the fat ducks," leaving all the others to waste.[87]

There wasn't a post office on St. Joseph Island. To justify one, US postal service regulations required a town, an inconvenience club members remedied by creating Sport, Texas. The town of Sport encompassed only one dwelling, the Tarpon Club, where postmaster Carl R. Evans handled mail delivered from Rockport. Instead of letters and newspapers, however, Evans was kept busy with

COPANO AND ARANSAS BAYS → 249

Sport, Texas *mail boat, arriving at the Tarpon Club pier, St. Joseph Island. The Lydia Ann Lighthouse on Harbor Island is in background. (Courtesy Jim Moloney)*

gourmet foods, fine liquors, and wine sent south from throughout the United States.[88]

As rapidly as it rose, the fabled but short-lived club was in decline by 1904. That year the post office closed, and in 1905 the magnificent structure was torn down, the pieces of a once opulent sporting lifestyle transported by barge to Corpus Christi. Club manager Brice followed and went to work as manager of the Seaside Hotel. Within a few decades only a handful of fishing shacks stood on the once storied grounds.[89]

St. Joseph Island hunting history in the early 1900s was dominated by the Wood family. T. D. Wood, with Samuel Allyn, first purchased land on St. Joseph in the 1880s. By the turn of the century Wood's son Richard hosted prominent sporting visitors such as Governor Thomas M. Campbell, who appointed Richard the second game, fish and oyster commissioner of Texas in 1907. The island was always at the mercy of Gulf weather, and waves from the hurricane of 1919 that washed over it killed nearly six thousand of Wood's cattle. Their carcasses lined the beach from Lamar to Corpus Christi, where a Hereford bull washed into the lobby of the Nueces Hotel.[90]

Fort Worth oilman Sid Richardson bought the entirety of St. Joseph Island in 1936. One of the wealthiest men in the nation, Richardson was known as much for his philanthropy as for his disdain of publicity, and the solitude of the island fitted him perfectly. Richardson gave the task of building a lodge to his nephew, Perry Bass Sr., who brought in carpenters and laborers who lived in tents during the lodge's construction. It was called simply "the ranch house," but its bright green lawn, palm trees, and landing strip stood in marked contrast to the surrounding sand scrub. Richardson ranch house over the years was host to the likes of President Franklin D. Roosevelt, the president's son Elliott, and Richardson's

ROCKPORT FISHERMAN *and hunting guide William "Big Willie" Sherman Close Jr.* (center) *on the deck of his boat* Katy, *late 1930s. To the right is his son Robert Longley Close, and a Mr. Smith is on the left. (Courtesy Fred Close)*

lawyer, John Connally. When Sid Richardson died at the lodge of a heart attack in 1959, ownership of St. Joseph Island shifted to Perry Bass.[91]

During Perry Bass's tenure came the proliferation of airboats that could push further—and more noisily—into the marsh than wooden skiffs had ever done. Tired of it, Perry offered James Fox exclusive rights to the parts of St. Joseph Island near his ranch house. James first started hunting in the 1940s with his mentors Henry Ballou and his uncle Little Willie Close. He guided in 1953 for the St. Charles Bay Hunting Club, then went out on his own with Fox's Guide Service in 1969.

To reach St. Joseph Island, James crossed Aransas Bay by outboard to a barge he maintained at Allyn's Bight, or Bayou, where he kept two airboats. Hunting around Allyn's Lake, James and his customers shot mostly pintails, wigeons, teal, and redheads. He watched for days when the water rose as far as the *Salicornia* sand flats and followed the pintails as they congregated in the shallow water. As the water level dropped, he followed them again to the bay shore, where they fed on submerged grasses over the muddy bottom. Looking south from his blinds, James always anticipated when Pop Spears would fire up his airboat and return from his hunts at South Bay Hunting Club, jumping so many birds "we'd see the sky just fill up with just waves of ducks. And they'd come right down the [shore] line."

Houston art dealer Meredith Long introduced James to artist John P. "Jack" Cowan in 1970, and for years James took Jack around Aransas estuaries to photograph scenes that would become subjects of his famous paintings. James has been featured in several, including *Early Limits* (1969) and *Fox's Blind* (1973) on Fence Lake. The story of James's rescue of Cowan and his son, Joe Allen, artist Herb Booth, and Booth's son during a winter storm is the stuff of legend.

In James's telling of the adventure, "Cowan had just built a tunnel-hulled jet boat he named *Scooter*." Its inaugural sail was

> a fishing trip on New Years Eve, 1973, when a northwester blew in that dropped the temperature from 72 to 36 degrees in a few hours, and Cowan was dressed for 72-degree weather. Winds gusted to sixty-five miles an hour, and waves on the south side of St. Joe's were up to five feet. Herb Booth was hunting in the grass. He saw Cowan's flare when his engine wouldn't start and the boat couldn't handle the waves. Booth tried to make the rescue, but his small boat had four people and two dogs and was taken bow over stern by a large wave. I headed out that afternoon and saw the head of a black Labrador swimming for shore. I knew something had gone terribly wrong. I got the dog and found Booth wading for shore. I went back for the others that stayed with the boat. I took everyone to Bass's ranch house.
>
> Jack Cowan's son had remained in the blind, but it was impossible to pick him up because the waves were breaking big, and right on the shoreline. I called the Coast Guard to dispatch a helicopter. They said, 'We'll send a boat.' I told them if they did, they'd have more than one dead person on their hands. Send a chopper. They did.

That duck blind has been forever immortalized by Cowan in his painting the *Helicopter Blind.* Cowan expressed his thanks to Fox with an original painting that hangs in his Rockport home, inscribed with, "To Fox—thank God you were there!"

James quit bay hunting in the late 1980s. Business suffered during the Texas oil and banking crisis, and the bag limit was dropped from up to ten birds a day to a maximum of three. Then there was the 1988 sting, with Fox charged with illegal transportation of waterfowl and conspiracy. He says his defense nearly broke him financially and spiritually. Fox guided a few more years for Brian Dunn at Fennessey Ranch and then quit the sport.[92]

Generations of Rockport families made the Aransas Bay crossing to hunt ducks on St. Joseph Island each fall. Johnny Atwood made his first trip when he was seven. "Daddy would come and take us out of school. A southeast wind and overcast, that's all that had come together. We'd load the shrimp boat and towed a net-skiff." They anchored the big boat, rowed to shore, then poled the flats. "We put out forty or fifty handmade decoys that we made from balsa taken from old life jackets. They had a head on a string that was removable." After a hunt, "we went home in the afternoon and picked ducks all night. All pintails. We didn't throw a thing away."

On a hunt with his father and brother at Mud Island, Johnny recalls, "We had probably fourteen ducks out of a fifteen-duck limit, and we were tryin' to get that last duck. We killed mostly pintails, and redheads we'd passed up. There was a bunch of redheads came down from the north, and as redheads will do, they just sort of dove to the ground level and they got in a long line and started at us. All three of us shot into those damn ducks and we had nineteen of them on the ground. We didn't know what we were gonna do with 'em. Daddy breasted 'em out and filled empty pecan cans with duck breasts. On the way back he lit up the Coleman stove on the boat, and we ate those things fried—and you talk about good."[93]

After sails were forever furled in the early 1900s, sportsmen who crossed Aransas Bay to St. Joseph Island by gasoline engine found an island that looked very much as it did to the first settlers—Lafitte's pirates after they hurriedly abandoned the Texas upper coast—and later ship captains, bar pilots, and lightermen. The only difference was that wildfowl no longer blackened the sky.

CHAPTER 13

SOUTH BAY to CORPUS CHRISTI BAY

Aransas Bay forms a narrow neck as it approaches Corpus Christi Bay, the constriction between the mainland and St. Joseph and Mustang Islands marked by South Bay and Redfish Bay. Gulf waters ebb and flow by wind-driven tides through Aransas Pass, its constantly changing channel shaping the southern tip of St. Joseph Island and winding around Harbor Island before reaching Corpus Christi Bay to the south. Towns that call this part of the Texas coast home are Aransas Pass and Port Aransas.

HARBOR ISLAND

Harbor Island has gone by different names; it was Curlew Island in the 1830s, and after the Civil War, market hunters knew it as the Big Flats. Located at the convergence of Aransas, South, Redfish, and Corpus Christi Bays, Harbor Island is a tidal delta of winding bayous through black mangroves thick with shoal grass, turtle grass, and manatee grass. There the sea can seem alive with mullet, redfish, and dolphins, the sky a swirling mass of motion and color with roseate spoonbills, herons, pelicans, seagulls, and redheads in flocks that still cover the horizon, punctuated by the graceful dance of pintails and determined flights of wigeons.[1]

Harbor Island was a nationally known gunning destination. A big part of its attraction was the numbers of wintering canvasbacks, with the flats around Harbor Island in the late 1890s touted as "the best canvasback water left open to the public in the United States." According to Robin Doughty, Harbor Island hunters killed so many ducks that, between the island and Port Aransas inlet, sharks congregated to feast on floating birds before they could be retrieved.[2]

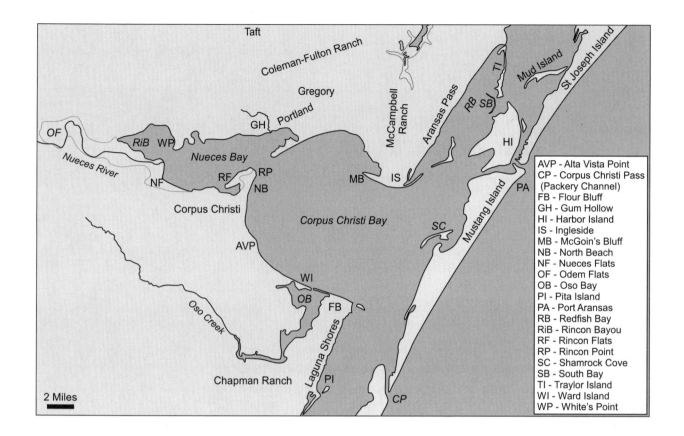

Corpus Christi Bay *as it looked in the early 1900s, before the Intracoastal Canal and other ship channels.*

TOWN OF ARANSAS PASS

On the mainland between Rockport and Corpus Christi, the town of Aransas Pass grew in the late 1800s along the SA&AP rail line, later the Southern Pacific. Trains brought land speculators, politicians, and railroad officials who combined business with the pleasure of good duck shooting. A party of Ohio and Chicago politicians in 1899 wrote, "We were so favorably situated that our party, in three days, killed over 500 [ducks]. It was not a remarkable killing when you consider the great number that came in at that time." Another group killed seven hundred ducks in two days.[3]

Aransas Pass was situated near inland prairie freshwater ponds, Harbor Island, and St. Joseph and Mustang Islands. Promotional material published by the railroad company and chamber of commerce called the Aransas Pass area the "finest hunting and fishing on the continent," with "canvasback and redhead ducks in abundance." Another brochure advertised how, just outside of town, "at times the entire country as far as the eye can reach appears to be covered with . . . Canada honkers, the Hutchins goose, snow goose, and brant."[4]

Aransas Pass in 1903 had only eight families, but the population swelled each winter with arriving hunters. Aransas Pass Gun Club, opened in 1911 by a Mr. Vernor from San Antonio, was the town's first advertised private club. Most visitors hired local guides, and they had plenty of options. In the 1910s and '20s the

POSTCARD PROMOTING *waterfowl hunting in the town of Aransas Pass, 1910. (Courtesy Jim Moloney)*

CYRUS E. FARLEY (left) *and R. E. Farley (right) with San Antonio customers Mr. Eichlizt and Jim Simpson and two Chesapeake Bay retrievers, late 1910s to 1920s. (Courtesy Bruce Baker)*

list included Walter Brauer, with his shallow-draft sailboat and rowing skiff; a Mr. Butcher, whose clients included Oklahoma governor J. B. A. Robertson; Mike Covington, who hunted on Harbor Island; and Robert Ellington Farley and his son Cyrus E. Farley. By the mid-1920s the town's best-known guides included William Craven and Byrd Minter.[5]

Robert Ellington "Bob" Farley settled in Port Aransas in 1890 and moved to the town of Aransas Pass after he lost everything in the 1919 hurricane. Family historian Bruce Baker recalls that Bob guided duck hunters in both towns and had regular clients, many from San Antonio, who returned year after year. In Aransas Pass they stayed at his house, which he called his hunting lodge, where they slept on the screened porch that wrapped around the building.[6]

ARANSAS PASS *guide Cyrus E. Farley* (far right) *late 1910s to 1920s. The number of canvasbacks in the photo suggests the hunt might have been on Harbor Island.* (Courtesy Bruce Baker)

Bob was a self-made naturalist who built the coastal Texas collection of mounted bird specimens and eggs for the Texas State Museum in Austin and the Smithsonian Institution. Family members recall the gallon jars of eggs Bob stacked in his garage next to his piles of wooden decoys, his uncanny ability to predict weather, and his logbooks filled with bird counts and accounts of natural history. Inspired by the decline in fish and game he witnessed during his years on the coast, he became a state game warden in the late 1920s.

Bob's son Cyrus, born in 1895, earned a living as a fishing guide, commercial snapper fisherman, and shrimper. He guided duck hunters from the 1910s through at least the 1920s and continued to guide family friends until the 1940s. Nearly a hundred years later locals still tell the story of how game warden Bob Farley fined his own son for hunting without a license, the event duly noted in his logbooks.[7]

Aransas Pass grocer William "Old Man" Craven built his duck blinds on the northwest side of Harbor Island, towing customers in a line of skiffs behind his twenty-six-foot runabout with its old Biltwell engine. Harbor Island waters were too shallow for his big boat, so Craven attached a solid brass propeller to his boat's driveshaft to carve a cut into the island's mangroves from the Morris-Cummins channel. His ditch appears on maps today as Craven Cut. Ohio's W. B. Haynes, a customer in the 1920s, thought Craven was one of the best duck shooters he ever knew. Craven's 1930s clients reached his blinds, towed by "a speedy motorboat . . . at 20 mph."[8]

The modern face of Texas had begun to etch itself into Harbor Island when Craven started hunting. The Aransas Harbor Terminal Railroad, which ran down the spine of the island, carried cars to the ferry landing as boat traffic waited in

A PARTY OF *Byrd Minter hunters with pintails and redheads at Aransas Pass, 1920s to early 1930s. (Courtesy Byrd Minter Jr.)*

the Morris-Cummins channel for the bridge tender to raise the hand-cranked drawbridge. Boats and barges from a developing oil industry came and went from terminal docks on the west side of the island. On the south side, dredge boats were busy digging the Corpus Christi Ship Channel through the flats at Turtle Cove.[9]

With a tripod-mounted 8-gauge shotgun, Granville Elias "Bill" Minter shot ducks for the market on freshwater ponds north of the town of Aransas Pass. He opened Minter's Fish House in 1909, shipping ducks surreptitiously along with his fish to Saint Louis.

Bill's son Byrd first hunted ducks for the market with his father, brother, and fish house employees. While still in high school in the 1920s, Byrd started a guiding business by hauling skiffs behind his father's shrimp boat to blinds on Harbor Island. By the 1930s his customers were ferried in a twenty-eight-foot cabin boat built by Albert "One Arm" Farley of Aransas Pass. As business grew, Byrd's duck blinds eventually covered two miles of Harbor Island shoreline on the East Flats on the south side of the causeway to Port Aransas. Byrd added a thousand used decoys to his inventory and hired several guides, including Pappy Freeze, who worked with Byrd for as long as he was in business.[10]

Byrd had every duck blind ready before the opening of duck season one year in the mid-1940s, but no ducks. He telephoned his customers and advised them to come another day. That evening he took his sons to a football game, and with a light rain falling, he began to hear large flights of ducks overhead. As the wind switched hard from the north, the migrating birds fighting it started to fly lower and lower. Their path took them below the level of the stadium lights, and they began to land, exhausted, on the playing field. The game was canceled when too many redheads and pintails piled up between goal posts. Byrd went home and telephoned his customers, who all had splendid hunts the next day.

Byrd's was an operation he never had to advertise. Part of the reason was the free coverage he got from outdoors writers Andy Anderson of the *Houston Press* and Dick Freeman of the *Houston Chronicle,* both regular customers. The list of well-known clients also included champion shotgunner Grant Ilseng, the Peckmeckys of Austin's Peckmecky Sporting Goods, five-star general Hap Arnold, Mississippi senator John Stennis, Texas senator Ralph Yarborough, a young schoolteacher by the name of Lyndon Johnson, and the Hunt family. One of the Hunts' lawyers was the first of five generations who were guided by Byrd Minter.

Minter family stories live on through the young boy at that football game, Byrd Lee Minter Jr. Byrd Jr. tagged along with his father on bay hunts to Harbor Island and "blackland mud-style hunts" for geese in the fields around Tivoli, and says his father's customers were a big influence on him as he was growing up. The double-barreled L. C. Smith .410 that he and his brother used when they rode bicycles to hunt freshwater ponds near town was a gift from regular client Grant Ilseng, who taught them both how to shoot. Byrd remembers that Grant, an exhibition shooter, once snuck a 10-gauge into his blind, annoying his brother-in-law in another duck blind by shooting ducks at long distances that were headed for the brother-in-law's decoys. Byrd says his father may have been the only guide on the coast with a supply of shotgun shells during World War II, largely because Grant, who worked for Peters Ammunition, brought them.

In the 1940s the Minters each year participated in Andy Anderson's popular Annual Wild Game Dinner for Disabled Veterans, supplying birds for the Naval Hospital in Corpus Christi. Although the limit was ten ducks a person, Byrd Jr. recalls a hunt at which they shot one thousand birds for Andy's worthy cause. The hunting party included a chief state game warden as well as a federal game warden.

Customers' ducks were cleaned at Gladys's Café, a large warehouse north of the railroad tracks. Byrd Jr. has vivid memories of the twenty or so African Americans who made up Gladys's extended family as they picked ducks, danced, drank beer, and ate barbecue—all at the same time—as the piles of duck feathers grew deeper. Cleaned ducks were delivered to Byrd and the other operations in the area by local taxi drivers. Although she worked late into the night, Gladys always met Byrd and his customers early the next morning at the Bakery Café in Aransas Pass to prepared their breakfast.[11]

Byrd Jr. and his brother painted their father's twelve hundred decoys every summer for almost fifteen years. They painted them one last time in 1952 when renowned big game sport fishing and hunting guide Byrd Minter Sr. retired his duck hunting operation and sold his decoys and blinds to Dick Fox and the Texas Eastern Company.[12]

When Dick Fox settled in Aransas Pass in the early 1940s there were only seven houses on the seawall south of the railroad tracks to Harbor Island. He lived in one of the houses and managed hunting clubs from two others: the Mission Lodge and the Jess Edwards lodge, which later became Teal Lodge. By the early 1950s, Teal Lodge was purchased by Texas Eastern Gas Pipeline Co. Dick took his Texas Eastern hunters by launch to the old terminal docks at Morris-Cummins channel, then ferried them to the shallows of Harbor Island on the first airboat in the area.[13]

Gordon Sims "Pop" Spears Jr., in faded blue overalls and boat shoes with no socks, and his South Bay Hunting Club were synonymous with Aransas Pass waterfowl hunting for more than forty years. Pop was born in 1927 on the family farm on the south shore of Port Bay, where, near its hundred-acre lake, the family shot geese and sandhill cranes by the light of the moon. Pop's great-uncle Edward shot canvasbacks on the lake for Corpus Christi markets and earned extra income by guiding sportsmen at his Uncle Ed's Hunting Camp. When they couldn't pay taxes on the land after the Depression, they lost it.[14]

The Spears family resettled in Aransas Pass, where eight-year-old Pop earned money rowing customers for William Craven. The young boy soon graduated to guiding, bringing home as many as fifty birds a day to clean for extra cash. Pop did the plucking while his parents singed pin feathers over a kerosene stove, and often they were still at work when the sun came up. They were paid ten cents for the "easy birds"—the puddle ducks—and fifteen cents for the "tough" birds—canvasbacks, redheads, and bluebills.[15]

Pop Spears opened South Bay Hunting Club in 1965 with sons Mike and Gordon, and later youngest son Jamie. They built their first bay shrub boat blinds on Harbor Island and charged thirty dollars a gun to guide hunters from wooden skiffs with 10-horsepower Johnson outboards. When the Spears brothers saw Dick Fox roar across the South Bay flats in the Teal Lodge airboat, they were determined to own one as well and soon had a sixteen-foot jonboat with 110-horsepower Corvair engine.[16]

South Bay Hunting Club, like most of the lower coast outfitters, maintains its blinds on state-owned tidal waters through a gentlemen's agreement with other gunners. Sometimes it hasn't been so gentlemanly. The "BBQ blind" got its name when Gordon and Jamie built too close to one of Kirk Pruitt's blinds, and he burned theirs down; all that remained were four smoking pilings. When they told Pruitt they were going to retaliate by burning one of his blinds, Pruitt replied, "Well, you can do that, but remember, you've got twenty blinds and I got only four, so whose gonna lose more?" They called a truce.

Dick Fox of the Teal Lodge also thought the Spears brothers had built a blind too close to one of his, and to let them know it, he dropped an old refrigerator outside their decoy spread. Gordon, with Jamie and Pop's brother Roy, dragged the contraption over to one of Fox's blinds and banged holes in it with a pickax, leaving Mr. Fox to contend with ducks that flared off his decoy spread at the sight of the sinking refrigerator among his decoys.

Sometimes when they drop off customers, the Spearses find other hunters in their blinds. Jamie says, "We try to give them a little latitude and let them shoot it if we have another blind we can go to. Now cousin Craig "Moose" Kidd, if he needs to hunt a blind, he asks 'em nicely to move on, and if they don't, well, he always brings a can of lighter fluid and a lighter. He pours the stuff all around the blind. Then he stands there with his lighter—he's a big guy—and tells them they have two choices, one of which is to move on."

Pop was the second of five generations of Spearses to hunt waterfowl in Aransas Pass, and his sons Jamie and Gordon today carry on the South Bay Hunting Club tradition. The club still averages almost five thousand birds from over one thousand hunters per year. Pintails at times rise in bunches of two thousand to three thousand, and flocks of redheads still darken the sky. Wigeons follow the redheads, and there are fair numbers of gadwalls, teal, bluebills, buffleheads, and goldeneyes. Snow geese following a front occasionally overshoot the coast, turning around at daybreak, where they "just drop right in to the first [decoy] spread they spot."

In his lifetime Pop Spears saw a lot of changes come to Harbor Island. The canvasbacks disappeared. Snow goose shooting on those rare but special days when they piled into duck decoys on a blue norther was prohibited on north Harbor Island for protection of any wandering whooping cranes. Sons Jamie and Gordon now offer only a ferry service to their blinds; they stopped guiding as a result of the 1988 federal sting operation that netted them along with dozens of other guides along the Texas Gulf Coast. "Nowadays," Jamie says, "If my customers try to come in to my boat with one bird over the limit, I just call the game warden, and tell 'im I'm coming in with one. It's not good for business, but I have to do it."[17]

For Pop Spears, South Bay Hunting Club and Harbor Island were a special place where, tucked into the edge of the mangroves on a secluded pond in the "family blind," he passed on stories to his sons and then their sons. He died in 2008.

PORT ARANSAS

Hunters who made their way to the north end of Mustang Island in the 1850s found only a single dwelling, the El Mar Rancho of Robert A. Mercer. The settlement that grew up around it went by the town names of Ropesville, Tarpon, and finally, in 1910, Port Aransas. Tarpon fishing made the town famous, but winter duck shooting was every bit as good. Those that came to hunt for the market or sport used steamers and sailing scows to hunt Harbor Island and the back side of St. Joseph and Mustang Islands, or they borrowed horses to find freshwater

THE TARPON INN *at Port Aransas in the early 1900s. (Mathews Collection, courtesy Port Aransas Museum, File No. sc0065af41)*

inland ponds on Mustang Island, such as the sandy slough known for years as the Graveyard Hole.[18]

Land speculation and the taming of Aransas Pass for a deepwater port increasingly brought people to the Mustang Island fishing village in the late 1800s. Their accommodations and sporting needs were handled by Captain Frank Stephenson at the Tarpon Inn, built in 1886. The only other buildings around the inn were the Aransas lifesaving station and a few fishermen's cottages scattered among oleander and rose bushes. Despite the long journey to reach it, Tarpon Inn established a national reputation for sport, hospitality, and a dining room that provided local fish, crabs, turtles, and oysters and winter feasts of ducks, geese, and shorebirds.[19]

In 1925, Tarpon Inn owner J. M. Ellis rebuilt the inn as a forty-room, two-story building that stands today. Son Bill Ellis arranged the duck hunting. As late as the 1940s he raised flags, each with a different color or number, to let local guides know they were needed for an arriving party. Guides didn't have to spend the day watching the flagpole; the town was small enough that "everybody on the island would tell them, 'Bill's looking for you.'" Ellis and the Tarpon Inn provided guided hunts for redheads and pintails for $12.50 throughout the late 1950s.[20]

A large number of guiding operations and private sporting cubs opened in the town that grew up around the Tarpon Inn. Writer and historian Rick Pratt says that by World War I, "It seemed like everyone in town was a guide." Most of the well-known island fishing families, called boatmen in Port Aransas, took duck hunting parties in winter, including several generations of the "local" Roberts, "Florida" Roberts, Studeman, Brundrett, Mathews, Dryer, and Farley families.[21]

The earliest known private hunting club on Mustang Island was Port Aransas Club, started by Waco sportsmen in 1924. With charter members from Boston to San Francisco, the club built the Krazy Kat Inn and a dozen cottages and provided

> **DUCKS**
> ARE PLENTIFUL
> AT
> **ARANSAS PASS**
>
> Good rooms and Meals, Fast Speed Boats, Experienced Guides and an organization intent upon giving the very best service.
>
> *Rates Reasonable*
>
> **KRAZY KAT INN**
>
> Aransas Pass, Texas
> Phone or write for reservation.

(Modified from *San Antonio Express*, Jan. 13, 1928)

speedboats night and day to ferry hunters from the club wharf at Aransas Pass. Members and guests paid $12.50 a day for lodging, meals, and a guide to take them to one of the hundred duck blinds. Serious about their sport, the club hired C. W. Grubbs, a famous name in decoy manufacturing, to repair their thirty dozen decoys and organize duck calling classes for guides. One of those guides was Barney Farley, who in 1937 gained a national reputation as one of President Roosevelt's tarpon fishing guides.[22]

Port Aransas Club made a moving picture of a duck hunt in the late 1920s, featured today at the Port Aransas Museum. A rare image of the place and times, the movie shows Farley-built launches towing skiffs to blinds on Harbor Island and big groups of pintails coming in to stools of wooden decoys. The star of the film was club member Gail Borden Munsill, president of the Aransas Holding Company. Before he died at age twenty-nine in 1934, Munsill had brought electric lights, telephones, and the causeway to the island. While the buildings remained for many decades, Port Aransas Club faded from the historical record in the 1930s.[23]

Railroad executive George Myer chartered Aransas Pass Sporting Club in 1927 and sold one-hundred-dollar charter memberships to five hundred "northern capitalists." Myer's plans included building a nine-hole golf course and a grand four-story clubhouse on the beach with 150 guest rooms, café, auditorium, gymnasium, bowling alley, and billiard room. James Ed Cotter, whose résumé included working for the Tarpon Club on St. Joseph Island, was elected chairman of the board. Whether any part of the club was ever built is lost to history, for its groundbreaking coinciding with the start of the Great Depression.[24]

Port Aransas hosted a large number of guiding operations available to the public. Tarpon Inn was first, joined in the early 1900s by Cline's Resort. Built by Edward A. Cline across from the Tarpon Inn, it featured a hotel, a restaurant, and a long fishing pier where guides and hunters congregated early each morning. Cline's Resort was destroyed by the 1919 hurricane, and the family moved to Corpus Christi, where they opened another waterfowl hunting service.[25]

The Port Aransas boat basin was the center of most of the town's fishing and hunting activity. Dredged in the 1910s, it was lined with wharves, fish houses, and duck picking sheds. Sportsmen went there to arrange their hunts or to have their catches of tarpon or big game fish mounted at Ancel Brundrett and Alfred Roberts's taxidermy shop. Nearby were the Farley boat builders, who first built tarpon skiffs and then their famous narrow-hulled, open cockpit launches.[26]

Guides at the harbor included Barney Farley, who started his long career as a tarpon and duck hunting guide from a rowing skiff in the 1910s. In 1930 he opened Barney's Place, where he sold fishing tackle and ran his charter business. Although best known as one of the guides on President Roosevelt's tarpon fishing trip to Port Aransas in 1937, he was an equally proficient waterfowl guide, considered "the local authority on . . . duck hunting between Corpus Christi and

BARNEY FARLEY JR. (front, left), and Ray Farley (front, right) with Braniff airline hostesses on a hunt at Barney's Place in 1939. (Courtesy Barney Farley III)

MATHEWS'S PLACE, for a time also Barney's Place, at Port Aransas harbor. (Mathews Collection, courtesy Port Aransas Museum, File No. sc0007a81c)

Aransas Bays." Barney made newspapers throughout Texas when he guided four Braniff airline hostesses in 1939.[27]

By the late 1920s the harbor was home to Johnny Mathews, who ran his guiding business from the Silver King Café and later Mathews Place, the white building with the cupola on top advertising, "Everything for the Sportsman." Johnny in the 1950s was called the "grand old man of [Port Aransas] duck guiding" by customers who paid $12.50 a day for a tow boat service and guide at one of his thirty-two bay blinds.[28]

THIS 1930 *to 1940s Port Aransas photo is thought to show A. E. Keisling* (seated) *and his son, Roy A. Keisling. According to historian Mark Creighton, Keisling built the Delmar Yacht Basin and drowned when his skiff capsized in a storm in 1942. (Henry Studeman Collection, courtesy Port Aransas Museum, File No. 9–1)*

Other early town guides were Shorty Smith, Mac MacAuley, Henry Studeman, and Ed Tarrant. Ed opened a fishing and hunting guiding service at A. E. Keisling's Delmar Yacht Basin on Cline's Point in the 1930s and was in business for over thirty years under different names, including Skelly's and Del Mar. Fisherman's Wharf opened in the 1940s with thirty-five bay blinds managed by Winfield Hamlin and later Red Rodgers. Salt Lake Hunting Club in the 1950s rented motorboats and offered guided airboat hunts for ten dollars a day. For an additional fee sportsmen could even lease a trained retriever.[29]

Sportsmen from the 1940s to the '60s still met their guides at the harbor, but they could also arrange hunts in town at Bilmore and Son Hardware on Alister Street or at Ed Tarrant's sporting goods store. Tarrant's sign overhead read "Drug Store"—it was a drug store before he bought it, but he never bothered to take down the sign. Duck cleaning was available at Mathews Place, from Hop Roberts at the Roberts Fish Company, and at L. N. Welch's L&N Fish House. Edgar Dryer cleaned ducks at "Uncle Edgar's" pink trailer on Main Street in the 1960s and '70s. Rick Pratt recalls, "You'd take your ducks to him and he would give you half back. I don't know what he did with the other half, but I do know that if you needed ducks, you could buy his extras. His TV was always blaring, and there were feathers from floor to ceiling."[30]

Over the years the town on Mustang Island bore witness to the change from sail and steam to naphtha and gasoline engines. With motors, guides no longer had to row their clients in small skiffs from sunrise to sunset in search of tarpon. The tarpon, though, began to disappear from Port Aransas waters in the 1950s. Huge flocks of pintails and redheads could still be found on Harbor Island, but bag limit reductions in the early 1960s convinced the same guides who retired their tarpon rigs to put away their decoys. In the 1970s a limit of ten pintails breathed new life to the island's duck hunting, and some of the guides returned.

Today, most of the inland freshwater ponds at Port Aransas are gone, and new houses march over their geomorphic footprint. Harbor Island, like a scarred wetland warrior, has born channels and industrial violations with dignity, and parts of it look as it did when the market hunters first gunned there. Somewhere in the pass, in the waters once traversed by the Mercer family of bar pilots and by innumerable guides in their Farley boats, a sportsman hooks a tarpon. Behind him is the Tarpon Inn, and if his eyes weren't glued to his line, he would have seen a big knot of redheads overhead, diving for the mangroves behind the lighthouse at Harbor Island.

CORPUS CHRISTI BAY

Productive waterfowl habitat surrounded the town of Corpus Christi on Corpus Christi and Nueces Bays. At Rincon Bayou by the mouth of the Nueces River east of town, hunters who braved the mud found swarms of puddle ducks in a maze of reed and sedge-lined marsh ponds. Wet seasons brought wild cranberries, and with them, large concentrations of mallards. During periods of high water, sportsmen continued upriver to Odem Flats, a wide part of the floodplain, to shoot geese and cranes. Further upriver the floodplain narrowed between inland terraces, its banks covered by elm, hackberry, ash, and palmetto, their limbs cloaked in Spanish moss that completely blocked the sunlight.[31]

Flat-bottomed scows took hunters northeast of town to Old Ingleside and ranch lands that became Portland, or sportsmen instead went by wagon, fording the narrow oyster reef at the mouth of Nueces Bay at low tide. South of town they frequented Cayo del Oso, which separated the mainland from the peninsula of Flour Bluff. At its mouth was a two-mile-wide silled estuary constricted by white sands and brush-covered, high dunes of Ward Island, a duck hunter's paradise where a sportsman said he never brought home fewer than a hundred ducks a day.[32]

Turning the corner of Corpus Christi Bay brought the hunter to Laguna Madre by way of Laguna Shores, with its irregularly shaped shoreline of inland scrub oaks and cactus where prevailing onshore winds brought the smell of salt and decaying shoal grass. Every curve in the shoreline held diving ducks and wigeons joined by pelicans, seagulls, shorebirds, herons, and egrets. Each flock was an outburst of color and movement, the shorebirds and wigeons in constant motion, the pelicans and divers more subdued.

Sailing scows took hunters across the bay to the lee side of Padre Island, a carpet of sea oats and seacoast bluestem grasses before the Gulf side, which was stacked with drift and floating timbers poking from brilliant white sand dunes. Miles of shin oaks loaded with acorns brought whooping and sandhill cranes, and the periodic island depressions between were filled with clear fresh water and were black with ducks. Puddle ducks roosted in the maze of cuts and islands behind the promontory of Shamrock Peninsula, sheltered by thick stands of bay brush and *Spartina* grasses on high ground and the black mud of the flats marked

A Padre Island *hunt, 1901. Left to right: San Antonio hunter C. F. Michael, Archie Hall of Corpus Christi, and Corpus Christi customs agent Max Luther. (Corpus Christi Public Library, Special Collection F5, Folder No. 2.81, Item 2)*

by *Salicornia*. Big flocks of divers, pintails, and wigeons fed on the seagrass flats between Dead Man's Hole and Night Hawk Bay.[33]

The only sign of civilization on Padre Island was Patrick Dunn's cattle. Sportsmen were welcomed as long as they got permission from Dunn's offices in Corpus Christi or Brownsville or went to Padre Island next to Packery Channel to Dunn's one-story, shellcrete ranch house tucked into the live oaks behind a wood corral. Edmund C. Westervelt had Dunn's consent to hunt the island in the early 1900s, and to get there he paddled a canoe across Laguna Madre. It usually took him only two hours to kill seventy-five ducks.[34]

Sportsmen visiting Corpus Christi after the Civil War relied on stage coach service or rode horseback along old trading routes from San Antonio. By water they had a number of choices: steamers of the Morgan's Louisiana and Texas Railroad and Steamship Company, which left Galveston every Tuesday and Friday, or the mail boat from Indianola, which sailed to Corpus Christi three times a week. With favorable winds, the schooner *Hettie May* could make the trip between Point Isabel and Corpus Christi in twenty hours. When the SA&AP railroad came to town in the 1880s, it changed everything.[35]

The SA&AP recognized the value of sportsmen to its business. The railroad published regular hunting and fishing reports and ran advertisements such as, "A few days of duck hunting will do you good." Special hunters' tickets, priced at four cents a mile, were available in 1890 from San Antonio to Aransas Pass, Rockport, and Corpus Christi. Along the route, engineers dropped hunters off and later picked them up by the side of the tracks. According to local historian Murphy Givens, "Boys who had been hunting ducks on the Portland side would cross [the wooden trestle bridge across the narrows of Nueces Bay]. If a train arrived, they would drop down and hold on to the ties until it passed over."[36]

DUCK HUNTERS *crossing the SA&AP railroad trestle to Corpus Christi, 1903. Ducks and gear were hauled using a cart built to the gauge of the rail tracks. (Courtesy Jim Moloney)*

With rail access, the Corpus Christi area became a popular destination for both Texas and northern sportsmen. Newspapers sang the praises of its bays, "in which the redhead duck, the pintail, the canvasback, mallard, and green-winged teal come in thousands." Author Emerson Hough wrote in *Forest and Stream* of exceptional canvasback shooting in the late 1800s. So many ducks covered Corpus Christi Bay in December 1905 they formed a floating island, a "phenomenon" ten miles long. Swans were common in hunters' bags before the turn of the century. San Patricio and Aransas County rancher George W. Fulton Jr. killed nine of the great white birds and ninety-eight geese on the north shore of Corpus Christi Bay in 1887, and a swan shot south of town in 1892 had a wingspan of seven feet.[37]

In the late 1800s, hotels such as the Alexander, Crescent, Constantine, and St. James arranged sporting excursions for out-of-town guests. The Constantine, run by "old time hotel man" Nic Constantine, was the gathering place for duck hunters and boat captains who traded yarns by the hotel fireplace. The meeting place of Colonel Patrick Dunn and his cronies was the St. James Hotel. Having grown weary of exaggerated sporting stories told around the bar, they founded the Mysterious 8 Club, a social club in which the only by-law was truth-telling in Corpus Christi fishing and hunting pursuits.[38]

Only a few organized hunting clubs appear to have been in operation on Corpus Christi and Nueces Bays during the late 1800s; their heyday was not until after World War I. The first hugely popular commercial operation was not a club

TRAVELING HUNTERS *at the SA&AP rail depot in Corpus Christi, 1907. (Courtesy Bell/Whittington Library, Portland, Texas, File No. 104945)*

A PROMOTIONAL POSTCARD *of a Corpus Christi Bay duck hunt, 1900. The party was made up of Tennessee and Wisconsin sportsmen aboard the schooner* Lloyd Van Hook. *Corpus Christi Captain J. W. Long is in far back, and the deaf mute deck hand "Dummy" is to far left. (Corpus Christi Public Library, Special Collection F6, Folder No. 2.09, Item 1; caption from Institute of Texan Cultures, San Antonio, File No. 80–147).*

at all and had no fancy lodge or annual dues—it was a cattle tank on Gum Hollow Creek. Located in San Patricio County, Gum Hollow was known throughout Texas and the United States in the late 1800s.

East of Corpus Christi on the Coleman-Fulton Pasture Company (CFP) Picatche Pasture, Gum Hollow Creek formed a small, arcuate sand delta where it drained into the north side of Nueces Bay. Saltwater intermittently intruded long distances up its floodplain, and the mesquite and scrub prairie on its banks was home to antelope, jackrabbits, and rattlesnakes. It would have been hard to imagine this landscape as one of Texas's most famous duck hunting habitats. But when CFP built an earthen dam across the creek in the late 1800s, it created a one-hundred-acre cattle tank, a freshwater oasis that attracted huge circling flocks of redheads, sprigs, bluebills, and late-season canvasbacks.[39]

Sportsmen followed the birds, first on horseback and then by the SA&AP railway with connections in San Antonio, Corpus Christi, and later Portland. Visitors camped or rented rooms at Melissa Ann Smith's Portland boarding house and

Two well-dressed *hunters and their guide* (right) *returning from Gum Hollow. (Courtesy Bell/ Whittington Library, Portland, Texas, File No. 104939)*

made their way to Gum Hollow dam by horse and wagon. Gunners never needed decoys or blinds; they simply stood in thick cane that grew on the dam and shot passing ducks. Enterprising local boys made good money by fetching and cleaning birds, which were iced and shipped from the Portland SA&AP depot.[40]

Corpus Christi and San Antonio hunters ruled Gum Hollow's roost in the 1890s. On one shoot, San Antonio Gun Club members killed 927 ducks, bested only by Corpus Christi hunters with their total of over 1,000 ducks on an 1898 outing. Visiting Texas gunners who descended on Gum Hollow included hunters from Austin, Waco, Fort Worth, and Dallas. One Dallas entourage arrived in a special car so luxuriously fitted that they had "every comfort aboard that one would enjoy at home."[41]

Hunters from throughout the country made the pilgrimage to Gum Hollow as well. Orator and statesman William Jennings Bryan hunted there with Texas senator John Willacy. Samuel Clemens boarded a train bound for Portland, forgoing the attention he would have garnered if he had used his pen name Mark Twain. Executives from Parker Brothers Gun Company came in 1896, and when "champion one-barrel shot" Pete Murphy visited from Philadelphia, San Antonio hunters named a narrow spit in Gum Hollow Lake after him. John Mackie, of the Peters Cartridge Company, planned a three-day trip that was cut short when he used up all his ammunition in a single day, the ducks "thick as flies." When a party of New York bankers arrived in their private car, San Antonio pundits reported the ducks were quite safe, as the hunters fired a lot of ammunition but could "scarcely wing a bird."[42]

Increasingly annoyed at the crowds, San Antonio hunters complained when eighteen shooters on the dam on a Sunday morning "blazed away at every duck

Hunters on *the dam at Gum Hollow with a pile of diving ducks, probably mostly redheads, early 1900s. Note the bird dogs, which were likely used for retrieving duties. (Courtesy Bell/Whittington Library, Portland, Texas, File No. 104942)*

in sight" and made the ducks wild, their shooting "difficult." Four San Antonio gunners were said to "have held the dam against all comers" in 1897 and had the good fortune to fire one thousand rounds. In an effort to control the volume of sportsmen, CFP superintendent C. E. H. Glazebrook required visitors to apply for a hunting permit and posted regulations in San Antonio papers. One rule read: "No gun shall be fired before sun-up or after sun-down, and shooting [is] to be confined to the flight of birds over the dam." More hunters brought more restrictions, and in 1899 Glazebrook added that ducks could be taken only on the wing. When he limited the number that could be killed to fifty per gun, his may have been the first daily bag limit in Texas.[43]

By the early 1900s a small, single-story lodge was built for hunters, managed by Edwin C. "Ed" and George Fisher. A hired game warden collected a fee of a dollar a day. Hunters were required to sign the new state game law affidavit that they did not kill more than the recently mandated daily limit of twenty-five ducks. Ducks were still so plentiful that "within an hour or so" it was not a problem for the sportsman to "kill his limit of 25 birds."[44]

When President Taft came to town in 1909, visiting hunters were no longer welcome at Gum Hollow. Ranch hunting became a strictly private affair, and a very well appointed one. George W. Fulton, who had first brought his thirsty cows to the gully on the bay only a few decades earlier, would not have recog-

A LARGE BAG *of mostly pintails and redheads at Delmar Place, early 1900s. Corpus Christi's Roy Aldridge (seated, front center) was a captain and owner of the Delmar guest cottages. The only others identified are Craig, in the white shirt, and Everhart, in the white hat. (Corpus Christi Public Library, Special Collection F6, Folder No. 2.09, Item 3)*

nized his ranch, renamed Taft Ranch as the town of Taft was carved from the prairie in preparation for the president's visit. A thirty-five-room mansion was built with a garage to house six new automobiles. An electric light and ice plant was constructed, a new yacht ordered from the Great Lakes, and a golf course sculpted from the scrub. In Gregory, the Hotel Green was built for the president's entourage and connected to the ranch's ten miles of new gravel roads by a boulevard with four hundred palm trees planted along it. The ducks came along with the president in October 1909, but the shocked *San Antonio Light and Gazette* proclaimed that Taft "Will Not Shoot Ducks." He preferred golf.[45]

The next year, duck shooting at Gum Hollow was used to lure investors to the new luxurious "seaside and winter resort" of Portland. The reign of the once popular hunting spot ended a few years later when a storm washed out Gum Hollow dam.[46]

From the dam at Gum Hollow, San Antonio sportsman Oscar Guessaz watched as flights of ducks headed east to the T. P. McCampbell Ranch. When Gum Hollow closed, Guessaz, with a group of San Antonio, Dallas, and Waco sportsmen, chartered the new Ingleside Gun and Rod Club on McCampbell Ranch. The club property extended from the coast several miles inland and, like Gum Hollow, included freshwater cattle tanks. A modern clubhouse built in 1911 accommodated one hundred guests and had an eighteen-hole golf course.[47]

Closer to Corpus Christi, duck hunts and "sea side outings" were advertised at Delmar Place, on what is now Ocean Drive. South of the city, hunters followed a shell road to the grand Alta Vista Hotel, with its fifteen-hundred-foot dock,

UNDATED PHOTO *of Corpus Christi hunters aboard a finely fitted motor yacht. Note the bay laurels on the upper deck used for skiff blinds. (Corpus Christi Public Library, Special Collection F1, Folder No. 24.11, Item 5)*

two-story pavilion, fleet of steam launches, and custom fishing tackle and gun room. Sporting parties from the north sometimes stayed for months at a time. The hotel provided skiffs, ammunition, and decoys and hired Captain Andrew Anderson for hunting excursions to Padre and Mustang Islands. The grounds were still so wild in 1908 that a three-foot "leopard cat" was killed near the hotel. By 1913 visiting sportsmen found respite at the elegant Nueces Hotel on the bay.[48]

Duck hunting and private sporting clubs were a critical part of advertising schemes used to attract investors to the Corpus Christi Bay area. In 1890 Elihu Ropes, the man who first tried to build a channel across Mustang Island, promoted his new development at Flour Bluff by advertising abundant ducks, geese, snipes, plovers, and green sea turtles. In 1911 Harbor City Development built Ingleside Inn and offered duck blinds in front of the property. When demand was too great for the number of available rooms, guests stayed in fifty two-room tents. One of the last developments to advertise waterfowl hunting to encourage land sales was Remington Lodge on Flour Bluff, where H. H. Friar in 1927 built a hunting lodge, one hundred cottages, manicured shell streets, a pier, and a number of duck blinds. Remington Lodge and its subdivision survived the Great Depression but were condemned by the government in 1941 for the naval air training station at Flour Bluff.[49]

By the turn of the century sailing scows were joined on Corpus Christi waterways each winter by private yachts sailed south by wealthy sportsmen. Joseph

> ## *Hunting—Fishing*
>
> The best fishing on the coast on Padre Island at the Pass and the Shell Banks. The best duck and goose shooting at the south end of Mustang and adjacent islands.... and a smooth beach over 100 miles long, the ideal outing grounds of the southwest.
>
> **Tickets on sale at the Causeway.**
>
> Open Day and Night
> THE PICNIC GROUND
> OF ALL SOUTHWEST
>
> **Padre Island Causeway Company**

(Modified from *Corpus Christi Times,* Dec. 3, 1927)

Pulitzer Jr. of the Saint Louis and New York publishing family brought his gasoline launch *Granada II* for winter duck hunting trips between 1911 and 1918. Like Pulitzer, a group of Oklahoma businessmen kept their yacht, the *Tawnie,* in the Corpus Christi turning basin for winter hunting and year-round fishing.[50]

By the 1920s the automobile began to have as big an impact on sport hunting as the SA&AP railway did forty years earlier. City hunters and their automobiles became inseparable, their cars taking them around Corpus Christi and Nueces Bays and across the new Don Patricio Causeway to Padre Island, where hunting permits were sold by the Padre Island Causeway Company. Hunters in cars following narrow wooden tracks over the bay found it took "very little effort to bag the limit of ducks and some geese during a few hours of hunting." Reed Automobile Company even sold used cars by explaining to hunters that mud and salt air could ruin the family car, their logic being that it was best to buy a "reconditioned" one for hunting.[51]

Restaurants and diners catered to local sportsmen. Nixon's Café, for example, during the 1930s offered to cook wild ducks that customers brought in. Duck picking businesses opened, the largest being "the sanitary plant" of Williams Poultry and Egg Co. Local newspapers heralded the arrival of the outdoor sports writer, and Corpus had some of the best. "Uncle Jeff" in the 1920s and '30s wrote hunting and fishing articles for the *Corpus Christi Times;* he was followed by Byron B. Buzbee and his column, "Buzzin' Outdoors Sports." Writers for the *Corpus Christi Caller-Times* in the 1940s and '50s were Buster Haas, author Hart Stilwell, and for a long time Roy Swann, who six days a week put his stories together within the yellow walls of Vernon's BBQ. Today sportsmen follow the writing of Davis Sikes.[52]

The list of Corpus Christi Bay area sporting operations in the 1920s was long. Ernest Powell offered goose hunting near the Don Patricio Causeway, with guided duck shoots at Shamrock Cove. Outfitter Rex Allen advertised "real shooting and finest accommodations" at Little Duck Lake on the north end of Padre Island. Flour Bluff was home to guides Sam Jeletich and the Edward A. Cline family. Located on Concrete (Oso) Road, the Clines provided decoys and boats with bay duck hunts and goose shooting at Alta Vista Point.

Guide Randolph Carter made newspapers across Texas in 1930 when his client, Dr. Bullard of the US Veterans' Hospital, was hit in the head by a falling duck and knocked unconscious. The party, which at first thought him to be dead, was much relieved when the initial diagnosis proved to be wrong. Carter was still taking parties in the years before World War II, hunting near Allen's Wharf and Pita Island off Flour Bluff.[53]

E. B. "Red" Tyler started Red's Place in 1948 at Laguna Shores with three rental boats and a bait house. By 1955 he had sixty-three skiffs and a boat harbor. Red dug a channel to Pita Island, where, for $3.50 a day, hunters were towed to bay blinds for redheads, pintails, and wigeons. Red's Place offered goose hunting on the southeast side of Chapman Ranch, where customers were instructed to meet each morning at the King Ranch fence.[54]

In the late 1940s Laguna Madre Sportsman's Club built a fishing and hunting lodge with cabins, boats, and duck blinds on Flour Bluff near the Humble Channel. George E. Gibbons Jr. offered day hunting on his farm at the end of Staples Road on the Chapman Ranch side of Oso Creek. George didn't charge a fee, sportsmen needed only to get permission at his office on North Port Street. Because of its sandy bluffs and freshwater pond fed by a windmill, puddle ducks gathered there in good numbers, and on windy days redheads came from the bay. Grandson Billy Sheka, who runs Bill Sheka Jr. Outdoors, says as Corpus Christi grew, the pond was so close to town "it must have been the most poached spot in Corpus."[55]

By the 1950s Wright's Duck Hunting Service on Padre Island provided tow boats to their bay blinds, each provisioned with twenty-four decoys, for ten dollars per gun. A&H Sporting Goods hunted Padre Island, ferrying customers by airboat to salt flats on the west side of the island. Guests of the Robert Driscoll Hotel downtown arranged duck hunts through the concierge, where fourteen dollars covered lodging and blinds on Laguna Shores, with decoys provided. The commander of the Corpus Christi Naval Air Station (NAS) had a dozen duck blinds built for active and retired military on Laguna Madre in 1954. The NAS Boat Club ran a boat shuttle service for hunters, who were provided with a bright orange flag to hoist when they were ready to leave the blind.[56]

Many Corpus Christi guides shuttered their doors when the season was closed on redheads in 1957 and again for four years between 1960 and 1963. The local boys kept hunting, and Billy Sheka remembers that during the 1960s, high

> **CLINE'S FLOUR BLUFF**
>
> 12 miles on concrete road. Phone 9010-F2 for reservations Good bags the rule. Rates reasonable. Guides, decoys, boats furnished.

(Modified from *Corpus Christi Times*, Dec. 21, 1932)

> **DUCK HUNTING**
>
> Rates: $5.00 half a day, with guide, one or two people. $8.00 all day, one or two people.
>
> **RANDOLPH CARTER**
> ALLEN'S WHARF,
> PITA ISLAND

(Modified from *Corpus Christi Times*, Nov. 1, 1940)

school boys after classes hunted some of the old duck blinds that still remained along Laguna Shores. "There were so many ducks," he says, "it was ridiculous." After a hunt they took their harvest to the staff of the Corpus Christi Country Club "until we gave them so many they stopped taking them."[57]

Although liberal bag limits returned in the late 1960s, guided hunting was slow to rebound. When Doug Bird came south from Canada in the 1960s, he couldn't believe the number of ducks around Corpus Christi and was puzzled that hardly anyone hunted them. He opened Doug's Guide Service in 1968 and took customers to Night Hawk Bay on the flats behind Padre Island. When he bought his first airboat, he hunted the flats behind Pita Island at the end of Laguna Shores, where Red Tyler once guided.[58]

At his peak Doug had five guides, expanding the operation to include a camp south of Baffin Bay at the farthest end of the Upper Laguna Madre, called the Graveyard, or Nine Mile Hole. Doug offered two-day packages in which every other morning he loaded his Robalo 23 with gunning and fishing gear, diesel fuel, water, and eight to ten hunters for the thirty-mile crossing. It was worth the journey; there were so many ducks that, if he could convince his hunters not to shoot endless decoying redheads, he delivered straps of ten pintails for each customer.

Though the greater Canada geese were gone, inland farmers still had trouble keeping specklebellies and lesser Canadas out of their pea fields. Doug followed those geese nearly to San Antonio. He remembers one of the largest roosts was at A. A. McGregor's place at Odem Flats on the Nueces River floodplain, where, among the saltgrass and mosquitoes, there were "so many rattlesnakes you were not allowed on the ranch unless you drove or rode a horse." Hunters could still book with Doug's Guide Service until 2007, although Doug had to quit guiding in 1997 for health reasons related to his service in the Vietnam War.[59]

As in Houston on the upper coast, Corpus Christi's mad rush for deepwater ports, industry, and development has come at the expense of most of its spectacular wildfowl habitat. On the edge of Nueces Bay, North Beach was cut off by a deepwater port, and the flats at Rincon Point became the Nueces Bay causeway landing. The shooting grounds east of downtown, all the way to the upper Laguna Madre, are now concrete, and new land development extends south past Oso Creek and west up the Nueces River to the wind farms at Odem Flats. Padre Island National Seashore provides respite, but not without having to dodge proposals to use it as a navy bombing range and as a giant spaceport. Corpus Christi sportsmen have lost something very special.[60]

CHAPTER 14

LAGUNA MADRE

Bordered by the mainland on one side and by over a hundred miles of Padre Island white sand on the other, the hypersaline lagoon of Laguna Madre was a continuous body of water until wind-blown Holocene sand deposits—the Coastal Sand Sheet—divided it into upper and lower water bodies. Duck hunters familiar with the marsh grass and mud of the rest of the Texas coast found Laguna Madre an entirely different place. Its waters were crystal clear, three feet deep in most places, with a hard bottom and little boot-sucking mud. The water's edge in many places was lined with high dunes of clay and sand. For a long time there were no large towns between Corpus Christi and Brownsville, and sportsmen shared the coast with more cattle than people.[1]

Laguna Madre's underwater garden of widgeon, shoal, turtle, and manatee grasses brought more redheads than any other place in the United States; waterfowl biologists estimated over a million redheads wintered on Laguna Madre before the 1950s. Bart Ballard, of the Texas A&M University–Kingsville Caesar Kleberg Wildlife Institute, still sees flocks five miles long, with wintering numbers of three hundred thousand to eight hundred thousand ducks. Redhead concentrations are so large, Bart says, that they uproot acres of seagrass that, collecting in huge floating islands, are blown ashore and provide pintails, wigeons, and even more redheads with a second opportunity to feed.[2]

In some places, particularly around Arroyo Colorado, there were sometimes as many pintails as redheads. Robert Singleton, chief of coastal waterfowl studies for the Texas Game and Fish Commission, observed a single flock of half a million pintails in the mid-1950s. The profusion of ducks on the Arroyo Colorado shoreline was often joined by geese and cranes that crossed Laguna Madre from their roosts on Padre Island.[3]

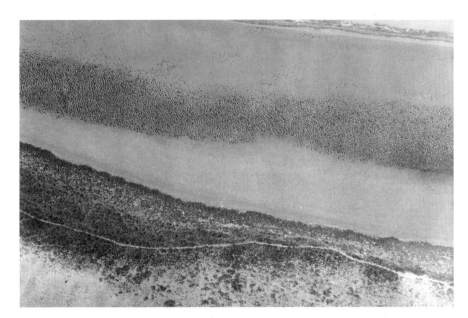

A Bob Singleton *aerial photo, from the early 1950s, of pintails concentrated in Laguna Madre. (Courtesy Charles Stutzenbaker)*

Too many *bluebills and redheads to count on Arroyo Colorado, 1950. (Courtesy Shannon Tompkins)*

Waterfowl traditionally left Laguna Madre feeding grounds to access inland freshwater ponds intermittently filled by only rainfall or natural springs. When James C. Fulton of Aransas Steam Mills dug the first wind-powered wells to water cattle in 1885, he created a source of abundant fresh water on the edge of Laguna Madre. Fulton's Portales Tanks south of Oso Creek, for example, were a quarter of a mile wide by half a mile long and usually covered bank to bank with waterfowl. As grass plains were converted to croplands, the new food supply provided wildfowl with another reason to move inland.[4]

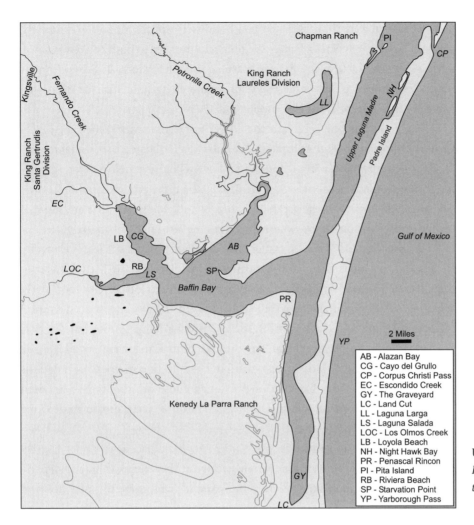

Upper Laguna Madre *and* Baffin Bay *as they appeared around the turn of the twentieth century.*

UPPER LAGUNA MADRE

North to south, Upper Laguna Madre extends from Corpus Christi Bay to the Coastal Sand Sheet. Areas bounding Upper Laguna Madre encompass a wide variety of habitat, including Padre Island freshwater ponds, the saline waters of Baffin Bay, and the prairie, pasture, and cattle tanks of King and Chapman Ranches.

The 34,631-acre Phillip Chapman Ranch was carved from the King Ranch Laureles Division in 1919. Chapman Ranch cattle lands were quickly converted to food crops, with thousands of acres of peas, corn, and winter wheat irresistible to greater and lesser Canada, snow, and specklebelly geese. By the 1930s farmers complained of crop destruction by the feeding birds, and their hired hands patrolled farm roads to drive geese away with rifles. The farmer's loss was the sportsman's gain, and for the next four decades Chapman Ranch was a premier goose hunting locality that by the 1950s had attracted thousands of hunters.[5]

Passing miles of truck crops interrupted by small, hipped-roof tenant houses, Chapman Ranch hunters saw long lines of geese—so many that sports writers used words such as "hordes" and "goose-infested" to describe their numbers. Corpus Christi's Billy Sheka Jr. says the only requirement to hunt them was a permit that was available at ranch headquarters, the ranch store, or Eweul Prince's house, where Prince "answered the door with a shotgun at his side [that] you could see through the wooden Venetian slats."[6]

The bounty of inland geese was shared by most of the nearby ranches. At Luby Farm near Robstown, San Antonian Kate Luby Shaffer hosted the annual Johnny Shaffer memorial hunt, a social and outdoor event held every November. According to San Antonio outdoor writer Fred Maly, the most common goose in their bag during the 1950s was the greater Canada. By 1966 Maly didn't see any more of the big birds. He didn't know where they went, he just knew they were gone.[7]

A decade after Maly saw his last greater Canadas, most of the lesser Canadas, snows, and specklebellies had disappeared as well. Driving the back roads over the scrub first walked by Mifflin Kenedy a hundred years earlier, outdoor writer Roy Swann remarked that the number of geese didn't "raise the interest in wading into the mud and black goo." By 1977 Chapman Ranch goose hunting was written about in the past tense, as "once noted for its Canada and lesser Canada goose concentrations." Most people attribute the decline in goose populations south of Corpus Christi, like that of the famed goose hunting region between Austwell and Tivoli, to fall tilling of cropland. The birds, according to guide Doug Bird, simply had nothing to eat.[8]

Between Corpus Christi Bay and Baffin Bay and adjacent to upper Laguna Madre is Laguna Larga. The first people to gaze at this extensive inland depression were Native Americans, followed by Spaniards who came to water herds of cattle and mustangs. Laguna Larga was originally covered by the Spanish land grant Rincon de los Laureles, and in 1868 it became part of Mifflin Kenedy's Laureles Ranch. Later it was owned by Texas Land and Cattle Company (TLC), and finally, the King Ranch Laureles Division.[9]

Early travelers to the huge freshwater basin found no mesquite and huisache shrubs, only open bluestem grasslands. Natural fires that swept the land every few years restricted the shinnery oaks, now a continuous belt to Baffin Bay, to only scattered mottes. The lake in wet years could cover sixteen square miles, and some years it went dry. Rain brought rejuvenation, and with it spike rush, widgeon grass, and stands of bulrushes and cattails returned.[10]

Laguna Larga held every duck known to the Central Flyway as well as geese and sandhill and whooping cranes. The only sportsmen to witness its immense flights of wildfowl in the late 1800s were guests of Captain John Tod, manager of TLC. By the early 1900s, guests were invited by King Ranch manager Richard Mifflin Kleberg Sr. In Kleberg's days only a few whooping cranes remained, but snow geese were abundant enough that a visitor in 1919 thought the lakeshore was covered in snow. Along with the thousands of snow geese were greater and lesser Canada geese, but among the flocks of white in 1921 was only one blue goose.[11]

Goose hunt *in 1928 on the King Ranch Laureles Division. Hunters on the trip were John R. Allen, A. Wakinner, Frank Sparks, John R. Tompkins, Frank Moffett, and Frank Williamson. (Corpus Christi Public Library, Special Collection F1, Folder No. 24.11, Item 3)*

One visitor said Kleberg harvested snow geese on ranch pastures "by taking his big Packard car and run[ning] towards them on the prairies at 60 mph." Kleberg over the years maintained a suitable fleet of vehicles for the task, including his 1949 Buick Eight equipped with a special transmission, oversized tires, radio-telephone, barometer, gun racks, and a bar. The beige car, affectionately named El Kineño, had leather jump seats affixed to the front fenders with seat belts to secure shooters during mad dashes around Laguna Larga.[12]

Decades later, Laguna Larga still held huge numbers of snow geese. Waterfowl biologist Bart Ballard once saw flocks not in the open pastures but deep in the scrub, and they had to dodge mesquite trees to come into his decoys. He had never seen anything like it in his life.[13]

Steamboat captain Richard King started what became the giant King Ranch near Santa Gertrudis Creek in 1853. When King first arrived, ducks mostly congregated on natural drainage systems of Petronila, Escondido, Salada, and Los Olmos Creeks, their narrow floodplains etched into low, sandy bluffs covered with yucca and sea ox-eye daisy. That changed when King built dams to water his cattle and created the huge waterfowl roosting areas of Tranquitas and Escondido Lakes. Pastures adjacent to the roosts brought flocks of snow geese, and when King Ranch's Mexican cowboys, or vaqueros, wanted birds for the pot, they galloped into the geese and, using long, plaited rawhide whips, killed several on the wing as they rose in front of the horses.[14]

Kingsville, founded in 1904 as a depot for the first trains between Houston and Brownsville, was headquarters for King Ranch sporting guests. In the 1940s, King Ranch offered the public limited duck and goose hunting opportunities; the ranch even provided vehicles and employees as guides. In the early 1950s, one-day hunting invitations were extended to Kleberg County residents, and the ranch's "sportsmen guests" one year harvested more than six hundred geese and nearly seven hundred ducks. The Kingsville Naval Auxiliary Air Station (NAAS) Sportsman's Association was given access to hunt waterfowl on the ranch in the 1950s.[15]

Shallow Laguna Madre waters meet Baffin Bay between Point of Rocks and Penascal Rincon. Against yellow and gray bluffs of sand and clay, the shallow shorelines of Baffin and Alazan Bays, Cayo del Grullo, and Laguna Salada were once black with ducks, especially at the mouths of mud flats and adjacent inland freshwater ponds. Encompassed by King and Kenedy Ranches, and far from any large towns, Baffin Bay heard scarcely a shot near the turn of the century—a time when sportsmen's guns were roaring on the Texas upper coast.

The first commercial hunting service on Baffin Bay was likely Theodore F. Koch's two-story Buena Vista Hotel, built in 1908 on Ebony Hill overlooking Laguna Salada. Dubbed "Headquarters for Hunters," the resort hotel brought guests from as far away as Chicago on the new Baffin Bay and Western Railroad, a spur track off the main Saint Louis, Brownsville & Mexico Railway. Guides rowed customers out in skiffs from the long hotel pier for shoots of redheads, pintails, wigeons, and mottled ducks. The magical days of the Buena Vista Hotel and its railroad were short-lived, and the resort hotel fell victim to hurricanes in 1916 and 1919.[16]

It was another thirty years before Pete Riskin opened Loyola Hunting Club on Baffin Bay. By then, oars were replaced by outboard motors, with Riskin providing a tow boat service to his blinds in the 1940s and early '50s. Most mornings the only guns his hunters heard were their own. By 1957, hunters rented boats from Alvie and Cleo Kraatz at Kraatz Boat and Bait Camp, located on the grounds of the old Buena Vista Hotel.[17]

The west and south sides of Baffin Bay are part of the Kenedy La Parra Ranch. Before wind farms, the horizon was covered in oak mottes and solitary stands of Spanish bayonet in a medley of wiregrass, bluestem, and cactus. Prairie playa potholes speckled the landscape, in wet years holding huge numbers of pintails, wigeons, and occasional mallards. It was not an area the public often got a chance to hunt. The only known commercial guide was W. Randall of Falfurrias, who brought hunters by wagon to hunt shorebirds and geese in the early 1900s.[18]

From Baffin Bay to the southern boundary of King Ranch at Port Mansfield, Laguna Madre waters begin to lose the battle with the Coastal Sand Sheet. Duck hunters found this piece of coastline very different from anywhere else in Texas. There was a grain to the land formed by topographic ridges of wind-blown sand and clay. Global adventurer and writer Van Campen Heilner, who hunted here in the 1930s, thought the sand hills stretched "to eternity." Shallow evaporative ponds between ridges of oak trees and grassland held big numbers of ducks during wet years, their waters changing color with the amount of blue green algae left by wind-blown tides.[19]

The last gasp of Upper Laguna Madre waters and shallow sand tidal flats goes by the name Graveyard, or Nine Mile Hole. Here, the bay laps onto sand dunes and high mud hills, called *lomas* and *potreros,* without the wide growths of marsh grass present nearly everywhere else in Texas where water meets land. Corpus Christi guide Doug Bird hunted the Graveyard and remembered sometimes endless numbers of redheads, pintails, and wigeons. Billy Sheka, running his boat wide open at night, reached out and caught a low-flying redhead. Bart Ballard once figured he saw a million and a half shorebirds mixed in with a flock of eighty thousand redheads, the sweeping, swirling mass of birds covering eight miles.[20]

LOWER LAGUNA MADRE

Past the Graveyard, the Coastal Sand Sheet extends through the King Ranch Norias Division and Redfish Bay, gradually giving way to Arroyo Colorado floodplain and delta deposits. An ancient arm of the Rio Grande, Arroyo Colorado was once deep enough for sloops to travel upstream to Harlingen. South of Arroyo Colorado, the north–south trending Lower Laguna Madre is crossed by delta sediments of the Rio Grande. The verdant freshwater corridor of the Rio Grande stands in marked contrast to the sand dunes of South Padre Island, where Laguna Madre waters make their way to the Gulf through Brazos Santiago Pass.[21]

Long lines of redheads and pintails crossed bluestem grasses, cactus, oak mottes, and brilliant white sand dunes as they headed for freshwater ponds and cattle tanks on the King Ranch Norias Division. Norias patriarch Caesar Kleberg was usually the only person hunting them. When Kleberg had company from outside the ranch, they had to come by horseback or stagecoach, a long journey before the Kings and Klebergs, among others, brought the Saint Louis, Brownsville and Mexico Railway through the ranch in 1904.[22]

When the first train pulling six varnished private cars arrived at Norias, it at last provided visiting sportsmen with a modern form of transportation. The depot and its new hotel bustled in winters with guests of Caesar Kleberg and the King Ranch. The sporting list was impressive, made up of railroad barons; naturalists from the American Museum of Natural History in New York City; military officers; politicians, such as Texas governor Neff and William Jennings Bryan; humorist Will Rogers; and Hollywood stars who included Roy Rogers.[23]

From the Norias social and sporting oasis it was easy to forget that well into the 1900s a war was being waged between King Ranch fence riders and cattle rustlers and bandits. King Ranch riders enforced not only Texas law but also King Ranch law, and history had taught them to expect the worst. In the 1930s, when many of those crossing King Ranch fences were no longer stealing cattle but instead poaching, the stage was set for violent confrontation. Three hunters disappeared or were found dead in the mid-1930s. In 1936, San Perlita farmers

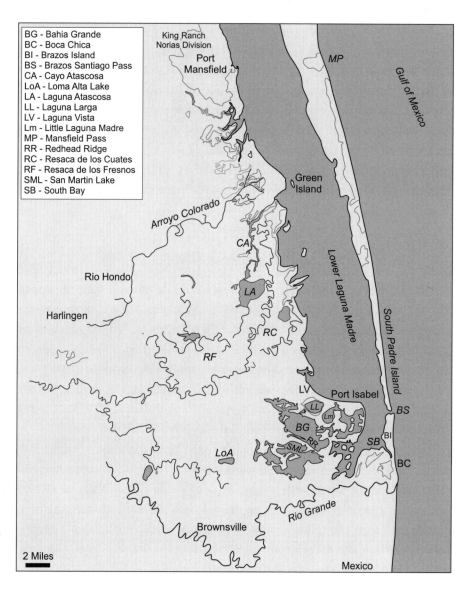

Lower Laguna Madre *and Rio Grande before dredging of the Intracoastal Canal and Brownsville Ship Channel.*

Luther and John Blanton crossed the King Ranch fence to hunt ducks and were never seen again.[24]

The case of the missing duck hunters was intensely followed in Texas and throughout the nation. A 1936, *Time* magazine reported that area citizens, tired of King Ranch and South Texas justice, took matters into their own hands and gathered arms, intent on invading the ranch. It took Texas Ranger captain William McMurray to convince them to declare a truce.[25]

State newspapers tried to make sense of the case as it wound its way through odd twists and turns. A Texas Ranger named Louis Lamadrid announced he would head the investigation, but it was discovered that he was an imposter. Two suspects were rounded up by legitimate lawmen, but when a Raymondville judge imposed a fine and jail sentence, it was not against the suspects but the legitimate lawmen, for contempt of court. The case was never solved. Local sympathy for the poachers withered two years later when one shot and killed Game Warden Dawson R. Murchison while he was patrolling the ranch.[26]

A hundred years after rail delivered Caesar Kleberg's guests to the Norias Division, Bart Ballard saw firsthand what they must have witnessed. Hunting a four-acre pond, he watched a line of redheads—fifty birds wide and a mile and a half long—come inland from the Laguna Madre nearly nonstop for thirty minutes. Bart put down his gun and watched as each bird touched down for no more than half a minute, then departed to make room for the next wave of birds.[27]

It took days by wagon at the turn of the century to reach the southern end of King Ranch at Redfish Landing, later Port Mansfield. When the first automobile traveled here in 1907, vaqueros tied ropes to their saddle horns to pull the car through deep sand. The first paved road reached the twenty cottages of what would be Port Mansfield after the hurricane of 1933. Visiting sportsmen had to find a local waterman willing to guide them on shoots until the 1950s, when San Antonian Clyde Conoly opened Redfish Courts. Conoly offered tourist cottages with ten duck blinds on Redfish Bay on the edge of Laguna Madre and took goose hunters inland to truck farms.[28]

South of Port Mansfield a new sporting destination, served by the depot towns of Raymondville and Harlingen, was opened when the Saint Louis, Brownsville and Mexico Railway connected Cameron County with the rest of Texas in the spring of 1904. It had been a hard land to civilize, a haven for outlaws, Civil War deserters, and cattle rustlers from both sides of the border. As late as the 1900s, game wardens assigned to the region called it the "lawless corridor."[29]

Before it was called Harlingen it was a mesquite thicket, then, with a few houses and saloons, it became "Six Shooter Junction" and "Rattlesnake Junction." Leonidas C. "Lon" Hill, founder and the "father of Harlingen," was a devoted duck and goose hunter who courted investors on hunting excursions to Brownsville, Point Isabel, and the Arroyo Colorado. He provided local sportsmen with access to his Rincon Ranch, where for two dollars a day they hunted Tule Lake and even over plots of experimental rice.[30]

Hill had one foot in the Old West and one in the future. The two revolvers he wore wherever he went were not just for show; he was known to draw them, as in 1906, when he shot and killed nemesis Theodore Dix. Hill the sportsman hunted by horseback until the first automobiles huffed and puffed into the Valley, and from then on he was one of the automobile's biggest fans. He brought the first gasoline motor launch to the area in 1906 for a duck hunt on Arroyo Colorado. Newspaper articles in the early 1900s regularly followed Hill's activities as he headed off by automobile or boat to someplace "where ducks are plentiful."[31]

By the 1930s native grasses and inland depressions were almost entirely replaced by crops of citrus, cotton, and corn that hugged the coast from Raymondville to Harlingen. Geese came to the patchwork of truck farms, grain crops, and pastures, and the once natural ponds, altered by levees for irrigation, still held fair numbers of ducks. State game warden Charlie Jones reported that "Canadian honkers" were common in the 1940s, but by the '50s they began to disappear, the gap filled with growing flocks of snow, blue, specklebelly, and lesser Canada geese.[32]

Billy Sheka Jr. followed the geese to South Texas from Corpus Christi in the 1960s. He remembers flocks that flew over his grandfather's Triple Seven Ranch ranch house for hours at a time, the sound sometimes deafening. For Billy and his friends those geese were sport, but to his grandfather, George Gibbons, they were a nuisance that destroyed his crops. George in the 1960s posted a plea in the *Valley Morning Star* for gunners to come shoot the marauding geese. He finally resorted to filing crop destruction permits that allowed his hands to kill any number of birds at any time, as long as they didn't retrieve them. Billy remembers people kept track of where the dead birds were, later picking them up to feed local farming communities.[33]

Lush Arroyo Colorado delta deposits were a welcome change from inland mesquite-chaparral bush and winding white, blue, and gray tidal flats of the Laguna Madre coastline. Here the landscape was green in places, dense with ebony, hackberry, ash, and a tangle of thorn bushes and cactus. Sportsmen shared the lakes, meandering streams, and oxbows—called *resacas*—with ocelots and rattlesnakes. Late winter canvasbacks came to the large lake of Laguna Atascosa, and at the old Arroyo Colorado delta mouth, gunners followed flocks of redheads, bluebills, buffleheads, pintails, wigeons, and teal.[34]

So many birds wintered on Arroyo Colorado that, as late as 1955, a single flock reportedly covered four miles. *Field and Stream* editor Van Campen Heilner described a hunt at the mouth of the Arroyo Colorado in his *A Book on Duck Shooting*. To get there he took the train to Harlingen, drove to Rio Hondo, and then traveled by launch before walking three miles. It was a place, he wrote, where cattle and man stranded in a quicksand of thick clay, with pintails in such numbers they "spread out across the sky with absolutely no end."[35]

Heilner's South Texas guides were San Benito's Stuart Atkins and R. J. "Monty" Montgomery, a trophy big-game fisherman and later mayor of Rio Hondo. Monty also guided Eltinge F. Warner, publisher of *Field and Stream,* when he came to Lower Laguna Madre to make the film *Texas Redheads* in the 1940s. The movie attracted substantial local attention, and the press enthused that it would provide the Lower Rio Grande Valley with "a tremendous amount of favorable geese and duck hunting publicity."[36]

The freshwater Rio Grande delta, at the southern end of Texas between Brownsville and Point Isabel, was once a waterfowl paradise. Huge flocks swirled over its freshwater and coastal wetlands. They produced a riot of color: red, black, and white markings of redheads and canvasbacks; the flashy colored speculums of cinnamon, blue-winged, and green-winged teal; white and chestnut-colored pintails; the brilliant green that adorned mallards, shovelers, and wigeons; and

A MIXED BAG *of canvasbacks, redheads, gadwalls, coots, curlews, quail, and a shoveler. Year unknown, but likely between 1900 and 1920. (Runyon [Robert] Photograph Collection, Center for American History, UT–Austin, File No. di-04314)*

A HARVEST *of Canada geese and a few ducks from the Rio Grande valley between 1900 and 1920. The hunter in the center is holding a live Canada goose, possibly a live decoy. (Runyon [Robert] Photograph Collection, Center for American History, UT–Austin, File No. di-04317)*

the shades of black and gray of bluebill, mottled, ruddy, and whistling ducks. Greater Canada geese and swans frequented shoreline marshes, inland pastures, and growths of "wild cranberries" along the river.[37]

It could be a long journey for sportsmen to reach the end of Texas in the years following the Civil War. Rail went only as far as Galveston, where they boarded one of Colonel Morgan's steamships bound for the port of Brazos Santiago and waited for a schooner to take them to the Point Isabel wharf. When the cactus and mesquite plains of South Texas were crossed by the tracks of the Saint Louis, Brownsville and Mexico Railway, sportsmen arrived in such numbers that the rail company provided special trains and routing for hunting parties. "American coke king" Paul Rainey was like many moneyed sportsmen who brought a secretary and six servants by private rail car, with a separate one for his hunting horses and dogs.[38]

A short wagon trip from Brownsville in the 1800s put sportsmen in a labyrinth of lakes and *resacas* deep in Tamaulipan thorn scrub, mesquite-palmetto scrub, and a canopy of ebony-anacua woods. Waterfowl abounded on Loma Alta Lake and Adams Gardens Lake, the latter covered in late-season canvasbacks before it was drained for agricultural use in the 1930s. On the outskirts of town, Fort Brown Resaca after the turn of the century was full of mallards and redheads, and they stood thick on its banks. Once, during a cold front, flocks of migrating ducks and geese were so dazzled by Brownsville city lights that, for hours, hundreds of confused birds circled the town until "they made their escape."[39]

South Texas politician Judge James B. Wells was host to many of Brownsville's important visitors. His catered hunting excursions were complete with local oysters, fish, green turtles, and wild game. Wells's notables and politicos in 1893 shot 160 ducks, and another party killed sixty redheads in just a few hours. Political opponents smirked when newspapers reported that, on one hunt, Wells stalked a flock of ducks that turned out to be tame, later paying restitution to a fuming farmer of $1.25 for each bird he killed.[40]

The Brownsville Fishing and Hunting Club, founded in the late 1800s, was probably Rio Grande Valley's first organized sporting club. After the turn of the century, Brownsville residents located most of their clubs closer to the coast. The Ramireno Duck Club, formed in 1921, was one of the few later clubs based in the city; its members paid a carefully calculated annual fee of $21.40. Ramireno was organized by R. D. Camp, a highly regarded conservationist and naturalist who carried the title of both state and federal warden. B. G. Eubank opened a guiding service headquartered in Brownsville in 1933. Combining fishing and hunting trips, he advertised "a strike every cast and an abundance of duck and geese."[41]

Batsell-Wells Sportsman's Headquarters, also called Batsell-Wells Sporting Goods Store, was a Brownsville institution. According to grandson Barry Batsell, owner J. H. Batsell started the business in 1927 because he couldn't find the sporting supplies he needed in the far corner of Texas. J. H. Batsell had a major influence on the waterfowling culture of the Rio Grande Valley. He cultivated relationships with local ranchers and convinced them to provide affordable public hunting rather than lease to private clubs, and he kept sportsmen informed of fish and fowl through regular columns he wrote for the *Brownsville Herald*.[42]

Between Brownsville and Point Isabel, the Rio Grande finished its journey to the Gulf by way of distributary channels, wind tidal flats, playa lakes, and shallow lagoons separated by clay ridges. Popular shooting localities were at Redhead Ridge on Bahia Grande, Boca Chica Flats, and the black mangroves of South Bay. Other nearby hunting grounds included Redfish Bay and Holly Beach, the shallow flats of Laguna Vista Cove, and the high ridges of Loma de la Grulla.[43]

Brownsville sportsmen after 1872 crossed the Rio Grande floodplain to Point Isabel on the wood-burning locomotive of the Rio Grande Railroad. Traveling a narrow-gauge track, trains on the original route crossed the waters of Bahia Grande via the "Long Bridge." Brownsville sportsman Efren Champion remembered that Bahia Grande "was a duck hunter's paradise," and he was like many who got off the train to hunt and waited for it to pick him up on the return trip. Efren recalled ducks so plentiful along the tracks that "poor Mexican folks who could not afford a gun would hide near a *barranco* [gully] and kill ducks with a stick."[44]

Cameron County Clerk H. D. Seago remembered hunters shot ducks from the moving train, and it would roll to stop so they could retrieve their kill. Sportsmen shared their bounty with "bridge-walkers," who carried wooden barrels of water to douse fires started by coals and cinders belched from the locomotive. Bridge-walkers were less successful in keeping livestock off the tracks; the Long Bridge was locally dubbed Buey Muerto, or "dead ox."[45]

Along the route of the Rio Grande Railroad was Redhead Ridge. Like Lake Surprise, Morgan's Point, Gum Hollow, and Harbor Island, the name Redhead Ridge invoked images of endless ducks to waterfowlers from throughout the United States. Located on the Esperanza tract, Redhead Ridge was a narrow, natural topographic high five miles long that separated saltwater Bahia Grande from freshwater San Martin Lake. Elevations of over twenty feet above the surrounding flats and lagoons gave sportsmen a commanding view of "never-ending waves" of redheads as they passed low over the ridge between the two lakes.[46]

Thousands of hunters paid homage to the flocks of redheads at Redhead Ridge, traveling to hunt them first by rail from Brownsville and then by automobile. Between 1915 and 1930 as many as four hundred cars lined the road on weekend mornings. Sportsmen could not describe Redhead Ridge without hyperbole. One wrote, "You can go down there and see almost all the redheads there are in the world," with "redheads stretched out across the skies a mile wide and no end to them ahead and behind." Hart Stilwell, who as a boy hopped off the train to hunt, included a chapter on Redhead Ridge in his *Hunting and Fishing in Texas.* He wrote that Redhead Ridge once hosted one of the greatest concentrations of redheads in the nation, "a sight a man ought not to miss."[47]

Redhead Ridge was free to the public until 1931, when it became part of the twenty-five-thousand-acre Boca Chica Shooting Preserve and Esperson Duck and Goose Hunting Preserve. Permits to both preserves were available from a caretaker's shack on Boca Chica Highway and at Batsell-Wells Sporting Goods Store. The two-dollar-a-day fee, or ten dollars for a season pass, allowed access to Redhead Ridge, San Martin Lake, and South Bay.[48]

While redheads got most of the attention, adjacent ponds and pastures held large numbers of lesser and greater Canada, snow, and specklebelly geese. Esperson Duck and Goose Hunting Preserve kept track of the goose harvest, and in the 1930s hunters took about four hundred geese each season. Brownsville's best known goose hunters were Sam Norman and Nig Johnson, who often returned to town with forty to fifty geese a day. Local sportsman Earl Hunter became a local legend when he killed two geese with one shot from a .410.[49]

At the south end of Laguna Madre, Point Isabel near the turn of the century had only one "rickety hotel and some run-down hovels." Waterfowl were so plentiful that a visitor wrote he could "stand up in his skiff and slaughter canvasback, and all kinds of ducks, geese, flamingoes [roseate spoonbills], cranes six feet high, curlews and snipes . . . no further than one or two miles from the wharf." Weekends saw rail cars of the Rio Grande Railroad laden with Brownsville excursionists. The *Brownsville Herald* dutifully listed traveling parties and details of their hunts, such as a group in 1906 that returned to the city with 190 redheads, fourteen Canada geese, and, using names for wildfowl today unrecognizable, "one polywompos and 13 Lula birds."[50]

When the Saint Louis, Brownsville, and Mexico Railway reached South Texas, it brought an explosion in new hotels and hunting clubs to Point Isabel. The chairman of the railroad company, Sam Fordyce, opened Point Isabel Fishing and Hunting Club and built the nearby Beebe Hotel as a "Hunter's Paradise." Other railroad investors, including Robert J. Kleberg and Jeff N. Miller, chartered the Point Isabel Tarpon and Fishing Club. That club's board of directors voted unanimously in 1907 to run the train from Brownsville three times a week to their new club. Headquarters was Jeff Miller's Jefferson Inn, built "especially for the sportsman." Club member Judge Wells, always the consummate host, welcomed orator and politician William Jennings Bryan for a duck hunt in 1911.[51]

Waterfowl hunting was one of the main selling points for Dr. H. W. Taylor, who arrived from California in 1907 and purchased three miles of Laguna Madre beach front near Laguna Larga to open Laguna Vista resort. He promoted his venture as a sporting haven with "myriads of teal, canvas back, redheads, and other choice ducks, and wild geese . . . [that] show their appreciation of the balmy climate by wintering there." Taylor guided many prospective investors himself. By 1910 the club resort had eighty members and several hunting lodges.[52]

The sporting reputation of Point Isabel grew through the 1910s to the late 1920s. Captain Wallace of the coast guard station on Brazos Island in 1917 claimed that the huge volume of visiting hunters killed "millions of ducks." President-elect Warren Harding came for a vacation in 1920 and was afforded all the sporting luxuries of the times. The *Galveston Daily News* reported, under the headline "Power boats will be used in fishing and hunting ducks," that the Texas Game, Fish, and Oyster Commission had loaned the distinguished visitor a captain and the commission's gasoline launch *Jim Duke.* North of Point Isabel, the

> **Duck & Goose**
> Hunting Preserve
> **Esperson Tract**
> 25,000 acres below Brownsville, including Mouth of River and Red Head Ridge.
> — • —
> **Rates 50c per day or $1.00 for Season**
> — • —
> See us for permits
> **Batsell-Wells**
> **Sporting Goods**
> Brownsville, Texas

> **The Beebe Hotel**
> Hunter's Paradise
> **Sam Fordyce, Texas**
> C. P. Welles, Prop. and Mgr.
> **Best Rooms and Meals in Town**
> YOUR PATRONAGE SOLICITED

(Modified from *Brownsville Daily Herald*, Mar. 25, 1907)

(Modified from *Valley Star-Monitor-Herald*, Nov. 13, 1938)

San Antonio–based Holly Beach Company broke ground in 1929 for the resort city of Holly Beach, building a hunting and fishing lodge "of the highest type." The operation was managed by James B. Sorenson, son of Rockport's renowned sportsman Andrew Sorenson.[53]

Across Laguna Madre from Point Isabel, winter wildfowl migrations to the barrier islands of South Padre and Brazos Island were followed by gunners from as far away as the Great Lakes and New England in the late 1800s. Many arrived by steamer to the mouth of the Rio Grande before heading north to Brazos Santiago Pass and the southern tip of South Padre. Brownsville hunters reached the coast by wagon, following a winding route across salt flats and ridges to Brazos Island.

At the turn of the century wealthy northern sportsmen often brought their own steam yachts and hunted for months at a time. Colonel Edward H. R. Green of Massachusetts was one, and from the deck of his yacht he once "filled the saluting cannon with two pounds of shot and a pound and a half of powder, and fired at a flock of ducks, killing 121." With schemes to deepen Brazos Santiago Pass, Green foresaw the future when he wrote, "I am afraid . . . that if the harbor is deepened it will spoil the duck shooting. If the bar is cut away and steamers make it easy to come and go the ducks will go." Green was best known to Texas sportsmen for his extravagant Tarpon Club on St. Joseph Island across from Port Aransas.[54]

Point Isabel hotels served as the starting point for sportsmen who hunted the back side of the islands, crossing the shallow southern end of Laguna Madre in small sloops. A group from Brownsville who boarded at the Isabel Hotel made an excursion to South Padre Island in 1907, their trials and tribulations common to urban sport hunters of the period. One hunter reached down to retrieve a duck and was startled to find that he had grabbed a huge rattlesnake instead. In the hands of an inexperienced hunter, an "automatic gun" unexpectedly discharged, but its owner was "taking care it was not pointed at anyone."[55]

George Sim started the Tarpon Beach resort development on South Padre Island overlooking Brazos Santiago Pass in 1907. Targeting the "great numbers of sportsmen of the wealthy class from the north," Sim advertised the new clubhouse where "fall and winter hunting is unexcelled, [with] millions of ducks and wild fowl making their home." A boat service was provided to ferry members and guests from Point Isabel to the club's new landing piers, boathouses, and boardwalk in a setting of California fan palms, oleanders, and salt cedars. The age of the automobile was coming, with Sim certain that the 125-mile-long shell road planned along the length of Padre Island would attract investors. Tarpon Beach owners deeded William Jennings Bryan his own lot with the hope that the famous politician's endorsement would promote sales.[56]

In 1926 another group of investors planned a grand "Valley playground" on Brazos Island, complete with a causeway joining the clubhouse with their shooting preserve on the mainland. Even more ambitious was the Rio Grande Valley Rod and Gun Club, started by Frank Faurote the same year on ten thousand acres of Laguna Madre bayfront. Kansas City, Washington, DC, and Texas businessmen planned a three-story clubhouse, golf course, and trap shooting range along with fifty cabins, a fleet of fishing boats, and several cabin cruisers. Colonel Robertson's "famous beach speedway" passed in front of the club property, where arriving visitor's could fulfil their "dream of speeding with safety." The Rio Grande Valley Rod and Gun Club did not survive the Great Depression.[57]

In the years before and just after World War II, the face of the Rio Grande corridor from Brownsville to renamed Port Isabel began to show signs of wear. In the late 1930s the Long Bridge across Bahia Grande was gone; only its pilings remained, stretching "for three miles like bleached bones." Giant Canada geese that followed blue northers were an infrequent visitor by the 1940s, and a decade-long drought reduced the volume of wintering ducks on the Rio Grande delta to as few as twenty-five hundred in 1945.[58]

Under the heading "Famed Duck Paradise Bows to March of Development," the *Brownsville Herald* in 1935 followed Redhead Ridge, the "famed hill," as it marched towards extinction. Sportsmen stood on the banks of the Bahia Grande and watched as a fifteen-hundred-pound charge of dynamite leveled the south plunge of the hill to make way for the Brownsville ship channel. Hart Stilwell wrote tersely that "cutting the Brownsville ship channel drained our duck lakes, and ruined Redhead Ridge." The waters were indeed gone, and the sky that had once been filled with clouds of redheads was instead filled with clouds of wind-borne dust.[59]

Fresh water was the lure for immense wintering flocks of wildfowl to the Rio Grande delta, and it was becoming in short supply. Dams and irrigation projects continued to drain the lifeblood from the Rio Grande until one day it, too, went dry. Up the coast, the Arroyo Colorado had long since stopped flowing into Laguna Madre. Some respite from modern ravages was provided when state and federal refuges were purchased along the Rio Grande at Boca Chica and at Laguna Atascosa. Sixty years after Bahia Grande moved from wetlands to desert, eight state and federal entities combined to bring water back to the coastal depression. Through their efforts, the day may come again when a sportsman stands atop Redhead Ridge and sees "all the redheads there are in the world."[60]

PART THREE

NORTH, WEST, and EAST INLAND SPORT HUNTING

CHAPTER 15

BIG PRAIRIE and EAGLE LAKE

It was a blurred boundary, mostly just a change in the course of the Brazos River, that separated Colorado County's Big Prairie from Houston Prairie. Big Prairie geographic names such as Lissie, Eagle Lake, Garwood, and Canebrake Prairie came later as settlements were built over its rich organic soils. The lake and town that shared the name Eagle Lake were in the heart of Big Prairie, sixty miles west-southwest of Houston. Fed by Moore's Branch Slough to the northwest, the fifteen-hundred-acre lake was called the Big Lake. Its waters were covered with aquatic vegetation, giant cut grass, bulrushes, and cane, with oak trees rimming the shoreline once home to dozens of migrating eagles from which the town took its name.[1]

EAGLE LAKE

The town of Eagle Lake, proclaimed "Goose Capital of the World" in the 1960s, didn't start that way. It was ducks, particularly mallards, that put the town on the sporting map. An early destination for sportsmen, the town was linked to Houston and Galveston before the Civil War by the first railroad in Texas, the Buffalo Bayou, Brazos, and Colorado Railroad, and in the late 1800s by the SA&AP Railway. Along the route, hunters after the Civil War found it "very painful" to look out from the train windows "upon the big white cranes," greater Canada geese, swans, ducks, and prairie-chickens that covered Big Prairie.[2]

Horses and wagons took sportsmen from train depot to lake, often with a stop at E. L. Mooney's Hardware to purchase supplies that included shotguns, live decoy ducks, and duck and goose calls. Most hunters camped on the lakeshore for days at a time, renting boats or hiring a local guide for shoots where

Jim Douglass (front left), *Duke Eggers* (front right), *Ray Munn Fitzgerald* (back left) *and Howard Strahan in downtown Eagle Lake, 1920s. The town would later be famous for snow and specklebelly geese, but in the early 1900s hunters shot only greater Canada geese. Note the mud chains on the running boards. (Courtesy David and Eula Wintermann Library, Eagle Lake, Texas)*

skiffs and canoes were simply pulled into the grass. One well-known early guide was G. Y. Morgan, who built cypress canoes so well suited to Eagle Lake waters that his design was later adopted by Eagle Lake Rod and Gun Club and is still in use.[3]

The first sporting lodge built on the lake was Eagle Lake Hunting Club, in business by 1890, whose members stayed in tents on the club grounds. C. L. Bering of Houston's C. L. and Theo Bering Hardware and Sporting Goods belonged to the club, and on a three-day trip in 1903 he shot 310 teal, ruddy ducks, canvasbacks, and mallards. Another private club, the Eagle Lake Gun Club, opened in 1906 but evidently was not long-lived. Conductors of the Santa Fe Railway organized the Sportsman's Club around the turn of the century. On one hunt, Sportsman's Club members shot so many ruddy ducks, shovelers, teal, canvasbacks, and mallards that they had to cool their gun barrels in lake water. Shooting well past sunset, they got lost and spent a long night wading in circles. Their duck boat, decoys, and ammunition were never found.[4]

Rice, the grain that was to have a profound effect on waterfowl patterns in Texas, was first planted in Colorado County by Captain William Donovant in the 1890s. Donovant owned the rights to Eagle Lake waters, and when he was shot in the back in 1905, water title shifted to B. L. Vineyard and Rudolph T. Wintermann, then to Oscar Wintermann and his Lakeside Irrigation Company. Eagle Lake water was crucial to the increasing volume of rice, but the crop eventually required more water than the lake could provide. For several years the lake was pumped dry until a canal was dug from the Colorado River in 1907.[5]

Ducks found water and rice a perfect combination, and they roosted by day on Eagle Lake and swarmed to nearby rice fields by night. Harvey S. Vineyard

PRAIRIE DUCK *hunt in Colorado County, early 1900s. Left to right: Doc Welch (with beard), unidentified, and Dick Byars. Note the large numbers of mallards. (Courtesy Nesbitt Memorial Library, Columbus, Texas, File No. 00965)*

returned from a rice field hunt in the 1910s, his wagon loaded with 150 ducks and fifteen geese. In 1913, when rains postponed the rice harvest, Lakeside Irrigation Co. manager C. P. Hoyo remarked, "The birds and ducks are simply swamping some of the fields, and in some cases [they] have ruined and torn all to pieces large numbers of shock standing in the fields." It was the same in 1922 and again in 1925. That year local game warden Tom Waddell received letters from dozens of farmers who complained ducks were "simply eating up their rice crops, unable to be threshed on account of the continued rains."[6]

Rice field hunting did not start as sport but as a necessity to reduce crop destruction. Eagle Lake's Davis Waddell says, "My grandfather [William Waddell] used to give my dad and his brothers a case of shells and tell 'em to go out and shoot the ducks at night. They hated it." Bill Blair remembers his grandfather A. Helmer "Pappy" Seaholm, who farmed near Bonus, "couldn't keep the ducks out of shocked rice. They used coal oil lanterns at night to try and keep them out."[7]

In the late 1920s Pappy got some help with rice crop ducks when he formed Bonus Hunting Club. Headquartered in Eagle Lake's White House Hotel, his day hunting operation was probably the first in the area. Bill Blair says his grandfather started it when "a fella came to town sellin' baby grand pianos, and he asked if Grandpa would take him hunting." From that, word spread, "and Grandpa bought one of his pianos, too." At first Pappy worked only for tips, then in the early 1930s he advertised guided duck hunts for three dollars a day. One customer described Pappy's ponds with "millions of . . . greenheads all bunched together," and his property, called the Flats, was "so literally covered with ducks you couldn't see the water. With a roar like a big whirlwind they would leave the ponds. Ducks would rise and form black clouds in the skies."[8]

BIG PRAIRIE AND EAGLE LAKE   ➔   301

On both the lake and rice fields, hunters went to the ducks by sneaking them, and then took the shot on the water before the birds took flight. It was called pot shooting, and Bill Blair says of the practice: "Those days were very different than now. The rice stubble was waist high. There were prairie ponds and the edges were covered with high reeds. They would sneak ducks with side by side shotguns with two shells loaded, and keep two in their mouth and two in the fingers of one hand. That way they could kill 50 to 70 ducks on one sneak. They said they whistled to get their heads up. After a sneak, they'd throw them in the wagon or Model T and drive to town."[9]

Local newspapers kept track of the pot shooters' scores, always seeking the ones who killed the most birds. Eagle Lake's Tom and J. E. Roberts held the record in 1912 with 31 ducks killed with a single volley. Three Houston gunners in 1920 crawled up to the Eagle Lake shore and emptied their side-by-side double-barrels, killing 76. The undisputed champion pot hunters in 1923 were four duck hunters from Weimar who fired into a single flock, killing 143 and finishing the day with 190 ducks. In 1928, Oscar J. Wintermann and three friends snuck the lake and fired seventeen rounds, with the number killed 85 "large ducks, with twenty teals."[10]

In a 1990s interview with Texas Parks and Wildlife's David Lobpries, Oscar's son David Wintermann said pot shooting was the only way locals knew how to hunt. But when Arkansas guide Jimmy Reel came to town in the 1930s, he introduced the community to duck blinds and retrievers. "People quit crawling on ponds," Wintermann said, as hunting began to evolve into more of "a gentleman's sport."[11]

Sportsmen had to find another place at the end of World War I when Eagle Lake was used by Ellington Field aviators as a bombing range for two years. The town on its shores thought it was a small sacrifice for the war effort and wisely considered it dangerous to have a duck boat on the lake during bombing practices. They saw a bigger change in 1920 when pharmacist S. C. "Jake" Smothers, who for years had dreamed of operating a world-class hunting club, was granted the entirety of Eagle Lake by Oscar Wintermann to open Eagle Lake Rod and Gun Club.[12]

Houston's Gervais Bell, past president of Eagle Lake Rod and Gun Club and a member for about thirty-five years, says Jake traveled to Houston to solicit interest in forming the club. Original incorporators were W. A. Sherman, James P. Houstoun, and J. H. Pittman, with Howard Hughes Sr. a founding member. After choosing the site where the town's pavilion once stood, club members hauled the two-story boarding house of the nearby Lakeside Sugar Refinery to the lakeshore with a team of oxen. Jake Smothers and his wife moved in upstairs and stayed for the next fifty years.[13]

Many early club members came by train and were ferried from the depot by the club truck. Their drive down the dirt road to Eagle Lake Rod and Gun Club

The Eagle Lake *Rod and Gun Club lodge, originally part of the Lakeside Sugar Refinery, has looked much the same since the 1920s. (Courtesy Jerry Sims)*

Eagle Lake *Rod and Gun Club truck, ca. 1930. (Courtesy Nesbitt Memorial Library, Columbus, Texas, File No. 01629)*

ended at the large main building with green trim and a screened front porch above a lawn that sloped to the lake under a canopy of moss-covered oak trees. On the grounds were a garden, Jake's father's blacksmith shop, and a live mallard decoy pen by the boat shed. Inside they were well served by a white-uniformed staff that included Sherma and Willie Davis, and the cook, Miss Mahalis. Food and hospitality were as celebrated as duck hunting. *New York Sun* correspondent Bob Davis, a guest in 1931, wrote, "I have never sat one table where there were so many high-class gentlemen, so much good cooking, and so many able gunners as I encountered at the Eagle Lake Rod and Gun Club."[14]

Jake had a tradition in which, each winter, he delivered mallards to the *Eagle Lake Headlight* newspaper staff. Whenever they wanted ducks, a short note appeared in the newspaper, such as one in 1936 that warned that if no mallards were forthcoming, Jake was in danger of "breaking an established record of fifteen years." The newspaper noted visits to the club from luminaries such as Will

Rogers and writer Irvin S. Cobb, who wrote letters describing his hunts for local readers. In one, he quipped, "I shall miss the charming companionship of the club members—and God knows I missed most of the ducks that I shot at," and, "When I hit a duck it is an emotional shock to both of us." He expressed relief when the limit was dropped from twenty-five to fifteen birds because "now I only have to think up fifteen alibis instead of twenty five." Cobb may not have been exaggerating. Guide Jimmy Reel often poled him across the lake for hours while Cobb shot a couple hundred shells at rising ducks, although he "usually had two teal to show for it.[15]

A morning hunt at the club started with a short walk to the boathouse after Mr. Jake finished organizing guides and blinds "as closely as a stockbroker pursuing stock selections." Guides picked up some of the English callers from the duck pen and loaded them, along with hunters and wooden decoys, into one of the club's cypress canoes. Built by G. Y. Morgan, the club's canoes were twelve feet long and three feet wide, with galvanized tin tacked around the bottom. When they were fully loaded, only inches of freeboard remained between boat and water.[16]

Guides used push poles to follow a maze of trails through tall cattails, bulrushes, and cut grass. The northwest part of the lake was, in places, too dense to hunt, and longtime guide Charlie Braden says they used dynamite to make trails to the duck hunting holes. For many years members did not hunt from blinds, instead poling canoes into a wide area of water, where they shot from the boat. It was a rare morning that they didn't return with a limit of twenty-five birds each, and Charlie remembers the ritual when, at the end of a hunt, members carefully arranged their kill on the side of their automobiles for bragging rights on the return trip.[17]

Arkansas native Jimmy Reel was head guide until 1940, when E. J. "Ed" Braden took the job. Club historian Jerry Sims says Ed was a gifted storyteller whose animated tales were usually illustrated with cuss words. He lived in a frame house by the entrance to the club, raising four boys who all became club guides. Between Ed and his son Charlie, there was a Braden guiding at the club for nearly seventy years. Charlie was born in 1921 and grew up on the lake before there were any houses on its shore. Crossing the lake in an outboard, he once hit an alligator and was thrown from his boat. With it going in circles around him, he grabbed a gunwale and hauled himself back in. Charlie was eighty years old, still five years away from retirement.[18]

Guides such as Charlie with decades of tenure were the rule rather than the exception. Club historian Jerry Sims provides a rich image of thirty-year veteran Dale "Buddy" Stapleton, who started in the 1940s. Buddy, Sims writes, wore a black slicker and rain hat, rain or shine, and was always smoking a hand-rolled Bull Durham cigarette. He called mallards like he talked—real slow, so slow that his high ball cadence "never got [all the way] up to the high notes." A former rail-

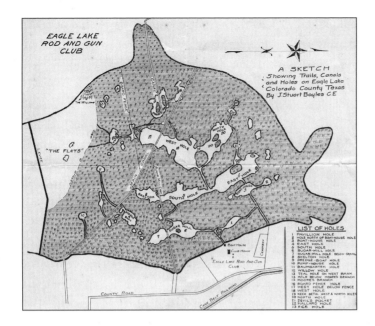

UNDATED MAP *of Eagle Lake with the names of Eagle Lake Rod and Gun Club duck blinds. Note the density of vegetation in areas that today are all open water. (Courtesy Agnes Reel Strauss)*

road man, he was as strong as he was tough. When he got bitten on both hands by a water moccasin, he didn't even bother to go to a doctor.[19]

Jerry Sims's mother first packed him off from Houston on the train to Eagle Lake, and his guiding career began when club member Virgil Scott drew last for a guide in 1950. Club members did not choose the fourteen-year-old boy often. Jerry's regular charge was Mr. Jake, and he made a lasting impression on the aging club manager when, on their first hunt, he knocked down seven ducks with one shot. Jerry came from a good bloodline—his uncle was Ed Braden, and in keeping with club tradition, his brothers James and Carlton became guides, and later his son Jerry Jr.[20]

As late as the 1950s there were only three club outboard motors, and guides like Jerry carried on the tradition of push-poling Morgan canoes, an excruciating job in hard winds. Often the best way from blind to lodge was not a straight line but a route around the lake along the leeward shore. Charlie Braden, in typical understatement, says sometimes on a "hard norther waves would get pretty big."[21]

Getting to and from the hunt is the stuff of legend. As Houston grocery store owner and club member C. G. Pillot grew older, guides built a chair for him in the bow of a club canoe and pointed him toward the decoys to shoot. Old man G. Y. Morgan was guiding him when the top-heavy vessel turned over, and Charlie remembers, "You could hear 'em hollerin' all the way at the club house. They were in water up to their necks in a canal with just their heads stickin' up." Guide Terry Landry set the club record for getting lost when he set out in the fog for the lake's south side, running aground forty-five minutes later on the north side. He set off again to the south and landed again on the north shore. Canoes shared the predawn darkness on the way to the blind with alligators, though Charlie says,

BIG PRAIRIE AND EAGLE LAKE → 305

"We would hunt and wade with the alligators, and they would never bother us." Water moccasins were a different story. "Moore's Branch blind was one—snakes were bad in it. The first thing you do when you get in the blind, you better shake it first."[22]

Club duck blinds were named for members or for ducks, such as Blue Wing and Mallard Hole, and some were named for geography, such as Town Hole, Little and Big Board Fence, East Hole, and West Hole. Charlie remembers the most productive blinds were Brett, Danor, and Hunt. David Wintermann had a couple of special blinds, Charlie says, and "after Dizzy Dean hunted, club members wanted to hunt in the blind that Dizzy Dean hunted. They didn't care if they killed anything, they just wanted to hunt where Dizzy Dean hunted." Sometimes the duck blinds weren't where they left them the day before, having been mistakenly built on floating islands that gave Jake Smothers "no end of trouble."[23]

The fluid magnet that was Eagle Lake was once winter home to "a black cloud of ducks, resembling hundred and hundreds of blackbirds." Twice in the 1920s Eagle Lake Rod and Gun Club killed over 9,000 ducks in a winter, and on opening day of the 1929 season, twenty-five gunners shot 599. Growing up on its banks, Charlie remembers how, at night, roosting ducks left the lake in "just droves, goin' to the rice fields to feed. I'd always find some fast ducks, little ducks [that would] fly into the power line, and kill themselves. They'd be coming out of the lake and they'd fly into that wire." Jake Smothers once sat on the front porch of the lodge at night and listened to the sound of hundreds of mallards as they waddled up on the shoreline to feed on acorns. As late as the 1950s, mallard shooting at Eagle Lake Rod and Gun Club was still compared to that of legendary Stuttgart, Arkansas.[24]

By the 1960s there were fewer ducks and a lot more open water. The giant cut grass, bulrushes, and cane were disappearing, the lake's clear waters turning muddy from suspended sediment. While the causes were many, an important one was the introduction of nutria. With their voracious appetites, nutria were initially brought in to open up areas of dense vegetation, and the club was so protective of its transplants that signs were posted advising members not to shoot them. In his interview with TPWD's David Lobpries, David Wintermann admitted, "I made the mistake of putting five nutria in the lake in 1951. The man assured me there would be no problem."[25]

The nutria population exploded. Colorado County game warden Tom Waddell, who helped with eradication efforts, reported killing fourteen thousand of them within only seven years after they were introduced. Jake Smothers said the toothy South American rodents not only destroyed vegetation but also ate duck decoys, and they were known even to raze duck blinds. Poisoning efforts were not very successful. Ed Braden mixed batches of arsenic with sweet potatoes, but son Charlie says, "Hell, it made 'em fat. They'd sit there and wait for them in the morning to bring that stuff, and they'd eat. It didn't kill a one of 'em."[26]

The nutria were not alone in their attack. In the 1940s water pumped from the Colorado River begin to fill Eagle Lake with sand. More levees were built, and a canal dug around the lake perimeter allowed water to be maintained at a relatively constant level, a process biologist Charles Stutzenbaker says drowned standing grasses. "People maintain it was the nutria," he says, "but the nutria only helped." The sixty sportsmen who today make up Eagle Lake Rod and Gun Club have adapted to changes in the lake through management of habitat projects along its shores, including sloughs and depressions south and west of the lake.[27]

Eagle Lake was once an important part of the social fabric of the town that took its name from its waters. In the 1800s they fished it, hunted it, were baptized in it, and held picnics and dances on the old covered pavilion on the shore. When lake access was restricted in the 1920s, townspeople could only watch as summer storms billowed in or when the lake sometimes froze in winter. They watched at a distance as flames lit the night sky when the western bank of the lake caught fire during the drought of 1950, and they watched, too, as each winter clouds of ducks dropped from the sky.[28]

Poking up from the open waters of Eagle Lake are a few pilings, all that remain of the club's old duck blinds, once hidden in high grass. They were the haunts of old Mr. Morgan with his cypress canoes, Jake Smothers, Jimmy Reel, David Wintermann, the Bradens, the Simses, and a host of others who are the hunting history of Eagle Lake Rod and Gun Club.

Sportsman and benefactor David Wintermann was the third generation of Wintermanns to control Eagle Lake waters. Born in 1911, he was eight years old when he made his first duck hunt with Jake Smothers, his first duck a pintail shot with a .22 rifle. He hunted ducks from then on, the rifle replaced by a Fox double-barreled 20-gauge. The limit then was twenty-five, and he said, "Generally we got our limit."[29]

David Wintermann over the years kept good company: sportsmen such as Jimmy Reel and Cal Gersten; politicians George H. W. Bush and James Baker III; Danbury rancher Jack Garrett; artist John P. "Jack" Cowan; art gallery owner Meredith Long; Andy Sansom, when he was with TPWD and the Nature Conservancy; and Ducks Unlimited president John E. Walker. The social center for Wintermann's sporting circle was Cal Gersten's one-room quail farm office next door to David Wintermann's house, the little green structure dubbed the Thanatopsis Literary and Drinking Society. Its by-laws included no neckties or women and a five-dollar fine imposed for shooting a hen duck. The latter was enforced by Jimmy Reel, who collected the money and stuffed it into a slit in the side of a Clorox bottle; the proceeds were mailed each year to Ducks Unlimited.[30]

Many of the famous sporting works of art by Jack Cowan, Herb Booth, and Steve Russell feature David Wintermann and his hunting entourage around Eagle Lake. Cowan painted a classic Eagle Lake shoot over old-style rags, called

Dawn Flight, and Herb Booth's *Finishing Up* featured both Jimmy Reel and David Wintermann. In Peter Johnson's globetrotting book on hunting called *The World of Shooting,* the section on Eagle Lake was prompted by an invitation from David Wintermann.[31]

David turned the shoreline of his home overlooking Eagle Lake into a refuge for ducks. Charlie Braden says, "Mr. Wintermann used to feed five to ten thousand birds along the bank in front of his house, and he was very particular about those ducks. We used to have a rover and he'd go around and scare up the ducks [for the Eagle Lake Rod and Gun Club]. I had Marshall Lewis roving one day and he didn't know we wasn't supposed to come over here to this side of the lake. Every [club] boat came in within 30 minutes and had a limit of blue-winged teal. Wintermann came calling down at the clubhouse, and says, 'I've got a good mind to shut you down, you're not supposed to do that.' He was upset."[32]

David Wintermann was a sportsman, a conservationist, and a generous benefactor to his Eagle Lake hometown and Texas waterfowling. He was a Ducks Unlimited trustee in the 1960s and lifetime contributor as trustee emeritus. Each winter he sponsored hunts with the proceeds directed to his favorite causes. Before Davis died in 1997, he donated the land that became the 245-acre Wintermann Wildlife Management Area.[33]

Before the turn of the century, Eagle Lake hunting excursions required a trip of several days by horse and buggy and later, train. With the automobile, sportsmen between world wars could make a hunt and return to Houston the same day. The modern era of waterfowl hunting was in full swing, and one of the first in Eagle Lake to capitalize on it was James Richard "Jimmy" Reel.

Jimmy first hunted on his father's farm in northern Arkansas. He was eleven years old when he fired one shot into a flock of ducks and killed eighteen. His father, who had told him never to pot shoot ducks, cut a switch and whipped him. Jimmy quit school in the seventh grade and organized his first fishing and hunting club on his father's farm when he was fourteen. Houston sportsman Alex Wolff says that, during the Depression, Jimmy spent two years "riding the freight trains and looking for employment." His coming to Eagle Lake wasn't planned; Alex says "Jimmy fell off a freight train in the thirties." The man who was to become one of Texas's best known waterfowl guides at first ran a pool hall on Eagle Lake's Main Street. Jimmy started his Texas guiding career at Eagle Lake Rod and Gun Club in 1933, and in 1939 he founded the J. R. "Jimmy" Reel Hunting Club, which he would lead for the next forty years.[34]

At first Jimmy didn't make enough money as a guide to raise his young family, and he left Eagle Lake in 1940 bound for Houston to work as a rice buyer for Pfeffer Rice Milling Company. In 1944 Jimmy and his wife, Lucille, moved back to Eagle Lake, and to make ends meet he started the private Lower Lake Hunting Club, opened the nearby Silver Creek Hatchery, and worked as a rice buyer for the River Brand Mills.[35]

DAVID R. WINTERMANN (front), *Andy Sansom (center), and Davis Waddell. (Courtesy Davis Waddell)*

As an Eagle Lake Rod and Gun Club guide, Jimmy had watched as mallards dropped into the boggy land south of the Big Lake where William Donovant had planted his first few acres of rice in 1896. Over the years the depression was known as Frazer or Terrell Lake. Its owner, W. R. Terrell, approached Jimmy in 1941 with the idea of forming a private club. Offering him a ten-year lease for six thousand dollars a year, Terrell agreed to construct a water gap to control water levels and pay Jimmy five hundred dollars a year to manage it. Jimmy began writing letters to sportsmen from Houston to New York, and in 1942 he found twelve members willing to pay five hundred dollars each.[36]

There was trouble from the start. Terrell had also leased the renamed Lower Lake to a Houston company, and Jimmy gave up half his lease for a year to appease them. The next year he nearly closed the club down, writing letters to return members' deposits that for some reason he never had to mail. Then in 1944 the Gulf, Colorado, and Santa Fe Railway Company served notice that Jimmy's water structures encroached on their right-of-way. Perhaps his biggest hurdle was

FIRST WATER *on Jimmy Reel's new duck ponds at Lower Lake Hunting and Fishing Club, 1942. (Courtesy Agnes Reel Strauss)*

JIMMY AND LUCILLE REEL *in front of the Lower Lake Hunting and Fishing Club clubhouse, 1942. (Courtesy Agnes Reel Strauss)*

the five-year running battle with adjoining property owner C. E. Everitt that culminated in a 1947 lawsuit seeking a court order to remove Lower Lake dam.[37]

Between obstacles, Jimmy built a duck club. He had planned his lake carefully; the spillway from the big lake and his concrete dam to the south created two hundred acres of shallow water. Members reached the club by a drive on Farm-to-Market Road 102 past Eagle Lake Rod and Gun Club, then up a small knoll in a stand of scrub oak. In its first year, new white paint covered the one-story clubhouse, which had once been the Lakeside Sugar Refinery company office. Lucille Reel took charge of the books and the kitchen; Essie Ham did the cooking; James Gordon and Henry P. Ham maintained the lodge, grounds, and

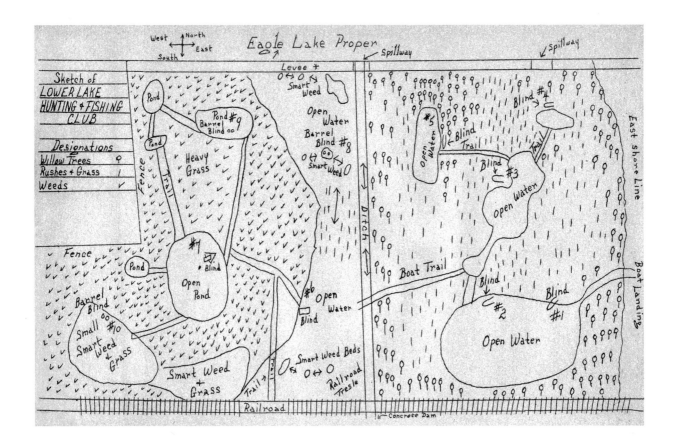

LOWER LAKE *Hunting and Fishing Club as it looked in 1947. The map was drawn by Brandon Fitzpatrick in 1947 for C. E. Everitt's lawsuit. (Courtesy Agnes Reel Strauss)*

boathouse; and Bill Mason built and brushed duck blinds. The piers of Jimmy's boat landing were filled with new Hudson Bay poling boats. Through correspondence with Terrell's Aquatic Nurseries in Wisconsin, Jimmy learned about aquatic vegetation—duck food—and by 1944 he planted bur reed roots, one thousand wild celery winter buds, and hundreds of pounds of wild duck millet seed and smartweed seed.[38]

Jimmy wrote the first club by-laws. In a sign of changing times, one of his rules—"Any member leaving decoys in water at blind shall be fined 50 cents to have same picked up, which shall be done by negro boy on place"—was edited by the membership with the words *negro boy* replaced by *caretaker*. The club grew from twelve to twenty members in a year, and by 1947 it was incorporated as Lower Lake Inc. with forty members More lease land was added in 1949 at Skull Creek, a place excitedly described in club correspondence as "predominantly mallards, [that] usually do not hit the coastal country until a real norther kicks them out of the grain belt."[39]

Jimmy's lifetime friend Lou Lewis, of Lewis Food Market, was a club member, and Lou's son Barry recalls his days at the club as a boy in the mid-1940s. Before each hunt, he says, members drew for blinds, with the lowest number getting the first pick. Over fifty years later he remembers the best blinds were numbers 11, 2, and 7. After the draw, "you took your car from the clubhouse down to the boat

BIG PRAIRIE AND EAGLE LAKE → 311

landing. The lake back then didn't look anything like it looks now. There was a lot of grass, duck weed, and reeds, and you had to work your way through, weaving your way down these boat lanes in the grass to get to your blind. You had to know the area."[40]

Barry recalls, "We had mallards, pintails, and teal and some gadwalls. I remember a Thanksgiving. We were out in the blind with Jimmy and we killed our limit of pintails. We just sat there and watched Jimmy just whistle in the pintails. No [duck] calls, he just whistled. And they'd all light and then he'd get up and he'd say, 'Shoo!' and they'd fly away. Then he'd wait about four or five minutes and the pintails would come back. He'd start whistlin' them in again and they'd just circle and circle and circle and light in the decoys. That was just unbelievable."[41]

Barry has fond memories of members Dr. Mylie Durham Sr., for whom Houston's Durham Street was named; Dr. F. O. McGehee; Dr. Lucien Bukowsky; and many of the others. Legendary wildcatter Glen McCarthy was a frequent guest. McCarthy, whose empire included Houston's Shamrock Hotel, was known for driving his "royal blue Cadillac at 100 mph, often with a whiskey bottle at his side" and had "a longshoreman's uninhibited propensity for barroom fights." Barry heard similar stories from his father. "Glen McCarthy was so dapper, but at the club he'd have one too many and they'd get into fights. Then in the morning it was all over, and they'd all get up and go hunting together. Those people had so much fun."[42]

Jimmy had a noticeable scar right across his nose, and Barry is one of the few people who knows how he got it. "My older brother Gene spent a few weeks one summer down at Lower Lake helping Jimmy repair the blinds and a water turkey flew by. Jimmy said, 'Gene, see if you can kill that water turkey.' Gene shot, and the water turkey was comin' down and they watched it and the water turkey hit Jimmy right in the nose. And that's how he got that scar. He carried it all his life with him. Why he didn't duck, I've never been able to figure out."[43]

Lower Lake Club was where Jimmy first cajoled his membership into shooting mostly drakes so that a larger number of hens could return to the spring nesting grounds. More hens meant more ducks the next season. He was so serious about the practice that he fined club members who shot hens and donated the proceeds to Ducks Unlimited. In his 1949 letter to DU with a check for $48.93, Jimmy wrote that the amount was "accumulated by fining members 50 cents each for each hen mallard and hen sprig killed during the season." It was a tradition Jimmy upheld until he died.[44]

Jimmy and Lucille Reel ran Lower Lake Club as part of the Eagle Lake community, inviting the town to weekend barbecues, picnics, and skeet shoots. Jimmy Reel left Lower Lake Hunting and Fishing Club in 1952, and it was next managed by E. F. "Abbey" Abercrombie. Abercrombie supervised the draining of Lower Lake to improve habitat in 1954 and was surprised by the number of water moccasins, killing 175 in two days. Abercrombie left Lower Lake in 1958 to

> **Veteran Guide Jimmy Reel Offers**
>
> # Duck & Goose
>
> **Day Hunting – Season Leases**
>
> Meet at Campbell's Café in Eagle Lake — Hunting on Eagle Lake, Lissie and Garwood Prairies.
>
> **Hunting Every Day Until Noon**
> **BLINDS and WHITE SPREAD SHOOTING**
>
> Decoys and Guides Furnished
>
> **FOR RESERVATIONS:**
>
> # PH. CE4-2062
>
> Eagle Lake or Write Box 756

(Modified from *Eagle Lake Headlight,* Oct. 27, 1966)

manage Lakeside Hunting Club, located on land adjacent to Lower Lake Club and owned by Jimmy's old nemesis, C. E. Everitt.[45]

Jimmy opened a guided day hunting service during his Lower Lake Club tenure. Called the J. R. "Jimmy" Reel Hunting Club, it became one of the best known guided hunting operations in the nation. But in his early days, before all the recognition, Jimmy did all his business by means of handwritten letters, responding to inquiries such as this one from the late 1940s, original punctuation preserved: "Is there any chance for you to get my boy and self a duck hunt in the lake I would be glad to pay for both of us, but it had to be on a sat. or Sunday cause the boy is still this year going to school."[46] Correspondence came often, but by the late 1940s it was increasingly typewritten and under the letterhead of prominent businesses and national sporting companies.

Hunts with Jimmy became known throughout the continent for huge numbers of geese, mallards, and pintails that set their wings for his white decoy spreads. From the 1950s to the 1970s he was featured in national sporting magazines and newspaper columns, and he became a spokesman for Peters ammunition. The array of writers who paid homage to white spread hunts with Jimmy Reel were convinced it was his calling, or his decoys, that produced those marvelous hunts. In part, it was, but Jimmy knew the main reason had more to do with roost ponds. They covered the prairie, and he started them.

Jimmy had watched in the 1930s as ducks began to disappear as farming consumed prairie pothole ponds. He thought that pumping water on fallow and harvested rice fields might, in part, offset the loss, and he approached David

Wintermann with the idea. Wintermann remembered, "Jimmy Reel told me 'we've got to do something about the ducks,'" and they did, by building the first Colorado County roost ponds where ducks were allowed to rest undisturbed from hunting pressure. Two roosts were built south of Eagle Lake, including the sixty-two-acre Timber Lake pond. North of town the old Seaholm Lake became a forty-acre roost, and they converted a fourth from an old catfish farm.[47]

Through relationships established with local landowners in his rice buying job, Jimmy had access to land eventually covering one hundred thousand acres in three counties. The largest tracts included David Wintermann's Eagle Lake holdings, Tom Haley's Vineyard Ranch, the Lehrer family's properties in Garwood, and Hancock Rock near Provident City. Jimmy covered much of that land with roost ponds. Alex Wolff was one of Jimmy's season hunters in the late 1940s, and from his Lucky Seven lease on Duncan Lane near Altair, he watched as Jimmy's prairie roost ponds started holding not only ducks, but also large numbers of geese.[48]

Despite all the geese, Jimmy Reel at heart remained a duck hunter. Guide Clifton Tyler says, "Jimmy wanted to create Stuttgart Arkansas here in Eagle Lake and was not interested in the geese, but he saw later on there was money in it." Alex Wolff remembers, "Jimmy didn't even like goose hunting. He let somebody else do the goose hunting." For many years that person was Marvin Tyler, who got his guiding start with Jimmy at Lower Lake Club about 1950.[49]

The place where Jimmy Reel came closest to creating his "little Stuttgart" on the Texas prairie was called the Timber Hole, or Timber Lake, where he and David Wintermann built a levee and flooded a stand of post oaks. Timber Lake was one of the few places where, because of the trees, snow geese wouldn't congregate, and its clear water provided abundant food for ducks. A classic photo taken by *Houston Post* outdoor writer Harv Boughton shows Jimmy standing in the trees, the sky in front of him black with mallards, pintails, teal, and gadwalls funneling in to the decoys. Jimmy is turned to the camera, smiling ear to ear.[50]

Jimmy Reel was one of the best duck and goose callers on the Texas prairie and used an Illinois-style mallard call, but for pintails he just "whistled them in." Bob Brister wrote that Jimmy would keep his highball going long after mallards and pintails had lit on the water, only "10 yards away [and] answering him." Jodie Socha, who learned the guiding trade from Jimmy in the 1960s, says on most afternoons Jimmy drove the prairie in his Chevy Impala with his golden retriever Ginger by his side, and snuck to the edge of roost ponds to listen to ducks. He could name every species by its call. When Bill Appelt started hunting in Eagle Lake, Jimmy told him to do the same thing, and Bill learned how to call "by going down to the flats at night and listening to the ducks."[51]

Jimmy held strong convictions about the right way to hunt waterfowl. He never hunted after noon and eschewed taking long, potentially crippling, shots. Clifton Tyler says Jimmy "was the epitome of a sportsman. When the limit was only five ducks, he always took out six [shotgun] shells. Never more." Jimmy shot a Remington Model 1148 28-gauge, using only 7½ shot for both ducks and geese. Bob Brister was on a hunt with Jimmy and Olympic shooting champion Tom Garrigus, and everyone in the party shot a 20-gauge except Bob. Jimmy admonished Bob with, "If I hadn't had a certain sportswriter along with that cannon, I might have been able to get you boys a fairly decent goose shot." Louis Schorlemmer, who worked with Jimmy from 1967 to 1976, jokes, "When I bought a new 12-gauge shotgun, I did not tell Jimmy Reel about it."[52]

J. R. "Jimmy" Reel Hunting Club, over its almost forty-year tenure, provided dozens of local boys and men employment as guides. African American Bill Mason started at Lower Lake Club and remained with Jimmy until he died. Leo Kuhlanek, best known as Leo the Bohemian, started in 1952. Bill Blair remembers how, before a hunt, Leo would sit in the back of the Sportsman's Inn and not speak a word to anyone. Customers who asked him how he thought they were going to do that day received his standard reply, in his old school accent: "Well, if you shoot one goose you did good. If you shoot two geese you done twice as good." A few of the other many guides included Louis Schorlemmer, Bill Appelt, Jim Longtin, and friends such as Cal Gerston and brother-in-law Frank Hough Jr.[53]

The short, thin man with his trademark canvas hunting cap and a golden retriever by his side died in 1976. A gaping hole was left in the prairie, and the family and community worked together to pick up the hunting pieces. Wife Lucille ran the J. R. "Jimmy" Reel Hunting Club for a year, then daughter Agnes, who later sold it to guide Bill Appelt. Bill, who moved to town as a football coach in 1971, handled J. R. "Jimmy" Reel Hunting Club for twenty years before turning it over to Davis Waddell.[54]

Jim Longtin looks back on his days with Jimmy Reel and says, "You have to understand what kind of a guide he was. I remember once he came in with a party and they had a limit of ducks. They had a limit of geese. And an eight-point buck. There was nobody like Jimmy Reel." Jimmy is buried in Eagle Lake, where each winter tens of thousands of snow geese pass overhead, looking for, and finding, big roost ponds. So too do the pintails, though not in the numbers they once did. Jimmy Reel's once abundant mallards, however, are gone.[55]

Marvin Tyler and his Blue Goose Hunting Club, west of Eagle Lake, were as much a Colorado County waterfowling landmark as Jimmy's J. R. "Jimmy" Reel Hunting Club. Marvin's son Clifton says his father got his start as a duck hunting guide for Jimmy at Lower Lake Club in the 1940s. Together, they watched as the numbers of geese in Eagle Lake continued to grow, "and it just awed them." They wanted to hunt them, and Clifton says it was Marvin who figured out how to do it. Within a few years Marvin opened Marvin's Restaurant and Blue Goose Hunting Club with Jimmy Reel, who remained a partner until the mid-1960s.[56]

Clifton says Marvin's Restaurant was born when his father inherited an acre of land in Altair from his grandfather, left his job in Houston, and built "a beer

> **BLUE GOOSE HUNTING CLUB**
>
> **MARVIN TYLER**　　　　　　　　　**J. R. REEL**
> Phone CE 4-2156 (Eagle Lake)　　　Phone CE 4-2062
> Altair, Texas　　　　　　　　500 W. Prairie, Eagle Lake, Texas
>
> **OVER 20,000 ACRES UNDER LEASE**
> EAGLE LAKE, LISSIE & GARWOOD PRAIRIES
>
> **PARKAS—WHITE SPREADS—DECOYS FURNISHED**
>
> MINIMUM 3 GUNS TO SPREAD
> MORNING HUNTING ONLY—DEPOSITS FOR WEEKENDS
>
> *Welcome Goose Hunters To*
>
> **MARVINS OF ALTAIR**
> MARVIN AND PHYLLIS TYLER—OWNERS
>
> **FAMILY STYLE BREAKFAST**
> **STEAKS—THICK & SIZZLING**
>
> LIMITED CABIN ACCOMMODATIONS AVAILABLE
> BOX 306, ALTAIR, TEXAS　　　　　　　PHONE CE 4-2156

(Modified from *San Antonio Light,* Oct. 6, 1963)

joint and a liquor store. It was a hell of a honky tonk." Marvin grew his honky tonk on Highway 90 into a prairie dining and hunting oasis that he ran for over thirty years as the social center for the sporting and local community. Clifton recalls, "All the landowners would come to Dad's restaurant and eat, and it was all credit. And they wined and dined and ran up the bills and he could sometimes trade hunting for food bills. I don't think they cared whether he paid them or not as long they were wined and dined at that restaurant."[57]

Marvin's wife, Phyllis, ran the kitchen on weekends, with her meals of steaks and seafood served to diners by headwaiter and restaurant fixture Shorty Stewart. Shorty started with Marvin as a guide in the 1950s, and when a hunter missed a bird he would tell them, "Good shot, boss, you missed only by a little bit." Hunters could stay in one of Marvin's nineteen cabins, meeting at the restaurant at 4:00 a.m., where they paid ten dollars to hunt with Tyler or one of his guides. "My father would meet them all at the door," Clifton says. "In the morning the first thing hunters saw was my father and that big ol' hand stuck out to shake hands with all of them, he'd shake hands with every hunter. And he'd find out who they were and then he'd yell out for their guide."[58]

Blue Goose Hunting Club had a sporting shop where customers bought so many Lohman brand goose calls that the company developed a special Marvin Tyler call, one with four Xs across the barrel. He started selling packaged goose hunts so customers could write one check that covered the hunt, lodging, food, and cleaned birds. Sometimes delivering those cleaned birds was harder then shooting them. "The first pickers," Clifton says, "were black families in Altair. They had wood fires under the big old pots that they dipped the birds in. Kids, parents, aunts, and uncles, everybody would help. Mother would pay them every week or so. Every few years they'd boycott, wanted more money. They'd say, 'We're not gonna pick any more geese,' and that put us in a bind. My mother finally had enough and went and bought pickin' machines and hired our own crew."[59]

The first property Marvin leased was with Jimmy Reel at the famous Vineyard Ranch southeast of Eagle Lake. It was on the Vineyard that Marvin built his first goose roost in 1959, one continually maintained for another fifty years by Jimmie Thomas and Eagle Lake's Steve Balas. Within a few short years Marvin leased thousands of acres around Eagle Lake, Lissie, and Garwood and in Provident City. In those early years Marvin hauled tow sacks filled with white cloth decoys to the field, then hid his hunters under white bed sheets. Soon Marvin, with golden retriever Major at his side, decked his hunters out in white parkas, hoods, and face masks. Alex Wolff says he "even painted his boots white."[60]

Russell Tinsley wrote the first promotional article on Marvin for *Texas Fish & Game* magazine, and it immediately improved business. Marvin never forgot the help, Clifton says, and from then on "Tinsley hunted every opening weekend with Dad and Tom Haley at the spot called the Knob [at the Vineyard in Eagle Lake]. We called it Haley's Knob." Appreciating the publicity, Marvin reserved the first Monday of each season for the Outdoor Sportswriters Association, providing food and lodging for as many as forty writers at a time. Year after year they reciprocated with dazzling articles describing the numbers of geese and dizzying flights of pintails, mallards, mottled ducks, and teal that decoyed to a Marvin Tyler rag spread.[61]

Marvin celebrated the end of each hunting season with an annual wild game dinner for local landowners, club guides, and assorted sports writers. Festivities in 1964 were hosted by the Tylers and Jimmy and Lucille Reel, with the main dining hall decked out in a theme like a white decoy spread. Two hundred guests were entertained with live music, hunting movies, awards for best guides, and a duck calling contest with an intimidating list of contestants that included Jimmy Reel, Arthur Hudgins, and Jake Smothers. Special guests at the eighteenth annual dinner in 1968 were Bob Brister and his wife. Those were heady times on the prairie, with a lot to celebrate—that year at the Blue Goose they killed nearly ten thousand ducks and geese.[62]

Then came Andy Griffith. In November 1969, ABC's *American Sportsman* rolled into town to film a segment with TV personality Griffith and golfer Sam Snead. Clifton remembers they hunted for four days and that "my father and Andy Griffith got along like born brothers. They would tell jokes nonstop, and they would sing gospel songs out there in the spread." On the last evening Marvin Tyler characteristically hosted a party for the stars and crew at the restaurant.[63]

After the *American Sportsman* footage aired, the boom to Marvin's business was louder than a 10-gauge on a foggy morning. Sportsmen flocked to Eagle Lake; Marvin's business doubled the first year, then tripled the next. In only two short years he went from eight guides to twenty-five and from ten thousand acres

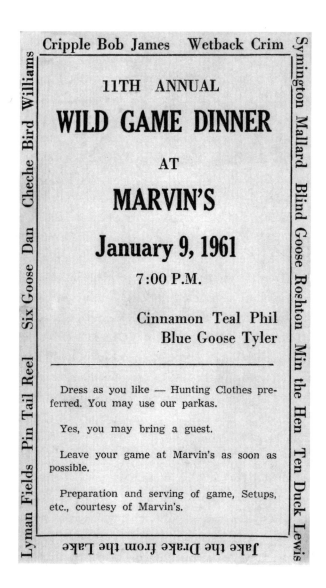

INVITATION TO *Marvin Tyler's wild game dinner, 1961. (Courtesy Agnes Reel Strauss)*

under lease to one hundred thousand. The ripple effect benefited local businesses and the boys and men who earned a living as guides. Clifton, who started guiding for his father at the age of six, says "goose hunting allowed me to go to college," but "the more important thing that the goose hunting industry did in this area was that it paid the way to college for a lot of young men."[64]

Three of Marvin's top guides were John Fields, Herman "Major" Benge, and Mike Baird. Clifton says 1968 was a really tough year on the prairie because of a poor snow goose hatch, and Mike Baird had "zeroed" seven days in a row. "He walked into the restaurant and threw his calls on the floor and said, 'Marvin, I quit.' Turned around and walked out. But he was back a few days later." Tyler's guides knew every bird on the Texas prairie but not, evidently, from every flyway. "In 1964 trumpeter swans for some reason came through here. And this guide came in with these four trumpeter swans that they'd shot and carried them right in the restaurant. Wanted to know what they were. My father didn't know what

ANDY GRIFFITH (left), *Marvin Tyler* (center), *and Sam Snead on the 1969 hunt in Altair filmed for the* American Sportsman *television series. (Courtesy Nesbit Memorial Library, Columbus, Texas, File No. 01952)*

they were, and all the guides were impressed with the great big old geese. Jimmy Reel walked in and he just stopped and braced himself at the front door and he said, 'Y'all get those things out of here,' and he told everybody what they were."[65]

In 1983 Marvin sold his Blue Goose Hunting Club to long-time guide John Fields. Marvin's tradition of putting out hundreds of three-foot by three-foot pieces of white cloth on the ground is still practiced in Eagle Lake, and that's the way his son Clifton hunts today.

Throughout the 1950s and '60s, the combination of rice and roost water brought not just big numbers of geese, but also hunters. The number of hunting guides in Eagle Lake and other Colorado County towns such as Lissie and Garwood grew as well. During the late 1950s ten dollars covered the cost to hunt with the town's biggest outfitter, Jimmy Reel, at his Epps Café headquarters, or with his partner Marvin Tyler in Altair. Retired game warden Tom Waddell opened Lissie Prairie Club in 1954 on twenty thousand acres between Egypt and Lissie, and the next year Tom brought in partner Arthur B. Hudgins. Peter D. "Dan" Gerston opened Bar-D Hunting Club and met his hunters at the "Lissie store." Other guides were Abbey Abercrombie of Lakeside Hunting Club, Albert Dutcher of the W Bar-D Club, Leroy Biggs, Bill Thomas Jr., and V. R. Corman's J. C. Hunting Club in Lissie.[66]

The revenue hunters brought to the area was not small. Recognizing the value of sport hunting, the *Eagle Lake Headlight* in 1962 dubbed Eagle Lake the "Goose Capital of the World," and the new slogan was used in advertising campaigns throughout Texas and the United States. More guides hung their shingles in the 1960s, including Cal Gerston, W. A. "Bill" Adams at Eagle Lake Sportsman's Club, and Anderson Hunting between Lissie and Chesterville. Arthur B. Hudgins, who met his hunters at Joe's Café in Hungerford, saw his business grow from ten hunters a day to one hundred in just a few years. Jimmie Thomas bought the Vineyard property near town in 1964 and started Vineyard Hunting Club, and Gardner Seaholm opened an Eagle Lake day hunting service in 1968. By the 1970s two of the biggest names in town were Clifton Tyler and Davis Waddell.[67]

Clifton Tyler tagged along on his father's hunts at Blue Goose Club when he was six. By the time he was eleven, his father put him in his customers' cars, and in the predawn darkness the boy pointed the way down winding farm roads toward ponds and blinds. Clifton was instructed to walk up and down each of the prairie ponds before daylight, muddying up the water to make it look as if ducks had been feeding. In his pocket he carried a bag of rocks, and he tossed them into the water to make the decoys appear to be swimming.[68]

Clifton started Clifton Tyler Goose Hunting Club in 1975, with headquarters in the 1912 Farris Hotel. Outdoor writer Russell Tinsley, who wrote the first article on Marvin's Blue Goose Club, did the same for Clifton. In addition to day hunts, Clifton offered "executive" hunts, on which his guides put out the decoys before his clients arrived and provided breakfast and coffee in the field and later a tailgate bar. Port Bay Club member John Cook made a few of these hunts with his friend John E. Walker and remembers, "I asked Clifton, 'So what's the "executive" part of the hunt?' He set up a card table and put the hunters' white parkas over it as a tablecloth, and he served us smoked salmon and raw oysters."[69]

Clifton becomes animated when he recalls hunts that produced, as guides refer to them, "the funnel," in which dozens of small and large flocks join into a tornado of thousands of birds that circle, drop, cross, and whiffle, seemingly decoying from every direction. Clifton says, "I've called a shot on a funnel before and nobody ever pulled the trigger, they just watched. It was too beautiful." He and guide Davis Waddell had a group coming in like that once when "one guy shot a single before he was told to. I yelled, 'You shot too soon!' He said, 'Clifton I didn't shoot too soon, you'd called the shot too late!'"[70]

Clifton is walking the rice stubble, reaching into a large linen sack and dropping torn bed sheets one at a time. His hunters dutifully trudge behind him, spreading them out, making them look as much as possible like a flock of geese on the ground. It's the classic Texas white rag spread, and when dawn comes it may bring specks, Canadas, snows, or Ross's geese. The air is filled with the sound of thousands of snow geese roosting to the north on Vineyard pond, the place where, a half-century before, Clifton's father flooded his first roost pond with Jimmy Reel.

Davis Waddell guided for Bill Appelt and Clifton Tyler before he opened Prairie Waterfowl Hunts, and he later took over the J. R. "Jimmy" Reel Hunting Club.

Davis's list of clients included a Nixon cabinet member, a former commander at West Point, and the McIlhenny family, of Tabasco fame, who returned each year for over twenty-six years. Like a lot of young men, Davis knew more about waterfowl than politics, and one morning when he picked up his hunters, he was intercepted by a guy in a suit, who he learned later was a Secret Service agent. A few minutes later, he was sitting in a chair reading the paper when Secretary of State James A. Baker III arrived. Davis had no idea who he was; he just stuck his hand over the top and kept reading.[71]

Clifton and Davis guided in the years when the list of Colorado County guide services reached its peak of about eighteen, in 1990. Today there are fewer guides in Eagle Lake, less rice, and fewer geese. But the sign on the way into town still reads "Goose Capital of the World."

SKULL CREEK

It might have been the acorns, or maybe it was the dam built in the early 1900s that created half-mile-wide Griffin Lake. Either way, Skull Creek was magic to mallards. Game warden Thomas Waddell in the 1940s saw a flock on Griffin Lake he estimated at 150,000 ducks—nearly half mallards. Chief state game warden E. T. Dawson reported a "freakish concentration" of mallards and pintails in 1943. Their numbers so muddied the water that the turbidity killed every fish in the lake.[72]

Jimmy Reel leased Skull Creek in the 1950s and '60s, and Barry Lewis hunted it with him. Barry remembers "if it was a very windy, bad weather day, Jimmy knew where all the mallards would be. They'd all be rafted up on Skull Creek." Barry found a two-acre pond tucked into the oak trees where it seemed to him that "every mallard that came through that part of the country came down."[73]

C. E. "Ed" Johnson's Skull Creek Motel, on the road west from Eagle Lake between Columbus and Altair, overlooked the creek's timbered floodplain. With its cabins, skeet shooting range, and restaurant, it was always full of hunters in the 1960s and '70s. The mallards and hunters disappeared when Johnson sold Skull Creek to Parker Brothers, who brought in giant earth moving machinery and dug gravel pits. The scarred earth remains today.[74]

GARWOOD

The part of the Big Prairie south and west of the Colorado River at the turn of the century was known as Garwood or Goldenrod Prairie. There, farmers and ranchers shot greater Canada geese from horseback, or ducks along the river bottoms, or they went south to hunt Nada Lake before it was drained for agriculture. Rice became big business in the town of Garwood during the early 1900s, and when snow geese made their journey inland, those thousands of acres of rice put the crossroads at Garwood on the hunting map.[75]

In the 1950s Garwood rice stubble hosted Jimmy Reel, Marvin Tyler, and a number of private hunting clubs and leases. For ten dollars Leonard "Lefty" Burton provided a taxi service to Garwood for as many as fifteen hunters who he delivered from Columbus. Adolph Korenek had a day hunting operation in Nada during the 1960s and charged ten dollars a gun. One of the best known private clubs was the Garwood Lease, organized in the 1960s by Houston's Fred Buxton, with rice fields and flooded prairie leased from the Kalina family.[76]

The name synonymous with big rice holdings in southern Colorado County was the Lehers, and David Lobpries remembers "when you could visit the Leher ranch headquarters, sign a waiver, and hunt almost anywhere for free." David's family owned Harry Café, a fixture for Garwood hunters from the 1950s and for the next forty years. David says, "Ewey Keeney Sr. was one of the first to come from Houston, and he asked my mother to open early for breakfast, and it grew to the picking business." Before mechanical pickers, local black families hand-picked birds and sold the feathers to a buyer in New York. Harry closed for a while when his wife died and reopened as Rosie's Picking Parlor.[77]

Garwood is well known in sporting circles as home to the Bucksnag Hunting Club, located in the old Chapman Hotel. It wasn't planned as a hunting club; it started instead in 1968 as a dining club opened by the Raley, Leher, and Reel families. With business slow, Jimmy Reel and his partners were forced to come up a new idea, and Bucksnag was born the next year. The private club's original roster was composed of fifteen members, all either Jimmy's friends or favorite clients from his day hunting business. The list included Texas governor William P. "Bill" Clements, Barnes "Barney" Donnelly, and Alex Wolff, the eldest of three generations of Wolffs who have hunted the club.[78]

Bucksnag never had to advertise, although it got some free publicity when G. Bradford Cook Jr. brought a few Nixon administration people as guests in the 1970s. Alex Wolff's son David says, "The story goes that during Watergate, there is testimony in the congressional record that a lot of the break-in and cover-up planning was done 'in a duck blind in Texas.' That duck blind was at the Bucksnag."[79]

In Bucksnag's first year, former Houston police captain Dave Hadley managed the lodge, with Leo Kuhlanek as head guide. Other guides were Bill Mason, Louis Schorlemmer, Jimmy's son Loudon, and future son-in-law Mike Strauss. Guide Jim Longtin did the paintings that today hang in the lodge near the fireplace, and Al Bisbey, who like Jim hunted for many years on Katy Prairie, was a guide and member. Jodie Socha is head guide today. His sons Ronnie and Randy started guiding at Bucksnag when they were twelve, and now Jodie's grandsons guide there as well.[80]

Jodie got his start guiding 1967, when Jimmy Reel came into Pat Norton's Evinrude dealership in El Campo where Jodie was working. "Jimmy asked me what I did on weekends. I said, 'Well, I don't do a heck of a lot.' He asked me if I wanted to learn how to guide, and the pay was twenty dollars a day. 'Well I don't know—wadda I gotta do?' Jimmy said, 'I'll send you out with some of the other guys. See if you like it.'" Jodie went out for four weekends and liked it so much that he started gathering his own white rag spread. He first took his mother's bed sheets, then proceeded to buy, borrow, and steal enough to build a spread of two hundred rags. "We carried 'em out to the field in six-foot-long plastic bags, and it was a lot of work at the time. But every time we went out we killed five snow geese each."[81]

What Jimmy Reel had learned over the years about putting water on the prairie he perfected at Bucksnag at the club's South Benches roost. Jim Longtin says the geese at South Benches didn't come in all at once, "they came in wave after wave." Jimmy estimated its 165 acres of roosting water, at their peak, held 250,000 geese. Rice, roosts, and guides provided Bucksnag members with some marvelous hunting. Alex Wolff remembered in the first year of the club he shot a limit of geese thirteen hunts in a row.[82]

Alex, who died in 2009, had a long history on the prairie, and Jodie Socha remembers him fondly. "Mr. Wolff shot a 20-gauge, and I remember he would lie down [in the field] and just go to sleep. Every time." Jodie took him on his last hunt, the first year of the 'white geese only' conservation season when only snow and blue geese were legal kills. "We had a big flock come in, and after a volley we had some seven to eight [snow] geese down. There was one spec in the whole thing, and that spec flew right by him at twenty feet. Mr. Wolff shot that goose, and then lays his gun down and goes back to sleep. When it was time to go, he asks me, 'Jodie, did you get my blue goose?' And I said, 'Yessir, Mr. Wolff, I got your blue goose.' That was the last hunt Mr. Wolff ever made, and the last goose he ever killed was an illegal goose. I'll never forget it, and I don't think anybody's ever told him." That morning they shot 113 geese, "but Alex remembers the hunt was 112 because we left his speck in the field."[83]

After Jimmy died in 1976, Louis Schorlemmer and Jimmy's wife, Lucille, daughter Agnes, and son Loudon kept Bucksnag running. Agnes and her husband, Mike Strauss, led it for another twenty years before the lodge was bought by members of the club. Today Jodie and his sons maintain the South Benches roost the same way Jimmy did almost half a century earlier, and the staff inside the "Hunting Hotel" keep members comfortable and well fed. The club looks a lot like it did when Jimmy ran it. The only thing that he might not recognize is that now the South Benches no longer hold a quarter million geese; it's more like twenty-five thousand to thirty-five thousand.[84]

CHAPTER 16

KATY PRAIRIE

WHEN SETTLERS FIRST CROSSED "THE PRAIRIE," THEY FOUND high-standing grasses of bluestem, switchgrass, yellow Indian grass, and eastern grama in a gentle topography of knolls and natural ponds. Legend has it the ponds were wallowed by buffaloes, the great herds once covering the countryside. Near where the town of Katy would come to be, high stands of cane covered the banks of Cane Creek on its way to Buffalo Bayou. Rainwater runoff was so slow that early ranching families said the prairie would "bog a snipe down if he was standing on a saddle blanket."[1]

Covering over a thousand square miles, the Prairie was bordered to the north by pineywoods from Tomball to Prairie View and to the west by hardwood bottoms of the Brazos River. The south boundary went as far as a meander in the Brazos River at Fulshear Plantation, then west to Bovine Bend, later called Wallis, and once extended to the east to Buffalo and Brays Bayous. It was just "the Prairie" at first, then Houston Prairie, and as communities were established on either side of Cypress Creek, locally it became Hockley-Cypress and Katy-Brookshire Prairies. Finally it was just Katy Prairie, and, according to TPWD biologist David Lobpries, it was once the densest inland wetlands in Texas.[2]

HOCKLEY-CYPRESS PRAIRIE

In the early 1850s Captain John W. Warren's stagecoach brought Houston sportsmen to Houseville, later Hockley. Within only a few years wagon wheel ruts were traversed by iron and steel tracks of the Houston and Texas Central Railway. Warren, a former gamekeeper in his native England, opened the Warren Hotel for railroad men and traveling sportsmen. There, he leased hunting dogs and horses and buggies. Evening meals at the boarding house were supplied by the venison, ducks, prairie-chickens, plovers, and snipes harvested on trips afield.[3]

Twelve-year old-George Ellis lived in the Warren Hotel in 1857 and later became Warren's son-in-law, a Hockley constable, and proprietor of Hockley Sportsman's Clubhouse. Opened in the 1880s, Ellis's "fine hunting-grounds" and Sportsman's Clubhouse were on the agenda of the sporting wealthy from Houston, Galveston, and Dallas. Ellis once entertained the Earl of Aylesford on a snipe shoot, a railroad company placing a private rail car at his disposal. Hockley was a small town with a big reputation, earning mention in 1883 in Charles Hallock's prestigious *Sportsman's Directory to the Principal Resorts for Game and Fish in North America*.[4]

Hockley Sportsman's Clubhouse was a regular destination for the Houston Gun Club. Its members made weekend excursions for pigeon shoots, waterfowl, and the popular prize hunts in which teams competed for the highest kill of wild birds using a point system assigned to different bird species. On one prize hunt, Houston Gun Club and their hosts netted nearly one thousand birds. George Ellis later became sheriff of Harris County and moved to Houston, and he continued to hunt ducks south of town at Morgan's Point.[5]

The prairie corridor northwest of Houston was home to several other private clubs in the 1800s, including Hockley's Lone Star Gun Club, Cypress Gun Club, Cypress Gun and Rifle Club, and the Cypress Top Gun Club in the 1890s. To the southwest, the town of Katy was not yet on any Texas map.[6]

KATY-BROOKSHIRE PRAIRIE

Katy, originally called Cane Island, in the 1890s was a small depot town with a little over a hundred residents and two hotels along the Missouri-Kansas-Texas Railroad line. On the route between Galveston and Dallas, Katy became headquarters for sportsmen who arrived on the *Katy Flyer* to hunt along the banks of Cypress Creek. Looking out the train window at the turn of the century, they saw rice crops begin to replace prairie wetlands and native grasses and watched sweeping prairie fires that still burned in the fall.[7]

Three generations of Jordan men—Hank, Chester, and Lyle—farmed the Katy Prairie beginning in 1913. Coming from Oklahoma, the Jordans found only a few scattered rice farms, those of the Woods, Longenbaugh, and Stockdick families. Lyle Jordan says, "When Dad came there it was nothing but sod grass, red wolf, buffalo wallows, prairie-chickens, and ducks."[8]

Born in 1935, Lyle is a bridge between the Katy Prairie of the past and what it is today. He says that between Katy and downtown Houston there was nothing but a little store in Barker and Addicks, and "goin' to Houston was an all day affair." In the late 1930s Chester Jordan moved his family from Katy to Brookshire. One of

Lyle's first recollections was, at two years old, looking out the window of the two-room tin shack "with ice all over everything, and it was just clouds of ducks."

Lyle says Katy Prairie ponds held water year-round. Most were less than an acre in size and filled with "crawdads longer than your hand," softshell turtles, water moccasins, clams, alligator turtles, bullfrogs by the thousands, "millions of mallards," plovers, curlews, clappers, and little Sonora rails. Sandhill cranes were "so thick in that prairie that they'd eat up pasture, and people would shoot at them with deer rifles to get 'em out of their pasture land." On the high ground there were thousands of prairie-chickens and quail and "millions of jack rabbits on the knolls."

The locals called winter storms "blue tail northers," and the sleet, freezing temperatures, and wind often killed their cattle. Lyle remembers that, after one of these storms, a sheet of ice covered a barbed wire fence from top wire to the bottom. It was like a pane of glass, he says, and "I [saw] mallard ducks for a mile and a half standing on the other side of that sheet of ice, trying to get out of that cold wind." Lyle once set his watch as a cloud of ducks first started splashing into a knoll pond on Ray Woods's farm, and it was an hour and fifteen minutes later before the last bird hit the water. Charles Cardiff, whose family came to the Katy area in 1923, scouted the prairie on horseback, then crawled prospective ponds. On one sneak, with ducks grouped up after a blue norther, Charles shot two or three times and picked up sixty-six ducks, mostly sprigs.[9]

Farmers relied only on rainfall to irrigate their first crops of rice, peanuts, and corn. Harvested rice shocked and left to cure in the field brought ducks by the thousands, mostly pintails, mallards, and teal. Charles Cardiff remembers so many ducks they created a "big roar" when they rose. Sometimes during the day farmers didn't see a duck, but the characteristic orange-tinted belly of pintails killed by moonlight was good evidence the birds were roosting by day in the coastal marsh, flying some fifty miles inland to rice fields after dark.[10]

Prairie ducks were important to the area's farming families, who cured the meat and saved feathers for mattresses and pillows. "People," Lyle says, "put ducks up for the year." He remembers they usually tried to shoot about a hundred ducks a shoot, and afterwards family and ranch hands would "go to pickin' ducks" in the bunkhouse. Ducks were split, boiled, quartered, and put in quart jars with water poured water over them, then the top was sealed.[11]

Ranch families and their hands crawled through tall prairie grass or hunted from horseback and over steers trained to be steady on the shot. Jim Warren, fourth-generation Hockley rancher and great-grandson of John W. Warren, says, "My father in the '30s and '40s hunted waterfowl from horseback. He'd just go out on his horse 'Andy Brown,' an old bay horse. You could shoot a shotgun off of him. He'd walk up on a pond and get his ducks, then go back to the house. It wasn't sport, it was just out getting food." Lyle says of those days: "We didn't know what getting in a blind was, or a decoy. You shot ducks to eat, not for fun."[12]

It was a cold, rainy day when Jordan farmhands collected seven-year-old Lyle and headed to one of the forty-foot-high rice straw haystacks used for cattle feed. Mallards hurtled out of the field as they approached. Climbing on top of the stack, they dug chest-deep holes, loaded their double-barrels, and waited for the ducks to return. "And here would come those ducks back," Lyle recalls. "Now that's something to see. Bunches of mallard ducks, 15, 20, at a time would come in and land below you, and start walkin' to that haystack, and start eatin' rice." They waited until the ducks were thick before making the shot. "Then it was slidin' down that ol' slick hay stack, get to the bottom and catchin' cripple ducks. Then it was back to the bunkhouse, back to pickin' ducks."[13]

Night hunting was another efficient and practical means to put food on the table. Lyle made his first night hunt with Ed Comeaux and his brother-in-law Bill Faulk, who brought their families from South Louisiana to work the Jordan rice farm. Crossing a flooded rice field with Faulk's yard dog in tow, Lyle saw hordes of ducks silhouetted against clouds and moon just a few feet away. When Faulk's dog saw or heard a duck, Lyle says, "The ol' chow dog would sit on the levee and throw her ears up. When the dog did that, [Faulk] would blow his duck call." Honing in on the sound, they took their shots during the brief moment ducks were outlined against the moon. Then the Cajuns "would count the [number of] plops on the water, then walk out and pick up that many ducks."[14]

Ducks were food, but they were also a source of revenue from visiting sportsmen. In an interview with Texas Parks and Wildlife, Chester Jordan said his father Hank started "a little hunting operation with a steer" on their land south of Brookshire in the late 1920s. For a fee of five dollars, hunters, mostly from Houston, loaded into wagons behind a team of mules with the ox tied alongside, scouting ducks over the tall grass by standing in the wagon. When a flock was located, they made a sneak, by which two to three men walked behind the steer and circled the pond, closer with each pass. "Then you'd stop and let the steer keep walking. There's nothing that has any more of a surprised look on their face than a bunch of ducks sitting there and all of a sudden they see three guys standing there with shotguns." At the end of a successful hunt, proud sportsmen showed off their ducks strapped over their Model T.[15]

Other Katy ranchers who hunted over trained steers include Charles C. Cardiff, George Nelson, and Joe Beckendorff. Joe rented his steers to sportsmen from Katy to the upper coast, and his trained ox Oscar was often featured in local newspapers. Oscar spent most of the winter of 1933 on Jackson Ranch in Chambers County, earning a grateful Beckendorff over one hundred dollars. Lyle Jordan remembers the last known hunting steer on the prairie belonged to George Nelson and was named Leo after Texas radio personality and politician W. Lee "Pappy" O'Daniel. By then laws were passed outlawing the use of hunting steers, and although Leo was hard to hide, Lyle says, "The game wardens never could catch George Nelson and his ox."[16]

There were only a few private clubs on the Katy Prairie before the 1930s. One was North Prairie Hunting and Fishing Club, which in the 1920s leased twenty-three thousand acres in Waller County and hired "three riders, chief of whom will be a deputy game warden" to patrol the preserve. A. L. Hawkins opened Hawks Hunting Club near Katy in the early 1930s, and its members built a clubhouse. Most city hunters, however, didn't join private clubs—they pitched tents by the side of the road. From there, Lyle says, "they would walk into the prairie for two to three miles," shooting mostly mallards.[17]

After World War II, Houstonians started to lease hunting land and paid twenty-five cents an acre. There were only a few day hunting operations. Lyle remembers Earl "Old Man" Roesner, who had a thirty-acre rice reservoir south of town with two duck blinds that he leased for five dollars a day in the 1950s. Rice crops had replaced nearly all of the Katy Prairie's natural ponds, and the Old Man had "the only water in the country." City sportsmen that came could "kill a mess of any kind of ducks."[18]

For years, Andy Anderson of the *Houston Press* traveled the coast soliciting sportsmen to raise money for charitable causes. Floyd Breedlove VFW Post and the Katy community in the late 1940s teamed up with Andy to organize a social and fundraising event called the Hunters Party and participated in Andy's statewide Annual Wild Game Dinner for Disabled Veterans.

Katy's first Hunters Party, in 1950, was promoted as the VFW-COTFAG Hunters Party and State Championship Duck Calling Contest. It was a celebration of people and sport, attended by Houston sports writers Andy Anderson, Jimmy Lingan, and Bill Walker, with Bill Cardiff the master of ceremonies. National skeet shooting champion Grant Ilseng hosted a shooting exhibition, using Hank Jordan's expensive Stetson hat as a target. Duck calling contests were judged by former Houston duck call manufacturer C. A. Oliveras, Baytown's Watty Watkins, Jim "Spoonbill" Rose, and Joe Beckendorff. The annual Hunters Party fundraiser was part of the local scene for five years and raised thousands of dollars for charity before the festivities ended in 1955.[19]

Equally successful was the Annual Wild Game Dinner for Disabled Veterans, started by Andy Anderson in 1949. It took the energetic newspaperman very little effort to convince local landowners to agree to open their ranches on the last weekend of every hunting season for sportsmen willing to donate their harvest to the cause. Participating ranches included the great Katy Prairie families of the era: the Warrens, Beckendorffs, Stockdicks, Peeks, Mortons, Longenbaughs, Jordans, Cardiffs, Woodses, and Hoyts, the Wheelesses of Cinco Ranch, and the Huggins family of Fulshear.[20]

In its first year, Katy Prairie hunters sent 473 wild ducks to the naval hospital in Houston, and by the early 1950s the number grew to 800 a year. When the benefit started, only a few geese had arrived on the prairie; the most they collected was 30. But by 1956 more geese were donated than ducks, the number reaching 432.

> **YOU'VE DONE A SWELL JOB, VETS**
> We Wish You Every Success On Your
> **KATY V. F. W.-COFTAG**
> **DUCK CALLING CONTEST**
> and
> **BARBECUE**
>
> **AMERICAN RICE GROWERS ASSOCIATION**
> Katy, Texas

(Modified from *Brookshire Times*, Oct. 20, 1950)

Support from the extended community was huge. State game wardens checked in participants, ranchers guided hunters to their roost ponds, VFW volunteers manned duck cleaning areas, and state highway patrolmen hauled the ducks to the old VFW barn. Houston's Harvey Evans brought the Houston Retriever Club to collect downed birds."[21]

State game warden Thomas Waddell shot his benefit birds over a trained steer, and legend has it that the "last day of the season the ox fell over dead." Tom's great-nephew Davis Waddell jokes that Katy ranchers probably brought his uncle along so they didn't have to follow legal limits. It didn't help. Harvey Evans says that the ducks were piled high one year when federal wardens made a visit. "The day the Fed showed up, the word just spread right down the levee, from one person to the other: 'Fed's here and they're gonna make everybody have a limit of ducks.' Well, there wasn't any way we could do that, so we sent the word back around, 'Go stop those cars!' We had to stop a bunch of people, and told 'em what was goin' on and got 'em to come in there and count 'em as hunters." They did not find enough cars. "So the Feds stopped our hunt right there."[22]

The benefit hunts got more bad press in 1956 when undercover agent Anthony Stefano filed charges against several Katy hunters for selling their wild ducks. In his prosecution of sixty-seven-year-old E. M. East, Stefano told the Houston judge: "We heard rumors that many ducks which should have gone to the Veterans Hospital were being diverted for private sale to market hunters around Katy." East was sentenced to ninety days in jail for selling twenty-eight ducks.[23]

By the time Andy Anderson died in 1956, his Annual Wild Game Dinner for Disabled Veterans had spread throughout Texas. But the end was in sight. In Katy, only 150 ducks and 27 geese were collected for charity in 1958. People were concerned that, with game in short supply, the popular event was doomed. It was, and rancher Bill Cardiff explained why: "Most of the hunting lands are now leased to Houston hunters and sportsman," he said, and with hunting pressure so unbearable, "virtually all of the game is driven out of the area shortly after the season opens."[24]

KATY PRAIRIE'S *Chester Jordan (right) in 1931 with his father, Hank, and greater Canada geese. (Courtesy David Lobpries)*

Until the late 1940s, greater Canadas were the most common geese on the prairie, with most found in the knoll country around Hockley. Each winter when the Canadas arrived, families "would go sneak 'em. It was an event." They used longhorn steers, and after the hunt, they tied the geese together and let them hang over the steer's back.

Snow geese were rare. Charles Cardiff didn't see his first snows until the early 1930s, and Chester Jordan only heard them as they flew over on their way to the coast. His son Lyle adds, "We didn't know what a white goose was." By the late 1940s, as small flocks began to move inland from the coast to feed, "people asked, 'What kind of birds are these?' They called 'em white or blue brant. Everybody decided to go out and kill one, see how they tasted."[25]

After World War II, tractors replaced mules, and combines made threshers obsolete. To increase irrigation efficiency, fields were leveled by fresnos, iron boxes pulled by mules or tractors. The buffalo wallows, once prime duck habitat, disappeared, filled with soil from leveled knolls. Rice cultivation was good for geese, but bad for ducks and worse on prairie-chickens. Lyle Jordan remembers, "Once the sod was gone so were the chickens. When they used to shock rice, they would be up on top of the shocks by the hundreds. And they would drum. The plow pushed it all out."[26]

By the late 1950s the thousands of acres of prairie rice brought immense flocks of snow, specklebelly, and lesser Canada geese. At first they flew inland from the coast, and then they began to roost on artificial reservoirs used to irrigate rice fields. The first Katy Prairie roost ponds were on farms owned by Richard Woods and the Longenbaughs and on Warren Ranch. Ducks, much like the geese, adapted to the man-made changes, and though they never returned

Lyle Jordan *of Texas Safaris, Katy Prairie, 1960s. (Courtesy Lyle and Pat Jordan)*

to the prairie in their former numbers, they began to share roosting water with geese. On Warren Ranch reservoir, Jim Warren remembers nights when "it would be just wave after wave [of ducks] goin' over. You couldn't see 'em but you could hear 'em. They would either be comin' or goin,' depending on what kind of moon you got. I can hear it right now as if it were still happenin.'"[27]

Landowners started to promote goose hunting along with ducks. Chester Jordan, who for years advertised only duck ponds east of Brookshire at Jordan Farms, was probably the first to lease rice fields for goose hunting in the late 1950s. Over the next few decades the sport grew into a major outdoor industry, and most give credit for its commercial start to Chester's son, Lyle Jordan.[28]

Lyle first hunted ducks by crawling ponds like everyone else, his gun a 16-gauge Winchester Model 12 with the plug out. When he blew the end of the barrel off his gun—twice—he kept using it. It just got shorter. Lyle says he first learned there was more to the sport than crawling from Ed Comeaux and his brother-in-law Bill Faulk, who hunted over handmade decoys and used cane reed duck calls.[29]

Lyle was married and running the Katy Poultry House when a Houston businessman came through the door with a convincing argument for why they should partner in a commercial hunting operation. It was 1961, and the next year South Texas Hunters' Club was born. The first year was nearly Lyle's last when his new partner pocketed all the money.[30]

Lyle and his wife, Pat, decided to give the business another try. He got advice on running a guiding business from Jimmy Reel, and through trade, barter, and a generous extended family he opened Texas Safaris on twelve hundred acres of Jordan and Woods farmland. When Lyle went to Houston to solicit customers, he says, "I only had one ol' western suit and a cowboy hat and a pair of boots. Pat, every three or four days, had to sew up the pockets."[31]

KATY PRAIRIE'S *Lyle Jordan preparing snow goose decoys for the season, late 1960s. (Courtesy Lyle and Pat Jordan)*

TEXAS SAFARIS *advertisment, 1966. (L. to R.) Lyle Jordan, Jim Longtin, Hugh Russell (courtesy Jim Longtin).*

Lyle first hunted snow geese by spreading pages from the *Houston Chronicle* over rice stubble. He covered his head with a white sheet, the practice that led locals to call snow goose shooting "ghost hunting." Down the road, Eagle Lake hunters were decoying geese using scraps of white cloth, including diapers and tablecloths—the Texas white spread. Lyle embraced the idea, at first setting out small spreads of 150 decoys. He put a stick in the ground or dirt clod at a fair shooting distance; if geese passed that line, they were in range.[32]

"We experimented every day," Lyle recalls. He filled in rag spreads with anything white, including foam, bird-shaped kites. He ran a string across stakes, tied rags on it, and pulled on the end—pintails loved it. Cloth rags were later switched to white plastic banquet cloth, with some turned into wind socks by attaching them to welded washers on rods. When Lyle went to bigger spreads, he used fifteen hundred trash cans cut in half and staked. Lyle's white spreads decoyed snows, blues, Canadas, and specks, big numbers of wigeons, pintails, black mallards, and teal. By 1965 his customers took an unprecedented four thousand birds, and it was just the beginning.[33]

Lyle knew that roosting water was the key to prairie waterfowl hunting, but convincing rice farmers to put water on their land was not easy. "Duck hunting was Christmas money," he says. "Farmers did not like to hold water on their land," as it took grazing land out of rotation and encouraged weeds. By the 1970s Katy Prairie had what Lyle calls "the ten big roosts." His uncle Richard Woods was first with a thirty-acre roost. It was followed by Longenbaugh Farm roost and Welch Lake, both about fifty acres. Others were on Cinco Ranch, the McMillan rice farm, and Warren Reservoir near Hockley. The largest area roost was the Big Three Reservoir on Freeland land next to the Bollinger roost. Lyle, who was responsible for convincing the Freelands to flood Big Three, built a couple of other roosts on Jordan land.[34]

Lyle offered corporate memberships and season leases and built the business to twenty-five to thirty companies a year. Members made half-day hunts, meeting in the early morning at the shed behind Lyle's house, where they picked locations on a wooden board with a map drawn on it, placing washers on nails to reserve their spot. He grew the business to include Brazos River bottom hunting, Texas Hill Country deer and antelope, hunts in Mexico, and offshore fishing. Katy-Brookshire was the center for geese, ducks, doves, quail, and snipes. Lyle didn't like the headaches of guided day hunting, but he finally relented in 1971. He figured if he charged the exorbitant fee of fifteen dollars a gun with a guide extra, it would discourage business. It didn't.[35]

The Texas Safaris waterfowl piece supported six to eight guides. Arkansas's Jim Longtin was one of the first. When Lyle caught Brooks Brewer and Richard Smith poaching, he turned them into guides instead of the law, both before they were old enough to drive. Richard Smith, who "probably killed more snow geese than any guide in the state," worked fifteen years for Lyle, and when Texas Safaris closed he moved to Larry Gore's Eagle Lake and Katy Prairie Outfitters.[36]

Houston Chronicle outdoor writer Doug Pike and World Champion goose caller James Prince both got their guiding starts at Texas Safaris. James, then a freshman in high school, remembers a quiet Monday morning at the hunting shed when Lyle suggested he round up all the Sunday papers he could find, ball up the pages, and put them in a garbage bag. Lyle told him to "carry the bag down to the flats and toss the balls on the water—they'll open up and look like ducks.

You'll kill pintails." That day James didn't shoot a duck. He just watched—the volume of decoying birds was too spectacular. Doug Pike later wrote what Lyle thought was the best description of him: the "guide that smelled like smoke that got a red Cadillac."[37]

On the front cover of the *Houston Chronicle Texas Magazine* in 1968, a threatening sky forms the backdrop to a white spread, and the lone figure of Patsy "Pat" Jordan is walking the field. It was the first of several articles written about Pat, who guided for her husband for ten years. She started by taking visiting hunters' wives, then began filling in when Lyle had more hunters than guides to take them. It wasn't long before Pat was in more demand than many of her male counterparts.[38]

Lyle Jordan developed a keen waterfowl knowledge over the years. Mallards, he says, normally had orange skin, but "If you put that mallard on peanuts, he will turn as white as snow, and when you pick 'im your hands is like you had Vaseline hair tonic all over. It just comes out of their skin. There is nothing that will equal a bird that's fed on peanuts." He advises not to kill ducks after January, when they fed on "the new grass," as "they get brassy and not worth eating. You'd throw 'em away." In high winds he says to watch the first goose that leaves the roost, because "that first goose would show you what direction they were all gonna go." He once hauled a fifty-five-gallon drum filled with syrup to one of his roosts and poured it on the water because he heard it made the ducks taste sweet.

Lyle's Katy Prairie education was hard-earned knowledge. The only way into a field was by walking, packing in decoys through plowed, often muddy fields on cold, wet mornings. Hunts in late winter were nearly always made with frozen hands and feet. Small comfort was provided when "we'd go to dry cleaners and get dry cleaning bags to wear to fight the wind." There were hunts in mud so thick that Lyle sat on a board so he "wouldn't sink so far down."

A few of the hundreds of yarns from the days of Texas Safaris live on through Lyle and his guides. Lyle remembers he let his regular customers, astronauts Gus Grissom, Ed White, Wally Schirra, and Deke Slayton, hunt all day on the back of his property, Gus always accompanied by "his half of a half pint of white lightning." Singer and songwriter John R. Lee preferred shooting red-eared turtles for turtle soup over hunting geese.[39]

With newspaper deadlines looming, *Houston Chronicle* writer Joe Doggett thought it would be "irrational and irresponsible, totally lacking in professional judgment," to accept Lyle's offer to hunt on a soggy January day in 1973. Joe was there before sunrise. The sportswriter, who had missed a few close shots on decoying pintails and wigeons, later joked he felt cheated not having shot a mallard. Lyle didn't hesitate, saying he "did not deserve a mallard and hinted that maybe even a spoonbill was asking too much."[40]

One corporate hunter showed up to hunt alone. Not knowing much about the sport, he hung rag decoys on a barbed wire fence by the road. Lyle says when he went to check on him, he "was in the canal ditch, waiting on geese. Four wires of fence he had covered in rags. Heck with going out in that field, he's gonna get 'em from the road!" More than one novice hunter returned home thinking he had a limit of greenheads, succumbing to the old guide's trick of "pulling out a pocket knife, trimming the bill of a spoonbill, so they think it's a mallard." The "poverty weeds" Lyle used to brush his blinds were dry one late-season day—so dry that the black plume of smoke he saw from the house was from hunters who had brought a portable heater to the blind and had burned it down.[41]

Texas Safaris closed its doors in 1984. Lyle says he "was standin' in Big Three Reservoir, the best place on the prairie," when he decided to retire to the Hill Country. He called Larry Gore and offered him all his leases. Looking back on his times with Jimmy Reel, Joe Lagow, Marvin Tyler, and O. D. LaBove, the guide that smelled like smoke and got a red Cadillac says, "I'll see 'em somewhere on the other side."[42]

The opening of Lyle Jordan's business was the start of the big boom of Katy Prairie goose hunting, when thousands of geese flocked to Katy Prairie and hunters followed in equally impressive numbers. Along with Lyle's, some of the first day hunting operations were Joe Weaver's near Brookshire, Vernon Jurries's in Pattison, and Freddie D. Hoyt's Circle H Hunting and Fishing Club on Katy-Hockley Road. Hoyt had goose and duck blinds on three lakes, and among his customers in 1963 were astronauts Walter Schirra, Neil Armstrong, and Deke Slayton. The next year, Hoyt turned the operation into a private resort for Houston's wildcatter and Shamrock Hotel owner Glenn McCarthy and his partners, calling it MCM Hunting Ranch.[43]

By the late 1960s and early '70s there were about ten Katy and Hockley Prairie hunting operations. Goose hunters in cars and pickup trucks converged on Katy in the predawn hours, meeting at restaurants that catered to hunters. At 3:00 a.m., hunters met at Katy Restaurant and Fort Bend Steak House, headquarters for Sportsmen's Day Hunting Club and Guzman's Day Hunting of Katy. Guzman advertised that if you forgot to make reservations, "Meet at the Ft. Bend Steak House at 4:30 and I will take you out." By the 1980s the mecca for Katy hunters became Kountry Kitchen.[44]

Guiding legends were born on the prairie during those early years. Lyle Jordan says of those early guides, "We was coon hunters and fox hunters and people thought we was crazy when we started guiding waterfowl." They went from crazy to recognized as their names began appearing in outdoor newspaper columns and sporting magazines. One name featured as early as Lyle's was that of Jim Longtin.[45]

Arkansas native Jim Longtin started hunting at Tri-County Duck Club on the Arkansas River when he was nine. Those were the days, Jim remembers, when huge reservoirs were filled with hundreds of thousands of mallards that decoyed into timber lakes a hundred at a time. Jim moved to Houston in the ninth grade

A YOUNG *Jim Longtin after a Lake Charlotte hunt. (Courtesy Jim Longtin)*

and got his start during high school as a freelance guide. Over his forty-two-year career he guided more than thirty thousand people, including two presidents and an Arabian king.[46]

During his high school freelance years, Jim was hunting on Old and Lost Rivers when he saw clouds of birds circling over the Trinity River treeline south of Lake Charlotte. He followed them, wading through the cypress trees as "the whole place exploded with mallards." It reminded him of his native Arkansas, and he hunted that flooded timber for years.[47]

During college Jim worked for Lyle Jordan at Texas Safaris, and in 1964 started Katy Prairie Day Hunting with his headquarters at Gene's Sport Shop. Adding a deepwater fishing charter service the next year, Jim changed the name to Fish and Fowl. Fish and Fowl offered a wide range of sporting services—his waterfowl piece alone featured prairie, Trinity River timber, and coastal hunting. Blackie Tyler joined him in 1967, then took over the business two years later.[48]

In the late 1960s and 1970s Jim guided for another great Arkansas duck caller, Jimmy Reel, in Eagle Lake and Garwood. He founded Spindletop Rod and Gun Club next to Pipkin's Ranch, near Winnie, in 1979. Two years later he lost the club when one of his corporate clients offered the landowner twice the money. He returned to Katy Prairie, where he opened Paddlefoot Places on fifteen thousand acres of Jordan Farms on Woods Road, and he ran it until he retired in 1994.[49]

> **KATY PRAIRIE DAY HUNTING**
> **DECOY SPREADS FURNISHED**
> RICE FIELDS · PONDS · PLOWED GROUND
> HUNTING BY RESERVATION ONLY
> **JIM LONGTIN–BLACKY TYLER**
> **UL2-7407≡UL2-4503≡GY2-9098**
> (KATY)   (HOUSTON)

(Modified from *Brookshire Times,* Nov. 16, 1967)

Jim's list of accomplishments and contributions to the sport is long. As a boy, he learned how to sound exactly like the ducks he hunted, and by the time he was thirteen he had placed in duck calling contests that included the Junior World. He continued to win local, state, and regional calling contests throughout his adult life and gave calling lessons in sporting goods stores around Houston. Back in the days of record players, Jim was the featured duck caller on the *Fowl Talk* instructional record.[50]

A passion for waterfowl led Jim to a degree in wildfowl biology and another in art. His wildfowl paintings were featured in magazines and art shows, and two oil paintings still hang in the den of Garwood's Bucksnag Club. Jim, with outdoor writer John Wootters, started the Texas Outdoor Academy in Houston, with classes on calling and waterfowl hunting. Avian cholera struck Katy Prairie roost ponds in the late 1980s, and for three years he worked as a volunteer with TPWD biologists to contain the outbreak. Overworked biologists during those troubling years will never forget him.[51]

Jim experimented with everything that had to do with the sport, designing camouflage patterns for outdoor clothing and making some of the first goose decoy kites and "flyers" used on the Texas prairie. He even convinced a toy company to create balloons shaped like geese. Filled with helium, they worked great until the weather got cold, Jim says, and then they sank to the ground. Asked about hunting in his good old days, he shakes his head. "You wouldn't understand it. Nobody could understand it that hadn't seen it. It was just that good."[52]

David Jenkins was another of the early day hunting guides, getting his start in the early 1960s. For years he hunted on Bud Southard's ranch across from Warren Reservoir, and with early guide Jimmy Clapp he charged twenty dollars for a guide, rag spreads, and white parkas. Jenkins produced the *Fowl Talk* calling instructional record for geese and ducks with Jim Longtin. Jim, who spent long days in the field with Jenkins remembers him as "an awfully good shot."[53]

Lyle Jordan did the hunting reports on radio for Ford and Lone Star beer with Jenkins. Lyle had to think hard about what to say for the "where to hunt in the morning" forecast, but Jenkins, he says, gave the same response nearly every week. "Dave would come and he'd say, with his deep voice, 'Where I would hunt in the morning would be either in the plowed ground, rice field or duck pond.' Well, there wasn't anything else!"[54]

Jenkins guided until 1988, when, caught in a USFWS undercover operation, he faced thirteen charges that included shooting over the limit, using lead shot, shooting after dark, transportation of illegal birds, and sale of migratory birds. Legend has it that he fled to South America to avoid facing charges.[55]

Guide Blackie Tyler drove a rice truck on Katy Prairie, a job that gave him the opportunity to meet nearly every farmer in the area. Those connections helped him to acquire lease land, first for Jim Longtin and later when he took over Jim's Fish and Fowl business. By the early 1970s Blackie guided as many as fifty hunters a day. Two of his young guides, Butch Wagner and Larry Gore, went on to open their own successful operations. Blackie had the dubious honor of putting a huge rag spread out the night before a hunt in 1973 for *Houston Chronicle* outdoor writer Bob Brister, only to arrive in the morning to find other hunters had stolen every one of his decoys.[56]

Al Bisbey got his start with Rocky and Perry Robertson at Robertson Rice Farm as a day hunting guide in the late 1960s. He met his hunters each morning at the Massey Ferguson shop in Katy, and Al remembers for "$5.00 you could hunt a pond, and $15 got you a guide. I was the only guide at the time." Al next moved to Dennison and Hegar rice farms before taking over David Jenkins's Hockley operation in 1975.[57]

By then Al's customers met at the Kountry Kitchen in Katy, and he says, "Every table was filled with [Larry] Gore hunters, but Larry always saved one for me." Will Beaty, owner of CFO Outfitters and Marsh Point in Chambers County, was fifteen years old when he guided for Al, and because he was too young to drive, Al came to the house to pick him up before each hunt. Will guided over huge goose spreads, sometimes with up to four thousand decoys that they cut from rolls of plastic banquet sheets from the Popcorn Factory in Houston.[58]

Al's big rag spreads and his mouth calling produced hugely successful goose and duck hunts. James Prince remembers watching him call pintails to big spreads on the McMillan Carnation Pond, with its hard sand bottom and blinds built into the levee. His hunters nearly always shot a limit of the white and brown birds. Al often hosted Houston sportswriters, and once, when he brought Bob Brister, they found the pile of rags he always left in the field frozen into a six- by twelve-foot solid mass that never thawed in time for the hunt. Outdoor writer Stan Slaten once put his cameras in a decoy bag, and "We floated those bags across the pond. We didn't know his cameras were in there. He poured the water out of 'em."[59]

If there is one outfitter whose tenure reflects the lofty levels Katy Prairie goose hunting reached at its peak, it would be Larry Gore and his Eagle Lake and Katy Prairie Outfitters. The Wyoming native hatched his business in 1977 while still a high school student in Sugar Land. First called Larry Gore Guide Service, the business started as an assignment for Larry's agricultural co-op class, devised primarily as a way for the high school boy to hunt more often and at better places.

Larry's high school class project combined elements from other area guiding operations. From Lyle Jordan he borrowed the season lease model. From David Jenkins he added a day hunting piece, and he looked to Marvin Tyler for the idea of controlling so much land his hunters could go wherever the birds went. From the very beginning he advertised in national sporting magazines, an idea Larry credits to growing up seeing Gary Conner's Top of Texas Guiding Service advertisements in *Field and Stream*.

The first landowner Larry approached with his business model was George Nelson, who leased Nelson Farms to his father. Next, he knocked on doors. His was a slow start, the only clients at first being friends and coworkers, and Blackie Tyler offered him a job while he built up his business. By 1980 it was showing promise. That year Larry Gore Guide Service was renamed Katy Prairie Outfitters, with the word *outfitter* added, rather than *guide* or *club,* as a nod to his Wyoming roots.

Larry worked with local landowners, cajoling and paying them to pump water for roost ponds. More water meant more birds, he explained, and for him that meant more customers. The landowner-outfitter partnership became so successful that he eventually maintained one hundred ponds. The number of geese on his Katy Prairie roosts surpassed even Larry's expectations and became, he says, "a spectacle." Roost water brought back "the good ol' days for ducks as well. Those birds came and they stayed, and stayed."[60]

For more than three decades, every day during the season a procession of cars made the predawn pilgrimage from Houston to Larry's headquarters at Kountry Kitchen, filling tables with hunters. At the end of the hunt those cars and trucks formed a parade line from the restaurant parking lot to Katie Blaze's picking house, which had the word *geese* spelled wrong on its sign.[61]

By the 1990s Larry's tightly run business grew to about a hundred goose hunters a day for an average of five thousand guided hunter days a year, plus another three hundred club members. He employed forty guides, twelve full-time, and had seven office personnel. James Prince, who worked for Larry beginning in 1987, says during his eleven-year tenure he did twenty-eight television shows with Larry. In the late 1990s, when the *Houston Chronicle* waterfowl directory featured more than thirty outfitters on Katy Prairie, Larry's high school project had become an institution, arguably the best known guided hunting operation in the nation.[62]

Dark clouds formed on the Katy horizon in the 1990s. After the gravel road between Houston and Katy became an interstate highway, asphalt and suburbs began to cover the prairie where buffaloes once wallowed. An international airport was planned on Freeman's Big Three Reservoir. When Larry saw it coming, he expanded his acreage to Eagle Lake, changing the name of his business in 1988 to Eagle Lake and Katy Prairie Outfitters. When Lyle Jordan saw it coming, he left town.

Lyle says, "It happened so fast. I used to pack decoys and make a spread and kill a lot of geese right where Igloo plant is sitting right now, between Katy and Brookshire. I can remember when that prairie used to be so dark that whenever Exxon opened up the Katy gas field out there, north of 90, they had a flare burning. There were people that wanted to sue because they was keeping 'em awake, they had the lights burnin' all times of night, and they couldn't sleep at night. 'Course it ruined all the night duck hunting, they couldn't compete with that flare."[63]

CHAPTER 17

SHORT STORIES from FARTHER AFIELD

From the Panhandle to Caddo Lake in East Texas and from the upper coastal prairies north to the Red River, inland Texas waterfowlers share a heritage as deep as that from the coast. Compared to the coast, their hunting was in some ways very different, their pursuits taking them to flooded river bottoms, natural lakes, agricultural lands, and later man-made water impoundments. But in other ways their sport was strikingly similar; they hunted many of the same birds, suffered similar discomforts, and had to rely upon knowledge of their surroundings—or a guide or club—to enjoy a day of gunning.

PANHANDLE

For good waterfowl shooting around the Panhandle towns of Lubbock and Amarillo, hunters in the late 1800s relied on rainfall to bring playa lakes and intermittent streams to life. When the plow first brought agriculture to the prairie—wheat, "green" or winter wheat, corn, and peanuts—birds started coming to the northwest corner of Texas in such numbers that farmers no longer considered hunting a sport, but a necessity. As the sky above their crops began to go black with circling waterfowl, whole families gathered their guns.[1]

Newspapers followed flocks as they routinely destroyed entire crops of peanuts and corn, with headlines such as "Wild Ducks Ravage Castro County Grain" or "Ducks Destroy Corn Crop." Under the heading "Many Wild Ducks Menace Plains Farmers," pintails, teal, mallards, and even redheads plagued the Panhandle's standing corn crop in 1924, when "wild ducks in great swarms that darken the skies" poured into the Panhandle.[2]

Even more birds came as water was added to row crops and cereal grains by means of large-scale irrigation projects. Northwest of Amarillo in Bailey County, Goose and Bull Lakes in the 1930s supported forty thousand wintering mallards. In 1940, White Lake reservoir, on the Muleshoe watershed project, held two hundred thousand ducks, mostly mallards. At the Palo Duro Club in 1942, the canyons of Palo Duro Canyon were said to be "a duck haven with clouds of the migratory fowl . . . affording members their bag limits with ease."[3]

Greater Canada geese followed the ducks in the 1920s. North of Lubbock, "great droves" of geese frequented Running Water Draw near Plainview. During the 1930s and '40s, large goose concentrations were found in lakes around Adrian and the Canadian River streams above Old Tascosa, northwest of Amarillo. To the southwest, roosting water at Tule Lake and adjacent cornfields made a perfect combination for geese and mallards. Nearby Tierra Blanca Creek couldn't have looked more different from the Gulf Coast, with highland shortgrass prairie dissected by canyons and ephemeral creeks. But after Buffalo Lake was built in the 1930s, it wintered as many as fifty thousand greater Canada geese and more than one hundred thousand ducks. Geese feeding in the winter wheat fields surrounding the lake gave farmers fits but provided hunters with great sport.[4]

SAN ANTONIO

San Antonio sportsmen had a big influence on coastal Texas duck hunting, particularly around Aransas Bay, where they organized many of the Coastal Bend's earliest hunting clubs. Duck hunting was so imbued in the city's culture that the *San Antonio Light* carried a special "Fowling and Fowlers" section that followed city sportsmen around the state in the 1890s. The tally of their harvest, in those days considered the sporting measure of men and women, was dutifully reported in the weekly newspaper column.[5]

Among the first organized Alamo City sporting clubs were the San Antonio Sportsman's Club, Alamo Gun Club, and Mitchell Lake Club, all founded in the early 1880s. John Gilbert, A. B. Critzer, and Oscar Guessaz started the venerable San Antonio Gun Club in 1888, its one hundred members hunting on lakes near the city, with excursions to the coast by train. Bexar County Country and Sportsmen's Club was chartered in 1898 on two thousand acres outside the city, its primary purpose to attract investors to San Antonio. Clubs had well-rounded outdoor agendas that included shooting contests and pursuit of practically every game fish and animal in the Lone Star State. When they hunted waterfowl, most went south to Mitchell Lake.[6]

Mitchell Lake, on the floodplain where the Medina River joins the San Antonio River, was the city's premier fowling destination. Hunters found the lake a six-hundred-acre jungle of "man-high swamp reed," cattails, and wild coffee weeds, with mallards, canvasbacks, teal, scaup, pintails, gadwalls, redheads, ruddy

> **DUCK HUNTERS!**
> JOIN
> **Mitchell Lake Club**
> Best shooting in state. Apply A. V.
> Holland, treasurer. Cr. 952, Box 1107.

(Modified from *San Antonio Light,* Oct. 29, 1926)

ducks, wigeons, geese, curlews, snipes, Canada geese, and swans. Spaniards who watered their longhorns on the lake's moss-covered oak and hackberry shores in the 1700s called it Laguna de los Patos—"lake of the ducks."[7]

As San Antonio went from mission to city, the lakeshore remained largely uninhabited, in part because of mosquitoes so thick it was said they drove "herds of cattle through barbed-wire fences." Market hunters who fed the growing town shared the winter wildfowl migration with sport hunters, both returning to the city with waterfowl by the wagonload. In the 1870s so many hunters camped along the lake's perimeter that the night sky seemed ablaze from the light of their campfires.[8]

Most private San Antonio clubs with lake access improved its natural habitat. Along shoreline depressions called "the outside ponds," they constructed levees and drilled artesian wells to create impoundments planted with wild celery and rice. Club sportsmen shot a remarkable volume and diversity of puddle ducks, diving ducks, geese, swans, and cranes. Highly regarded local sportsman August Ohnesorge usually shot only mallards, returning from one hunt with seventy-five. Undeterred by ice a week later, he killed fourteen by walking out on the frozen lake and knocking birds on the head with his ramrod.[9]

The first shooting preserve located on Lake Mitchell was Mitchell Lake Club, formed before 1885. Its sixty members built a lodge on the edge of the lake and posted a gamekeeper at the gate, primarily to keep out market hunters. The club's secretary and treasurer was writer, sportsman, and Texas game law proponent Oscar Guessaz. Hardin "Hardy" Adams was manager. Access to the grounds was by gate key and membership cards available from Charles Hummel's gun store downtown.[10]

In the 1920s, Rudy Strohmeyer and Jules Appler opened Mitchell Lake Gun Club, with a lodge, boathouse, and fifty skiffs. By the time postal clerk David A. Mahavier took over the club in the late 1930s, man-made changes to Mitchell Lake and years of drought in the northern United States and Canada had taken a toll on waterfowl populations. The 2,250 ducks Mahavier's seventy-five members harvested in the 1939 season hardly compared to the 7,576 only nine years earlier. By then nearly all of the swans were gone, and greater Canada geese were becoming rare.[11]

Ike Eisenhower hunted Mitchell Lake Gun Club nearly every morning when he was stationed at Fort Sam Houston. David Mahavier received a note from the front lines during World War II in which the general apologized for being too busy to hunt that season. Mahavier is credited with opening the first public day hunting operation on Mitchell Lake, and he later opened a guiding service with properties in Seadrift, Austwell, and Port O'Connor. He sold Mitchell Lake Gun Club to A. B. Edwards in 1945, and it closed in the late 1950s.[12]

East of Mitchell Lake, William Cassin ran private Cassin Lake in the early 1900s, with season hunting permits available from Charles Hummel's gun shop and D. & A. Oppenheimer's bank. North of Mitchell Lake, Canvasback Lake was home to the Canvasback Club and Mitchell Lake Hunting Preserve in the 1930s. The Sportsman's Club was chartered as a social, business, and conservation organization in 1935. Headquartered in the downtown Plaza Hotel, its advisory board included A. L. Huber and Armstrong B. Weakley who were among the original incorporators of the St. Charles Bay Hunting Club.[13]

Blue Wing Hunting and Fishing Club was organized in 1910 at Blue Wing Lake on South Flores Road, with forty members who constructed a private fifty-acre water impoundment. One of the club organizers was Ed Rand, also a charter member of Rockport's Port Bay Club and an early supporter of Oscar Guessaz's crusade to pass state game laws. Armstrong B. Weakley, an incorporator of St. Charles Bay Hunting Club, was an early member. Blue Wing Club is still in existence.[14]

Southwest of the city, Lost Lake Hunting Club was founded on the Medina River. Club proprietors Jack Thurman and William Mussey constructed two freshwater lakes and offered annual memberships for seventy-five dollars in the late 1920s. Other popular duck hunting localities included Lake Elmendorf, southeast of the city, and by the early 1900s man-made Medina Lake. Dr. R. Menger shot a whistling swan with a seven-foot wingspan on the lake in 1917, and a party in 1920 killed twenty-seven canvasbacks out of their bag of ninety-five ducks.[15]

VICTORIA

Situated where the high prairie meets the Guadalupe River floodplain before San Antonio Bay, this inland gateway to the Gulf earned Victoria a mention in *The Sportsman's Guide to the Hunting and Shooting Grounds of the United States and Canada* in the late 1800s for its volume of mallards, wood ducks, Canada geese, and cranes. Listed gunning destinations were Mill Bottom, Wood Lake, Jones Bayou, and Rupley's Lake between Victoria and Goliad. Southwest of town, along the steep bluffs of the San Antonio River, thousands of ducks wintered on the shoreline of Milpita Lake, or Mill Peat Lake, on O'Connor Ranch.[16]

Hunters who frequented the Guadalupe River followed it south to Green Lake and the Guadalupe Delta on Lavaca Bay by way of Adler, Pridham (Manchola),

DUCKS, SQUIRRELS, *and a sandhill crane shot near Victoria, late 1800s, with Jim Rose (left) and Louis F. Jecker (right). The other man is unidentified.* (Victoria Regional History Center, Victoria College/University of Houston–Victoria Library, File No. 493)

Stubbs, Linn, and Cypress Lakes. Another popular spot was Traylor Lake on the Guadalupe floodplain at the crossing of the Pan American Railway near Bloomington, about twelve miles from town. Typical was the party of seven hunters who bagged enough ducks and geese to fill six large barrels, or about 360 ducks. Traylor Lake disappeared from maps in about 1914.[17]

The largest Victoria hunting clubs in the early 1900s were Rathborne Sporting Club and Sitterles Hunting Club. Members of H. E. Rathborne's club were mostly bankers, oilmen, lawyers, and railroad officials from Dallas, Houston, and Victoria. The club, incorporated in 1907, hunted locally on land owned by Victoria's John Welder and on his Green Lake property and made shooting trips to Rockport, Aransas Pass, Bayside, and Port O'Connor.[18]

The hunting prowess of Victoria's O. Z. Dahlberg made the local newspaper in 1915 on one of these coastal sojourns. Spotting a flock of ducks, Dahlberg snuck them for half a mile over rocks, thorns, and mud. When he opened fire, not a bird rose. Certain he had killed a great number, he raced back to camp for help to bring in the harvest. On his return, a "considerably peeved" rancher demanded to know "who in thunder has shot all my decoys to pieces." Dahlberg paid for the damages, then "beat a retreat back to camp and to Victoria."[19]

Membership of the Sitterles Hunting Club, run by the Sitterles family, was made up of ranchers, farmers, and working men. The club hunted along the Guadalupe River corridor from Schiers Bottom to Pridham Lake and south to Hog Bayou on the west bank of Green Lake. Huge camps were set up for each outing, with cooks preparing the site several days in advance. Supplies were brought in by mule-drawn wagons, and for refrigeration the crew dug a hole large enough for a three-hundred-pound block of ice insulated with wood shavings and covered with a wagon sheet. When the hunters arrived, big pots of wild game stew were already simmering on the fire.[20]

FORT BEND COUNTY

The Gulf, Colorado, and Santa Fe train deposited Houston and Galveston sportsmen along the flooded timber, lakes, and oxbows of the Brazos River corridor in the coastal prairie of Fort Bend County as early as the 1870s. Many made their way to the oak-lined banks of Big Creek, one of the best spots west of Houston for congregating mallards. Oscar "Pop" Scott, who ran the store in nearby Thompson, remembered that Big Creek in the 1880s had so many mallards, "they were just feedin' over each other." Oscar's party on one hunt "got down on our knees and let 'em feed up to just the right range," and with two side-by-side 12 gauges, they picked up one hundred mallards.[21]

North of Big Creek, Dry Creek drained into the fourteen-hundred- to twenty-two-hundred-acre Smithers Lake on the Davis-Ryon Ranch, renamed George Ranch when it was run by Albert P. George. The George Foundation's Orin Covell says when Albert took charge of the ranch, he was appalled at the volume of ducks killed by the lake's two market hunters, and he ran them off. Albert substituted the ranch's commercial gunners with two sporting clubs, Booth Hunting Club and Gulf Coast Hunting Club, in 1901.[22]

The membership of both George Ranch hunting clubs was mostly from Houston and Galveston. Galveston hunters traveled in style, arriving in well-appointed passenger cars on the Santa Fe train to nearby Thompson's Switch, often accompanied by a small orchestra and a separate refrigerated car filled with fresh seafood. Lodges were built on both the north and south sides of the lake, where, during the off-season, the clubs held gatherings such as Albert George's annual Washington's Birthday barbecue and oyster roast.[23]

Club members set their own hunting season between Thanksgiving and February 22 until 1913, when the first mandated seasons came into existence, and they limited themselves to no more than 150 ducks per blind. Galveston's J. H. Fosgard hunted the lake in 1907 and was like most Smithers Lake gunners who, for several days in a row, shot his limit of 25 ducks each day.[24]

Guides and helpers, mostly black men who worked cattle on the ranch the remainder of the year, were hired to build and brush cypress wood duck blinds, pole shooters to their locations, retrieve birds, and set decoys. Most of the wooden decoy spreads were mixed with live English callers kept in a cage on the edge of the lake. Richmond's Hilmar G. Moore hunted with the last of the ranch's black guides, "Cripple" Joe Holden. Joe, he says, called ducks with his mouth and had charge of the live decoys that, by then, were raised in a pen near the main house. Joe always hunted with a drake in the blind and put two hens in the decoy spread.[25]

George Ranch *North Camp, 1915. (Courtesy George Ranch Museum, File No. 2000.080.024)*

The morning's *harvest at the George Ranch South Camp, early 1900s, included mallards, mottled ducks, and canvasbacks. Hunters are unidentified. (Courtesy George Ranch Museum, File No. 2000.080.062)*

A number of private clubs were founded on other natural lakes near George Ranch, including rush-covered, horseshoe-shaped Tom Booth Lake, Vine Lake, and the large Worthington Lake. Hale Ranch, where Big Creek drains into the Brazos River, was the hunting preserve of Herman Hale, Joe Wesendoff, and Houston's Pilant Club. Frank Hoot and his son Frank Jr. were guides there for many years. Hale Ranch is now part of Brazos Bend State Park, a rare bright spot in an area consumed by development, with a new toll road planned through the heart of once famous duck country.[26]

Moore Ranch, founded in 1824, was north of George Ranch and west of Richmond. Part of Moore Ranch included the eighteen-hundred-acre Orchard Lake, which, Charles Stutzenbaker says, was "historically one of the most important winter waterfowl locations along the Texas coast, and very likely wintered more birds than Eagle Lake." According to Hilmar G. Moore, grandson of Moore Ranch founder John Moore Sr., the lake's banks were covered in rushes and cattails, its waters clear and shallow except for alligator holes that were "over your head."[27]

A STOOL OF *wooden decoys in 1917 at Orchard Lake, northwest of Rosenberg in Fort Bend County. (John Winter Collection, courtesy Cliff Fisher)*

Hilmar remembers clouds of ducks, mostly mallards and teal, with cinnamon teal "all over the place" before the 1950s. The most common goose on the lakeshore was the greater Canada, he says, and "when my father wanted a goose, he'd let my mother drive the buggy and he'd just step out and let her keep driving and he'd get down on a knee and shoot one with a rifle." After World War II Hilmar never saw more than a dozen of the big birds again, but he began seeing his first blue geese.[28]

With access by rail, sportsmen came to Orchard Lake from all parts of Texas. Fifty Brenham Gun and Rod Club hunters made a trip in 1902 and shot three hundred ducks before scrambling back to the train during a wet norther. On a Thanksgiving Day shoot in 1905, they returned with "a croaker sack full" of ducks. Houston hunter John Winter guided parties on Orchard Lake in the 1920s, and over wooden and live decoys brought back dozens of mallards.[29]

Hilmar recalls that visiting sportsmen "would make arrangements for the farmers to pick 'em up on Friday—the train came out of Houston on Friday—and take 'em to the lodge they built for hunting, then the farmers would then take them back to the train on Sunday evenings." Charles Stutzenbaker, who grew up nearby, adds that area farm boys made extra income as guides and cleaned birds "for the affluent who came to the lake to hunt." Orchard Lake's mallard magic ended when Gulf Oil discovered commercial hydrocarbons below the lake and drained its waters through a canal dredged to the Brazos River in 1926.[30]

BRENHAM

Perched on the northern edge of the Great Prairie, small lakes along the Yegua, Navasota, and Brazos Rivers dotted the landscape around Brenham. The Stone

BILL KIEL SR. *with a limit of mallards from Flag Pond Hunting and Fishing Club, Brenham. (Courtesy Bill and Jean Kiel)*

BILL KIEL JR. *readying for the hunt in one of Flag Pond Hunting and Fishing Club's square-ended pirogues. (Courtesy Bill and Jean Kiel)*

family founded Brenham Gun and Rod Club on Stone Lake, three miles from town, in the early 1900s. The club's twenty-five charter members built a lodge, boathouses, cottages, and a keeper's cottage for manager T. A. Low Jr. Members hunted mostly mallards and teal on wild rice that grew on the flats on the lake's north end. Stone Lake was famous for its huge "rabbit-eating bass," which were known, as well, to pull coots from the water's surface. The club maintained a special Pullman car for their shooting excursions to Houston, Galveston, Eagle Lake, Orchard Lake, and Port Lavaca.[31]

Near Burton, west of Brenham, the Flag Pond Hunting and Fishing Club opened in 1926. Bill Kiel Sr. was a founding member, and son Bill Jr. recalls the club was run by the "one-eyed bachelor" Theodore Pfundt. Flag Pond was shallow and went dry every few years. Numbered duck blinds were reached by square-ended pirogues push-poled across the lake. Bill Jr. says the pirogues, made at the Burton Lumber Company, "leaked like a sieve" until the wooden planks swelled

SHORT STORIES FROM FARTHER AFIELD

after being in the water for a while. Over wooden blocks they ordered from Sears, club members shot pintails, wigeons, mallards, wood ducks, bluebills, redheads, and canvasbacks. Cottages were built along the Flag Pond shore, and the one Bill Sr. "and the Fisher boys" built is still in the family nearly a century later.[32]

AUSTIN

The most popular destination for Austin waterfowlers in the late 1800s was Lake McDonald, a thirty-mile-long waterway created by a granite dam built across the Colorado River. Rail led to the lake from the city, and a resort grew on its shores, complete with camp houses, a post office, a grocery store, and a restaurant. Hunters chartered boats for days at a time, with one of the most elegant being the sixty-foot steam launch *Belle of Austin*. Austin hunters cultivated crops of wild rice and celery around the lake, where wild ducks were said to be "very abundant and offer great sport." The lake disappeared when the flood of April 1900 breached the dam.[33]

WACO

Located on the floodplain of the Brazos River, Waco had an early organized sporting history, beginning with the influential Waco Gun Club, founded in the 1870s. Although the club was best known for its influential role in early Texas conservation efforts, its members could be found in every corner of the state in pursuit of fish and game.[34]

The most popular Waco gunning spot close to town was Dry Pond, located on the river about a mile outside the city limits. With its banks and knolls covered in post oaks, the depression, two and one-half miles wide, brought immense flocks of mallards and wood ducks. Waco residents, tired of Dry Pond waters flooding the city, drained it in 1892. Every sportsman in town took the SA&AP train south in 1903 when a wet winter left miles of standing water on the prairie along the train tracks, deep enough that it "afford[ed] swimming for waterfowl." The Waco train station was packed with gunners, and most returned with "grain sacks full of ducks."[35]

MEXIA

River bottoms east of Waco were home to Mexia Fishing and Hunting Club, founded in the 1890s, and the Mexia Gun and Fishing Club, organized in 1912. Near Coolidge, the Cooledge Lake Club opened in the 1920s on what was called R.R. Lake. Its proprietor warned members that their annual membership fee of five dollars would be revoked if they didn't retrieve all the ducks they shot. Both the town and the club spelled their name wrong until 1930, when the name was changed to Coolidge.[36]

CORSICANA

Across Central Texas in the late 1800s, man-made water impoundments in the form of cattle tanks and reservoirs for city drinking water began holding large numbers of geese and ducks. Quick to embrace nature's new bounty, Corsicana sportsmen opened several fishing and hunting resorts on man-made water structures after the turn of the century.

Corsicana Rod and Gun Club on the Beaton Tank and Burk Fishing and Hunting Club on the Burk Tank were both founded about 1906. Woodlie, built on three lakes six miles northeast of the city, and the Waterworks Club were other popular clubs on town reservoirs. Mallards were the prized quarry at the "famous resort" on Fish Tank No. 1. The resort closed in 1917 when the tank was drained and converted to cropland. The Fish Tank No. 2 Club, with its modern clubhouse, closed in 1916 when it became the Corsicana Country Club.[37]

DALLAS

In the 1840s a traveler to the upper reaches of the Trinity River found a blind Scotsman named Campbell who lived in a hut on the riverbank. Each morning Campbell went hunting, his daughter Nelly picking him up and dropping him off in a small sailing sloop. The blind man sat and listened for feeding ducks, then mounted his fowling piece and fired in the direction of the sound. He waited patiently for Nelly's return to retrieve the fruits of his labor.[38]

The city of Dallas was founded not far from Campbell's hut. Sportsmen from the young city in the late 1800s rode horses to rolling hills and creeks of the Trinity River headlands, their approach accompanied by the roar of thousands of ducks that jumped from pecan-covered timber bottoms. Wooden decoys were set and black powder smoke wafted through the trees as mallards, sprigs, and wood ducks returned to the feeding areas. Dallas hunters also found wide places in the Trinity, sometimes filling their hard-chined, pointed rowboats with so many canvasbacks, redheads, and bluebills that only inches of freeboard remained between gunwales and water. Whether from flooded timber or open water, it was not unusual for hunters to return to Dallas with wagonloads of ducks.[39]

Dallas outdoor enthusiasts opened sporting clubs near the city, along the coast, and throughout the rivers and flooded timber of North and East Texas to Caddo Lake. The earliest club was Dallas Fishing and Hunting Club, which, according to Clare G. Weakley Jr., was also Texas's first country club. Chartered by confederate Civil War veterans Colonel John T. Trezevant and Captain William H. "Billy" Gaston, the club was located south of town near Hutchins at Doddy's ferry landing on the Trinity River. Twenty-five charter members paid a five-thousand-dollar stock subscription, constructing buildings and docks on two lakes. Members hunted from wooden rowing skiffs and duck blinds, adding live decoys to their blocks from the club's two dozen penned mallards.[40]

In its first year the club planted ten bushels of experimental wild rice. Twenty years later the crop covered tens of acres and attracted hundreds of fat, rice-fed mallards. Experiments with wild celery were equally successful in attracting big flocks of canvasbacks, and the club's improved habitat also held mottled ducks, redheads, teal, wigeons, bluebills, and spoonbills. When the twenty-five-duck limit was mandated in 1907, sportsmen could "go out any old morning and bag 25 to the gun before breakfast."[41]

Dallas Fishing and Hunting Club in the early 1900s grew to over forty members who paid six hundred dollars a share with thirty-dollar annual dues. Among the prominent members were W. G. Sterrett, an early member of the Texas Fish, Game and Oyster Commission. The Dallas Fishing and Hunting Club is still in operation today.[42]

South of the city, the Fin and Feather Club of Dallas was "carved from the wild and dense Trinity River bottoms" in 1893. Fifty original members each purchased three hundred dollars of stock and built a three-hundred-acre lake with a boathouse for twenty-five skiffs. An earlier building on the grounds was used as the men's clubhouse, and a two-story ladies lodge was added. The Fin and Feather Club quickly became known for flocks of thousands of ducks, particularly canvasbacks, mallards, and teal. Travel was by the Hutchins road, and because it was often impassable after heavy rains, club members still used horse and buggy years after the arrival of the automobile.[43]

Koon Kreek (Coon Creek) Klub, called "the mecca of Dallas sportsmen on the account of abundant fish and game," formed in 1902. Located nine miles south of Athens in Henderson County, the club was originally named for Coon Creek, which ran through the property. One hundred charter members paid one hundred dollars a share to purchase seven thousand acres. They built a dam across the creek to create an eight-hundred-acre lake and built a nineteen-room clubhouse. With both timber and open-water hunting, one Koon Kreek Klub member killed 365 ducks in a single day. When limits were mandated in the early 1900s, Blind No. 9 on the main lake could produce up to eight limits of twenty-five ducks in a single morning. Member D. O. Mills killed three swans on one hunt.[44]

Sportsmen first reached the club's lodge on the Athens-Palestine wagon road by horseback, then in 1910 they paid $2.75 for a round-trip ticket on the Texas and New Orleans Railroad. Guests came from throughout the country, and the citizens of Athens organized brass bands to meet their trains. An invitation was extended to "bully" sportsman Theodore Roosevelt and other dignitaries in November 1910 to attend the exhibition of the "fabulously trained horse" King George, touted as capable of retrieving ducks and catching fish.[45]

Koon Kreek Klub was probably the first in Texas to employ a full-time biologist to manage wildlife and improve habitat. Professor Bagwell, hired in the

J. E. R. Chilton's *limit of twenty-five pintails from the Fin and Feather Club of Dallas, 1910. (Courtesy Rich Flaten)*

1930s, was provided a house on the club grounds with a research laboratory for "testing of water, fish, and foods." By 1962 a Koon Kreek Klub membership cost six thousand dollars, with one hundred sportsmen on a waiting list that averaged ten years. Like the Dallas Fishing and Hunting Club and the Fin and Feather Club, Koon Kreek Klub is still in operation, although the spelling of its name is now Coon Creek Club.[46]

The Hollywood Country Club opened in 1924 a few miles from Koon Kreek Klub. Creeks on the Trinity River were dammed for four artificial lakes, with one set aside as a permanent refuge in an effort to "prevent many of the ducks from flying on to the coast." Three hundred Dallas sportsmen joined the club the first year and built a large lodge with dining and sleeping quarters that accommodated 250 guests.[47]

PARIS

South of Red River, the response of waterfowl to the first man-made lake on the North Texas prairie around Paris was immediate. In the 1890s "thousands of big greenhead mallards" congregated on the new Paris city reservoir. Hunting permits were sold until 1916, when the city council, concerned about contamination of its drinking water supply, banned sportsmen from all public waterworks.[48]

On the outskirts of town, geese followed new grain crops and impounded irrigation water, with local newspapers noting that, although geese were hard to kill with shotguns, hunters with rifles were doing quite well. Paris sportsmen traveled by wagon north to the Red River, where, on autumn nights, roosting ducks exploded from the timber in numbers so immense that Paris hunters stopped bothering to load and instead used their guns as clubs. When Paris in 1903 illuminated the night sky with electric lights, large bunches of bewildered snipes and killdeers landed in town square.[49]

EAST TEXAS

In East Texas pineywoods country, mallards and wood ducks darkened the sky over flooded pine, oak, maple, dogwood, and gum forests along densely forested creeks of the Trinity, Neches, Angelina, and Sabine Rivers. Local sustenance hunters and sportsmen at the turn of the century began to share the waterfowl bounty with private hunting clubs, most started by Dallas sportsmen in partnership with men from booming East Texas railroad towns. Generations of Dallas and East Texas sportsmen made up the membership of two long-lived clubs, the Little Sandy Hunting and Fishing Club and Ferndale Club.

The Little Sandy Club was founded by N. H. Lassiter in 1907 with twenty-seven Fort Worth and Dallas members. The club flooded hundreds of acres of hardwood timberlands of the upper Sabine River Basin, which provided habitat for a dizzying number of mallards and wood ducks. Weekends saw the city's Texas and Pacific Railroad depot filled with sportsmen headed to Mineola on the edge of the club grounds. Faced in the 1980s with losing their spectacular habitat to a proposed reservoir, the club donated its land to the US Fish and Wildlife Service as a conservation easement. Although the move ignited a federal court battle with the Sabine River Authority, the thirty-eight-hundred-acre Little Sandy NWR results from their dogged efforts.[50]

The Ferndale Club was organized by Dr. J. B. Florence of Leesburg in 1909. Florence was an influential country doctor who area residents relied on not only for their health, but also for advice on "what to plant, [and] how to vote." Collecting fifty dollars from fifty original members, Florence built a dam over Flat Ford on North Lilly Creek near the town of Pittsburg. Within three years the new hunting and fishing preserve boasted 350 acres of flooded timber and a two-story clubhouse in the pine trees. By 1959 club membership grew to 185, and it remains open today.[51]

Caddo Lake, situated on the Texas-Louisiana border, was the jewel of nineteenth-century East Texas duck hunting. Places on Caddo Lake's west shore—Taylor Island, Uncertain Ranch, Goose Prairie, and Long Point—became synonymous with seemingly unlimited flights of mallards, bluebills, canvasbacks, redheads, teal, and pintails. Canada geese, "dark brant" and occasionally snow geese roosted on Broad or Big Lake and fed on the shallow flats at Goose Prairie, Harrison Bayou, and Jackson's Arm between Uncertain and Mossy Brake.[52]

The lake was called the sinking bayou by the Caddo Indians, and according to legend it was formed when the New Madrid earthquake of 1811–12 caused the Red River to run backwards and its waters poured into Big Cypress Creek and adjacent lowlands. Others prefer the explanation that the lake originated from a log jam that formed on the Red River. Early gunners weren't concerned where the water came from, only that each winter clouds of mallards and wood ducks came to the flooded tupelo, oak, and bald cypress for duck potato and acorns, and canvasbacks congregated on the open waters of Big Lake to feed on eelgrass.[53]

Caddo Lake's fish and fowl were an important food source to cotton plantation workers and those engaged in lake commerce, with steamboats calling on a growing network of port towns from the 1830s. Those were the days of long-barreled, muzzle-loading shotguns, when the only practical way to hunt ducks was to wait for a large flock to group on the water before making the shot. In the winter of 1855–56, John Haywood and Port Caddo blacksmith James Penny killed 133 ducks with only two shots. Another group of four hunters returned every afternoon with between 250 and 400 ducks, and they, too, claimed they never fired more than two shots.[54]

The number of ducks killed in a single volley on Caddo Lake remained a topic of Texas sportsmen throughout the 1800s. Dallas sportsman Captain Ben Melton, debating the verity of forty-nine ducks killed with one shot in the 1880s, did not think it newsworthy, as any number could be killed by those with the courage "to acknowledge the corn"—a reference to big flocks that grouped on the water while feeding on bait. Called upon to comment on another kill of seventy-six ducks with only two shots, sportsman and Marshall senator William H. Pope deemed it true, adding that the gun used was already famous for the "destruction of life," its discharge having broken the ranks of a Federal army during the Civil War, allowing Texas Ranger and Confederate general Ben McCulloch to put the enemy to flight.[55]

With huge numbers of ducks and railroad access to nearby Marshall, Caddo Lake in the last decades of the 1800s firmly established its reputation as a sporting resort of nearly mythical proportions. A Dallas party returned from a hunt in 1886 with 361 ducks, reporting skies filled with clouds of waterfowl. Texas governor Hogg traveled to Port Caddo in 1891, accompanied by newspapermen as anxious to report on his shooting prowess as his politics. Newspapers across the eastern part of the state advised whenever the mast was unusually heavy, as in the fall of 1897, when abundant acorns brought ducks in "large droves."[56]

The backbone of Caddo Lake sport hunting was its guides, called oarsmen, whose job was rowing clients—locally called "making a pull"—to blinds or "shooting points." Guides brought hunters to the deep waters of Big Lake and to the remote, cypress-studded backwaters and all points between. Most disorienting was flooded timber, which, it was said, "no Dallas men and few Marshall men ever got in and out of" without a guide. It was also a place where guides sometimes got lost while they were looking for lost guides.[57]

The Big Lake was not for the novice boatsman. Geographic senses could be dulled by a fog that rolled in and might remain for days. Caddo Lake watermen drowned with frightening regularity when broad water turned from a gentle inland sea to an angry froth with only scant warning. When a search for a missing party yielded somber clues but no bodies, families and lawmen yielded to the inevitable and waited. They knew that within a few days to as long as a month, most of the dead would float to the surface, or "come up," as it was called.[58]

Both private and public hunting clubs were founded on Caddo Lake shores after the turn of the century. Among the best known were Jennings Taylor Island Lodge, Johnson Brothers Ranch, Dallas Caddo Hunting and Fishing Club, and the Texas and Pacific Railway clubhouse on Big Lake.[59]

Former *Marshall Morning Star* editor R. L. Jennings built a lodge in 1905 on Taylor Island and made it open to the public. Jennings's land purchase was not without controversy. The land had long been held by fishing guide and local butcher Gotlieb Boehringer, and when he lost the title in a lawsuit, he was forced to pack up his wife and six children and live in a tent. The feud with Jennings ended when, on a lonely road on a lonely night, Boehringer was shot from his wagon. Jennings was arrested for the murder but he was not found guilty.[60]

Less blood was shed when Johnson Brothers Ranch was established in 1908. Located in Uncertain, the ranch catered to the public, providing customers with "live and block" decoys, cabins, and guides. Otto and Burt Johnson ran the business until 1937, when, seeking to put an end to their bouts of malaria, they sold everything and left East Texas. By then the Johnsons had entertained sixty thousand sportsmen, with nearly half of them from Dallas and Fort Worth alone. Johnson Ranch Marina is still in business today and is the oldest inland marina in Texas.[61]

The longest-lived private club on Caddo Lake is Dallas Caddo Hunting and Fishing Club, founded by T. S. Root in 1909 on Uncertain Ranch. Charter members were enticed to pay $210 a share with the promise of a portion of any oil wealth found on club lands. A two-story, fourteen-room clubhouse, tucked into the trees on the edge of the lake, was built in 1913. By the 1930s club membership grew to 110, with most from Dallas and nearby Marshall. When the venerable old lodge was struck by lightning and burned down in 1941, members promptly built a new one, and it remains in operation today.[62]

A visit to towns and landings around Caddo Lake in the early 1900s provided a diversity of images: worn out fishing and hunting shacks, fishing boats with steam boilers or one- or two-cylinder gasoline inboards, cypress pirogues and flat-bottomed bateaux, piers piled with gill nets, trotlines, hoop nets, and, nearby, occasional piles of mussel shells left by pearl hunters. Every yard seemed to have chickens and tame ducks strutting by skinny dogs stretched out in the sun. Handmade signs with some of the words misspelled advertised camps, guides, or live decoys and duck blinds for rent.

In winter, ducks were in the air and hanging from houses. Writer Fred Dahmer's uncle covered his two-story log house with the ducks he shot, gutted and hung from pegs to cure during the days before widely available refrigeration. At waterman and historian Wyatt Moore's Karnack store, a duck often hung from every wooden plank around it. Moore's family knew when the hunting would be good by the number of sportsmen who drove by their house. They would, he said, "Hear of a norther comin' over the Western Union [telegraph in Marshall] then there'd be an exodus of Model Ts to the lake that night."[63]

In an area where squatter camps, bootlegger stills, and questionable pasts melted into the depths of the cypress brakes, law of any type was not warmly embraced by the community. The first state game wardens who came to Caddo Lake in 1913 hadn't been on the lake for more than a few months when their boat was stolen. When outlaw duck hunter Joe Dixon saw Game Warden Goodfellow snooping around his property, he shot him. His gun, loaded with bird shot, didn't kill the lawman, but Joe was sure he'd think twice before prowling around his property again.[64]

Descriptions of the people who made up the local outdoor community usually include the word *character* or *colorful.* The unique culture of Caddo Lake outdoorsmen started early, personified by Captain Amory Starr and his plantation on Goose Prairie. Legend has it that Starr in the 1800s was rowed around the lake in an ancient galley ship powered by the sweat of a crew of black oarsmen. At the end of his seafaring forays he had wagonloads of fish and game delivered to his friends in Marshall. Starr lives on in Texas sporting history as the man who, in the 1880s, organized the first bird dog field trials in the state.[65]

By the 1920s the Caddo culture thrived in lake guides and camp operators. The sport hunting business by then was booming, with special rail coach cars from Marshall and automobiles from nearby Karnack delivering so many sportsmen they were said to be as plentiful as ducks. Fishing and hunting camps sprang up around the shoreline to serve the growing demand; the 1938 *Caddo Lake Handbook* listed at least twenty-three camps that leased boats and cottages.[66]

George Murata, who first opened Jap's Place in a tent left by an oil company on the north shore of the Big Lake at Potters Point, rented skiffs to fishermen and duck hunters. Murata was a colorful Caddo Lake personality rumored to have found a buried treasure, and his resumé included a stint as a lake pearl fisherman, with trips to Tiffany's in New York to sell the Caddo Lake pearls. Murata was once called to testify about a murder he witnessed, but he was suddenly unable to speak any language other than his native Japanese. The defendant was freed.[67]

Albright's Camp, located near Karnack, was one of the many camps on the lake's east shore that offered guides and boats. Owner Daniel Albright made extra income driving the back roads selling fish and "liked his whiskey and patronized the bootleggers a little bit too much." Better known as Dummy, Albright was a deaf-mute who wrote stunning poetry inspired by his quiet outdoor world.[68]

Floyd "Crip" Haddock, who ran Crip's Camp, was another lake legend. Although polio confined him to a wheelchair from a young age, it hardly seemed to slow him down. Crip bought Johnson Ranch in 1937 and hired ten guides, all local African Americans, and from his wheelchair he organized customers using a loudspeaker. In 1949 he opened a second Crip's Camp on Goose Prairie with seven cabins and thirty-five boats.[69]

Crip was a familiar site on the lake, his guides accompanying him on hunting trips and lifting him in and out of boats and duck blinds. It was a cold December day in 1957 when Crip and one of his guides, Starling Hood Jr., failed to return from an afternoon duck hunt. His "double first cousin," Wyatt Moore, joined the search, and in a 1983 interview with Thad Sitton, Moore remembered it vividly. Crip, he said, had set out with a new Evinrude three-horsepower engine on his boat, which was, as usual, overloaded with a Coleman stove, toolbox, and "enough shells to last 'im a month." Evidently the last thing Crip had done before the boat overturned, drowning both men, was shoot a duck. The man who pulled Crip from the lake after he "come up" later drowned as well. Caddo was just that kind of lake.[70]

Most of the geese on Caddo Lake disappeared when the dam built to control water levels eliminated the shallow flats where they fed. By the 1960s, most of the big flights of canvasbacks were gone as well. There were still days with plenty of mallards, but not as often as there once had been. Although the era of exclusive, private resorts had ended, the sporting hospitality was carried on by public camps, hunting clubs, and day hunting businesses.[71]

There are duck blinds today on Caddo Lake that have been in the same location for over a hundred years. If they could speak, they would tell tales of generations of Caddo Lake sportsmen, with the words *colorful* and *character* likely resonating from their wooden walls.

EPILOGUE

By the turn of the century the population of several species of waterfowl had dropped dramatically throughout the United States. The causes were many, but a major one was national demand for waterfowl in the marketplace that, by the early 1900s, had reached dizzying levels. There is little doubt that the market hunter's gun led to the near extinction of plumage-bearing wading birds and the demise of the Eskimo curlew. Once numbering in the millions, the Eskimo curlew was already rare in the 1890s. Some of the last known sightings were in the Galveston area in the 1960s.[1]

Whether it was the gun or other influences is debatable, but the whooping crane nearly followed the path of the Eskimo curlew. Still common in hunters' bags in the late 1800s, the white crane disappeared entirely from the Rio Grande Valley in the 1920s and the upper coast and King Ranch on the Upper Laguna Madre in the 1930s. By the time Aransas National Wildlife Refuge on Blackjack Peninsula was established in 1937, the wintering population was reduced to fourteen birds. The sandhill crane population was in a similar situation; when the manager of the Tremont Hotel in Galveston shot one in 1909, it was by then considered "a very rare specimen of game bird as a trophy."[2]

The once animated skies over Texas's rich land and water resources began to empty of even more species in the twentieth century. The gun could no longer be blamed for the decline; passage of state and federal game laws between 1903 and 1918 and a growing awareness of conservation had, in most instances, reduced its impact. The cause was mostly man-made change to migratory bird nesting grounds and their Gulf Coast wintering areas.

A SHIFT FROM THE COAST

Texans once saw uncountable numbers of waterfowl wintering on their rivers and bays. Although the great flocks are gone, the Lone Star State still holds more than 70 percent of the Central Flyway waterfowl counted in midwinter surveys. But there has been a shift of populations away from the Texas coast. There, sportsmen still see remarkable concentrations of teal, pintails, gadwalls, wigeons, wood ducks, redheads, and bluebills, among others, but substantially fewer of other once abundant species, notably mallards, mottled ducks, and canvasbacks.[3]

Huge flocks of mallards once graced Texas's inland prairies and fresh- to brackish-water marshes from Orange to Calhoun Counties, and at times as far south as the Rio Grande. Mallards made up almost half of the ducks killed on the upper coast as late as the 1930s and '40s. By the late 1950s coastal concentrations began to dwindle, and by the 1970s they were uncommon in hunter's bags.[4]

It wasn't until 1889 that the mottled duck was first identified as a species, and for years it was called a black duck, summer mallard, or black mallard. It was first thought to be migratory, and early observers were puzzled by huge flocks in the marshes during August, believing they portended an early and harsh winter. But this was Texas's and Louisiana's duck, resident to the Gulf Coast. Ducks Unlimited biologist Todd Merendino once said that the mottled duck was the best barometer of the health of Texas's coastal ecosystem. The barometer is falling.[5]

From Sabine to Brownsville, canvasbacks frequented inland lakes and parts of the coast, where they found wild celery or eelgrass. Lake Surprise in Chambers County once held so many of the big divers that their rising "shook the air, sounding like the roar of a freight train crossing a wooden trestle." Other canvasback concentrations referenced in 1800s sporting accounts were on Lost and Keith Lakes in Jefferson County, Sweetwater Lake on Galveston Island, and the San Jacinto River on Galveston Bay. Along the middle coast they were on Hynes Bay by Guadalupe Delta and Swan Lake on Copano Bay and between St. Joseph and Mustang Islands at Harbor Island. Only Corpus Christi Bay was regularly mentioned on the lower coast.[6]

The distribution of geese, swans, and cranes has changed as well, a wild mix of successes and failures. The greater Canada goose began disappearing from the coast between the 1950s and the 1970s. During the same time period the numbers of snow geese increased to a peak of 1.1 million. Both trumpeter and tundra, or whistling, swans were once harvested by hunters from Sabine Lake to the Rio Grande delta and by inland sportsmen across the state. They were uncommon by the 1920s. Whooping cranes today maintain only a tenuous hold on survival along the Coastal Bend. Wildfowl biologists and sportsmen, however, deserve credit for the success story of the sandhill crane; its numbers on the Central Flyway have increased since the 1930s.[7]

PROGRESS

Modern trends in waterfowl populations are a result of alteration of migratory bird nesting grounds, Gulf Coast wintering areas, and creation of new habitat—inland artificial water impoundments and the planting of grain crops—in nontraditional wintering areas. It started early.

Large portions of Texas's river floodplains were stripped of their timber during the 1800s. Coastal and inland prairies were being converted to agriculture, the slow percolation of their surface waters altered by the dredging of channels, their natural lakes pumped dry for irrigation. Wetlands were not spared either; their demise was considered of "incalculable value in reclaiming thousands of acres of the low coast lands that are now only capable of producing mosquitoes and alligators." With man's hunger for deepwater commerce, channels were dredged across fresh and brackish bay waters. As early as the 1890s a sportsman worried that the rapid pace of habitat destruction would lead to the extermination of all wild game.[8]

The 1900s brought more diversion of freshwater rivers for crop irrigation and the building of dams for agriculture and power. Meandering river courses were straightened and deepened. Construction of the IC, eventually linking Sabine Lake to Brownsville, provided a direct conduit for saltwater to reach coastal wetlands; TPWD estimates the IC accounted for destruction of over one hundred thousand acres of wetlands. When the nutria was introduced to the Texas coast in the 1950s, it too came with consequences. The large South American rodent consumed large volumes of vegetation that anchored wetlands, accelerating rates of coastal subsidence and erosion.[9]

Entire estuaries, in particular Galveston and Nueces Bays, are now entirely consumed by urbanization. Too, petroleum extraction, refineries, and the petrochemical industries have replaced coastal wetlands with the trappings of heavy industry and the discharge of its by-products. In the 1920s, oil floating on the water at the mouth of the San Jacinto River caught fire. Oil leaking from the Friendswood Field killed as many as six thousand ducks on Galveston Bay in the 1940s. Diving ducks foraging on the bottom of Lavaca Bay continue to pull up plants lodged in bottom sediments contaminated by mercury, discharged by Alcoa at Point Comfort and permitted by the State of Texas.[10]

As the coast lost food and roosting habitat, both were being created in other parts of Texas and the continental United States. The result was a major shift in wintering patterns of waterfowl. The first influence on coastal waterfowl populations began as native prairie was converted to rice in the late 1800s. Waterfowl were quick to take advantage of the new food source, at first only having to move short distances inland to feed.

Snow geese followed rice to the upper prairie in the late 1940s and early '50s, returning nightly to the coast to roost. With construction of prairie water impoundments, geese began remaining inland overnight. Eagle Lake's Clifton Tyler recalls, "At first, we had no idea that geese roosted at night. As the duck ponds got bigger, they became goose roosts, and then it dawned on us that we could put up holding ponds and somewhat control the geese." Clifton's father Marvin said, "It took time, but more geese started staying here all winter." Texas rice and roosts had created a wintering flyway shift.[11]

A bigger impact was made by waterfowl refuges built along the Central Flyway, called "duck ports." Their construction coincided with the Dust Bowl years, with 223 refuges built in forty-three states in just one year. They were originally intended to aid waterfowl on their routes to and from traditional wintering grounds, but an unintended consequence was the holding of waterfowl for extended periods during winter. The alteration of established patterns was called short-stopping, or its more formal term, suspension.[12]

Charles Stutzenbaker says Texas and Louisiana biologists saw a direct correlation between the disappearance of the greater Canada goose on the Gulf Coast and construction of the big refuges up north. By the late 1960s they also found over a third of Central and Mississippi Flyway snow and blue geese showed signs of suspension. The primary culprits were three northern refuges: Sand Lake Refuge in South Dakota, DeSoto Refuge in Iowa, and Squaw Creek Refuge in Missouri. Squaw Creek, for example, had no snow geese in 1940. By 1960 its wintering population reached 150,000.[13]

Midcontinent refuges were not alone. In North Texas and the Panhandle, row crops, cereal grains, and impounded irrigation water brought ducks that "darken[ed] the skies." Reservoirs such as Lake Texoma, built in the 1940s, provided entirely new roosting habitat. By 1947 the lake was holding an estimated sixty-five thousand mallards that left each day to feed on peanut crops around nearby Denison. TPWD's Brian Sullivan and Melissa Morin compiled band data that documented the decline of lesser and greater Canada geese along the coast. Coastal birds, they found, had moved to the upper forks of the Brazos River north of Abilene, along with impoundments and intermittently wet playa lakes of the Texas Panhandle.[14]

Ducks and geese received another push from the coast as rice production declined in the 1980s. From a high of 700,000 acres, it plummeted to 140,000 acres by the 1990s. Competition for water from cities and industry will continue to impact rice production. Further, Bill Stransky of the Texas Rice Coalition for the Environment explains that some of the rice now grown is a high-yield, hybrid seed rice, with much of the crop volume of only limited food value. It is also harvested in summer, without the "second crop" that has traditionally greeted waterfowl in early fall.[15]

Efficiency of modern agriculture practices has also meant less food on the ground. Fields are sprayed with herbicides that prevent seed plants from growing after the harvest. Sometimes crops are sprayed with saltwater, which kills the plant quickly and discourages volunteer rice. Farmers, too, are encouraged to disk fields as soon a possible after the growing season. Less grain means fewer birds. Texas once wintered as many as 1.1 million snow geese, but the number has dipped to as low as 300,000 in the last few years.[16]

Freddie Abshier has lived long enough to see first mallards, then geese, disappear from the upper coast marsh. He says, "The last three or four years right here, if I hear a snow goose, specklebelly goose or a Canada goose fly over this place three times during the hunting season, well I think I've heard something. Used to be they'd come out of the marsh by the thousands in the morning, come back from the high ground in the evening by the thousands, and I'm talking thirty, forty, fifty minutes to an hour [of] solid geese. The sky would be just dark with 'em. It's hard to explain it. Now we don't have enough geese down here now to make a gumbo out of."[17]

BACK TO THE FUTURE

The decline of waterfowl in parts of Texas is not unique. There are entire ecosystems in the United States, notably on the east and west coasts, where once grand waterfowl habitat lies buried beneath the mantle of progress. If the past is the key to the present, Texas might well join them. But there are glimmers of hope.

Texas hunters have long been leaders in efforts to preserve waterfowl and their habitat. It was sportsmen who first fought fiercely to outlaw market hunting, influencing and drafting laws in an effort to prevent wildfowl going the way of the Carolina parakeet and passenger pigeon. Before the turn of the century, Texans from all major cities, particularly Waco, San Antonio, Houston, Galveston, and Dallas, were active in a growing number of national conservation organizations and founded many state and county chapters.[18]

During the Dust Bowl years, King Ranch's Richard M. Kleberg was one of the sponsors of the Duck Stamp Law, which mandated a one-dollar license fee to hunters, with the proceeds used, in part, to create waterfowl habitat. Texans were instrumental during those years in their support of More Game Birds in America and DU. Local sportsmen's clubs by the 1950s extended from Orange to Brownsville and played an important role in lobbying legislators and raising money for conservation causes.[19]

TPWD remains, today, the leading agency for statewide waterfowl, wetlands, and conservation initiatives. The department is joined by USFWS, DU, Nature Conservancy, and the Texas Land Conservancy, along with numerous smaller agencies and private landowners who continue to preserve habitat through land purchases and conservation easements. Groups such as the Texas Rice Coalition for the Environment, under the leadership of Bill Stransky, are successfully restoring huge wetland areas. Bill Gammel and his Worldwide Wetlands, with Marty Briggs, are focusing on ways to bring the mottled duck back.

    These are just a few of the agencies and people all working to preserve pieces of the Texas outdoors. Some of them are duck hunters, many are not. They are the modern heroes of Texas waterfowl.

NOTES

INTRODUCTION

1. *Dallas Morning News,* Jan. 10, 1909.

2. "Corpus Christi—The City of Destiny and of Your Destination," promotional brochure (ca. 1910s) in private collection of Jim Moloney, 9.

3. *San Antonio Daily Express,* Jan. 4, 1893; *Dallas Morning News,* Sept. 25, 1898.

4. *Galveston Daily News,* Jan. 2, Feb. 22, 1884; Mar. 10, 1889.

5. Ibid., Jan. 2, Feb. 23, 1884; Mar. 10, 11, 1889; Edward T. Martin, "Snipe and Snipe Shooting," *Outing* 74, no. 1 (1919):163–64.

6. *Galveston Daily News,* May 1, 1885; Apr. 4, 1887.

CHAPTER 1. SPORT HUNTING IN TEXAS

1. "The Feathered Game of Texas," *Bailey's Magazine of Sports and Pastimes* 6 (1863):195; C. R. Tinan, "The Wild Goose," in *Shooting on Upland, Marsh, and Stream,* ed. William Bruce Leffingwell (New York: Rand McNally, 1890), 341.

2. W. L. McAtee, "Winter Ranges of Geese on the Gulf Coast," *The Auk: A Quarterly Journal of Ornithology* 28, no. 2 (1911):272–74; J. R. Singleton, *Texas Coastal Waterfowl Survey,* FA Report Series no. 11 (Austin: Texas Game and Fish Commission, 1953), 22; Kenneth Foree, "Geese, Smart Men Alter Town's Life," *Dallas Morning News,* Nov. 3, 1964; Charles Stutzenbaker, pers. comm., Feb. 18, 2010.

3. H. P. Attwater, "Southwestern Game," *Ornithologist and Oologist* 16, no. 7 (1891):109–10; McAtee, "Winter Ranges," 272; Freddie Abshier interview, Feb. 6, 2009, Anahuac, TX; Francis H. Kortright, *The Ducks, Geese and Swans of North America* (Washington, DC: American Wildlife Institute, 1943), 148.

4. Foree, "Geese, Smart Men"; *Galveston News,* Oct. 17, 1939; *San Antonio Express,* Nov. 11, 1952; Col. Geo. A. McCall, "Some Remarks on the Habits, etc., of Birds Met With in Western Texas, between San Antonio and the Rio Grande, and in New Mexico; With Descriptions of Several Species Believed to Have Been Hitherto Undescribed," *Proceedings of the Academy of Natural Sciences of Philadelphia* (Philadelphia: Merrihew and Thompson, 1852), 5, 223–24; Spencer F. Baird, "Birds of the Boundary," *Report of the United States and Mexican Boundary Survey* (Washington, DC: A. O. P. Nicholson, 1859), 2, 26; Elizabeth H. Smith, "Redheads and Other Wintering Waterfowl," in *The Laguna Madre of Texas and Tamaulipas* (College Station: Texas A&M University Press, 2002), 177.

5. McAtee, "Winter Ranges," 273; *Eagle Lake Headlight,* Oct. 27, 1934.

6. John K. Strecker Jr., *The Birds of Texas: An Annotated Checklist,* Baylor University Bulletin, vol. 40, no. 1 (Waco: Baylor University Press, 1912), 15.

7. Robin W. Doughty, *Return of the Whooping Crane* (Austin: University of Texas Press, 1989), 18; Captain Frank W. Flack, *A Hunter's Experiences in the Southern States of America: Being an Account of the Natural History of Various Quadrupeds and Birds Which Are the Objects of Chase in Those Countries* (London: Longmans, Green and Co., 1866), 277; Charles B. Cory, *The Birds of Illinois and Wisconsin,* Field Museum of Natural History Publication 131, Zoological Series, vol. 9 (Chicago: The Museum, 1909):376; *San Antonio Daily Light,* June 15, 1896.

8. Neltje Blanchan, *Birds That Hunt and Are Hunted* (New York: Doubleday and McClure, 1899), 229; "Resorts of Game," in *Fur, Fin, and Feather: A Compilation of the Game Laws of the Principal States and Provinces of the United States and Canada* (New York: M. B. Brown and Co., 1872), 235–44; Emerson Hough, "Plover-Shooting,"

and Thomas C. Abbott, "Snipe and Snipe-Shooting," in *Shooting on Upland, Marsh, and Stream*, ed. William Bruce Leffingwell (New York: Rand McNally, 1890), 208 and 257; *Dallas Morning News,* Nov. 22, 1903; *Fort Worth Morning Register,* Aug. 27, 1899; H. E. Dresser, "On the Birds of Southern Texas," *The Ibis: Quarterly Journal of Ornithology* 49 (1866):39, www.archive.org/stream/ibis02brit/ibis02brit_djvu.txt.

9. *Dallas Morning News,* Nov. 24, 1895.

10. *Galveston Daily News,* Nov. 12, 1905.

11. Charles Stutzenbaker interview, Oct. 24, 2008, Port Arthur, TX.

12. Ralph Semmes Jackson, *Home on the Double Bayou: Memories of an East Texas Ranch* (Austin: University of Texas Press, 1961), 94; *Galveston Daily News,* Oct. 28, 1879; *Galveston Tri-Weekly News,* Dec. 13, 1869; *Brownsville Herald,* Oct. 24, 1940.

13. *San Antonio Daily Express,* Jan. 4, 1893.

14. *San Antonio Light,* Dec. 24, 1899; Emerson Hough, "Goose Shooting on the Gulf Coast," *Outing* 37 (1901):702–6.

15. Lyle Jordan recorded narratives, 2001, in private collection of Doug Pike; *San Antonio Light,* Oct. 13, 1938.

16. Kem Dean, letter in "News from the Classes," *Technology Review: Relating to the Massachusetts Institute of Technology* 23 (1921):103.

17. *San Antonio Express,* June 10, 1936; *Dallas Morning News,* Feb. 1, 1913; "Automobiles in Texas," *1941–42 Texas Almanac,* Portal to Texas History, www.texasalmanac.com/history/early/1911Automobiles.pdf.

18. "The Motor Car as an Aid to Hunting in Texas," *The Horseless Age* 18, no. 14 (1906):9; *Galveston Daily News,* Oct. 24, 1922; July 7, 1938.

19. *San Antonio Express,* June 10, 1936; Marshall Hayes interview, Jan. 22, 2010, Markham, TX.

20. *Freeport Facts,* Jan. 24, 1946; Ronnie Luster, pers. comm., Dec. 8, 2009; Jim Mills interview, Mar. 28, 2010, Seadrift, TX; *Corpus Christi Caller-Times,* Nov. 3, 1957; Bill Kiel interview, Mar. 4, 2010, Kingsville, TX.

21. Bobby LeBlanc, pers. comm., May 25, 2010; Errol "E. J." Fournet, pers. comm., May 27 and July 13, 2009.

22. "A Week's Sport in Texas," *The New Monthly Magazine* 145 (1869):21.

23. Stephen M. Miller, *Early American Waterfowling, 1700s–1930* (Chicago: Winchester Press, 1986), 162; *Galveston Daily News,* Oct. 5, 1885.

24. *Galveston Daily News,* Dec. 5, 1887.

25. "Ducks on the Texas Coast," *Hunter-Trader-Trapper* 17, no. 3 (1908):75–76.

26. Harris M. Brown, "With the Ducks on the Texas Coast," *Sportsman Magazine,* Mar. 1897, 493.

27. Robert Milner, "History of the Labrador Retriever," *Ducks Unlimited* 74, no. 5 (2010):80.

28. Lyle Jordan recorded narratives; *Pampa Daily News,* Dec. 27, 1929.

29. *Galveston Daily News,* Feb. 20, 1878; *Brownsville Herald,* Jan. 8, 1946; Freddie Abshier interview.

30. Peter Stines interview, Sept. 5, 2008, Wallisville, TX; "A Week's Sport in Texas," 20–31; Texas Historical Marker Application, n. 11, Sept. 1988, in collection of Port Arthur Public Library, Port Arthur, TX; *Brownsville Daily Herald,* July 12, 1902.

31. *Port Arthur News,* Oct. 24, 1930; Dec. 7, 1937.

CHAPTER 2. DECOYS AND DUCK CALLS

1. Freddie Abshier interview, June 13, 2008, Anahuac, TX; Joe Whitehead, "Ducks," manuscript, in private collection of Joe Whitehead, Smith Point, TX.

2. Fred Dahmer oral history interview with David Todd, June 7, 1997, Uncertain, TX, Conservation History Association of Texas, Texas Legacy Project, Reel No. 1010; Wyatt Moore oral history interview with Thad Sitton, Feb. 7, 1983, Tape No. 150, File No. OH 150-3, James Gilliam Gee Library, Texas A&M University–Commerce; *Galveston Daily News,* Dec. 31, 1897; Nov. 6, 1921; Jan. 31, 1932; *San Antonio Express,* Oct. 27, 1925; *Dallas Morning News,* Nov. 11, 1929; *Amarillo Globe,* Oct. 30, 1930.

3. Homer Harmon interview with Royce A. Strickland, July 4, 1999; Dahmer interview with Todd; Jack Holland, manuscript presented to the author, Oct. 17, 2008.

4. *Port Arthur News,* Oct. 29, 1933; Nov. 3, 1974.

5. Charles Stutzenbaker interview, Oct. 24, 2008, Port Arthur, TX; Davis R. Waddell, pers. comm., June 27, 2009.

6. John M. Weathersby, "Lindsey Dunn of Delhomme," *Ducks Unlimited,* Nov.–Dec. 1991, 63.

7. Palmer and Talley Melton interview, July 17, 2009, Houston, TX.

8. Walsh, *Outlaw Gunner,* 41; H. M. Brown, letter to the editor, *Recreation* 13, no. 1 (1900):59; Ted Bates interview, Dec. 19, 2009, Palacios, TX; *Brownsville Herald,* Sept. 19, 1922; *Valley Star-Monitor-Herald,* Oct. 10, 1937; Mills family album, in collection of Aransas County Historical Society, Rockport, TX.

9. Holland manuscript.

10. *Galveston Daily News,* Mar. 28, 1931; June 30, 1932; Aug. 17, 1935; *Port Arthur News,* July 22, 1932; *Dallas Morning News,* Aug. 2, 1935; Earl Porter interview with Royce A. Strickland, Feb. 23, 2001.

11. Charles Stutzenbaker interview; Abshier interview.

12. Davis R. Waddell interview, Apr. 25, 2009, Eagle Lake, TX; William F. Mackey, *American Bird Decoys* (New York: Bonanza Books, 1965), 33.

13. Carlos Smith interview, Apr. 26, 2009, LaPorte, TX.

14. Charles Stutzenbaker interview; Bill Provine, pers. comm., May 14, 2011; Becky Stutzenbaker interview, May 30, 2009, Port Arthur, TX.

15. *Houston Chronicle,* Dec. 25, 1960; Harmon interview with Strickland; Abshier interview.

16. Kendon L. Clark, pers. comm., Dec. 2009.

17. Royce A. Strickland, pers. comm., May 3, 2010; Shannon Tompkins, pers. comm., Aug. 2, 2010.

18. Johnnie Dutton interview, June 6, 2009, Baytown, TX.

19. *Baytown Sun,* May 2, 1966; "Texas Artists," *Texas Parks & Wildlife,* Feb. 1986; Royce A. Strickland interview, May 31, 2009, Baytown, TX; Gordon LeCompte interview, Feb. 13, 2010, Sargent, TX.

20. Newspaper clipping, *Baytown Sun,* 1993, in private collection of Royce A. Strickland; LeCompte interview.

21. Royce A. Strickland, pers. comm., Feb. 14, 2010.

22. *Victoria Advocate,* Sept. 4, 1953; *Baytown Sun,* Nov. 24, 1959; "Texas Artists"; newspaper clipping, *Baytown Sun,* 1993; LeCompte interview.

23. LeCompte interview; Royce A. Strickland, pers. comm., Feb. 14, 2010.

24. Marshall Hayes interview, Jan. 22, 2010, Markham, TX; Rick Pratt, pers. comm., Jan. 25, 2010; decoys in private collection of Joe Whitehead.

25. Mills family album; Fred Close interview, Apr. 4, 2009, Rockport, TX; Ed Duvall interview, June 21, 2008, Rockport, TX.

26. Gordon Stanley interview, Feb. 21, 2009, Rockport, TX.

27. Rick Pratt interview, Sept. 24, 2009, Port Aransas, TX.

28. Ron Gard, pers. comm., Mar. 25, 2011.

29. Dr. Thomas H. Nelson, pers. comm., Mar. 25 and 26, 2011; Dr. Thomas Nelson, "Doc's Deke's," *Ducks Unlimited,* May–June 1981, 18; Ron Gard, pers. comm., Mar. 22, 2011.

30. Joe Whitehead interview, June 14, 2008, Smith Point, TX; *Corpus Christi Caller-Times,* Oct. 31, 1943.

31. Dutton interview; Ron Gard, pers. comm., Dec. 7, 2009.

32. William J. Mackey Jr., *American Bird Decoys* (New York: Bonanza Books, 1965), 208–9; Kenneth L. Trayer, *North American Factory Decoys: A Pictorial Directory and Reference Guide* (Lancaster, PA: Reyart Pub., 2003), 170; *Galveston Daily News,* Jan. 30, 1907; Jan. 6, 1924.

33. "Charles Grubbs: Decoy Carver, Call Maker, Duck Hunter," in private collection of Gary Chambers; Trayer, *North American Factory Decoys,* 170–71; *San Antonio Express,* Oct. 17, 1928.

34. Abshier interview.

35. Archie Johnson, *Canvas Decoys of North America* (Lewes, DE: Decoy Magazine, 1994), 158–59; Chester Barker interview, May 9, 2009, Houston, TX.

36. *Galveston Daily News,* Aug. 1, 1928; *Port Arthur News,* Jan. 28, 1929; Bob Brister, "Those Good Old Days for Geese Still Here," *Houston Chronicle,* Nov. 20, 1988.

37. Prentice Holder interview, July 31, 2010, Baytown, TX; *Baytown Sun,* Dec. 7, 1953; "Ghostly Goose Hunters in Texas," *Life,* Dec. 7, 1953.

38. Alex Wolff interview, June 28, 2008, Houston, TX.

39. Halton Henderson, "Go White for Snows," *Field and Stream* 77, no. 5 (1972):138; Jim Longtin, pers. comm., Feb. 28, 2011; Bob Brister, *Houston Chronicle,* undated, in private collection of Agnes Reel Strauss.

40. Larry Hodge, "From Rags to Riches," *Texas Parks & Wildlife,* Sept. 2003, www.tpwmagazine.com/archive/2003/sept/legend/; Bob Brister, "Smarter Than a Goose," *Argosy* 347, no. 4 (1958):91.

41. Clifton Tyler interview, Jan. 25, 2009, Eagle Lake, TX; Hodge, "From Rags to Riches."

42. Tyler interview; *Houston Chronicle,* Nov. 20, 1997.

43. Wayne Waldrop, "Pioneer of the Prairie," *Waterfowl Magazine* 22, no. 6;Texas Goose Hunting, Clifton Tyler Goose Hunting Club, www.gooseshoot.com/; Chuck Barry, pers. comm., June 22, 2009.

44. Chuck Barry, pers. comm., June 22, 2009.

45. *Port Arthur News,* Nov. 3, 1974; Dec. 19, 1976; Bobby and Billy LeBlanc interview, Feb. 7, 2009, Port Arthur, TX; *Baytown Sun,* Nov. 19, 1971; Jerry Lynn Ayers interview, June 29, 2008, Houston, TX.

46. Howard L. Harlan and W. Crew Anderson, *Duck Calls, an Enduring American Folk Art* (Nashville: Harlan Anderson Press, 1988), 3; *Galveston Daily News,* Jan. 30, 1907; Strickland interview; John M. Taylor, pers. comm., Mar. 19, 2009; LeBlanc interview.

47. *Eagle Lake Headlight,* Jan. 7, 1911, to Dec. 21, 1912, microfilm image 65, Eula and David Wintermann Library, also Oct. 24, 1925, and May 13, 1933; Waddell interview; *Galveston Daily News,* Dec. 20, 1925.

48. Johnson *Canvas Decoys of North America,* 158; Barker interview.

49. Bill Quick, pers. comm., Mar. 31, 2009; *Port Arthur News,* Dec. 19, 1976.

50. James Fernandez interview, Dec. 22, 2008, Port Arthur, TX.

51. *Port Arthur News,* Dec. 23, 1973.

52. Fernandez interview.

53. *Port Arthur News,* Oct. 13, 1966.

54. Fernandez interview.

55. Henry Stowers, "Fowl Weather Friend," *Big Spring Daily Herald,* Oct. 31, 1971; Henry Stowers, "He Walks on Water," *Dallas Morning News,* Sept. 19, 1975.

56. Gary Chambers, pers. comm., Oct. 19, 2010; Lyle Jordan recorded narratives, 2001, in private collection of Doug Pike; Tyler interview.

57. *Port Arthur News,* Feb. 26, 1928.

58. *Lubbock Avalanche Journal,* Apr. 25, 1948; *Galveston Daily News,* May 2, 1948; *Baytown Sun,* Oct. 19, 1949; *Brookshire Times,* Oct. 13 and 27, 1950.

59. *San Antonio Express,* Sept. 27, 1953; July 6, 1955.

60. *Port Arthur News,* Nov. 3, 1974.

CHAPTER 3. HUNTING LAWS: RULES OF THE GAME

1. H. P. N. Gammel, ed., *The Laws of Texas, Supplemental Volume to the Original Ten Volumes, 1822–1897* (Austin: Gammel's Book Store, 1907), vol. 13, 254, Gammel's The Laws of Texas, http://texashistory.unt.edu/ark:/67531/metapth6719/; Early history of the Fish Commission and Game, Fish and Oyster Commission, manuscript, courtesy of Texas Parks and Wildlife Dept.

2. *Corpus Christi Times,* Mar. 2, 1938.

3. *Dallas Morning News,* Nov. 1, 1903; *Galveston Daily News,* Nov. 15, 1908.

4. *Dallas Morning News,* Jan. 18, 1909; Joe Brown, "Hunting History: Licenses First Issued in 1909," *Wichita Falls Times Record News,* Jan. 30, 2008, Wichita Falls Online, www.timesrecordnews.com/news/2008/jan/30/hunting-history/.

5. *Wichita Falls Daily Times,* Jan. 29, 1915; *San Antonio Light,* Mar. 21, 1915.

6. *San Antonio Light,* Aug. 25, 1918; *Galveston Daily News,* Mar. 19, 1925; Nov. 27, 1937; *Dallas Morning News,* Sept. 4, 1927.

7. *Victoria Daily Advocate,* Dec. 19, 1916; *San Antonio Light,* Nov. 17, 1918; *San Antonio Express,* Oct. 24, 1922; *Brownsville Herald,* Dec. 23, 1910; *Galveston Daily News,* July 3, 1911; Aug. 28, 1921; *San Antonio Evening, News,* Dec. 3, 1918.

8. Gammel, *Laws of Texas,* 13:281, http://texashistory.unt.edu/ark:/67531/metapth6719/; *Galveston Daily News,* July 18, 1894; Apr. 19, 1896.

9. *Victoria Daily Advocate,* Sept. 9, 1913; *Dallas Morning News,* Jan. 10, 1925.

10. *Galveston Daily News,* Nov. 1, 1930; *Dallas Morning News,* Sept. 21, 1934.

11. *Dallas Morning News,* Aug. 2, 1935; Aug. 15, 1936; *Galveston Daily News,* Aug. 3, 1935; *Corpus Christi Times,* Dec. 25, 1936.

12. *Dallas Morning News,* Aug. 15, 1936.

13. Ray Osborne, "Four-Legged Duck Blinds Are Banned," *Dallas Morning News,* Aug. 24, 1941; *Galveston Daily News,* June 11, 1946.

14. *Galveston Daily News,* Jan. 21 and Feb. 10, 1894; George Bird Grinnell, *American Duck Shooting* (New York: Forest and Stream Publishing, 1901), 598.

15. Charles Stutzenbaker, pers. comm., Jan. 16, 2011.

16. C. D. Stutzenbaker, "Nontoxic Steel Shot: A Solution to Lead Poisoning," *Texas Parks & Wildlife,* Aug. 1981, 12–15; Charles Stutzenbaker interview, May 30, 2009, Port Arthur, TX.

CHAPTER 4. SABINE ESTUARY

1. *Port Arthur Herald,* Dec. 1, 1898; Jim Sutherlin interview, Oct. 23, 2008, Port Arthur, TX; J. R. Singleton, *Texas Coastal Waterfowl Survey,* FA Report Series no. 11 (Austin: Texas Game and Fish Commission, 1953), 13.

2. *Port Arthur News,* July 1, 1923.

3. *Port Arthur Herald,* Feb. 24, 1898; Oct. 14, 1899; *Galveston Daily News,* Nov. 10, 1893; Feb. 6 and Sept. 5, 1897.

4. *Dallas Morning News,* Dec. 13, 1892.

5. *Galveston Daily News,* Nov. 25, 1884; Nov. 30, 1896.

6. Bill Quick, pers. comm., Mar. 31, 2009; *Port Arthur Herald,* Feb. 24, 1898; *Sabine Pass News,* Jan. 5, 1899.

7. Bill Quick, pers. comm., Mar. 31, 2009.

8. *Port Arthur News,* July 19, 1925; Yvonne Sutherlin, pers. comm., Dec. 22, 2008.

9. *Port Arthur News,* July 19, 1925; Charles Stutzenbaker interview, Oct. 24, 2008, Port Arthur, TX; *Port Arthur Herald,* Nov. 21, 1903; Jim Sutherlin, pers. comm., Oct. 23, 2008.

10. Jim Sutherlin, pers. comm., Oct. 23, 2008; *Port Arthur News,* July 19, 1925.

11. *Port Arthur News,* Aug. 24, 1975; *Galveston Daily News,* Dec. 3, 1907; Feb. 28, 1909.

12. *Port Arthur Herald,* Nov. 21, 1903; *Galveston Daily News,* Jan. 25, 1903.

13. Diana J. Kleiner, "Jefferson County," Handbook of Texas Online, www.tshaonline.org/handbook/online/articles/hcj05.

14. McFaddin Ranch land plat map, 1931, McFaddin-Ward House House collection, Beaumont, TX; Sutherlin interview; Charles Stutzenbaker, pers. comm., May 12, 2009.

15. Charles Stutzenbaker interview, June 20, 2009, Needmore Ranch, TX.

16. Bill Wilson interview, June 30, 2009, Needmore Ranch, TX; Gerry Cordts interview, July 10, 2009, Winnie, TX.

17. Cordts interview; Rosine Wilson interview, June 30, 2009, Needmore Ranch, TX.

18. Gerry Cordts, pers. comm., June 29, 2009.

19. *Weimar Mercury,* Nov. 14, 1958.

20. Bobby LeBlanc, unpublished family history, Feb. 2011.

21. Ibid.

22. Bobby and Billy LeBlanc interview, Feb. 7, 2009, Port Arthur, TX.

23. *Victoria Advocate,* Mar. 12, 1969; *San Antonio Express and News,* July 30, 1972; *Galveston Daily News,* Nov. 18, 1933; *Port Arthur News,* Oct. 30, 1934; Craig LeBlanc, pers. comm., Dec. 23, 2008; Bobby and Billy LeBlanc interview.

24. Bobby and Billy LeBlanc interview, Feb. 7, 2009, Port Arthur, TX; Bobby LeBlanc interview, Mar. 27, 2009, Port Arthur, TX; Bobby LeBlanc, pers. comms., Dec. 14, 2008, and Mar. 12, 2011; Bobby LeBlanc, unpublished family history, Feb. 2011.

25. James Fernandez interview, Dec. 22, 2008, Port Arthur, TX.

26. *Port Arthur News,* Dec. 13, 1968, and undated; Craig LeBlanc interview, Feb. 7, 2009, Port Arthur, TX; Bobby and Billy LeBlanc interview.

27. Mark Foreman, pers. comm., June 21, 2009.

28. Ray Sasser, "Sunday Outdoors," *Port Arthur News,* Nov. 9, 1975; Hayes Mendoza interview, May 1, 2009, Port Arthur, TX.

29. Mark Foreman, pers. comm., May 9, 2009; Coty Foreman interview, May 1, 2009, Port Arthur, TX; Leo Foreman interview, May 1, 2009, Port Arthur, TX.

30. Mendoza interview.

31. Ed Holder, "Sunday Outdoors," *Port Arthur News,* Dec. 22, 1968; *Corpus Christi Caller-Times,* Dec. 5, 1971; George Kellam, "To Get Goose Limit, Bark Like Canine," *Fort Worth Star-Telegram,* undated.

32. Randy Foreman, pers. comm., Nov. 7, 2010; Randy Foreman interview, May 1, 2009, Port Arthur, TX.

33. Randy Foreman interview.

34. Ibid.; Coty Foreman interview, May 1, 2009, Port Arthur, TX; Mark Foreman, pers. comm., May 9, 2009.

35. Randy Foreman interview; Coty Foreman interview; Mark Foreman, pers. comm., May 9, 2009 Mendoza interview; Leo Foreman interview.

36. Leo Foreman interview; Coty Foreman interview; Randy Foreman interview.

37. *Sabine Pass News,* Nov. 17, 1897; *Galveston Daily News,* Apr. 28, 1902; *Port Arthur Herald,* Sept. 30, 1905.

38. *Galveston Daily News,* Aug. 17, 1913; *Port Arthur News,* June 17, 1928.

39. *Brookshire Times,* Dec. 28, 1917; *Galveston Daily News,* Nov. 12, 1915; Aug. 25, 1922; *Port Arthur News,* Nov. 30, 1924; Dec. 13, 1925.

40. *Port Arthur News,* Oct. 31, 1924; Oct. 11, 1925; July 27, 1969; Stutzenbaker interview, Oct. 24, 2008.

41. *Port Arthur News,* Oct. 29, 1929; Wayne Stupka, pers. comm., June 26, 2009; *Corpus Christi Caller-Times,* Jan. 22, 1956.

42. *Port Arthur News,* Oct. 23, 1939; Nov. 20, 1946; Mar. 30, 1947; Stutzenbaker interview, Oct. 24, 2008; Bobby and Billy LeBlanc interview; Walter J. Stone to W. P. McFaddin Jr., Oct. 25, 1955, in private collection of Gerry Cordts.

43. McFaddin Ranch lease ledger, in private collection of Bobby LeBlanc; George T. Camp to J. C. L. McFaddin, Oct. 27, 1952, in private collection of Gerry Cordts; Mike Cooper interview, July 10, 2009, Port Arthur, TX; J. C. L. McFaddin to Harry A. Hebert, Nov. 6, 1957, in private collection of Gerry Cordts.

44. O. V. Kibbe Jr. to J. C. L. McFaddin, Oct. 24, 1956, in private collection of Gerry Cordts; *Port Arthur News,* Sept. 28, 1941; Henry LeBlanc to Russell McGuire, Jan. 3, 1956, in private collection of Gerry Cordts; Stutzenbaker interview, June 20, 2009; *Corpus Christi Caller-Times,* Aug. 8, 1961; *Amarillo Globe-Times,* Jan. 6, 1961.

45. Bobby and Billy LeBlanc interview; Fernandez interview.

46. Greg Keddy interview, Aug. 9, 2008, High Island, TX; *Beaumont Enterprise,* Nov. 7, 1971; Bobby and Billy LeBlanc interview; *Port Arthur News,* Nov. 24, 1965; Buddy Gough, "Sixty Years Ago—There Was a Zillion Ducks," *Beaumont Enterprise Journal,* Nov. 11, 1973.

47. *Beaumont Enterprise,* Nov. 7, 1971; Keddy interview; Ed Holder, "The Great Outdoors" *Port Arthur News,* undated clipping in Port Arthur Public Library; *Port Arthur News,* May 11, 1967; *Beaumont Enterprise,* Nov. 7, 1971.

48. *Galveston Daily News,* Oct. 18, 1922.

49. *Port Arthur News,* Dec. 7, 1937; Oct. 30, 1943; Nov. 2, 1945; Nov. 12, 1965; Apr. 27, 1968.

50. Ed Holder, "The Great Outdoors," *Port Arthur News,* Nov. 13, 1966; Fernandez interview.

51. Roy Swan, "Texas' Newest State Park," *San Antonio Express and News,* July 30, 1972; *Port Arthur News,* Oct. 17 and 20, 1973; Sept. 8, 1975; May 29, 1977; Fernandez interview.

52. Gerry Cordts, pers. comm., Mar. 16, 2010; Stutzenbaker interview, Oct. 24, 2008; Randy Foreman interview.

53. Stutzenbaker interview, Oct. 24, 2008; Holder, "The Great Outdoors," *Port Arthur News,* Nov. 13, 1966; Jim Sutherlin, pers. comm., Sept. 29, 2009.

54. Henry Stowers, "Fowl Weather Friend," *Big Spring Daily Herald,* Oct. 31, 1971; *Port Arthur News,* Oct. 16, 1977; Mar. 13, 1985; Bobby and Billy LeBlanc interview.

55. *Port Arthur News,* Jan. 19, 1975; Oct. 16, 1977; Stutzenbaker interview, Oct. 24, 2008; Keddy interview; Holder, "The Great Outdoors," *Port Arthur News,* Nov. 13, 1966.

56. Henry Stowers, "He Walks on Water," *Dallas Morning News,* Sept. 19, 1975; *Port Arthur News,* Mar. 24, 1976; Oct. 16, 1977; Keddy interview.

57. *Port Arthur News,* Nov. 4, 1927; Oct. 16, 1977; Ray Sasser, "Hunters to Fight City Limit," *Port Arthur News,* Dec. 16, 1977.

58. Lillian C. Richard interview, Mar. 27, 2009, Port Neches, TX; Brook Chatagnier interview, Mar. 27, 2009, Port Neches, TX.

59. Stutzenbaker interview, Oct. 24, 2008; Errol "E. J." Fournet, pers. comm., May 26, 2009.

60. Chatagnier interview.

61. Jim Arledge, "Trails and Trout," *Beaumont Enterprise,* Nov. 3, 1966.

62. *Port Arthur News,* Jan. 1, 1931; Charles Stutzenbaker interview, May 30, 2009, Port Arthur, TX.

63. Stutzenbaker interview, Oct. 24, 2008.

64. Errol "E. J." Fournet interview, May 1, 2009, Nederland, TX; Errol "E. J." Fournet, pers. comm., May 27, 2009.

65. Jim Sutherlin interview, Oct. 24, 2008, Port Arthur, TX; Craig LeBlanc, pers. comm., Oct. 23, 2008; Randy Foreman interview.

66. Fournet interview.

67. Sutherlin interview, Oct. 24, 2008; Stutzenbaker interview, Oct. 24, 2008; Fernandez interview.

68. Richards interview; Randy Chatagnier interview, Mar. 27, 2009, Port Neches, TX.

69. Stutzenbaker interview, Oct. 24, 2008; Charles Stutzenbaker, pers. comm., Oct. 22, 2009.

70. Rosine McFaddin Wilson, "The McFaddin Family," *Texas Gulf Historical and Biographical Record* 16, no. 1 (1980):38.

71. *Port Arthur News,* Nov. 29, 1936; *Galveston Daily News,* Jan. 1, 1950; Bobby LeBlanc, unpublished family history, Feb. 2011.

72. *Weimar Mercury,* Nov. 14, 1958; *Port Arthur News,* Aug. 28, 30, 1974; John Marks, "McFaddin Ranches," , manuscript, 1991, 8, McFaddin-Ward House collection, Beaumont, TX.

73. Marks, "McFaddin Ranches," 8; *Port Arthur News,* May 29, 1977.

74. Billy LeBlanc interview, Feb. 7, 2009, Port Arthur, TX; Ray Sasser, "Outdoors," *Port Arthur News,* Sept. 11, 1977; Ray Sasser, "Sunday Outdoors," *Port Arthur News,* June 19, 1977.

75. Shannon Tompkins, pers. comm.; *Port Arthur News,* Aug. 5, 1977; Sasser, "Sunday Outdoors," *Port Arthur News,* June 19, 1977; Ray Sasser, "Hunters Fire Away at Fed Refuge Plan," *Port Arthur News,* June 8, 1977; Leo Foreman interview.

76. *Port Arthur News,* Feb. 11, 1969; Fernandez interview; Randy Foreman interview.

77. *Port Arthur News,* Aug. 5, Sept. 4, 1977.

78. Ray Sasser, "Outdoors," *Port Arthur News,* Oct. 2, 1977; *Galveston Daily News,* Apr. 4, 1979; *Deer Park Progress,* Aug. 7, 1980; Keddy interview.

79. Sutherlin interview; Stutzenbaker interview, Oct. 24, 2008.

CHAPTER 5. EAST BAY

1. W. T. Block, "A History of Jefferson County, Texas, from Wilderness to Reconstruction," Early Transportation and Commerce, History, www.wtblock.com/wtblockjr/History%20of%20Jefferson%20County/Introduction.htm.

2. Ralph Semmes Jackson, *Home on the Double Bayou: Memories of an East Texas Ranch* (Austin: University of Texas Press, 1961), 12; Mickie Baldwin, "James Taylor White," Handbook of Texas Online, www.tshaonline.org/handbook/online/articles/WW/fwh21.html; Pat A. Daniels, "High Island, TX," Handbook of Texas Online, www.tshaonline.org/handbook/online/articles/HH/hlh44.html.

3. *Galveston Daily News,* Nov. 14, 1914; Daniels, "High Island, TX," Handbook of Texas Online; Thomas Selkirk, "Reminiscences of Hunter's Paradise," *Dallas Morning News,* Feb. 5, 1922.

4. *Galveston Daily News,* Nov. 14, 1914; Selkirk, "Reminiscences of Hunter's Paradise."

5. Melanie Wiggins, *They Made Their Own Law* (Houston: Rice University Press, 1990), 52; Margaret S. Henson and Kevin Ladd, *Chambers County, a Pictorial History* (Norfolk, VA: Donning Publishers, 1988), 268; *Galveston Daily News,* Feb. 19, 1910; Nov. 11, 1920; Dec. 2, 1923.

6. *Galveston Daily News,* Nov. 3, 1934; Nov. 13, 1942; Oct. 31, 1943; *Port Arthur News,* undated; Nov. 19, 1935; Nov. 28, Dec. 5, 1937; Nov. 22, 1938; Claud Kahla interview, June 6, 2009, High Island, TX.

7. Kahla interview.

8. Ibid.; *Galveston Daily News,* Nov. 1, 1910.

9. *Port Arthur News,* Oct. 23, 1966; Bobby LeBlanc, pers. comm., Feb. 27, 2009; Bill Gammel, pers. comm., Dec. 1, 2009; Wayne Stupka, pers. comm., June 26, 2009.

10. *Galveston Daily News,* May 17, 1930; Dec. 30, 1938.

11. *Galveston Daily News,* July 27, 1876; Oct., 5, 1885; May 17, 1930; Wiggins, *They Made Their Own Law,* 48.

12. Charles Hallock, *The Sportsman's Gazetteer and General Guide to the Game Animals, Birds and Fishes of North America: Their Habits and Various Methods of Capture,* Part 2, *A Sportsman's Directory to the Principal Resorts for Game and Fish in North America* (New York: Orange Judd Company, 1883), 154; *Galveston Daily News,* Oct., 5, 1885; Mar. 19, 1905; Wiggins, *They Made Their Own Law,* 52–53.

13. *Galveston Daily News,* July 25, 1897; Jan. 27, 1905; Mar. 31, 1932; "Game Laws in Brief and Woodcraft Magazine," *The Brief's Directory of Fish and Game Resorts* (New York: Forest and Stream Publishing, 1899) 1, no. 1:148.

14. Wiggins, *They Made Their Own Law,* 151–52.

15. Ibid., 139, 260; *Galveston Daily News,* June 15, 1977.

16. *Port Arthur News,* July 19, 1925; *Galveston Daily News,* Aug. 8, 1924; May 17, 1930; Kahla interview.

17. Wiggins, *They Made Their Own Law,* 99–100, 166.

18. Kahla interview; *Port Arthur News,* Mar. 7, 1942; Thelma Berwick Black interview, June 6, 2009, High Island, TX.

19. Clyde "Boots" Faggard, pers. comm., Apr. 18, 2009; Wiggins, *They Made Their Own Law,* 100; Joe Faggard interview, June 6, 2009, High Island, TX; *Galveston Daily News,* Feb. 17, 1946.

20. *Galveston Daily News,* Nov. 12, 1947; Oct. 24, 1957; Oct. 18, Nov. 25, Dec. 24, 1959; Melanie Wiggins, pers. comm., Oct. 2008; Boots Faggard, pers. comm., Apr. 18, 2009; *San Antonio Light,* Oct. 26, 1958; Oct. 27, 1960.

21. *Galveston Daily News,* Dec. 2, 1974; Feb. 24, 1985.

22. Forrest West, pers. comm., Sept. 7, 2008.

23. Melanie Wiggins, pers. comm., Oct. 2008.

24. Joe Doggett, "West, Mallards are Hard to Beat," *Houston Chronicle,* Jan. 7, 1993; Melanie Wiggins, pers. comm., Oct. 2008.

25. Forrest West, pers. comm., Sept. 7, 2008.

26. Joe Doggett, "Right on Target: Opening of Duck Season a Fun Time as Trip to High Island Scores a Perfect 10," *Houston Chronicle,* Nov. 7, 2002; Forrest West, pers. comm., Sept. 7, 2008.

27. Paul McDonald, pers. comm., Sept. 12, 2008; Forrest West, pers. comm., Sept. 7, 2008; Boots Faggard, pers. comm., May 13, 2009; Doggett, "Right On Target."

28. Chet Beaty interview, May 26, 2008, Hempstead, TX.

29. Joe Doggett, "Marsh Madness: Bogged Buggy Can't Spoil this Trek for Ducks," *Houston Chronicle,* Oct. 29, 1988; Joe Doggett, "Day-Hunt Outfitters Ease Burden," *Houston Chronicle,* Nov. 13, 2003.

30. Forrest West, pers. comm., Sept. 7, 2008.

31. Joe Whitehead interview, June 14, 2008, Smith Point, TX.

32. *Galveston Daily News,* Feb. 10, 1894; Whitehead interview; Wayne Capooth, *Waterfowling America* (Memphis: privately printed, 2008), 2:426; Charles Stutzenbaker interview, Oct. 24, 2008, Port Arthur, TX.

33. *Galveston Daily News,* Dec. 29, 1907; Jan. 30, 1909; "Observations at Fort Anahuac," *Dallas Morning News,* Mar. 25, 1899; *Dallas*

Morning News, Dec. 30, 1895; Gary Cartwright, *Galveston: A History of the Island* (New York: Atheneum, 1991), 56; Forest W. McNeir, *Forest McNeir of Texas* (San Antonio: Naylor, 1956), 73, 84–85.

34. *Dallas Morning News,* Jan. 20, 1903; Dec. 29, 1907; Jan. 30, 1924.

35. Ibid., Dec. 30, 1895.

36. Ibid.; McNeir, *Forest McNeir of Texas,* 86; "Observations at Fort Anahuac"; *Galveston Daily News,* Nov. 11, 1901.

37. McNeir, *Forest McNeir of Texas,* 79; Stutzenbaker interview, Oct. 24, 2008; Hilmar G. Moore interview, Aug. 4, 2009, Richmond, TX.

38. "Education: Neff to Baylor," Time Magazine Online, www.time.com/time/magazine/article/0,9171,743595,00.html.

39. *Dallas Morning News,* Feb. 1, 1924; *Galveston Daily News,* Dec. 29, 1907; Jan. 30, 1926.

40. McNeir, *Forest McNeir of Texas,* 74, 93; *Galveston Daily News,* July 9, 1954.

41. McNeir, *Forest McNeir of Texas,* 86; *Dallas Morning News,* Mar. 25, 1899.

42. *Galveston Daily News,* Oct. 11, 1907; Nov. 7, 1909; *Denton Record-Chronicle,* Sept. 21, 1950; *Galveston Daily News,* Nov. 7, 1909.

43. Henson and Ladd, *Chambers County,* 194–95.

44. Ralph Semmes Jackson, *Home on the Double Bayou: Memories of an East Texas Ranch* (Austin: University of Texas Press, 1961), 71–72, 75.

45. Henry Melton, 1935 Houston radio address, reprinted by *Houston Chronicle,* Nov. 3, 2000.

46. Jim Bob Jackson interview, Aug. 16, 2009, Baytown, TX; Palmer and Talley Melton interview, July 17, 2009, Houston, TX.

47. Mary Jean Abshier interview, June 13, 2008, Anahuac, TX; Freddie Abshier interview, Dec. 28, 2009, Anahuac, TX.

48. Freddie Abshier interview, June 13, 2008, Anahuac, TX; Jim Bob Jackson interview; Jim Bob Jackson, *JHK Ranch, 1940–1963* (Baytown TX: privately printed, 2010), 22.

49. *Galveston Daily News,* Dec. 14, 1926; *Port Arthur News,* Nov. 18, 20, 1932.

50. Mary Jean Abshier interview, Feb. 6, 2009, Anahuac, TX; Jackson Ranch day hunting pass, private collection of Mary Jean Abshier; Jim Bob Jackson interview.

51. Alex Wolff interview, June 28, 2008, Houston, TX.

52. Jim Bob Jackson interview; Jackson, *JHK Ranch,* 22.

53. Jim Bob Jackson interview; Joe Whitehead, "Ducks," manuscript; Whitehead interview.

54. Mary Jean Abshier interview, Feb. 6, 2009.

55. Jim Bob Jackson interview.

56. Whitehead, "Ducks."; Jim Bob Jackson interview.

57. Whitehead "Ducks."

58. Freddie Abshier interview, Feb. 6, 2009, Anahuac, TX.

59. Freddie Abshier interview, June 13, 2008.

60. Whitehead, "Ducks."

61. Melton interview.

62. Jim Bob Jackson, pers. comm., May 23, 2010; Jim Bob Jackson interview.

63. Kevin Ladd, "Barrow, Benjamin," Handbook of Texas Online, www.tshaonline.org/handbook/online/articles/fbabh.

64. Stutzenbaker interview; Kahla interview.

65. "Duck Hunting in Chambers County," interview with Joe Lagow, unknown author, May 22, 1985 manuscript in Wallisville Heritage Center collection, Wallisville, TX; Jack Holland interview, Oct. 18, 2008, Rockport, TX; Freddie Abshier interview; David Byford, "Veteran Guides Aid an Enjoyable Outing," *Baytown Sun,* Dec. 27, 1984.

66. Janet and Jean Lagow interview, Aug. 9, 2008, Winnie, TX.

67. Ibid.; Shannon Tompkins, "Gone Goose: Largest of Canada Geese Abandon Texas, Wintering Farther North," *Houston Chronicle,* Jan. 20, 2000; Janet Lagow, pers. comm.

68. Bob Brister, "Barrow's Memories Rekindled: Ranch Won Fame as Ideal Hunting Area," *Houston Chronicle,* Aug. 13, 1992.

69. *Beaumont Enterprise-Journal,* Jan. 27, 1980; Jack Holland interview, Oct. 18, 2008, Rockport, TX; Janet and Jean Lagow interview.

70. *San Antonio Light,* Oct. 27, 1960; *Dallas Morning News,* Nov. 4, 1950; Nov. 4, 1952; Janet and Jean Lagow interview.

71. Janet and Jean Lagow interview; Gordon LeCompte interview Feb. 13, 2010, Sargent, TX.

72. Brister, "Barrow's Memories"; *Weimar Mercury,* Dec. 1, 1939.

73. Brister, "Barrow's Memories"; Gordon LeCompte interview Feb. 13, 2020, Sargent, TX.

74. Holland interview; Bob Brister, "Where Have the Ducks Gone?" *San Antonio Light,* Dec. 4, 1966; Tompkins, "Gone Goose."

75. Forrest West, pers. comm; Shannon Tompkins, pers. comm.; Gene Campbell interview, May 2, 2009, Anahuac, TX; Dave Wilcox, pers. comm., Mar. 4, 2009; Clyde "Boots" Faggard interview, June 6, 2009, High Island, TX.

76. Hart Stilwell, "Outdoor Texas," *Houston Post,* fall 1962, in private collection of Mary Jean Abshier; Janet and Jean Lagow interview; Joe Doggett, "Lagow Leaves Waterfowl Legacy," *Houston Chronicle,* June 19, 1996; Aubrey Jones interview, Aug. 10, 2008, Anahuac, TX.

77. Janet and Jean Lagow interview; Freddie Abshier interview, Feb. 6, 2009.

78. "Duck Hunting in Chambers County," manuscript; Campbell interview.

79. *Galveston Daily News,* Sept. 23, ca. 1970; *Beaumont Enterprise,* Oct. 27, 1952; Cindy Horswell, "Storm Is Brewing over Peaceful Conservation Land: Conservation Pioneer's Family Continues Tradition of Protecting Wildlife on Ranch," *Houston Chronicle,* June 4, 2000.

80. Janet and Jean Lagow interview; Charles Stutzenbaker interview, Feb. 6, 2009, Port Arthur, TX.

81. David Byford, "Veteran Guides Aid an Enjoyable Outing," *Baytown Sun,* Dec. 27, 1984; Dave Wilcox, pers. comm.; Gordon LeCompte interview, Feb. 13, 2010, Sargent, TX.

82. Byford, "Veteran Guides Aid an Enjoyable Outing"; Jean Lagow interview, Sept. 5, 2008, Wallisville, TX; Shannon Tompkins, pers. comm.

83. Holland interview.

84. Walter Besser interview, July 11, 2008, Angleton, TX; Holland interview.

85. Holland interview.

86. Whitehead interview; Joe Whitehead interview, Aug. 9, 2008, Smith Point, TX.

87. Whitehead, "Ducks."

88. Joe Whitehead, pers. comm., July 26, 2010; Whitehead "Ducks."

89. Whitehead, "Ducks."

90. Freddie Abshier interview, June 13, 2008.

91. Ibid.

92. Freddie Abshier interview, Feb. 6, 2009.

93. Karla Jackson Dean interview, July 10, 2009, Anahuac TX.

94. *Galveston Daily News,* June 6, 1937; Dean interview; *Seguin Gazette,* Oct. 16, 1975.

95. Arthur James Jackson interview, July 10, 2009, Anahuac, TX.

96. Ibid.; Quinten Jackson interview, July 10, 2009, Anahuac, TX.

97. Holland interview; Arthur James Jackson interview; Dean interview.

98. Dean interview.

99. Ibid.; Felix Jackson, pers. comm., Aug. 5, 2008.

100. Whitehead, "Ducks"; Whitehead interview.

101. Ralph Leggett interview, May 2, 2009, Anahuac, TX.

102. Ibid.; "Duck Hunting in Chambers County."

103. Cliff Fisher interview, Mar. 8, 2009, Houston, TX; Leggett interview.

104. Leggett interview; Joe Whitehead, pers. comm., July 26, 2010.

105. "Duck Hunting in Chambers County"; Leggett interview.

106. Steve Kole Jr., pers. comm., May 23, 2009; Kole family website, https://picasaweb.google.com/mollie.c.bridges/HistoricalDocuments?authkey=GvIsRgCIDS8oy9k9a9wAE#5237705307205994914.

107. Steve Kole Jr., pers. comm., May 23, 2009.

108. Ibid.; Kole family website, https://picasaweb.google.com/mollie.c.bridges/HistoricalDocuments?authkey=GvIsRgCIDS8oy9k9a9wAE#5030112965303543490.

109. Aubrey Jones interview, Aug. 10, 2008, Anahuac, TX.

110. Will Beaty interview, July 25, 2008, Hempstead, TX.

CHAPTER 6. TRINITY RIVER DELTA

1. Charles Hallock, *The Sportsman's Gazetteer and General Guide to the Game Animals, Birds, and Fishes of North America: Their Habits and Various Methods of Capture,* Part 2, *A Sportsman's Directory to the Principal Resorts for Game and Fish in North America* (New York: Orange Judd Company, 1883), 154; Ike Handy, "Reflective Historical Narrative," ca. 1960s, in Royce A. Strickland, *Ridgehaven and a Dunn Marsh Legacy: Photojournal of Texas Coastal Outdoorsman Lindsey H. Dunn, Jr.* (Baytown, TX: privately printed, 2004).

2. Kendon L. Clark, *Marshman! Wildlife Experiences of Manson L. Clark of Cove, Texas* (Ozark, MO: Yates Publishing, 1983), 108; Damon McKay interview with Royce A. Strickland, Jan. 6, 2001, Cove, TX; Captain Frank W. Flack, *A Hunter's Experiences in the Southern States of America: Being an Account of the Natural History of Various Quadrupeds and Birds Which Are the Objects of Chase in Those Countries* (London: Longmans, Green and Co., 1866), 274.

3. *Galveston Daily News,* Oct. 17, 1875; Fred Badger, "On the Gulf Coast," *Outing: Sport, Adventure, Travel, Fiction* 39 (Oct. 1901–Mar. 1902):334.

4. Royce A. Strickland interview, May 31, 2009, Baytown, TX; Handy "Reflective Historical Narrative," 4; *Dallas Morning News,* Jan. 10, 1925.

5. Kendon L. Clark, *Diamond in the Rough: A History of Cove, Texas* (Ozark, MO: Yates Publishing, 1982), 2:85–86; Clark, *Marshman!* 110; Strickland interview.

6. Handy, "Reflective Historical Narrative," 1; Clark, *Diamond in the Rough,* 2:85.

7. Earl Porter interview with Royce A. Strickland, Feb. 23, 2001; McKay interview with Strickland.

8. McKay interview with Strickland.

9. Homer Harmon interview with Royce A. Strickland, July 4, 1999.

10. Porter interview with Strickland; Harmon interview with Strickland.

11. Porter interview with Strickland.

12. *San Antonio Light,* Oct. 26, 1958.

13. L. A. Williams interview with Royce A. Strickland, Apr. 10, 1993.

14. Clark, *Marshman!* 6–21.

15. Ibid., 11–25.

16. Kendon L. Clark, "Memoirs, or, Fulfilling My Obligation," manuscript, in private collection of Kendon L. Clark, 78–159; Clark, *Marshman!* 22.

17. Clark, *Marshman!* 22–111; Clark, "Memoirs," 160; Wade Clark, manuscript, undated, in Wallisville Heritage Center collection; Chester Rogers, [title illegible], *Houston Chronicle Magazine,* Oct. 27, 1946, in Wallisville Heritage Center collection.

18. Johnnie Dutton interview, June 6, 2009, Baytown TX.

19. Porter interview with Strickland.

20. Handy, "Reflective Historical Narrative," 1–3; John Winter photo albums, in private collection of Cliff Fisher.

21. John M. Weathersby, "Lindsey Dunn of Delhomme," *Ducks Unlimited,* Nov.–Dec. 1991, 58; Clark, *Diamond in the Rough,* 2:86;

Lindsey Dunn photographic collection, courtesy of Royce A. Strickland.

22. Lindsey Dunn Jr. interview with Strickland, June 17, 1990.

23. Ibid.; Strickland interview.

24. Royce A. Strickland, pers. comm., June 18, 2009.

25. Clark, Kendon L., *Diamond in the Rough,* 2:86; Cliff Fisher interview, Mar. 8, 2009, Houston, TX; Handy, "Reflective Historical Narrative," 4.

26. Clark, *Marshman!,* 78–87; Handy, "Reflective Historical Narrative," 5; David Wilcox, pers. comm., Mar. 4, 2009.

27. David Wilcox, pers. comm., Aug. 12, 2009; Steve Wilburn, pers. comm., Aug. 11, 2008.

28. Walter Besser interview, July 11, 2008, Angleton, TX.

29. *San Antonio Light,* Oct. 27, 1960; *Baytown Sun,* Dec. 10, 1954; *Galveston Daily News,* Dec. 13, 1955; David Wilcox interview, May 2, 2009, Anahuac, TX.

30. Shannon Tompkins, pers. comm., Feb. 6, 2009.

31. Bob Brister, "Of Memories and Mallards," *Houston Chronicle,* Dec. 25, 1960; Harvey Evans interview, Feb. 20, 2010, Portland, TX.

32. Sylvia Lamb interview, Aug. 8, 2008, Wallisville, TX.

33. Fisher interview; Besser interview.

34. *Houston Chronicle,* Dec. 25, 1960; Bob Brister, "A Lifetime of Hunting: Wallisville Guide Speaks Duck Lingo," *Houston Chronicle,* Nov. 24, 1955; Fisher interview.

35. Brister, "A Lifetime of Hunting"; *Houston Chronicle,* Dec. 25, 1960; Mickey Lamb, pers. comm., Aug. 8, 2008, Wallisville, TX; Bob Brister, "The Huntingest Gentleman of the Upper Coastal Marsh, *Houston Chronicle,* ca. 1981.

36. Royce A. Strickland, pers. comm., June 6, 2009.

37. Shannon Tompkins, "Nothing Like Hunting in Timber: Taking Ducks Just a Small Part of Experience," *Houston Chronicle,* Dec. 28, 2008; Porter interview with Strickland.

38. James Tilton to Shannon Tompkins, pers. comm., undated; Prentice Holder interview, July 31, 2010, Baytown, TX; Joe Doggett, pers. comm., June 4, 2009; Shannon Tompkins, pers. comm., June 6, 2009.

39. Forrest West, pers. comm., Sept. 7, 2008; Joe Doggett, "A Greenhead That Lives On," *Houston Chronicle,* Dec. 8, 1989; Joe Doggett, pers. comm., June 4, 2009; Los Patos promotional brochure, private collection of Shannon Tompkins; John P. Cowan, *A Texas Treasure* (Dallas: Collectors Covey, 1992), 68.

40. Bill Gammel, pers. comm., Jan. 15, 2010.

41. Royce A. Strickland, pers. comm., June 18, 2009; Bill Gammel, pers. comm., Jan. 15, 2010; Gordon LeCompte interview, Feb. 13, 2020, Sargent, TX; Shannon Tompkins, pers. comm., June 6, 2009.

42. Holder interview; Bill Gammel, pers. comm., Jan. 15, 2010; LeCompte interview.

CHAPTER 7. SAN JACINTO RIVER

1. William C. Harris, ed., *The Sportsman's Guide to the Hunting and Shooting Grounds of the United States and Canada* (New York: Anglers Publishing, 1888), 166; Wayne Capooth, *Waterfowling America* (Memphis: privately printed, 2008), 2:421; *Galveston Daily News,* Nov. 20, 1891; Oct. 26, 1893; Nov. 17, 1909.

2. *Galveston Daily News,* June 6, 1907; Liston Roberts, pers. comm., 2008.

3. *Galveston Daily News,* June 30, 1890; State of Texas, *Biennial Report of the Secretary of State of the State of Texas, 1914* (Austin: Von Boeckmann-Jones, 1914), 47; *Galveston Daily News,* May 16, 1878; May 15, 1896; June 6, 1907.

4. Forest McNeir, *Forest McNeir of Texas* (San Antonio: Naylor, 1956), 57; Nash Buckingham, *Mr. Buck: The Autobiography of Nash Buckingham* (New York: Countrysport Press, 1900), 180; *Galveston Daily News,* Dec. 4, 1898; Oct. 30, 1905.

5. Edward T. Martin, "The Two Extremes," *Hunter-Trader-Trapper* 41, no. 1 (1920):30; Andrew Forest Muir, "Destiny of Buffalo Bayou," *Southwestern Historical Quarterly* 47, no. 2 (1943):91, Southwestern Historical Quarterly Online, texashistory.unt.edu/ark:/67531/metapth146054/m1/109/?q=andrew forest muir; *Galveston Daily News,* June 25, 1885; B. R. Brunson and Andrew Forest Muir, "Morgan, James," Handbook of Texas History Online, www.tshaonline.org/handbook/online/articles/fm050 ; Ann Macklin Peel, ed., *To Become A Texian: The Letters and Journeys of Caroline Cox Morgan and Her Family, 1839–1857* (Frankfort: Kentucky Color Publishing, 1997), 2, Portal to Texas History, http://texashistory.unt.edu/ark:/67531/metapth26718/.

6. *Houston Telegraph and Texas Register,* Oct. 22, 1845; *Galveston Daily News,* Oct. 22, 1865; Aug. 21, 1898; Brunson and Muir, "Morgan, James," Handbook of Texas History Online.

7. Edward T. Martin, "Pintail Shooting in the Days Long Ago," *Hunter-Trader-Trapper* 32, no. 4 (1916):21; Edward T. Martin, "The Two Extremes," *Hunter-Trader-Trapper* 41, no. 1 (1920):30–31; *Galveston Daily News,* Jan. 16, 1886.

8. *Galveston Daily News,* July 23, 1890; Dec. 31, 1892; Sept. 20, 1893; Nov. 25, 1894; *Dallas Morning News,* Mar. 9, 1893; *Houston Daily Post,* Jan. 20, 1900, Library of Congress, Chronicling America, http://chroniclingamerica.loc.gov/lccn/sn86071197/1900-01-20/ed-1/seq-7/.

9. *Galveston Daily News,* Jan. 11, 1891; May 29, 1892; Jan. 5, 1893; Sept. 22, 1895; W. J. McDonald, *Biennial Report of the State Revenue Agent, 1906–08* (Austin: Von Boeckmann-Jones, 1909), 27.

10. Nash Buckingham, *Mr. Buck: The Autobiography of Nash Buckingham* (New York: Countrysport Press, 1900), 180; *Baytown Sun,* Nov. 5, 1953; *Galveston Daily News,* Sept. 3, Oct. 24, 1920.

11. *Victoria Weekly Advocate,* Feb. 6, 1909; *Galveston Daily News,* Dec. 31, 1922.

12. "The Motor Car as an Aid to Hunting in Texas," *The Horseless Age* 18, no. 14 (1906):9.

13. *Houston Daily Post,* Nov. 28, 1902, 5, Library of Congress, Chronicling America, http://chroniclingamerica.loc.gov/lccn/sn86071197/1902-11-28/ed-1/seq-5, and Jan. 30, 1903, 4, Library of Congress, Chronicling America, http://chroniclingamerica.loc.gov/lccn/sn86071197/1903-01-30/ed-1/seq-4; *Galveston Daily News,* July 10, 1906; Sept. 3, 1920.

14. Damon McKay interview with Royce A. Strickland, Jan. 6, 2001.

15. John Winter photo albums, in private collection of Cliff Fisher.

16. Ibid.; Charles Stutzenbaker, pers. comm., May 30, 2009.

17. John Winter photo albums.

18. Ibid.; Lee Smith, pers. comm., June 9, 2009.

19. John Winter photo albums.

20. Ibid.; Errol "E. J." Errol Fournet, pers. comm., Apr. 27, 2009; Oddjob Motors, www.oddjobmotors.com/elto.htm.

21. John Winter photo albums; Cliff Fisher interview, Mar. 8, 2009, Houston, TX.

22. *Houston Chronicle,* Sept. 25, 1953; Chet Beaty interview, May 26, 2008, Hempstead, TX.

23. John Winter photo albums.

24. Undated newspaper clipping from ibid.

25. Ibid.

26. Ibid.; "Hints to Duck Hunters," *Sports Round-Up,* Dec. 1946, 10-14, John Winter photo albums.

27. Palmer and Talley Melton interview, July 17, 2009, Houston, TX; Shannon Tompkins, "Ghost Dance: Visions of the Waterfowling World in the Early 1900s Are Surreal, Haunting," *Houston Chronicle,* Nov. 2, 2000.

28. Melton interview.

29. Henry Melton, 1935 Houston radio address, reprinted by *Houston Chronicle,* Nov. 3, 2000.

30. Tompkins, "Ghost Dance."

31. *Galveston Daily News,* July 7, 1934; Clifton Tyler interview, Jan. 25, 2009, Eagle Lake, TX.

32. Bob Brister, "A Semi Swan Song: Bob Brister Reflects on Nearly 40 Years as Outdoors Editor," *Houston Chronicle,* Jan. 28, 1993.

33. Ibid.; Rick Pratt, "Bob Brister's Long Shadow," *Shooting Sportsman* 17, no. 6 (2005): 14-15.

34. Pratt, "Bob Brister's Long Shadow"; Forrest West, pers. comm., Sept. 7, 2008; *Galveston Daily News,* Jan. 27, 1941; June 14, 1987.

35. J. C. Clopper, "J. C. Clopper's Journal and Book of Memoranda for 1828," *Texas Historical Association Quarterly* 13, no. 1 (1909):44-80, Southwestern Historical Quarterly Online, http://texashistory.unt.edu/ark:/67531/metapth101051/m1/52/; Buck A. Young, "Baytown, TX," Handbook of Texas Online, www.tshaonline.org/handbook/online/articles/hdb01; *Baytown Sun,* Jan. 11, 1950; Jan. 18, 1951; Sept. 11, 1974; Nov. 15, 1984.

36. Brian Hightower, pers. comm., July 31, 2009; *Galveston Daily News,* Apr. 12, 1984.

37. Royce A. Strickland interview, May 31, 2009, Baytown, TX; *Baytown Sun,* Nov. 24, 1959; May 2, 1966; Gordon LeCompte interview, Feb. 13, 2010, Sargent, TX.

38. *Baytown Sun,* Nov. 24, 1959; LeCompte interview.

39. Mike Leebron interview, Feb. 13, 2010, Sargent, TX.

40. *Baytown Sun,* May 26, 1977; "Ghostly Goose Hunters in Texas," *Life,* Dec. 7, 1953.

41. *Baytown Sun,* Aug. 3, 1986.

42. Prentice Holder interview, July 31, 2010, Baytown, TX.

43. Gary Chambers, pers. comm.; Royce A. Strickland, pers. comm., Feb. 14, 2010; *Baytown Sun,* Oct. 28, 1959.

44. *Baytown Sun,* Dec. 28, 1949; Oct. 19, 1950; Sept. 25, 1968.

45. *Baytown Sun,* May 26, 1977; Brister, "Semi Swan Song."

CHAPTER 8. WEST GALVESTON BAY

1. "Galveston, Houston and Henderson Railroad," Handbook of Texas Online, www.tshaonline.org/handbook/online/articles/eqg07; *Galveston Daily News,* Dec. 27, 1873; Apr. 2, 1878.

2. *Galveston Daily News,* Jan. 12, 1887; Mar. 13, 1893; Nov. 24, 1895; Aug. 22, 1907.

3. Ibid., July 10, 1906; Apr. 25, 1907; July 5, 1911; *Houston, A History and Guide* (Houston: Anson Jones, 1942), 218, Portal to Texas History, http://texashistory.unt.edu/ark:/67531/metapth5865/m1/282/; *Fort Worth Star-Telegram,* May 14, 1907.

4. *Galveston Daily News,* Oct. 29, 1896; Priscilla Myers Benham, "Texas City, TX," Handbook of Texas Online, www.tshaonline.org/handbook/online/articles/hdt03.

5. *Galveston Daily News,* Sept. 16, 1879; Mar. 13, 1893.

6. Ibid., Apr. 2, 1878; Oct. 28, 1879; Dec. 6, 1886.

7. Ibid., Dec. 6, 1886.

8. *Galveston City Gazette,* Oct. 28, 1843; *Telegraph and Texas Register,* Oct. 22, 1845; Matilda C. Houstoun, "Texas and the Gulf of Mexico, or, Yachting in the New World," *Home and Travellers Library* (Philadelphia: G. B. Zieber, 1845), 1:137.

9. *Galveston Daily News,* Oct. 5, 1885; May 27, 1917.

10. Gary Cartwright, *Galveston, A History of the Island* (New York: Atheneum, 1991), 119; *Galveston Daily News,* Feb. 20 1886; Nov. 8, 1893; Jan. 21, 1909.

11. *Galveston Daily News,* Sept. 16, 1929.

12. Ibid., June 5, 1879; Aug. 9, 1884; Dec. 20, 1895; Jan. 19, 1897; Nov. 15, 1899; July 13, 1902.

13. Cartwright, *Galveston, A History of the Island,* 160-64.

14. *Dallas Morning News,* Jan. 10, 1901; *Galveston Daily News,* Dec. 16, 1900.

15. *Galveston Daily News,* Aug. 14, 1901; Sept. 18, 1904.

16. Ibid., Nov. 26, 1901; Dec. 7, 1907.

17. Ned Hardy, "When the Ducks Begin to Fly," *Dallas Morning News,* Sept. 27, 1908; *Galveston Daily News,* Dec. 29, 1905; Sept. 8, 1908; Oct. 5, 1913.

18. Hardy, "When the Ducks Begin to Fly"; *Galveston Daily News,* Dec. 1, 1916; Nov. 1, 1930; Dec. 23, 1941.

19. *Galveston Daily News,* Sept. 5, 1936; Oct. 3, 1939; *Port Arthur News,* June 24, 1924.

20. *Galveston Daily News,* Nov. 30, 1902; Jan. 7, 1912; Aug. 18, 1929.

21. Ibid., Oct. 31, Dec. 2, 1923; Nov. 16, 1931; Nov. 4, Dec. 23, 1941; Nov. 6, 1942.

22. Ibid., Mar. 16, 1972; Nov. 19, 1982; Kevin Ladd, pers. comm. A. C. Becker, *Waterfowl in the Marshes* (South Brunswick and New York: A. S. Barnes, 1969), 155.

23. *Galveston Daily News,* Feb. 13, 1940; Oct. 11, 1941.

24. Ibid., Nov. 12, 1947; Nov. 1 and 4, 1949.

25. *Abilene Reporter-News,* Dec. 21, 1946; *Brazosport Facts,* July 11, 1972.

26. *Galveston Daily News,* Oct. 1, 1928.

27. James Smock, pers. comm., Jan. 22, 2009.

28. *Galveston Daily News,* Oct. 26, 1958; Oct. 18, 1959.

29. *San Antonio Light,* Oct. 27, 1960; Halls Bayou Ranch Hunting Club, www.hallsbayou.com/club%20info/hbr_hunting_club_information.html; *Galveston Daily News,* Oct. 27, 1959; Oct. 27, 1960; A. C. Becker Jr., "The Outdoorsman," *Galveston Daily News,* Oct. 15, 1969; Marshall Hayes interview, Nov. 12, 2009, Markham, TX.

30. Stewart Campbell interview, Apr. 3, 2009, Port O'Connor, TX; Halls Bayou Ranch Hunting Club, www.hallsbayou.com/club%20info/hbr_hunting_club_information.html.

31. *Denton Record-Chronicle,* Sept. 21, 1950; George L. Flynn, "San Luis Pass during the Civil War and the 1800s," manuscript, 1996, Brazoria County Historical Museum; *Freeport Facts,* Nov. 3, 1963.

32. US Fish and Wildlife Service, *Wetlands Preservation Program: Texas Gulf Coast—Category 8,* updated (Albuquerque: USFWS, Department of the Interior, 1981), A-33.

CHAPTER 9. BRAZOS AND SAN BERNARD RIVERS TO THE GULF

1. *Galveston Daily News,* Mar. 9, 1894; Mar. 24, 1897.

2. *Brazosport Facts,* Dec. 26, 1965; July 11, 1972.

3. Light Townsend Cummins, *Emily Austin of Texas, 1795–1851* (Fort Worth: TCU Press, 2009), 194.

4. *Brazosport Facts,* July 24, 1966; Feb. 18, 1968.

5. *Galveston Daily News,* Oct. 12, 1895; Jan. 18, 1896; Sept. 9, 1891.

6. *Dallas Morning News,* Aug. 26, 1906.

7. *Galveston Daily News,* Aug. 31, 1893.

8. *Brazosport Facts,* Feb. 4, 1957; *Galveston Daily News,* Nov. 6 1907.

9. *Biennial Report of the Secreatry of State of the State of Texas* (Austin: Von Boeckmann-Jones, 1914), 117; *Galveston Daily News,* Dec. 1, 1901; Oct. 8, 1913; Aug. 25, 1943; *Brazosport Facts,* Dec. 12, 1967.

10. *Galveston Daily News,* Aug. 25, 1943; *Brazosport Facts,* Dec. 26, 1965; Sept. 20, 1970; Harv Boughton, "The Outdoors with Rod, Gun and Camera," *Houston Post,* Nov. 20, 1966.

11. *Freeport Facts,* Nov. 1, 1945; Dec. 5, 1946; Dec. 30, 1952.

12. Ibid., Sept. 14, 1944.

13. *Galveston Daily News,* Nov. 20, 1945; *Freeport Facts,* Jan. 24, 1946; Jan. 15, 1948.

14. *Brazosport Facts,* Dec. 26, 1965; *Freeport Facts,* July 4, 1946; Aug. 19, 1948.

15. *Brazosport Facts,* July 21, 1959; Nov. 30, 1962; Bill Stransky interview, Feb. 14, 2010, Angleton, TX; Al Bisbey, pers. comm., Apr. 3, 2010.

16. *Brazosport Facts,* Jan. 30, 1966; Nov. 19, 1968; Sept. 28, 1972; David Hailey, pers. comm., Aug. 9, 2010.

17. James B. Blackburn Jr., *The Book of Texas Bays* (College Station: Texas A&M University Press, 2004), 29, 97–101; George C. Werner, "Houston Tap and Brazoria Railway," Handbook of Texas Online, www.tshaonline.org/handbook/online/articles/eqh13.

18. Captain Frank W. Flack, *A Hunter's Experiences in the Southern States of America: Being an Account of the Natural History of Various Quadrupeds and Birds Which Are the Objects of Chase in Those Countries* (London: Longmans, Green and Co., 1866), 274–78.

19. Charles Stutzenbaker interview, Oct. 15, 2009, Port Arthur, TX; Brazoria County Historical Museum map collection, Angleton, TX; *Galveston Daily News,* Sept. 21, 1893; Bill Womack interview, Nov. 4, 2009, West Columbia, TX; Mary Jean Renfro Romero, pers. comm., Jan. 28, 2010.

20. Peter S. Steigerwald to Mary Jean Renfro Romero, Dec. 20, 2009; Mary Jean Renfro Romero, pers. comm., Jan. 28, 2010.

21. Mary Jean Renfro Romero, pers. comm., Jan. 28, Feb. 1, 13, 2010; W. H. Steigerwald diary, Nov. 8, 1943, in private collection of Mary Jean Renfro Romero.

22. Mary Jean Renfro Romero, pers. comm., Nov. 10, 2009.

23. Mary Jean Renfro Romero, pers. comm., Feb. 27, 2010; Steigerwald diary, Nov. 8, 1943.

24. Bert C. Hess to Jimmy Reel, Jan. 14, 1948, in private collection of Agnes Reel Strauss; Gordon Stanley, pers. comm., Oct. 17, 2008; Charlie Braden interview, June 27, 2009, Eagle Lake, TX.

25. Steigerwald diary, Apr. 12, 1947; Mary Jean Renfro Romero, pers. comm., Jan. 28 and Mar. 16, 2010; Steigerwald diary, undated, ca. 1943.

26. Steigerwald diary, Nov. 7, 1944.

27. Ibid., and Nov. 8, 1943.

28. Ibid., July 12, 1944; Bill Womack, pers. comm., Sept. 22, 2009; Mary Jean Renfro Romero, pers. comms., Dec. 2, 2009, and Apr. 23, 2010.

29. Womack interview.

30. Mike Wicker, pers. comm., Aug. 30, 2009; Womack interview.

31. Jim Dailey interview, Apr. 11, 2009, Palacios, TX; Mary Jean Renfro Romero, pers. comm., Jan. 12, 2009; Womack interview; Gary Cole interview, Dec. 12, 2009, Sargent, TX.

32. *Brazosport Facts,* July 19, 1964.

33. Ibid., Aug. 19, 1976; *Port Arthur News,* July 28, 1977.

34. *Brazosport Facts,* Aug. 20, 25, 1965; June 5, 1977; Charles Stutzenbaker interview, Oct. 15, 2009, Port Arthur, TX, and pers. comm., Jan. 16, 2011; David Hailey, pers. comm., Aug. 9, 2010.

35. Larry Goodbread, pers. comm., Oct. 2, 2009; US Fish and Wildlife Service, *Wetlands Preservation Program,* 18.

CHAPTER 10. MATAGORDA BAY

1. Keith Guthrie, *Texas Forgotten Ports* (Austin: Eakin Press, 1988), 5.

2. *The Caney Run,* Texas Sesquicentennial pamphlet (Palacios, TX: City by the Sea Museum, 1986), www.rootsweb.ancestry.com/~txmatago/caney_run.htm; Robert S. Gray, ed., *A Visit to Texas in 1831* (Houston: Cordovan, 1975), 122.

3. Will Branch, "Sargent, TX," Handbook of Texas Online, www.tshaonline.org/handbook/online/articles/hns21; J. R. Singleton, *Texas Coastal Waterfowl Survey,* FA Report Series no. 11 (Austin: Texas Game and Fish Commission, 1953), 26; Charles Stutzenbaker, pers. comm., Sept. 21, 2009; *Galveston Daily News,* Aug. 8, 1893; Sept. 22, 1912.

4. *Galveston Daily News,* Dec. 15, 1911.

5. Diana J. Kleiner, "Bay City, TX," Handbook of Texas Online, www.tshaonline.org/handbook/online/articles/heb02; *Galveston Daily News,* Jan. 1, 1895; Nov. 26, 1901; *Dallas Morning News,* Nov. 2, 1902; *Victoria Advocate,* Dec. 12, 1908.

6. *Galveston Daily News,* Nov. 10, 1894; Jan. 15, 1895; Barbara Smith, pers. comm., Dec. 2, 2010.

7. *Galveston Daily News,* Sept. 8, 1926; Newspaper clipping, undated, in private collection of Will Blackbird; *Llano News,* Sept. 7, 1933; *Galveston Daily News,* July 13, 1933.

8. Todd Merendino interview, July 4, 2009, Matagorda TX; Jim Dailey interview, Apr. 11, 2009, Palacios, TX; *Galveston Daily News,* Feb. 10, 1895.

9. *Galveston Daily News,* Nov. 14, 1875; *Dallas Morning News,* Feb. 8, 1906.

10. *Galveston Daily News,* Nov. 19, 1896; Jan. 28, 1912; *Brownsville Daily Herald,* Jan. 16, 1897.

11. William C. Harris, ed., *The Sportsman's Guide to the Hunting and Shooting Grounds of the United States and Canada* (New York: Anglers Publishing, 1888), 167; Keith Guthrie, *Texas Forgotten Ports* (Austin: Eakin Press, 1988), 148; *Eagle Lake Headlight,* May 1, 1903, to Dec. 22, 1906, microfilm image 514, Eula and David Wintermann Library.

12. *Galveston Daily News,* Dec. 3, 1901; Dec. 7, 1909; *San Antonio Express,* Dec. 11, 1911; *San Antonio Light and Gazette,* Dec. 12, 1909.

13. *Galveston Daily News,* Aug. 26, Oct. 19, Nov. 4, and Nov. 20, 1905.

14. Ibid., Nov. 20 and Dec. 8, 1905; *San Antonio Daily Light,* Nov. 12, 1905.

15. *Galveston Daily News* Oct. 30 and Nov. 5, 1905.

16. *Dallas Morning News,* Nov. 7, 1906; *Galveston Daily News,* Dec. 23, 1911; May 17, 1921.

17. *San Antonio Express,* Dec. 16, 1923; *Eagle Lake Headlight,* Aug. 11, 1923.

18. Hilmar G. Moore interview, Aug. 4, 2009, Richmond, TX; *Galveston Daily News,* Dec. 13, 1922.

19. Henry Melton photo albums, private collection of Palmer and Talley Melton.

20. Charles Stutzenbaker interview, May 30, 2009, Port Arthur, TX; Raymond Cox interview, Aug. 15, 2010, Matagorda, TX; *Brazosport Facts,* Nov. 14, 1958.

21. Marc Ealy interview, Aug. 23, 2009, Matagorda, TX.

22. Ibid.

23. Dailey interview.

24. Charles Stutzenbaker interview, Feb. 7, 2009, Port Arthur, TX; Ealy interview.

25. *Galveston Daily News,* Dec. 13, 1922; Nov. 1, 1928; Nov. 18, 1929.

26. Ted Bates interview, Apr. 11, 2009, Palacios, TX.

27. Jim Mills interview, May 16, 2009, Port Lavaca, TX; Cox interview.

28. Moore interview; Gordon LeCompte interview, Feb. 13, 2010, Sargent, TX.

29. Mary L. Griffin, "Palacios, TX," Handbook of Texas Online, www.tshaonline.org/handbook/online/articles/hfp01; Dailey interview.

30. "Luther Hotel," Palacios Area Historical Association City by the Sea Museum, www.citybytheseamuseum.org/luther.html; *Images of America Matagorda County,* Matagorda Museum Association, (USA: Arcadia Publishing, 2008), 112; *Galveston Daily News,* Jan. 9, 25, 1907.

31. *Galveston Daily News,* Oct. 1, 1922; Ted Bates Jr. interview, Apr. 11, 2009, Palacios, TX.

32. Bates interview.

33. Marvin Strakos interview, Jan. 31, 2012, Port O'Connor, TX.

34. *Galveston Daily News,* Nov. 21, 1895.

35. Carlos Smith interview, Apr. 26, 2009, LaPorte, TX.

36. Dailey interview.

37. *Victoria Advocate,* Nov. 8, 1970; J. C. Melcher interview, Mar. 19, 2009, Port Lavaca, TX; *Galveston Daily News,* Feb. 13, 1910.

38. Melcher interview; *Victoria Daily Advocate,* Oct. 1, 1903.

39. William C. Harris, ed., *The Sportsman's Guide to the Hunting and Shooting Grounds of the United States and Canada* (New York: Anglers Publishing, 1888), 167; *Galveston Daily News,* Dec. 3, 1901.

40. *Galveston Daily News,* Feb. 18, 1905.

41. *Dogdom: Official Paper of the American Toy Dog Club* 8, no. 1 (Mar. 1907):892; *Galveston Daily News,* Jan. 30, 1907.

42. *Victoria Advocate,* Mar. 2, 1907; *Galveston Daily News,* Apr. 24, 1907; *San Antonio Light,* May 7, 1907; *Dogdom* 8, no. 1 (Mar. 1907):892; *Victoria Advocate,* Mar. 2, 1907.

43. *San Antonio Light,* May 5, 1912; *Victoria Daily Advocate,* Jan. 29, 1912.

44. Melcher interview; *San Antonio Express,* Sept. 20, 1936.

45. *Shifting Sands of Calhoun County* (Port Lavaca, TX: Calhoun County Historical Commission, 1980), 10; *Weimar Mercury,* Dec. 14, 1923.

46. *Corpus Christi Times,* May 26, 1954; *Galveston Daily News,* Feb. 10, 1916; Melcher interview; *San Antonio Express,* Dec. 18, 1933; *Victoria Advocate,* Dec. 18, 1933.

47. *Daily Advocate,* July 17, 195, 1915; *Shifting Sands of Calhoun County* (Port Lavaca, TX: Calhoun County Historical Commission, 1980), 248; Carlos Smith, pers. comm., Mar. 23, 2009.

48. Smith interview.

49. Ibid.

50. *Mexia Evening News,* June 3, 1921; Smith interview.

51. Carlos Smith, pers. comm., Mar. 23, 2009.

52. Smith interview.

53. *Galveston Tri-Weekly News,* Oct. 24, 1863.

54. *Galveston Daily News,* Feb. 28, 1887; *San Antonio Light,* Dec. 20, 1924.

55. *Victoria Advocate,* Jan. 28, 1973; *San Antonio Light,* Oct. 24, 1955; Steve Fisher interview, Nov. 18, 2009, Port Lavaca, TX.

56. *Victoria Advocate,* Nov. 22, 1972; Jan. 28, 1973.

CHAPTER 11. ESPIRITU SANTO AND SAN ANTONIO BAYS

1. Keith Guthrie, *Texas Forgotten Ports* (Austin: Eakin Press, 1988), 192.

2. *Galveston Daily News,* Jan. 10, 1896; Mar. 4, 1897; *Victoria Daily Advocate,* Oct. 24, 1901; *Shifting Sands of Calhoun County* (Port Lavaca, TX: Calhoun County Historical Commission, 1980), 13; *San Antonio Daily Express,* Aug. 19, 1910; Dr. R. Held Johnson and Edward Baldwin Rice, eds., *The Angler's and Sportsman's Guide* (New York: Field and Stream Publishing, 1912), 205.

3. *Galveston Daily News,* Oct. 22, 30, 1910; Dec. 8, 1920; *Victoria Daily Advocate,* Dec. 5, 1914.

4. *Kerrville Mountain Sun,* Mar. 19, 1925; *Brownsville Herald,* Jan. 8, 1928; Stewart Campbell interview, Apr. 3, 2009, Port O'Connor, TX.

5. Harvey Evans interview, Feb. 20, 2010, Portland, TX.

6. *San Antonio Light,* Mar. 11, 1951; Nov. 20, 1958; Feb. 25, 1962; Evans interview; Bob Brister, "Where Have the Ducks Gone?" *San Antonio Light,* Dec. 4, 1966; Campbell interview; *San Antonio Express and News,* Oct. 23, 1960.

7. Wayne Stupka interview, July 10, 2009, Pleasure Island, TX; Shannon Tompkins, pers. comm., Feb. 25, 2009.

8. Jim Dailey interview, Apr. 11, 2009, Palacios, TX.

9. Francis Parkman, *The Works of Francis Parkman* (Boston: Little, Brown and Co., 1869), 7:119; Guthrie *Texas Forgotten Ports,* 192–96; *Galveston Civilian and Gazette,* Dec. 15, 1857; Wayne H. McAlister, *Life on Matagorda Island, Texas* (College Station: Texas A&M University Press, 2004), 225.

10. *San Antonio Express,* Dec. 21, 1924.

11. *Dallas Morning News,* Oct. 7, 1934; undated newspaper clipping from John Winter photo albums, in private collection of Cliff Fisher.

12. Undated newspaper clipping from John Winter photo albums; Rick Pratt interview, Sept. 24, 2009, Port Aransas, TX.

13. *San Antonio Express,* Dec. 28, 1930; *Western Aerospace* 14 (1934):3; *Galveston Daily News,* Jan. 22, 1933.

14. John Winter photo albums.

15. *Victoria Advocate,* Nov. 30, 1956.

16. *San Antonio Express,* Jan. 29, 1952; Ronnie O. Luster, pers. comm., Feb. 11, 2010.

17. *Victoria Advocate,* Nov. 30, 1956; *San Antonio Express and News,* Jan. 6, 1974; *Corpus Christi Times,* July 16, 1975; *San Antonio Express,* Feb. 1, 1972; Forrest Hawes, pers. comm., Oct. 11, 2010.

18. Campbell interview.

19. Bob Brister and John P. Cowan, *The Golden Crescent* (Houston: Zephyr Press, 1969), 73–76; Campbell interview.

20. John P. Cowan, *A Texas Treasure* (Dallas: Collectors Covey, 1992), 92; Stewart Campbell interview, Apr. 3, 2009, Port O'Connor, TX.

21. Mary Martha Adolphus Shivers Culpin, pers. comm., Apr. 23, 2009; McAlister, *Life on Matagorda Island, Texas,* 226–27.

22. Al Johnson interview, Feb. 20, 2009, Rockport, TX; McAlister, *Life on Matagorda Island, Texas,* 228; Dailey interview.

23. Johnson interview.

24. Dailey interview; Chris Martin interview, Apr. 3, 2009, Seadrift, TX; *Abilene Reporter-News,* Nov. 16, 1960.

25. Chris Martin interviews, Mar. 13 and Apr. 3, 2009, Seadrift, TX.

26. Johnson interview.

27. *Victoria Daily Advocate,* Nov. 12, 1903; Martin interviews, Mar. 13 and Apr. 3, 2009; Campbell interview.

28. Campbell interview.

29. Martin interview, Apr. 3, 2009.

30. *Shifting Sands of Calhoun County,* 13; Rebecca Rubert, "Seadrift, TX," Handbook of Texas Online, www.tshaonline.org/handbook/online/articles/hjs12; *Victoria Daily Advocate,* Nov. 20, 1917.

31. *San Antonio Express and News,* July 3, 1955; Nov. 6, 1960; J. C. Melcher interview, Mar. 19, 2009, Port Lavaca, TX; *San Antonio Light,* Oct. 27, 1960.

32. *Shifting Sands of Calhoun County,* 8; Jim Wayne Johnson interview, Mar. 28, 2010, Seadrift, TX; *Corpus Christi Times,* Jan. 15, 1960.

33. *Victoria Advocate,* Dec. 6, 1907; Mar. 14, 1908; *Galveston Daily News,* June 23, 1887; Sept. 13, 1894; Nov. 20, 1896.

34. *San Antonio Daily Express,* Mar. 11, 1908; *Victoria Advocate,* Mar. 14, 1908; *Port Arthur News,* June 18, 1945; Indianola Company correspondence, Oct. 18, 1985, in private collection of Coco Blackbird.

35. Jim Wayne Johnson interview.

36. J. C. Melcher, pers. comm., June 4, 2010; Jim Wayne Johnson interview.

37. *Galveston Daily News,* Apr. 9, 1906; *Victoria Advocate,* Dec. 5, 1971.

38. Joe Ray Custer, pers. comm., Sept. 6, 2010; Jim Mills interview, May 16, 2009, Port Lavaca, TX.

39. *Galveston Daily News,* Nov. 16, 1895; Mills interview.

40. *Victoria Daily Advocate,* Oct. 21, 1910; Dec. 3, 1922; A. E. Amerman Jr. to Howard Kenyon Jr., Mar. 25, 1946, and A. T. Mullins to A. E. Amerman Jr., May 21, 1958, in private collection of Coco Blackbird; *San Antonio Express,* May 16, 1930; *Galveston Daily News,* Dec. 15, 1928; *Denton Record-Chronicle,* Jan. 14, 1931.

41. *Corpus Christi Times,* Apr. 29, 1960; Coco Blackbird interview, May 28, 2010, Seadrift, TX.

42. Blackbird interview.

43. A. E. Amerman Jr. to Howard Kenyon Jr., Mar. 25, 1946; Blackbird interview; Jim Mills interview, May 28, 2010, Seadrift TX.

44. Mills interview, May 28, 2010.

45. Joe Ray Custer, pers. comm., Sept. 6, 2010; *San Antonio Express,* Nov. 14, 1934.

46. *Port Arthur News,* Nov. 19, 1933; *San Antonio Light,* Nov. 19, Dec. 3, 1939; Dec. 6, 1942.

47. Mills interview, May 16, 2009; Marvin Strakos interview, Jan. 31, 2012, Port O'Connor, TX.

48. Ibid.

49. Ibid., and Mills interview, May 28, 2010.

50. Roy Swann, "Early Hunter Found Game," *Corpus Christi Caller Times,* Jan. 18, 1959; W. B. Leffingwell, "Shooting on the Gulf Coast," *Outing: An Illustrated Monthly Magazine of Sport, Travel, and Recreation* 33 (1899):509.

51. Hobart Huson, *Refugio: A Comprehensive History of Refugio County from Aboriginal Times* (Houston: Guardsman Publishing, 1953), 2, 328; *Victoria Daily Advocate,* Nov. 13, 1915.

52. Johnny Atwood interview, Apr. 3, 2009, Rockport, TX; Alex H. Halff, *St. Charles Bay Hunting Club: Sport, Tradition, and Camaraderie* (Houston: Gulfstream Graphics, 2003), 95.

53. *San Antonio Express,* Dec. 19, 1950.

54. *San Antonio Express,* Nov. 6, 1954; *Corpus Christi Caller-Times,* Jan. 22, Nov. 1, 1956; Atwood interview; Coco Blackbird, pers. comm., June 3, 2010.

CHAPTER 12. COPANO AND ARANSAS BAYS

1. Brian Preston interview, June 22, 2008, Aransas Pass, TX.

2. Fred Close interview, Apr. 4, 2009, Estes Flats, TX; Alex H. Halff, *St. Charles Bay Hunting Club: Sport, Tradition, and Camaraderie* (Houston: Gulfstream Graphics, 2003), 42.

3. *Galveston Daily News,* Oct. 25, 1879; Dec. 13, 1896; Wayne Capooth, *Waterfowling America* (Memphis: privately printed, 2008), 2:424; William Allen and Sue Allen Taylor, *Aransas: The Life of a Texas Coastal Community* (Austin: Eakin Press, 1997), 179.

4. *San Antonio Light,* Jan. 19, 1869; Feb. 15, 1890.

5. *Galveston Daily News,* Mar. 21, 1885; Feb. 10, 1887; Capooth, *Waterfowling America* 2:439–40.

6. *The Texarkana Gateway to Texas and the Southwest* (Saint Louis: Woodward and Tiernan, 1896), 216.

7. Hobart Huson, *History of Refugio County* (Houston: Guardsman Publishing Co., 1956), 2:172; *San Antonio Daily Express,* Sept. 28, 1888; *Galveston Daily News,* Jan. 16, Feb. 22, 1898.

8. *Dallas Morning News,* Nov. 15, 1892; Feb. 5, 1897; *San Antonio Daily Express,* Jan. 24, 1893; Nov. 23, 1899; *San Antonio Light,* June 26, 1898; Dec. 9, 1900.

9. *San Antonio Express,* Oct. 29, 1929; *Dallas Morning News,* Nov. 25, 1892; Nov. 24, 1895.

10. Kathleen Huson Maxswell, ed., *Hobart Huson: A Texas Coastal Bend Trilogy* (Austin: Eakin Press, 1994), 7; Halff, *St. Charles Bay Hunting Club,* 4.

11. Huson, *History of Refugio County,* 2:171; *Galveston Daily News,* Oct. 25, 1879; Maxwell, *Hobart Huson,* 21; Halff, *St. Charles Bay Hunting Club,* 4.

12. *Galveston Daily News,* Oct. 11, 1902; Apr. 23, 1917.

13. W. B. Leffingwell, "Shooting on the Gulf Coast," *Outing: An Illustrated Monthly Magazine of Sport, Travel, and Recreation* 33 (1899):506–9.

14. *Galveston Daily News,* Oct. 1, 1899; Tom A. Marshall, "A Texas Duck Hunt and a New Kind of Retriever," in *Ducking Days: Narratives of Duck Hunting, Studies of Wildfowl Life, and Reminiscences of Famous Marksmen on the Marshes and at the Traps.* Ed. Charles B. Morss and William Chester Hazelton (Chicago: n.p., 1918), 123; *San Antonio Evening News,* Sept. 20, 1919.

15. *Victoria Daily Advocate,* Jan. 25, 1915; *Galveston Daily News,* Apr. 23, 1917.

16. *San Antonio Light and Gazette,* Mar. 25, 1911; Clark McAdams, "Following the Redheads to the Gulf Coast," in *Ducking Days,* 27.

17. Stephen M. Miller, *Early American Waterfowling, 1700s—1930* (Chicago: Winchester Press, 1986), 163–69.

18. Ibid., 169; Betty Armstrong Adams, pers. comm., Feb. 20, 2011.

19. *Galveston Daily News,* Nov. 19, 1905; *San Antonio Express,* Oct. 29, 1929; *San Antonio Express and News,* Sept. 30, 1956; Gulf Coast Immigration Company, *Rockport, Texas, the New Deep Water Harbor on the Gulf of Mexico* (N.p.: 1905), 5; Gulf Coast Immigration Company, *Rockport, Queen of the Gulf* (N.p.: 1910), 1–31.

20. *San Antonio Light,* July 11, 1898.

21. Ibid., Jan. 2, July 11, 1898; *San Antonio Light,* Nov. 26, 1899; *San Antonio Daily Express,* Nov. 16, 1901.

22. William Allen and Sue Allen Taylor, *Aransas: The Life of a Texas Coastal Community* (Austin: Eakin Press, 1997), 169; *Dallas Morning News,* May 21, 1912; J. A. Allen, ed., *The Auk: A Quarterly Journal of Ornithology* 28, no. 2 (1911):272.

23. *Dallas Morning News,* Nov. 24, 1895; *San Antonio Express,* Feb. 26, 1925; *San Antonio Express and News,* Sept. 30, 1956; Allen and Taylor, *Aransas,* 299.

24. *Galveston Daily News,* Nov. 19, 1905; *San Antonio Express,* Oct. 29, 1929; *San Antonio Express and News,* Sept. 30, 1956; *San Antonio Light,* Jan. 7, 1913; *Dallas Morning News,* Sept. 18, Dec. 24, 1906; Dec. 19, 1912.

25. *San Antonio Light,* June 13, 1912; Jan. 7, 1913; *San Antonio Daily Express,* Mar. 19, 1897; Sept. 14, 1902; *San Antonio Express,* Dec. 14, 1924; Sept. 15, Oct. 29, 1929; *Galveston Daily News,* Apr. 7, 1912; Dec. 8, 1920.

26. Barbara Armstrong, "Texas State Historical Markers" manuscript, Aransas County Public Library, 1; The Port Bay Hunting and Fishing Club, www.portbayclub.com/.

27. Elaine Vandeveer interview, Oct. 18, 2008, Rockport, TX.

28. Armstrong, "Texas State Historical Markers," 1.

29. Allen and Taylor, *Aransas,* 213.

30. *Galveston Daily News,* Dec. 15, 1929; Aug. 29, 1965.

31. *San Antonio Express* Dec. 14, 1931; Allen and Taylor, *Aransas,* 213; Armstrong, "Texas State Historical Markers," 1; Vandeveer interview.

32. Vandeveer interview.

33. Ibid.

34. Armstrong, "Texas State Historical Markers," 4.

35. Jerry Lynn Ayers interview, June 29, 2008, Houston, TX.

36. Ibid.

37. Ed Duvall, pers. comm., Oct. 17, 2008; Ayers interview.

38. Jerry Ayers to Ed Duvall, May 2008.

39. Ed Duvall, pers. comm., Oct. 17, 2008; Ed Duvall, John Cook, George King, and Jeff Kucera interview, June 21, 2008, Rockport, TX.

40. Duvall, Cook, King and Kucera interview.

41. The Port Bay Hunting and Fishing Club, www.portbayclub.com/; Duvall, Cook, King, and Kucera interview; "Ducks Unlimited Institute for Wetland and Waterfowl Research Announces Fellowship Competitions for 2006," Ducks Unlimited Canada, www.ducks.ca/conserve/research/proposals/pdf/flship.pdf.

42. Duvall, Cook, King, and Kucera interview, June 21, 2008, Rockport, TX.

43. *Dallas Morning News,* Jan. 29, 1922.

44. *Galveston Daily News,* June 2, 1923; Halff, *St. Charles Bay Hunting Club,* 5–38; *Corpus Christi Caller-Times,* Jan. 22, 1956.

45. Halff, *St. Charles Bay Hunting Club,* 13–119; James Fox interview, Oct. 17, 2008, Rockport, TX.

46. Halff, *St. Charles Bay Hunting Club,* 18–95; David and Jim Herring interview, Apr. 3, 2009, Rockport, TX; David Herring, "Duck Hunting in the Old Days," manuscript, in private collection of David Herring, Rockport, TX.

47. David and Jim Herring interview.

48. Herring, "Duck Hunting in the Old Days"; Halff, *St. Charles Bay Hunting Club,* 95.

49. David Herring, pers. comm., Aug. 13, 2009; Johnny Atwood interview, Apr. 3, 2009, Rockport, TX; Herring, "Duck Hunting in the Old Days."

50. Herring, "Duck Hunting in the Old Days"; Halff, *St. Charles Bay Hunting Club,* 92, David and Jim Herring interview.

51. David and Jim Herring interview; Herring, "Duck Hunting in the Old Days."

52. Halff, *St. Charles Bay Hunting Club,* 109; Herring, "Duck Hunting in the Old Days."

53. Halff, *St. Charles Bay Hunting Club,* 38–92; Atwood interview.

54. Halff, *St. Charles Bay Hunting Club,* 95, 71.

55. Ibid., 64–97; Bob Brister, "Hunters are Hit by Freeze, Flak," *Houston Chronicle,* Feb. 12, 1989.

56. Brister, "Hunters are Hit by Freeze, Flak"; Halff, *St. Charles Bay Hunting Club,* 72.

57. Halff, *St. Charles Bay Hunting Club,* 95; *Corpus Christi Times,* Nov. 20, 1931; Al Johnson interview, Feb. 21, 2009, Rockport, TX.

58. Jim Mills interview May 16, 2009, Port Lavaca, TX.

59. Ibid.; Undated newspaper clipping in Mills family album, Aransas County Historical Society; Johnson interview; Narrative for 2011 Subject Marker Nomination, Mills Wharf, courtesy Jim Mills.

60. Undated newspaper clipping in Mills family album; *San Antonio Evening News,* Nov. 17, 1939; *Corpus Christi Caller-Times,* Oct. 31, 1943; Johnson interview; Gordon Stanley, pers. comm.

61. Undated newspaper clipping in Mills family album, Aransas County Historical Society, Rockport, TX; Jim Mills interview; *Brownsville Herald,* Dec. 9, 1947.

62. Jim Mills interview.

63. C. H. "Burt" Mills Jr., pers. comm., Nov. 14, 2008; Jim Mills interview.

64. Jim Mills interview.

65. Ibid.; C. H. "Burt" Mills Jr. interview, Oct. 17, 2008, Rockport, TX.

66. Jim Mills interview; C. H. "Burt" Mills Jr. interview.

67. Mary Ann Cavazos, "Aransas County to Get $75M Project," *Corpus Christi Caller,* July 14, 2007, www.caller.com/news/2007/jul/14/sea-gun-sports-inn/; *Corpus Christi Caller-Times,* Aug. 11, 1963; "Historic Sea Gun Structure Leveled," *Rockport Pilot,* www.rockport-pilot.com/articles/2008/06/11/news/news00.txt; Fred Maly, "Angling Around," *San Antonio Light,* Oct. 26, 1966.

68. *Corpus Christi Times,* June 26, 1926; *San Antonio Light,* Nov. 1, 1970; John Silberisen and Jo Silberisen, "A Blue Norther," manuscript, in private collection of John and Jo Silberison.

69. Jim Herring interview, Apr. 3, 2009, Rockport, TX.

70. Siberisen and Silberisen, "A Blue Norther."

71. *San Antonio Light,* Sept. 30, 1956; Jo Silberisen, pers. comm., Feb. 25, 2009.

72. Siberisen and Silberisen, "A Blue Norther."

73. John Silberisen, pers. comm., Feb. 25, 2009.

74. Allen and Taylor, *Aransas,* 334; Close interview.

75. Fox interview; Close interview.

76. Mary Martha Adolphus Shivers Culpin, pers. comm., Apr. 23, 2009; *Corpus Christi Times,* Aug. 25, 1936; Jim Herring interview.

77. *Corpus Christi Times,* Oct. 26, 1934; May 22, 1947; David and Jim Herring interview; *Corpus Christi Caller-Times,* Nov. 1, 1956; Jim Mills interview.

78. *San Antonio Express,* Nov. 1, 1953; *Corpus Christi Times,* Apr. 8, 1957; Feb. 10, 1959; *San Antonio Light,* Oct. 30, 1956.

79. Close interview; Jim Mills interview; David Herring, pers. comm., Mar. 17, 2009.

80. Atwood interview; Close interview.

81. Marshall, "A Texas Duck Hunt and a New Kind of Retriever," 125.

82. *San Antonio Light,* Sept. 11, 1898; *Dallas Morning News,* Sept. 25, 1898.

83. *San Antonio Light,* Sept. 11, 1898; *Dallas Morning News,* June 29, 1898; *San Antonio Daily Express,* June 18, 1899.

84. *Dallas Morning News,* June 29, 1898; *Brownsville Daily Herald,* Oct. 13, 1904; *San Antonio Daily Express,* June 27, 1898.

85. *Corpus Christi Caller-Times,* Jan. 18, 1959; *Dallas Morning News,* Jan. 11, 1899.

86. *Dallas Morning News,* Sept. 25, 1898.

87. Ibid., June 29, 1898; "Ducks on the Texas Coast," *Hunter-Trader-Trapper* 17, no. 3 (1908):76.

88. *Galveston Daily News,* Apr. 2, 1899; Guthrie Ford, pers. comm., Sept. 26, 2009; *San Antonio Daily Light,* Mar. 3, 1899.

89. *Dallas Morning News,* Nov. 27, 1904; Guthrie Ford, pers. comm., Sept. 26, 2009; *Galveston Daily News,* Feb. 7, 1905; *Brownsville Daily Heral*d, Oct. 13, 1904.

90. *Rockport Pilot,* Mar. 22, 1995; W. W. Wood, "History of Rockport, Fulton, Lamar and El Copano" manuscript, 1953, Aransas County Library, 72.

91. Wood, "History of Rockport, Fulton, Lamar and El Copano," 72; Guthrie Ford, pers. comm., Jan. 21, 2010; Charles Stutzenbaker interview, Oct. 15 2009, Port Arthur, TX; *Galveston Daily News,* Dec. 30, 1938; *El Paso Herald,* Mar. 10, 1973; *Odessa American,* Oct. 6, 1959; *San Antonio Express and News,* Sept. 15, 1973.

92. Fox interview.

93. Atwood interview.

CHAPTER 13. SOUTH BAY TO CORPUS CHRISTI BAY

1. C. Herndon Williams, *Texas Gulf Coast Stories* (Charleston, SC: History Press, 2010), 46; "Ducks on the Texas Coast," *Hunter-Trader-Trapper* 17, no. 3 (1908):75–76; James B. Blackburn Jr., *The Book of Texas Bays* (College Station: Texas A&M University Press, 2004), 200.

2. Robin W. Doughty, *Return of the Whooping Crane* (Austin: University of Texas Press, 1989), 14; *Dallas Morning News,* Sept. 25, 1898.

3. Gen. F. S. Monnett, letter to the editor, *Recreation: A Monthly Magazine of Everything the Name Implies* 13, no. 6 (1900):460; Charles Thomas Logan, "Quaint San Antonio," *Frank Leslie's Popular Monthly* 46, no. 1 (1898):93.

4. San Antonio and Aransas Pass Railway advertisement, *American Angler* 29, no. 1 (1899):4; *Aransas Pass Texas: Where Sails Meet Rails* (Port Aransas, TX: Chamber of Commerce, 1912), 27, in collection of Larry Ray.

5. *Corpus Christi Caller-Times,* Nov. 9, 1947; *San Antonio Light,* Oct. 12, 1911; *Corpus Christi Times,* Sept. 8, 1953; *Dallas Morning News,* Jan. 12, 1922; Byrd Minter Jr., pers. comm., Dec. 17, 2010.

6. Pat Farley, pers. comm., Mar. 26, 2011; Bruce Baker, pers. comm., Mar. 27, 2011.

7. Bruce Baker, pers. comm., Mar. 27, 2011.

8. David Sikes, "Family Business: Spears Clan the Grandfather of Coastal Bend Outfitters," *Corpus Christi Caller-Times,* Nov. 10, 2002; Jamie Spears and Gordon Spears III interview, June 22, 2008, Port Aransas, TX; *Corpus Christi Caller-Times,* Dec. 12, 1954; *Freeport Facts,* Jan. 19, 1933.

9. J. G. Ford, *A Texas Island* (Port Aransas, TX: Huraah Publishing, 2008), 25; Byrd Minter Jr., pers. comm., Feb. 8, 2011.

10. Byrd Minter Jr. interview, Feb. 18, 2011, Port Aransas, TX; Mark Creighton, "Byrd Minter: 1906–1997, Charter and Lifetime Member Hall of Fame, Port Aransas Boatmen, Inc.," *Port Aransas Preservation and Historical Association Newsletter* 4, no. 6 (2010),2; Byrd Minter Jr., pers. comm., Dec. 17, 2010.

11 Byrd Minter Jr., pers. comms., Dec. 17, 2010; Feb. 8, Mar. 16, 2011.

12. Minter interview; Creighton, "Byrd Minter," 2.

13. Minter interview; Spears and Spears interview, June 22, 2008.

14. Spears and Spears interview, June 22, 2008.

15. Ibid.; Sikes, "Family Business."

16. Jamie Spears and Gordon Spears III interview, Nov. 12, 2008, Port Aransas, TX; Sikes, "Family Business."

17. Spears and Spears interviews, June 22, Nov. 12, 2008, Port Aransas, TX.

18. *Corpus Christi Times,* Aug. 6, 1957; Ford, *A Texas Islan*d, 55; *Corpus Christi Caller-Times,* Feb. 12, 1956.

19. Tarpon Inn Historical Marker (1979), Travel South Texas, www.stxmaps.com/go/texas-historical-marker-tarpon-inn.html; *San Antonio Light,* Oct. 16, 1904.

20. *Corpus Christi Times,* Aug. 6, 1957; *San Antonio Express,* Mar. 1, 1925; Rick Pratt interview, Sept. 24, 2009, Port Aransas, TX; *San Antonio Light,* Oct. 26, 1958.

21. Rick Pratt interview, Sept. 24, 2009, Port Aransas, TX.

22. *San Antonio Light,* Dec. 19, 1924; *San Antonio Express,* Oct. 31, 1927; Oct. 17, 1928; Barney Farley, *Fishing Yesterday's Gulf Coast* (College Station: Texas A&M University Press, 2002), 3.

23. *San Antonio Light,* Feb. 26, 1928; *San Antonio Express,* Oct. 12, 1934.

24. *San Antonio Light,* Apr. 3, 1927; *San Antonio Light,* Nov. 20, 1927.

25. "Name of New Project Evokes E. A. Cline Saga," *Port Aransas Preservation and Historical Association Newsletter* 4, no. 4 (2010):2.

26. Pratt interview; William Allen and Sue Allen Taylor, *Aransas: The Life of a Texas Coastal Community* (Austin: Eakin Press, 1997), 291.

27. *Galveston Daily News,* Apr. 6, 1962; Byron B. Buzbee, "Buzzin' Outdoors," *Corpus Christi Times,* Dec. 11, 1936; *San Antonio Light,* Nov. 15, 1939.

28. *San Antonio Light,* June 1, 1941; Sept. 30, 1956; Nov. 20, 1958; *San Antonio Express and News,* Oct. 18, 1959.

29. *Corpus Christi Caller-Times,* Jan. 15, Feb. 12, 1956; Mark Creighton, pers. comm., Feb. 1, 2010; *San Antonio Light,* June 1, 1941; Oct. 30, 1956; July 15, 1957; *Corpus Christi Caller-Times,* Nov. 2, 1958; *San Antonio Express and News,* Oct. 18, 1959.

30. *Corpus Christi Times,* Mar. 29, 1962; *Dallas Morning News,* Nov. 21, 1952; *Corpus Christi Caller-Times,* Jan. 29, 1956; Pratt interview.

31. *Corpus Christi Times,* Oct. 30, 1931; *Corpus Christi Caller-Times,* Jan. 15, 1956; A. C. Peirce, *A Man from Corpus Christi,* rev. ed. (1894; reprint, Rockport: Copano Bay Press, 2008), 181.

32. Peirce, *A Man from Corpus Christi,* 181; *Corpus Christi Caller-Times,* Sept. 28, 1947.

33. Vernon Bailey, *Biological Survey of Texas,* North America Fauna no. 25 (Washington: Government Printing Office, 1905), 24; T. E. Fulbright and Fred C. Bryant, "The Wild Horse Desert: Climate and Ecology," in *Ranch Management: Integrating Cattle, Wildlife, and Range,* ed. C. A. Forgason, F. C. Bryant, and P. C. Genho (Kingsville: King Ranch Institute, 2003), 35–58.

34. Roy Swann, "Early Hunter Found Game," *Corpus Christi Caller Times,* Jan. 18, 1959; David Sikes, pers. comm.; Murphy Givens and Jim Moloney interview, Feb. 19, 2010, Corpus Christi, TX.

35. *Galveston Daily News,* Sept. 18, 1881; Murphy Givens, pers. comm., Feb. 19, 2010; *Brownsville Daily Herald,* Sept. 4, 1895.

36. *San Antonio Daily Express,* Nov. 18, 1910; Murphy Givens, "Oyster Reef Road Was Used for Seven Decades," *Corpus Christi Caller-Times,* June 15, 2005, www.caller.com/news/2005/jun/15/oyster-reef-road-was-used-for-seven-decades/.

37. "Duck Shooting on the Coast," *Shields' Magazine* 5, no. 5 (1907):313; Roy Swann, "Early Hunter Found Game," *Corpus Christi Caller Times,* Jan. 18, 1959; *Galveston Daily News,* Dec. 5, 1887; Dec. 4, 1905; *Brownsville Daily Herald,* Nov. 30, 1892.

38. *San Antonio Daily Light,* Oct. 20, 1893; Givens and Moloney interview; *Laredo Times,* Dec. 21, 1903; H. S. Canefield, "The Death of the Red-Winged Mallard," *Outing* 37, no. 4 (1901):427; *Brownsville Daily Herald,* Nov. 3, 1905.

39. Keith Guthrie, *The History of San Patricio County* (Austin: Nortex Press, 1986), 174; *San Antonio Light,* Nov. 29, 1896; *San Antonio Daily Light,* Dec. 17, 1905.

40. *San Antonio Light,* Nov. 12, 1899; A. Ray Stephens, *The Taft Ranch: A Texas Principality* (Austin: University of Texas Press, 1964), 133.

41. *Galveston Daily News,* Jan. 25, 1896; Nov. 20, 1898; *San Antonio Light,* Jan. 2, 1898.

42. *San Antonio Light,* Nov. 22, 1908; Guthrie, *History of San Patricio County,* 174; *San Antonio Daily Light,* Jan. 19, Dec. 20, 1896; Mar. 21, 1897; Dec. 11, 1899.

43. *San Antonio Daily Light,* Dec. 20, 1896; Jan. 17, 1897; Nov. 12, 19, 1899.

44. Guthrie, *History of San Patricio County,* 174; *San Antonio Daily Light,* Dec. 17, 1905.

45. *Victoria Advocate,* Sept. 10, 1909; *Dallas Morning News,* Aug. 29, 1909; *San Antonio Light and Gazette,* Oct. 20, 1909.

46. *Victoria Advocate,* Sept. 10, 1910; Stephens, *The Taft Ranch,* 133.

47. *San Antonio Light,* Sept. 19, 1911.

48. *San Antonio Light and Gazette,* July 27, 1909; *Galveston Daily News,* Feb. 6, 1905; *San Antonio Light,* Dec. 7, 1908; *Brownsville Herald,* Mar. 18, 1913; Clark McAdams, "Following the Redheads to the Gulf Coast," in *Ducking Days: Narratives of Duck Hunting, Studies of Wildfowl Life, and Reminiscences of Famous Marksmen on the Marshes and at the Traps,* ed. Charles B. Morss and William Chester Hazelton (Hazelton, PA: W. C. Hazelton, 1918), 27.

49. *San Antonio Daily Light,* Dec. 26, 1890; *San Antonio Light,* Mar. 24, Nov. 6, 1913; Jan. 23, 1941; *San Antonio Express,* July 6, 1911; *Corpus Christi Times,* Oct. 4, 1927.

50. McAdams, "Following the Redheads," 27; *Corpus Christi Times,* Nov. 27, 1936.

51. *Corpus Christi Times,* Oct. 28, 1926; Dec. 3, 28, 1927.

52. *Corpus Christi Times,* Nov. 20, Dec. 3, 1931; Doug Bird interview, Feb. 19, 2010, Corpus Christi, TX.

53. *Corpus Christi Times,* Oct. 30, Nov. 20, Dec. 2, 1931; Nov. 1, 1940; *Corpus Christi Caller-Times,* Dec. 12, 1954; *Port Arthur News,* Jan. 19, 1930.

54. *Corpus Christi Caller-Times,* Nov. 7, 1954; Apr. 4, 1955; *San Antonio Light,* Sept. 30, 1956; *San Antonio Express and News,* Oct. 18, 1959.

55. *Corpus Christi Caller-Times,* June 10, 1951; Billy Sheka interview, Feb. 19, 2010, Corpus Christi, TX.

56. *San Antonio Light,* Sept. 30, 1956; *Corpus Christi Caller-Times,* Nov. 3, 1957; *San Antonio Express and News,* Oct. 18, 1959; *Corpus Christi Times,* Oct. 4, 1954.

57. Alex H. Halff, *St. Charles Bay Hunting Club: Sport, Tradition, and Camaraderie* (Houston: Gulfstream Graphics, 2003), 118–19; Sheka interview.

58. Bird interview.

59. Ibid.; Doug Bird, pers. comm., Feb. 8, 2010.

60. James B. Blackburn Jr., *The Book of Texas Bays* (College Station: Texas A&M University Press, 2004), 215, 218.

CHAPTER 14. LAGUNA MADRE

1. David A. McKee, *Fishes of the Texas Laguna Madre,* Gulf Coast Studies no. 14 (College Station: Texas A&M University Press, 2008), 1.

2. James B. Blackburn Jr., *The Book of Texas Bays* (College Station: Texas A&M University Press, 2004), 248; *Brownsville Herald,* Feb. 4, 1968; Bart Ballard interview, Mar. 5, 2010, Kingsville, TX.

3. *Corpus Christi Caller-Times,* Dec. 19, 1954.

4. *Galveston Daily News,* Feb. 25, 1884; Mar. 21, 1885; Wayne Capooth, *Waterfowling America* (Memphis: privately printed, 2008), 2:439.

5. Chapman Ranch, Texas Historical Marker, www.stxmaps.com/go/texas-historical-marker-chapman-ranch.html; Doug Bird, pers. comm., Feb. 8, 2010; *San Antonio Express,* Oct. 24, 1934; *Corpus Christi Times,* Oct. 21, 1936; Apr. 29, 1977.

6. Doug Bird, pers. comm., Feb. 8, 2010; Billy Sheka interview, Feb. 19, 2010, Corpus Christi, TX.

7. *San Antonio Light,* Nov. 16, 1959; Fred Maly, "Angling Around," *San Antonio Light,* Nov. 21, 1966.

8. *Corpus Christi Times,* Nov. 26, 1976; Apr. 29, 1977; Doug Bird interview, Feb. 19, 2010, Corpus Christi, TX.

9. Untitled map, Corpus Christi Museum of Science and History, Corpus Christi, TX; Jane C. Monday and Betty Bailey Colley, *Voices from the Wild Horse Desert* (Austin: University of Texas Press, 1997), 1; *San Antonio Light,* Feb. 20, 1886.

10. Tim Fulbright, pers. comm., Apr. 12, 2010; Bart Ballard, pers. comm., Mar. 5, 2010; Butch Thompson, pers. comm., July 7, 2009; Charles Stutzenbaker interview, Oct. 24, 2008, Port Arthur, TX.

11. Witmer Stone, ed., *The Auk: A Quarterly Journal of Ornithology* 39, no. 3 (1922):412–13; *San Antonio Light,* Feb. 20, 1886; A. C. Bent, *Life Histories of North American Wild Fowl,* US National Museum Bulletin 130 (Washington, DC: Government Printing Office, 1925; reprint, New York: Dover Publications, 1987), 171.

12. Bent, *Life Histories of North American Wild Fowl,* 171; *Beaumont Journal,* undated clipping, ca. 1954, in private collection of Gerry Cordts.

13. Ballard interview.

14. Murphy Givens, pers. comm., Sept. 7, 2010; Ballard interview; Murphy Givens, "Rawhide Artists," transcript, KEDT radio, Sept. 17, 2010, pers. comm.

15. Byron Bushart, and Mattie Bailey Bushart, *Byron's Texas Gulf Coast Guide: Hunting and Fishing Tourist,* 1941–42 edition (N.p: n.p., 1941–42), 49; *San Antonio Express and News,* Mar. 11, 1956; *Brownsville Herald,* Aug. 22, 1946; *Corpus Christi Caller-Times,* Jan. 15, 1956.

16. *Corpus Christi Caller-Times,* Apr. 25, 1954; Jan. 18, 1959; Misc. undated newspaper clippings, Baffin Bay Café, Riviera, TX.

17. *San Antonio Light,* Nov. 2, 1949; *Corpus Christi Caller-Times,* Feb. 26, 1961.

18. "Where to Go," *Field and Stream,* Aug. 1912, 438.

19. Van Campen Heilner, *A Book on Duck Shooting* (New York: Alfred A. Knopf, 1946), 120; John W. Tunnell Jr., "Geography, Climate, and Hydrology," in *The Laguna Madre of Texas and Tamaulipas* (College Station: Texas A&M University Press, 2002), 15; James B. Blackburn Jr., *The Book of Texas Bays* (College Station: Texas A&M University Press, 2004), 217.

20. Walt Kittelberger, pers. comm., Feb. 23, 2010; Bird interview; Billy Shika, pers. comm., Jan. 31, 2010; Ballard interview.

21. *Corsicana Daily Sun,* Oct. 26, 1925; Bill Kiel interview, Mar. 4, 2010, Kingsville, TX.

22. Eileen Mattei, "King of Conservation," *Texas and Parks & Wildlife,* May 2010, 49.

23. *Brownsville Daily Herald,* Mar. 9, 1930; Mattei, "King of Conservation," 49, 51; *Brownsville Herald,* Dec. 7, 1914; Dec. 24, 1922; Jan. 14, 1923; *San Antonio Light,* Dec. 17, 1915; *Galveston Daily News,* Jan. 1, 1911.

24. *San Antonio Light,* May 3, 1937; *Port Arthur News,* Nov. 28, 1936.

25. "Texas: King Ranch Mystery," *Time,* Dec. 7, 1936, www.time.com/time/magazine/article/0,9171,757065,00.html.

26. Ibid.; *Corpus Christi Times,* July 13, 1937; *Big Spring Daily Herald,* July 14, 1937; "Game Warden Dawson R. Murchison," Officer Down Memorial Page, www.odmp.org/officer/15952-game-warden-dawson-r-murchison.

27. Ballard interview.

28. Kiel interview; "History of Port Mansfield," Port Mansfield, Texas, www.port-mansfield.com/history.htm; *San Antonio Light,* Oct. 30, 1956.

29. J. R. Singleton, *Texas Coastal Waterfowl Survey,* FA Report Series no. 11 (Austin: Texas Game and Fish Commission, 1953), 20; *Brownsville Daily Herald,* Mar. 9, 1930; "Hidalgo County, TX," Handbook of Texas Online, www.tshaonline.org/handbook/online/articles/hch14; Mike Bradshaw, *Texas Game Warden Chronicles* (Carrizo Springs, TX: Mesquite Bean Press, 2009), 11.

30. *Brownsville Herald,* July 12, 1932; Norman Rozeff, pers. comm., Sept. 10, 2010; *Valley Star-Monitor-Herald,* Oct. 10, 1937; *Brownsville Herald,* Sept. 19, 1922; Nov. 18, 1938; *Brownsville Daily Herald, Brownsville Daily Herald,* Jan. 25, 1908; Jan. 3, 1910.

31. *Brownsville Herald,* Mar. 12, 1906; Nov. 18, 1938; *Brownsville Daily Herald,* Oct. 13, 1906; Oct. 1, 1910.

32. *Valley Morning Star,* Nov. 14, 1947; Singleton, *Texas Coastal Waterfowl Survey,* 20.

33. Billy Sheka, pers. comm., Jan. 9, 2011.

34. Robin W. Doughty, *Wildlife and Man in Texas: Environmental Change and Conservation* (College Station: Texas A&M University Press, 1983), 81; Blackburn, *Book of Texas Bays,* 252.

35. *Corpus Christi Caller-Times,* Feb. 13, 1955; Heilner, *Book on Duck Shooting,* 118–20.

36. Hart Stilwell, "Outdoors in the Valley," *Brownsville Herald,* Dec. 13, 1938; *Valley Morning Star,* Oct. 16, 1948; *Brownsville Herald,* Dec. 3, 1947.

37. *Brownsville Daily Herald,* Feb. 13, 1895; *Brownsville Herald,* Oct. 31, 1937.

38. *Galveston Daily News,* Dec. 26, 1877; Jan. 30, 1910; *Brownsville Daily Herald,* Sept. 13, 1894; Jan. 27, 1896.

39. Dan E. Klepper, "Resaca Rebirth," *Texas Parks & Wildlife,* Oct. 2008, 34; *Brownsville Herald,* Dec. 21, 1937; *Brownsville Herald,* Sept. 19, 1922; *Brownsville Herald,* Oct. 9, 1917.

40. *Brownsville Daily Herald,* Jan. 23, 1893; Sept. 13, 1894; Feb. 17, 1896.

41. *Dallas Morning News,* Mar. 19, 1898; *Brownsville Herald,* Oct. 13, 1922; Jan. 14, 1923; Bushart and Bushart, "Byron's Texas Gulf Coast Guide," 76.

42. Barry Batsell, pers. comm., Aug. 27, 2010.

43. Tunnell, "Geography, Climate, and Hydrology," 15; *Brownsville Herald,* Oct. 31, 1937.

44. *Brownsville Herald,* Oct. 24, 1940; Sept. 19, 1943.

45. Ibid., Sept. 19, 1943.

46. Ibid., Nov. 13, 1931; Hart Stilwell, *Hunting and Fishing in Texas,* rev. ed. (1946; reprint, Dallas: Collectors Covey, 2005), 168–73.

47. *Brownsville Herald,* Nov. 13, 1931; Heilner, *Book on Duck Shooting,* 118; *San Antonio Light,* June 10, 1969; Stilwell, *Hunting and Fishing in Texas,* 167.

48. *Brownsville Herald,* Nov. 11, 13, 1931; Oct. 30, 1940.

49. Ibid., Nov. 27, Dec. 27, 1933; Nov. 4, 10, 1934; Nov. 1, 1942;.

50. Edward L. N. Glass, ca. 1914, reprinted in *Tidbits,* ed. Robert B. Vezzetti, Brownsville Historical Association, undated, 50, courtesy of Norm Rozeff and Cameron County Historical Association; *Galveston Daily News,* Nov. 6, 1904; *Brownsville Daily Herald,* Feb. 21, 1906.

51. *Brownsville Daily Herald,* Nov. 21, 1906; Mar. 13, July 12, 1907; Nov. 16, 1908; Herbert Whyte, "Herbert Whyte and His Answers," *Outing* 54 (1909):509; *Galveston Daily News,* Nov. 22, 1907; *Brownsville Herald,* Jan. 28, 1911.

52. *Brownsville Daily Herald,* May 21, Nov. 18, 1907; Jan. 12, 1910.

53. *Brownsville Herald,* Feb. 16, 1917; *Galveston Daily News,* Nov. 9, 1920; *San Antonio Express,* Sept. 15, 1929.

54. *Galveston Daily News,* Feb. 11, 1900.

55. *Brownsville Herald,* Nov. 7, 1907.

56. *Brownsville Daily Herald,* Nov. 9, 22, 1907; Jan. 1, 1908; *Galveston Daily News,* May 16, 1907.

57. *San Antonio Light,* Sept. 7, Nov. 16, Dec. 5, 1926.

58. *Brownsville Herald,* Sept. 19, 1943; Oct. 16, 1944; Elizabeth H. Smith, "Redheads and Other Wintering Waterfowl," in *The Laguna Madre of Texas and Tamaulipas,* 171–72.

59. *Brownsville Herald,* Mar. 10, 1935; Stilwell, "Outdoors in the Valley," *Brownsville Herald,* Feb. 28, 1941; Blackburn, *Book of Texas Bays,* 225; US Fish and Wildlife Service, Laguna Atascosa, Bahia Grande, www.fws.gov/southwest/refuges/texas/STRC/laguna/Bahia%20Grande_Laguna.html.

60. Blackburn, *Book of Texas Bays,* 200; Bahia Grande: Wetland Restoration Project; Heilner, *Book on Duck Shooting,* 118.

CHAPTER 15. BIG PRAIRIE AND EAGLE LAKE

1. Keith Guthrie, *Texas Forgotten Ports: Mid-Gulf Coast Ports from Corpus Christi to Matagorda Bay* (Austin: Eakin Press, 1988), 124; Unpublished Eagle Lake map drawn by Jake Smothers, 1936, in private collection of Jerry Sims; Charles Stutzenbaker interview, Feb. 6, 2009, Port Arthur, TX; P. Briscoe, "The First Texas Railroad," *Southwestern Historical Quarterly* 7, no. 4 (1904):279–85, http://texashistory.unt.edu/ark:/67531/metapth101030/m1/287/.

2. Kenneth Foree, "Geese, Smart Men Alter Town's Life," *Dallas Morning News,* Nov. 3, 1964; Briscoe, "First Texas Railroad," 279–85; "Eagle Lake," *Houston Daily Post,* Dec. 27, 1895, Library of Congress, Chronicling America, http://chroniclingamerica.loc.gov/lccn/sn86071197/1895-12-27/ed-1/seq-11; *Galveston Tri-Weekly News,* Dec. 13, 1869.

3. *Eagle Lake Headlight,* Jan. 12, 1907, to Dec. 21, 1912, microfilm images 534 and 915, Eula and David Wintermann Library; *Houston Daily Post,* Nov. 26, 1899, Library of Congress, Chronicling America, http://chroniclingamerica.loc.gov/lccn/sn86071197/1899-11-26/ed-1/seq-7/; *Eagle Lake Headlight,* May 1, Aug. 7, 1909; Charlie Braden, pers. comm., Sept. 7, 2009.

4. *Galveston Daily News,* Mar. 18, 1894; "A Good Duck Hunt," *Houston Daily Post,* Jan. 30, 1903, Library of Congress, Chronicling America, http://chroniclingamerica.loc.gov/lccn/sn86071197/1903-01-30/ed-1/seq-4; *Eagle Lake Headlight,* May 1, 1903, through Dec. 22, 1906, microfilm image 11, Eula and David Wintermann Library; *Galveston Daily News,* Nov. 20, 1908.

5. David Wintermann, "History of Eagle Lake," manuscript, 1962, in private collection of Jerry Sims; *San Antonio Daily Light,* May 14, 1905; *Eagle Lake Headlight,* July 1, 8, 1976; Charlie Braden interview, June 27, 2009, Eagle Lake, TX.

6. *Houston Daily Post,* Jan. 30, 1903, Chronicling America, http://chroniclingamerica.loc.gov/lccn/sn86071197/1903-01-30/ed-1/seq-4; *Weimar Mercury,* Nov. 14, 1913; Feb. 6, 1914; Jan. 21, 1944; *Colorado (TX) Citizen,* Nov. 12, 1925.

7. Davis R. Waddell interview, Apr. 25, 2009, Eagle Lake, TX; Bill Blair, pers. comm., May 9, 2009.

8. *Eagle Lake Headlight,* Oct. 27, 1934; Nov. 22, 1935; Bill Blair, pers. comm., June 23, 2009.

9. Bill Blair, pers. comm., May 9, 2009.

10. *Weimar Mercury,* Dec. 20, 1912; Jan. 5, 1923; *Colorado (TX) Citizen,* Nov. 15, 1928.

11. David Wintermann interview with David Lobpries, undated, in private collection of David Lobpries.

12. *Eagle Lake Headlight,* Sept. 7, 1918; Apr. 25, 1957; Oct. 23, 1969.

13. Gervais Bell interview, Mar. 9, 2009, Houston, TX; *Galveston Daily News,* June 25, 1920; Eagle Lake Rod and Gun Club rule book, 1986, 10; *Eagle Lake Headlight,* June 5, 1952; July 31, 1975; Charlie Braden, pers. comm., June 16, 2009; Braden interview.

14. Braden interview; *Eagle Lake Headlight,* Jan. 9, 1932.

15. *Eagle Lake Headlight,* Jan. 13, 1923; Jan. 9, 1932; Nov. 1, 1934; Dec. 25, 1936; Howard Briscoe, *Houston Post Tempo Magazine,* 1968, Hunting and Fishing Collection, Eula and David Wintermann Library, Eagle Lake, TX.

16. Jerry Sims, "Eagle Lake, 1950–1995," manuscript, in private collection of Jerry Sims; Braden interview; Charles Stutzenbaker, pers. comm., June 23, 2009.

17. Sims, "Eagle Lake, 1950–1995"; Braden interview; Wintermann interview with Lobpries; *Eagle Lake Headlight,* Dec. 15, 1928.

18. Braden interview; Sims, "Eagle Lake, 1950–1995"; Jerry Sims interview, July 1, 2009, Houston, TX.

19. Braden interview; Sims, "Eagle Lake, 1950–1995."

20. Sims, "Eagle Lake, 1950–1995."

21. Braden interview.

22. *Galveston Daily News,* Oct. 29, 1896; Sims, "Eagle Lake, 1950–1995"; Braden interview.

23. Braden interview; Sims, "Eagle Lake, 1950–1995"; William Henry Harrison Sr., *A History of Eagle Lake Texas* (Austin: Eakin Press, 1987), 22.

24. *Eagle Lake Headlight,* Nov. 13, 1942; Sims, "Eagle Lake, 1950–1995"; Braden interview; Fred Maly, "Outdoor Page," *San Antonio Express,* Nov. 1, 1952.

25. Jerry Sims interview, June 27, 2009, Eagle Lake, TX; Wintermann interview with Lobpries.

26. *Dallas Morning News,* Mar. 18, 1956; Apr. 27, 1958; Braden interview.

27. Braden interview; Wintermann interview with Lobpries; Stutzenbaker interview; Bell interview.

28. *Eagle Lake Headlight,* Dec. 27, 1924; Feb. 8, 1951.

29. Wintermann interview with Lobpries.

30. Waddell interview; Bob Brister, "Outdoors," *Houston Chronicle,* Dec. 28, 1968.

31. Clifton Tyler interview, Jan. 25, 2009, Eagle Lake, TX.

32. John P. Cowan, *A Texas Treasure* (Dallas: Collectors Covey, 1992), 61; Bob Brister, "Herb Booth, 1989 Channel 8 TeleAuction Artist," manuscript, in private collection of Agnes Reel Strauss; Braden interview.

33. John Hart, undated newspaper clipping, in collection of Eagle Lake Prairie Edge Museum, Eagle Lake, TX.

34. *Eagle Lake Headlight,* June 16, 1955; Oct. 31, 1968; Agnes Reel Strauss interview, Aug. 16, 2010, Cat Spring, TX; Alex Wolff interview, June 28, 2008, Houston, TX.

35. C. Gibson to Jimmy Reel, Houston, Jan. 2, 1941, in private collection of Agnes Reel Strauss; *Eagle Lake Headlight,* June 21, 1951; June 16, 1955; Jan. 6, 1950 to Dec. 28, 1951, microfilm image 456, Eula and David Wintermann Library.

36. *Eagle Lake Headlight,* Dec. 25, 1958; July 1, 1976; Tom Waddell to Jimmy Reel, Mar. 11, 1941; W. R. Terrell to Jimmy Reel, Feb. 11, 1942 and May 15, 1942; and C. Gibson to Jimmy Reel, Mar. 11, 1941, all in private collection of Agnes Reel Strauss.

37. O. J. Jenson, Layne-Texas Company, to Jimmy Reel, Aug. 28, 1942; Jimmy Reel to Lower Lake Club Membership (draft letters never mailed), Apr. 28, 1943; C. S. Neal to Jimmy Reel, June 12, 1944; and miscellaneous notes (including an eighteen-page handwritten summary of events by Jimmy Reel), all in private collection of Agnes Reel Strauss; *Eagle Lake Headlight,* Oct. 10, 1947.

38. Lower Lake Club ledgers, Feb. 1, 1943; Jimmy Reel to S. C. Smothers, Aug. 15, 1942; and Jimmy Reel to Lower Lake Club membership, Jan. 18, 1943, all in private collection of Agnes Reel Strauss; Barry Lewis interview, July 1, 2008, Houston, TX.

39. Jimmy Reel, "Form of Suggested Rules and Regulations Governing Members and Their Guests of the Lower Lake Hunting and Fishing Club"; "By-Laws of the Lower Lake Hunting and Fishing Club, Season 1942–43"; Jimmy Reel to Lower Lake Club membership, Mar. 12, 1943; H. K. Arnold to Stockholders of Lower Lake Club, Dec. 11, 1947; and J. E. Suttles to Lower Lake Club membership, Oct. 13, 1949, all in private collection of Agnes Reel Strauss.

40. Barry Lewis interview, July 1, 2008, Houston, TX.

41. Ibid.

42. "Texas: King of the Wildcatters," *Time,* Feb. 13, 1950, www.time.com/time/magazine/article/0,9171,811889,00.html; Lewis interview.

43. Lewis interview.

44. H. K. Arnold to R. A. King, Jan. 3, 1949, in private collection of Agnes Reel Strauss.

45. *Eagle Lake Headlight,* Aug. 8, 1947; Oct. 30, 1952; Apr. 1, 1954; Oct. 23, 1958.

46. A. C. Appelt to Jimmy Reel, Dec. 4, 1948, in private collection of Agnes Reel Strauss.

47. Wintermann interview with Lobpries.

48. Jim Longtin, pers. comm., Apr. 21, 2009; Jodie Socha interview, May 31, 2008, Sugar Land, TX; David Lobpries interview, Oct. 9, 2008, Wharton, TX; Tyler interview; Wolff interview.

49. Tyler interview; Wolff interview; Clifton Tyler, pers. comm., June 21, 2009.

50. Bob Brister, "Outdoors," *Houston Chronicle,* Dec. 28, 1968; Harv Boughton, "The Outdoors with Rod, Gun and Camera," *Houston Post,* Jan. 2, 1966.

51. Wolff interview; Brister, "Outdoors," Dec. 28, 1968; Socha interview; Bill Appelt, pers. comm., Apr. 5, 2010.

52. Fred Maly, "Angling Around," *San Antonio Light,* Nov. 28, 1966; Tyler interview; Bob Brister, "Outdoors," *Houston Chronicle,* Dec. 1, 1968; Louis Schorlemmer interview, Apr. 1, 2010, Eagle Lake, TX.

53. Agnes Reel Strauss interview, Aug. 16, 2010, Cat Spring, TX; Bill Blair, pers. comm., June 23, 2009; *Eagle Lake Headlight,* Nov. 1, 1962; Harv Boughton, "The Outdoors with Rod, Gun and Camera," *Houston Post,* Nov. 20, 1966.

54. *Eagle Lake Headlight,* Oct. 18, 1990; Bill Appelt, pers. comm., Apr. 5, 2010; Waddell interview.

55. Jim Longtin, pers. comm., Apr. 21, 2009.

56. Tyler interview; *Eagle Lake Headlight,* Nov. 1, 1962; Oct. 28, 1965.

57. Tyler interview.

58. *Eagle Lake Headlight,* Jan. 5, 1961, to Dec. 27, 1962, microfilm image 645, Eula and David Wintermann Library; Tyler interview.

59. Tyler interview.

60. Ibid.; Wolff interview.

61. Tyler interview.

62. *Eagle Lake Headlight,* Jan. 9, 1964; Jan. 26, 1967.

63. Tyler interview; *Eagle Lake Headlight,* Nov. 13, 1969.

64. Wayne Waldrop, "Pioneer of the Prairie," *Waterfowl Magazine* 22, no. 6, Texas Goose Hunting, Clifton Tyler Goose Hunting Club, www.gooseshoot.com/; Tyler interview.

65. Tyler interview.

66. *Eagle Lake Headlight,* Jan. 5, 1961, to Dec. 27, 1962, microfilm image 645, Eula and David Wintermann Library; Henry Stowers, "Perfect Goose Hunting Trip," *Dallas Morning News,* Nov. 10, 1966; *Eagle Lake Headlight,* Oct. 30, 1958; Oct. 27, 1966.

67. Harrison, *History of Eagle Lake Texas,* 534; Special goose hunter's section, *Eagle Lake Headlight,* Oct. 29, 1964; Oct. 31, 1968, 10; Stowers, "Perfect Goose Hunting Trip"; Tyler interview; *Eagle Lake Headlight,* Nov. 1, 1962; Dec. 23, 1976.

68. Tyler interview.

69. Ibid.; John Cook interview, June 21, 2008, Rockport TX.

70. Tyler interview.

71. Waddell interview.

72. *San Antonio Light,* Dec. 17, 1943; *Weimer Mercury,* Jan. 21, 1944.

73. Lewis interview.

74. Wolff interview; Lewis interview.

75. Charles Stutzenbaker, pers. comm., Feb. 18, 2010; David Lobpries, pers. comm., Aug. 1, 2009.

76. *Cuero (TX) Record,* Nov. 6, 1957; *San Antonio Express,* Nov. 22, 1968; Bell interview.

77. David Lobpries interviews, Oct. 19, 2008, Wharton, TX, and Mar. 19, 2010, Hockley, TX; David Wolff, pers. comm., May 17, 2010; Agnes Reel Strauss, pers. comm., June 2, 2010.

78. Strauss interview; Linda Gillan Griffin, "Hunting at the Bucksnag," *Houston Chronicle Magazine, Texas,* Dec. 9, 1990, 12–15; David Wolff, pers. comm., May 17, 2010.

79. Wolff interview.

80. David A. Wolff, pers. comm., May 18, 2010; Wolff interview; Jim Longtin, pers. comm., Apr. 21, 2009; Socha interview.

81. Socha interview.

82. Jim Longtin, pers. comm., Apr. 21, 2009; Wolff interview.

83. Socha interview.

84. Griffin, "Hunting at the Bucksnag"; Agnes Reel interview, Aug. 16, 2010, Cat Spring TX; "The History of Bucksnag Hunting Club," www.bucksnag.com/history.htm; Socha interview.

CHAPTER 16. KATY PRAIRIE

1. Jim Warren interview, Mar. 19, 2010, Hockley, TX; David Lobpries, pers. comm., Mar. 19, 2010; Jim Longtin, pers. comm., Mar. 7, 2009; Lyle Jordan recorded narratives, 2001, in private collection of Doug Pike; Chester Jordan interview with Vernon Bevill, Bob Spain, and David Lobpries, Mar. 1994, tape 7329, Texas Parks and Wildlife Department archives, Austin, TX.

2. E. G. Wermund, "Geology and Physical Features of the Katy Prairie," Katy Prairie Conference, Apr. 29–30, 1994, 1; Charles Christopher Jackson, "Wallis, TX," Handbook of Texas Online, www.tshaonline.org/handbook/online/articles/WW/hjw2.html; *Galveston Daily News,* Apr. 14, 1877; Jim Warren, pers. comm., July 20, 2010; Warren interview; David Lobpries, pers. comm., Mar. 19, 2010.

3. Warren interview; Jim Warren, pers. comm., Mar. 30, 2010; *Galveston Daily News,* Nov. 9, 1878; Samuel Oliver Young, *True Stories of Old Houston and Houstonians: Historical and Personal Sketches* (Galveston: Oscar Springer, 1913), 35.

4. Jim Warren, pers. comm., Mar. 30, 2010; *Galveston Daily News,* Aug. 21, 1878; Oct. 31, 1882; Sept. 27, 1885; Apr. 13, 1886; Feb. 22, 1894; Charles Hallock, "A Sportsman's Directory to the Principal Resorts for Game and Fish in North America," in *The Sportsman's Gazetteer and General Guide* (New York: Orange Judd, 1883), 155.

5. *Galveston Daily News,* Jan. 2, Sept. 14, 1884; Nov. 20, 1886; Nov. 30, 1895.

6. Ibid., May 15, 1896; June 3, 1897; Mauri Lynn Smith, "Cypress, TX (Harris County)," Handbook of Texas Online, www.tshaonline.org/handbook/online/articles/CC/hlc66.html.

7. *Galveston Daily News,* Feb. 27, 1893; Feb. 3, 1901; Roverta Wright Rylander, "Katy, TX," Handbook of Texas Online, www.tshaonline.org/handbook/online/articles/KK/hfk1.html; Chester Jordan interview with Bevill, Spain, and Lobpries, tape 7329.

8. Chester Jordan interview with Bevill, Spain, and Lobpries, tape 7328; Lyle Jordan recorded narratives.

9. Lyle Jordan recorded narratives; Charles Cardiff interview with Vernon Bevill, Bob Spain, and David Lobpries, Mar. 1994, tape 7326, Texas Parks and Wildlife Department archives, Austin, TX.

10. Cardiff interview with Bevill, Spain, and Lobpries, tape 7326; Lyle Jordan recorded narratives.

11. Lyle Jordan recorded narratives.

12. Ibid.; Chester Jordan interview with Bevill, Spain, and Lobpries, tape 7329; Jim Warren interview, Mar. 19, 2010, Hockley, TX.

13. Lyle Jordan recorded narratives.

14. Ibid.

15. Chester Jordan interview with Bevill, Spain, and Lobpries, tape 7328; Lyle Jordan recorded narratives; Cardiff interview with Bevill, Spain, and Lobpries, tape 7326.

16. Cardiff interview with Bevill, Spain, and Lobpries, tape 7326; *Port Arthur News,* Jan. 20, 1933; Lyle Jordan, pers. comm., May 1, 2010.

17. *Victoria Advocate,* Sept. 20, 1922; *Brookshire Times,* Nov. 25, 1932; Lyle Jordan recorded narratives.

18. Lyle Jordan recorded narratives.

19. *Brookshire Times,* Oct. 13, 27, 1950; Oct. 13, 1955.

20. Ibid., Dec. 30, 1949.

21. Ibid.; Dec. 22, 1950; Dec. 18, 1952; Jan. 12, 1956; Harvey Evans interview, Feb. 20, 2010, Portland, TX.

22. Davis Waddell, pers. comm., Jan. 22, 2010; Evans interview.

23. *Del Rio News-Herald,* May 22, 1956.

24. *Baytown Sun,* Nov. 28, 1953; *Brookshire Times,* Jan. 2, 16, Dec. 18, 1958.

25. Lyle Jordan recorded narratives; Chester Jordan interview with Bevill, Spain, and Lobpries, tapes 7328 and 7329; Cardiff interview with Bevill, Spain, and Lobpries, tape 7327.

26. Pat Jordan, pers. comm., Apr. 28, 2010; Lyle Jordan recorded narratives.

27. Larry Gore interview with Todd Steele, July 15, 2009, Katy, TX; Warren interview.

28. *Brookshire Times,* Sept. 26, 1957; Nov. 5, 1959; Doug Pike, "Mankind, Waterfowl Coexisting Thus Far," *Houston Chronicle,* Nov. 26, 1989; James Prince, pers. comm., Mar. 21, 2010.

29. Pat Jordan, pers. comm., Mar. 21, 2010; Lyle Jordan recorded narratives.

30. *Brookshire Times,* Dec. 6, 1962; Pat Jordan, pers. comm., Mar. 21, 2010.

31. Lyle Jordan recorded narratives.

32. Ibid.

33. Byron W. Dalrymple, "Gimmicks for Geese," *Field and Stream,* Feb. 1974; Pat Jordan, pers. comm., Mar. 25, 2010; *Brookshire Times,* Nov. 10, 1966.

34. Lyle Jordan recorded narratives; Lyle Jordan, pers. comm., May 1, 2010; Jim Warren, pers. comm., May 2, 2010.

35. James Prince, pers. comm., Mar. 21, 2010; Texas Safaris promotional brochure, in private collection of Lyle and Pat Jordan; *San Antonio Light,* Oct. 31, 1971.

36. Lyle Jordan interview with Todd Steele, July 23, 2009, Kerrville, TX; James Prince, pers. comm., Mar. 21, 2010.

37. James Prince, pers. comm., Mar. 21, 2010; Lyle Jordan recorded narratives.

38. Josie Weber, "Goose on the Loose," *Houston Chronicle Magazine, Texas,* Dec. 29, 1968, 6–9; Byron W. Dalrymple, "This Most Unusual Guide," *Outdoor Life,* Jan. 1973.

39. Lyle Jordan recorded narratives.

40. Undated clipping from *Houston Chronicle,* Jan. 1973, in private collection of Lyle and Pat Jordan.

41. Lyle Jordan recorded narratives.

42. Pat Jordan, pers. comm., Mar. 17, 2010; Lyle Jordan recorded narratives.

43. *Brookshire Times,* Nov. 10, 1960; Nov. 23, 1961; Jan. 24, 1963.

44. Ibid., Nov. 10, 1966; Oct. 24, 1968.

45. Lyle Jordan, pers. comm., May 1, 2010.

46. Jim Longtin, pers. comm., Mar. 7, 2009; Private collection of Jim Longtin.

47. Jim Longtin, pers. comm., Jan. 29, 2011.

48. *Brookshire Times,* Jan. 9, 1969; Jim Longtin, pers. comm., Mar. 7, 2009.

49. Jim Longtin, pers. comm., Jan. 29, 2011.

50. Undated newspaper article in private collection of Jim Longtin; *Fowl Talk,* sound recording, 45 rpm, in private collection of Jim Longtin.

51. Jim Longtin, pers. comms., Mar. 7, 2009, and Feb. 28, 2011; David Lobpries interview, Mar. 19, 2010, Hockley, TX.

52. Jim Longtin, pers. comms., Mar. 7, 2009, and Feb. 28, 2011.

53. Lyle Jordan recorded narratives; *San Antonio Light,* Nov. 2, 1969; Jim Longtin, pers. comm., Jan. 29, 2011.

54. Lyle Jordan recorded narratives.

55. Miscellaneous Records of Texas Waterfowl, US Fish and Wildlife Service, Southern District, including excerpts (undated) from Grand jury indictment, *United States of America vs. Dave Jenkins,* US District Court, Southern District of Texas, Victoria Division, in private collection of Shannon Tompkins.

56. Jim Longtin, pers. comm., Jan. 29, 2011; *Brookshire Times,* Oct. 8, 1970; James Prince, pers. comm., Mar. 21, 2010; *Port Arthur News,* Nov. 1, 1973.

57. Al Bisbey, pers. comm., Apr. 3, 2010.

58. Ibid.; Will Beaty interview, 25 July 2008, Hempstead, TX.

59. James Prince, pers. comm., Mar. 21, 2010; Al Bisbey, pers. comm., Apr. 3, 2010.

60. Larry Gore, pers. comm., Mar. 23, 2010.

61. Al Bisbey, pers. comm., Apr. 3, 2010.

62. *Houston Chronicle,* Oct. 23, 2003; Gore interview with Steele; James Prince, pers. comm., Mar. 21, 2010; *Houston Chronicle,* Oct. 28, 1999.

63. Lyle Jordan recorded narratives.

CHAPTER 17. SHORT STORIES FROM FARTHER AFIELD

1. *Amarillo Globe,* Dec. 12, 1924; W. S. Adair, "Early Days in Texas," *Dallas Morning News,* Jan. 29, 1933.

2. *Port Arthur News,* Jan. 9, 1924; Oct. 30, 1925; *Lubbock Morning Avalanche,* Aug. 31, 1924.

3. *Lubbock Avalanche-Journal,* Feb. 17, 1935; Feb. 25, 1940; *Amarillo Daily News,* Nov. 25, 1942.

4. *Amarillo Globe,* Dec. 12, 1924; *Amarillo Daily News,* Nov. 25, 1942; Dec. 18, 1947; *Amarillo Globe-News,* Dec. 21, 1947.

5. *San Antonio Light,* Jan. 2, 1898.

6. Ibid., July 7, 1884; Dec. 30, 1886; July 7, 1892; *San Antonio Light,* Sept. 1, 1895; *San Antonio Daily Express,* Oct. 13, 1885; July 5, 1888; Dec. 12, 1898; *Galveston Daily News,* Jan. 25, 1896.

7. *San Antonio Light,* Dec. 12, 1898; "Mitchell Lake," Wikipedia, http://en.wikipedia.org/wiki/Mitchell_Lake.

8. *San Antonio Light,* Oct. 18, 1924; *San Antonio Light and Gazette,* Nov. 30, 1909; *San Antonio Express,* Dec. 12, 1876.

9. *San Antonio Daily Light,* Aug. 27, 1894; Dec. 6, 1898; *San Antonio Daily Express,* Dec. 12, 1898.

10. *San Antonio Daily Express,* Oct. 13, 1885; *San Antonio Daily Light,* Aug. 27, 1894; Nov. 18, 1896; *San Antonio Light,* June 25, 1895; Aug. 21, 1904.

11. *San Antonio Light,* Sept. 8, Oct. 22, 1929; Nov. 12, 1939; *San Antonio Express,* Nov. 4, 1930; Oct. 15, 1940.

12. *San Antonio Light,* May 6, 1945; Nov. 11, 1957; Oct. 19, 1958.

13. Ibid., Aug. 28, 1908; May 30, 1936; Nov. 12, 1939; *San Antonio Express,* Sept. 29, 1935.

14. *Victoria Advocate,* Dec. 3, 1910; *San Antonio Express and News,* Feb. 21, 1954; *Galveston Daily News,* June 2, 1923; *San Antonio Express,* Sept. 17, 1938; Alex Halff, pers. comm., Apr. 21, 2009.

15. *San Antonio Light,* Jan. 7, 1917; Nov. 7, 1920; Nov. 23, 1929; *San Antonio Express,* Nov. 2, 1930; *San Antonio Evening News,* Oct. 18, 1920.

16. William C. Harris, ed., *The Sportsman's Guide to the Hunting and Shooting Grounds of the United States and Canada* (New York: Anglers' Publishing, 1888), 168; *Victoria Advocate,* Oct. 10, 1933.

17. *Victoria Advocate,* Oct. 30, 1977; *Victoria Daily Advocate,* Jan. 19, 1911; Dec. 5, 1914.

18. *Victoria Daily Advocate,* Jan. 18, 1905; Dec. 6, 1907; *Victoria Advocate,* Oct. 26, 1907; Sidney Weisiger, "Vignettes of Old Victoria, Hunting-Fishing Clubs," *Victoria Advocate,* Nov. 5, 1972.

19. *Victoria Daily Advocate,* Dec. 11, 1915.

20. Weisiger, "Vignettes of Old Victoria, Hunting-Fishing Clubs."

21. *Galveston Daily News,* Oct. 28, 1879; Hilmar G. Moore interview, Aug. 4, 2009, Richmond, TX.

22. *Galveston Daily News,* Nov. 26, 1901; Oct. 5, 1913; Orin Covell interview with Todd Steele, Aug. 8, 2008, Richmond, TX.

23. Covell interview with Steele; *Galveston Daily News,* Feb. 26, 1909.

24. *San Antonio Light,* Mar. 21, 1915; *Galveston Daily News,* Nov. 5, 1907; Jan. 7, 1912.

25. Hilmar G. Moore interview.

26. Covell interview with Steele; Hilmar G. Moore, pers. comm., July 30, 2009.

27. Charles Stutzenbaker, pers. comm., Aug. 19, 2009; Hilmar G. Moore interview.

28. Hilmar G. Moore interview.

29. *Galveston Daily News,* Nov. 18, 1902; Dec. 2, 1905; John Winter photo albums, in private collection of Cliff Fisher.

30. Hilmar G. Moore interview; Charles Stutzenbaker, pers. comm., Aug. 19, 2009.

31. *Galveston Daily News,* Dec. 24, 1902; Oct. 27, 1905; May 14, 1909; Jan. 15, 1911.

32. Ibid., Dec. 9, 1926; Bill Kiel interview, Mar. 4, 2010, Kingsville, TX; Bill Kiel Jr., pers. comm., Jan. 31, 2010.

33. *Dallas Morning News,* June 20, 1909; William C. Harris, ed., *The American Angler and Sportsman Tourist* 27, no. 11 (1897):278; *San Antonio Daily Express,* May 12, 1900.

34. *Galveston Daily News,* Dec. 27, 1877.

35. *Dallas Morning News,* Dec. 23, 1892; Mar. 5, 1903; *Galveston Daily News,* Jan. 20, May 26, June 4, 1885.

36. *San Antonio Evening News,* Oct. 28, 1899; *Mexia Evening News,* Aug. 20, 1921; *Mexia Daily News,* Apr. 8, 1924; Nov. 5, 1926; Vivian Elizabeth Smyrl, "Coolidge, TX," Handbook of Texas Online, www.tshaonline.org/handbook/online/articles/CC/hlc49.html.

37. *Dallas Morning News,* June 23, 1906; Jan. 24, 1909; *Corsicana Daily Sun,* Apr. 24, 1909; Nov. 16, 1916; Oct. 24, 1917; *Corsicana Semi-Weekly Light,* Oct. 26, 1916.

38. *Wisconsin Democrat,* Feb. 7, 1846.

39. *Dallas Morning News,* Nov. 25, 1891; Dec. 16, 1900; Oct. 22, 1904.

40. Clare G. Weakley Jr., "Texas' First Country Club," Dallas County Pioneer Association, http://dallaspioneer.org/stories/historical.php?ID=47.

41. *Dallas Morning News,* Oct. 23, 1885; Oct. 22, 1904; Jan. 1, Dec. 31, 1905.

42. Ibid., Jan. 1, 1905; Weakley, "Texas' First Country Club."

43. *Dallas Morning News,* July 9, 1896; Mar. 22, July 7, 1903; Jan. 20, 1915; Rich Flaten, pers. comm., Mar. 22, 2011.

44. *Dallas Morning News,* Mar. 2, 1904; Dec. 24, 1905; Sept. 7, 1924; Feb. 11, 1962; Kenneth Foree, "Red Book Glows of 1902 Fishing," ibid., June 23, 1963.

45. *Galveston Daily News,* Apr. 6, 1906; *Dallas Morning News,* May 22, 1910; Feb. 11, 1962.

46. *Dallas Morning News,* Jan. 10, 1939; Feb. 11, 1962; Ron Gard, pers. comms., Aug. 13, 2010; Mar. 4, 2011.

47. *Dallas Morning News,* Sept. 7, 1924.

48. Ibid., Sept. 27, 1899; Aug. 23, 1916.

49. Ibid., Mar. 6, Nov. 27, 1903; Feb. 20, 1905.

50. *Fort Worth Star-Telegram,* Mar. 28, 1911; *Dallas Morning News,* Aug. 4, 1907; *New Braunfels Herald-Zeitung,* July 12, 1989.

51. *Winnsboro News,* June 25, 1959; *Dallas Morning News,* June 18, 1909; Ron Gard, pers. comm., July 7, 2011.

52. *Caddo Lake Handbook,* 1938, reprinted by Johnson's Ranch Marina, 2010.

53. *Galveston Daily News,* Oct., 16, 1921; *Houston Chronicle,* Apr. 15, 1993; Jaques D. Bagur, *A History of Navigation on Cypress and the Lakes* (Denton: University of North Texas Press, 2001), 7; Shannon Tompkins, "Caddo Lake's History is the Stuff of Legend," *Houston Chronicle,* Dec. 13, 2009; *Houston Chronicle,* Jan. 1, 1998.

54. Bagur, *History of Navigation,* 118; *Dallas Morning News,* Jan. 30, 1890.

55. *Dallas Morning News,* Jan. 19, 1890.

56. Ibid., Nov. 29, 1886; Nov. 21, 1891; Nov. 22, 1897.

57. Walter Martin, pers. comm., Mar. 6, 2011; J. A. Phillips, "Bygone Days on Caddo Lake," *Forest and Stream* 89 (1919):157; *Galveston Daily News,* Oct. 16, 1921.

58. Wyatt Moore interview with Thad Sitton, Feb. 2, 1983, Tape no. 150, File no. 150-1, James Gilliam Gee Library, Texas A&M University-Commerce.

59. Fred Dahmer interview with David Todd, June 7, 1997, Uncertain, TX, Texas Legacy Project, Reel No. 1010, Conservation History Association of Texas.

60. *Dallas Morning News,* Oct. 21, 1905; June 2, Nov. 10, 1910.

61. *Caddo Lake Handbook; Dallas Morning News,* Nov. 11, 1924; Oct. 25, 1932; *Dallas Morning News,* May 30, 1954; Walter and Brenda Martin, pers. com., Apr. 5, 2011.

62. *Dallas Morning News,* May 21, 1889; June 7, 1913; Jan. 10, 1915; Aug. 7, 1941; *Galveston Daily News,* Oct. 16, 1921; Walter Martin, pers. comm., Mar. 6, 2011.

63. Dahmer oral history interview with Todd; Moore oral history interview with Sitton, Feb. 12, 1983, Tape no. 150, File no. OH 150-5.

64. William Sterrett, *Game, Fish and Oyster Commission of Texas for the Period Ending Aug. 31, 1914* (Austin: E. L. Steck Press, 1914), 27; Moore oral history interview with Sitton, Feb. 2, 1983, Tape no. 150, File no. 150-1.

65. Phillips, "Bygone Days on Caddo Lake"; *Caddo Lake Handbook; Dallas Morning News,* Jan. 3, 1909.

66. *Dallas Morning News,* Dec. 5, 1937; *Caddo Lake Handbook.*

67. *Caddo Lake Handbook; Dallas Morning News,* July 5, 1925; Fred Dahmer, *Caddo Was . . . : A Short History of Caddo Lake* (Austin: University of Texas Press, 1989), 40; Wyatt Moore oral history interview with Sitton, Feb. 2, 1983, Tape no. 150, File No. 150-1.

68. Dahmer oral history interview with Todd; Dahmer, *Caddo Was . . . ,* 65.

69. *Dallas Morning News,* May 30, 1954; *Caddo Lake Handbook.*

70. *Dallas Morning News,* May 30, 1954; *San Antonio Light,* Dec. 4, 1957; Wyatt Moore oral history interview with Sitton, Feb. 2, 1983, Tape no. 150, File no. 150-1.

71. Moore oral history interview with Sitton, Feb. 12, 1983, Tape no. 150, File no. OH 150-5; Shannon Tompkins, pers. comm., Mar. 26, 2011.

EPILOGUE

1. *Big Spring Herald,* Mar. 21, 1976; Frank Moore Colby, ed., *The New International Year Book* (New York: Dodd, Mead and Co., 1915), 473.

2. "General Notes," *The Auk: A Quarterly Journal of Ornithology* 39, no. 3 (1922):412-13; Robin W. Doughty, *Wildlife and Man in Texas: Environmental Change and Conservation* (College Station: Texas A&M University Press, 1983), 181; William Allen and Sue Allen Taylor, *Aransas: The Life of a Texas Coastal Community* (Austin: Eakin Press, 1997), 179, 358; *Galveston Daily News,* Dec. 14, 1909.

3. Dave Morrison, pers. comm., Nov. 15, 2010.

4. J. R. Singleton, *Texas Coastal Waterfowl Survey,* FA Report Series no. 11 (Austin: Texas Game and Fish Commission, 1953), 60.

5. N. S. Goss, "The Mottled Duck in Kansas," *The Auk: A Quarterly Journal of Ornithology* 7, no. 1 (1890):88; Christine Rappleye, "Coastal Mottle Ducks Show Impressive Growth," *Beaumont Enterprise,* Nov. 22, 2007.

6. Forest W. McNeir, *Forest McNeir of Texas* (San Antonio: Naylor, 1956), 74.

7. Shannon Tompkins, "This Season is for the Birds," *Houston Chronicle,* Jan. 21, 2010; "The Cranes: Status Survey and Conservation Action Plan: Sandhill Crane," US Geological Survey, Northern Prairie Wildlife Research Center, www.npwrc.usgs.gov/resource/birds/cranes/gruscana.htm.

8. *Galveston Daily News,* Jan. 18, 1896; *Dallas Morning News,* Mar. 25, 1899.

9. US Fish and Wildlife Service, *Wetlands Preservation Program: Texas Gulf Coast—Category 8,* updated (Albuquerque: USFWS, Department of the Interior, 1981), 19.

10. *Baytown Sun,* May 26, 1977; *San Antonio Light,* Mar. 21, 1944; James B. Blackburn Jr., *The Book of Texas Bays* (College Station: Texas A&M University Press, 2004), 156.

11. Charles Stutzenbaker interview, Oct. 24, 2008, Port Arthur, TX; Clifton Tyler interview, Jan. 25, 2009, Eagle Lake, TX; Larry Hodge, "From Rags to Riches," *Texas Parks & Wildlife,* Sept. 2003,www.tpwmagazine.com/archive/2003/sept/legend/.

12. *Dallas Morning News,* Aug. 8, 1936; *Galveston Daily News* June 22, 1935; C. D. Stutzenbaker, "Distribution Dilemma," *Texas Parks & Wildlife* 28, no. 12 (1970):12-14.

13. Stutzenbaker, "Distribution Dilemma."

14. *Lubbock Morning Avalanche,* Aug. 31, 1924; *Lubbock Avalanche-Journal,* Dec. 21, 1947; Shannon Tompkins, "Gone Goose: Largest of Canada Geese Abandon Texas, Wintering Farther North," *Houston Chronicle,* Jan. 20, 2000.

15. William C. Hobaugh, Charles D. Stutzenbaker, and Edward L. Flickinger, "The Rice Prairies," in *Habitat Management for Migrating and Wintering Waterfowl in North America,* ed. L. M. Smith Jr., R. L. Pederson, and R. M. Kaminski (Lubbock: Texas Tech University Press, 1989), 392; David Lobpries interview, Oct. 9, 2008, Wharton, TX; Bill Stransky, pers. comm., Dec. 9, 2010.

16. Shannon Tompkins, pers. comm., Dec. 28, 2010; Bill Stransky, pers. comm., Sept. 21, 2009; Tompkins, "This Season is for the Birds."

17. Freddie Abshier interview, June 13, 2008, Anahuac, TX.

18. *Dallas Morning News,* Aug. 1, 1926.

19. Ibid, Feb. 5, 1936; *Galveston Daily News,* May 23, 1937.

INDEX

Abercrombie, E. F. "Abbey," 312
A Book on Duck Shooting (Heilner), 288
Abshier, Freddie
    at Anahuac NWR, 106
    on Barrow's Ranch, 107
    biography, 117-20
    on blue geese, 8
    on decline of waterfowl, 365
    on decoys, 23, 34
    on fog, 21
    on handmade wood decoys, 28
    on JHK Ranch, 105
    on Joe Lagow, 111
    on sand hazards, 101
access to hunting
    airboats, 16-18, 68-70, 76, 80, 107-8, 207, 211-12, 232-33
    marsh buggies, 16, 17, 78, 95, 119, 136, 137
    overview, 10-18
    See also automobiles and access to hunting; boat access to hunting; railroads, and access to hunting
Adolphus, A. J. "Moose," 246, 247
aerial bird shooting, 52
African American guides and workers, 112-13, 181, 230, 315, 348
agriculture, impact on hunting, 148, 156, 219-20, 282, 313-14, 331, 363, 364-65
airboats, 16-18, 68-70, 76, 80, 107-8, 207, 211-12, 232-33
airplanes, 52, 154, 191, 209, 241
Alamo Beach, 197-98

Alamo Beach Game Preserve, 198
Albright, Daniel "Dummy," 360
Aldridge, Ray, 273
alligator buggies, 69
Alligator Head Ranch, 205
alligators, 20, 191, 305-6
Alta Vista Hotel, 243-74
Alvin, Texas, 163
Amarillo, Texas, 343
American Sportsman (TV program), 317
Anahuac, Texas, 87, 112, 140
Anahuac National Wildlife Refuge, 106, 111
Anderson, Andy, 41-42, 156, 260, 329-30
Anderson, Jake, 69
Anderson, Tom, 188-89
Angelina River, 356
Annual Wild Game Dinner for Disabled Veterans, 329-30
Appelt, Bill, 314, 315
Aransas and Copano Bays
    overview, 221
    Rockport area, clubs and guides, 226-47
    Rockport area, early years, 221-26
    St. Joseph Island, 247-53
Aransas National Wildlife Refuge, 239, 361
Aransas Pass, 256-62
Aransas Pass Gun Club, 256
Aransas Pass Sporting Club, 264
Armstrong, Charles L., 34, 38
Armstrong, Neil, 336
Armstrong, William and Clarence, 224
Armstrong Featherweight Decoys Inc., 38, 50
Army Hole, 210

Arnold, Henry "Hap," 118, 260
Arroyo Colorado, 279, 285, 288, 295
art, sporting themed, 143, 156, 211-12, 251-52, 307-8, 322, 338
astronauts, 335, 336
Atkins, Stuart, 288
Atwood, Johnny, 247, 252-53
Austin area hunting, 352
automobiles, hunting from/with, 52, 148, 283
automobiles and access to hunting, 13, 14, 81, 91-92
    Corpus Christi area, 275
    Galveston, 166
    Laguna Madre, 287, 291
    Matagorda Bay, 189-90
    Port O'Connor, 207
    San Jacinto River area, 148, 152
    Trinity River delta, 134
avian cholera, 338

Babineaux, Max, 111
Badgley, Abe and Babe and family, 143-44, 159
Baffin Bay, 284
bag limits, 52-53, 54-55, 252, 266, 272, 277
Bahia Grande, 291, 294
Baird, Mike, 318
baiting, prohibition of, 54
Ballard, Bart, 283, 285, 287
Ballou, Henry, 237, 238-39
balsa wood decoys, 28, 31, 47
banding programs, 200, 229
Barber, Dan, 195

barges, 91, 147, 212, 217, 249
Barney's Place, 264
Barrow's Ranch and family, 106-12, 106-15, 151
Barry, Chuck, 36
bartering, 74, 80, 118, 123
Bass, Perry, Sr., 250, 251
Bates, Ted and family, 12, 27, 194-95
Batsell, J. H., 290
Batsell-Wells Sporting Goods Store, 290, 291, 293
Bauer, Frank, 199-200
Baughman, Sonny, 93-94
Bay City, Texas, 186
Bay Flats Lodge, 213
Baytown, Texas, 157-60
Baytown Sun, 157, 159
Beach Hotel, 197, 198
Beaty, J. M., 62
Beaty, Will, 124-25, 339
Beckendorff, Joe, 328
Becker, Adolf C., 168
Beebe Hotel, 292, 293
Bell, Ed, 202
Bell, Gervais, 302
Benge, Herman "Major," 318
Bering, C. L. and Theo, 148-50, 300
Berwick family, 92
Besser, Walter, 139-40, 141-42
Big Creek, 348
Big Lake, 358
Big Prairie. See Eagle Lake
Big Three Reservoir, 334
Bird, Doug, 277, 282
bird banding programs, 200
The Birds of Texas (Strecker), 9
Bisbey, Al, 178, 339
black lab retrievers, 19-20
black powder guns, 18, 77, 357
Blair, Bill, 301
blind (sightless) hunting, 353
blinds
    brush, 12, 18, 191, 194, 201, 245, 336
    livestock, hunting over, 13, 14, 54, 99, 328, 330
    overview, 18, 19
    rice stacks, 328
    sunken, 88, 122, 208, 211
bluebills, 8, 43, 279-80
blue goose, 8-9, 282
Blue Goose Hunting Club, 315-19
Blue Wing Hunting and Fishing Club, 346
boat access to hunting
    airboats, 16-18, 68-70, 76, 80, 107-8, 207, 211-12, 232-33

barges, 91, 147, 212, 217, 249
overview, 12-13, 15
Sabine estuary, 60
San Jacinto River area, 152
sloops/schooners, 12-13, 18, 152, 164, 174-75, 223-26, 224
tow boats, 152, 237-38, 242-43, 245
See also motorized boats, introduction of
Boca Chica Shooting Preserve, 291
Boehringer, Gotlief, 358
Bolivar Peninsula, 90-96
Bonus Hunting Club, 301
Booth, Herb, 307
Booth Hunting Club, 165-66, 348
Boughton, Harv, 156
Boyd, J. L., 75
Braden, Charlie and family, 304, 305-6, 308
brant, overview, 8
Brays Bayou, 146
Brazoria County area
    hunting clubs, coastal, 176-83
    overview, 173-76
    sporting culture of, 183-84
Brazoria National Wildlife Refuge, 184
Brazos Bend State Park, 349
Brazos Island, 293, 294
Brazos River, 173, 299, 348, 350, 352
Brazos Santiago Pass, 294
breech-loading shotguns, 18
Brenham area hunting, 350-52
Brenham Gun and Rod Club, 351
Brewer, Walter, 30-31, 44
"Bridge to Nowhere," 210
"bridge-walkers," 291
Brister, Bob
    on Barrow's Ranch and Joe Lagow, 108-9
    at Blue Goose Hunting Club, 317
    and Freddie Abshire, 118-19
    at Hall's Bayou, 170
    on Jimmy Reel, 118-19, 314
    on pollution in Houston Ship Channel, 159-60
    on rag spread hunting, 36
    and Stewart Campbell, 211
    on whooping crane shooting, 239
    writing and hunting career, 156-57
Brooks Field Hunting and Fishing Lodge, 209
Broussard and Hebert Ranch, 75, 79
Brown, H. Lutcher and family, 217-18
Brown and Root, 122, 182-83
Brown's Camp, 88-89

Brownsville, Texas, 288, 290
Brownsville Fishing and Hunting Club, 290
Brownsville Herald, 290, 292, 294
Brundrett Ranch, 212
brush blinds, 12, 18, 191, 194, 201, 245, 336
Bryan, William Jennings, 96-97, 271, 285, 292, 294
Buckingham, Nash, 148
Bucksnag Hunting Club, 322, 338
Buena Vista Hotel, 284
Buffalo Bayou, 145-46
buffleheads, overview, 8
Bukowsky, Lucien, 312
Bureau of Biological Survey, 200, 229
burning off of vegetation, 64, 68, 73, 87, 217
Burton, A. C., 199-200
Burton, Leonard "Lefty," 322
Busch Landing, 157
Bush, George H. W., 307

Caddo Lake, 356-60
Cade, C. T. and Cade Marsh, 91, 94
Calhoun County, 98, 197, 199, 205, 210
calling competitions, 40-41, 41-42, 157, 329, 338
calling/whistling by mouth, 41, 71, 72, 79, 153, 157-58, 242, 314, 339, 348
Cameron County, 287
Campbell, Stewart, 170, 210-11, 213
Camp Hunt, 208
Canada geese
    decoys, 32, 48, 49
    hunting highlights, 105-6, 116, 218-19
    Katy Prairie, 331
    Laguna Madre, 282
    as live decoys, 27
    Matagorda Bay, 192, 199, 200
    overview, 8, 9, 362
    Panhandle, 344
Canada Ranch and family, 116, 122-23
Cane Island, 326
Caney Creek, 185
canon, hunting with, 293
Canvasback Club, 166
canvasbacks
    bag limits, reduction in, 54-55
    decoys, 46
    hunting highlights, 18-19, 63, 75, 96-99, 218-19
    overview, 8, 362
Carancahua Bay, 196
Cardiff, Bill, 329, 330
Cardiff, Charles, 327
Carlton, B. H. "Hardy" and family, 178

Carter, Randolph, 276, 277
carved decoys. See wood decoys
Casa de los Patos, 142–43
"Cat-A-Gators," 78
causeways
    Aransas Bay, 240, 246
    Nueces Bay, 277
    Padre Island, 275, 276
    Port Aransas, 264
    Port Bay, 228
Cedar Bayou, 150, 157, 248
Cedar Lake, 174, 175
celery, wild, 98, 122, 164, 166, 311, 354
Central Flyway, 7, 362–63, 364
Cessac Café, 92
Cessac family, 78, 79
chain of lakes, Chambers County, 96–99
Chamberlain, Wilt, 121
Chambers Country Club, 139
Chambers County, 19, 53, 55, 59, 63, 96, 102, 117, 122, 362
Chambliss, Jack, 118–19
Champion Lake, 142–43, 144
Champion Paper and Fibre Company, 94, 142–43
Chapman Ranch, 276, 281–82
charity events, 121–22, 177, 260, 329
Charles W. Grubbs Manufacturing Company, 33–34, 38, 49
Chatagnier family, 80, 83
cheniers, 59
Chesapeake Bay retrievers, overview, 19
Chinese tallow trees, 171
Chocolate Bay (Brazoria County), 168–71
cholera, avian, 338
church services for hunters, 82–83
Circle H Hunting and Fishing Club, 336
City Café, Rockport, 244
Civilian and Galveston City Gazette, 163
C. L. and Theo Bering Hardware and Sporting Goods, 129, 148–50, 300
Clark, Kendon L. and family, 29, 30, 134–35
Clark Rice and Irrigation Company, 196, 197
Clear Lake, 161–63
Clemens, Samuel, 271
Clements, William P. "Bill," 322
Cleveland, Grover, 248
Cline, Joseph, 164–65
Cline's Resort, 264, 277
Clopper's Point (Morgan's Point), 145, 146–48
Close, William Sherman, "Big Willie" and family, 246, 247
cloth spreads, 34–38, 159, 218, 317, 319, 320, 323, 333–34

coastal floodplain forest, 179
Coastal Sand Sheet, 279, 281, 284, 285
coastal Texas
    ecology overview, 7, 362–63
    and flyway shift, 363–65
    map, xiv
Cobb, Irvin S., 304
Coleman-Fulton Pasture Company (CFP), 222, 226, 270
Colorado County, 299
Colorado River, 185, 186, 300, 307
    See also Matagorda Bay
Connally, John, 251
Connolly, John, 122–23
Conoly, Clyde, 287
conservation
    emergence of, 51
    modern initiatives, 365–66
    See also refuges, wildlife
conservationists, hunters as
    Bob Farley, 258
    David Wintermann, 308
    Henry LeBlanc, 71
    Joe Lagow, 112
    Joe Matthews, 143–44
    Peg Melton, 155–56
    Pop Sorenson, 226
    Waco Gun Club, 352
Conservation of Texas Fish and Game, Inc. (COTFAG), 41–42
Cook, John, 233
Cooley, Denton, 114
Coon Creek Club, 354–55
Copano and Aransas Bays
    overview, 221
    Rockport area, clubs and guides, 226–47
    Rockport area, early years, 221–26
    St. Joseph Island, 247–53
Corpus Christi area
    Aransas Pass, 256–62
    Corpus Christi Bay, 267–78
    Harbor Island, 255
    Port Aransas, 262–67
Corpus Christi Bay
    1800s, 267–72
    1900s, 272–78
Corpus Christi Ship Channel, 259
Corpus Christi Times, 275
Corsicana area hunting, 353
Cotter, James "Ed," 248
cotton farming, 217
Cotton Lake, 134–35
cottonmouths, 21, 76–77, 120, 306, 312
Cove (Winfree's Cove), 29, 129–35, 151

Cove Hunting and Fishing Club, 129
Covell, Orin, 348
Cowan, John P. "Jack," 143, 156, 211–12, 251–52, 307
cranes, wintering
    Corpus Christi Bay, 267
    Laguna Madre, 282
    overview, 9, 362
    protection of, 52
    See also sandhill cranes; whooping cranes
Craven, William "Old Man," 258–59
crawlers (marsh buggies), 69
Creekmore, H. B. "Bowie," 31, 44, 110
Crip's Camp, 360
crop destruction by waterfowl
    Eagle Lake, 301
    Laguna Madre, 281, 288
    Matagorda Bay, 197
    Panhandle area, 343
Cullen, Hugh "Roy," 192
culture of waterfowling, 80–84, 183–84
curlews, 9, 52
Curry, Arthur Richard and family, 229–32
cypress wood decoys, 28, 29, 30, 31, 43, 46, 49

Dahlberg, O. Z., 347
Dahmer, Fred, 359
Dailey, Jim, 196, 208
Dallas area hunting, 353–55
Dallas Caddo Hunting and Fishing Club, 358
Dallas Fishing and Hunting Club, 353–54
Dallas Morning News, 248, 249
dams
    Big Caney Creek, 142
    Brays Bayou, 146
    Caddo Lake, 360
    Colorado River, 186, 352
    Copano Bay area, 222
    and destruction of habitat, 363
    Gum Hollow Creek, 270–73
    King Ranch, 283
    Lavaca River, 196
    Trinity River, 355
dangers to hunters
    drownings, 226, 360
    mud hazards, 70, 78, 90, 95, 101, 176–77, 335
    overview, 21–22
    shootings, accidental, 21–22, 102
    See also deaths of hunters; snakes, dangerous; weather dangers
Davis, Bob, 303
Davis, Dave "Bubba," 31, 46, 232, 233

day hunting
- Eagle Lake, 301, 313
- East Bay area, 88-89, 101, 102, 107
- and internal combustion engines, 15
- Katy Prairie, 329, 334, 336-37
- Sabine estuary, 77-80
- San Antonio area, 346
- Trinity River delta, 141-42
- West Galveston Bay area, 169-70

Dean, C. L., 223-24
Dean, Dizzy, 64, 111, 118, 306
deaths of hunters
- boat mishaps, 21
- drownings, 226, 360
- King Ranch poaching incident, 285-87
- lost, 21
- shootings, accidental, 21-22, 102
- weather-related, 98, 102, 110

DeBakey, Michael, 114
declines in waterfowl
- agriculture, 148, 156, 219-20, 282, 313-14, 331, 363
- deepwater ports, 159-60, 259, 263, 277-78, 294, 363
- drought, effects of, 53
- drought and waterfowl decline, 15, 19, 53, 220, 294, 345
- hunting pressure, 220, 330, 361
- industrial/residential development, 140, 144, 159-60, 171, 247, 266-67, 341, 363-65
- lead poisoning, 54, 55-56
- nutria, 90, 306
- sedimentation, 307
- subsidence, 90
- See also conservation

decoys, 43-50
- factory, 33-34, 49, 50
- giant, 216
- goose, 333
- live, 23-28, 54, 132, 303
- newspaper spreads, 34, 35, 334-35
- overview, 23
- pasteboard, 9
- tin silhouette, 32, 33, 48
- white rag spreads, 34-38, 159, 218, 317, 319, 320, 323, 333-34
- wind sock, 36
- wood, handmade, 28-33, 159

Decrow's Point, 187
deepwater ports, 159-60, 259, 263, 277-78, 294, 363
Deepwater Rice Farm, 145-46
Delhomme, C. B., 138, 139, 153

Delmar Place, 273
diapers in rag spreads, 35, 37, 218, 333
diving ducks
- bluebills, 43, 279-80
- overview, 8
- ring-necked ducks, 48
- scaup (lesser), 137-38
- See also canvasbacks; redheads

Dix, Theodore, 287
Dixon, Joe, 359
Doggett, Joe, 95, 142, 143, 156, 335
dogs (retrievers), 19-21, 95, 114, 121
Donnelly, Barnes "Barney," 322
Donovant, William, 300, 308
Don Patricio Causeway, 275
Doug's Guide Service, 277
dredging
- Colorado River, 186
- Corpus Christi Ship Channel, 259
- Matagorda Bay, 210
- Port Aransas, 264
- Rockport, 246
- See also deepwater ports; Intracoastal Canal (IC), impact of

driftwood decoys, 28, 32, 47
drought and waterfowl decline, 15, 19, 53, 220, 294, 345
drownings, 226, 360
Dry Pond, 352
duck calls/calling, 38-41, 50, 72, 142, 159, 314, 338
- See also mouth calling/whistling
"duck ports," 364
ducks, resident, 362
- See also mottled ducks
ducks, wintering
- hunting highlights, 104-5, 116, 269, 271, 293, 306, 357
- as live decoys, 23-28
- overview, 7-8
- wood decoys, handmade, 28-33
- See also diving ducks; individual species

Duck Stamp Law, 365
duck stamps, 184
Ducks Unlimited, 112, 124-25, 139, 365
DuNah, George W., 215
Duncan Ranch and family, 217
Dunn, Lindsay and family, 26, 136-39, 153
Dunn, Patrick, 268
DuPont plant, 80
Durham, Mylie, Sr., 312
Dust Bowl, 15, 53-54, 364
Dutton, Doris Daniel and family, 30, 33, 49, 136

Eagle Lake and Katy Prairie Outfitters, 340-41
Eagle Lake area
- Blue Goose Hunting Club, 315-19
- David Wintermann, 307-8
- decline of waterfowl, 306-7
- Eagle Lake Rod and Gun Club, 302-6, 309
- early profile, 299-300
- Garwood, 321-23
- hunting clulture, 319-20
- Jimmy Reel, 308-15
- pot shooting, 302
- rice crops, 300-301
- Skull Creek, 321

Eagle Lake Headlight, 303-4, 319
Eagle Lake Hunting Club, 300
Eagle Lake Rod and Gun Club, 300, 302-6
Eagle Nest Lake, 179
Eagle Nest & Maner Lake Fish and Game Preserve, 179-82
East Bay area
- Barrow's Ranch and Joe Lagow, 106-12
- Bolivar Peninsula, 90-96
- JHK Ranch, 99-106
- Lake Surprise/chain of lakes, 96-99
- White's Ranch, 87-90

East Bay Lodge, 122-23
East Texas hunting, 356-60
ecosystem management. See conservation; habitat management; water management
education programs for hunters, 184
Eisenhower, Ike, 346
Ellis, George, 326
Ellis, J. M. and family, 263
English callers as live decoys, 23-24, 25
Esperson Duck and Goose Hunting Preserve, 291, 292
Espiritu Santo Bay area
- Matagorda Island, 208-13
- overview, 205
- Port O'Connor, 205-8

etiquette, hunting, 82, 119-20
Evans, Harvey, 140, 330
Everitt, C. E., 309, 311, 312
E. W. Rice & Irrigation Co., 189
Exxon, 341
The Eyes of Texas (TV show), 135

factory decoys, 33-34, 49, 50
Faggard, Clyde "Pop" and family, 92-93
Farley, Barney, 264-65
Farley, Robert Ellington "Bob" and family, 257-58

Farley boats, 264
Faurote, Frank, 294
federal appropriation/purchase of land, 84–85, 106, 209–10
    See also military confiscation of hunting lands
federal land, hunting on, 85
Federal Migratory Bird Act, 52
Fernandez, James "Cowboy"
    on agency land appropriation/purchase, 85
    duck calls by, 39–41
    on marsh buggy cruising, 83
    at Port Arthur Hunting Club, 71
    Sea Rim Marsh, 78
    at Shell Lake Hunting Club, 76–77
Ferndale Club, 356
ferry operations
    Aransas Pass, 258–59
    Bolivar Peninsula, 92, 166
    Brazos River, 176
    Lynchburg, 146
Field and Stream, 156, 288
Fields, John, 318, 319
Fin and Feather Club of Dallas, 354
firearms
    capacity restrictions on, 54
    hazards of, 21–22
    muzzle-loaders, 77, 357
    overview, 18
Fisher, Cliff, 141, 142
Flack, Frank W., 179
Flag Pond Hunting and Fishing Club, 351–52
flavor of birds (table appeal), 8
Fleischman, Max, 229
Florence, J. B., 356
Flour Bluff, 274, 277
fog hazard, 21, 120, 238, 305, 358
Fordyce, Sam, 292
Foreman, Ezra D. "Easy" and family, 71–74
Fort Bend County hunting, 348–50
Fowl Talk (recording), 338
Fox, Dick, 260–62
Fox, James, 250–52
Frandolig, Jim, 47
Freeman, Dick, 260
Freeport, Texas, 176
Freeport Boating and Hunting Club, 177
Freeport Facts, 177
Freeport Sulphur Company, 176, 178
Fulton, George W., 222, 269, 272–73
Fulton, James C., 280
fund raising. See philanthropy of hunters

"the funnel," 320
Futch, Ed, 233

gadwalls, overview, 8
Galveston, Texas, 164
Galveston Bay, 145, 146, 161
Galveston County, 24, 163
Galveston Daily News, 34, 166, 188, 189, 202, 292
Galveston Gun Club, 164
Galveston Hunting Club, 165
Galveston Island, 163–68
    See also Bolivar Peninsula
gambling, 180, 182, 216
Gammel, Bill, 366
Ganado, Texas, 199
Gard, Ron, 32
Gardner, Phil, 114
Gaston, William H. "Billy," 353–54
gate fees, 77, 78, 101, 111, 142
Gates, John Warne, 61–63
gauge limits, 54
geese
    crop destruction by, 281, 288
    hunting highlights, 79, 99–100, 243, 281–82, 292, 331–32, 344
    as live decoys, 24, 27, 28
    overview, 8–9, 362
    See also individual species
George, Albert P., 348
George, J. W. "Jack," 236
George Ranch, 25, 166, 348, 349
Gersten, Cal, 307
"ghost hunting," 333–34
Gibbons, George E., Jr., 276, 288
Givens, Murphy, 268
Glazebrook, C. E. H., 272
The Golden Crescent (Brister), 156, 211
goldeneyes, overview, 8
goose calls/calling, 41, 157–58, 314
"Goose Capital of the World," 299
Goose Creek, 157–60
Goose Prairie, 359, 360
Goose Roost Hunt Club, 158
goose roosts, 105, 110, 123, 277, 317, 364
Gore, Larry, 339, 340–41
Graveyard, 285
Great Depression, 15–16, 264, 294
greater Canada geese. See Canada geese
Green, Edward H. R. "Eddie," 13, 248–50, 293
Green Head Guide Service, 114
Green Lake, 214–15
Griffin Lake, 321
Griffith, Andy, 317, 319

Griffith, Linzie, 139
Grissom, Gus, 335
grit/gravel, 79, 90, 116, 219
Grubbs, Charles W., 33–34, 38, 39, 41, 198, 264
Guadalupe River and delta, 214, 215–18, 346–48
Guessaz, Oscar, 55, 273, 345
Gulf Coast Hunting Club, 165–66, 348
Gulf Oil, 80, 350
Gum Hollow, 270–73
Haas, Buster, 275
habitat management
    Dallas area, 354–55
    Eagle Lake, 311
    East Bay area, 122
    Matagorda Island, 208
    Panhandle, 345
    Sabine estuary, 63, 64, 68, 73–74
    See also conservation; water management
Haddock, Floyd "Crip," 360
Halff, Alex, 234, 236, 239
Halliburton, 122, 182–83
Hallock, Charles, 326
Hall's Bayou, 168, 169
hammerless shotguns, 18
Harbor Island, 255
Harbour, Jeff, 159
Harding, Warren, 292
Hardy, Ned, 169
Hardy, Nick, 166
Hargraves Hunting Camp, 140
Harlingen, 287
Harmon, Homer and family, 29, 132–33
Harrell, Milton and family, 232–33
Harris County, 145
Hartzog, Howard, 210
Hasselmann Bay Club, 212
hazards. See dangers to hunters
Hebert, Clifton "Pappy," 102
Heilner, Van Campen, 284, 288
Heldenfels, Walter, 235
Herring, David and Jim, 234, 235, 237, 238, 244
Hess, C. F. "Bert," 181
High Island, 87–88
High Island Café, 92
High Island Hunting Club, 87–88
Hill, Leonidas C. "Lon," 287
Hockley, Texas, 325–26
Hockley-Cypress Prairie, 325–26
Hockley Sportsman's Clubhouse, 326
Hogg, James H., 97
Holden, "Cripple" Joe, 348

Holder, Prentice, 144, 159
Holland, Jack and family, 27-28, 113-15
Holloman, Gus, 121
Holly Beach, 283
Home Place reservoir, 110, 111, 112
honkers, overview, 8
horses, hunting over/from, 54, 327
Hoskins Mound, 178
Hotel Palacios, 193-94
hotels of note
    Brazoria County, 175-76
    Corpus Christi area, 263-64, 269, 273-74
    Eagle Lake, 301
    East Bay area, 91, 92
    Galveston, 164
    Katy Prairie, 325-26
    Laguna Madre, 284, 292, 293-94
    Matagorda Bay, 193-94, 197-98
    Rockport area, 223, 227-28, 234, 243
    Sabine estuary, 61, 62
    San Antonio Bay area, 219
    West Galveston Bay area, 161-62
    See also lodges of note
Hough, Emerson, 12-13, 218, 269
Houston, Texas, 145, 161
Houston Audubon Society, 239
Houston Chronicle, 156, 260, 340
    See also Brister, Bob
Houston Fishing and Hunting Club, 162
Houston Gun Club, 145-46, 148, 326
Houston Lighting and Power Co., 140
Houston Post, 156
Houston Press, 156, 260
Houston Ship Channel, 159
Houston Telegraph and Texas Register, 163
Houstoun, Matilda, 163-64
Hoyt, Freddie D., 336
Hughes Hunting and Fishing Club, 178
Humble Oil, 157
Humphreys, Albert E., 201
Hunt, Wilkins W., 154, 208
Hunters Party event, 329
Hunting and Fishing in Texas (Stilwell), 291
hunting licenses, 52
hunting lore and storytelling
    Brazoria County, 9, 182-83
    Eagle Lake, 305
    East Bay area, 95, 98, 110
    Katy Prairie, 335-36
    Port O'Connor, 207
    Rockport area, 233
    Sabine estuary, 70
    San Jacinto River area, 159
    Trinity River delta, 133-34
    Victoria area, 347
hunting seasons, 52, 53, 54-55, 201, 348
hunting zones, 52, 53
hurricanes
    1875, 115, 187, 208
    1886, 202, 208
    1900, 88, 98, 165
    1915, 88
    1916, 284
    1919, 231, 250, 257, 264, 284
    Carla 1961, 29, 66, 124, 139, 207
    Ike 2008, 67, 125
Hynes Bay, 218-20

illegal hunting practices, 80, 102, 252, 262, 330, 339
Ilseng, Grant, 260, 329
Indianola, 193, 202-3
industrial development and decilne in waterfowl, 140, 144, 159-60, 171, 247, 266-67, 341, 363-65
Ingleside Ridge, 95-96, 115
injuries, overview, 21-22
    See also dangers to hunters
Intracoastal Canal (IC), impact of, 64, 65, 92, 173, 191, 246, 363

Jackson, Elmer "Crack Corn," 112-13
Jackson, Guy Cade and family, 102-3, 106
Jackson, James and family, 99, 101
Jackson Brothers Ranch and family, 120-22
J. D. Murphree WMA, 65
Jefferson County, 59, 64, 74-77
    See also Sabine estuary
Jefferson Inn, 292
Jenkins, David, 338-39
Jennings, R. L., 358
JHK Ranch, 99-106
Jimmy's Duck Hunting Camp, 243-46
Johnson, Al, 213
Johnson, Jimmy Wayne "J. W.," 215
Johnson, Lyndon, 122-23, 260
Johnson, Nig, 292
Johnson, Peter, 307
Johnson, Rob S., 235, 237
Johnson, Theodore "Charlie," 224
Johnson Brothers Ranch, 358
Jordan, Henry "Hank," 14, 326-28, 331, 332-36
Jordan, Lyle, 20, 41, 326-37, 339, 341
J. R. "Jimmy" Reel Hunting Club, 308, 313-15

Kahla, Claud and family, 89-90
Kahla's High Island Hotel, 92
Kamey Island and family, 216
Karnack, Texas, 359-60
Katy-Brookshire Prairie
    post WWII, 329-41
    pre WWII, 326-29
Katy Prairie
    ecology overview, 325
    Hockley-Cypress Prairie, 325-26
    Katy-Brookshire Prairie post WWII, 329-41
    Katy-Brookshire Prairie pre WWII, 326-29
Katy Prairie Day Hunting, 337
Katy Prairie Outfitters, 340-41
Keisling, A. E. and family, 266
Keller Bay, 196
Kemp's Duck Preserve, 226, 228
Kenedy, Mifflin, 282
Kenedy La Parra Ranch, 284
Kenyon Island and family, 216-17
Kiel, Bill Sr. and family, 351-52
Kilgore, John E., 215
killdeers, overview, 10
King, Richard, 283
King Ranch
    Laureles Division, 281, 282
    Norias Division, 285-87
    origins of, 283-84
Kingsville, Texas, 283-84
Kleberg, Caesar, 285
Kleberg, Richard Mifflin, Sr., 282-83, 365
Kleberg, Robert J., 292
Kleberg County, 283-84
Koch, Theodore F., 284
Kole Farm/Reservoir and family, 123-25
Koon Kreek Klub, 354-55
Kountry Kitchen, 336, 339, 340
Krajka, Rudolph, 138, 139
Krazy Kat Inn, 263-64
Kuhlanek, Leo, 315

LaBove, O. D., 79-80
Labrador retrievers, overview, 19-20
LaFour, Morgan and family, 29, 43, 140-42
Lagow, Joe, 108-12, 113-14
Laguna Larga, 282-83
Laguna Madre
    ecology overview, 267, 279-80
    lower, 285-95
    military recreation on, 276
    upper, 281-85
Laguna Madre Sportsman's Club, 276
Laguna Vista Resort, 292
Lake Charlotte, 128, 140

Lake McDonald, 352
Lake Placedo, 196
Lakeside Irrigation Company, 300, 301
Lake Surprise, 63, 96–99, 362
Lake Texoma, 364
Lamar Peninsula, 28, 31, 221, 234, 235, 238, 239–40
Lamb, Mickey, 142
Landry, Terry, 305
LaSalle Lodge, 206
LaSalle Ranch, 206, 207
Lassiter, N. H., 356
Laureles Ranch, 282
Lavaca Bay/River, 196, 346–47
Lawrence's Marsh, 136
laws, hunting, 28, 51–56, 52–53, 132, 252, 266, 272, 277
lead poisoning in birds, 54, 55–56
League City, Texas, 162
LeBlanc, Billy, 65, 69–70
LeBlanc, Bobby, 65, 67, 71
LeBlanc, Henry Joseph, 17, 65–71, 84
Lechenger, Ralph B., 129
LeCompte, Rudolph "Rudy" J. and family
    at Barrow's Ranch, 110
        biography, 157–58
        decoys by, 30–31, 44, 144, 158
        duck calling competitions, 42, 157
Leebron, Mike, 158
Leffingwell, W. B., 224
Left-Hand Hunting, Fishing, and Carnival Club, 148
Leggett, Ralph, 122–23
Leher family, 322
Leiter, Joseph, 188
Lewis, Barry, 321
Lewis, Charlotte, 120
Lewis, Lou and Barry, 311–12
Lewis Marine Station, 207
licenses, hunting, 52
Life, 158–59
Lillard, D. C., 102
Lingan, Jimmy, 153, 156
Little Sandy Hunting and Fishing Club, 356
Little Sandy National Wildlife Refuge, 356
live decoys, 23–28, 54, 132, 303
livestock, hunting over, 13, 14, 54, 99, 121, 327, 328, 330
Lobpries, David, 55, 306, 322
lodges of note
    Brazoria County, 180
    Caddo Lake, 358
    Corpus Christi area, 273
    Eagle Lake, 305

    East Bay area, 94, 96
    Matagorda Bay, 191
    Matagorda Island, 208–9, 212
    Port O'Connor, 206
    Rockport area, 248–50
    Sabine estuary, 61, 63, 75
    Trinity River delta, 142–43
logging industry, 94
Lone Star Sportsman (television show), 80
"Long Bridge," 291
Longtin, Jim, 315, 336–38
lore and storytelling
    Brazoria County, 9, 182–83
    Eagle Lake, 305
    East Bay area, 95, 98, 110
    Katy Prairie, 335–36
    Port O'Connor, 207
    Rockport area, 233
    Sabine estuary, 70
    San Jacinto River area, 159
    Trinity River delta, 133–34
    Victoria area, 347
Los Patos Guide Service/Lodge, 94
lost hunters, 21, 61, 110, 177, 300, 305, 358
    See also fog hazard
Lost Lake (Sabine estuary), 15, 62–63, 75, 76
Lost Lake (Trinity River delta), 130
Lost Lake Hunting Club, 346
Lower Lake Hunting and Fishing Club, 308, 310, 311, 312–13
Loyola Hunting Club, 284
Lubbock, Texas, 343
Luster, Ronnie, Sr., 177
Lynchburg ferry, 146, 149

Mack, Connie, 229
Mackey, William F., 29
Mackie, John, 271
Mad Island Game Preserve, 189
Mad Island Slough, 191
magazine capacity limits, 54
Mahavier, David, 345, 346
"making a pull," 357–58
malaria, 358
Maley, Joe, 29, 30
mallards
    decoys, 25, 26, 27, 28, 43, 44, 45, 49, 50
    hunting highlights, 119, 299, 301, 327, 348
    overview, 7, 362
Maly, Fred, 282
Maner/Manor Lake, 179
Manor Lake Hunting and Fishing Club, 179–82
mansion lodges. See lodges of note

maps
    Brazoria County, 175
    coastal Texas, xiv
    Copano and Aransas Bays, 222
    Corpus Christi Bay, 256
    Eagle Lake, 305
    East Bay area, 89
    Laguna Madre, lower, 286
    Laguna Madre, upper, 281
    Matagorda Bay, 187
    Sabine estuary, 60
    San Antonio/Espiritu Santo Bay, 206
    San Jacinto River area, 146
    Trinity River delta, 128
market hunting
    and bag limits, 52
    and conservation movement, 51
    George Ranch, 348
    hunting pressure of, 51–52, 361
    and Moody family operation, 97–98
    Morgan family, 140
    Whitehead family, 115
Mark Twain, 271
Marshall, Texas, 357
marsh buggies, 16, 17, 78, 95, 119, 136, 137
Marshman! Wildlife Experiences of Manson L. Clark of Cove, Texas (Clark), 134
Marsh Point, 124–25
Martin, Chris, 212–13, 213–14
Martin, Edward T., 147
Marvin's Restaurant, 315–16, 317–18
Mason, Bill, 315
Matagorda, Texas, 188
Matagorda Bay
    Carancahua and Keller Bays, 196
    ecology overview, 185–88
    Indianola and Powderhorn Lake, 202–3
    Matagorda, 188–92
    Palacios, 193–96
    Port Lavaca, 196–202
Matagorda County, 154, 188, 189
Matagorda Island, 205, 208–13, 241
Matagorda Island Lodge, 209
Matagorda Peninsula, 187–88
Mathews, Johnny and Mathew's Place, 265
Matranga, Donald, 141
Matthews, Joseph E., 143–44
Mays, Willie, 121
McAdams, Clark, 225–26
McCampbell Ranch, 273
McCarthy, Glen, 312, 336
McFaddin National Wildlife Refuge, 67, 71
McFaddin Ranch and family, 63–65, 77
    See also Port Arthur Hunting Club

INDEX → 397

McGehee, F. O., 312
McGregor, A. A., 277
McIlhenny family, 321
McKay, Robert Freeman and family, 131–32
McKinley, William, 248
MCM Hunting Ranch, 336
McMurray, William, 286
media coverage
    Brazoria County, 177
    Corpus Christi area, 269
    Eagle Lake, 317, 320
    of federal land appropriations, 84
    Galveston, 167
    of hunting lore, 159
    Matagorda Bay, 188, 197
    overview, 2
    of rail access to Texas hunting, 11
    San Jacinto River area, 156, 157
      (See also outdoor writers)
    of William Jennings Bryan, 96–97
    See also outdoor writers
Medina River/Lake, 344, 346
Meitzen, Red, 45
Melcher, J. C. and family, 197, 214
Melton, Ben, 357
Melton, Henry Palmer "Peg"
    biography, 155–56
    at JHK Ranch, 100–101, 106
    and live decoys, 27
    at Matagorda Bay, 190
Mendoza, Hayes, 72
Mercer, John G., 47
mercury, 363
mergansers, overview, 8
Mertz, Albert, 229, 230
Mexia area hunting, 352
Middleton, Dave, 94
Migratory Bird Treaty Act (1918), 52
military confiscation of hunting lands
    bombing ranges, 106, 209–10, 212, 302
    naval air station, 274
military recreation, 108, 191, 209–10, 276, 284
Miller, Jeff N., 292
Mills, Jim, 218
Mills, John Howard "Cap" and family
    live decoys, 27
    Mill's Wharf, 219–20, 240–43, 243
    silhouette decoys by, 32, 33
    at St. Charles Bay Hunting Club, 235, 236, 237
    wood decoys by, 31, 32
Minter, Granville Elias "Bill" and family, 259–60

Mitchell, Billy, 153
Mitchell Lake, 344–46
Mitchell Lake Club, 345
Mitchell Lake Gun Club, 345–46
Montgomery, R. J. "Monty," 288
Moody family
    Galveston lodge, 170
    Lake Surprise, 63, 96–99
    LaSalle Lodge, 206
    at Port Bay Club, 229
Moore, Hilmar G., 192, 349–50
Moore, Wyatt, 359
Moore Ranch, 349–50
More Game Birds in America, 365
Morgan, G. Y./Morgan canoes, 300, 304, 305
Morgan's Point, 145, 146–48
morning only shooting, 112
mosquitos, nuisance of, 21, 176, 178, 212, 345
motorized boats, introduction of
    C. B. Delhomme, 139
    and ease of access, 13, 15
    Galveston Bay area, 166–67
    hunting from, 52
    Laguan Madre, 287
    Rockport area, 224
    San Jacinto River area, 154
mottled ducks
    decoys, 27–28, 31, 44, 45
    overview, 7, 362
mouth calling/whistling, 41, 71, 72, 79, 153, 157–58, 242, 314, 339, 348
movies, hunting, 177, 264, 288
mud hazards, 70, 78, 90, 95, 101, 176–77, 335
mules, hunting over, 121
Munsill, Gail Borden, 264
Murata, George, 359–60
Murchison, Clinton, 212, 246
Murchison, Dawson R., 287
Murphy, Pete, 271
muskrat trapping/shacks, 81–82, 83, 140
Mustang Island, 262–67
muzzle-loaders, 18, 77, 357
Myer, George, 264
Mysterious 8 Club, 269

Namath, Joe, 121
Nature Conservancy, 85, 365
Navasota River, 350
Neches River, 356
Needmore Ranch, 63–65
Neff, Pat, 98
Negley, William and Carolyn (nee Brown), 217–18
Nelson, George, 328

Nelson, Jim and family, 32–33, 34–35, 48, 158–59
newspaper spread decoys, 34, 35, 334–35
nicknames of bird species, 7–10
night hunting, 52, 99–100, 102, 328
nontoxic shot laws, 56
Norman, Sam, 292
North Prairie Hunting and Fishing Club, 329
Nueces Bay/River, 267
nutria nuisance, 90, 111, 132, 139–40, 306–7

Oak Shore Club, 227–28
oarsmen of Caddo Lake, 357–58
O'Connor, Thomas, 205
O'Daniel, W. Lee "Pappy," 328
Offats Bayou, 167, 168
oil industry and hunting
    East Bay area, 92
    Fort Bend County, 350
    impact overview, 363
    Jackson Brothers, 120
    Katy Prairie, 341
    Sabine estuary, 63, 80
    San Jacinto River area, 157
Old River Club, 148
Oliverus, Constant A., 34, 38, 50
Orange, Texas, 60, 76
    See also Sabine estuary
Orange County, 59, 76
    See also Sabine estuary
Orchard Lake, 349–50
Osceola Plantation, 179
Oshman, Ansell, 40
Oshman's Sporting Goods, 40, 181
outboard motors, introduction of. See motorized boats, introduction of
Outdoors with Brister (TV show), 156
outdoor writers, 156–57, 168, 177, 260, 275, 317, 329
    See also individual writers
oxen, hunting over, 13, 14, 54, 99, 328, 330
Oyster Lake, 187, 190

Padre Island, 267, 268
    See also Laguna Madre
Padre Island Causeway Company, 275
Palacios, Texas, 193–96
Palacios Point, 186
Palo Duro Canyon, 344
Panhandle hunting, 343–44
paper spread decoys, 34, 35, 334–35
Paris, Texas area hunting, 355–56
Pastime Hunting and Fishing Club, 165
Paul Webber's Duck School, 184

Payne Boat Docks, 207
Peach Point Plantation, 174
Peach Point Wildlife Mangement Area, 184
peanuts, 215, 335
Peck, G. W., 229
pelicans, 123, 139, 233
Peninsula Club and Hotel, 234
Permanent Game Law and Game Warden Act (1907), 51
Permanent Wild Life Protection Fund, 52
Perry Ranch, 178
Pherobe (yacht), 96, 97
philanthropy of hunters, 121–22, 177, 260, 329
Pickett's Bayou Hunting Club, 143–44
Pierce, G. N., 229
Pike, Doug, 334–35
Pilant Club, 124
Pillot, C. G., 305
pintails (Northern)
    decoys, 28, 31, 43, 46, 47
    hunting highlights, 105, 133, 231, 279–80
    overview, 7
Pipkin's Hunting Ranch and family, 77–78
plastic cloth spreads, 36, 339
plastic decoys, 34
plovers, overview, 9–10
poachers, 65, 113–14, 218, 285–87
Point Isabel, Texas, 288, 292–93
Point Isabel Fishing and Hunting Club, 292
Point Isabel Tarpon and Fishing Club, 292
poker, 180, 182, 216
politics and hunting, 84, 85, 122–23
    See also promotion of development through hunting
pollution, industrial, 159–60, 247, 363
Pool Ranch, 178, 184
Pope, William H., 357
Port Aransas, 262–67
Port Aransas Club, 263–64
Port Arthur, Texas, 60, 61, 63
    See also Sabine estuary
Port Arthur Hunting Club, 65–71, 84
Port Arthur News, 34, 80
Port Bay Club, 228–34
Porter, Earl, 136
Port Isabel, Texas, 294
    See also Point Isabel, Texas
Portland, Texas, 267, 270–71, 273
Port Lavaca, Texas, 196–202
Port Lavaca Fishing and Hunting Club, 198
Port Lavaca Gun Club, 198–99
Port Mansfield, 284, 287
Port O'Connor, Texas, 201, 205–8

Port O'Connor Hunting and Fishing Lodge, 154, 208, 209
Portsmouth Ranch, 190–91
Post, Wiley, 102
Potlikker's Club, 129, 136, 139
pot shooting, 302
Powderhorn Lake, 202–3
prairie chickens, 11, 331
Prairie Waterfowl Hunts, 320–21
Pratt, Rick, 163
preservation of duck/goose meat, 82, 327
Price, Bob, 194
Prince, James, 334–35, 340
promotion of development through hunting, 2, 215, 222, 273, 274, 344
Proxmire, William, 210
puddle ducks, 7–8
Pulitzer, Joseph, Jr., 225–26, 244, 274–75
Pullman cars, private, 10–11
pump shotguns, 18

Quintana, Texas, 174–75

rabbits, 74
rag spreads, 34–38
rail cars, private, 10–11
railroads, hunting zones based on, 52
railroads and access to hunting
    Brazoria County, 175
    Corpus Christi area, 256, 258–59, 268–69, 270
    Eagle Lake, 299
    East Bay area, 87–88, 91
    Fort Bend County, 348, 350
    Katy Prairie, 326
    Laguan Madre, 284
    Laguna Madre, 285, 290, 291
    Matagorda Bay, 188, 189, 193–94, 197
    overview, 10–12
    Port O'Connor, 205–6
    Rockport area, 222–23
    Sabine estuary, 59, 62
    West Galveston Bay area, 161, 163
railroads/trains, hunting from, 11–12, 291
Rand, Ed, 229, 346
Raney, M. C., 177
Rathborne Sporting Club, 347
rattlesnakes, 21, 169, 170, 177, 178, 196, 212, 277, 294
rat (muskrat) trapping/shacks, 81–82, 83, 140
Read, William A., 34–35, 158–59
recordings, duck call, 72, 338
Redfish Bay, 255
    See also Corpus Christi area

Redhead Ridge, 291, 294
redheads
    closed seasons, 54–55, 276
    decoys, 28
    hunting highlights, 279, 280, 287, 291
    overview, 8
Red River, 355
Red's Place, 276
Reel, James Richard "Jimmy," 35, 302, 304, 307, 308–15, 321, 322–23
refuges, wildlife
    agency appropriation/purchase of land, 84–85, 106, 184
    Anahuac National Wildlife Refuge, 106, 111
    Aransas National Wildlife Refuge, 239, 361
    Brazoria National Wildlife Refuge, 184
    hunter's support of, 156
    impact of and short-stopping, 364
    Laguna Atascosa National Wildlife Refuge, 295
    Las Palomas Wildlife Management Area–Boca Chica Unit, 295
    Little Sandy National Wildlife Refuge, 356
    McFaddin National Wildlife Refuge, 67, 71
    San Bernard National Wildlife Refuge, 184
Refugio County, 220
regulations, hunting. See laws, hunting
Renfro, John Roger "Jack," 179–82
repeating shotguns, 18, 54
retrievers, 19–21, 95, 114, 121
rice, wild, 351, 352, 354
rice crops, impact on hunting
    Brazos County, 176
    Eagle Lake area, 300–301, 321–22
    Katy Prairie, 327, 331
    Matagorda Bay, 186, 194, 196–97
    modern rice farming practices, 364
    rag spreads over, 34, 36
    rice straw blinds, 105
Richard, Lillian Chatagnier, 80, 83
Richardson, Sid, 246, 250–51
Ridgehaven and Delhomme hunting preserve, 153
Rincon de los Laureles, 282
Rincon Ranch, 287
ring-necked ducks, 8, 48
ringnecks, overview, 8
Rio Grande, 285, 288–89, 290–91, 295
Rio Grande Valley Rod and Gun Club, 294

Ripley's Believe It or Not, 242, 243
Riskin, Pete, 284
Robinson Lake, 122
Rockport area
    clubs and guides, 226–47
    early years, profile, 221–26
Roesner, Earl "Old Man," 329
Rogers, Roy, 285
Rogers, Will, 102, 285, 304
Romero, Claude, 83
Roosevelt, Franklin D., 250
roost ponds, 277, 313–14, 334, 340, 364
    See also goose roosts
Ropes, Elihu, 274
Ross's goose, 8–9
ruddy ducks, overview, 8
Russell, Steve3, 307
Ryan, Nolan, 114

Sabine, Texas, 60, 61
    See also Sabine estuary
Sabine estuary
    agency appropriation/purchase of land, 84–85
    day hunting and guides, 77–80
    hunting and development promotion, 61–63
    hunting culture, 80–84
    Jefferson County clubs, 74–77
    McFaddin Ranch, 63–65
    overview and ecology, 59–61
    Port Arthur Hunting Club, 65–71
Sabine River, 356
saltwater incursion into freshwaters, 64, 98, 124, 218, 363
Saluria, Texas, 208
San Antonio area hunting, 344–46
San Antonio Bay area
    Green Lake, 214–15
    Guadalupe River delta, 215–18
    hunting overview, 213–14
    Hynes Bay, 218–20
    Matagorda Island, 205, 208–13
    Port O'Connor, 205–8, 208–13
San Antonio Express, 188
San Antonio Light, 226
San Bernard National Wildlife Refuge, 184
San Bernard River, 164
    See also Brazoria County area
sandhill cranes, 9, 52, 193, 202, 213, 219, 361
San Jacinto Battlegrounds, 148
San Jacinto River area
    early 1900s, 148–56
    ecology and early hunting, 145–48

    Goose Creek and Baytown, 157–60
    outdoor writers, 156–57
San Luis Pass, 170
San Patricio County, 270
Santa Fe Hunting Club, 165–66
Sargent, George, 185
Sasser, Ray, 84, 85
scaup (lesser), 8, 137–38
Schirra, Wally, 335, 336
Schmidt family. See Smith, Harry C. and family
Schnieder, Charles "Pappy," 232
schooners/sloops, 12–13, 18, 152, 164, 174–75, 224
Schorlemmer, Louis, 315
Scott, Oscar "Pop," 348
Seabrook Fishing and Hunting Club, 162, 163
Seadrift, Texas, 213, 214
Sea Gun Inn, 243
Seaholm, A. Helmer "Pappy," 301
Sea Rim Marsh, 78
Sea Rim State Park, 78
Sea View Hotel, 90, 91
Secrets of Duck Calling (recording), 72
Selkirk family, 87–88
selling of game, illegal, 330, 339
semiautomatic shotguns, 18
Shearer, A. R., 53
Sheka, Billy, Jr., 288
Shell Hotel, 227–28
shell limits, 54
Shoal Point, 162
shootings, accidental, 21–22, 102
shorebirds, overview of wintering species, 9–10
short-stopping, 364
Shotgunning: The Art and the Science (Brister), 156
shotguns, overview, 18
shovelers, overview, 8
Sikes, Davis, 275
Silberisen, Jimmy and John, 237, 243–46
silhouette decoys, 32, 33, 48
Sim, George, 294
Sims, Jerry, 304, 305
Singleton, Robert (Bob), 8
sink boxes, 18–19, 20, 54
Sitterles Hunting Club and family, 347–48
Slaten, Stan, 156, 339
Slayton, Deke, 335, 336
Slick, Tom, 237
sloops/schooners, 12–13, 18, 152, 164, 174–75, 223–26, 224
Slop Bowl, 176–77

Smith, Carlos. See Smith, Harry C. and family
Smith, Charles "Smitty," 24–25, 38, 72
Smith, Harry C. and family, 29, 196, 198, 199
Smith, R. E. "Bob," 191
Smithers Lake, 25, 166, 348
Smith Point, 115
Smock, Rip, 169, 170
Smothers, S. C. "Jake" and family, 302–3, 305
snakes, dangerous
    rattlesnakes, 21, 169, 170, 177, 178, 196, 212, 277, 294
    water moccasins, 21, 76–77, 120, 306, 312
Snead, Sam, 317, 319
sneak boats, restrictions on, 54
sneak hunting, 11, 72, 302, 327
snipe, 9, 129
snow geese
    decoys, 49
    hunting highlights, 105, 282–83
    as live decoys, 27
    overview, 8, 362
Socha, Jodie, 322–23
Sonnier, Pop, 82
Sontag, Joe "Uncle Billy," 242
Sontag, Les, 46
Sorenson, Andrew "Pop" and family, 226–27, 228–29, 293
Sorenson's Camp, 226–27
South Bay, 255
    See also Corpus Christi area
South Bay Hunting Club, 261–62
South Benches roost, 323
Southern Pacific resort (Matagaorda), 188–89
South Padre Island, 293–94
South Texas Hunter's Club, 332
Sparks, Sam, 162
Speaker, Tris, 229
Spears, Gordon Sims "Pop" and family, 261–62
species protection laws, 52–53
specklebellies/specks, 8, 9, 49
Spindletop Oil Field, 63
Spindletop Rod and Gun Club, 337
spoonbills, overview, 8
Sport, Texas, 249–50
Sportsman's Club, 300
Sportsman's Directory to the Principal Resorts for Game and Fish in North America (Hallock), 326
Sports Round-Up, 154
spread hunting, 34–38
sprigs. See pintails (Northern)

Standard Brass Camp, 66–71
Standard Brass Manufacturing Company, 65
Stapleton, Dale "Buddy," 304–5
Star Brand Ranch, 212
Starr, Amory, 359
state parks, hunting in, 78
state regulations/agencies, 51, 52, 78, 84–85, 365
   See also laws, hunting
St. Charles Bay Hunting Club, 28, 234–40
steel shot, 55
steers, hunting over, 13, 14, 54, 99, 328, 330
Stefano, Anthony, 330
Steigerwald, Walter H. "Stag," 179
Stennis, John, 260
Stephenson, Bob, 114
Stephenson, Frank, 263
Stewart, Shorty, 316
Stillwell, Hart, 118, 291
Stilwell, Hart, 275
St. Joseph Island, 239, 244, 247–53
Stone family, 350–51
stranding incidents, 21, 153
Strecker, John, 9
Strickland, Royce, 136–38
Stubbs, M. E. "Ras," 129, 130
Stutzenbaker, Charles
   decoys by, 43
   on Eagle Lake water management, 307
   and lead poisoning in birds, 54, 55
   on live decoys, 25
   on McFaddin Ranch, 63
   on muskrat trapping, 81–82
   on Orchard Lake, 349, 350
   on rail access, 11
   on suspension at refuges, 364
subsidence, 90, 111, 218, 363
subsistence hunting, [ ], 121, 215, 327–28
sulfur industry, 176, 178
Sulphur Company Club, 178
Sunday hunting, 51–52, 163
Sure Shot Game Calls, 40
suspension (at refuges), 364
Swan Lake, 196
Swan Lake Hunting Club, 227
Swan Lake Ranch, 217–18
Swann, Roy, 275
swans, wintering
   Corpus Christi Bay, 269
   Eagle Lake, 318–19
   Galveston Bay, 165
   overview, 9, 362
   protection of, 52
   Trinity River delta, 127

Sweetware Lake Hunting Club, 166
Swickheimer, David, 186
synthetic decoys, 34

table appeal (flavor), 8
table linens in rag spreads, 35–36, 333
Taft, Howard, 272–73
Taft Ranch, 272–73
tallow trees, 171
Tarpon Beach, 294
Tarpon Club, 74–75, 248–50
Tarpon Inn (Freeport), 176
Tarpon Inn (Port Aransas), 263
taste of birds (table appeal), 8
Taylor, H. W., 292
Taylor Island, 358
teal, 8, 43
Teal Lodge, 261
Teeple, Frad H., 205–6
Terrell, W. R., 309
Texaco, 80, 178
Texas Audubon Society, 365
Texas City, Texas, 162
Texas Fish & Game, 317
Texas Game, Fish, and Oyster Commission (GFOC), 51
Texas Land and Cattle Company (TLC), 282
Texas Land Conservancy, 365
Texas Outdoor Academy, 338
Texas Parks and Wildlife Department (TPWD), 51, 78, 84–85, 365
Texas Rice Coalition for the Environment, 366
Texas Safaris, 332–36
Thanatopsis Literary and Drinking Society, 307
They Made Their Own Law (Wiggins), 91
Thurmond, I. C., 229, 230
Tilton, Amos, 29–30, 43
Timber Hole/Lake, 314
Time, 286
tin silhouette decoys, 32, 33, 48
Tinsley, Russell, 317, 320
Tod, John, 282
tollers, 27
Tompkins, Shannon, 110, 113, 142, 143–44, 155–56
tow boat access, 152, 237–38, 242–43, 245
Townley, A. L., 38, 50
Townsend, Oliver, 31, 45
traffic law for hunters, 82
trains. See railroads and access to hunting
transportation. See access to hunting; railroads

Traylor, W. B., 215
Traylor Lake, 347
Traylor's Cut, 216, 217
Tres Palacios Bay, 186–87, 193
tresspassers, 66, 67
Trezavant, John T., 353–54
Trinity River and delta, 15, 26
   Dallas area, 353
   east of river, 140–44
   ecology overview, 127–29
   west of river, 129–40
trumpeter swans, 9
tupelo wood decoys, 28
Turtle Bay, 128, 140, 195
Twain, Mark, 271
Tyler, Blackie, 339
Tyler, Clifton
   Clifton Tyler Goose Hunting Club, 320
   on father, Martin's business, 315–16, 317
   on goose roosts, 364
   on Jimmy Reel, 314
   on white rag spreads, 36
   on working as guide, 318
Tyler, E. B. "Red," 276
Tyler, Marvin, 35–36, 315–19

Uncertain Ranch, 358
United Carbon Company, 247
urbanization and decline in waterfowl, 140, 266–67, 363–65
Urschel, Charles, 237
US Fish and Wildlife Service, 54, 84–85, 365

Valley Morning Star, 288
Velasco, Texas, 174–75
Velasco Hotel, 175
Venado Lakes, 196
veterans' benefits, [ ], 329–30
Victoria, Texas, 215
Victoria area hunting, 346–48
Vineyard, Harvey S., 300–301
Vineyard Ranch, 317
Vingt'-une Islands, 153

Waco area hunting, 352
Waco Gun Club, 352
Waddell, Davis, 320–21
Waddell, Thomas (Tom) and family, 25, 301, 306, 330
Walker, Bill, 156
Waller County, 329
Walton, Ike, 168
Waraken, E. R., 98
Warner, Eltinge F., 288

Warren, John W. and family, 325-26, 327
Warren Hotel, 325-26
Washington, Jocko, 181, 182
waterfowl, overview of wintering species, 7-10
water management
    Copano Bay area, 222
    East Bay area, 122, 123
    Matagorda Bay, 191
    Matagorda Island, 208, 212
    Sabine estuary, 64, 68, 73-74
    Trinity River delta, 136
water moccasins, 21, 76-77, 120, 306, 312
Watkins, Elbert "Watty," 159
weather dangers
    East Bay area, 97, 98, 102
    Katy Prairie, 327
    overview, 21
    Rockport area, 238-39, 245-46, 252
    Sabine estuary, 60-61, 70
    San Antonio Bay area, 218-19
    Trinity River delta, 134, 135
Weeks-McLean Law, 52
Weingarten, Joe, 181
Welder, John J. and Ranch, 201, 213, 215
Welder Flats, 213-14
Wells, James B. (Judge), 290, 292
Wells, W. C., 47
Wells Court, 240
West, Forrest, 93-95, 110, 143, 157-58
West Galveston Bay area
    Chocolate Bayou/Bay, 168-71
    Clear Lake to Virginia Point, 161-63
    Galveston Island, 163-68
wetland preservation/restoration, 85, 144, 365-66
Wet Marsh Pond, 129, 136, 139, 140
whips, hunting with, 283
whistling ducks, overview, 8
whistling swans, 9
White, Ed, 335
white brant, overview, 8
white-fronted geese, 8, 9
Whitehead, Joe and family, 33, 48, 115-17
White House Hotel, 301
white hunting outfits, 35, 37, 159, 317
white rag spreads, 34-38, 159, 218, 317, 319, 320, 323, 333-34
White's Ranch Station, 87-90
whooping cranes
    Copano Bay area, 222
    Laguan Madre, 282
    overview, 9
    protection of, 52, 210, 361, 362-63
    shooting, 83, 239
wigeons, 8, 45
Wiggins, Melanie, 91, 94
wild celery, 98, 122, 164, 166, 311, 354
wildlife restocking, 112
wild rice, 351, 352, 354
Williams, Larenzie Aubrey "Dee," 133-34
Williams, Ted, 114
Wilson, Rosine McFaddin, 64
wind sock decoys, 36
Windsor Hotel, 61, 62
Winfree's Cove (Cove), 129-35
Winter, John, 128, 129, 150-54, 208, 209-10
Winterman, David, 302, 307, 309, 313-14
Wintermann, Oscar J., 300, 302
Wolf, Bobby, 64
Wolff, Alex, 102, 314, 322, 323
Wood, T. D. and family, 250
wood decoys, handmade, 28-33, 159
    See also decoys
wood ducks, 8, 48
Wooden Shoe Hunting and Fishing Club, 163
The World of Shooting (Johnson), 307
World War II rationing, 15-16
Worldwide Wetlands, 366
wounded birds as decoys, 27
writers, outdoor, 156-57, 168, 177, 260, 275, 317, 329
    See also individual writers
Wynne, Toddie Lee, 212, 243

Yarborough, Ralph, 260
Yegua River, 350
Yellow Rose of Texas, 148
Yentzen, George, 39-40, 41, 76
Yzaguirre, Mario, 239

OTHER TITLES IN THE GULF COAST BOOKS SERIES

Lighthouses of Texas
    Baker and Holland

The Laguna Madre of Texas and Tamaulpas
    Tunnell and Judd

Life on Matagorda Island
    McAlister and McAlister

The Book of Texas Bays
    Blackburn and Olive

Plants of the Texas Coastal Bend
    Lehman and White

Galveston Bay
    Sally E. Antrobus

Crossing the Rio Grande: An Immigrant's Life in the 1880s
    Gómez and Valdez

Birdlife of Houston, Galveston, and the Upper Texas Coast
    Eubanks and Behrstock

The Formation and Future of the Upper Texas Coast
    John B. Anderson

Finding Birds on the Great Texas Coastal Birding Trail
    Eubanks and Behrstock

Texas Coral Reefs
    Cancelmo and Earle

Fishing Yesterday's Gulf Coast
    Farley and McEachron

Fishes of the Texas Laguna Madre
    McKee and Compton

The Louisiana Coast: Guide to an American Wetland
    Gay M. Gomez

Storm over the Bay: The People of Corpus Christi and Their Port
    Mary Jo O'Rear

After Ike: Aerial Views from the No-Fly Zone
    Bryan Carlile

Kayaking the Texas Coast
    John Whorff

Glory of the Silver King: The Golden Age of Tarpon Fishing
    Hart Stilwell, edited by Brandon Shuler

River Music: An Atchafalaya Story
    Ann McCutchan

Del Pueblo: A History of Houston's Hispanic Community
    Thomas H. Kreneck

Letters to Alice: Birth of the Kleberg-King Ranch Dynasty
    Monday and Vick